T0226929

Principles of Data Integration

Principles of Data Integration

AnHai Doan
University of Wisconsin, Madison, Wisconsin

Alon Halevy
Google Inc., Mountain View, California

Zachary Ives
University of Pennsylvania, Philadelphia, Pennsylvania

AMSTERDAM • BOSTON • HEIDELBERG • LONDON
NEW YORK • OXFORD • PARIS • SAN DIEGO
SAN FRANCISCO • SINGAPORE • SYDNEY • TOKYO

Morgan Kaufmann is an imprint of Elsevier

ELSEVIER

Acquiring Editor: Andrea Dierna
Development Editor: Alex Burack
Project Manager: Danielle S. Miller
Designer: Kristen Davis

Morgan Kaufmann is an imprint of Elsevier
225 Wyman Street, Waltham, MA 02451, USA

Library of Congress Cataloging-in-Publication Data
Application submitted.

British Library Cataloguing-in-Publication Data
A catalogue record for this book is available from the British Library.

ISBN: 978-0-12-416044-6

For information on all MK publications
visit our website at *www.mkp.com*

Typeset by: diacriTech, India

Printed and bound by CPI Group (UK) Ltd, Croydon, CR0 4YY

Transferred to digital print 2012

Working together to grow
libraries in developing countries

www.elsevier.com | www.bookaid.org | www.sabre.org

ELSEVIER   BOOK AID International   Sabre Foundation

We would like to dedicate this book to our students.

Contents

Preface

Over the past 20 years, the role of the database, and especially of database techniques, has changed dramatically. We have moved from a world in which an enterprise or organization had one central, relatively closed database for all record-keeping to a Web-dominated world in which many different databases and other sources of structured information must interact and interoperate, ideally in a way that gives users a fully integrated view of the world.

This book focuses on that latter world. It shows how database ideas have been broadened and deepened to accommodate external sources of information, to handle the distributed aspects of the Web and the issues that arise from mutual information sharing, and especially to deal with heterogeneity and uncertainty. We see such topics as a natural extension of the topics covered in a typical university-level database course. Hence, the book is primarily intended as a text for an advanced undergraduate or graduate course that follows the undergraduate database class present in many curricula. Additionally, the book is suitable as a reference and tutorial for researchers and practitioners in the database and data integration fields.

The book is divided into three main parts. Part I builds upon the topics covered in a database course and focuses on the foundational techniques used in data integration: techniques for manipulating query expressions, for describing data sources, for finding matches across heterogeneous data and schemas, for manipulating schemas, for answering queries, for extracting data from the Web, and for warehousing and storing integrated data. Part II focuses on extended data representations that capture properties not present in the standard relational data model: hierarchy (XML), ontological constructs from knowledge representation, uncertainty, and data provenance. Part III looks at novel architectures for addressing specific integration problems, including diverse Web sources, keyword queries over structured data that have not been fully integrated, peer-to-peer methods of data integration, and collaboration. We conclude with a brief overview of promising future directions for the field.

A range of supplementary, Web-based material is available for the book, including problem sets, selected solutions, and lecture slides.

Acknowledgments

Many people gave us helpful feedback on earlier versions of the book. We are extremely grateful to Jan Chomicki and Helena Galhardas, who were among the first to use the book in their courses and to give us feedback. Others who gave us fantastic feedback included Mike Cafarella, Debby Wallach, Neil Conway, Phil Zeyliger, Joe Hellerstein, Marie-Christine Rousset, Natasha Noy, Jayant Madhavan, Karan Mangla, Phil Bernstein, Anish Das Sarma, Luna Dong, Rajeev Alur, Chris Olston, Val Tannen, Grigoris Karvounarakis, William Cohen, Prasenjit Mitra, Lise Getoor, and Fei Wu. The students in the CS 784 course on advanced data management at Wisconsin and the CIS 550 course on database and information systems at Penn have read various chapters of the book over several semesters and provided great comments. We especially thank Kent Chen, Fei Du, Adel Ardalan, and KwangHyun Park for their help.

Portions of the content in this book were derived from the authors' work in collaboration with many colleagues and students. We would like to acknowledge and thank them for their contributions.

Finally, we are extremely grateful to our families, who sacrificed a good deal of quality time so that we could complete this manuscript.

AnHai Doan
Alon Halevy
Zachary Ives

1

Introduction

The invention of the Internet and the emergence of the World Wide Web revolutionized people's access to digital data stored on electronic devices. Today, we take for granted the ability to specify a search query into a browser or smartphone and tap into millions of documents and into databases of local businesses, recommendations, and coupon offers. Similarly, we also assume we can order a computer configured just the way we want and receive it within *days*, even if the computer requires assembling parts from dozens of companies scattered around the world. To provide such services, systems on the Internet must efficiently and accurately process and serve a significant amount of data. But unlike traditional data management applications, such as maintaining a corporation's payroll, the new services require the ability to *share* data among multiple applications and organizations, and to *integrate* data in a flexible and efficient fashion. This book covers the principles of *data integration*, a set of techniques that enable building systems geared for flexible sharing and integration of data across multiple autonomous data providers.

1.1 What Is Data Integration?

We illustrate the need for data integration with two examples, one representing a typical scenario that may occur within a company and the other representing an important kind of search on the Web.

■ ■ ■

Example 1.1

Consider FullServe, a company that provides Internet access to homes, but also sells a few products that support the home computing infrastructure, such as modems, wireless routers, voice-over-IP phones, and espresso machines. FullServe is a predominantly American company and recently decided to extend its reach to Europe. To do so, FullServe acquired a European company, EuroCard, which is mainly a credit card provider, but has recently started leveraging its customer base to enter the Internet market.[1]

The number of different databases scattered across a company like FullServe could easily reach 100. A very simplified version of FullServe's database collection is shown in Figure 1.1. The Human Resources Department has a database storing information about each employee,

---

[1] The names of these companies and the combination of businesses in which they are involved are purely fictional, but not unimaginable in today's economy.

1

Employee Database
FullTimeEmps(ssn, empID, firstName,
    middleName, lastName)
Hire(empID, hireDate, recruiter)
TempEmployees(ssn, hireStart,
    hireEnd, name, hourlyRate)

Resume Database
Interviews(interviewDate, pID, recruiter,
    hireDecision, hireDate)
CVs(ID, resume)

Training Database
Courses(courseID, name, instructor)
Enrollments(courseID, empID, date)

Services Database
Services(packName, textDescription)
Customers(name, ID, zipCode, streetAdr,
    phone)
Contracts(custID, packName, startDate)

Sales Database
Products(prodName, prodID)
Sales(prodID, customerID,
    custName, address)

HelpLine Database
Calls(date, agent, custID, text, action)

FIGURE 1.1 Some of the databases a company like FullServe may have. For each database, we show some of the tables and for each table, some of its attributes. For example, the Employee database has a table FullTimeEmps with attributes ssn, empID, firstName, middleName, and lastName.

separating full-time and temporary employees. They also have a separate database of resumes of each of their employment candidates, including their current employees. The Training and Development Department has a database of the training courses (internal and external) that each employee went through. The Sales Department has a database of services and its current subscribers and a database of products and their customers. Finally, the Customer Care Department maintains a database of calls to their help-line center and some details on each such call.

Upon acquiring EuroCard, FullServe also inherited their databases, shown in Figure 1.2. EuroCard has some databases similar to those of FullServe, but given their different location and business focus, there are some obvious differences.

There are many reasons why data reside in multiple databases throughout a company, rather than sitting in one neatly organized database. As in the case of FullServe and EuroCard, databases are acquired through mergers and acquisitions. When companies go through internal restructuring they don't always align their databases. For example, while the services and products divisions of FullServe are currently united, they probably didn't start out that way, and therefore the company has two separate databases. Second, most databases originate from a particular group in a company that has an information need at a particular point in time. When the database is created, its authors cannot anticipate all information needs of the company in the future, and how the data they are producing today may be used differently at some other point in time. For example, the Training database at FullServe may have started as a small project by a few employees in the company to keep track of who attended certain training sessions in the company's early days. But as the company grew, and the Training and Development Department was created, this database needed to be broadened quite a bit. As a result

Employee Database
Emp(ID, firstNameMiddleInitial,
   lastName, salary)
Hire(ID, hireDate, recruiter)

Resume Database
Interviews(ID, date, location,
   recruiter)
CVs(candID, resume)

Credit Card Database
Cards(CustID, cardNum,
   expiration, currentBalance)
Customers(CustID, name,
   address)

HelpLine Database
Calls(date, agent, custID,
   description, followup)

FIGURE 1.2 Some of the databases of EuroCard. Note that EuroCard organizes its data quite differently from FullServe. For example, EuroCard does not distinguish between full-time and part-time employees. FullServe records the hire data of employees in the Resume database and the Employee database, while EuroCard only records the hire date in the Employee database.

of these factors and others, large enterprises typically have dozens, if not hundreds, of disparate databases.

Let us consider a few example queries that employees or managers in FullServe may want to pose, all of which need to span *multiple* databases.

- Now that FullServe is one large company, the Human Resources Department needs to be able to query for all of its employees, whether in the United States or in Europe. Because of the acquisition, data about employees are stored in multiple databases: two databases (for employees and for temps) on the American side of the company and one on the European side.
- FullServe has a single customer support hotline, which customers can call about any service or product they obtain from the company. It is crucial that when a customer representative is on the phone with a customer, he or she sees the entire set of services the customer is getting from FullServe, whether it be Internet service, credit card, or products purchased. In particular, it is useful for the representative to know that the customer on the phone is a big spender on his or her credit card, even if he or she is calling about a problem with his or her Internet connection. Obtaining such a complete view of the customer requires obtaining data from at least three databases, even in our simple scenario.
- FullServe wants to build a Web site to complement its telephone customer service line. On the Web site, current and potential customers should be able to see all the products and services FullServe provides, and also select bundles of services. Hence, a customer must be able to see his or her current services and obtain data about the availability and pricing of any other services. Here, too, we need to tap into multiple databases of the company.
- To take the previous example further, suppose FullServe partners with a set of other vendors to provide *branded* services. That is, you can get a credit card issued by your favorite sports team, but the credit card is actually served by FullServe. In this case, FullServe needs to provide a Web service that will be accessed by other Web sites (e.g., those of the sports teams) to provide a single login point for customers. That Web service needs to tap into the appropriate databases at FullServe.
- Governments often change reporting or ethic laws concerning how companies can conduct business. To protect themselves from possible violations, FullServe may want to be proactive. As

a first step, the company may want to be aware of employees who've worked at competing or partner companies prior to joining FullServe. Answering such a query would involve combining data from the Employee database with the Resume database. The additional difficulty here is that resumes tend to be unstructured text, and not nicely organized data.

- Combining data from multiple sources can offer opportunities for a company to obtain a competitive advantage and find opportunities for improvement. For an example of the former, combining data from the HelpLine database and the Sales database will help FullServe identify issues in their products and services early on. Discovering trends in the usage of different products can enable FullServe to be proactive about building and maintaining inventory levels. Going further, suppose we find that in a particular area of the country FullServe is receiving an unusual number of calls about malfunctions in their service. A more careful look at this data may reveal that the services were installed by agents who had taken a particular training course, which was later found to be lacking. Finding such a pattern in the data requires combining data from the Training database, HelpLine database, and Services database, all residing in very different parts of the company.

■ ■ ■

Example 1.2

Consider a very different kind of example where data integration is also needed. Suppose you are searching for a new job, and you'd like to take advantage of resources on the Web. There are thousands of Web sites with databases of jobs (see Figure 1.3 for two examples). In each of these sites, you'd typically see a form that requires you to fill out a few fields (e.g., job title, geographical location of employer, desired salary level) and will show you job postings that are relevant to your query. Unfortunately, each form asks for a slightly different set of attributes. While the Monster form on the left of Figure 1.3 asks for job-related keywords, location, company, industry, and job category, the CareerBuilder form on the right allows you to select a location and job category from a menu of options and lets you further specify your salary range.

Consequently, going to more than a handful of such Web sites is tiresome, especially if you're doing this on a daily basis to keep up with new job postings. Ideally, you would go to a *single* Web site to pose your query and have that site integrate data from all relevant sites on the Web.

More generally, the Web contains millions of databases, some of which are embedded in Web pages and others that can be accessed through Web forms. They contain data in a plethora of domains, ranging from items typically found in classified ads and products to data about art, politics, and public records. Leveraging this incredible collection of data raises several significant challenges. First, we face the challenge of schema heterogeneity, but on a much larger scale: millions of tables created by independent authors and in over 100 languages. Second, extracting the data is quite difficult. In the case of data residing behind forms (typically referred to as the *Deep Web* or *Invisible Web*) we need to either crawl through the forms intelligently or be able to pose well-formed queries at run time. For data that are embedded in Web pages, extracting the tables from the surrounding text and determining its schema is

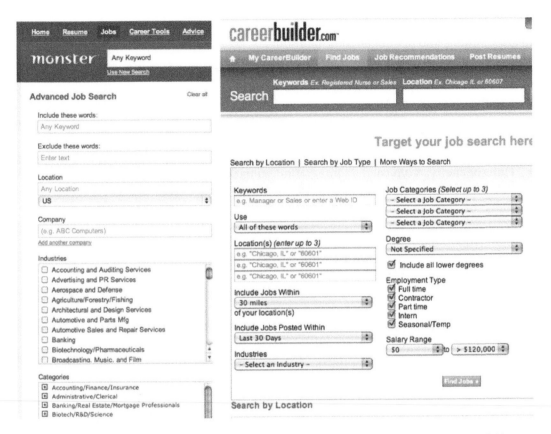

FIGURE 1.3 Examples of different forms on the Web for locating jobs. Note that the forms differ on the fields they request and formats they use.

challenging. Of course, data on the Web are often dirty, out of date, and even contradictory. Hence, obtaining answers from these sources requires a different approach to ranking and data combination. ■ ■ ■

While the above two examples illustrate common data integration scenarios, it is important to emphasize that the problem of data integration is pervasive. Data integration is a key challenge for the advancement of science in fields such as biology, ecosystems, and water management, where groups of scientists are independently collecting data and trying to collaborate with one another. Data integration is a challenge for governments who want their different agencies to be better coordinated. And lastly, mash-ups are now a popular paradigm for visualizing information on the Web, and underlying every mash-up is the need to integrate data from multiple disparate sources.

To summarize, the goal of a data integration system is to offer uniform access to a set of autonomous and heterogeneous data sources. Let us expand on each of these:

- **Query**: The focus of most data integration systems is on querying disparate data sources. However, updating the sources is certainly of interest.
- **Number of sources:** Data integration is already a challenge for a small number of sources (fewer than 10 and often even 2!), but the challenges are exacerbated when the number of sources grows. At the extreme, we would like to support Web-scale data integration.
- **Heterogeneity:** A typical data integration scenario involves data sources that were developed independently of each other. As a consequence, the data sources run on different systems: some of them are databases, but others may be content management systems or simply files residing in a directory. The sources will have different schemata and references to objects, even when they model the same domains. Some sources may be completely structured (e.g., relational databases), while others may be unstructured or semi-structured (e.g., XML, text).
- **Autonomy:** The sources do not necessarily belong to a single administrative entity, and even when they do, they may be run by different suborganizations. Hence, we cannot assume that we have full access to the data in a source or that we can access the data whenever we want, and considerable care needs to be given to respecting the privacy of the data when appropriate. Furthermore, the sources can change their data formats and access patterns at any time, without having to notify any central administrative entity.

1.2   Why Is It Hard?

In order to approach the problem of data integration effectively, it is important to first examine the reasons for which it is hard. Later in the book we cover these challenges in more detail, but here we give a high-level description of the challenges. We classify the reasons into three different classes: systems reasons, logical reasons, and social reasons. We examine each one separately.

1.2.1 Systems Reasons

The systems challenges that occur in data integration are quite obvious and appear very early in the process of trying to build an integration application. Fundamentally, the challenge is to enable different systems to talk seamlessly to one another. Even assuming that all systems are running on the same hardware platform and all the sources are relational database systems supporting SQL standard and ODBC/JDBC, the problem is already not easy. For example, while SQL is a standard query language for relational databases, there are some differences in the way different vendors implement it, and these differences need to be reconciled.

Executing queries over multiple systems efficiently is even more challenging. Query processing in distributed databases (i.e., databases where the data are partitioned into multiple nodes) is already a hard problem. The saving grace in distributed databases is that the data are *a priori* distributed to the different nodes by one entity and in an organized and known fashion. In data integration we are faced with a preexisting collection of sources, and the organization of the data in the sources is much more complex and not necessarily well known. Furthermore, the capabilities of each of the data sources in terms of the query processing powers they have can be very different. For example, while one source may be a full SQL engine and therefore may be able to accept very complex queries, another source may be a Web form and therefore only accept a very small number of query templates.

1.2.2 Logical Reasons

The second set of challenges has to do with the way data are logically organized in the data sources. For the most part, structured data sources are organized according to a schema. In the common case of relational databases, the schema specifies a set of tables, and for each table a set of attributes with their associated data types. In other data models the schema is specified by tags, classes, and properties.

Human nature is such that if two people are given *exactly* the same requirements for a database application, they will design very different schemata.[2] Hence, when data come from multiple sources, they typically look very different.

We can see several differences when we compare the schemata of the databases of FullServe and EuroCard:

- EuroCard models temporary employees and full-time employees in the same database table, while FullServe maintains two separate tables. This may be because FullServe uses an outside agency to contract and manage its temporary employees.
- Even when modeling employees, FullServe and EuroCard do so differently and cover slightly different attributes. For example, EuroCard uses IDs (corresponding to national ID cards) to identify employees, while FullServe records the social security number but also assigns an employee ID (since social security numbers may not be used as IDs in certain cases, for privacy reasons). FullServe records the hireDecision and hireDate attributes in their Resume database, but EuroCard simply assumes these attributes can be obtained by querying the Employee database with the appropriate ID. On the other hand, EuroCard records *where* each interview was conducted, whereas FullServe does not.
- Even when modeling the exact same attribute, FullServe and EuroCard may use different attribute names. For example, the HelpLine database of FullServe uses the attributes text and action to record the same as the attributes description and followup in EuroCard's database.

---

[2]This aspect of human nature is well known to database professors and is often used to detect cheating.

Finally, the representation of the data can be significantly different as well. For example, in FullServe's Employee database, the company records the first, middle, and last name of every employee in a separate field. In the Training database, it only records the full name of the employee in a single field, and as a result, names often occur in various formats, such as (First, Last) or (Last, First Initial). Consequently, it may be hard to match records from these two databases. The same problem occurs between the Sales and Services databases. While the Sales database only records a field for the name and a field for the address, the Services database records much finer-grained information about each subscriber. Of course, the units of measure will differ as well: FullServe uses American dollars for prices, while EuroCard uses Euros. Since the exchange rate between the currencies constantly changes, the correspondence between the values cannot be set *a priori*.

Data from multiple sources can only be integrated if we bridge this so-called *semantic heterogeneity*. In fact, semantic heterogeneity turns out to be a major bottleneck for data integration.

1.2.3 Social and Administrative Reasons

The last set of reasons we mention are not so technical as the previous ones, but are often as hard and can easily be the reason a data integration project fails. The first challenge may be to *find* a particular set of data in the first place. For example, it may turn out that EuroCard did not save the resumes of their employees electronically, and a special effort is required to locate and scan them all.

Even when we know where all the data are, owners of the data may not want to cooperate with an integration effort. When owners come from different companies or universities, there are some obvious reasons for not wanting to share, but even within an enterprise, owners are often reluctant. In some cases, the reason is that their data are part of a carefully tuned and mission-critical function of the enterprise. Allowing additional queries from the data integration system can put a prohibitively heavy load on their system. In other cases, the reason is that some data can only be viewed by particular people within the enterprise, and the data owners are worried (for a good reason!) that the data integration system will not be able to enforce these restrictions. Finally, in some cases people create *data fiefdoms* — here, access to the data means more power within the organization. For example, the head of the Sales Department may not want to share the data on sales representatives' work, as it may reveal some internal problems.

It is worth noting that in a few circumstances — for instance, those involving medical records or law enforcement — there may be legitimate legal reasons why a data owner cannot share data. Because such situations arise, the problem of anonymizing data remains a hot topic in computer science research.

While we cannot expect to solve the social problems with technology alone, technology can help data owners capitalize on some of the benefits of data integration, thereby providing additional incentives to participate. For example, an important benefit of participating in a data integration project is that one's data can be reached by many more people and have a broader impact (e.g., if the data are included in relevant search results by a Web search engine). As another example, a data integration system can be designed so that the attribution of the data is always clear (even when results are assembled from multiple sources), therefore ensuring that appropriate credit is given to the data owners.

1.2.4 Setting Expectations

Data integration is a hard problem, and some say it will never be completely solved (thereby guaranteeing a steady stream of readers for this book). Before we can discuss solutions to different aspects of data integration, it is important to set the expectations appropriately.

In the ideal world, we would like to provide a data integration system access to a set of data sources and have the system automatically configure itself so that it can correctly and efficiently answer queries that span multiple sources. Since this ideal goal is unlikely to be achieved, we focus on two more modest goals. Our first goal is to build tools that *reduce the effort* required to integrate a set of data sources. For example, these tools should make it easy to add a new data source, relate its schema to others, and automatically tune the data integration system for better performance.

Our second goal is to improve the ability of the system to answer queries in uncertain environments. Clearly, if the data integration system must always return correct and complete answers, then uncertainty cannot be tolerated at all. But in applications where data integration facilitates exploratory efforts (e.g., on the Web), the system should be able to answer queries under uncertainty. For example, when we look for jobs on the Web, it's okay to find 29 out of 30 relevant sources, or to return answers that don't completely satisfy the user query.

In some sense, user effort and accuracy are competing goals in setting up a data integration application. The more time we spend, the more accurate our system is going to be. Hence, in cases where we are willing to trade off lower accuracy for decreased setup time and labor, our goal can be stated as follows: *reduce the user effort needed to obtain high-quality answers from a data integration system.*

1.3 Data Integration Architectures

As background for the discussion later in the book, we briefly describe the architecture of a data integration system. There are a variety of possible architectures for data integration, but broadly speaking, most systems fall somewhere on the spectrum between *warehousing* and *virtual integration*. In the warehousing end of the spectrum, data from the indvidual data sources are loaded and materialized into a physical database (called a *warehouse*), where queries over the data can be answered. In virtual integration, the data remain in the sources and are accessed as needed at query time. Despite the differences in approach, many of the hard challenges are shared across these architectures.

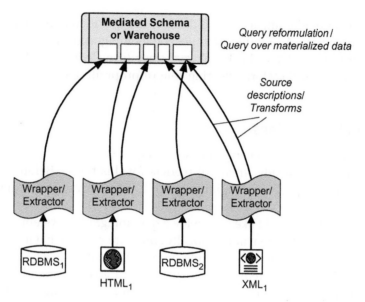

FIGURE 1.4 The basic architecture of a general-purpose data integration system. Data sources can be relational, XML, or any store that contains structured data. The *wrappers* or *loaders* request and parse data from the sources. The *mediated schema* or central *data warehouse* abstracts all source data, and the user poses queries over this. Between the sources and the mediated schema, *source descriptions* and their associated *schema mappings*, or a set of *transformations*, are used to convert the data from the source schemas and values into the global representation.

1.3.1 Components of the Data Integration System

Figure 1.4 shows the logical components of both kinds of data integration systems. We now describe each of these components, beginning with the components used in the virtual approach to integration. We contrast the warehouse model afterwards.

On the bottom of the figure we see the *data sources*. Data sources can vary on many dimensions, such as the data model underlying them and the kinds of queries they support. Examples of structured sources include database systems with SQL capabilities, XML databases with an XQuery interface, and sources behind Web forms that support a limited set of queries (corresponding to the valid combinations of inputs to its fields). In some cases, the source can be an actual application that is driven by a database, such as an accounting system. In such a case, a query to the data source may actually involve an application processing some data stored in the source.

Above the data sources are the programs whose role is to communicate with the data sources. In virtual data integration, these programs are called *wrappers*, and their role is to send queries to a data source, receive answers, and possibly apply some basic transformations on the answer. For example, a wrapper to a Web form source would accept a query and translate it into the appropriate HTTP request with a URL that poses the query on the source. When the answer comes back in the form of an HTML file, the wrapper would extract the tuples from the HTML file.

The user interacts with the data integration system through a single schema, called the *mediated schema*. The mediated schema is built for the data integration application and contains *only* the aspects of the domain that are relevant to the application. As such, it does not necessarily contain all the attributes we see in the sources, but only a subset of them. In the virtual approach the mediated schema is not meant to store any data. It is purely a logical schema that is used for posing queries by the users (or applications) employing the data integration system.

The key to building a data integration application is the *source descriptions*, the glue that connects the mediated schema and the schemas of the sources. These descriptions specify the properties of the sources that the system needs to know in order to use their data. The main component of source descriptions is the *semantic mappings*, which relate the schemata of the data sources to the mediated schema. The semantic mappings specify how attributes in the sources correspond to attributes in the mediated schema (when such correspondences exist), and how the different groupings of attributes into tables are resolved. In addition, the semantic mappings specify how to resolve differences in how data values are specified in different sources. It is important to emphasize that the virtual data integration architecture only requires specifying mappings between the data sources and the mediated schema and not between every *pair* of data sources. Hence, the number of mappings we specify is the same as the number of sources and not the square of that number. Furthermore, the semantic mappings are specified *declaratively*, which enables the data integration system to reason about the contents of the data sources and their relevance to a given query and optimize the query execution.

In the warehousing approach, instead of a mediated schema the user poses queries in terms of the warehouse schema. In addition to being a schema that contains the necessary attributes from the sources, the warehouse schema is also a physical schema with an underlying database instance. Instead of wrappers, the system includes *ETL* or extract-transform-load tool pipelines that periodically extract data from the sources and load them into the warehouse. Unlike wrappers, ETL tools typically apply more complex transformations to the data that may involve cleaning, aggregation, and value transformations. These transformations play the role of schema mappings in the virtual data integration architecture, but tend to be more procedural in nature.

Some of the properties of data warehousing stem from the fact that these systems were not originally developed for the purpose of data integration. Instead, they were developed as a tool for performing deeper analysis, such as uploading data from transactional systems (e.g., databases recording every sale made at a store) into a database where the data is aggregated and cleaned so decision support queries can be posed (e.g., sales of particular products by region). Converting data from the transactional systems to the warehouse can involve rather sophisticated transformations and aggregation. We discuss data warehousing and some of its variants in detail in Chapter 10, but the vast majority of the book discusses data integration in terms of the

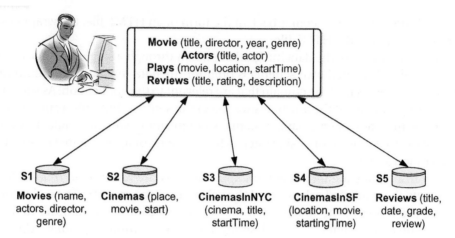

FIGURE 1.5   An example data integration scenario. Queries about movies are answered using a combination of sources on movie details, cinema listings, and review databases.

virtual data integration approach because it best illustrates the main concepts of data integration.

1.3.2 Example Data Integration Scenario

The following example, shown in Figure 1.5, illustrates a complete data integration scenario.

Data Sources and Mediated Schema

In the example, we have five data sources. The first one on the left, S1, stores data about movies, including their names, actors, director, and genre. The next three sources, S2–S4, store data about showtimes. Source S2 covers the entire country, while S3 and S4 consider only cinemas in New York City and San Francisco, respectively. Note that although these three sources store the same type of data, they use different attribute names. The rightmost source, S5, stores reviews about movies.

The mediated schema includes four relations, Movie, Actors, Plays, and Reviews. Note that the Review in the mediated schema does not contain the date attribute, but the source storing reviews does contain it.

The semantic mappings in the source descriptions describe the relationship between the sources and the mediated schema. For example, the mapping of source S1 will state that it contains movies, and that the attribute name in Movies maps to the attribute title in the Movie relation of the mediated schema. It will also specify that the Actors relation in the mediated schema is a *projection* of the Movies source on the attributes name and actors.

Similarly, the mappings will specify that tuples of the Plays relation in the mediated schema can be found in S2, S3, or S4, and that the tuples in S3 have their location city set to New York (and similarly for San Francisco and S4).

In addition to the semantic mappings, the source descriptions also specify other aspects of the data sources. First, they specify whether the sources are *complete* or not. For example, source S2 may not contain all the movie showtimes in the entire country, while source S3 may be known to contain *all* movie showtimes in New York. Second, the source descriptions can specify limited access patterns to the sources. For example, the description of S1 may specify that in order to get an answer from the source, there needs to be an input for at least one of its attributes. Similarly, all the sources providing movie playing times also require a movie title as input.

Query Processing

We pose queries to the data integration system using the terms in the mediated schema. The following query asks for showtimes of movies playing in New York and directed by Woody Allen.

```
SELECT title, startTime
FROM Movie, Plays
WHERE Movie.title = Plays.movie AND location="New York"
  AND director="Woody Allen"
```

As illustrated in Figure 1.6, query processing proceeds in the following steps.

Query reformulation. As described earlier, the user query is posed in terms of the relations in the mediated schema. Hence, the first step the system must do is *reformulate* the query into queries that refer to the schemas of the data sources. To do so, the system uses the source descriptions. The result of the reformulation is a set of queries that refer to the schemata of the data sources and whose combination will yield the answer to the original query. We refer to the result of reformulation as a *logical query plan*.

The following would be derived during reformulation:

- Tuples for Movie can be obtained from source S1, but the attribute title needs to be reformulated to name.
- Tuples for Plays can be obtained from either source S2 or S3. Since the latter is complete for showings in New York City, we choose it over S2.
- Since source S3 requires the title of a movie as input, and such a title is not specified in the query, the query plan must first access source S1 and then feed the movie titles returned from S1 as inputs to S3.

Hence, the first logical query plan generated by the reformulation engine accesses S1 and S3 to answer the query. However, there is a second logical query plan that is also correct (albeit possibly not complete), and that plan accesses S1 followed by S2.

Query optimization. The next step in query processing is query optimization, as in traditional database systems. Query optimization takes as input a logical query plan and produces a *physical query plan*, which specifies the exact order in which the data sources are accessed, when results are combined, which algorithms are used for performing operations on the data (e.g., join between sources), and the amount of resources allotted to

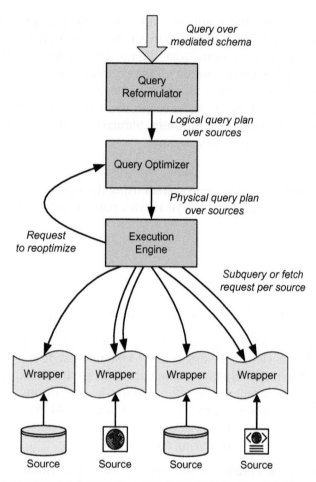

FIGURE 1.6 Query processing in a data integration system differs from traditional database query processing in two main ways. First, the query needs to be reformulated from the mediated schema to the schema of the sources. Second, query execution may be adaptive in that the query execution plan may change as the query is being executed.

each operation. As described earlier, the system must also handle the challenges that arise from the distributed nature of the data integration system.

In our example, the optimizer will decide which join algorithm to use to combine results from S1 and S3. For example, the join algorithm may stream movie titles arriving from S1 and input them into S3, or it may batch them up before sending them to S3.

Query execution. Finally, the execution engine is responsible for the actual execution of the physical query plan. The execution engine dispatches the queries to the individual sources through the wrappers and combines the results as specified by the query plan.

Herein lies another significant difference between a data integration system and a traditional database system. Unlike a traditional execution engine that merely executes the query plan given to it by the optimizer, the execution engine of a data integration system may decide to ask the optimizer to reconsider its plan based on its monitoring of the plan's progress. In our example, the execution engine may observe that source S3 is unusually slow and therefore may ask the optimizer to generate a plan that includes an alternate source.

Of course, an alternative would be for the optimizer to already build certain contingencies into the original plan. However, if the number of unexpected execution events is large, the original plan could grow to an enormous size. Hence, one of the interesting technical challenges in designing the query processing engine is how to balance the complexity of the plan and its ability to respond to unexpected execution events.

1.4 Outline of the Book

The remainder of this book will elaborate on each of the components and processes described above. The following outlines some of the main topics covered by each chapter.

Chapter 2 lays a few theoretical foundations that are needed for later discussions. In particular, the chapter describes algorithms for manipulating and reasoning about query expressions. These algorithms enable us to determine whether one query is *equivalent* to a second query even if they are written differently and to determine whether a query can be answered from previously computed views on the database. These algorithms will be essential for query reformulation and optimization in data integration, but are also useful in other data management contexts.

Chapter 3 describes the formalisms proposed for specifying source descriptions and in particular the semantic mappings. We describe two languages that use query expressions for specifying semantic mappings—Global-as-View (GAV) and Local-as-View (LAV)—and the GLAV language that combines the two. For each of these languages, we describe the appropriate query reformulation algorithms. We also describe how we can handle information about source completeness and about limitations on accessing data in sources.

In Chapter 4 we begin our discussion of techniques for *creating* semantic mappings. As it turns out, creating mappings is one of the main bottlenecks in building data integration applications. Hence, our focus is on techniques that reduce the time required from a person to create mappings. Chapter 4 discusses the fundamental problem of determining whether two strings refer to the same real-world entity. String matching plays a key role in matching data and schema from multiple sources. We describe several heuristics for string matching and methods for scaling up these heuristics to large collections of data. We then discuss the problems of creating mappings at the schema level (Chapter 5). One of the interesting aspects of these techniques is that they leverage methods from machine learning, enabling the system to improve over time as it sees more correct schema and object matchings.

Beyond the problem of establishing mappings between schemas, there are a variety of other operations one performs on metadata. Chapter 6 discusses general schema manipulation or *model management operators*, which can be incredibly useful in comparing and composing schemas and mappings.

Next we consider techniques for identifying mappings or entity correspondences at the data level (Chapter 7). Again, as with the schema mapping problem, machine learning techniques prove useful.

Chapter 8 discusses query processing in data integration systems. The chapter describes how queries are optimized in data integration systems and query operators that are especially appropriate for this context. The important new concept covered in this chapter is *adaptive query processing*, which refers to the ability of a query processor to change its plan during execution.

Chapter 9 then discusses how Web information extractors or *wrappers* are constructed, in order to acquire the information to be integrated. Wrapper construction is an extremely challenging problem, especially given the idiosyncrasies of real-world HTML. It typically requires a combination of heuristic pattern matching, machine learning, and user interaction.

Chapter 10 reviews *data warehousing* and its variants. The main advantage of data warehousing is that it can support complex queries more efficiently. We also discuss *data exchange*, an architecture in which we have a *source* database and our goal is to translate the data and store them in a *target* database that has a different schema, and answer queries over the target database.

Part II of the book focuses on richer ways of representing the data, incorporating hierarchy, class relationships, and annotations. Chapter 11 discusses the role of XML in data integration. XML has played an important role in data integration because it provides a syntax for sharing data. Once the syntax problem was addressed, people's appetites for sharing data in semantically meaningful ways were whetted. This chapter begins by covering the XML data model and query language (XQuery). We then cover the techniques that need to be developed to support query processing and schema mapping in the presence of XML data.

Chapter 12 discusses the role of knowledge representation (KR) in data integration systems. Knowledge representation is a branch of artificial intelligence that develops languages for representing data. These languages enable representing more sophisticated constraints than are possible in models employed by database systems. The additional expressive power enables KR systems to perform sophisticated reasoning on data. Knowledge representation languages have been a major force behind the development of the *Semantic Web*, a set of techniques whose goal is to enrich data on the Web with more semantics in order to ultimately support more complex queries and reasoning. We cover some of the basic formalisms underlying the Semantic Web and some of the challenges this effort is facing.

Chapter 13 discusses how to incorporate uncertainty into data integration systems. When data are integrated from multiple autonomous sources, the data may not all be correct or up to date. Furthermore, the schema mappings and the queries may also be approximate. Hence, it is important that a data integration system be able to incorporate these types of uncertainty gracefully. Then Chapter 14 describes another form of annotation: data provenance that "explains," for every tuple, how the tuple was obtained or derived. We describe the close relationship between provenance and probabilistic scores.

Finally, Part III discusses some new application contexts in which data integration is being used and the challenges that need to be addressed in them. Chapter 15 discusses the kinds of structured data that are present on the Web and the data integration opportunities that arise there. The Web offers unique challenges because of the sheer number and diversity of data sources.

Chapter 16 considers how one can combine ideas from keyword search and machine learning to provide a more lightweight form of integration "on demand": even in the absence of preexisting mappings and mediated schemas, a system can find ways of joining sources' data to "connect" data values matching search terms, thus answering ad hoc queries. The system might even use machine learning techniques to refine its results. This is a form of "pay as you go" data integration that may be useful in domains where little administrator input is available.

Chapter 17 describes a peer-to-peer (P2P) architecture for data sharing and integration. In the P2P architecture, we don't have a single mediated schema, but rather a loose collection of collaborating peers. In order to join a P2P data integration system a source would provide semantic mappings to *some* peer already in the system, the one for which it is most convenient. The main advantage of the P2P architecture is that it frees the peers from having to agree on a mediated schema in order to collaborate.

Chapter 18 describes how ideas from Web-based data integration and P2P data sharing have been further extended to support collaborative exchange of data. Key capabilities in collaborative systems include the ability to make annotations and updates to shared views of data.

Finally, we conclude with a brief look at some of the directions that seem especially open for high-impact developments in the data integration field.

Bibliographic Notes

Data integration has been a subject of research since the early 1980s, beginning with the Multi-Base System [366]. Since then, there has been considerable research and commercial development in the area. The paper on *mediators* [571] helped fuel the field and ultimately obtain more government funding for research in the area. The emergence of the World Wide Web and the large number of databases available online led to considering large-scale data integration [229]. Özsu and Valduriez provide a book-length treatment of distributed databases [471].

Since the late 1990s, data integration has been a well-established field in the enterprise market typically referred to as *Enterprise Information Integration* (EII) [285]. There is also a significant market for data integration on the Web. In particular, numerous companies created domain-specific interfaces to a multitude of data sources in domains such as jobs, travel, and classifieds. These sites integrate data from hundreds to thousands of sources. Chaudhuri et al. [123] provide a good overview of the state of the art of business intelligence and of the data integration challenges that arise there.

This chapter offered only a very cursory introduction to the relational data model and query languages. We refer the reader to standard database textbooks for further reading on the topic [245, 489]. For a more theoretical treatment of query languages and integrity constraints, we refer the reader to [7], and for a comprehensive treatment of datalog, see [554].

Foundational
Data Integration Techniques

2

Manipulating Query Expressions

The first step in answering a query posed to a data integration system is selecting which data sources are most relevant to the query. Making this decision relies on a set of methods for manipulating queries and reasoning about relationships between queries. This chapter covers such reasoning techniques in detail. While these techniques are very useful in data integration, they are also of independent interest and have been used in other contexts as well, such as query optimization and physical database design.

Section 2.1 begins with a review of database concepts that are used throughout the book. Section 2.2 describes techniques for *query unfolding*, where the goal is to reformulate a query, possibly posed over *other* queries or views, so that it refers only to the database relations. In the context of query optimization, query unfolding may let a query optimizer discover more efficient query processing plans because there is more freedom deciding in which order to perform join operations. In the context of data integration, query unfolding will be used to reformulate a query posed over a mediated schema into a query referring to data sources (Section 3.2.2).

Section 2.3 describes algorithms for *query containment* and *query equivalence*. Query containment is a fundamental ordering relationship that may hold between a pair of queries. If the query Q_1 contains the query Q_2, then the answers to Q_1 will always be a superset of the answers of Q_2 *regardless* of the state of the database. If two queries are equivalent, then they always produce the same answers, even though they may look different syntactically. We will use query containment and equivalence to decide whether two data sources are redundant with each other and whether a data source can be used to answer a query. In the context of query optimization, we use query equivalence to verify that a transformation on a query preserves its meaning.

Section 2.4 describes techniques for *answering queries using views*. Intuitively, answering queries using views considers the following problem. Suppose you have stored the results of several queries into a set of views over a database. Now you receive a new query and you want to know whether you can answer the query using *only* the views, without accessing the original database. In the context of query optimization, finding a way to answer a query using a set of views can substantially reduce the amount of computation needed to answer the query. As we describe in Section 3.2.3, in the context of data integration we often describe a set of data sources as views over a mediated schema. User queries are formulated using the terms in the mediated schema. Hence, answering queries using views is necessary in order to reformulate user queries to refer to the data sources.

2.1   Review of Database Concepts

We begin with a review of a few basic terms and concepts from the database literature related to data modeling and querying.

2.1.1 Data Model

Data integration systems need to handle data in a variety of data models, be it relational, XML, or unstructured data. We review the basics of the relational data model here, and introduce other data models later in the book. In particular, Chapter 11 discusses XML and its underlying data model, as it plays a key role in many data integration scenarios.

A relational database is a set of *relations*, also called *tables* (see Figure 2.1). A *database schema* includes a *relational schema* for each of its tables and a set of *integrity constraints* that we describe a bit later.

A *relational schema* specifies the set of attributes in the table and a data type for each attribute. The *arity* of a relation is the number of attributes it has. For example, in Figure 2.1, the arity of the Interview relation is 5 and its schema is:

candidate: string   date: date
recruiter: string   hireDecision: boolean
grade: float

In a sense, the schema describes how the database author decided to organize the data, what aspects of the data she chose to model, and the distinctions she wished to make. For example, the Interview table does not include an attribute for the location of the interview

Interview

candidate	date	recruiter	hireDecision	grade
Alan Jones	5/4/2006	Annette Young	No	2.8
Amanda Lucky	8/8/2008	Bob Young	Yes	3.7

EmployeePerformance

empID	name	reviewQuarter	grade	reviewer
2335	Amanda Lucky	1/2007	3.5	Eric Brown
5443	Theodore Lanky	2/2007	3.2	Bob Jones

Employee

empID	name	hireDate	manager
2335	Amanda Lucky	9/13/2005	Karina Lillberg
5443	Theodore Lanky	11/26/2004	Kasper Lillholm

FIGURE 2.1 The Interview table stores the employment candidates and the result of their interviews. The EmployeePerformance table describes the quarterly evaluation score of each employee.

or the position for which the candidate was interviewing. The EmployeePerformance table only provides a single grade, and does not model the fact that this grade may be the composition of several more specific performance measures. One of the challenges we face in data integration is that different sources organize their data differently, and these differences need to be reconciled.

A relational table includes a finite number of rows, called *tuples* (or *records*). A tuple assigns a value to each attribute of the table. If the relation being discussed is clear from the context, we denote its tuples with its values in parentheses, e.g.,

(Alan Jones, 5/4/2006, Annette Young, No, 2.8)

If not, we denote it as a *ground atom*:

Interview(AlanJones, 5/4/2006, AnnetteYoung, No, 2.8)

In some cases, we describe a tuple with a mapping from attribute names to values, such as:

{candidate→ Alan Jones, date → 5/4/2006, recruiter→ Annette Young, hireDecision→ No, grade → 2.8}

We pay special attention to the NULL value in a database. Intuitively, NULL means that the value is not known or may not exist. For example, the value of an age attribute may be NULL if it's not known, whereas the value of spouse could be either unknown or may not exist. The important property to keep in mind about the NULL value is that an equality test involving a NULL returns NULL. In fact, even *NULL = NULL* returns NULL. This makes intuitive sense because if two values are not known, we certainly do not know that they are equal to each other. We can test explicitly for NULL with the predicate is NULL.

A *state* of the database, or *database instance*, is a particular snapshot of the contents of the database. We distinguish between *set* semantics of databases and *multi-set* semantics. In set semantics, a database state assigns a set of tuples to each relation in the database. That is, a tuple can only appear once in a relation. In multi-set semantics, a tuple can appear any number of times in each relation, and hence a database instance is an assignment of a multi-set of tuples to each relation. Unless we state otherwise, our discussion will assume set semantics. Commercial relational databases support both semantics.

We use these notations throughout the book.

- We denote a database instance with D (possibly with subscripts).
- We denote attributes with letters from the beginning of the alphabet, e.g., A, B, C. We denote sets or lists of attributes with overbars, e.g., $\bar{A}$.
- We denote relation names with the letters R, S, and T and sets or lists of relations with overbars, e.g., $\bar{R}$.
- We denote tuples with the lowercase letters, e.g., s, t.
- If $\bar{A}$ is a set of attributes and t is a tuple in a relation that has the attributes in $\bar{A}$, then $t^{\bar{A}}$ denotes the restriction of the tuple t to the attributes in $\bar{A}$.

2.1.2 Integrity Constraints

Integrity constraints are a mechanism for limiting the possible states of the database. For example, in the employee database, we do not want two rows for the same employee. An integrity constraint would specify that in the employee table the employee ID needs to be unique across the rows. The languages for specifying integrity constraints can get quite involved. Here we focus on the following most common types of integrity constraints:

- **Key constraints:** A set of attributes $\bar{A}$ of a relation R is said to be a key of R if there do not exist a pair of tuples $t_1, t_2 \in R$ such that $t_1^{\bar{A}} = t_2^{\bar{A}}$ and $t_1 \neq t_2$. For example, the attribute candidate can be a key of the Interview table.
- **Functional dependencies:** We say that a set of attributes $\bar{A}$ functionally determines a set of attributes $\bar{B}$ in a relation R if for every pair of tuples $t_1, t_2 \in R$, if $t_1^{\bar{A}} = t_2^{\bar{A}}$, then $t_1^{\bar{B}} = t_2^{\bar{B}}$.

  For example, in the EmployeePerformance table, empID and reviewQuarter functionally determine grade. Note that a key constraint is implies a functional dependency where the key attributes determine all of the other attributes in the relation.
- **Foreign key constraints:** Let S be a relation with attribute A, and let T be a relation whose key is the attribute B. The attribute A is said to be a foreign key of attribute B of table T if whenever there is a row in S where the attribute A has the value v, then there must exist a row in T where the value of the attribute B is v. For example, the empID attribute of the EmployeePerformance table would be a foreign key of the Employee table.

GENERAL CONSTRAINT EXPRESSIONS

Tuple-generating dependencies (TGDs) and equality-generating dependencies (EGDs) offer a general formalism for specifying a wide class of integrity constraints. As we see in subsequent chapters, TGDs are also used to specify schema mappings.

Tuple-generating dependencies are formulas of the form

$$(\forall \bar{X}) s_1(\bar{X}_1), \ldots, s_m(\bar{X}_m) \rightarrow (\exists \bar{Y}) t_1(\bar{Y}_1), \ldots, t_l(\bar{Y}_l)$$

where $s_1, \ldots, s_m$ and $t_1, \ldots, t_l$ are relation names. The variables $\bar{X}$ are a subset of $\bar{X}_1 \ldots \cup \ldots \bar{X}_m$, and the variables $\bar{Y}$ are a subset of $\bar{Y}_1 \ldots \cup \ldots \bar{Y}_l$. The variables $\bar{Y}$ do not appear in $\bar{X}_1 \ldots \cup \ldots \bar{X}_m$. Depending on the context, the relation names on the left- and right-hand side of the dependency may refer to relations in the same schema or may refer to different databases.

Equality-generating dependencies are similar, except that the right-hand side contains only equality atoms:

$$(\forall \bar{Y}) t_1(\bar{Y}_1), \ldots, t_l(\bar{Y}_l) \rightarrow (Y_i^1 = Y_j^1), \ldots, (Y_i^k = Y_j^K)$$

where all the variables on the right-hand side appear on the left-hand side. We note that in practice, the quantifiers ($\forall \bar{X}$ and $\exists \bar{Y}$) are often omitted. In these cases, all the variables that appear on the left-hand side are assumed to be universally quantified (∀) and the variables appearing only on the right-hand side are assumed to be existentially quantified (∃).

As we illustrate below, we can use these formalisms to express the contraint classes mentioned above.

The attribute candidate is a key of the Interview table: (the following formula specifies a key constraint assuming set semantics for the table)

$$(\forall C_1, D_1, R_1, H_1, G_1, D_2, R_2, H_2, G_2)$$
$$\text{Interview}(C_1, D_1, R_1, H_1, G_1), \text{Interview}(C_1, D_2, R_2, H_2, G_2) \rightarrow$$
$$D_1 = D_2, R_1 = R_2, H_1 = H_2, G_1 = G_2$$

The attributes empID and reviewQuarter functionally determine grade in the EmployeePerformance table:

$$(\forall I, N_1, R, G_1, Re_1, N_2, G_2, Re_2)$$
$$\text{EmployeePerformance}(I, N_1, R, G_1, Re_1), \text{EmployeePerformance}(I, N_2, R, G_2, Re_2)$$
$$\rightarrow G_1 = G_2$$

The recruiter attribute of the Interview table is a foreign key of the EmployeePerformance table:

$$(\forall I, N, R, Gr, Re)\ \text{EmployeePerformance}(I, N, R, Gr, Re) \rightarrow (\exists Na, Hd, Mg)\ \text{Employee}(I, Na, Hd, Ma)$$

2.1.3 Queries and Answers

Queries are used for several purposes in data integration systems. As in database systems, queries are used in order to formulate users' information needs. In some cases, we may want to reuse the query expression in other queries, in which case we define a named *view* over the database, defined by the query. If we want the database system to compute the answer to the view and maintain the answer as the database changes, we refer to the view as a *materialized view*.

In data integration systems, we also use queries to specify *relationships* between the schemata of data sources. In fact, as we discuss in Chapter 3, queries form the core of the formalisms for specifying semantic mappings.

We distinguish between *structured* queries and *unstructured* queries. Structured queries such as SQL queries over relational databases or XQuery queries over XML databases are the ones we work hard to support in database systems. Unstructured queries are the ones we are most familiar with on the Web: the most common form of an unstructured query is a list of keywords.

We use two different notations for queries over relational databases throughout the book. The first is SQL, which is the language used to query relational data in commercial relational systems. Unfortunately, SQL is not known for its aesthetic aspects and hence not convenient for more formal expositions. Hence, in some of the more formal discussions, we use the notation of *conjunctive queries*, which is based on (a very simple form of) mathematical logic.

SQL is a very complex language. For our discussion, we typically use only its most basic features: selecting specific rows from a table, selecting specific columns from a table, combining data from multiple tables using the join operator, taking the union of two tables, and computing basic aggregation functions. For example, the following queries are typical of the ones we see in the book.

■ ■ ■ ━━━

Example 2.1

```
SELECT recruiter, candidate
FROM Interview, EmployeePerformance
WHERE recruiter = name AND EmployeePerformance.grade < 2.5
```

━━━ ■ ■ ■

■ ■ ■ ━━━

Example 2.2

```
SELECT reviewer, AVG(grade)
FROM EmployeePerformance
WHERE reviewQuarter = "1/2007"
```

━━━ ■ ■ ■

The query in Example 2.1 asks for pairs of recruiters and candidates where the recruiter got a low grade on their performance review. The answer to this query may reveal candidates who we may want to reinterview. The query in Example 2.2 asks for the average grade that a reviewer gave in the first quarter of 2007.

Given a query Q and a database D, we denote by $Q(D)$ the result of applying the query Q to the database D. Recall that $Q(D)$ is also a relation whose schema is defined implicitly by the query expression.

2.1.4 Conjunctive Queries

We briefly review the formalism for conjunctive queries. A conjunctive query has the following form:

$$Q(\bar{X}) \text{:-} R_1(\bar{X}_1), \ldots, R_n(\bar{X}_n), c_1, \ldots, c_m$$

In the query, $R_1(\bar{X}_1), \ldots, R_n(\bar{X}_n)$ are the *subgoals* (or *conjuncts*) of the query and together form the *body* of the query. The R_i's are database relations, and the $\bar{X}$'s are tuples of variables and constants. Note that the same database relation can occur in multiple subgoals. Unless we explicitly give the query a different name, we refer to it as Q.

The variables in $\bar{X}$ are called *distinguished variables*, or *head variables*, and the others are *existential variables*. The predicate Q denotes the answer relation of the query. Its arity is the number of elements in $\bar{X}$. We denote by *Vars(Q)* the set of variables that appear in its head or body.

The c_j's are *interpreted atoms* and are of the form $X \; \theta \; Y$, where X and Y are either variables or constants, and at least one of X or Y is a variable. The operator θ is an interpreted predicate such as $=, \leq, <, !=, >,$ or $\geq$. We assume the obvious meaning for the interpreted predicates, and unless otherwise stated, we interpret them over a dense domain.[1]

The semantics of a conjunctive query Q over a database instance D is as follows. Consider any mapping ψ that maps each of the variables in Q to constants in D. Denote by $\psi(R_i)$ the result of applying ψ to $R_i(\bar{X}_i)$, by $\psi(c_i)$ the result of applying ψ to c_i, and by $\psi(Q)$ the result of applying ψ to $Q(\bar{X})$, all resulting in ground atoms. If

- each of $\psi(R_1), \ldots, \psi(R_n)$ is in D, and
- for each $1 \leq j \leq m$, $\psi(c_j)$ is satisfied,

then (and only then) $\psi(Q)$ is in the answer to Q over D.

To illustrate the correspondence between SQL queries and conjunctive queries, the following conjunctive query is the same as the SQL query in Example 2.1:

$Q_1(Y, X)$:- Interview(X, D, Y, H, F), EmployeePerformance(E, Y, T, W, Z), $W \leq 2.5$

Note that the join in the conjunctive query is expressed by the fact that the variable Y appears in both subgoals. The predicate on the grade is expressed with an interpreted atom.

Conjunctive queries must be *safe*; that is, every variable appearing in the head also appears in a non-interpreted atom in the body. Otherwise, the set of possible answers to the query may be infinite (i.e., the variable appearing in the head but not in the body can be bound to any value).

We can also express disjunctive queries in this notation. To express disjunction, we write two (or more) conjunctive queries with the same head predicate.

■ ■ ■ ▬▬▬▬▬▬▬▬▬▬▬▬▬▬▬▬▬▬▬▬▬▬▬▬▬▬▬▬▬▬▬▬▬▬▬▬

Example 2.3

The following query asks for the recruiters who performed the best *or* the worst:

$Q_1(E, Y)$:- Interview(X, D, Y, H, F), EmployeePerformance(E, Y, T, W, Z), $W \leq 2.5$
$Q_1(E, Y)$:- Interview(X, D, Y, H, F), EmployeePerformance(E, Y, T, W, Z), $W \geq 3.9$

▬▬▬▬▬▬▬▬▬▬▬▬▬▬▬▬▬▬▬▬▬▬▬▬▬▬▬▬▬▬▬▬▬ ■ ■ ■

We also consider conjunctive queries with negated subgoals, of the form

$$Q(\bar{X}) :\text{-} R_1(\bar{X}_1), \ldots, R_n(\bar{X}_n), \neg S_1(\bar{Y}_1), \ldots, \neg S_m(\bar{Y}_m)$$

For queries with negation, we extend the notion of safety as follows: any variable appearing in the head of the query must also appear in a *positive* subgoal. To produce an answer for the query, the mapping from the variables of Q to the constants in the database must satisfy $\psi(S_1(\bar{Y}_1)), \ldots, \psi(S_m(\bar{Y}_m)) \notin D$.

---

[1]The alternative would be to interpret them over a discrete domain such as the integers. In that case we need to account for subtle inferences such as implying $X = 4$ from the conjunction $X > 3, X < 5$.

In our discussions, the term *conjunctive queries* will refer to conjunctive queries *without* interpreted predicates or negation. If we allow interpreted or negated atoms, we will explicitly say so.

2.1.5 Datalog Programs

A datalog program is a set of rules, each of which is a conjunctive query. Instead of computing a single answer relation, a datalog program computes a set of *intensional* relations (called IDB relations), one of them being designated as the *query predicate*. In datalog, we refer to the database relations as the *EDB relations* (extensional database). Intuitively, the extensional relations are given as a set of tuples (also referred to as ground facts), while the intensional relations are defined by a set of rules. Consequently, the EDB relations can occur in only the body of the rules, whereas the IDB relations can occur both in the head and in the body.

■ ■ ■ ▬▬▬▬▬▬▬▬▬▬▬▬▬▬▬▬▬▬▬▬▬▬▬▬▬▬▬▬▬▬▬▬▬▬

Example 2.4

Consider a database that includes a simple binary relation representing the edges in a graph: edge(X,Y) holds if there is an edge from X to Y in the graph. The following datalog query computes the paths in the graph. edge is an EDB relation and path is an IDB relation.

r_1 path(X,Y) :- edge(X,Y)
r_2 path(X,Y) :- edge(X,Z), path(Z,Y)

The first rule states that all single edges form paths. The second rule computes paths that are composed from shorter ones. The query predicate in this example is path. Note that replacing r_2 with the following rule would produce the same result.

r_3 path(X,Y) :- path(X,Z), path(Z,Y)

▬▬▬▬▬▬▬▬▬▬▬▬▬▬▬▬▬▬▬▬▬▬▬▬▬▬▬▬▬▬ ■ ■ ■

The semantics of datalog programs are based on conjunctive queries. We begin with empty extensions for the IDB predicates. We choose a rule in the program and apply it to the current extension of the EDB and IDB relations. We add the tuples computed for the head of the rule to its extension. We continue applying the rules of the program until no new tuples are computed for the IDB relations. The answer to the query is the extension of the query predicate. When the rules do not contain negated subgoals, this process is guaranteed to terminate with a unique answer, independent of the order in which we applied the rules.

■ ■ ■ ▬▬▬▬▬▬▬▬▬▬▬▬▬▬▬▬▬▬▬▬▬▬▬▬▬▬▬▬▬▬▬▬▬▬

Example 2.5

In Example 2.4, suppose we begin with a database that contains the tuples edge(1,2), edge(2,3), and edge(3,4). When we apply r_1 we will obtain path(1,2), path(2,3), and path(3,4). The first time we apply r_2 we obtain path(1,3) and path(2,4). The second time we apply r_2 we obtain path(1,4). Since no new tuples can be derived, the evaluation of the datalog program terminates.

▬▬▬▬▬▬▬▬▬▬▬ ■ ■ ■

In data integration we are interested in datalog programs mostly because they are sometimes needed in order to compute all the answers to a query from a set of data sources (see Sections 3.3 and 3.4). Readers who are familiar with the Prolog programming language will notice that datalog is a subset of Prolog. The reader should also note that not all SQL queries can be expressed in datalog. In particular, there is no support in datalog for grouping and aggregation and for outer joins. SQL does support limited kinds of recursion but not arbitrary recursion.

2.2 Query Unfolding

One of the important advantages of declarative query languages is *composability*: you can write queries that refer to views (i.e., other named queries) in their body. For example, in SQL, you can refer to other views in the FROM clause. Composability considerably simplifies the task of expressing complex queries, because they can be written in smaller fragments and combined appropriately. Query unfolding is the process of undoing the composition of queries: given a query that refers to views, query unfolding will rewrite the query so it refers only to the database tables.

Query unfolding is conceptually quite simple. We iteratively unfold a single view in the definition of the query until no more views remain. The following describes a single unfolding step. Like all other algorithms in this chapter, we describe them using the notation of conjunctive queries (see Section 2.1). We typically restrict our discussion to algorithms for manipulating conjunctive queries, and in some cases describe some important extensions. The bibliographic references contain pointers to algorithms that cover more complex queries.

UNFOLDING A SUBGOAL

Let Q be a conjunctive query of the form

$$Q(\bar{X}) :\text{-} \ p_1(\bar{X}_1), \ldots, p_n(\bar{X}_n)$$

where p_1 is itself a relation defined by the query

$$p_1(\bar{Y}) :\text{-} \ s_1(\bar{Y}_1), \ldots, s_m(\bar{Y}_m)$$

We assume without loss of generality that $\bar{Y}$ is a tuple of variables, and each variable occurs in the tuple at most once. The other subgoals of Q may also be defined by other queries or be database relations.

A single unfolding step is performed as follows. Let ψ be the variable mapping that maps $\bar{Y}$ to $\bar{X}_1$ and maps the existential variables in p_1 to new variables that do not occur anywhere else. To unfold $p_1(\bar{X}_1)$, remove $p_1(\bar{X}_1)$ from Q and add the subgoals $s_1(\psi(\bar{Y}_1)), \ldots,$ $s_m(\psi(\bar{Y}_m))$ to the body of Q.

We repeat the above procedure until all of the subgoals in Q refer to database relations.

■ ■ ■ ▬▬▬▬▬▬▬▬▬▬▬▬▬▬▬▬▬▬▬▬▬▬▬▬▬▬▬▬

Example 2.6

Consider the following example, where Q_3 is defined in terms of Q_1 and Q_2. The relation Flight stores pairs of cities between which there is a direct flight, and the relation Hub stores the set of hub cities of the airline. The query Q_1 asks for pairs of cities between which there is a flight that goes through a hub. The query Q_2 asks for pairs of cities that are on the same outgoing path from a hub.

$Q_1(X, Y) :\text{-} \ \text{Flight}(X, Z), \text{Hub}(Z), \text{Flight}(Z, Y)$

$Q_2(X, Y) :\text{-} \ \text{Hub}(Z), \text{Flight}(Z, X), \text{Flight}(X, Y)$

$Q_3(X, Z) :\text{-} \ Q_1(X, Y), Q_2(Y, Z)$

The unfolding of Q_3 is

$Q_3'(X, Z) :\text{-} \ \text{Flight}(X, U), \text{Hub}(U), \text{Flight}(U, Y), \text{Hub}(W), \text{Flight}(W, Y), \text{Flight}(Y, Z)$

▬▬▬▬▬▬▬▬▬▬▬▬▬▬▬▬▬▬▬▬▬▬▬▬▬▬▬ ■ ■ ■

There are a few points to note about query unfolding. First, the resulting query may have subgoals that seem redundant. The next section will describe a set of algorithms for removing redundant subgoals by leveraging techniques for query containment. Second, the query and the view may each have *interpreted predicates* (recall from Section 2.1.4) that are satisfiable in isolation, but after the unfolding we may discover that the query is unsatisfiable and therefore the empty answer can be returned immediately. This, of course, is an extreme example where unfolding can lead to significant optimization in query evaluation.

It is also interesting to note that through repeated applications of the unfolding step, the number of subgoals may grow exponentially. It is quite easy to create an example of n queries defining a query Q, such that unfolding Q yields 2^n subgoals.

Finally, we emphasize that unfolding does not necessarily yield more efficient ways to execute the query. In fact, in Section 2.4 we do exactly the opposite—we try to rewrite queries so they *do* refer to views in order to speed up query processing. Unfolding merely allows the query processor to explore a wider collection of query plans by considering a larger set of possible orderings of the join operations in the query, and by considering the complete set of constraints expressed with interpreted predicates holistically. Of course, the ability to unfold queries is crucial when queries are written in a compositional fashion, which is one of the main benefits of declarative querying.

2.3 Query Containment and Equivalence

Let us reconsider the unfolding of the query Q_3 in Example 2.6:

$Q_3'(X,Z)$:- Flight(X, U), Hub(U), Flight(U, Y), Hub(W), Flight(W, Y), Flight(Y, Z)

Intuitively, this query seems to have more subgoals than necessary. Specifically, the subgoals Hub(W) and Flight(W, Y) seem redundant, because whenever the subgoals Hub(Z) and Flight(Z, Y) are satisfied, then so must Hub(W) and Flight(W, Y). Hence, we would expect the following query to produce exactly the same result as Q_3':

$Q_4(X,Z)$:- Flight(X, U), Hub(U), Flight(U, Y), Flight(Y, Z)

Furthermore, if we consider the following query, which requires *both* intermediate stops to be hubs:

$Q_5(X,Z)$:- Flight(X, U), Hub(U), Flight(U, Y), Hub(Y), Flight(Y, Z)

then we would expect the set of answers to Q_4 to always be a *superset* of the answers to Q_5.

Query containment and equivalence provide a formal framework for reaching the conclusions we described above. Reasoning in this way enables us to remove subgoals from queries, thereby reducing the computation needed to execute them. As we will see in the next chapter, query containment and equivalence provide the formal framework for comparing different results of query reformulation in data integration systems.

2.3.1 Formal Definition

We begin with the formal definition. Recall that $Q(D)$ denotes the result of the query Q over the database D. The arity of a query refers to the number of arguments in its head.

Definition 2.1 (Containment and Equivalence). *Let Q_1 and Q_2 be two queries of the same arity. We say that Q_1 is contained in Q_2, denoted by $Q_1 \sqsubseteq Q_2$, if for any database D, $Q_1(D) \subseteq Q_2(D)$. We say that Q_1 is equivalent to Q_2, denoted by $Q_1 \equiv Q_2$, if $Q_1 \sqsubseteq Q_2$ and $Q_2 \sqsubseteq Q_1$.* □

The important aspect of the above definition is that containment and equivalence are properties of the queries, and not the current state of the database. The relationship needs to hold for *any* database state. In fact, determining query containment and equivalence can be viewed as a problem of logical deduction specialized to query expressions.

In our discussion, we do not consider the data types of individual columns of database relations. However, in practice we would only consider containment between pairs of queries that are union compatible, i.e., each of the columns of their head predicates are compatible. In what follows, we describe query containment (and hence equivalence) algorithms for common classes of queries. The bibliographic references point out additional cases that have been studied and indicate where to find the full details of the algorithms we describe.

2.3.2 Containment of Conjunctive Queries

We begin by discussing the simplest case of query containment: conjunctive queries with no interpreted predicates or negation. In our discussion we will often refer to *variable mappings*. A variable mapping ψ from query Q_1 to query Q_2 maps the variables of Q_1 to either variables or constants in Q_2. We also apply variable mappings to tuples of variables and to atoms. Hence, $\psi(X_1, \ldots, X_n)$ denotes $\psi(X_1), \ldots, \psi(X_n)$, and $\psi(p(X_1, \ldots, X_n))$ denotes $p(\psi(X_1), \ldots, \psi(X_n))$.

In the case of conjunctive queries with no interpreted predicates or negation, checking containment amounts to finding a *containment mapping*, defined next.

Definition 2.2 (Containment Mapping).   *Let Q_1 and Q_2 be conjunctive queries. Let ψ be a variable mapping from Q_1 to Q_2. We say that ψ is a containment mapping from Q_1 to Q_2 if*

- $\psi(\bar{X}) = \bar{Y}$, *where $\bar{X}$ and $\bar{Y}$ are the head variables of Q_1 and Q_2, respectively, and*
- *for every subgoal $g(\bar{X}_i)$ in the body of Q_1, $\psi(g(\bar{X}_i))$ is a subgoal of Q_2.*   □

The following theorem shows that the existence of a containment mapping is a necessary and sufficient condition for containment.

Theorem 2.1.   *Let Q_1 and Q_2 be two conjunctive queries. Then, $Q_1 \sqsupseteq Q_2$ if and only if there is a containment mapping from Q_1 to Q_2.*   □

Proof. Suppose Q_1 and Q_2 have the following form:

$$Q_1(\bar{X}) :\text{-} \; g_1(\bar{X}_1), \ldots, g_n(\bar{X}_n)$$
$$Q_2(\bar{Y}) :\text{-} \; h_1(\bar{Y}_1), \ldots, h_m(\bar{Y}_m)$$

For the *if* direction, suppose there is a containment mapping, ψ, from Q_1 to Q_2 and suppose that D is an arbitrary database instance. We need to show that if $\bar{t} \in Q_2(D)$, then $\bar{t} \in Q_1(D)$.

Suppose $\bar{t} \in Q_2(D)$; then there is a mapping, ϕ, from the variables of Q_2 to the constants in D such that

1. $\phi(\bar{Y}) = \bar{t}$, and
2. $h_i(\phi(\bar{Y}_i)) \in D$ for $1 \leq i \leq m$.

Now consider the composition mapping $\phi \circ \psi$ that maps the variables of Q_1 to constants in D (i.e., the mapping that first applies ψ and then applies ϕ to the result). Since ψ is a containment mapping, the following conditions, necessary to show that $\bar{t} \in Q_1(D)$, hold:

- $\phi \circ \psi(\bar{X}) = \bar{t}$ because $\psi(\bar{X}) = \bar{Y}$ and $\phi(\bar{Y}) = \bar{t}$.
- For every $1 \leq i \leq n$, $g_i(\psi(\bar{X}_i))$ is a subgoal of Q_2, and therefore $g_i(\phi \circ \psi(\bar{X}_i)) \in D$.

Therefore, $\bar{t} \in Q_1(D)$.

For the *only if* direction, assume that $Q_1 \sqsupseteq Q_2$, and we will show that there is a containment mapping from Q_1 to Q_2.

Let us consider a special database, D_C, that we call the *canonical database* of Q_2, and is constructed as follows. The constants in D_C are the variables or constants appearing in the body of Q_2. The tuples of D_C correspond to the subgoals of Q_2. That is, for every $1 \leq i \leq m$, the tuple $\bar{Y}_i$ is in the relation h_i.

Clearly, $\bar{Y} \in Q_2(D_C)$, simply by the definition of Q_2. Since $Q_1 \sqsupseteq Q_2$, $\bar{Y}$ must also be in $Q_1(D_C)$, and therefore there is a mapping ψ from the variables of Q_1 to the constants in Q_2 such that

- $\psi(\bar{X}) = \bar{Y}$, and
- for every $1 \leq i \leq n$, $g_i(\psi(\bar{X}_i)) \in D_C$.

It is easy to see that ψ is a containment mapping from Q_1 to Q_2.   □

The important aspect of the above proof is the concept of a canonical database. We were able to show that if $Q_1(D_C) \sqsupseteq Q_2(D_C)$, then containment holds on *any* database. Hence, we obtain Algorithm 1 for checking containment.

Algorithm 1. CQContainment: Query containment for conjunctive queries.

Input: conjunctive query Q_1; conjunctive query Q_2. **Output:** returns **true** if $Q_1 \sqsupseteq Q_2$.

    Let Q_1 be of the form $Q_1(\bar{X})$:- $g_1(\bar{X}_1), \ldots, g_n(\bar{X}_n)$

    Let Q_2 be of the form $Q_2(\bar{Y})$:- $h_1(\bar{Y}_1), \ldots, h_m(\bar{Y}_m)$

    // Freeze Q_2:

    Create a database D_C where the constants are the variables and constants in Q_2

    for every $1 \leq i \leq m$ **do**

        add the tuple $\bar{Y}_i$ to the relation h_i

    end for

    Evaluate Q_1 over D_C

    return true if and only if $\bar{X} \in Q_1(D_C)$.

■ ■ ■ ▬▬▬

Example 2.7

Recall the queries we considered earlier:

$Q_3'(X, Z)$:-   Flight(X, U), Hub(U), Flight(U, Y), Hub(W), Flight(W, Y), Flight(Y, Z)

$Q_4(X_1, Z_1)$:- Flight(X_1, U_1), Hub(U_1), Flight(U_1, Y_1), Flight(Y_1, Z_1)

The following containment mapping shows that $Q_3' \sqsupseteq Q_4$:

$$\{X \rightarrow X_1, Z \rightarrow Z_1, W \rightarrow U_1, Y \rightarrow Y_1\}$$

▬▬▬▬▬▬▬▬▬▬▬▬▬▬▬▬▬▬▬▬▬▬▬▬▬▬▬▬▬▬▬▬▬▬▬▬▬▬ ■ ■ ■

As we will see soon, a single canonical database will not always suffice as we consider queries with interpreted predicates or negation, but we will be able to remedy the situation by considering multiple canonical databases.

COMPUTATIONAL COMPLEXITY

Deciding whether $Q_1 \sqsupseteq Q_2$ is NP-complete in the size of the two queries. In practice, however, this is not a concern for multiple reasons. First, we are measuring the complexity in terms of the size of the queries, not the size of the data, and queries tend to be relatively small (though not always!). In fact, the algorithm above evaluates a query over an extremely small database. Second, in many practical cases, there are polynomial-time algorithms for containment. For example, if none of the database relations appears more than twice in the body of one of the queries, then it can be shown that containment can be checked in time that is polynomial in the size of the queries.

2.3.3 Unions of Conjunctive Queries

Next, we consider containment and equivalence of unions of conjunctive queries. Recall that unions are expressed as multiple rules with the same relation in the head.

■ ■ ■ ▬▬▬▬▬▬▬▬▬▬▬▬▬▬▬▬▬▬▬▬▬▬▬▬▬▬▬▬▬▬▬▬▬▬▬

Example 2.8

The following query asks for the pairs of cities that (1) are either connected by one-stop flight, or (2) both have a flight into the same hub.

$Q_1(X, Y)$:- Flight(X, Z), Flight(Z, Y)
$Q_1(X, Y)$:- Flight(X, Z), Flight(Y, Z), Hub(Z)

Suppose we want to decide whether the following query is contained in Q_1:

$Q_2(X, Y)$:- Flight(X, Z), Flight(Z, Y), Hub(Z)

▬▬▬▬▬▬▬▬▬▬▬▬▬▬▬▬▬▬▬▬▬▬▬▬▬▬▬▬▬▬▬ ■ ■ ■

The following theorem shows a very important property: if Q_2 is contained in Q_1, then there must be a single conjunctive query in Q_1 that contains Q_2 on its own. In other words, two conjunctive queries in Q_1 cannot "gang up" on Q_2.

Theorem 2.2. *Let* $Q_1 = Q_1^1 \cup \ldots \cup Q_1^n$ *be a union of conjunctive queries and let* Q_2 *be a conjunctive query. Then* $Q_1 \sqsupseteq Q_2$ *if and only if there is an* $1 \leq i \leq n$, *such that* $Q_1^i \sqsupseteq Q_2$. □

Proof. The *if* direction is obvious. If one of the conjunctive queries in Q_1 contains Q_2, then clearly $Q_1 \sqsupseteq Q_2$.

For the *only if* direction, we again consider the canonical database created by Q_2, D_C. Suppose the head of Q_2 is $\bar{Y}$. Since $Q_1 \sqsupseteq Q_2$, then $\bar{Y}$ should be in $Q_1(D_C)$, and therefore there is some $1 \leq i \leq n$, such that $\bar{Y} \in Q_1^i(D_C)$. It is easy to see that $Q_1^i \sqsupseteq Q_2$. □

In Example 2.8, containment holds because Q_2 is contained in the first rule defining Q_1.

An important corollary of Theorem 2.2 is that the algorithm for checking containment of queries with union is a slight variation on the previous algorithm. Specifically, we create a canonical database from the body of Q_2. If $\bar{X}$ is in the answer to Q_1 over the canonical database, then $Q_1 \sqsupseteq Q_2$. In the case that Q_2 is a union of conjunctive queries, $Q_1 \sqsupseteq Q_2$ if and only if Q_1 contains each of the conjunctive queries in Q_2. Hence, the complexity results for conjunctive queries transfer over to queries with unions.

2.3.4 Conjunctive Queries with Interpreted Predicates

We now consider conjunctive queries with interpreted predicates, which have the form:

$$Q(\bar{X}) :\!\text{-}\ R_1(\bar{X}_1), \ldots, R_n(\bar{X}_n), c_1, \ldots, c_m$$

where c_j's are *interpreted atoms* (we often call them *comparisons*), and are of the form $X\theta Y$, where X and Y are either variables or constants (but at least one of them must be a variable). The operator θ is an interpreted predicate such as $=, \leq, <, \neq, >$, or $\geq$. We assume the obvious meaning for the interpreted predicates, and unless otherwise stated, we interpret them over a dense domain.

Conjunctive queries allow conjunctions of interpreted atoms. In some of our reasoning, we will also manipulate Boolean formulas that include disjunctions. We use the standard notation for logical entailment. Specifically, if C is a Boolean formula over interpreted atoms, and c is an interpreted atom, then $C \models c$ means that any variable substitution that satisfies C also satisfies c. For example, $\{X \leq Y, Y \leq 5\} \models X \leq 5$, but $\{X \leq Y, Y \leq 5\} \not\models Y \leq 4$. Checking whether $C \models c$ can be done in time quadratic in the sizes of C and c.

The following definition extends the notion of containment mappings to queries with interpreted predicates.

Definition 2.3 (Containment Mapping with Interpreted Predicates). *Let Q_1 and Q_2 be conjunctive queries with interpreted atoms. Let C_1 (resp. C_2) be the conjunction of interpreted predicates in Q_1 (resp. Q_2). Let ψ be a variable mapping from Q_1 to Q_2. We say that ψ is a containment mapping from Q_1 to Q_2 if*

- *$\psi(\bar{X}) = \bar{Y}$, where $\bar{X}$ and $\bar{Y}$ are the head variables of Q_1 and Q_2, respectively,*
- *for every non-interpreted subgoal $g(\bar{X}_i)$ in the body of Q_1, $g(\psi(\bar{X}_i))$ is a subgoal of Q_2, and*
- *$C_2 \models \psi(C_1)$.* □

It is easy to verify that one direction of Theorem 2.1 extends to queries with interpreted predicates. That is, if there is a containment mapping from Q_1 to Q_2, then $Q_1 \sqsupseteq Q_2$. However, as the following example shows, the converse is not true.

■ ■ ■ ▬▬▬▬▬▬▬▬▬▬▬▬▬▬▬▬▬▬▬▬▬▬▬▬

Example 2.9

$Q_1(X, Y) :- R(X, Y), S(U, V), U \leq V$

$Q_2(X, Y) :- R(X, Y), S(U, V), S(V, U)$

It is easy to see that $Q_1 \sqsupseteq Q_2$ because in either alternative, $U \leq V$ or $U > V$, the S subgoal in Q_1 will be satisfied. However, there is no containment mapping with interpreted predicates from Q_1 to Q_2.

▬▬▬▬▬▬▬▬▬▬▬▬▬▬▬▬▬▬▬▬▬▬▬▬ ■ ■ ■

In fact, the reasoning that shows that $Q_1 \sqsupseteq Q_2$ in Example 2.9 is the key to developing a containment algorithm for conjunctive queries with interpreted predicates. In the example, suppose we rewrite Q_2 as the following union:

$Q_2(X, Y) :- R(X, Y), S(U, V), S(V, U), U \leq V$
$Q_2(X, Y) :- R(X, Y), S(U, V), S(V, U), U > V$

Now it is fairly easy to verify using containment mappings that Q_1 contains each of the two conjunctive queries in Q_2. The following discussion will make this intuition precise.

We first introduce *complete orderings* that are refinements of a set of conjunctive comparison atoms. Specifically, a conjunction of comparison predicates, C, may still only specify partial knowledge about the orderings of the variables in C. For example, $\{X \geq 5, Y \leq 8\}$ does not entail $X \leq Y$, $X \geq Y$, or $X = Y$. The complete orderings originating from C are the sets of comparisons that are consistent with C, but also completely determine all the order relations between pairs of variables. Naturally, there are multiple complete orderings consistent with a given conjunction, C.

Definition 2.4 (Complete Ordering and Query Refinements). *Let Q be a conjunctive query whose variables are $\bar{X} = X_1, \ldots, X_n$ and mentioning the constants $\bar{A} = a_1, \ldots, a_m$. Let C be the conjunction of interpreted atoms in Q. A complete ordering C_T on the variables $\bar{X}$ is a satisfiable conjunction of interpreted predicates, such that $C_T \models C$ and for every pair d_1, d_2, where $d_1, d_2 \in \bar{X} \cup \bar{A}$, one of the following holds:*

- $C_T \models d_1 < d_2$,
- $C_T \models d_1 > d_2$,
- $C_T \models d_1 = d_2$.

Given a conjunctive query

$Q(\bar{X}) :- R_1(\bar{X}_1), \ldots, R_n(\bar{X}_n), C$

let $c^1, \ldots, c^l$ be the complete orderings of the variables and constants in Q. Then

$$Q^1(\bar{X}) :\text{-} R_1(\bar{X}_1), \ldots, R_n(\bar{X}_n), c^1$$

$$\vdots$$

$$Q^l(\bar{X}) :\text{-} R_1(\bar{X}_1), \ldots, R_n(\bar{X}_n), c^l$$

are the complete query refinements of Q. Note that $Q \equiv Q^1 \cup \ldots \cup Q^l$.   □

To check that Q_1 contains Q_2, we need to find a containment mapping from Q_1 to each of the complete query refinements of Q_2. The following theorem states this intuition formally.

Theorem 2.3. *Let Q_1 and Q_2 be two conjunctive queries with interpreted predicates. Let $Q_2^1, \ldots, Q_2^l$ be the complete query refinements of Q_2. $Q_1 \sqsupseteq Q_2$ if and only if for every $1 \le i \le l$ there is a containment mapping from Q_1 to Q_2^i.*   □

Proof. The *if* direction is rather obvious since $Q \equiv Q^1 \cup \ldots \cup Q^l$ and because containment mappings are a sufficient condition for containment even with interpreted predicates.

For the *only if* direction, consider l canonical databases, $C_D^1, \ldots, C_D^l$, each constructed as before, except that the constants in C_D^i are rational numbers that satisfy the interpreted predicates in Q_2^i. Let t_i be an answer derived by Q_2^i from C_D^i. Since $Q_1 \sqsupseteq Q_2$, then $t_i \in Q_1(C_D^i)$. A similar argument to the proof of Theorem 2.1 shows that there is a containment mapping from Q_1 to Q_2^i.   □

The practical problem with the algorithm implied by Theorem 2.3 is that the number of complete query refinements of Q_2 can be quite large. In fact, the number of refinements can be exponential in the size of Q_2. Recall that the number of refinements corresponds to all the different orderings on constants and variables appearing in the query. As a result, the computational complexity of checking containment for conjunctive queries with interpreted predicates is Σ_2^p-complete, which is the class of problems described by formulas of the form $\forall X \exists Y P(X, Y)$, where P is a condition that can be verified in polynomial time. Here, X ranges over the set of refinements, Y ranges over the set of variable mappings, and P verifies that the variable mapping is a containment mapping.

Fortunately, in practice we do not need to consider all possible refinements of Q_2. Algorithm 2 describes, **CQIPContainment**, a more efficient algorithm for query containment with interpreted predicates.

Applying algorithm **CQIPContainment** to our example, we would evaluate Q_1 on the database D_C that contains the tuples $\mathbf{R}(X, Y), \mathbf{S}(U, V), \mathbf{S}(V, U)$. $Q_1(D_C)$ would contain the following pairs: $((X, Y), U \le V), ((X, Y), U \ge V)$. Hence, $C = U \le V \vee U \ge V = \textit{True}$. Since $C_2 = \textit{True}$, we get $C_2 \models C$, and therefore $Q_1 \sqsupseteq Q_2$.

2.3.5 Conjunctive Queries with Negation

Next, we consider queries with negation that have the following form:

$$Q(\bar{X}) :\text{-} R_1(\bar{X}_1), \ldots, R_n(\bar{X}_n), \neg S_1(\bar{Y}_1), \ldots, \neg S_m(\bar{Y}_m)$$

Algorithm 2. CQIPContainment: Query containment for conjunctive queries with interpreted predicates.

Input: conjunctive query Q_1; conjunctive query Q_2. **Output:** returns **true** if $Q_1 \sqsupseteq Q_2$.

Let Q_1 be of the form $Q_1(\bar{X}) :\text{-} g_1(\bar{X}_1), \ldots, g_n(\bar{X}_n)$

Let Q_2 be of the form $Q_2(\bar{Y}) :\text{-} h_1(\bar{Y}_1), \ldots, h_m(\bar{Y}_m)$

// Freeze Q_2:

Create a database D_C where the constants are the variables and constants in Q_2

for every $1 \leq i \leq m$ **do**

  add the tuple $\bar{Y}_i$ to the relation h_i

end for

Evaluate $Q_1'(\bar{X}) : -g_1(\bar{X}_1), \ldots, g_n(\bar{X}_n)$ over D_C

Every tuple in $Q_1'(D_C)$ can be described as a pair $(t, \phi(C_1))$, where ϕ is the variable mapping from Q_1' to D_C that satisfied all the subgoals of Q_1'

Let $C = c_1 \vee \ldots \vee c_k$, where $(\bar{Y}, c_1), \ldots, (\bar{Y}, c_k)$ are all the tuples in $Q_1'(D_C)$ with $\bar{Y}$ as their first component

return $Q_1 \sqsupseteq Q_2$ if and only if (1) there is at least one tuple of the form $(\bar{Y}, c) \in Q_1'(D_C)$ and (2) $C_2 \models C$

We require that the queries be *safe*, i.e., that any variable appearing in the head of the query also appear in a positive subgoal. For ease of exposition, we consider queries without interpreted predicates.

The natural extension of containment mappings to queries with negation ensures that positive subgoals are mapped to positive subgoals and negative subgoals are mapped to negative subgoals. The following theorem shows that containment mappings offer a sufficient condition for containment. We leave the proof to the reader, as it is an extension of the proof of Theorem 2.1.

Theorem 2.4. *Let Q_1 and Q_2 be safe conjunctive queries with negated subgoals. If there is a containment mapping ψ from Q_1 to Q_2 such that ψ maps the positive subgoals of Q_1 to positive subgoals of Q_2 and maps the negative subgoals of Q_1 to negative subgoals of Q_2, then $Q_1 \sqsupseteq Q_2$.* □

Here, too, containment mappings do not provide a necessary condition for containment. It is actually quite tricky to find an example where containment holds but there is no containment mapping, but the following example illustrates this case.

■ ■ ■ ▬▬▬▬▬▬▬▬▬▬▬▬▬▬▬▬▬▬▬▬▬▬▬▬▬▬▬▬▬

Example 2.10

Consider the queries Q_1 and Q_2. Note that they do not have head variables, and are therefore Boolean queries—they return true or false.

$Q_1() :\text{-} a(\mathsf{A}, \mathsf{B}), a(\mathsf{C}, \mathsf{D}), \neg a(\mathsf{B}, \mathsf{C})$

$Q_2() :\text{-} a(\mathsf{X}, \mathsf{Y}), a(\mathsf{Y}, \mathsf{Z}), \neg a(\mathsf{X}, \mathsf{Z})$

A little bit of thought will show that $Q_1 \sqsupseteq Q_2$; however, there is no containment mapping from Q_1 to Q_2.

∎ ∎ ∎

Recall that in the previous cases, the key to proving containment was to consider a very special canonical database (or set of databases). If containment was satisfied on all canonical databases, then we were able to derive that containment holds on *all* databases. In the case of queries with negated subgoals, the key to proving containment is to show that we only need to consider databases of a certain size.

Theorem 2.5. *Let Q_1 and Q_2 be two conjunctive queries with safe negated subgoals and assume they mention disjoint sets of variables. Let B be the total number of variables and constants in Q_2. Then, $Q_1 \sqsupseteq Q_2$ if and only if $Q_1(D) \supseteq Q_2(D)$ on all databases D that have at most B constants.*   □

Proof. Let Q_1 and Q_2 be of the following form (we omit the variables in the subgoals):

$$Q_1(\bar{X}) :\text{-} \ p_1, \ldots, p_n, \neg r_1, \ldots, \neg r_l$$
$$Q_2(\bar{Y}) :\text{-} \ q_1, \ldots, p_m, \neg s_1, \ldots, \neg s_k$$

The *only if* direction is obvious, so we consider the *if* direction. Suppose $Q_1 \not\sqsupseteq Q_2$. It suffices to show that there is a counterexample database with at most B constants.

Since $Q_1 \not\sqsupseteq Q_2$, there must exist a database D, a tuple $\bar{t}$, and a mapping ϕ from the variables of Q_2 to the constants in D, such that (1) $\phi(\bar{Y}) = \bar{t}$, (2) $\phi(q_i) \in D$, for $1 \leq i \leq m$, (3) $\phi(s_1), \ldots, \phi(s_k) \notin D$ for $1 \leq i \leq k$, and (4) $\bar{t} \notin Q_1(D)$.

Consider the database D' that includes only the tuples from D that either have only constants in the range of ϕ or have constants from Q_2.

First, we argue that $\bar{t} \in Q_2(D')$. This follows from the construction of D'. The range of ϕ is unaffected, and therefore the positive atoms that contributed to deriving $\bar{t}$ are in D' and the negative atoms certainly hold because D' is a subset of D. Hence, (2) and (3) above still hold. In fact, the same argument shows that $\bar{t} \in Q_2(D'')$ for any database D'' such that $D' \subseteq D'' \subseteq D$.

Second, we argue that we can build a database D'', where $D' \subseteq D'' \subseteq D$ and D'' is a counterexample. Furthermore, the number of constants in D'' is at most B. Note that the number of constants in D' is bounded by B.

Let us consider two cases. In the first case, there was no mapping, ψ, from the variables of Q_1 to D, such that $\psi(p_i) \in D$ for $1 \leq i \leq n$. In this case, there certainly is no such mapping from Q_1 to D', and therefore D' is a counterexample because $\bar{t} \notin Q_1(D')$.

In the second case, there may be mappings from the variables of Q_1 to D' that satisfy its positive subgoals. We construct D'' as following, after initializing it to D'.

Let ψ be a mapping from the variables of Q_1 to D', such that $\psi(p_i) \in D'$ for $1 \leq i \leq n$. There must be a j, $1 \leq j \leq l$, such that $\psi(r_j) \in D$. Otherwise, $\bar{t}$ would be in the answer to $Q_1(D)$. We add $\psi(r_j)$ to D'', and therefore ψ is no longer a variable mapping that would lead to $\bar{t}$ being in $Q_1(D'')$. Note that adding $\psi(r_j)$ to D'' did not change the number of constants in D'' because all the variables that occur in r_j must occur in one of the p_i's.

Since the number of tuples we may add to D'' in this way is bounded, we will ultimately not be able to add any more tuples. The database D'' has at most B constants, and $\bar{t} \notin Q_1(D'')$. Hence, D'' is a counterexample, establishing the theorem.   □

Theorem 2.5 entails that it suffices to check that containment holds on all databases with up to B constants (up to isomorphism). Since there are a finite number of such databases, we can conclude that query containment is decidable. In what follows we describe a strategy that is more efficient than naively enumerating all possible such databases.

Let C denote the variables appearing in Q_2. We construct a set of canonical databases whose constants are C. Intuitively, each canonical database corresponds to a set of equality constraints applied to the elements of C (in the same spirit of refinements in Section 2.3.4, but considering only the = predicate).

Formally, in each canonical database we apply a partition to elements of C. A partition of C maps the constants in C to a set of equivalence classes and applies a homomorphism to C where each constant is mapped to a unique representative of its equivalence class. Let k be the number of possible partitions of C, and ϕ_k the homomorphism associated with the kth partition. We create databases $D_1, \ldots, D_k$, where the database D_i includes the tuples $\phi_k(q_1), \ldots, \phi_k(q_m)$. For each D_i we construct a set of databases $\mathcal{D}_i$ as follows:

- If the body of Q_2 is not satisfied by D_i, we set $\mathcal{D}_i$ to be the empty set. Note that D_i may not satisfy the body of Q_2 because a negative subgoal of Q_2 may not be satisfied.
- If the body of Q_2 is satisfied by D_i, then $\mathcal{D}_i$ is the set of canonical databases that can be constructed from D_i as follows:
  - Add any subset of tuples to D_i that includes only constants from D_i, but do not add the $\phi_i(s_1), \ldots, \phi_i(s_k)$.

The containment $Q_1 \sqsupseteq Q_2$ holds if and only if for every i, $1 \leq i \leq k$ and for every $D \in \mathcal{D}_i$, $\phi_i(\bar{X}) \in Q_1(D)$.

■ ■ ■ ▬▬▬▬▬▬▬▬▬▬▬▬▬▬▬▬▬▬▬▬▬▬▬▬▬▬▬▬

Example 2.11

We illustrate the containment algorithm on the queries in Example 2.10. Q_2 includes four constants, A, B, C, and D.

We first consider the partition in which all variables in Q_2 are equated, yielding the database $D_1 = \{a(A, A)\}$. The body of Q_2 is not satisfied on D_1 because the negative subgoal is not satisfied. Hence, $\mathcal{D}_1$ is the empty set and containment holds trivially.

Now consider the other extreme, the partition in which each variable is in its own equivalence class, yielding the database $D_2 = \{a(A, B), a(C, D)\}$. Since Q_2 is satisfied in D_2, $\mathcal{D}_2$ includes any database that can be constructed by adding tuples to D_2 that have the constants A, B, C, and D, but *not* the atom $a(B, C)$. A case-by-case analysis verifies that Q_1 is satisfied in every database in $\mathcal{D}_2$.

In the same fashion, the reader can verify containment holds when we consider the other partitions of the variables in Q_2.

■ ■ ■

COMPUTATIONAL COMPLEXITY

The computational complexity of checking containment for conjunctive queries with negated subgoals is Σ_2^p-complete, which is the class of problems described by formulas of the form $\forall X \exists Y P(X, Y)$, where P is a condition that can be verified in polynomial time. Here, X ranges over the set of canonical databases $\mathcal{D}_1, \ldots, \mathcal{D}_k$, Y ranges over the set of variable mappings, and P is the function that verifies that the variable mapping is a containment mapping.

2.3.6 Bag Semantics, Grouping, and Aggregation

SQL queries operate, by default, on bags (multi-sets) of tuples, rather than sets of tuples. Answers to queries in SQL are also bags by default, unless the DISTINCT keyword is used. The key difference in bag semantics is that we also count the number of times a tuple appears in a relation (either the input or the result of a query). We refer to that number as the tuple's *multiplicity*. For example, consider the following query over the table in Figure 2.2:

$Q_1(X, Y) :- \text{Flight}(X, Z, W), \text{Flight}(Z, Y, W_1)$

Under set semantics, the answer to Q_1 would contain a single tuple (San Francisco, Anchorage). Under bag semantics, the tuple (San Francisco, Anchorage) appears in the answer with multiplicity 2, because there are two pairs of flights that connect San Francisco with Anchorage.

The topic of query containment and equivalence for queries with bag semantics is quite involved. Query containment and equivalence for queries with grouping and aggregation depend heavily on our understanding of containment for bags. This section gives an overview of the issues and some of the results known in this area.

To discuss containment of queries with aggregation, we first need to modify the definition of containment slightly to account for the different semantics. Specifically, we say that $Q_1 \sqsupseteq Q_2$ with bag semantics if for any database D and for any tuple $\bar{t}$, the multiplicity of $\bar{t}$ in

Flight

Origin	Destination	DepartureTime
San Francisco	Seattle	8AM
San Francisco	Seattle	10AM
Seattle	Anchorage	1PM

FIGURE 2.2 A simple flight table that illustrates the difference between set and bag semantics.

$Q_1(D)$ is at least as much as the multiplicity of $\bar{t}$ in $Q_2(D)$. As before, $Q_1 \equiv Q_2$ are equivalent if $Q_1 \sqsubseteq Q_2$ and $Q_2 \sqsubseteq Q_1$.

■ ■ ■ ▬▬▬▬▬▬▬▬▬▬▬▬▬▬▬▬▬▬▬▬▬▬▬▬▬▬▬▬▬▬▬▬▬▬▬▬

Example 2.12

As a trivial example showing that equivalence under set semantics does not imply equivalence under bag semantics, consider the following two queries:

$Q_1(X) :- P(X)$
$Q_2(X) :- P(X), P(X)$

Suppose an instance of P has n occurrences of a constant d. Then the result of Q_2 would contain n^2 occurrences of d, while Q_1 would only contain n occurrences of d. Hence, while Q_1 and Q_2 are equivalent under set semantics, they are not equivalent under bag semantics.

▬▬▬▬▬▬▬▬▬▬▬▬▬▬▬▬▬▬▬▬▬▬▬▬▬▬▬▬▬▬▬▬▬▬▬ ■ ■ ■

Query containment for conjunctive queries without interpreted predicates and without negation is not even known to be decidable. Furthermore, it is known that when interpreted predicates are allowed or when unions are allowed, query containment is undecidable. There is more known on query equivalence. In fact, the following theorem states that for two conjunctive queries to be bag-equivalent, they need to be isomorphic to each other. The bibliographic notes include a reference to the proofs of the theorems in this section.

Theorem 2.6. *Let Q_1 and Q_2 be conjunctive queries. Then, Q_1 and Q_2 are bag-equivalent if and only if there is a 1-1 containment mapping (i.e., isomorphism) from Q_1 to Q_2.*   □

QUERIES WITH GROUPING AND AGGREGATION

Conditions for equivalence for queries with grouping and aggregation highly depend on the specific aggregation function in the query. Some aggregation functions are sensitive to multiplicities (e.g., Average and Count), while others are not (e.g., Max and Min). The following are two examples of where precise conditions are known for equivalence of such queries.

COUNT QUERIES

These queries are of the form

$$Q(\bar{X}, count(\bar{Y})) :- R_1(\bar{X}_1), \ldots, R_n(\bar{X}_n)$$

The query computes the table specified by the body subgoals, groups the results by the variables in $\bar{X}$, and for every group outputs the number of different values for $\bar{Y}$.

The following theorem shows that count queries are sensitive to multiplicities. The theorem can be extended to queries with interpreted predicates using the concept of complete orderings we introduced earlier.

Theorem 2.7. *Let Q_1 and Q_2 be two count queries. The equivalence $Q_1 \equiv Q_2$ holds if and only if there is a variable mapping ψ from the variables of Q_1 to the variables of Q_2 that* *induces an isomorphism between the bodies of Q_1 and Q_2 and an isomorphism between the heads of Q_1 and Q_2.*   □

MAX QUERIES

It can be shown that max queries are *not* sensitive to multiplicities. A max query has the form

$$Q(\bar{X}, \mathsf{max}(Y)) :\text{-} R_1(\bar{X}_1), \ldots, R_n(\bar{X}_n)$$

The query computes the table specified by the body subgoals, groups the results by the variables in $\bar{X}$, and for every group outputs the maximum value of the variable Y. We define the *core* of a max query to be the query where the variable Y appears in the head without the aggregation function, i.e.,

$$Q(\bar{X}, Y) :\text{-} R_1(\bar{X}_1), \ldots, R_n(\bar{X}_n)$$

The following theorem establishes the property of max queries:

Theorem 2.8. *Let Q_1 and Q_2 be two max queries with no comparison predicates. The equivalence $Q_1 \equiv Q_2$ holds if and only if the core of Q_1 is equivalent to the core of Q_2.*   □

■ ■ ■ ▬▬

Example 2.13

The following example shows that Theorem 2.8 does not apply to queries with interpreted predicates.

$$Q_1(\mathsf{max}(Y)) :\text{-} \mathsf{p}(Y), \mathsf{P}(Z_1), \mathsf{p}(Z_2), Z_1 < Z_2$$
$$Q_2(\mathsf{max}(Y)) :\text{-} \mathsf{p}(Y), \mathsf{P}(Z), Z < Y$$

Both queries return answers if P contains at least two different constants. However, while Q_1 considers all tuples in P, Q_2 considers all the tuples except for the one with the smallest value. Hence, the maximum value is always the same (and hence, $Q_1 \equiv Q_2$), but the cores are not equivalent. Fortunately, there is a more elaborate condition for checking containment of max queries with interpreted predicates (see the bibliographic references for more details).

▬▬▬▬▬▬▬▬▬▬▬▬▬▬▬▬▬▬▬▬▬▬▬▬▬▬▬▬▬▬▬▬▬▬▬▬▬ ■ ■ ■

2.4 Answering Queries Using Views

In the previous section we described query containment, which is a fundamental relationship between a pair of queries. One of the important uses of query containment is that when we detect that a query Q_1 is contained in a query Q_2, we can often compute the answer to Q_1 from the answer to Q_2. In this section we are interested in the more general problem of when we can answer a query Q from a collection of views. The following example illustrates our goal.

■ ■ ■ ▬▬

Example 2.14

Consider the familiar movie domain with the following relations. In the relations, the first argument is a numerical ID of the movies in the database.

Movie(ID, title, year, genre)
Director(ID, director)
Actor(ID, actor)

Suppose a user poses the following query, asking for comedies produced after 1950 where the director was also an actor in the movie:

$Q(T, Y, D)$:- Movie(I, T, Y, G), $Y \geq 1950$, G="comedy", Director(I, D), Actor(I, D)

Suppose that, in addition, we have access to the following view over the database:

$V_1(T, Y, D)$:- Movie(I, T, Y, G), $Y \geq 1940$, G="comedy", Director(I, D), Actor(I, D)

Since the selection on year in V_1 is less restrictive than in Q, we can infer that $V_1 \sqsupseteq Q$. Since the year attribute is in the head of V_1, we can use V_1 to answer Q simply by adding another selection:

$Q'(T, Y, D)$:- $V_1(T, Y, D)$, $Y \geq 1950$

Answering Q using V_1 is likely to be more efficient than answering Q_1 directly from the database, because we do not need to perform the join operations in Q. However, suppose that instead of V_1 we only had access to the following views:

$V_2(I, T, Y)$:- Movie(I, T, Y, G), $Y \geq 1950$, G="comedy"
$V_3(I, D)$:- Director(I, D), Actor(I, D)

Neither V_2 nor V_3 contain Q, and therefore the same reasoning as above does not apply. However, we can still answer Q using V_2 and V_3 as follows, also leading to a more efficient evaluation plan in many cases:

$Q''(T, Y, D)$:- $V_2(I, T, Y)$, $V_3(I, D)$

■ ■ ■

The example above illustrates that deciding whether a query can be answered from a set of precomputed views is a more general problem than query containment, because we need to consider *combinations* of views. In data integration, such combinations will be quite important because we will consider combinations of data sources, each corresponding to a view, to answer a user query. This section describes algorithms for answering queries using views and provides a deeper understanding for when views can be used and when not.

2.4.1 Problem Definition

We begin by formally defining the problem of answering queries using views. Throughout this section we assume that we are given a set of views denoted as $V_1, \ldots, V_m$. Unless stated otherwise, we will assume that the language for specifying the query and the views is conjunctive queries.

Given a query Q and a set of view definitions $V_1, \ldots, V_m$, a rewriting of the query using the views is a query expression Q' that refers *only* to the views $V_1, \ldots, V_m$. In SQL, a query refers only to the views if all the relations mentioned in the FROM clause are views. In the notation of conjunctive queries, a query refers only to the views if all the subgoals are views with the exception of interpreted atoms. In practice, we may also be interested in rewritings that can also refer to the database relations, but all the algorithms we describe in this section can easily be extended to that case.

The most natural question to pose is whether there is an *equivalent* rewriting of the query that uses the views.

Definition 2.5 (Equivalent Query Rewritings).   *Let Q be a query and $V = \{V_1, \ldots, V_m\}$ be a set of view definitions. The query Q' is an equivalent rewriting of Q using V if*

* *Q' refers only to the views in V, and*
* *Q' is equivalent to Q.* $\square$

For example, the query Q'' in Example 2.14 is an equivalent rewriting of Q using V_2 and V_3. Note that when we consider the equivalence between a query Q and a rewriting Q', we actually need to consider the unfolding of Q' w.r.t. the views.

There may not always be an equivalent rewriting of the query using a set of views, and we may want to know what is the *best* we can do with a set of views. For example, suppose that instead of V_2 in Example 2.14, we had the following view that includes comedies produced after 1960:

$V_4(I,T,Y)$:- Movie(I,T,Y,G), $Y \geq 1960$, G="comedy"

While we can't use V_4 to completely answer Q_1, the following rewriting is the best we can do and may be our only choice if we do not have access to any other data:

$Q'''(T,Y,D)$:- $V_4(I,T,Y)$, $V_3(I,D)$

Q''' is called a *maximally contained* rewriting of Q using V_3 and V_4. Intuitively, Q''' is the best conjunctive query that uses the views to answer the query. If we also have the following view:

$V_5(I,T,Y)$:- Movie(PI,T,Y,G), $Y \geq 1950$, $Y \leq 1955$, G="comedy"

then we can construct a union of conjunctive queries that is the best rewriting we can find.

The following definition makes these intuitions precise. To define maximally contained rewritings, we first need to specify the exact language we consider for rewritings (e.g., do we allow unions, interpreted predicates?). If we restrict or otherwise change the language of the rewriting, the maximally contained rewriting may change. In the definition below, the query language is denoted by $\mathcal{L}$.

Definition 2.6 (Maximally Contained Rewritings).   *Let Q be a query, $V = \{V_1, \ldots, V_m\}$ be a set of view definitions, and $\mathcal{L}$ be a query language. The query Q' is a maximally contained rewriting of Q using V w.r.t. $\mathcal{L}$ if*

- Q' *is a query in* $\mathcal{L}$ *that refers only to the views in* $\mathcal{V}$,
- Q' *is contained in* Q, *and*
- *there is no rewriting* $Q_1 \in \mathcal{L}$, *such that* $Q' \sqsubseteq Q_1 \sqsubseteq Q$ *and* Q_1 *is not equivalent to* Q'.   □

When a rewriting Q' is contained in Q but is not a maximally contained rewriting we refer to it as a contained rewriting.

■ ■ ■ ▬▬▬▬▬▬▬▬▬▬▬▬▬▬▬▬▬▬▬▬▬▬▬▬▬▬▬▬▬▬▬▬▬▬▬

Example 2.15

If we consider the language of the rewriting to be unions of conjunctive queries, the following is the maximally contained rewriting of Q:

$Q^{(4)}(\mathsf{T},\mathsf{Y},\mathsf{D})$:- $V_4(\mathsf{I},\mathsf{T},\mathsf{Y})$, $V_3(\mathsf{I},\mathsf{D})$
$Q^{(4)}(\mathsf{T},\mathsf{Y},\mathsf{D})$:- $V_5(\mathsf{I},\mathsf{T},\mathsf{Y})$, $V_3(\mathsf{I},\mathsf{D})$

If we restrict $\mathcal{L}$ to be conjunctive queries, then either of the two rules defining $\mathbf{Q}^{(4)}$ would be a maximally contained rewriting. This example illustrates that the maximally contained rewriting need not be unique.

▬▬▬▬▬▬▬▬▬▬▬▬▬▬▬▬▬▬▬▬▬▬▬▬▬▬▬▬▬▬▬▬▬▬▬ ■ ■ ■

The algorithms for finding equivalent rewritings differ a bit from those for finding maximally contained rewritings. As we explain in Chapter 3, in the context of data integration, views describe the contents of the data sources. However, the sources may be incomplete and not contain all the data conforming to their descriptions. In addition, the sources together may not cover the entire domain of interest. In the rest of this chapter, unless otherwise mentioned, our goal is to find a union of conjunctive queries that is the maximally contained rewriting of a conjunctive query using a set of conjunctive views.

2.4.2 When Is a View Relevant to a Query?

Informally, a few conditions need to hold in order for a view to be useful for answering a query. First, the set of relations the view mentions should overlap with that of the query. Second, if the query applies predicates to attributes that it has in common with the view, then the view must apply either equivalent or logically weaker predicates in order to be part of an equivalent rewriting. If the view applies a logically stronger predicate, it may be part of a contained rewriting.

The following example illustrates some of the subtleties in answering queries using views. Specifically, it shows how small modifications to the views render them useless for answering a given query.

■ ■ ■ ▬▬▬▬▬▬▬▬▬▬▬▬▬▬▬▬▬▬▬▬▬▬▬▬▬▬▬▬▬▬▬▬▬▬▬

Example 2.16

Consider the following views:

$V_6(\mathsf{T},\mathsf{Y})$:- Movie$(\mathsf{I},\mathsf{T},\mathsf{Y},\mathsf{G})$, $\mathsf{Y} \geq 1950$, G="comedy"
$V_7(\mathsf{I},\mathsf{T},\mathsf{Y})$:- Movie$(\mathsf{I},\mathsf{T},\mathsf{Y},\mathsf{G})$, $\mathsf{Y} \geq 1950$, G="comedy", Award(I,W)

$V_8(I,T)$:- Movie(I,T,Y,G), $Y \geq 1940$, G="comedy"

V_6 is similar to V_1, except that it does not include the ID attribute of the Movie table in the head, and therefore we cannot perform the join with V_2. The view V_7 considers only the comedies produced in or after 1950 that also won at least one award. Hence, the view applies an additional condition that does not exist in the query and cannot be used in an equivalent rewriting. Note, however, that if we have an integrity constraint stating that every movie wins an award (unlikely, unfortunately), then V_7 would actually be usable. Finally, view V_8 applies a weaker predicate on the year than in the query, but the year is not included in the head. Therefore, the rewriting cannot apply the appropriate predicate on the year.

■ ■ ■

The next few sections will give precise conditions and efficient algorithms for answering queries using views.

2.4.3 The Possible Length of a Rewriting

Before we discuss specific algorithms for rewriting queries using views, a first question we may ask is: What is the space of possible rewritings we even need to consider? We now describe a fundamental result that shows that if a conjunctive query has n subgoals, then we need not consider query rewritings that have more than n subgoals. This result enables us to focus on the set of rewritings that have at most n subgoals, and find efficient ways of searching this set.

Theorem 2.9. *Let Q and $\mathcal{V} = \{V_1, \ldots, V_m\}$ be conjunctive queries without comparison predicates or negation, and let n be the number of subgoals in Q.*

- *If there is an equivalent conjunctive rewriting of Q using $\mathcal{V}$, then there is one with at most n subgoals.*
- *If Q' is a contained conjunctive rewriting of Q using $\mathcal{V}$, and has more than n subgoals, then there is a conjunctive rewriting Q'', such that $Q \sqsupseteq Q'' \sqsupseteq Q'$, and Q'' has at most n subgoals.* □

Proof. Let the query be of the form

$$Q(\bar{A}) :- e_1(\bar{A}_1), \ldots, e_n(A_n)$$

and suppose that

$$Q'(\bar{X}) :- v_1(\bar{X}_1), \ldots, v_m(X_m)$$

is an equivalent rewriting of Q using $\mathcal{V}$, where the v_i's are subgoals referring to view relations, and that $m > n$. Let the unfolding of Q' w.r.t. the view definitions be

$$\begin{aligned}
Q'_u(\bar{X}) :- \ & e_1^1(\bar{X}_1^1), \ldots, e_1^{j_1}(\bar{X}_1^{j_1}), \\
& e_2^1(\bar{X}_2^1), \ldots, e_2^{j_2}(\bar{X}_2^{j_2}), \\
& \vdots \\
& e_m^1(\bar{X}_m^1), \ldots, e_m^{j_m}(\bar{X}_m^{j_m})
\end{aligned}$$

Note that Q'_u is equivalent to Q'. Since $Q \sqsupseteq Q'$, there must be a containment mapping from Q to Q'_u. Let the containment mapping from Q to Q'_u be ψ. Since Q has only n subgoals, the image of ψ can only be present in at most n rows of the definition of Q'_u. Let us assume without loss of generality that these are the first k rows, where $k \leq n$. Now consider the rewriting Q'' that has only the first k subgoals of Q'. The containment mapping ψ still establishes that $Q \sqsupseteq Q''$, and since Q'' has a subset of the subgoals of Q', then clearly $Q'' \sqsupseteq Q'$, and hence $Q'' \sqsupseteq Q$. Consequently, $Q \equiv Q''$, and Q'' has at most n subgoals. The proof of the second part of the theorem is almost identical. □

Theorem 2.9 yields a first naive algorithm for finding a rewriting of a query given a set of views. Specifically, there are a finite number of rewritings of length at most n subgoals using a set of views $\mathcal{V}$, because there are a finite number of variable patterns we can consider for each view. Hence, to find an equivalent rewriting, the algorithm can proceed as follows:

- Guess a rewriting Q' of Q that has at most n subgoals.
- Check if $Q' \equiv Q$.

Similarly, the union of all rewritings Q' of length at most n subgoals, such that $Q' \sqsubseteq Q$ is a maximally contained rewriting of Q.

This algorithm shows that finding an equivalent rewriting of a conjunctive query using a set of conjunctive views is in NP. In fact, it can be shown that the problem is also NP-hard, and therefore NP-complete. Employing this algorithm is impractical because it means enumerating all possible rewritings of length at most n subgoals and checking equivalence of these rewritings to the query. The next sections describe algorithms for finding a maximally contained rewriting that are efficient in practice.

2.4.4 The Bucket and MiniCon Algorithms

This section describes two algorithms, the Bucket Algorithm and the MiniCon Algorithm, that drastically reduce the number of rewritings we need to consider for a query given a set of views. Broadly speaking, the algorithms first determine a set of view atoms that are *relevant* to each subgoal, and then consider only the combinations of these view atoms. The MiniCon Algorithm goes a step further and also considers some *interactions* between view subgoals, therefore further reducing the number of combinations that need to be considered.

The Bucket Algorithm

The main idea underlying the Bucket Algorithm is that the number of query rewritings that need to be considered can be drastically reduced if we first consider each subgoal in the query in isolation, and determine which views may be relevant to that subgoal. As we discuss later, the Bucket Algorithm is not guaranteed to find all the maximally contained rewritings. However, since the reduction in the number of rewritings is best illustrated when the query and views include interpreted predicates, we use them in our algorithm description and example.

The first step of the algorithm is shown in Algorithm 3. The algorithm constructs for each subgoal g in the query a bucket of relevant view atoms. A view atom is relevant if one of its subgoals can play the role of g in the rewriting. To do that, several conditions must be satisfied: (1) the view subgoal should be over the same relation as g, (2) the interpreted predicates of the view and the query are mutually satisfiable after the appropriate substitution is made, and (3) if g includes a head variable of the query, then the corresponding variable in V must also be a head variable in the view.

Algorithm 3. CreateBuckets: Creating the buckets.

Input: conjunctive query Q of the form $Q(\bar{X}) : -R_1(\bar{X}_1), \ldots, R_n(\bar{X}_n), c_1, \ldots, c_l$; a set of conjunctive views $\mathcal{V}$. **Output:** list of buckets.

for $1 \le i \le n$ **do**
    Initialize $Bucket_i$ to $\emptyset$
end for
for $i = 1, \ldots, n$ **do**
    for each $V \in \mathcal{V}$ **do**
        Let V be of the form: $V(\bar{Y}) : -S_1(\bar{Y}_1), \ldots, S_m(\bar{Y}_m), d_1, \ldots, d_k$
        for $j = 1, \ldots, m$ **do**
            if $R_i = S_j$ **then**
                // Let ψ be the mapping defined on the variables of V as follows:
                Let y be the bth variable in $\bar{Y}_j$ and x be the bth variable in $\bar{X}_i$
                if $x \in \bar{X}$ and $y \notin \bar{Y}$ **then**
                    ψ is undefined and move to the next j
                else if $y \in \bar{Y}$ **then**
                    $\psi(y) = x$
                else
                    $\psi(y)$ is a new variable that does not appear in Q or V
                end if
                // Let Q' be the query defined as follows:
                $Q' : -R_1(\bar{X}_1), \ldots, R_n(\bar{X}_n), c_1, \ldots, c_l, S_1(\psi(\bar{Y}_1)), \ldots, S_m(\psi(\bar{Y}_m)), \psi(d_1), \ldots, \psi(d_k)$
                if Q' is satisfiable **then**
                    Add $\psi(V)$ to $Bucket_i$
                end if
            end if
        end for
    end for
end for
return $Bucket_1, \ldots, Bucket_n$

The second step of the Bucket Algorithm considers all the possible combinations of rewritings. Each combination that includes a view atom from each bucket (eliminating duplicate atoms if necessary). This phase of the algorithm differs depending on whether we are looking for an equivalent rewriting of the query using the views or the maximally contained rewriting:

- For an equivalent rewriting, we consider each candidate rewriting Q' and check whether $Q \equiv Q'$ or whether there are interpreted atoms C that can be added to Q' such that $Q \wedge C \equiv Q'$.
- For the maximally contained rewriting we construct a union of conjunctive queries by considering each conjunctive rewriting Q':
  - If $Q' \sqsubseteq Q$, then Q' is included in the union.
  - If there exist interpreted atoms C that can be added to Q' such that $Q' \wedge C \sqsubseteq Q$, then $Q' \wedge C$ is included in the union.
  - If $Q' \not\sqsubseteq Q$ but there exists a homomorphism, ψ, on the head variables of Q' such that $\psi(Q') \sqsubseteq Q$, then we include $\psi(Q')$ in the union.

■ ■ ■ ▬▬▬▬▬▬▬▬▬▬▬▬▬▬▬▬▬▬▬▬▬▬▬▬▬▬▬▬▬▬▬▬▬

Example 2.17

Continuing with the example from the movie domain, suppose we also have the relation Revenues(ID, Amount), describing the revenues each movie garnered over time, and suppose movie IDs are integers. Consider a query that asks for directors whose movies garnered a significant amount of money:

$Q(\text{ID}, \text{Dir})$:- Movie(ID, Title, Year, Genre), Revenues(ID, Amount), Director(ID, Dir),
$\qquad\qquad$ Amount $\geq$ \$100M

Suppose we have the following views:

$V_1(\text{I}, \text{Y})$ $\quad$:- Movie(I, T, Y, G), Revenues(I, A), I $\geq$ 5000, A $\geq$ \$200M
$V_2(\text{I}, \text{A})$ $\quad$:- Movie(I, T, Y, G), Revenues(I, A)
$V_3(\text{I}, \text{A})$ $\quad$:- Revenues(I, A), A $\leq$ \$50M
$V_4(\text{I}, \text{D}, \text{Y})$:- Movie(I, T, Y, G), Director(I, D), I $\leq$ 3000

In the first step the algorithm creates a bucket for each of the relational subgoals in the query in turn. The resulting contents of the buckets are shown in Table 2.1. The bucket of Movie(ID,Title,Year,Genre) includes views V_1, V_2, and V_4. Note that each view head in a bucket only includes variables in the domain of the mapping. Fresh variables (primed) are used for the other head variables of the view (such as A' in V_2(ID,A')).

The bucket of the subgoal Revenues(ID,Amount) contains the views V_1 and V_2, and the bucket of Director(ID,Dir) includes an atom of V_4. There is no atom of V_3 in the bucket of Revenues(I,A) because constraint on the revenues considered in V_3 is not mutually satisfiable with the predicates in the query.

In the second step of the algorithm, we combine elements from the buckets. The first combination, involving the first element from each bucket, yields the rewriting

$q_1'(\text{ID}, \text{Dir})$:- $V_1(\text{ID}, \text{Year})$, $V_1(\text{ID}, \text{Y}')$, $V_4(\text{ID}, \text{Dir}, \text{Y}'')$

Table 2.1   Contents of the Buckets*.

Movie(ID,Title,Year,Genre)	Revenues(ID,Amount)	Director(ID,Dir)
V_1(ID,Year)	V_1(ID,Y')	V_4(ID,Dir,Y')
V_2(ID,A')	V_2(ID,Amount)	
V_4(ID,D',Year)		

*The primed variables are those that are not in the domain of the unifying mapping.

However, while both V_1 and V_4 are relevant to the query in *isolation*, their combination is guaranteed to be empty because they cover disjoint sets of movie identifiers.

Considering the second elements in the two left buckets yields the rewriting

$$q_2'(\text{ID},\text{Dir}) \text{ :- } V_2(\text{ID},\text{A}'),\ V_2(\text{ID},\text{Amount}),\ V_4(\text{ID},\text{Dir},\text{Y}')$$

As is, this rewriting is not contained in the query, but we can add the predicate Amount $\geq$ \$100M, and remove one redundant subgoal $V_2(\text{ID},\text{A}')$ to obtain a contained rewriting

$$q_3'(\text{ID},\text{Dir}) \text{ :- } V_2(\text{ID},\text{Amount}),\ V_4(\text{ID},\text{Dir},\text{Y}'),\ \text{Amount} \geq \$100\text{M}$$

Finally, combining the last elements in each of the buckets yields

$$q_4'(\text{ID},\text{Dir}) \text{ :- } V_4(\text{ID},\text{D}',\text{Year}),\ V_2(\text{ID},\text{Amount}),\ V_4(\text{ID},\text{Dir},\text{Y}')$$

However, after removing the first subgoal, which is redundant, and adding the predicate Amount $\geq$ \$100M, we would obtain q_3' again, which is the only contained rewriting the algorithm finds.

■ ■ ■

The MiniCon Algorithm

The MiniCon Algorithm also proceeds in two steps. It begins like the Bucket Algorithm, considering which views contain subgoals that are relevant to a subgoal g in the query. However, once the algorithm finds a partial mapping from a subgoal g in the query to a subgoal g_1 in a view V, it tries to determine which *other* subgoals from that view must also be used in conjunction with g_1. The algorithm considers the join predicates in the query (which are specified by multiple occurrences of the same variable) and finds the minimal additional set of subgoals that need to be mapped to subgoals in V, given that g will be mapped to g_1. This set of subgoals and mapping information is called a *Mini-Con Description* (MCD) and can be viewed as a generalization of buckets. The following example illustrates the intuition behind the MiniCon Algorithm and how it differs from the Bucket Algorithm.

■ ■ ■

Example 2.18

Consider the following example over the same movie schema:

Q_1(Title,Year,Dir) :- Movie(ID,Title,Year,Genre), Director(ID,Dir), Actor(ID,Dir)
V_5(D,A)   :- Director(I,D), Actor(I,A)

$V_6(T, Y, D, A)$:- Director(I, D), Actor(I, A), Movie(I, T, Y, G)

In its first step, the Bucket Algorithm would put the atoms V_5(Dir,A') and V_5(D',Dir) in the buckets of Director(ID,Dir) and Actor(ID,Dir), respectively. However, a careful analysis reveals that these two bucket items cannot contribute to a rewriting. Specifically, suppose the variable Dir is mapped to the variable D in V_5 (see figure below). The variable ID needs to be mapped to the variable I in V_5, but I is not a head variable of V_5, and therefore we will not be able to join the Director subgoal of V_5 with the other subgoals in the query.

Q_1(Title, Year, Amount) :- Director(ID, Dir),Actor(ID,Dir),Movie(ID, Title, Year, Genre)

$\downarrow$ $\downarrow$

V_5(D,A)   :- Director(I, D)   Actor(I, A)

The MiniCon Algorithm realizes that V_5 cannot be used to answer the query and therefore ignores it. We now describe the details of the algorithm.

■ ■ ■

STEP 1: CREATING MCDs

A MCD is a mapping from a subset of the variables in the query to variables in one of the views. Intuitively, a MCD represents a fragment of a containment mapping from the query to the rewriting of the query. The way in which we construct the MCDs guarantees that these fragments can later be combined seamlessly.

In the algorithm description, we use the following terms. First, given a mapping τ from $Vars(Q)$ to $Vars(V)$, we say that a view subgoal g_1 *covers* a query subgoal g if $\tau(g) = g_1$. Second, we often need to consider *specializations* of a view, formed by equating some of the head variables of the view (e.g., V_6(T,Y,D,D) instead of V_6(T,Y,D,A) in our example). We describe these specializations with *head homomorphisms*. A head homomorphism h on a view V is a mapping h from $Vars(V)$ to $Vars(V)$ that is the identity on the existential variables, but may equate distinguished variables, i.e., for every distinguished variable x, $h(x)$ is distinguished, and $h(x) = h(h(x))$. We can now define MCDs formally.

Definition 2.7 (MiniCon Descriptions).   *A MCD C for a query Q over a view V is a tuple of the form $(h_C, V(\bar{Y})_C, \varphi_C, G_C)$ where*

- *h_C is a head homomorphism on V,*
- *$V(\bar{Y})_C$ is the result of applying h_C to V, i.e., $\bar{Y} = h_C(\bar{A})$, where $\bar{A}$ are the head variables of V,*
- *φ_C is a partial mapping from $Vars(Q)$ to $h_C(Vars(V))$, and*
- *G_C is a subset of the subgoals in Q that are covered by some subgoal in $h_C(V)$ using the mapping φ_C.*   □

In words, φ_C is a mapping from Q to the specialization of V obtained by the head homomorphism h_C. The main idea underlying the algorithm is to carefully choose the set G_C of subgoals of Q that we cover by the mapping φ_C. The algorithm will use only the MCDs that satisfy the following property:

Property 2.1. *Let C be a MCD for Q over V. The MiniCon Algorithm considers C only if it satisfies the following conditions.*

C1. *For each head variable X of Q that is in the domain of φ_C, $\varphi_C(X)$ is a head variable in $h_C(V)$.*

C2. *If $\varphi_C(X)$ is an existential variable in $h_C(V)$, then for every g, subgoal of Q, that includes X (1) all the variables in g are in the domain of φ_C, and (2) $\varphi_C(g) \in h_C(V)$.*

Clause C1 is also required by the Bucket Algorithm. Clause C2 captures the intuition we illustrated in our example. If a variable X is part of a join predicate that is not enforced by the view, then X must be in the head of the view so the join predicate can be applied by another subgoal in the rewriting. In our example, clause C2 would rule out the use of V_5 for query Q_1.

Algorithm 4 builds the MCDs. Note that the algorithm will not consider all the possible MCDs, but only those in which h_C is the least restrictive head homomorphism necessary in order to unify subgoals of the query with subgoals in a view.

Algorithm 4. FormMCDs: First phase of the MiniCon Algorithm. Note that condition (b) minimizes G_c given a choice of h_C and φ_C, and is therefore not redundant with condition (c).

Input: conjunctive query Q; set of conjunctive queries $\mathcal{V}$. **Output:** set of MCDs $\mathcal{C}$.

    Initialize $\mathcal{C} := \emptyset$

  for each subgoal $g \in Q$ **do**

    for view $V \in \mathcal{V}$ and every subgoal $v \in V$ **do**

      Let h be the least restrictive head homomorphism on V such that there exists a mapping φ, s.t. $\varphi(g) = h(v)$

      if h and φ exist **then**

        Add to $\mathcal{C}$ any new MCD C that can be constructed where:

        (a) φ_C (resp. h_C) is an extension of φ (resp. h),

        (b) G_C is the minimal subset of subgoals of Q such that G_C, φ_C, and h_C satisfy Property 2.1, and

        (c) it is not possible to extend φ and h to φ'_C and h'_C s.t. (b) is satisfied and G'_C, as defined in (b), is a subset of G_C

      end if

    end for

  end for

  return $\mathcal{C}$

■ ■ ■ ━━━

Example 2.19

In our example, after realizing that V_5 cannot be part of any MCD, the algorithm would create an MCD for V_6, whose components are

$$(A \rightarrow D, V_6(T, Y, D, D), \text{Title} \rightarrow T, \text{Year} \rightarrow Y, \text{Dir} \rightarrow D, \{1,2,3\})$$

Note that in the MCD the head homomorphism equates the variables D and A in V_6, and that the MCD includes all the subgoals from the query.

━━━ ■ ■ ■

STEP 2: COMBINING THE MCDs

In the second phase, the MiniCon Algorithm combines the MCDs to create conjunctive rewritings and outputs a union of conjunctive queries. Because of the way in which the MCDs were constructed, the second phase of the algorithm is actually simpler and more efficient than the corresponding one in the Bucket Algorithm. Specifically, any time a set of MCDs covers mutually disjoint subsets of subgoals in the query, but together cover all the subgoals, the resulting rewriting is guaranteed to be a contained rewriting. Hence, we do not need to perform any containment checks in this phase. Algorithm 5 combines MCDs.

MINIMIZING THE REWRITINGS

The rewritings resulting from the second phase of the algorithm may be redundant. In general, they can be minimized by techniques for conjunctive query minimization. However, one case of redundant subgoals can be identified more simply as follows. Suppose a rewriting Q' includes two atoms A_1 and A_2 of the same view V, whose MCDs were C_1 and C_2, and the following conditions are satisfied: (1) whenever A_1 (resp. A_2) has a variable from Q in position i, then A_2 (resp. A_1) has either the same variable or a variable that does not appear in Q in that position, and (2) the ranges of φ_{C_1} and φ_{C_2} do not overlap on existential variables of V. In this case we can remove one of the two atoms by applying to Q' the homomorphism τ that is (1) the identity on the variables of Q and (2) the most general unifier of A_1 and A_2.

CONSTANTS IN THE QUERY AND VIEWS

When the query or the view includes constants, we make the following modifications to the algorithm. First, the domain and range of φ_C in the MCDs may also include constants. Second, a MCD also records a (possibly empty) set of mappings ψ_C from variables in $Vars(Q)$ to constants.

When the query includes constants, we add the following condition to Property 2.1:

C3. If a is a constant in Q, it must be the case that either (1) $\varphi_C(a)$ is a distinguished variable in $h_C(V)$ or (2) $\varphi_C(a)$ is the constant a.

Algorithm 5. CombineMCDs: Second phase of the MiniCon Algorithm—combining the MCDs.

Input: MCDs $\mathcal{C}$, of the form $(h_C, V(\bar{Y}), \varphi_C, G_C, EC_C)$. **Output:** rewritten query.
  // Given a set of MCDs, $C_1, \ldots, C_n$, we define the function EC on $Vars(Q)$ as follows:
  if for $i \neq j$, $EC_{\varphi_i}(x) \neq EC_{\varphi_j}(x)$ **then**
    Define $EC_C(x)$ to be one of them arbitrarily, but consistently across all y for which $EC_{\varphi_i}(y) = EC_{\varphi_j}(x)$
  end if
  Initialize $Answer = \emptyset$
  for every subset $C_1, \ldots, C_n$ of $\mathcal{C}$ such that (1) $G_{C_1} \cup G_{C_2} \cup \ldots \cup G_{C_n} = subgoals(Q)$ and (2) **for** every $i \neq j$, $G_{C_i} \cap G_{C_j} = \emptyset$ **do**
    Define a mapping Ψ_i on the $\bar{Y}_i$'s as follows:
    if there exists a variable $x \in Q$ such that $\varphi_i(x) = y$ **then**
      Let $\Psi_i(y) = x$
    else
      Let Ψ_i be a fresh copy of y
      Create the conjunctive rewriting $Q'(EC(\bar{X}))$:- $V_{C_1}(EC(\Psi_1(\bar{Y}_{C_1}))), \ldots, V_{C_n}(EC(\Psi_n(\bar{Y}_{C_n})))$
      Add Q' to $Answer$
    end if
  end for
  return $Answer$

When the views have constants, we modify Property 2.1 as follows:

- We relax clause C1: a variable x that appears in the head of the query must either be mapped to a head variable in the view (as before) or be mapped to a constant a. In the latter case, the mapping $x \rightarrow a$ is added to ψ_C.
- If $\varphi_C(x)$ is a constant a, then we add the mapping $x \rightarrow a$ to ψ_C. (Note that condition C2 only applies to existential variables, and therefore if $\varphi_C(x)$ is a constant that appears in the body of V but not in the head, a MCD is still created.)

Next, we combine MCDs with some extra care. Two MCDs, C_1 and C_2, both of which have x in their domain, can be combined only if either they (1) both map x to the same constant, or (2) one (e.g., C_1) maps x to a constant and the other (e.g., C_2) maps x to a distinguished variable in the view. Note that if C_2 maps x to an existential variable in the view, then the MiniCon Algorithm would never consider combining C_1 and C_2 in the first place, because they would have overlapping G_C sets.

Finally, we modify the definition of EC, such that whenever possible, it chooses a constant rather than a variable.

COMPUTATIONAL COMPLEXITY

The worst-case computational complexity of the Bucket and MiniCon Algorithms is the same. In both cases the running time is $O(nmM)^n$, where n is the number of subgoals in the query, m is the maximal number of subgoals in a view, and M is the number of views.

2.4.5 A Logical Approach: The Inverse-Rules Algorithm

In this section we describe an algorithm for rewriting queries using views that takes a purely logical approach to the problem. The following example illustrates the intuition behind the algorithm.

■ ■ ■ ━━━━━━━━━━━━━━━━━━━━━━━━━━━━━━━━━━━━━━━

Example 2.20

Consider the view from our previous example:

$V_7(I, T, Y, G)$:- Movie(I, T, Y, G), Director(I, D), Actor(I, D)

Suppose we know that the tuple (79522, Manhattan, 1979, Comedy) is in the extension of V_7. Clearly, we can infer from it that Movie(79522, Manhattan, 1979, Comedy) holds. In fact, the following rule would be logically sound:

IN_1: Movie(I, T, Y, G) :- $V_7(I, T, Y, G)$

We can also infer from V_7(79522, Manhattan, 1979, Comedy) that some tuples exist in Director and Actor, but it's a bit trickier. In particular, we do not know which value of D in the database yielded V_7(79522, Manhattan, 1979, Comedy). All we know is that there is some constant, c, such that Director(79522,c), Actor(79522, c) hold. We can express this inference using the following rules:

IN_2: Director$(I, f_1(I, T, Y, G))$:- $V_7(I, T, Y, G)$
IN_3: Actor$(I, f_1(I, T, Y, G))$:- $V_7(I, T, Y, G)$

The term $f_1(I, T, Y, G)$ is called a *Skolem term* and denotes some constant that depends on the values I, T, Y, and G and the function name f_1. Given two nonidentical Skolem terms, we do not know whether they refer to the same constant in the database or not, only that they both exist.

The query rewriting produced by the Inverse-Rules Algorithm includes all the inverse rules we can write for each of the view definitions and the rule defining the query. In our example, the inverse rules are IN_1, IN_2, and IN_3. To illustrate, suppose our query asked for all movie titles, with their genres and years:

Q_2(Title, Year, Genre) :- Movie(ID, Title, Year, Genre)

Evaluating the inverse rules over the extension V_7(79522, Manhattan, 1979, Comedy) yields the tuples

Movie(79522, Manhattan, 1979, Comedy),
Director(79522, f_1((79522, Manhattan, 1979, Comedy))
Actor(79522, f_1((79522, Manhattan, 1979, Comedy)).

Evaluating Q_2 on that set of tuples would yield the answer Movie(Manhattan, 1979, Comedy).

━━━━━━━━━━━━━━━━━━━━━━━━━━━━━━━━━━━━━━ ■ ■ ■

Algorithm 6. CreateInverseRules: Inverse rule rewriting algorithm. Note that the answer contains the original query and the inverse rules $\mathcal{R}$.

Input: conjunctive query Q; set of conjunctive view definitions $\mathcal{V}$. **Output:** datalog program to answer Q.

  Let $\bar{R} = \emptyset$

  for every $V \in \mathcal{V}$ **do**

    Let V be of the form: $v(\bar{X}) \coloneq p_1(\bar{X}_1), \ldots, p_n(\bar{X}_n)$ and suppose the existential variables in V are $Y_1, \ldots, Y_m$

    for $j = 1, \ldots, n$ **do**

      LET $\bar{X}'_j$ be the tuple of variables created from $\bar{X}_j$ as follows:

      if $X = Y_k$ **then**

        X is replaced by $f_{v,k}(\bar{X})$ in $\bar{X}'_j$

      else

        X is unchanged in X'_j

      end if

      Add to $\mathcal{R}$ the inverse rule: $p_j(\bar{X}'_j) \coloneq v(\bar{X})$

    end for

  end for

  return $Q \cup \bar{R}$

Algorithm 6 creates the inverse-rule rewriting.

2.4.6 Comparison of the Algorithms

The strength of the Bucket Algorithm is that it exploits the comparison atoms in the query to prune significantly the number of candidate conjunctive rewritings that need to be considered. Checking whether a view should belong to a bucket can be done in time polynomial in the size of the query and view definition when the predicates involved are arithmetic comparisons. Hence, if the views are indeed distinguished by having different interpreted predicates, then the resulting buckets will be relatively small. This is a common scenario when we apply answering queries using views to integrating data on the World Wide Web, where sources (modeled as views) are distinguished by the geographical area they apply to or other interpreted predicates.

However, the Bucket Algorithm does not consider interactions between different subgoals in the query and the views, and therefore the buckets may contain irrelevant subgoals. The MiniCon Algorithm overcomes that issue. Furthermore, because of the way MCDs are built, the second phase of the MiniCon Algorithm does not require a containment check, and is thereby more efficient. In experiments, the MiniCon Algorithm is uniformly faster than the Bucket Algorithm.

The main advantage of the Inverse-Rules Algorithm over the Bucket and MiniCon algorithms is its conceptual simplicity, being based on a purely logical approach to inverting the view definitions. Because of this simplicity, the algorithm can also be applied when the query Q is recursive and, as we discuss in Chapter 3, to cases where there are known functional dependencies. In addition, the inverse rules can be created in time that is polynomial in the size of the view definitions. Note that the algorithm does not tell us whether the maximally contained rewriting is equivalent to the original query (and hence avoids NP-hardness).

On the other hand, the rewriting produced by the Inverse-Rules Algorithm often leads to a query that that is more expensive to evaluate over the view extensions. The reason is that the Bucket and MiniCon Algorithms create buckets and MCDs in a way that considers the context of the query Q, while the inverse rules are computed only based on the view definition. In experiments, the MiniCon Algorithm has been shown to typically be faster than the Inverse-Rules Algorithm.

2.4.7 View-Based Query Answering

Thus far we have described algorithms for finding the maximally contained rewriting for a query given a set of views. However, these rewritings are maximal with respect to the query language we consider for the rewritings. In our discussion, we have considered rewritings that we can express as unions of conjunctive queries.

In this section we consider a more general question: Given a query Q, a set of view definitions $\mathcal{V} = V_1, \ldots, V_n$, and extensions for each of the views, $\bar{v} = v_1, \ldots, v_n$, what are all the answers to Q that can be inferred from $\mathcal{V}$ and $\bar{v}$? We begin by introducing the notion of *certain answers* that enables us to formally state the above question, and then describe some basic results on finding certain answers.

Given a database D and a query Q, we know with certainty all the answers to Q. However, if we are only given $\mathcal{V}$ and $\bar{v}$, then we do not precisely know the contents of D. Instead, we only have *partial information* about the real state of the database D. The information is partial in the sense that all we know is the answer to certain queries posed on D.

■ ■ ■ ▬▬▬

Example 2.21

Suppose we have the following views computing the set of actors and directors, respectively:

V_8(Dir)   :- Director(ID, Dir)
V_9(Actor) :- Actor(ID, Actor)

Suppose we are given the following view extensions:

v_8: {Allen, Coppola}
v_9: {Keaton, Pacino}

There are multiple databases that may have led to these view extensions. For example, in one, the pairs of director and actor would be ((Allen, Keaton), (Coppola, Pacino)), while in another it could be ((Allen, Pacino), (Coppola, Keaton)). In fact, the database that contains all the possible pairs would also lead to the same view extensions.

▬▬▬ ■ ■ ■

With partial information, all we know is that D is in some set $\mathcal{D}$ of *possible* databases. However, for each database in $D \in \mathcal{D}$, the answer to Q may be different. The *certain answers*, which we define below, are the ones that are answers to Q in *every* database in $\mathcal{D}$.

Before we can formally define certain answers, we need to be explicit about our assumptions about the *completeness* of the views. We distinguish between the *closed-world assumption* and the *open-world assumption*. Under the closed-world assumption, the extensions $\bar{v}$ are assumed to contain *all* the tuples in their corresponding views, while under the open-world assumption they may contain only a subset of the tuples in the views. The closed-world assumption is the one typically made when using views for query optimization, and the open-world assumption is typically used in data integration.

We can now formally define the notion of certain answers.

Definition 2.8 (Certain Answers).   *Let Q be a query and $\mathcal{V} = \{V_1, \ldots, V_m\}$ be a set of view definitions over the database schema $R_1, \ldots, R_n$. Let the sets of tuples $\bar{v} = v_1, \ldots, v_m$ be extensions of the views $V_1, \ldots, V_m$, respectively.*

The tuple $\bar{t}$ is a certain answer to the query Q under the closed-world assumption given $v_1, \ldots, v_m$ if $\bar{t} \in Q(D)$ for all database instances D such that $V_i(D) = v_i$ for every i, $1 \le i \le m$.

The tuple $\bar{t}$ is a certain answer to the query Q under the open-world assumption given $v_1, \ldots, v_m$ if $\bar{t} \in Q(D)$ for all database instances D such that $V_i(D) \supseteq v_i$ for every i, $1 \le i \le m$.

$\square$

■ ■ ■ ▬▬▬▬▬▬▬▬▬▬▬▬▬▬▬▬▬▬▬▬▬▬▬▬▬▬▬▬▬▬▬

Example 2.22

Consider the views

$V_8(\text{Dir})$:- Director(ID, Dir)
$V_9(\text{Actor})$:- Actor(ID, Actor)

Under the closed-world assumption, there is only a single database that is consistent with the view extensions. Hence, given the query

$Q_4(\text{Dir}, \text{Actor})$:- Director(ID, Dir), Actor(ID, Actor)

the tuple (Allen, Keaton) is a certain answer. However, under the open-world assumption, this tuple is no longer a certain answer because the view extensions may be missing the other actors and directors.

▬▬▬▬▬▬▬▬▬▬▬▬▬▬▬▬▬▬▬▬▬▬▬▬▬▬▬▬▬ ■ ■ ■

Certain Answers under the Open-World Assumption

Under the open-world assumption, when the query does not contain interpreted predicates, the union of conjunctive queries produced by the MiniCon and Inverse-Rules Algorithms are guaranteed to compute all the certain answers to a conjunctive query given a set of conjunctive views. The following theorem shows that the Inverse-Rules Algorithm produces all the certain answers.

Theorem 2.10. *Let Q be a conjunctive query and let $V = V_1, \ldots, V_n$ be conjunctive queries, where neither Q nor V contain interpreted atoms or negation. Let Q' be the result of the Inverse-Rules Algorithm on Q and V. Given extensions $\bar{v} = v_1, \ldots, v_n$ for the views in V, evaluating Q' over $\bar{v}$ will produce all the certain answers for Q w.r.t. V and $\bar{v}$.* ☐

Proof. Denote by $\mathcal{D}$ the set of databases that are consistent with the extensions $\bar{v}$. To prove the theorem, we need to show that if $\bar{t} \in Q(D)$ for every $D \in \mathcal{D}$, then $\bar{t}$ would be produced by evaluating Q' over $\bar{v}$.

Evaluating Q' on $\bar{v}$ can be divided into two steps. In the first, we evaluate all the inverse rules on $\bar{v}$ to produce a *canonical database* D'. In the second step, we evaluate Q on D'. The proof is based on showing that if $\bar{t}$ is a tuple of constants with no functional terms and $\bar{t} \in Q(D')$, then $\bar{t} \in Q(D)$ for every $D \in \mathcal{D}$.

Suppose $\bar{a} \in v_i$ where V_i is of the form

$$v(\bar{X}) \text{ :- } \mathsf{p}_1(\bar{X}_1), \ldots, \mathsf{p}_m(\bar{X}_m)$$

and the existential variables in V are $Y_1, \ldots, Y_k$. If $D \in \mathcal{D}$, then there must be constants, $b_1, \ldots, b_k$, and a variable mapping ψ that maps $\bar{X}$ to $\bar{a}$ and $Y_1, \ldots, Y_k$ to $b_1, \ldots, b_k$, such that $\mathsf{p}_i(\psi(\bar{X}_i)) \in D$ for $1 \leq i \leq n$.

Evaluating the inverse rules on $\bar{v}$ produces exactly these tuples, except instead of $b_1, \ldots, b_k$ we get $f_{v_i,1}(\bar{a}), \ldots, f_{v_i,k}(\bar{a})$. In fact, *all* the tuples in D' are produced in this way for some $\bar{a} \in v_i$, so there are no extra tuples in D' that are not required by some $v_i(\bar{a})$.

Hence, we can characterize the databases in $\mathcal{D}$ as follows. Every $D \in \mathcal{D}$ can be created from D' by mapping the functional terms in D' to constants (possibly equating two distinct functional terms) and adding more tuples. In other words, for every database $D \in \mathcal{D}$ there is a homomorphism, ϕ, such that $\phi(D) \supseteq D'$.

Consequently, it is easy to see that if $\bar{t} \in Q(D')$, then $\bar{t} \in Q(D)$ for every $D \in \mathcal{D}$, since any pair of constants that are equal in D' are guaranteed to be equal in D. ☐

Theorem 2.10 can be used to show that the MiniCon Algorithm produces all the certain answers under the same condition. We leave it to the reader to show that any answer produced by the Inverse-Rules Algorithm is also produced by the MiniCon Algorithm, and therefore it produces all the certain answers as well.

Corollary 2.1. *Let Q be a conjunctive query, and let $V = V_1, \ldots, V_n$ be conjunctive queries. The Inverse-Rules and MiniCon Algorithms produce the maximally contained union of conjunctive query rewriting of Q using V.* ☐

Certain Answers under the Closed-World Assumption

Under the closed-world assumption, finding all the certain answers turns out to be computationally much harder. The following theorem shows that finding all the certain answers is co-NP-hard in the size of the data. Hence, none of the query languages we considered for rewriting will produce all the certain answers.

Theorem 2.11. *Let Q be a query and $\mathcal{V}$ be a set of view definitions. The problem of determining, given a view instance, whether a tuple is a certain answer under the closed-world assumption is co-NP-hard.*   □

Proof crux. We prove the theorem by a reduction from the 3-colorability problem. Let $G = (V, E)$ be an arbitrary graph. Consider the view definitions

$v_1(\mathsf{X})$:- color(X, Y)
$v_2(\mathsf{Y})$:- color(X, Y)
$v_3(\mathsf{X}, \mathsf{Y})$:- edge(X, Y)

and consider the instance I with $I(v_1) = V$, $I(v_2) = \{red, green, blue\}$, and $I(v_3) = E$. It can be shown that under the closed-world assumption, the query

$q()$:- edge(X, Y), color(X, Z), color(Y, Z)

has a certain answer if and only if the graph G is not 3-colorable. Because testing a graph's 3-colorability is NP-complete, the theorem follows. Note that q is a query with arity 0, hence it has a certain answer if and only if for any database, there is at least one substitution that satisfies the body.   □

Certain Answers for Queries with Interpreted Predicates

When queries and views include interpreted predicates, the results on finding certain answers or maximally contained rewritings do not all carry over. In fact, the fundamental result on the limit on the size of rewritings (Theorem 2.9) does not hold any more.

   The hard case is when the query contains interpreted predicates. The following theorem shows that it suffices for the query to contain the $\neq$ predicate, and then the problem of finding all certain answers is co-NP-complete.

Theorem 2.12. *Let Q be a query and $\mathcal{V}$ be a set of view definitions, all conjunctive queries, but Q may have the $\neq$ predicate. The problem of determining, given a view instance, whether a tuple is a certain answer under the open-world assumption is co-NP-hard.*   □

Proof crux. We prove the theorem by a reduction from the problem of testing satisfiability of a CNF formula. Let ψ be a CNF formula with variables $x_1, \ldots, x_n$ and conjuncts $c_1, \ldots, c_m$. Consider the following conjunctive view definitions and their corresponding view instances:

$v_1(\mathsf{X}, \mathsf{Y}, \mathsf{Z})$:- p(X, Y, Z)
$v_2(\mathsf{X})$:- r(X, Y)
$v_3(\mathsf{Y})$:- p(X, Y, Z), r(X, Z)

$I(v_1) = \{(i, j, 1) \mid x_i \text{ occurs in } c_j\} \cup \{(i, j, 0) \mid \neg x_i \text{ occurs in } c_j\}$
$I(v_2) = \{(1), \ldots, (n)\}$
$I(v_3) = \{(1), \ldots, (m)\}$

Finally, consider the following query:

$q()$:- $r(X, Y)$, $r(X, Y')$, $Y \neq Y'$

It is possible to show that q has a certain answer under the open-world assumption if and only if the formula ψ is not satisfiable. Since the problem of testing satisfiability is NP-complete, the theorem follows.   □

Fortunately, there are two important cases where the algorithms we described still yield the maximally contained rewritings and all the certain answers:

- if the query does not contain interpreted predicates (but the views may), and
- if all the interpreted predicates in the query are semi-interval comparisons.

The proof is left as an exercise for the reader.

Bibliographic Notes

Query containment has been an active area of research for many years, beginning with Chandra and Merlin [114], who proved that query containment and equivalence are NP-complete for conjunctive queries. Sagiv and Yannakakis first considered queries with unions and negation [502]. Rarajaman and Chekuri [130] describe several cases where checking query containment can be done in time polynomial in the size of the queries. Saraiya shows that when predicates do not appear more than twice in a conjunctive query, query containment can be checked in polynomial time [505].

Containment for conjunctive queries with interpreted predicates was first considered by Klug [347] (establishing the upper bound) and van der Meyden [557] (establishing the lower bound). Afrati et al. [16] consider more efficient algorithms for testing containment with interpreted predicates. In [12], the authors present a thorough treatment of query containment and answering queries using views with arithmetic comparisons. The algorithm we describe in Section 2.3.4 and the algorithm for query containment with negated subgoals in Section 2.3.5 are from Levy and Sagiv [382]. Benedikt and Gottlob [64] show that query containment for nonrecursive datalog is complete for co-NEXPTIME. Containment for queries with bag semantics were first considered by Chaudhuri and Vardi [127], and then by [320, 332]. Cohen [142] surveys algorithms for query containment with grouping and aggregation. Green [267] describes containment results for queries over *annotated relations* that cover also queries over bag semantics.

Answering queries using views has been considered in the context of data integration, query optimization (e.g., [13, 63, 125, 259, 588]), and maintenance of physical data independence (e.g., [551, 586]). A survey of the main techniques for answering queries using views is described by Halevy [284]. The result on the length of a rewriting in Section 2.4.3 is from Levy et al. [398] and the Bucket Algorithm is a slightly modified version of the algorithm described in [381]. The MiniCon Algorithm [482] and the SVB Algorithm [439] are also complete and more efficient. In [12] the authors discuss the subtleties of answering queries using views in the presence of interpreted predicates in the query and the views, and they show why the Bucket Algorithm may not be complete in the presence of interpreted predicates. In [349] the authors describe a significant speedup compared to the MiniCon Algorithm. The Inverse-Rules Algorithm is from Duschka and Genesereth [198]. An approach for answering queries using views based on the Chase Algorithm is described in [480]. Several works (e.g., [108]) considered answering queries using views over description logics. Certain answers were introduced by Abiteboul and Duschka [6], as well as the basic complexity results we described. Libkin [389] describes a general framework for defining incomplete information in databases from which he derives several results concerning certain answers for relational data and for XML data.

3 ▪▪▪
  ▪▪▪
  ▪▪▪

Describing Data Sources

In order for a data integration system to process a query over a set of data sources, the system must know which sources are available, what data exist in each source, and how each source can be accessed. The *source descriptions* in a data integration system encode this information. In this chapter we study the different components of source descriptions and identify the trade-offs involved in designing formalisms for source descriptions.

To put the topic of this chapter in context, consider the architecture of a data integration system, redrawn in Figure 3.1. Recall that a user (or an application) poses a query to the data integration system using the relations and attributes of the mediated schema. The system then reformulates the query into a query over the data sources. The result of the reformulation is called a *logical query plan*. The logical query plan is later optimized so it runs efficiently. In this chapter we show how source descriptions are expressed and how the system uses them to reformulate the user's query into a logical query plan.

3.1 Overview and Desiderata

Before we begin our technical discussion of source descriptions, it is instructive to highlight the goals that these descriptions are trying to achieve and outline basic desiderata for a source description formalism.

To understand the requirements for source descriptions, we use a scenario that includes the mediated schema and data sources depicted in Figure 3.2. Note that the first data source contains four tables, while the others each contain a single table. We refer to a relation in a data source by the relation name, prefixed by the source name (e.g., S1.Movie).

A source description needs to convey several pieces of information. The main component of a source description, called a *schema mapping*, is a specification of *what* data exist in the source and how the terms used in the source schema relate to the terms used in the mediated schema. The schema mapping needs to be able to handle the following discrepancies between the source schemata and the mediated schema:

- **Relation and attribute names:** The relation and attribute names in the mediated schema are likely to be different from the names in the sources even if they are referring to the same concepts. For example, the attribute description in the mediated schema refers to the text description of a review, which is the same as the attribute review in source S4. Similarly, if the same relation or attribute names are used in the mediated schema and in the source, that does not necessarily entail that they mean

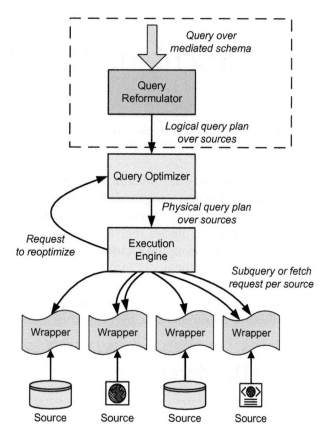

FIGURE 3.1 Query processing in a data integration system. This chapter focuses on the reformulation step, highlighted in the dashed box.

the same thing. For example, the attribute name appears in both the Actors relation in the mediated schema and in S3, but refers to actor names in one case and to cinema names in the other.

- **Tabular organization:** The tabular organization of data can be different between the mediated schema and the source. For example, in the mediated schema, the relation Actor stores the relationship between actor names and movie titles. In contrast, in source S1, actors are modeled with IDs, some of their data are stored in the relation Actor, and the relationship with movies is stored in the relation ActorPlays. Hence, the schema mapping needs to be able to specify that a join of two tables in the source corresponds to a relation in the mediated schema and vice versa.
- **Granularity level:** The coverage and level of granularity of the two schemas may differ. For instance, source S1 models actors in more detail than the mediated schema. The source models the year of birth and nationality of actors in addition to their name.

Mediated schema:

    Movie(title, director, year, genre)
    Actors(title, name)
    Plays(movie, location, startTime)
    Reviews(title, rating, description)

Data sources:

S1:

    Movie(MID, title)
    Actor(AID, firstName, lastName, nationality, yearOfBirth)
    ActorPlays(AID, MID)
    MovieDetail(MID, director, genre, year)

S2:

    Cinemas(place, movie, start)

S3:

    NYCCinemas(name, title, startTime)

S4:

    Reviews(title, date, grade, review)

S5:

    MovieGenres(title, genre)

S6:

    MovieDirectors(title, dir)

S7:

    MovieYears(title, year)

FIGURE 3.2 Example mediated schema and data sources.

One of the main reasons for differences in granularity level is that schemas are designed for different purposes. For example, the mediated schema may be designed for the sole purpose of serving as a back-end to an online shop, whereas the schema of S1 is designed for a detailed investigation of details about movies.

- **Data-level variations:** The schemas may be assuming different conventions for specifying data values. In the simple case, there may be a difference in the scales used to specify values (e.g, GPAs on a letter scale versus a numeric scale). In other cases, names of people or companies may be written differently. For example, in S1 names of actors are broken up into two columns, whereas in the mediated schema the full name is in one column.

Collectively, these differences between the mediated schema and the source schema (or between any pair of schema) are called *semantic heterogeneity*. Bridging semantic heterogeneity is considered to be one of the key challenges in data integration. We cover schema mappings in Section 3.2.

In addition to schema mappings, the source descriptions also specify information that enables the data integration system to optimize queries to the sources and to avoid illegal access patterns. Specifically, the following two are common.

ACCESS-PATTERN LIMITATIONS
Data sources may differ on which access patterns they support. In the best case, a data source is a full-fledged database system, and we can send it any SQL query. However, many data sources are much more limited. For example, a data source whose interface is a Web form constrains the possible access patterns. In order to get tuples from the source, the data integration system needs to supply some set of legal input parameters. We discuss limitations on access patterns to sources in Section 3.3. We postpone the discussion on leveraging processing power of data sources to Chapter 8.

SOURCE COMPLETENESS
It is often important to know whether a source is complete with respect to the contents it's purported to have. When a data source is known to be complete, the data integration system can save work by not accessing other data sources that have overlapping data. For example, if S2.Cinemas is known to have playing times of all movies in the country, then we can ignore S3 and S4 for many queries. In some cases, the data source may be complete w.r.t. a subset of its contents. For example, we may know that source S2 is complete with respect to movies in New York City and San Francisco. Given partially complete sources, we also want to know whether answers to our queries are guaranteed to be complete. As we see later, source completeness is expressed by the closed-world assumption we described in Section 2.4. We discuss how data integration handles knowledge about completeness in Section 3.5.

3.2 Schema Mapping Languages

Formally, a schema mapping is a set of expressions that describe a relationship between a set of schemata (typically two). In our context, the schema mappings describe a relationship between the mediated schema and the schema of the sources. When a query is formulated in terms of the mediated schema, we use the mappings to reformulate the query into appropriate queries on the sources. The result of the reformulation is a *logical query plan*.

Schema mappings are also used in other contexts. In the context of data exchange and data warehousing (which we discuss in Chapter 10), schema mappings express a relationship between a source database and a target database. There we use the schema mappings to map the data from the source database into the target database (which is often a data warehouse). A schema mapping may also be used to describe the relationship between two databases that store data, and the goal of the schema mapping is typically to merge the two databases into one. We discuss this case briefly in Chapter 6.

3.2.1 Principles of Schema Mapping Languages

In this chapter we use query expressions as the main mechanism for specifying schema mappings, and we leverage the algorithms described in Chapter 2 for query reformulation. In our description, we denote the mediated schema by G, and the source schemata by $S_1, \ldots, S_n$.

Semantics of Schema Mappings

The semantics of a schema mapping formalism are specified by defining which instances of the mediated schema are consistent with given instances of the data sources. Specifically, a semantic mapping M defines a relation M_R over

$$I(G) \times I(S_1) \times \ldots \times I(S_n)$$

where $I(G)$ denotes the possible instances of the mediated schema, and $I(S_1), \ldots, I(S_n)$ denote the possible instances of the source relations $S_1, \ldots, S_n$, respectively. If $(g, s_1, \ldots, s_n) \in M_R$, then g is a possible instance of the mediated schema when the source relation instances are $s_1, \ldots, s_n$. The semantics of queries over the mediated schema are based on the relation M_R.

Definition 3.1 (Certain Answers). *Let M be a schema mapping between a mediated schema G and source schemata $S_1, \ldots, S_n$ that defines the relation M_R over $I(G) \times I(S_1) \times \ldots \times I(S_n)$.*

Let Q be a query over G, and let $s_1, \ldots, s_n$ be instances of the source relations. We say that $\bar{t}$ is a certain answer of Q w.r.t. M and $s_1, \ldots, s_n$, if $\bar{t} \in Q(g)$ for every instance g of G such that $(g, s_1, \ldots, s_n) \in M_R$.   □

Logical Query Plans

To obtain the certain answers, the data integration system will create a logical query plan as a result of reformulation. The logical query plan is a query expression that refers only to the relations in the data sources. As we see later, it is not always possible to create a query plan that generates all the certain answers. Hence, in our discussion, we will analyze two different algorithmic problems: finding the *best* possible logical query plan and finding *all* the certain answers.

As we discuss the different schema mapping languages, we keep in mind the following important properties we would like the language to provide:

- **Flexibility:** Given the significant differences between disparate schemata, the schema mapping languages should be very flexible. That is, the language should be able to express a wide variety of relationships between schemata.

- **Efficient reformulation:** Since our goal is to use the schema mapping to reformulate queries, we should be able to develop reformulation algorithms whose properties are well understood and are efficient in practice. This requirement is often at odds with that of expressivity, because more expressive languages are typically harder to reason about.
- **Extensible to new sources:** For a formalism to be useful in practice, it needs to be easy to add and remove sources. If adding a new data source potentially requires inspecting all other sources, the resulting system will be hard to manage as it scales up to a large number of sources.

We discuss three schema mapping classes: Global-as-View (Section 3.2.2); Local-as-View (Section 3.2.3); Global-and-Local-as-View (Section 3.2.4), which combines the features of the two previous ones; and finally tuple-generating dependencies (Section 3.2.5), which use a different formalism but are equivalent in expressiveness to Global-and-Local-as-View. For historical reasons, the formalism names leave some room for further explanation, and we do so as we go along. We note that the topic of *creating* schema mappings is the subject of Chapter 5.

3.2.2 Global-as-View

The first formalism we consider, Global-as-View (GAV), takes a very intuitive approach to specifying schema mappings: GAV defines the mediated schema as a set of views over the data sources. The mediated schema is often referred to as a global schema, hence the name of the formalism.

Syntax and Semantics
The syntax of GAV source descriptions is defined as follows.

Definition 3.2 (GAV Schema Mappings). *Let G be a mediated schema, and let $\bar{S} = \{S_1, \ldots, S_n\}$ be schemata of n data sources. A Global-as-View schema mapping $\bar{M}$ is a set of expressions of the form $G_i(\bar{X}) \supseteq Q(\bar{S})$ or $G_i(\bar{X}) = Q(\bar{S})$, where*

- G_i *is a relation in G, and appears in at most one expression in $\bar{M}$, and*
- $Q(\bar{S})$ *is a query over the relations in $\bar{S}$.* □

Expressions with $\supseteq$ make the open-world assumption. That is, the data sources, and therefore the instances computed for the relations in the mediated schema, are assumed to be incomplete. Expressions with $=$ make the closed-world assumption in that the instances computed for the relations in the mediated schema are assumed to be complete. In Section 3.5 we show how to state more refined notions of completeness for data sources.

■ ■ ■

Example 3.1

The following is a GAV schema mapping for some of the sources in our running example. For readability, when illustrating GAV schema mappings, we typically abuse the notation by not showing the head of the query over the data sources, $Q(\bar{S})$, since it is the same as the relation G_i. Because of that, we also show union queries as multiple expressions (e.g., the first two statements below).

Movie(title, director, year, genre) ⊇ S1.Movie(MID, title),
                                    S1.MovieDetail(MID, director, genre, year)
Movie(title, director, year, genre) ⊇ S5.MovieGenres(title, genre),
                                    S6.MovieDirectors(title, director),
                                    S7.MovieYears(title, year)
Plays(movie, location, startTime) ⊇ S2.Cinemas(location, movie, startTime)
Plays(movie, location, startTime) ⊇ S3.NYCCinemas(location, movie, startTime)

The first expression shows how to obtain tuples for the Movie relation by joining relations in S1. The second expression obtains tuples for the Movie relation by joining data from sources S5, S6, and S7. Hence, the tuples that would be computed for Movie are the result of the union of the first two expressions. Also note that the second expression *requires* that we know the director, genre, and year of a movie. If one of these is missing, we will not have a tuple for the movie in the relation Movie. The third and fourth expressions generate tuples for the Plays relation by taking the union of S2 and S3.

■ ■ ■

The following definition specifies the relation M_R entailed by a GAV schema mapping M, thereby defining its semantics.

Definition 3.3 (GAV Semantics). *Let $\bar{M} = M_1,\ldots,M_l$ be a GAV schema mapping between G and $\bar{S} = \{S_1,\ldots,S_n\}$, where M_i is of the form $G_i(\bar{X}) \supseteq Q_i(\bar{S})$, or $G_i(\bar{X}) = Q_i(\bar{S})$.*

Let g be an instance of the mediated schema G and g_i be the set of tuples for the relation G_i in g. Let $\bar{s} = s_1,\ldots,s_n$ be instances of $S_1,\ldots,S_n$, respectively. The tuple of instances $(g,s_1,\ldots,s_n)$ is in M_R if for every $1 \leq i \leq l$, the following hold:

- *If M_i is a $=$ expression, then g_i is equal to the result of evaluating Q_i on $\bar{s}$.*
- *If M_i is a $\supseteq$ expression, then g_i is a superset of result of evaluating Q_i on $\bar{s}$.* ☐

Reformulation in GAV

The main advantage of GAV is its conceptual simplicity. The mediated schema is simply a view over the data sources. To reformulate a query posed over the mediated schema, we simply need to unfold the query with the view definitions (see Section 2.2). Furthermore, the reformulation resulting from the unfolding is guaranteed to find all the certain answers. Hence, the following theorem summarizes the complexity of reformulation and query answering in GAV.

Theorem 3.1. *Let $\bar{M} = M_1, \ldots, M_l$ be a GAV schema mapping between G and $\bar{S} = \{S_1, \ldots, S_n\}$, where M_i is of the form $G_i(\bar{X}) \supseteq Q_i(\bar{S})$, or $G_i(\bar{X}) = Q_i(\bar{S})$. Let Q be a query over G.*

If Q and the Q_i's in $\bar{M}$ are conjunctive queries or unions of conjunctive queries, even with interpreted and negated atoms, then the problem of finding all certain answers to Q is in PTIME in the size of the data sources, and the complexity of reformulation is in PTIME in the size of the query and source descriptions.   □

■ ■ ■ ▬▬▬▬▬▬▬▬▬▬▬▬▬▬▬▬▬▬▬▬▬

Example 3.2

Suppose we have the following query over the mediated schema, asking for comedies starting after 8 pm:

Q(title, location, st) :- Movie(title, director, year, "comedy"),
                     Plays(title, location, st), st $\geq$ 8pm

Reformulating Q with the source descriptions in Example 3.1 would yield the following four logical query plans:

Q'(title, location, st) :- S1.Movie(MID, title),
                    S1.MovieDetail(MID, director, "comedy" year),
                    S2.Cinemas(location, movie, st), st $\geq$ 8pm
Q'(title, location, st) :- S1.Movie(MID, title),
                    S1.MovieDetail(MID, director, "comedy" year),
                    S3.NYCCinemas(location, title, st), st $\geq$ 8pm
Q'(title, location, st) :- S5.MovieGenres(title, genre), S6.MovieDirectors(title, director),
                    S7.MovieYears(title, year), S2.Cinemas(location, movie, st),
                    st $\geq$ 8pm
Q'(title, location, st) :- S5.MovieGenres(title, genre), S6.MovieDirectors(title, director),
                    S7.MovieYears(title, year), S3.NYCCinemas(location, title, st),
                    st $\geq$ 8pm

We note two points about the above reformulation. First, the reformulation may not be the most efficient method to answer the query. For example, in this case it may be better to factor common subexpressions (namely, Movie and Plays) in order to reduce the number of joins necessary to evaluate the query. We discuss query optimization for data integration in Chapter 8.

Second, note that in the last two reformulations, the subgoals of S6.MovieDirectors and S7.MovieYears seem redundant because all we really need from the Movies relation is the genre of the movie. However, these subgoals are required because the mediated schema enforces that each movie have a known director and year.

▬▬▬▬▬▬▬▬▬▬▬▬▬▬▬▬▬▬▬▬▬ ■ ■ ■

Discussion

In terms of modeling, GAV source descriptions specify directly how to compute tuples of the mediated schema relations from tuples in the sources. We've already seen one limitation of GAV in Example 3.2 when we were not able to specify that the year or director of the movie be unknown. The following is a more extreme example of where translating data sources into the mediated schema is limiting.

■ ■ ■ ━━━

Example 3.3

Suppose we have a data source S8 that stores pairs of (actor, director) who worked together on movies. The only way to model this source in GAV is with the following two descriptions that use NULL liberally.

Actors(NULL, actor) ⊇ S8(actor, director)
Movie(NULL, director, NULL, NULL) ⊇ S8(actor, director)

Note that these descriptions essentially create tuples in the mediated schema that include NULLs in all columns except one. For example, if the source S8 included the tuples {Keaton, Allen} and {Pacino, Coppola}, then the tuples computed for the mediated schema would be

Actors(NULL, Keaton), Actors(NULL, Pacino)
Movie(NULL, Allen, NULL, NULL), Movie(NULL, Coppola, NULL, NULL)

Now suppose we have the following query that essentially recreates S8:

Q(actor, director) :- Actors(title, actor), Movie(title, director, genre, year)

We would not be able to retrieve the tuples from S8 because the source descriptions lost the relationship between actor and director.

━━ ■ ■ ■

A final limitation of GAV is that adding and removing sources involves considerable work and knowledge of the sources. For example, suppose we discover another source that includes only movie directors (similar to S6). In order to update the source descriptions, we need to specify exactly which sources it needs to be joined with in order to produce tuples of Movie. Hence, we need to be aware of all sources that contribute movie years and movie genres (of which there may also be many). In general, if adding a new source requires that we are familiar with all other sources in the system, then the system is unlikely to scale to a large number of sources.

3.2.3 Local-as-View

Local-as-View (LAV) takes the opposite approach to GAV. Instead of specifying how to compute tuples of the mediated schema, LAV focuses on describing each data source as precisely as possible and *independently* of any other sources.

Syntax and Semantics

As the name implies, LAV expressions describe data sources as views over the mediated schema.

Definition 3.4 (LAV Schema Mappings). *Let G be a mediated schema, and let $\bar{S} = \{S_1, \ldots, S_n\}$ be schemata of n data sources. A Local-as-View schema mapping M is a set of expressions of the form $S_i(\bar{X}) \subseteq Q_i(G)$ or $S_i(\bar{X}) = Q_i(G)$, where*

- Q_i *is a query over the mediated schema G, and*
- S_i *is a source relation and it appears in at most one expression in M.* ☐

As with GAV, LAV expressions with $\subseteq$ make the open-world assumption and expressions with $=$ make the closed-world assumption. However, LAV descriptions make completeness statements about data sources, not about the relations in the mediated schema.

■ ■ ■ ▬▬▬▬▬▬▬▬▬▬▬▬▬▬▬▬▬▬▬▬▬▬▬▬▬▬▬▬▬▬▬▬▬▬▬▬▬▬

Example 3.4

In LAV, sources S5–S7 would be described simply as projection queries over the Movie relation in the mediated schema. Note that here too we abuse the notation for clarity and omit the head of the Q_i's.

S5.MovieGenres(title, genre) $\subseteq$ Movie(title, director, year, genre)
S6.MovieDirectors(title, dir) $\subseteq$ Movie(title, director, year, genre)
S7.MovieYears(title, year) $\subseteq$ Movie(title, director, year, genre)

With LAV we can also model the source S8 as a join over the mediated schema:

S8(actor, dir) $\subseteq$ Movie(title, director, year, genre), Actors(title, actor)

Furthermore, we can also express constraints on the contents of data sources. For example, we can describe the following source that includes movies produced after 1970 that are all comedies:

S9(title, year, "comedy") $\subseteq$ Movie(title, director, year, "comedy"), year $\geq$ 1970

▬▬▬▬▬▬▬▬▬▬▬▬▬▬▬▬▬▬▬▬▬▬▬▬▬▬▬▬▬▬▬▬▬▬▬▬▬▬ ■ ■ ■

As with GAV, the semantics of a LAV schema mapping are defined by specifying the relation M_R defined by M.

Definition 3.5 (LAV Semantics). *Let $M = M_1, \ldots, M_l$ be a LAV schema mapping between G and $\bar{S} = \{S_1, \ldots, S_n\}$, where M_i is of the form $S_i(\bar{X}) \subseteq Q_i(G)$ or $S_i(\bar{X}) = Q_i(G)$.*

Let g be an instance of the mediated schema G and let $\bar{s} = s_1,\ldots,s_n$ be instances of $S_1,\ldots,$ S_n, respectively. The tuple of instances $(g,s_1,\ldots,s_n)$ is in M_R if for every $1 \leq i \leq l$, the following hold:

- *If M_i is a $=$ expression, then the result of evaluating Q_i over g is equal to s_i.*
- *If M_i is a $\subseteq$ expression, then the result of evaluating Q_i over g is a superset of s_i.*   □

Reformulation in LAV

The main advantage of LAV is that data sources are described in isolation and the system, not the designer, is responsible for finding ways of combining data from multiple sources. As a result, it is easier for a designer to add and remove sources.

■ ■ ■ ▬▬▬▬▬▬▬▬▬▬▬▬▬▬▬▬▬▬▬▬▬▬▬▬▬▬▬▬▬▬

Example 3.5

Consider the following query asking for comedies produced in or after 1960:

Q(title) :- Movie(title, director, year, "comedy"), year $\geq$ 1960

Using the sources S5–S7, we would generate the following reformulation from the LAV source descriptions:

Q'(title) :- S5.MovieGenres(title, "comedy"), S7.MovieYears(title, year), year $\geq$ 1960

Note that unlike GAV, the reformulation here did not require a join with the MovieDirectors relation in S6. Using the source S9, we would also create the following reformulation:

Q'(title) :- S9(title, year, "comedy")

Note that here the reformulation does not need to apply the predicate on year, because S9 is already known to contain only movies produced after 1970.

▬▬▬▬▬▬▬▬▬▬▬▬▬▬▬▬▬▬▬▬▬▬▬▬▬▬▬▬▬ ■ ■ ■

Of course, to obtain this flexibility, we need to develop more complex query reformulation algorithms. Fortunately, the techniques for answering queries using views (Section 2.4) give us a framework for establishing results for reformulation in LAV.

To see why answering queries using views applies in our context, simply consider the following. The mediated schema represents a database whose tuples are unknown. The data sources in LAV are described as view expressions over the mediated schema. The extensions of the views are the data stored in the data sources. For example, S8 is described as a join over the mediated schema. Hence, to answer a query formulated over the mediated schema, we need to reformulate it into a query over the known views, i.e., the data sources. Unlike the traditional setting of answering queries using views, here the original database (i.e., the mediated schema) never had any tuples stored in it. However, that makes no difference to the query reformulation algorithms.

The above formulation of the problem immediately yields a plethora of algorithms and complexity results regarding reformulation for LAV, as summarized by the following theorem. The proof of the theorem is a corollary of the results in Chapter 2.

Theorem 3.2. *Let* $M = M_1, \ldots, M_l$ *be a LAV schema mapping between G and* $\bar{S} = \{S_1, \ldots, S_n\}$, *where* M_i *is of the form* $S_i(\bar{X}) \subseteq Q_i(G)$ *or* $S_i(\bar{X}) = Q_i(G)$. *Let Q be a conjunctive query over G.*

- *If all the* Q_i's *in M are conjunctive queries with no interpreted predicates or negation, and all the* M_i's *are* $\subseteq$ *expressions, then all the certain answers can be found in time polynomial in the size of the data and in the size of M.*
- *If all the* Q_i's *in M are conjunctive queries with no interpreted predicates or negation, and some of the expressions in M are* $=$ *expressions, then finding all the certain answers to Q is co-NP-hard in the size of the data.*
- *If some of the* Q_i's *include interpreted predicates, then finding all certain answers to Q is co-NP-hard in the size of the data.* $\square$

We also note that finding all certain answers is co-NP-hard in the size of the data if the Q_i's include unions or negated predicates.

We generate logical query plans for LAV schema mappings using any of the algorithms described in Chapter 2 for finding a maximally contained rewriting of a query using a set of views. The computational complexity of finding the maximally contained rewriting is polynomial in the number of views and the size of the query. Checking whether the maximally contained rewriting is equivalent to the original query is NP-complete. In practice, the logical query plan created by the algorithm often finds all the certain answers even in cases where it is not guaranteed to do so.

Discussion

The added flexibility of LAV is also the reason for the increased computational complexity of answering queries. Fundamentally, the reason is that LAV enables expressing incomplete information. Given a set of data sources, GAV mappings define a *single* instance of the mediated schema that is consistent with the sources, and therefore query answering can simply be done on that instance. For that reason, the complexity of query answering is similar to that of query evaluation over a database. In contrast, given a set of LAV source descriptions, there is a *set* of instances of the mediated schema that are consistent with the data sources. As a consequence, query answering in LAV amounts to querying incomplete information, which is computationally more expensive.

Finally, we note a shortcoming of LAV. Consider the relations S1.Movie(MID, title) and S1.MovieDetail(MID, director, genre, year). The join between these two relations requires the MID key, which is internal to S1 and not modeled in the mediated schema. Hence, while it is possible to model the fact that MovieDetail contains directors, genres, and years of movies, LAV descriptions would lose the connection of those attributes with the movie title. The only way to circumvent that is to introduce an identifier for movies in the mediated schema. However, identifiers are typically not meaningful across multiple data sources, and hence we'd need to introduce a special identifier for every source where it is needed.

3.2.4 Global-and-Local-as-View

Fortunately, the two formalisms described above can be combined into one formalism that has the expressive power of both (with the sole cost of inventing another unfortunate acronym).

Syntax and Semantics
In the Global-and-Local-as-View (GLAV) formalism the expressions in the schema mapping include a query over the data sources on the left-hand side, and a query on the mediated schema on the right-hand side. Formally, GLAV is defined as follows.

Definition 3.6 (GLAV Schema Mapping). *Let G be a mediated schema, and let $\bar{S} = \{S_1, \ldots, S_n\}$ be schemata of n data sources. A GLAV schema mapping M is a set of expressions of the form $Q^S(\bar{X}) \subseteq Q^G(\bar{X})$ or $Q^S(\bar{X}) = Q^G(\bar{X})$ where*

* *Q^G is a query over the mediated schema G whose head variables are $\bar{X}$, and*
* *Q^S is a query over the data sources whose head variables are also $\bar{X}$.* ☐

■ ■ ■ ▬▬▬▬▬▬▬▬▬▬▬▬▬▬▬▬▬▬▬▬▬▬▬▬▬▬▬▬

Example 3.6

Suppose source S1 was known to have only comedies produced after 1970; then we could describe it using the following GLAV expression. Note that here too we abuse the notation by omitting the heads of the Q^G's and the Q^S's:

S1.Movie(MID, title), S1.MovieDetail(MID, director, genre, year) ⊆
                    Movie(title, director, "comedy", year), year ≥ 1970

▬▬▬▬▬▬▬▬▬▬▬▬▬▬▬▬▬▬▬▬▬▬▬▬▬▬▬ ■ ■ ■

The semantics of GLAV are defined by specifying the relation M_R defined by M.

Definition 3.7 (GLAV Semantics). *Let $M = M_1, \ldots, M_l$ be a GLAV schema mapping between G and $\bar{S} = \{S_1, \ldots, S_n\}$, where M_i is of the form $Q^S(\bar{X}) \subseteq Q^G(\bar{X})$ or $Q^S(\bar{X}) = Q^G(\bar{X})$.*

Let g be an instance of the mediated schema G, and let $\bar{s} = s_1, \ldots, s_n$ be instances of $S_1, \ldots, S_n$, respectively. The tuple of instances $(g, s_1, \ldots, s_n)$ is in M_R if for every $1 \leq i \leq l$, the following hold:

* *If M_i is a $=$ expression, then $S_i(\bar{s}) = Q_i(g)$.*
* *If M_i is a $\subseteq$ expression, then $S_i(\bar{s}) \subseteq Q_i(g)$.* ☐

Reformulation in GLAV

Reformulation in GLAV amounts to composing the LAV techniques with the GAV techniques. Given a query Q, it can be reformulated in the following two steps:

- Find a rewriting Q' of the query Q using the views $Q_1^G, \ldots, Q_l^G$.
- Create Q'' by replacing every occurrence of Q_i^G in Q' with Q_i^S and unfolding the result so it mentions only the source relations.

Applying Q'' to the source relations will yield all the certain answers in the cases specified in the theorem below. Consequently, the complexity of finding the certain answers and of finding a logical query plan in GLAV is the same as that for LAV.

Theorem 3.3. *Let $\bar{M} = M_1, \ldots, M_l$ be a GLAV schema mapping between a mediated schema G and source schemas $\bar{S} = \{S_1, \ldots, S_n\}$, where M_i is of the form $Q^S(\bar{X}) \subseteq Q^G(\bar{X})$ or $Q^S(\bar{X}) = Q^G(\bar{X})$, and assume that each relation in the mediated schema or in the sources appears in at most one M_i. Let Q be a conjunctive query over G.*

Assume that the Q_i^S's are conjunctive queries or unions of conjunctive queries, even with interpreted predicates and negated predicates.

- *If all the Q_i^G's in M are conjunctive queries with no interpreted predicates or negation, and all the M_i are $\subseteq$ expressions, then all the certain answers can be found in time polynomial in the size of the data and in the size of M, and the complexity of reformulation is polynomial in the number of data sources.*
- *If all the Q_i^G's in M are conjunctive queries with no interpreted predicates or negation, and some of the M_i's are $=$ expressions, then finding all the certain answers to Q is co-NP-hard in the size of the data.*
- *If some of the Q_i^G's include interpreted predicates, then finding all the certain answers to Q is co-NP-hard in the size of the data.* □

The reformulations created as described above produce only certain answers when some of the relations occur in more than one M_i, but may not produce all the certain answers. We note that in practice, the real power of GLAV is the ability to use both GAV and LAV descriptions, even if none of the source descriptions uses the power of both.

3.2.5 Tuple-Generating Dependencies

The previous three schema mapping languages are based on the notion of set inclusion (or equivalence) constraints: the query reformulation algorithm reasons about what query answers are certain, given source instances and the constraints.

An alternative language is derived from data dependency constraints, namely, *tuple-generating dependencies*, a formalism developed for the specification and analysis of integrity constraints in databases. Tuple-generating dependencies (or tgds) are equivalent in expressiveness to GLAV mappings.

Syntax and Semantics

We briefly introduced the tuple-generating dependency in Section 2.1.2, which discussed integrity constraints. We repeat the definition:

Definition 3.8 (Tuple-Generating Dependency). *A tuple-generating dependency (tgd) is an assertion about the relationship between a source data instance (in our case, a source database) and a target data instance (in our case, a central database or mediated schema). A tgd takes the form*

$$\forall \bar{X}, \bar{Y}(\phi(\bar{X}, \bar{Y}) \rightarrow \exists \bar{Z} \psi(\bar{X}, \bar{Z})) \tag{3.1}$$

where ϕ and ψ are conjunctions of atoms over the source and target instances, respectively. If the condition ϕ holds over the left-hand side (lhs) of the tgd, then condition ψ must hold over the right-hand side (rhs). □

Note that the above tgd is equivalent to the GLAV inclusion constraint:

$$Q^S(\bar{X}, \bar{Y}) \subseteq Q^T(\bar{Y}, \bar{Z})$$

where

$$Q^S(\bar{X}, \bar{Y}) :\text{-} \phi(\bar{X}, \bar{Y})$$
$$Q^T(\bar{Y}, \bar{Z}) :\text{-} \psi(\bar{Y}, \bar{Z})$$

■ ■ ■ ▬▬▬

Example 3.7

The GLAV description of Section 3.6 would be specified using a tgd as follows:

S1.Movie(MID, title) ∧ S1.MovieDetail(MID, director, genre, year) ⇒
Movie(title, director, "comedy", year) ∧ year ≥ 1970

▬▬▬▬▬▬▬▬▬▬▬▬▬▬▬▬▬▬▬▬▬▬▬▬▬▬▬▬▬▬▬▬▬▬▬▬▬▬▬ ■ ■ ■

Often we will omit the universal quantifiers from the description of the tgd, as they can be inferred from the variables used in the constraint. This allows us to rewrite the previous tgd as

$$\phi(\bar{X}, \bar{Y}) \rightarrow \exists \bar{Z} \psi(\bar{X}, \bar{Z})$$

Reformulation with tgds

Since tgds and GLAV mappings are equivalent in expressiveness, we can apply the reformulation algorithms discussed earlier on tgds. To reformulate tgds using the Inverse-Rules

Algorithm of Section 2.4.5, there is a more direct transformation. Given a tgd of the form

$$\phi(\bar{X}, \bar{Y}) \rightarrow \exists \bar{Z} \psi(\bar{X}, \bar{Z})$$

generate an inverse rules program P as follows:

- Replace each existential variable in the rhs, $z \in \bar{Z}$, with a new Skolem function over the variables shared between the lhs and rhs, namely, $f_z(\bar{X})$. Let the resulting rhs be $\psi(\bar{X}, \bar{Z}')$ where each term in Z' is now a Skolem function.
- For each relation atom $R_i(\bar{X}_{R_i})$ in $\psi(\bar{X}, \bar{Z}')$, define a new inverse rule:

$$R_i(\bar{X}_{R_i}) :- \phi(\bar{X}, \bar{Y})$$

Now evaluate the query over program P, as in Section 2.4.5.

■ ■ ■ ▬▬▬▬▬▬▬▬▬▬▬▬▬▬▬▬▬▬▬▬▬▬▬▬▬▬▬▬▬▬

Example 3.8

The tgd from Example 3.7 would result in the following inverse rule:

Movie(title, director, "comedy", year") :- S1.Movie(MID, title),
                                                      S1.MovieDetail(MID, director, genre, year)

▬▬▬▬▬▬▬▬▬▬▬▬▬▬▬▬▬▬▬▬▬▬▬▬▬▬▬▬ ■ ■ ■

Later in Section 10.2 we will see a more complex reformulation procedure called the *chase*, which is often used with tgds as well as another type of constraint called equality-generating dependencies (egds). We discuss the details of the chase with tuple-generating dependencies and equality-generating dependencies (egd's) in Section 10.2. We note here that the inverse-rules formulation described above has an exact correspondence to the execution of the chase, though only for the setting without egds.

3.3 Access-Pattern Limitations

Thus far, the logical plans we have generated assumed that we can access the relations in the data sources in any way we want. In particular, this means the data integration system can choose any *order* it deems most efficient to access the data sources and is free to pose any query to each source. In practice, there are often significant limitations on the allowable access patterns to data sources. The primary examples of such limitations involve sources served by forms on the Web and data available through specific interfaces defined by Web services. Typically, such interfaces define a set of required inputs that must be given in order to obtain an answer, and it is rarely possible to obtain *all* the tuples from such sources. In some other cases, limitations on access patterns are imposed in order to restrict the queries that can be asked of a source and therefore limit the load on the source.

This section begins by discussing how to model limitations on access patterns to data sources, and then describes how to refine a logical query plan into an *executable* plan that adheres to these limitations. We will see that access-pattern limitations can have subtle effects on query plans.

3.3.1 Modeling Access-Pattern Limitations

We model access-pattern limitations by attaching *adornments* to relations of data sources. Specifically, if a source relation has n attributes, then an adornment consists of a string of length n, composed of the letters b and f. The meaning of the letter b in an adornment is that the source *must* be given values for the attribute in that position. An f adornment means that the source does not need a value for that position. If there are multiple sets of allowable inputs to the source, we attach several adornments to the source.

■ ■ ■ ▬▬▬▬▬▬▬▬▬▬▬▬▬▬▬▬▬▬▬▬▬▬▬▬▬▬▬▬▬▬▬▬▬

Example 3.9

To illustrate the concepts in this section we use an example in the domain of publications and citations. Consider a mediated schema that includes the following relations: Cites stores pairs of publication identifiers (X, Y), where publication X cites publication Y, AwardPaper stores the identifiers of papers that received an award, and DBPapers stores the identifiers of papers in the field of databases.

The following LAV expressions also express the access-pattern limitations to the sources:

S1: CitationDB^{bf}(X,Y) $\subseteq$ Cites(X,Y)
S2: CitingPapers^{f}(X) $\subseteq$ Cites(X,Y)
S3: DBSource^{f}(X) $\subseteq$ DBpapers(X)
S4: AwardDB^{b}(X) $\subseteq$ AwardPaper(X)

The first source stores pairs of citations where the first paper cites the second, but requires that the citing paper be given as input (hence the *bf* adornment). The second source stores all the papers that cite some paper, and enables querying for all such papers. The third source stores papers in the database field, but does not have any access restrictions, and the fourth source stores all the papers that won awards, but requires that the identifier of the paper be given as input. That is, you can ask the source if a particular paper won an award, but cannot ask for all award papers.

▬▬▬▬▬▬▬▬▬▬▬▬▬▬▬▬▬▬▬▬▬▬▬▬▬▬▬▬▬▬▬ ■ ■ ■

3.3.2 Generating Executable Plans

Given a set of access-pattern limitations, we need to generate logical plans that are executable. Intuitively, an executable query plan is one in which we can always supply values to data sources when they are required. Hence, a key aspect of executable plans is the order of its subgoals. Formally, executable query plans are defined as follows.

Definition 3.9 (Executable Query Plans).   *Let $q_1(\bar{X}_1), \ldots, q_n(\bar{X}_n)$ be a conjunctive query plan over a set of data sources, and let BF_i be the set of adornments describing the access-pattern limitations to the source q_i.*

Algorithm 7. FindExecutablePlan: An algorithm for finding an executable ordering of a logical query plan.

Input: logical query plan Q of the form $g_1(\bar{X}_1), \ldots, g_n(\bar{X}_n)$; binding patterns $BF = BF_1, \ldots, BF_n$, where
BF_i is a set of adornments for g_i; **Output:** EP is the resulting plan.
    EP = empty list.
    for $i = 1, \ldots, n$ **do**
        Initialize $AD_i = BF_i$
        {As we add subgoals to the plan, AD_i records their new allowable access patterns}
    end for
    repeat
        Choose a subgoal $q_i(\bar{X}_i) \in Q$, such that AD_i has an adornment that is all f's and $q_i(\bar{X}_i) \notin EP$
        Add $q_i(\bar{X}_i)$ to the end of EP
        for every variable $X \in \bar{X}_i$ **do**
            if X appears in position k of $g_l(\bar{X}_l)$ and position k of an adornment $ad \in AD_i$ is b **then**
                change position k to f
            end if
        end for
    until no new subgoals can be added to EP
    if all the subgoals in Q are in EP **then**
        return EP as an executable plan
    else
        return No executable ordering
    end if

    We say that $q_1(\bar{X}_1), \ldots, q_n(\bar{X}_n)$ is an executable plan if there is a choice of adornments $bf_1, \ldots, bf_n$, such that

- *$bf_i \in BF_i$ and*
- *if the variable X appears in position k of $q_i(\bar{X}_i)$ and the kth letter of bf_i is b, then X appears in a subgoal $q_j(\bar{X}_j)$ where $j < i$.* □

Note that changing the order of the subgoals in the logical plan does not affect the results. Algorithm 7 shows how to find an executable reordering of a given logical query plan with a simple greedy algorithm. Intuitively, the algorithm orders the subgoals in the plan beginning with those that have a completely free adornment (i.e., all f's), and then iteratively adds subgoals whose requirements are satisfied by subgoals earlier in the plan. If the algorithm manages to insert all the subgoals into the plan, then it is executable. Otherwise, there is no executable ordering of the subgoals.

When we cannot find an executable ordering of the subgoals in a query plan, then the natural question that arises is whether we can *add* subgoals to make the plan executable, and whether the new plan is guaranteed to find all the certain answers.

■ ■ ■ ▬▬▬▬▬▬▬▬▬▬▬▬▬▬▬▬▬▬▬▬▬▬▬▬▬▬▬▬▬

Example 3.10

Consider the following query over our mediated schema, asking for all the papers that cite Paper #001:

$Q(X) :\text{-} \text{Cites}(X, 001)$

Ignoring the access-pattern limitations, the following plan would suffice:

$Q'(X) :\text{-} \text{CitationDB}(X, 001)$

However, that plan is not executable because CitationDB requires an input to its first field. Fortunately, the following longer plan is executable:

$q(X) :\text{-} \text{CitingPapers}(X), \text{CitationDB}(X, 001)$

■ ■ ■

The above example showed that it is possible to add subgoals to the plan to obtain an executable plan. The following example shows that there may not be any limit on the length of such a plan!

■ ■ ■ ▬▬▬▬▬▬▬▬▬▬▬▬▬▬▬▬▬▬▬▬▬▬▬▬▬▬▬▬▬

Example 3.11

Consider the following query, asking for all papers that won awards, and let's ignore S2 for the purpose of this example.

$Q(X) :\text{-} \text{AwardPaper}(X)$

Since the data source AwardDB requires its input to be bound, we cannot query it without a binding. Instead, we need to find candidate award papers. One way to find candidates is to query the source DBSource, obtaining all database papers, and feed these papers to the source AwardDB. Another set of candidates can be computed by papers cited by database papers, i.e., joining DBSource with the source CitationDB.

In fact, we can generalize this pattern. For any integer n, we can begin by finding candidate papers reachable by chains of citations starting from database papers and having lengh n. These candidates can be given as bindings to the AwardDB source to check whether they won an award. The query plans below illustrate the pattern. The problem, however, is that unless we have some unique knowledge of the domain, we cannot bound the value of n for which we need to create query plans.

$Q'(X) :\text{-} \text{DBSource}(X), \text{AwardDB}(X)$
$Q'(X) :\text{-} \text{DBSource}(X), \text{CitationDB}(V, X_1), \ldots, \text{CitationDB}(X_n, X), \text{AwardDB}(X)$

■ ■ ■

Fortunately, even if there is no bound on the length of a query plan, there is a compact *recursive* query plan that is executable and that will obtain all the possible answers. A recursive query plan is a datalog program whose base predicates are the data sources and that is allowed to compute intermediate relations in addition to the query relation. Let us first see how to construct a recursive plan for our example.

■ ■ ■ ───────────────────────────────────────

Example 3.12

The key to constructing the recursive plan is to define a new intermediate relation papers whose extension is the set of all papers reachable by citation chains from database papers. The papers relation is defined by the first two rules below. The third rule joins the papers relation with the AwardDB relation. Note that each of the rules in the plan is executable.

papers(X) :- DBSource(X)
papers(X) :- papers(Y), CitationDB(Y, X)
Q'(X) :- papers(X), AwardDB(X).

─────────────────────────────────────── ■ ■ ■

We now describe how to build such a recursive plan in the general case. We describe the construction for the case in which every source is represented by a relation with a single adornment, but the generalization for multiple adornments is straightforward. Given a logical query plan Q over a set of sources $S_1, \ldots, S_n$, we create an executable query plan in two steps.

Step 1: We define an intermediate (IDB) relation Dom that will include all the constants in the domain that we obtained from the sources. Let $S_i(X_1, \ldots, X_k)$ be a data source, and assume without loss of generality that the adornment of S_i requires that arguments $X_1, \ldots, X_l$ (for $l \leq k$) must be bound and the rest are free. We add the following rules, for $l + 1 \leq j \leq k$:

Dom(X_j) :- Dom(X_1),..., Dom(X_l), S_i($X_1, \ldots, X_k$)

Note that at least one of the sources must have an adornment that is all f's; otherwise, we cannot answer any query. Those sources will provide the base case rules for Dom.

Step 2: We modify the original query plan by inserting atoms of the Dom relation as necessary. Specifically, for every variable X in the plan, let k be the first subgoal in which it appears. If the adornment of $q_k(\bar{X}_k)$ has a b in any of the positions that X appears in $q_k(\bar{X}_k)$, then we insert the atom Dom(X) in front of $q_k(\bar{X}_k)$.

The above algorithm is obviously inefficient in many cases. In practice, the Dom relation need only include values for columns that need to be bound in some source. Furthermore, we can refine the Dom relation into multiple relations, each one containing the constants relevant to a particular column (e.g., we can create one relation for movie names and another for city names). In many application domains, such as geography (countries, cities) and movies, we have a reasonable list of constants. In these cases, we can use these lists in place of Dom.

3.4 Integrity Constraints on the Mediated Schema

When we design a mediated schema, we often have additional knowledge about the domain. We express such knowledge in the form of integrity constraints, such as functional dependencies or inclusion constraints. This section shows how the presence of integrity constraints on the mediated schema affects the query plans we need to create in order to obtain all certain answers. Integrity constraints affect both LAV and GAV source descriptions.

3.4.1 LAV with Integrity Constraints

The following example illustrates the complications that arise when we have integrity constraints in LAV.

■ ■ ■ ━━

Example 3.13

Consider a mediated schema that includes a single relation representing flight schedule information, including the pilot and aircraft that are planned for each flight.

schedule(airline, flightNum, date, pilot, aircraft)

Suppose we have the following functional dependencies on the Schedule relation:

Pilot → Airline and Aircraft → Airline

The first functional dependency expresses the fact that pilots work for only one airline, and the second specifies that there is no joint ownership of aircraft between airlines. Suppose we have the following LAV schema mapping of a source S:

S(date, pilot, aircraft) ⊆ schedule(airline, flightNum, date, pilot, aircraft)

The source S records the dates on which pilots flew different aircraft. Now suppose a user asks for pilots that work for the same airline as Mike:

q(p) :- schedule(airline, flightNum, date, "mike", aircraft), schedule(airline, f, d, p, a)

Source S doesn't record the airlines that pilots work for, and therefore, without any further knowledge, we cannot compute any answers to the query q. Nonetheless, using the functional dependencies of relation schedule, conclusions can be drawn on which pilots work for the same airline as Mike. Consider the database shown in Figure 3.3. If both Mike and Ann are known to have flown aircraft #111, then Ann works for the same airline as Mike because of the functional dependency Aircraft → Airline. Moreover, if Ann is known to have flown aircraft #222, and John has flown aircraft #222, then Ann and John work for the same airline because of the functional dependency Aircraft → Airline. Hence, because of the integrity constraint Pilot → Airline, we can infer that John and Mike work for the same airline. In general, we can consider any logical query plan, q'_n, of the following form:

$$q'_n(p) \text{ :- } S(D_1,\text{"mike"},C_1), \ S(D_2, p_2, C_1), \ S(D_3, p_2, C_2), \ S(D_4, p_3, C_2), \ \dots,$$
$$S(D_{2n-2}, p_n, C_{n-1}), \ S(D_{2n-1}, p_n, C_n), \ S(D_{2n}, p, C_n)$$

For any n, q'_n may yield results that shorter plans did not, and therefore there is no limit on the length of a logical query plan that we need to consider. Fortunately, as in the case of access-pattern limitations, recursive query plans come to our rescue. We now describe the construction of a recursive query plan that is guaranteed to produce all certain answers even in the presence of functional dependencies.

■ ■ ■

date	pilot	aircraft
1/1	Mike	#111
5/2	Ann	#111
1/3	Ann	#222
4/3	John	#222

FIGURE 3.3 A database of pilots' schedules.

The input to the construction is the logical query plan, q', generated by the Inverse-Rules Algorithm (Section 2.4.5). The inverse rule created for source S is shown below. Recall that f_1 and f_2 are Skolem functions, and they are used to represent objects about which we have incomplete information.

schedule(f_1(d,p,a), f_2(d,p,a), d, p, a) :- S(d, p, a)

The inverse rules alone don't take into account the presence of the functional dependencies. For example, applying the inverse rule on the table shown in Figure 3.3 would yield the following tuples:

schedule(f_1(1/1, Mike, #111), f_2(1/1, Mike, #111), 1/1, Mike, #111)
schedule(f_1(5/2, Ann, #111), f_2(5/2, Ann, #111), 5/2, Ann, #111)
schedule(f_1(1/3, Ann, #222), f_2(1/3, Ann, #222), 1/3, Ann, #222)
schedule(f_1(4/3, John, #222), f_2(4/3, John, #222), 4/3, John, #222)

Because of the functional dependencies on the schedule relation, it is possible to conclude that f_1(1/1, Mike, #111) is equal to f_1(5/2, Ann, #111), and that both are equal to f_1(1/3, Ann, #222) and f_1(4/3, John, #222).

We enable the recursive query plan to make such inferences by introducing a new binary relation e. The intended meaning of e is that e(c_1,c_2) holds if and only if c_1 and c_2 are equal constants under the given functional dependencies. Hence, the extension of e includes the extension of = (i.e., for every X, e(X,X)), and the tuples that can be derived by the following *chase rules* (e($\bar{A}$, $\bar{A}'$) is a shorthand for e(A_1,A'_1),...,e(A_n,A'_n)).

Definition 3.10 (Chase Rules). *Let $\bar{A} \to B$ be a functional dependency satisfied by a relation p in the mediated schema. Let $\bar{C}$ be the attributes of p that are not in $\bar{A}$, B. The chase rule* *corresponding to $\bar{A} \rightarrow B$ is the following:*

$$e(B,B') :\text{-} p(\bar{A},B,\bar{C}),\ p(\bar{A}',B',\bar{C}'),\ e(\bar{A},\bar{A}').$$

      ☐

Given a set of functional dependencies Σ on the mediated schema, we denote by *chase*(Σ) the set of chase rules corresponding to the functional dependencies in Σ. In our example, the chase rules are

    e(X,Y) :- schedule(X, F, P, D, A), schedule(Y, F', P', D', A'), e(A, A')
    e(X,Y) :- schedule(X, F, P, D, A), schedule(Y, F', P', D', A'), e(P, P')

The chase rules allow us to derive the following facts in relation e:

$e(f_1(1/1, \text{Mike}, \#111), f_1(5/2, \text{Ann}, \#111))$
$e(f_1(5/2, \text{Ann}, \#111), f_1(1/3, \text{Ann}, \#222))$
$e(f_1(1/3, \text{Ann}, \#222), f_1(4/3, \text{John}, \#222))$

The extension of e is reflexive by construction and is symmetric because of the symmetry in the chase rules. To guarantee that e is an equivalence relation, we add the following rule that enforces the transitivity of e:

    T: e(X,Y) :- e(X,Z), e(Z,Y).

The final step in the construction is to rewrite the query q′ in a way that it can use the equivalences derived in relation e. We initialize q″ to q′ and apply the following transformations:

1. If c is a constant in one of the subgoals of q″, we replace it by a new variable Z, and add the subgoal e(Z,c).
2. If X is a variable in the head of q″, we replace X in the body of q″ by a new variable X', and add the subgoal e(X′,X).
3. If a variable Y that is not in the head of q″ appears in two subgoals of q″, we replace one of its occurrences by Y', and add the subgoal e(Y′,Y).

We apply the above steps until no additional changes can be made to q″. In our example query q′ would be rewritten to

    q″(P) :- schedule(A, F, D, M, C), schedule(A′, F′, D′, P′, C′), e(M, "mike"),
             e(P′, P), e(A, A′)

The resulting query plan includes q″, the chase rules, and the transitivity rule T. It can be shown that the above construction is guaranteed to yield all the certain answers to the query in the presence of functional dependencies. The bibliographic notes include a reference to the full proof of this claim.

3.4.2 GAV with Integrity Constraints

A key property of GAV schema mappings is that unlike LAV mappings, they do not model incomplete information. Given a set of data sources and a GAV schema mapping, there is a single instance of the mediated schema that is consistent with the sources, thereby considerably simplifying query processing. With integrity constraints, as the following example illustrates, this property no longer holds.

■ ■ ■ ▬▬

Example 3.14

Suppose that in addition to the schedule relation, we also had a relation flight(flightNum, origin, destination) storing the beginning and ending points of every flight. In addition, we have the following integrity constraint stating that every flight number appearing in the schedule relation must also appear in the flight relation:

schedule(flightNum) $\subseteq$ flight(flightNum).

Assume that we have two sources, each providing tuples for one of the relations in the mediated schema (and hence the schema mappings are trivial). Consider the query asking for all flight numbers:

q(fN) :- schedule(airline, fN, date, pilot, aircraft), flight(fN, origin, destination)

In GAV we would answer this query by unfolding it and joining the two tables in Table 3.1, but only considering the tuples in the sources. Consequently, flight #111 that appears in the schedule relation but not in flight will not appear in the result.

The integrity constraint implies the existence of some tuples that may not appear explicitly in the source. In particular, while we do not know exactly the details of flight #111, we know it exists and therefore should be included in the answer to q. Note that this situation arises if we make the open-world assumption. If we made the closed-world assumption, the data sources in this example would be inconsistent with the schema mapping.

▬▬ ■ ■ ■

Table 3.1   Pilot and Flight Schedules

Flight		
FlightNum	**Origin**	**Destination**
222	Seattle	SFO
333	SFO	Saigon

Schedule				
Airline	**Flightnum**	**Date**	**Pilot**	**Aircraft**
United	#111	1/1	Mike	Boeing777-15
Singapore Airlines	#222	1/3	Ann	Boeing777-17

Using techniques similar to those in LAV, there is a way to extend the logical query plans to ensure that we obtain all the certain answers. We refer the reader to the bibliographic notes for futher details.

3.5 Answer Completeness

We've already seen that the schema mapping formalisms can express completeness of data sources, and we've also seen how completeness of data sources can affect the complexity of finding the certain answers. Knowing that sources are complete is useful for creating more efficient query answering plans. In particular, if there are several sources that contain similar data, then unless we know that one of them is complete, we need to query them all in order to get all the possible answers. This section considers a more refined notion of completeness, called *local completeness*.

3.5.1 Local Completeness

In practice, sources are often *locally* complete. For example, a movie database may be complete with regards to more recent movies, but incomplete on earlier ones. The following example shows how we can extend LAV expressions with local-completeness information. Similarly, we can also describe local completeness in GAV.

■ ■ ■ ▬▬▬

Example 3.15

Recall the LAV descriptions of sources S5–S7:

S5.MovieGenres(title, genre) $\subseteq$ Movie(title, director, year, genre)
S6.MovieDirectors(title, dir) $\subseteq$ Movie(title, director, year, genre)
S7.MovieYears(title, year) $\subseteq$ Movie(title, director, year, genre)

We can add the following local-completeness (LC) descriptions:

LC(S5.MovieGenres(title, genre), genre="comedy")
LC(S6.MovieDirectors(title, dir), American(director))
LC(S7.MovieYears(title, year), year $\geq$ 1980)

The above assertions express that S5 is complete w.r.t. comedies, S6 is complete for American directors (where **American** is a relation in the mediated schema), and that S7 is complete w.r.t. movies produced in 1980 or after.

▬▬▬▬▬▬▬▬▬▬▬▬▬▬▬▬▬▬▬▬▬▬▬▬▬▬▬▬▬▬▬▬▬▬▬▬▬ ■ ■ ■

Formally, we specify local-completeness statements by specifying a constraint on the tuples of a source.

Definition 3.11 (Local-Completeness Constraint).   *Let M be a LAV expression of the form* $S(\bar{X}) \subseteq Q(\bar{X})$, *where S is a data source and* $Q(\bar{X})$ *is a conjunctive query over the mediated* *schema. A local-completeness constraint C on M is a conjunction of atoms of relations in the mediated schema or of atoms of interpreted predicates that does not include relation names mentioned in Q. The atoms may include variables in $\bar{X}$ or new ones. We denote the complement of C by ¬C.* ☐

The semantics of the local-completeness expression LC(S, C) is that in addition to the original expression, we also have the following expression in the schema mapping. Note that we add the conjuncts of C to Q.

$$S(\bar{X}) = Q(\bar{X}), C$$

When schema mappings can include local-completeness statements, a natural question to ask is the following: Given a query over the mediated schema, is the answer to the query guaranteed to be complete?

■ ■ ■ ▬▬▬▬▬▬▬▬▬▬▬▬▬▬▬▬▬▬▬▬▬▬▬▬▬▬▬▬▬▬▬▬

Example 3.16

Consider the following two queries over the sources in Example 3.15:

q_1(title) :- Movie(title, director, genre, "comedy"), year $\geq$ 1990, American(director)
q_2(title) :- Movie(title, director, genre, "comedy"), year $\geq$ 1970, American(director)

The answer to q_1 is guaranteed to be complete because it only touches on complete parts of the sources: comedies by American directors produced after 1980. On the other hand, the answer to q_2 may not be complete if the source S7 is missing movies produced between 1970 and 1980.

▬▬▬▬▬▬▬▬▬▬▬▬▬▬▬▬▬▬▬▬▬▬▬▬▬▬▬▬▬▬▬ ■ ■ ■

Formally, we define answer completeness as follows. Intuitively, the definition says that whenever two instances of the data sources agree on the tuples for which the sources are known to be locally complete, they will have the same certain answers.

Definition 3.12 (Answer Completeness).   *Let M be a LAV schema mapping for sources $S_1, \ldots, S_n$ that includes a set of expressions of the form $S_i(\bar{X_i}) \subseteq Q_i(\bar{X_i})$, and a set of local-completeness assertions of the form $LC(S_i, C_i)$. Let Q be a conjunctive query over the mediated schema.*

The query Q is answer complete w.r.t. M if for any pair instances d_1, d_2 of the data sources, such that for every i, if d_1 and d_2 have the same tuples of S_i satisfying C_i, then the certain answers to Q over d_1 are the same as the certain answers to Q over d_2. ☐

3.5.2 Detecting Answer Completeness

We now describe an algorithm for deciding when a query is answer complete. To focus on the interesting aspects of the algorithm, we consider a simplified setting. We assume that data sources correspond directly to relations in the mediated schema, augmented with a

---

Algorithm 8. DecideCompleteness: An algorithm for detecting answer completeness of a query.

Input: conjunctive query over the sources $Q = S_1, \ldots, S_n$; M includes the LAV expressions $S_i(\bar{X}_i) \subseteq R(\bar{X}_i), C_i'$ and the local-completeness assertions $LC(S_i, C_i)$. **Output:** returns *yes* if and only if Q is answer complete w.r.t. M.

Let $E_1, \ldots, E_n$ be new relation symbols

Define the views $V_1, \ldots, V_n$ as follows:

$\quad V_i(\bar{X}_i) :\text{-} E_i(\bar{X}_i), \neg C_i$

$\quad V_i(\bar{X}_i) :\text{-} S_i(\bar{X}_i), C_i$

Let Q_1 be the query in which every occurrence of S_i in Q is replaced by V_i

return *yes* if and only if Q is equivalent to Q_1

---

conjunction of interpreted atoms. Specifically, we assume LAV expressions of the form

$$S_i(\bar{X}) \subseteq R_i(\bar{X}), C'$$

where R_i is a relation in the mediated schema and C' is a conjunction of atoms of interpreted predicates.

Algorithm 8 shows how to determine answer completeness by reducing it to the problem of query containment. The intuition behind the algorithm is the following. Since the sources S_i are complete for tuples satisfying C_i, the only tuples in S_i that may be missing are ones that satisfy $\neg C_i$. We define the view V_i to be the relation that includes the tuples of S_i that satisfy C_i and tuples that may be missing from S_i. The view V_i obtains the tuples satisfying C_i from S_i (since S_i has them all), and the tuples satisfying $\neg C_i$ from a new relation E_i whose tuples we don't know. Note that with appropriate extensions for the E_i's it is possible to create an instance of V_i that is equal to any possible instance of S_i.

The algorithm then compares the query Q with the query Q' in which occurrences of S_i are replaced with V_i. If the two queries are equivalent, then for any instance of the S_i's and the E_i's we obtain the same result. Since Q does not depend on the E_i's, this means that Q is completely determined by the tuples of S_i that satisfy C_i.

The following theorem establishes the correctness of algorithm **Decide-Completeness**.

Theorem 3.4. *Let M be a LAV schema mapping for sources $S_1, \ldots, S_n$ that includes the expressions $S_i(\bar{X}_i) \subseteq R(\bar{X}_i), C_i'$, and a set of local-completeness assertions $LC(S_i, C_i)$. Let Q be a conjunctive query over the mediated schema.*

Algorithm **Decide-Completeness** *returns* **yes** *if and only if Q is answer complete w.r.t. M.* □

Proof. For the first direction, suppose Q_1 is not equivalent to Q. We show that Q is not answer complete w.r.t. M.

Since $Q_1 \not\equiv Q$, there is a database instance d on which Q and Q_1 return different answers. Let d_1 be the instance of the data sources where the extension of S_i is its extension in d. Let d_2 be the instance of the data sources in which the extension of S_i is the extension of V_i in d. The instances d_1 and d_2 agree on the tuples of S_i that satisfy C_i, for $1 \leq i \leq n$, but do not agree on the certain answers to Q, and therefore Q is not answer complete w.r.t. M.

For the other direction, assume $Q_1 \equiv Q$. Let d_1 and d_2 be two instances of the sources that agree on the tuples of S_i that satisfy C_i. Define d_3 to be the restriction of d_1 (and hence also d_2) that include only the tuples of S_i that satisfy C_i. Since $Q_1 \equiv Q$ it is easy to see that $Q(d_1) = Q(d_3)$ and similarly that $Q(d_2) = Q(d_3)$. Hence, $Q(d_1) = Q(d_2)$.   □

3.6 Data-Level Heterogeneity

The schema mapping formalisms described thus far assumed that whenever an expression in the mapping requires joining tuples from different sources, then the join columns will have comparable values. For example, in the movie domain, we assumed that whenever a movie occurs in a source, it occurs with the same title string as in all other sources in which it appears.

In practice, sources not only differ on the structure of their schemas, but also differ considerably on how they represent values and objects in the world. We refer to these differences as *data-level heterogeneity*. Data-level heterogeneity can be broadly classified into two types.

3.6.1 Differences of Scale

The first kind of data-level heterogeneity occurs when there is some mathematical transformation between the values in one source and the other. Examples of this type of heterogeneity are when one source represents temperatures in Celsius while another does so in Fahrenheit, or when one source represents course grades on a numerical ladder while the other uses letter grades. In some cases the transformation may require values from different columns. For example, one source may represent first name and last name in two different columns, while another may concatenate them in one column. The latter example is one in which the transformation is not easily reversible. Consequently, it may not be possible to accurately retrieve the first name when the two names are concatenated. In other cases, the transformation may require deeper knowledge of the semantics. For example, in one database prices may include local taxes, while in another they do not. Some transformations may be time dependent. For example, the exchange rate between currencies varies constantly.

This kind of data-level heterogeneity can be reconciled by adding the transformation function to the expression in the schema mapping. For example, the first expression below translates the temperatures in the source from Fahrenheit to Celsius, and in the second expression, we adjust the price obtained from the source to include the local taxes.

S(city, temp - 32 * 5/9, month) ⊆ Weather(city, temp, humidity, month)
CDStore(cd, price) ⊆ CDPrices(cd, state, price * (1+rate)), LocalTaxes(state, rate)

Country GDPs	Country Water Access
Congo, Republic of the	Congo (Dem. Rep.)
Korea, South	South Korea
Isle of Man	Man, Isle of
Burma	Myanmar
Virgin Islands	Virgin Islands of the U.S.

FIGURE 3.4 Disparate databases often refer to the same real-world objects with different names. A concordance table provides the mapping between the different names.

3.6.2 Multiple References to the Same Entity

The second kind of data-level heterogeneity occurs when there are multiple ways of referring to the same object in the real world. Common examples of this case include different ways of referring to companies (e.g., IBM versus International Business Machines, or Google versus Google Inc.) and people (e.g., Jack M. Smith versus J. M. Smith). Reconciling multiple references to the same real-world entity gets more complicated when referring to complex objects. For example, a reference to a publication includes a list of references to authors, a title, a year of publication, and a reference to venue of the publication. Furthermore, data need not always be clean, complicating the reconciliation problem even further. In some cases, we don't even know the exact truth. For example, biologists have many ways of referring to genes or species and it's not even known how to resolve all the references.

To resolve this kind of heterogeneity we create a *concordance table*, whose rows include multiple references to the same object. Specifically, the first column includes references from the first source and the second includes references from the second source. When we join the two sources, we perform an intermediate join with the concordance table to obtain the correct answers. For example, Figure 3.4 shows a concordance table for two sources that describe different attributes of countries.

Clearly, the hard problem is to create the concordance table in applications where there are a large number of rows. We focus on the problem of automatic reference reconciliation in Chapter 7.

Bibliographic Notes

Global-as-View was used in the earliest data integration systems (e.g., Multi-Base [366]) and several systems since then [128, 230, 281, 533]. Local-as-View was introduced by the Information Manifold System [381] and used in [199, 361] and others. GLAV was introduced in [235] and is the main formalism used in data exchange systems (see Chapter 10). In fact, GLAV is essentially a formalism for specifying tuple-generating dependencies [7], and hence some of the theory on integrity constraints can be applied to data integration and exchange. The development of multiple schema mapping languages led to several comparisons between the formalisms [373, 379, 555]. Alexe et al. [24] describe a system for creating GLAV schema mappings by example.

Restrictions on access patterns were first discussed by Rajaraman et al. [488]. They considered the problem of answering queries using views when views have adornments describing the limitations on access patterns. They showed that in the case of looking for an *equivalent* rewriting of a query using views, the bound on the length of the rewriting established by [398] (namely, the number of subgoals in the query) no longer holds. Instead, they established a new bound that is the sum of the number of subgoals and of the number of variables in the query. Kwok and Weld [361] showed that if we are looking for the maximally contained rewriting of a query in the presence of access-pattern limitations, then there may be no bound on its length. The recursive query plan that generates all the certain answers was described by Duschka et al. [197, 200]. Friedman and Weld [234] and Lambrecht et al. [365] describe how to further optimize the recursive query plan. Manolescu et al. [228] show the effects of binding patterns on traditional System-R style query optimization. Levy et al. [381] describe a more complex model for access-pattern limitations, where in addition to modeling the input, we also model the output. Then, if the sources have more than one capability record, they show that the problem of finding an executable plan is NP-complete.

Integrity constraints in the mediated schema and their effects on finding the certain answers were first discussed in the context of LAV in Duschka et al. [197, 199]. There the authors show that it is possible to find all the certain answers to a query even if there are functional dependencies and/or full dependencies on the mediated schema. Our examples are taken from [197]. Integrity constraints on GAV were considered by Cali et al. [104], where the authors showed that it is possible to find all the certain answers in the presence of key constraints and inclusion dependencies.

The study of answer completeness in databases goes back to Motro [446]. Etzioni et al. [213] introduced the local-completeness notation in the context of information gathering agents and showed some of its basic properties. The completeness algorithm we described is based on [378], where it is shown that the problem of determining completeness can be reformulated as the problem of determining independence of queries from updates [89, 202, 203, 382], which, in turn, can be reduced to a containment checking problem. Razniewski and Nutt [495] extends the framework of local completeness and enables expressing local completness on *queries* in addition to portions of relations. Fan et al. [223] discuss query completeness in cases where some master data (which are complete and correct) exist in an enterprise. Floresecu et al. [227] described a formalism for expressing degree of completeness via a probability that a tuple will be in a source. Probabilistic approaches to schema mapping are now gaining attention again, and we discuss them further in Chapter 13. Naumann et al. [454] describe techniques for quantifying completeness of sources and query answers.

4

String Matching

String matching is the problem of finding strings that refer to the same real-world entity. For example, the string David Smith in one database may refer to the same person as David R. Smith in another database. Similarly, the strings 1210 W. Dayton St, Madison WI and 1210 West Dayton, Madison WI 53706 refer to the same physical address.

String matching plays a critical role in many data integration tasks, including schema matching, data matching, and information extraction. Consequently, in this chapter we examine this problem in depth. Section 4.1 defines the string matching problem. Section 4.2 describes popular similarity measures that can be used to compute a similarity score between any two given strings. Finally, Section 4.3 discusses how to efficiently apply such a measure to match a large number of strings.

4.1 Problem Description

The problem we address in this chapter is the following. Given two sets of strings X and Y, we want to find all pairs of strings (x, y), where $x \in X$ and $y \in Y$, such that x and y refer to the same real-world entity. We refer to such pairs as *matches*. Figure 4.1(a-b) shows two example databases representing sets of persons, and Figure 4.1(c) shows the matches between them. For example, the first match (x_1, y_1) states that strings Dave Smith and David D. Smith refer to the same real-world person.

Solving the matching problem raises two major challenges: accuracy and scalability. Matching strings accurately is difficult because strings that refer to the same real-world entity are often very different. The reasons for appearing different include typing and OCR errors (e.g., David Smith is misspelled as Davod Smith), different formatting conventions (10/8/2009 vs. Oct 8, 2009), custom abbreviation, shortening of strings or omission (Daniel Walker Herbert Smith vs. Dan W. Smith), different names or nicknames (William Smith vs. Bill Smith), and shuffling parts of the string (Dept. of Computer Science, UW-Madison vs. Computer Science Dept., UW-Madison). Additionally, in some cases the data source(s) do not contain enough information to determine whether two strings refer to the same entity (e.g., trying to decide whether two authors mentioned in two different publications are the same person).

To address the accuracy challenge, a common solution is to define a *similarity measure* s that takes two strings x and y and returns a score in the range $[0, 1]$. The intention is that the higher the score, the more likely that x and y match. We then say that x and y match if $s(x, y) \geq t$, where t is a prespecified threshold. Many similarity measures have been proposed, and we discuss the main ones in Section 4.2.

Set X	Set Y	Matches
x_1 = Dave Smith	y_1 = David D. Smith	(x_1, y_1)
x_2 = Joe Wilson	y_2 = Daniel W. Smith	(x_3, y_2)
x_3 = Dan Smith		
(a)	(b)	(c)

FIGURE 4.1 An example of matching person names. Column (c) shows the matches between the databases in (a) and (b).

The second challenge is to apply the similarity measure $s(x,y)$ to a large number of strings. Since string similarity is typically applied to data entries, applying $s(x,y)$ to all pairs of strings in the Cartesian product of sets X and Y would be quadratic in the size of the data and therefore impractical. To address this challenge, several solutions have been proposed to apply $s(x,y)$ only to the most promising pairs. We discuss the key ideas of these solutions in Section 4.3.

4.2 Similarity Measures

A broad range of measures have been proposed to match strings. A similarity measure maps a pair of strings (x,y) into a number in the range $[0,1]$ such that a higher value indicates greater similarity between x and y. The terms *distance* and *cost measures* have also been used to describe the same concept, except that smaller values indicate higher similarity.

Broadly speaking, current similarity measures fall into four groups: sequence-based, set-based, hybrid, and phonetic measures. We now describe each one in turn.

4.2.1 Sequence-Based Similarity Measures

The first set of similarity measures we consider views strings as sequences of characters and computes a cost of transforming one string into the other. We begin with a basic measure called *edit distance*, and then consider several more elaborate versions.

Edit Distance
The edit distance measure, also known as Levenshtein distance, $d(x,y)$, computes the *minimal* cost of transforming string x to string y. Transforming a string is carried out using a sequence of the following operators: delete a character, insert a character, and substitute one character for another. For example, the cost of transforming the string x = David Smiths to the string y = Davidd Simth is 4. The required operations are: inserting a d (after David), substituting m by i, substituting i by m, and deleting the last character of x, which is s.

It is not hard to see that the minimal cost of transforming x to y is the same as the minimal cost of transforming y to x (using in effect the same transformation). Thus, $d(x,y)$ is well-defined and symmetric with respect to both x and y.

Intuitively, edit distance tries to capture the various ways people make editing mistakes, such as inserting an extra character (e.g., Davidd instead of David) or swapping two characters (e.g., Simth instead of Smith). Hence, the smaller the edit distance, the more similar the two strings are.

The edit distance function $d(x,y)$ is converted into a similarity function $s(x,y)$ as follows:

$$s(x,y) = 1 - \frac{d(x,y)}{max(length(x), length(y))}$$

For example, the similarity score between David Smiths and Davidd Smith is

$$s(\text{David Smiths}, \text{Davidd Smith}) = 1 - \frac{4}{max(12,12)} = 0.67$$

The value of $d(x,y)$ can be computed using dynamic programming. Let $x = x_1 x_2 \dots x_n$ and $y = y_1 y_2 \dots y_m$, where the x_i and y_j are characters. Let $d(i,j)$ denote the edit distance between $x_1 x_2 \dots x_i$ and $y_1 y_2 \dots y_j$ (which are the ith and jth prefixes of x and y).

The key to designing a dynamic-programming algorithm is to establish a recurrence equation that enables computing $d(i,j)$ from previously computed values of d. Figure 4.2(a) shows the recurrence equation in our case. To understand the equation, observe that we can transform string $x_1 x_2 \dots x_i$ into string $y_1 y_2 \dots y_j$ in one of four ways: (a) transforming $x_1 x_2 \dots x_{i-1}$ into $y_1 y_2 \dots y_{j-1}$, then copying x_i into y_j if $x_i = y_j$, (b) transforming $x_1 x_2 \dots x_{i-1}$ into $y_1 y_2 \dots y_{j-1}$, then substituting x_i with y_j if $x_i \neq y_j$, (c) deleting x_i, then transforming $x_1 x_2 \dots x_{i-1}$ into $y_1 y_2 \dots y_j$, and (d) transforming $x_1 x_2 \dots x_i$ into $y_1 y_2 \dots y_{j-1}$, then inserting y_j. The value $d(i,j)$ is the minimum of the costs of the above transformations. Figure 4.2(b) simplifies the equation in Figure 4.2(a) by merging the first two lines.

Figure 4.3 shows an example computation using the simplified equation. The figure illustrates computing the distance between the strings $x = $ dva and $y = $ dave. We start with the matrix in Figure 4.3(a), where the x_i are listed on the left and the y_j at the top. Note that we have added x_0 and y_0, two null characters at the start of x and y, to simplify the implementation. Specifically, this allows us to quickly fill in the first row and column, by setting $d(i,0) = i$ and $d(0,j) = j$.

$$d(i,j) = \min \begin{cases} d(i-1, j-1) & \text{if } x_i = y_j \quad // \text{ copy} \\ d(i-1, j-1) + 1 & \text{if } x_i <> y_j \quad // \text{ substitute} \\ d(i-1, j) + 1 & // \text{ delete } x_i \\ d(i, j-1) + 1 & // \text{ insert } y_j \end{cases}$$

$$d(i,j) = \min \begin{cases} d(i-1, j-1) + c(x_i, y_j) & // \text{ copy or substitute} \\ d(i-1, j) + 1 & // \text{ delete } x_i \\ d(i, j-1) + 1 & // \text{ insert } y_j \end{cases}$$

$$c(x_i, y_j) = 0 \text{ if } x_i = y_j$$
$$1 \text{ otherwise}$$

(a)   (b)

FIGURE 4.2 (a) The recurrence equation for computing edit distance between strings x and y using dynamic programming and (b) a simplified form of the equation.

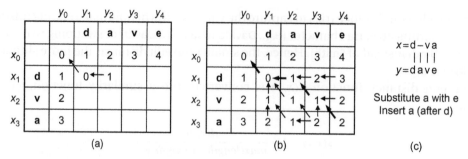

FIGURE 4.3 Computing the edit distance between **dva** and **dave** using the dynamic programming equation in Figure 4.2(b). (a) The dynamic programming matrix after filling in several cells, (b) the filled-in matrix, and (c) the sequence of edit operations that transforms **dva** into **dave**, found by following the bold arrows in part (b).

Now we can use the equation in Figure 4.2(b) to fill in the rest of the matrix. For example, we have $d(1,1) = \min\{0+0, 1+1, 1+1\} = 0$. Since this value is obtained by adding 0 to $d(0,0)$, we add an arrow pointing from cell $(1,1)$ to cell $(0,0)$. Similarly, $d(1,2) = 1$ (see Figure 4.3(a)). Figure 4.3(b) shows the entire filled-in matrix. The edit distance between x and y can then be found to be 2, in $(3,4)$, the bottom rightmost cell.

In addition to computing the edit distance, the algorithm also shows the sequence of edit operations, by following the arrows. In our example, since the arrow goes "diagonal," from $(3,4)$ to $(2,3)$, we know that x_3 (character a) has been copied into or substituted with y_4 (character e). The arrow then goes "diagonal" again, from $(2,3)$ to $(1,2)$. So again x_2 (character v) has been copied into or substituted with y_3 (character v). Next, the arrow goes "horizontal," from $(1,2)$ to $(1,1)$. This means a gap - has been inserted into x and aligned with a in y (which denotes an insertion operation). This process stops when we have reached cell $(0,0)$. The transformation is depicted in Figure 4.3(c).

The cost of computing the edit distance is $O(|x||y|)$. In practice, the lengths of x and y often are roughly the same, and hence we often refer to the above cost as quadratic.

The Needleman-Wunch Measure

The Needleman-Wunch measure generalizes the Levenshtein distance. Specifically, it is computed by assigning a score to each *alignment* between the two input strings and choosing the score of the best alignment, that is, the maximal score. An alignment between two strings x and y is a set of *correspondences* between the characters of x and y, allowing for *gaps*. For example, Figure 4.4(a) shows an alignment between the strings x = dva and y = deeve, where d corresponds to d, v to v, and a to e. Note that a gap of length 2 has been inserted into x, and so the two characters ee of y do not have any corresponding characters in x.

The score of an alignment is computed using a *score matrix* and a *gap penalty*. The matrix assigns a score for a correspondence between every pair of characters and therefore allows for penalizing transformations on a case-by-case basis. Figure 4.4(b) shows a sample score matrix where a correspondence between two identical characters scores 2,

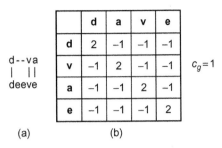

(a)   (b)

FIGURE 4.4 An example for the **Needleman-Wunch** function: (a) an alignment between two strings $x =$ **dva** and $y =$ **deeve**, with a gap in x, and (b) a score matrix that assigns to each pair of characters a score and a gap penalty c_g.

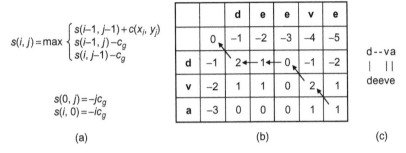

(a)   (b)   (c)

FIGURE 4.5 An example for the Needleman-Wunch function: (a) the recurrence equation for computing the similarity score using dynamic programming, (b) the dynamic-programming matrix between **dva** and **deeve** using the equation in part (a), and (c) the optimal alignment between the above two strings, found by following the arrows in part (b).

and -1 otherwise. A gap of length 1 has a penalty c_g (set to 1 in Figure 4.4). A gap of length k has a linear penalty of kc_g.

The score of an alignment is then the sum of the scores of all correspondences in the alignment, minus the penalties for the gaps. For example, the score of the alignment in Figure 4.4(a) is 2 (for correspondence d-d) + 2 (for v-v) −1 (for a-e) −2 (penalty for the gap of length 2) = 1. This is the best alignment between x and y (that is, the one with the highest score) and therefore is the Needleman-Wunch score between the two.

As described, the Needleman-Wunch measure generalizes the Levenshtein distance in three ways. First, it computes similarity scores instead of distance values. Second, it generalizes edit costs into a score matrix, thus allowing for more fine-grained score modeling. For example, the letter o and the number 0 are often confused in practice (e.g., by OCR systems). Hence, a correspondence between these two should have a higher score than one between a and 0, say. As another example, when matching bioinformatic sequences, different pairs of amino acids may have different semantic distances. Finally, the Needleman-Wunch measure generalizes insertion and deletion into gaps and generalizes the cost of such operations from 1 to an arbitrary penalty c_g.

The Needleman-Wunch score $s(x, y)$ is computed with dynamic programming, using the recurrence equation shown in Figure 4.5(a). We note three differences between the algorithm used here and the one used for computing the edit distance (Figure 4.2(b)). First, here we compute the *max* instead of *min*. Second, we use the score matrix $c(x_i, y_j)$ in the recurrence equation instead of the unit costs of edit operations. Third, we use the gap cost c_g instead of the unit gap cost. Note that when initializing this matrix, we must set $s(i, 0) = -ic_g$ and $s(0, j) = -jc_g$ (instead of i and j as in the edit distance case).

Figure 4.5(b) shows the fully filled-in matrix for $x = $ dva and $y = $ deeve, using the score matrix and gap penalty in Figure 4.4(b). Figure 4.5(c) shows the best alignment, found by following the arrows in the matrix of Figure 4.5(b).

The Affine Gap Measure

The affine gap measure is an extension of the Needleman-Wunch measure that handles longer gaps more gracefully. Consider matching $x = $ David Smith with $y = $ David R. Smith. The Needleman-Wunch measure can do this match very well, by opening a gap of length 2 in x, right after David, then aligning the gap with R. However, consider matching the same $x = $ David Smith with $y' = $ David Richardson Smith, as shown in Figure 4.6(a). Here the gap between the two strings is 10 characters long. Needleman-Wunch does not match very well because the cost of the gap is too high. For example, assume that each character correspondence has a score of 2 and that c_g is 1; then the score of the above alignment under Needleman-Wunch is $6 \cdot 2 - 10 = 2$.

In practice, gaps tend to be longer than one character. Hence, assigning a uniform penalty to each character in the gap in a sense will unfairly punish long gaps. The affine gap measure addresses this problem by distinguishing between the cost of *opening* a gap and the cost of *continuing* the gap. Formally, the measure assigns to each gap of length k a cost $c_o + (k-1)c_r$, where c_o is the cost of opening the gap (i.e., the cost of the very first character of the gap), and c_r is the cost of continuing the gap (i.e., the cost of the remaining $k-1$ characters of the gap). Cost c_r is less than c_o, thereby lessening the penalty of a long gap. Continuing with the example in Figure 4.6(a), if $c_o = 1$ and $c_r = 0.5$, the score of the alignment is $6 \cdot 2 - 1 - 9 \cdot 0.5 = 6.5$, much higher than the score 2 obtained under Needleman-Wunch.

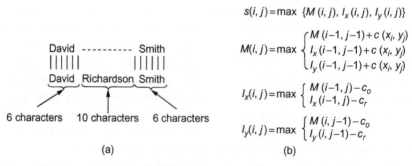

$$s(i, j) = \max \{M(i, j), I_x(i, j), I_y(i, j)\}$$

$$M(i, j) = \max \begin{cases} M(i-1, j-1) + c(x_i, y_j) \\ I_x(i-1, j-1) + c(x_i, y_j) \\ I_y(i-1, j-1) + c(x_i, y_j) \end{cases}$$

$$I_x(i, j) = \max \begin{cases} M(i-1, j) - c_o \\ I_x(i-1, j) - c_r \end{cases}$$

$$I_y(i, j) = \max \begin{cases} M(i, j-1) - c_o \\ I_y(i, j-1) - c_r \end{cases}$$

(a)   (b)

FIGURE 4.6 (a) An example of two strings where there is a long gap, (b) the recurrence equations for the affine gap measure.

Figure 4.6(b) shows the recurrence equations for the affine gap measure. Deriving these equations is rather involved. Since we now penalize opening a gap and continuing a gap differently, in every stage, for each cell (i,j) of the dynamic-programming matrix we keep track of three values:

- $M(i,j)$: the best score between $x_1 \ldots x_i$ and $y_1 \ldots y_j$ given that x_i is aligned to y_j
- $I_x(i,j)$: the best score given that x_i is aligned to a gap
- $I_y(i,j)$: the best score given that y_j is aligned to a gap

The best score for the cell, $s(i,j)$, is then the maximum of these three scores.

In deriving the above recurrence equations, we make the following assumption about the cost function. We assume that in an optimal alignment, we will never have an insertion followed directly by a deletion, or vice versa. This means we will never have the situation depicted in Figure 4.7(a) or Figure 4.7(b). We can guarantee this property by setting the cost $-(c_o + c_r)$ to be lower than the lowest mismatch score in the score matrix. Under such conditions, the alignment in Figure 4.7(c) will have a higher score than those to its left.

We now explain how to derive the equations for $M(i,j)$, $I_x(i,j)$, and $I_y(i,j)$ in Figure 4.6(b). Figure 4.8 explains how to derive the equation for $M(i,j)$. This equation considers the case where x_i is aligned with y_j (Figure 4.8(a)). Thus, $x_1 \ldots x_{i-1}$ is aligned with $y_1 \ldots y_{j-1}$. This can only happen in one of three ways, as shown in Figures 4.8(b)–(d): x_{i-1} is

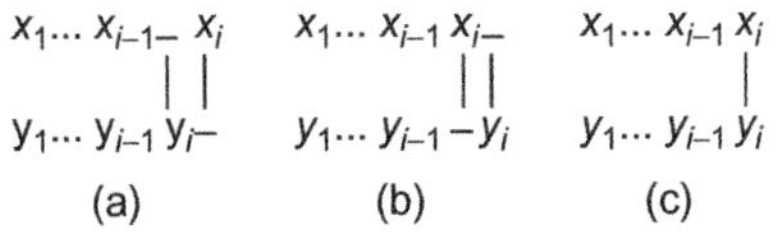

FIGURE 4.7 By setting the gap penalties and the score matrix appropriately, the alignment in (c) will always score higher than those in (a) and (b).

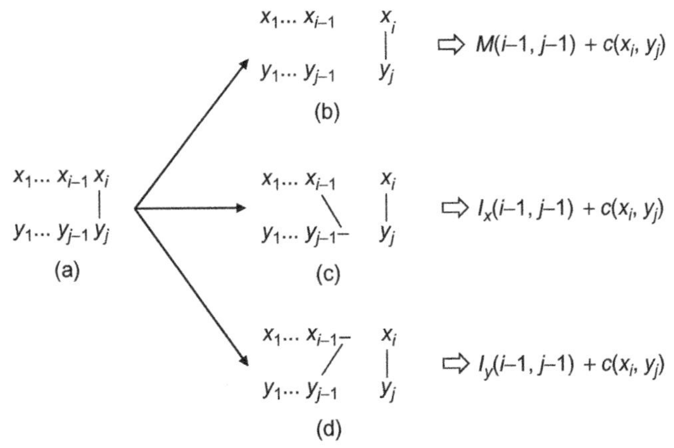

FIGURE 4.8 The derivation of the equation for $M(i,j)$ in Figure 4.6(b).

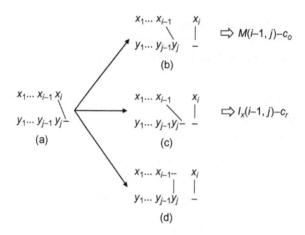

FIGURE 4.9 The derivation of the equation for $I_x(i,j)$ in Figure 4.6(b).

aligned with y_{j-1}, x_{i-1} is aligned into a gap, or y_{j-1} is aligned into a gap. These three ways give rise to the three cases in the equation for $M(i,j)$ in Figure 4.6(b).

Figure 4.9 shows how to derive the equation for $I_x(i,j)$ in Figure 4.6(b). This equation considers the case where x_i is aligned into a gap (Figure 4.9(a)). This can only happen in one of three ways, as shown in Figure 4.9(b)–(d): x_{i-1} is aligned with y_j, x_{i-1} is aligned into a gap, or y_j is aligned into a gap. The first two ways give rise to the two cases shown in Figure 4.6(b). The third case cannot happen, because it means an insertion followed directly by a deletion. This violates the assumption we described earlier. The equation for $I_y(i,j)$ in Figure 4.6(b) is derived in a similar fashion. The complexity of computing the affine gap measure remains $O(|x||y|)$.

The Smith-Waterman Measure

The previous measures consider *global* alignments between the input strings. That is, they attempt to match all characters of x with all characters of y.

Global alignments may not be well suited for some cases. For example, consider the two strings Prof. John R. Smith, Univ of Wisconsin and John R. Smith, Professor. The similarity score based on global alignments will be relatively low. In such a case, what we really want is to find two substrings of x and y that are most similar, and then return the score between the substrings as the score for x and y. For example, here we would want to identify John R. Smith to be the most similar substrings of the above two strings. This means matching the above two strings by ignoring certain prefixes (e.g., Prof.) and suffixes (e.g., Univ of Wisconsin in x and Professor in y). We call this *local alignment*.

The Smith-Waterman measure is designed to find matching substrings by introducing two key changes to the Needleman-Wunch measure. First, the measure allows the match to restart at any position in the strings (no longer limited to just the first position). The restart is captured by the first line of the recurrence equation in Figure 4.10(a). Intuitively, if the global match dips below zero, then this line has the effect of *ignoring the prefix*

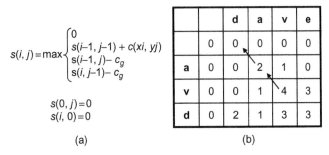

FIGURE 4.10 An example for the Smith-Waterman measure: (a) the recurrence equation for computing the similarity score using dynamic programming and (b) the dynamic-programming matrix between **avd** and **dave** using the equation in part (a).

and restarting the match. Similarly, note that all values in the first row and column of the dynamic-programming matrix are zeros, instead of $-ic_g$ and $-jc_g$ as in the Needleman-Wunsch case. Applying this recurrence equation to the strings avd and dave produces the matrix in Figure 4.10(b).

The second key change is that after computing the matrix using the recurrence equation, the algorithm starts retracing the arrows from the largest value in the matrix (4 in our example) rather than starting from the lower-right corner (3 in the matrix). This change effectively ignores suffixes if the match they produce is not optimal. Retracing ends when we meet a cell with value 0, which corresponds to the start of the alignment. In our example we can read out the best local alignment between avd and dave, which is av.

The Jaro Measure

The Jaro measure was developed mainly to compare short strings, such as first and last names. Given two strings x and y, we compute their Jaro score as follows.

- Find the common characters x_i and y_j such that $x_i = y_j$ and $|i - j| \leq \min \{|x|, |y|\}/2$. Intuitively, common characters are those that are identical and are positionally "close to one another." It is not hard to see that the number of common characters x_i in x is the same as the number of common characters y_j in y. Let this number be c.
- Compare the ith common character of x with the ith common character of y. If they do not match, then we have a transposition. Let the number of transpositions be t.
- Compute the Jaro score as

$$jaro(x,y) = 1/3[c/|x| + c/|y| + (c - t/2)/c]$$

As an example, consider x = jon and y = john. We have $c = 3$. The common character sequence in x is jon, and so is the sequence in y. Hence, there is no transposition, and $t = 0$. Thus, $jaro(x,y) = 1/3(3/3 + 3/4 + 3/3) = 0.917$. In contrast, the similarity score according to edit distance would be 0.75.

Now suppose $x =$ jon and $y =$ ojhn. Here the common character sequence in x is jon and the common character sequence in y is ojn. Thus $t = 2$, and $jaro(x,y) = 1/3(3/3 + 3/4 + (3 - 2/2)/3) = 0.81$.

The cost of computing the Jaro distance is $O(|x||y|)$, due to the cost of finding common characters.

The Jaro-Winkler Measure

The Jaro-Winkler measure is designed to capture cases where two strings have a low Jaro score, but share a prefix and thus are still likely to match. Specifically, the measure introduces two parameters: PL, which is the length of the longest common prefix between the two strengths, and PW, which is the weight to give the prefix. The measure is computed using the following formula:

$$jaro - winkler(x,y) = (1 - PL * PW) * jaro(x,y) + PL * PW$$

4.2.2 Set-Based Similarity Measures

The previous class of measures considers strings as sequences of characters. We now describe similarity measures that view strings as sets or multi-sets of *tokens*, and use set-related properties to compute similarity scores.

There are many ways to generate tokens from the input strings. A common method is to consider the *words* in the string (as delimited by the space character) and possibly stem the words. Common stop words (e.g., the, and, of) are typically excluded. For example, given the string david smith, we may generate the set of tokens {david, smith}.

Another common type of token is *q-grams*, which are substrings of length q that are present in the string. For example, the set of all 3-grams of david smith is {##d, #da, dav, avi, ..., ith, h##, th#}. Note that we have appended the special character # to the start and the end of the string, to handle 3-grams in these positions.

We discuss several set-based similarity measures. The bibliographic notes contain pointers to others that have been proposed in the literature. In our discussion we often assume *sets* of tokens, but we note that these measures have also been considered for the multi-set case, and what we discuss below can be generalized to that case.

The Overlap Measure

Let B_x and B_y be the sets of tokens generated for strings x and y, respectively. The overlap measure returns the number of common tokens $O(x,y) = |B_x \cap B_y|$.

Consider $x =$ dave and $y =$ dav; then the set of all 2-grams of x is $B_x = $ {#d, da, av, ve, e#} and the set of all 2-grams of y is $B_y = $ {#d, da, av, v#}. So $O(x,y) = 3$.

The Jaccard Measure

Continuing with the above notation, the Jaccard similarity score between two strings x and y is $J(x,y) = |B_x \cap B_y|/|B_x \cup B_y|$.

$$x=\text{aab} \Rightarrow B_x=\{a, a, b\}$$
$$y=\text{ac} \Rightarrow B_y=\{a, c\}$$
$$z=\text{a} \Rightarrow B_z=\{a\}$$

$$tf(a, x)=2 \quad idf(a)=3/3=1$$
$$tf(b, x)=1 \quad idf(b)=3/1=3$$
$$\dots \quad idf(c)=3/1=3$$
$$tf(c, z)=0$$

	a	b	c
v_x	2	3	0
v_y	3	0	3
v_z	3	0	0

(a)   (b)   (c)

FIGURE 4.11 In the TF/IDF measure (a) strings are converted into bags of terms, (b) TF and IDF scores of the terms are computed, then (c) these scores are used to compute feature vectors.

Again, consider $x =$ dave with $B_x =$ {#d, da, av, ve, e#}, and $y =$ dav with $B_y =$ {#d, da, av, v#}. Then $J(x,y) = 3/6$.

The TF/IDF Measure

This measure employs the notion of TF/IDF score commonly used in information retrieval (IR) to find documents that are relevant to keyword queries. The intuition underlying the TF/IDF measure is that two strings are similar if they share distinguishing terms. For example, consider the three strings $x =$ Apple Corporation, CA, $y =$ IBM Corporation, CA, and $z =$ Apple Corp. The edit distance and Jaccard measure would match x with y as $s(x,y)$ is higher than $s(x,z)$. However, the TF/IDF measure is able to recognize that Apple is a distinguishing term, whereas Corporation and CA are far more common, and thus would correctly match x with z.

When discussing the TF/IDF measure, we assume that the pair of strings being matched is taken from a *collection of strings*. Figure 4.11(a) shows a tiny such collection of three strings, $x =$ aab, $y =$ ac, and $z =$ a. We convert each string into a bag of terms. Using IR terminology, we refer to such a bag of terms as a *document*. For example, we convert string $x =$ aab into document $B_x = \{a, a, b\}$.

We now compute *term frequency* (TF) *scores* and *inverse document frequency* (IDF) *scores* as follows:

- For each term t and document d, we compute the term frequency $tf(t,d)$ to be the number of times t occurs in d. For example, since a occurs twice in B_x, we have $tf(a,x) = 2$.
- For each term t, we compute the inverse document frequency $idf(t)$ to be the total number of documents in the collection divided by the number of documents that contain t (variations of this definition are also commonly used, see below). For example, since a appears in all three documents in Figure 4.11(a), we have $idf(a) = 3/3 = 1$. A higher value of IDF means that the occurrence of the term is more distinguishing.

Figure 4.11(b) shows the TF/IDF scores for the tiny example in Figure 4.11(a).

Next, we convert each document d into a feature vector v_d. The intuition is that two documents will be similar if their corresponding vectors are close to each other. The vector of d has a feature $v_d(t)$ for each term t, and the value of $v_d(t)$ is a function of the TF and IDF scores. Vector v_d thus has as many features as the number of terms in the collection.

Figure 4.11(c) shows the three vectors v_x, v_y, and v_z for the three documents B_x, B_y, and B_z, respectively. In the figure, we use a relatively simple score: $v_d(t) = tf(t, d) \cdot idf(t)$. Thus, the score for feature a of v_x is $v_x(\mathsf{a}) = 2 \cdot 1 = 2$, and so on.

Now we are ready to compute the TF/IDF similarity score between any two strings p and q. Let T be the set of all terms in the collection. Then conceptually the vectors v_p and v_q (of the strings p and q) can be viewed as vectors in the $|T|$-dimensional space where each dimension corresponds to a term. The TF/IDF score between p and q can be computed as the cosine of the angle between these two vectors:

$$s(p, q) = \frac{\sum_{t \in T} v_p(t) \cdot v_q(t)}{\sqrt{\sum_{t \in T} v_p(t)^2} \cdot \sqrt{\sum_{t \in T} v_q(t)^2}} \tag{4.1}$$

For example, the TF/IDF score between the two strings x and y in Figure 4.11(a) is $\frac{2 \cdot 3}{\sqrt{2^2 + 3^2} \cdot \sqrt{3^2 + 3^2}} = 0.39$, using the vectors v_x and v_y in Figure 4.11(c).

It is not difficult to see from Equation 4.1 that the TF/IDF similarity score between two strings p and q is high if they share many frequent terms (that is, terms with high TF scores), unless these terms also commonly appear in other strings in the collection (in which case the terms have low IDF scores). Using the IDF component, the TF/IDF similarity score can effectively discount the importance of such common terms.

In the above example, we assumed $v_d(t) = tf(t, d) \cdot idf(t)$. This means that if we "double" the number of occurrences of t in document d, then $v_d(t)$ will also double. In practice this is found to be excessive: doubling the number of occurrences of t should increase $v_d(t)$ but not double it. One way of addressing this is to "dampen" the TF and IDF components by a logarithmic factor. Specifically, we can take

$$v_d(t) = log(tf(t, d) + 1) \cdot log(idf(t))$$

(In fact, $log(idf(t))$ itself is also commonly referred to as the inverse document frequency.) In addition, the vector v_d is often normalized to length 1, by setting

$$v_d(t) = v_d(t) / \sqrt{\sum_{t \in T} v_d(t)^2}$$

This way, computing the TF/IDF similarity score $s(p, q)$ as in Equation 4.1 reduces to computing the dot product between the two normalized vectors v_p and v_q.

4.2.3 Hybrid Similarity Measures

We now describe several similarity measures that combine the benefits of sequence-based and set-based methods.

The Generalized Jaccard Measure

Recall that the Jaccard measure considers the number of overlapping tokens in the input strings x and y. However, a token from x and a token from y have to be identical in order to be considered in the overlap set, which may be restrictive in some cases.

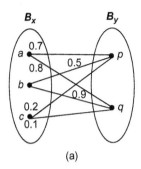 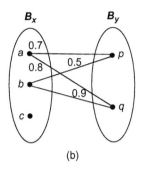 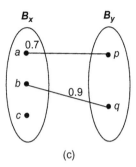

(a)   (b)   (c)

FIGURE 4.12 An example of computing the generalized Jaccard measure.

For example, consider matching the names of the nodes of two taxonomies describing divisions of companies. Each node is described by a string, such as Energy and Transportation and Transportation, Energy, and Gas. The Jaccard measure is a promising candidate for matching such strings because intuitively two nodes are similar if their names share many tokens (e.g., energy and transportation). However, in practice tokens are often misspelled, such as energy vs. eneryg. The generalized Jaccard measure will enable matching in such cases.

As with the Jaccard measure, we begin by converting the string x into a set of tokens $B_x = \{x_1, x_2, \ldots, x_n\}$ and string y into a set of tokens $B_y = \{y_1, y_2, \ldots, y_m\}$. Figure 4.12(a) shows two such strings x and y, with $B_x = \{a, b, c\}$ and $B_y = \{p, q\}$.

The next three steps will determine the set of pairs of tokens that are considered in the "softened" overlap set. First, let s be a similarity measure that returns values in the range $[0, 1]$. We apply s to compute a similarity score for each pair $(x_i \in B_x, y_j \in B_y)$. Continuing with the above example, Figure 4.12(a) shows all six such scores.

Second, we keep only those scores that equal or exceed a given threshold α. Figure 4.12(b) shows the remaining scores in our example, given $\alpha = 0.5$. The sets B_x and B_y, together with the edges that denote the remaining scores, form a bipartite graph G. In the third step we find the maximum-weight matching M in the bipartite graph G. Figure 4.12(c) shows this matching in our example. The total weight of this matching is $0.7 + 0.9 = 1.6$.

Finally, we return the normalized weight of M as the generalized Jaccard score between x and y. To normalize, we divide the weight by the sum of the number of edges in M and the number of "unmatched" elements in B_x and B_y. This sum is $|M| + (|B_x| - |M|) + (|B_y| - |M|) = |B_x| + |B_y| - |M|$. Formally,

$$GJ(x, y) = \frac{\sum_{(x_i, y_j) \in M} s(x_i, y_j)}{|B_x| + |B_y| - |M|}$$

Continuing with the above example, the generalized Jaccard score is $(0.7 + 0.9)/(3 + 2 - 2) = 0.53$.

The measure $GJ(x, y)$ is guaranteed to be between 0 and 1. It is a natural generalization of the Jaccard measure $J(x, y)$: if we constrain the elements of B_x and B_y to match only if they are identical, $GJ(x, y)$ reduces to $J(x, y)$. We discuss how to compute $GJ(x, y)$ efficiently later in Section 4.3.

The Soft TF/IDF Similarity Measure

This measure is similar in spirit to the generalized Jaccard measure, except that it uses the TF/IDF measure instead of the Jaccard measure as the "higher-level" similarity measure.

Consider an example with three strings $x =$ Apple Corporation, CA, $y =$ IBM Corporation, CA, and $z =$ Aple Corp. To match these strings, we would like to use the TF/IDF measure so that we can discount common terms such as Corporation and CA. Unfortunately, in this case the TF/IDF measure does not help us match x with z, because the term Apple in x does not match the misspelled term Aple in z. Thus, x and z do not share any term. As with the generalized Jaccard measure, we would like to "soften" the requirement that Apple and Aple match exactly, and instead require that they be similar to each other.

We compute the soft TF/IDF measure as follows. As with the TF/IDF measure, given two strings x and y, we create the two documents B_x and B_y. Figure 4.13(b) shows the documents created for the strings in Figure 4.13(a).

Next, we compute $close(x, y, k)$ to be the set of all terms in B_x that have at least one close term in B_y. Specifically, $close(x, y, k)$ is the set of terms $t \in B_x$ such that there exists a term $u \in B_y$ that satisfies $s'(t, u) \geq k$, where s' is a basic similarity measure (e.g., Jaro-Winkler) and k is a prespecified threshold. Continuing with our example in Figure 4.13(b), suppose $s'(a, a) = 1, s'(a, a') = 0.7, \ldots$, as shown in the figure. Then $close(x, y, 0.75) = \{a, b, c\}$. Note that $d \in B_x$ is excluded because the closest term to d in B_y is d', but d' is still too far from d (at a similarity score of 0.6).

In the final step, we compute $s(x, y)$ as in the traditional TF/IDF score, but giving a weight to each component of the TF/IDF formula according to the similarity score produced by s'. Specifically, let v_x and v_y be the feature vectors for x and y, as explained when we discussed the TF/IDF similarity measure. The vectors v_x and v_y are normalized to length 1, so that the traditional TF/IDF score can be computed as the dot product of the two vectors. Then we have

$$s(x, y) = \sum_{t \in close(x, y, k)} v_x(t) \cdot v_y(u_*) \cdot s'(t, u_*)$$

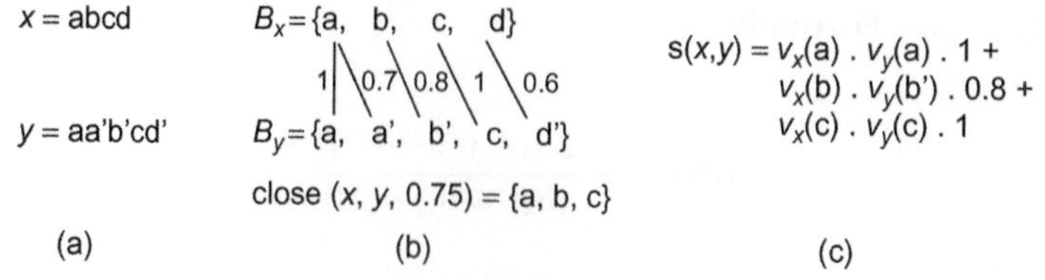

$x = abcd$ $B_x = \{a, \ b, \ c, \ d\}$

$\qquad\qquad\qquad\quad 1 \ \ 0.7 \ 0.8 \ \ 1 \ \ 0.6$

$y = aa'b'cd'$ $B_y = \{a, \ a', \ b', \ c, \ d'\}$

$close(x, y, 0.75) = \{a, b, c\}$

$s(x, y) = v_x(a) \cdot v_y(a) \cdot 1 +$
$\qquad\quad v_x(b) \cdot v_y(b') \cdot 0.8 +$
$\qquad\quad v_x(c) \cdot v_y(c) \cdot 1$

(a)   (b)   (c)

FIGURE 4.13 An example of computing soft TF/IDF similarity score for two strings x and y.

where $u_* \in B_y$ is the term that maximizes $s'(t, u)$ for all $u \in B_y$. Figure 4.13(c) shows how to compute $s(x, y)$ given the examples in Figures 4.13(a-b).

The Monge-Elkan Similarity Measure

The Monge-Elkan similarity measure can be effective for domains in which more control is needed over the similarity measure. To apply this measure to two strings x and y, first we break them into multiple substrings, say $x = A_1 \cdots A_n$ and $y = B_1 \cdots B_m$, where the A_i and B_j are substrings. Next, we compute

$$s(x,y) = \frac{1}{n} \sum_{i=1}^{n} \max_{j=1}^{m} s'(A_i, B_j)$$

where s' is a secondary similarity measure, such as Jaro-Winkler. To illustrate the above formula, suppose $x = A_1 A_2$ and $y = B_1 B_2 B_3$. Then

$$s(x,y) = \frac{1}{2} \left[\max\{s'(A_1, B_1), s'(A_1, B_2), s'(A_1, B_3)\} + \max\{s'(A_2, B_1), s'(A_2, B_2), s'(A_2, B_3)\} \right]$$

Note that we ignore the order of the matching of the substrings and only consider the best match for the substrings of x in y. Furthermore, we can customize the secondary similarity measure s' to a particular application.

For example, consider matching strings x = Comput. Sci. and Eng. Dept., University of California, San Diego and y = Department of Computer Science, Univ. Calif., San Diego. To employ the Monge-Elkan measure, first we break x and y into substrings such as Comput., Sci., and Computer. Next we must design a secondary similarity measure s' that works well for such substrings. In particular, it is clear that s' must handle matching abbreviations well. For example, s' may decide that if a substring A_i is a prefix of a substring B_j, such as Comput. and Computer, then they match, that is, their similarity score is 1.

4.2.4 Phonetic Similarity Measures

The similarity measures we have discussed so far match strings based on their *appearance*. In contrast, phonetic measures match strings based on their *sound*. These measures have been especially effective in matching names, since names are often spelled in different ways that sound the same. For example, Meyer, Meier, and Mire sound the same, as do Smith, Smithe, and Smythe. We describe the Soundex similarity measure, which is the most commonly used. We mention extensions of the basic Soundex measure in the bibliographic notes.

Soundex is used primarily to match surnames. It maps a surname x into a four-character code that captures the sound of the name. Two surnames are deemed similar if they share the same code. Mapping x to a code proceeds as follows. We use $x =$ Ashcraft as a running example in our description.

1. Keep the first letter of x as the first letter of the code. The first letter of the code for Ashcraft is A. The following steps are performed on the rest of the string x.

2. Remove all occurrences of W and H. Go over the remaining letters and replace them with digits as follows: replace B, F, P, V with 1; C, G, J, K, Q, S, X, Z with 2; D, T with 3; L with 4; M, N with 5; and R with 6. Note that we do not replace the vowels A, E, I, O, U, and Y. Continuing with our example, we convert Ashcraft into A226a13.
3. Replace each sequence of identical digits by the digit itself. So A226a13 becomes A26a13.
4. Drop all the nondigit letters (except the first one, of course). Then return the first four letters as the Soundex code. So A26a13 becomes A2613, and the corresponding Soundex code is A261.

Thus the Soundex code is always a letter followed by three digits, padded by 0 if there are not enough digits. For example, the soundex code for Sue is S000.

As described, the Soundex measure in effect "hashes" similar sounding consonants (such as B, F, P, and V) into the same digit, thereby mapping similar sounding names into the same soundex code. For example, it maps both Robert and Rupert into R163.

Soundex is not perfect. For example, it fails to map the similar sounding surnames Gough and Goff, or Jawornicki and Yavornitzky (an Americanized spelling of the former), into the same code. Nevertheless, it is a useful tool that has been used widely to match and index names in applications such as census records, vital records, ship passenger lists, and geneology databases. While Soundex was designed primarily for Caucasian surnames, it has been found to work well for names of many different origins (such as those appearing in the records of the U.S. Immigration and Naturalization Services). However, it does not work as well for names of East Asian origins, because much of the discriminating power of these names resides in the vowel sounds, which the code ignores.

4.3 Scaling Up String Matching

Once we have selected a similarity measure $s(x, y)$, the next challenge is to match strings efficiently. Let X and Y be two sets of strings to be matched, and t be a similarity threshold. A naive matching solution would be as follows:

for each string $x \in X$ **do**
    for each string $y \in Y$ **do**
        if $s(x, y) \geq t$ **then** return (x, y) as a matched pair
    end for
end for

This $O(|X||Y|)$ solution is clearly impractical for large data sets. A more commonly employed solution is based on developing a method FindCands that can quickly find the strings that *may* match a given string x. Given such a method, we employ the following algorithm:

for each string $x \in X$ **do**
    use method FindCands to find a candidate set $Z \subseteq Y$

for each string $y \in Z$ **do**
    if $s(x, y) \geq t$ **then** return (x, y) as a matched pair
  end for
end for

This solution, often called a *blocking solution*, takes $O(|X||Z|)$ time, which is much faster than $O(|X||Y|)$ because FindCands is designed so that finding Z is inexpensive and $|Z|$ is much smaller than $|Y|$. The set Z is often called the *umbrella set* of x. It should contain all true positives (i.e., all strings in Y that can possibly match x) and as few negative positives (i.e., those strings in Y that do not match x) as possible.

Clearly, the method FindCands lies at the heart of the above solution, and many techniques have been proposed for it. These techniques are typically based on indexing or filtering heuristics. We now discuss the basic ideas that underlie several common techniques for FindCands. In the following, we explain the techniques using the Jaccard and overlap measures. Later we discuss how to extend these techniques to other similarity measures.

4.3.1 Inverted Index Over Strings

This technique first converts each string $y \in Y$ into a document and then builds an inverted index over these documents. Given a term t, we can use the index to quickly find the list of documents created from Y that contain t, and hence the strings in Y that contain t.

Figure 4.14(a) shows an example of matching the two sets X and Y. We scan the set Y to build the inverted index shown in Figure 4.14(b). For instance, the index shows that the term area appears in just document 5, but the term lake appears in two documents, 4 and 6.

Given a string $x \in X$, the method FindCands uses the inverted index to quickly locate the set of strings in Y that share at least one term with x. Continuing with the above example,

Set X

1: {lake, mendota}
2: {lake, monona, area}
3: {lake, mendota, monona, dane}

Set Y

4: {lake, monona, university}
5: {monona, research, area}
6: {lake, mendota, monona, area}

Terms in Y	ID Lists
area	5
lake	4, 6
mendota	6
monona	4, 5, 6
research	5
university	4

(a)   (b)

FIGURE 4.14 An example of using an inverted index to speed up string matching.

given x = {lake, mendota}, we use the index in Figure 4.14(b) to find and merge the ID lists for lake and mendota, to obtain the umbrella set Z = {4, 6}.

This method is clearly much better than naively matching x with all strings in Y. Nevertheless, it still suffers from several limitations. First, the inverted list of some terms (e.g., stop words) can be very long, so building and manipulating such lists are quite costly. Second, this method requires enumerating all pairs of strings that share at least one term. The set of such pairs can still be very large in practice. The techniques described below address these issues.

4.3.2 Size Filtering

This technique retrieves only the strings in Y whose size make them match candidates. Specifically, given a string $x \in X$, we infer a constraint on the size of strings in Y that can possibly match x. We use a B-tree index to retrieve only the strings that satisfy the size constraints.

To derive the constraint on the size of strings in Y, recall that the Jaccard measure is defined as follows (where $|x|$ refers to the number of tokens in x):

$$J(x,y) = |x \cap y|/|x \cup y|$$

First, we can show that

$$1/J(x,y) \geq |y|/|x| \geq J(x,y) \tag{4.2}$$

To see why, consider the case where $|y| \geq |x|$. In this case, clearly $|y|/|x| \geq 1 \geq J(x,y)$. So we only have to prove $1/J(x,y) \geq |y|/|x|$, or equivalently that $|x \cup y|/|x \cap y| \geq |y|/|x|$. This inequality is true because $|x \cup y| \geq \max\{|x|, |y|\} = |y|$ and $|x \cap y| \leq \min\{|x|, |y|\} = |x|$. The case where $|y| < |x|$ can be proven similarly.

Now let t be the prespecified similarity threshold. If x and y match, then it must be that $J(x,y) \geq t$. Together with Equation 4.2, this implies that $1/t \geq |y|/|x| \geq t$ or, equivalently,

$$|x|/t \geq |y| \geq |x| \cdot t \tag{4.3}$$

Thus, given a string $x \in X$, we know that only strings that satisfy Equation 4.3 can possibly match x.

To illustrate, consider again the string x = {lake, mendota} (the first string in set X in Figure 4.14(a)). Suppose $t = 0.8$. Using the above equation, if $y \in Y$ matches x, we must have $2/0.8 = 2.5 \geq |y| \geq 2 \cdot 0.8 = 1.6$. We can immediately see that no string in the set Y in Figure 4.14(a) satisfies this constraint.

Exploiting the above idea, procedure FindCands builds a B-tree index over the sizes of strings in Y. Given a string $x \in X$, it uses the index to find strings in Y that satisfy Equation 4.3 and returns that set of strings as the umbrella set Z. This technique is effective when there is significant variability in the number of tokens in the strings of X and Y.

Set X
1: {lake, mendota}
2: {lake, monona, area}
3: {lake, mendota, monona, dane}

x: {lake, monona, area}
   ‾‾‾‾‾‾‾‾‾‾‾
       x'

y: {lake, mendota, monona, area}

Set Y
4: {lake, monona, university}
5: {monona, research, area}
6: {lake, mendota, monona, area}
7: {dane, area, mendota}

Terms in Y	ID Lists
area	5, 6, 7
lake	4, 6
mendota	6, 7
monona	4, 5, 6
research	5
university	4
dane	7

(a)   (b)   (c)

FIGURE 4.15 An example of using prefix filtering to speed up string matching.

4.3.3 Prefix Filtering

The basic idea underlying this technique is that if two sets share many terms, then large subsets of them also must share terms. Using this principle, we can reduce the number of candidate strings that may match a string x.

We first explain this technique using the overlap similarity measure and then extend it to the Jaccard measure. Suppose that x and y are strings that have an overlap of tokens $|x \cap y| \geq k$. Then it is easy to see that any subset $x' \subseteq x$ of size at least $|x| - (k-1)$ must overlap y. For example, consider the sets $x = \{$lake, monona, area$\}$ and $y = \{$lake, mendota, monona, area$\}$ in Figure 4.15(a). We have $|x \cap y| = 3 > 2$. Thus, the subset $x' = \{$lake, monona$\}$ in Figure 4.15(a) overlaps y (as does any other subset of size 2 of x).

We can exploit this idea in procedure FindCands as follows. Suppose we want to find all pairs (x, y) with overlap $O(x, y) \geq k$ (recall that $O(x, y) = |x \cap y|$ is the overlap similarity measure). Given a particular set x, we construct a subset x' of size $|x| - (k-1)$, and use an inverted index to find all sets y that overlap x'. Figures 4.15(b-c) illustrate this idea. Suppose we want to match strings in the sets X and Y of Figure 4.15(b), using $O(x, y) \geq 2$. We begin by building an inverted index over the strings in set Y, as shown in Figure 4.15(c). Next, given a string such as $x_1 = \{$lake, mendota$\}$, we take the "prefix" of size $|x_1| - 1$, which is $\{$lake$\}$ in this case, and let that be the set x'_1. We use the inverted index to find all strings in Y that contain at least one token in x'_1. This produces the set $\{y_4, y_6\}$. Note that if we use the inverted index to find all strings in Y that contain at least one token in x, we would end up with $\{y_4, y_6, y_7\}$, a larger candidate set. Thus, restricting index lookup to just a subset of x can significantly reduce the resulting set size.

Selecting the Subset Intelligently

So far we arbitrarily selected a subset x' of x and checked its overlap with the entire set y. We can do even better by selecting a *particular subset* x' of x and checking its overlap with only a *particular subset* y' of y. Specifically, suppose we have imposed an ordering $\mathcal{O}$ over

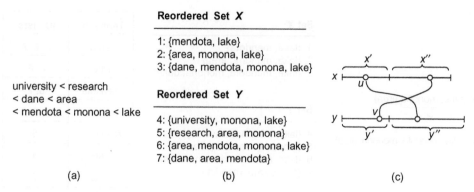

university < research
< dane < area
< mendota < monona < lake

Reordered Set X

1: {mendota, lake}
2: {area, monona, lake}
3: {dane, mendota, monona, lake}

Reordered Set Y

4: {university, monona, lake}
5: {research, area, monona}
6: {area, mendota, monona, lake}
7: {dane, area, mendota}

(a)   (b)   (c)

FIGURE 4.16 We can build an inverted index over only the prefixes of strings in Y, then use this index to perform string matching.

the universe of all possible terms. For example, we can order terms in increasing frequency, as computed over the union of sets X and Y of Figure 4.15(b). Figure 4.16(a) shows all terms found in $X \cup Y$ in this order.

We reorder the terms in each set $x \in X$ and $y \in Y$ according to the order $\mathcal{O}$. Figure 4.16(b) shows the reordered sets X and Y. Given a reordered set x, we refer to the subset x' that contains the first n terms of x as the prefix of size n (or the nth prefix) of x. For example, the 2nd prefix of x_3 = {dane, mendota, monona, lake} is {dane, mendota}. Given the above, we can establish the following property:

Proposition 4.1. *Let x and y be two sets such that $|x \cap y| \geq k$. Let x' be the prefix of size $|x| - (k-1)$ of x, and let y' be the prefix of size $|y| - (k-1)$ of y. Then x' and y' overlap.* ☐

Proof: Let x'' be the *suffix* of size $(k-1)$ of x (see Figure 4.16(c)). Clearly, $x' \cup x'' = x$. Similarly, let y'' be the suffix of size $(k-1)$ of y. Now suppose $x' \cap y' = \emptyset$. Then we must have $x' \cap y'' \neq \emptyset$ (otherwise, $|x \cap y| \geq k$ does not hold). So there exists an element u such that $u \in x'$ and $u \in y''$. Similarly, there exists an element v such that $v \in y'$ and $v \in x''$. Since $u \in x'$ and $v \in x''$, we have $u < v$ in the ordering $\mathcal{O}$. But since $v \in y'$ and $u \in y''$, we also have $v < u$ in the ordering $\mathcal{O}$, a clear contradiction. Thus, x' overlaps y'. ☐

Given the above property, we can revise procedure FindCands as follows. Suppose again that we consider overlap of at least k (that is, $O(x, y) \geq k$).

- We reorder the terms in each set $x \in X$ and $y \in Y$ in increasing order of their frequency (as shown in Figure 4.16(b)).
- For each $y \in Y$, we create y', the prefix of size $|y| - (k-1)$ of y.
- We build an inverted index over all the prefixes y'. Figure 4.17(a) shows this index for our example, assuming $O(x, y) \geq 2$.
- For each $x \in X$, we create x', the prefix of size $|x| - (k-1)$ of x, then use the above inverted index to find all sets $y \in Y$ such that x' overlaps with y'.

Terms in Y	ID Lists
area	5, 6, 7
mendota	6
monona	4, 6
research	5
university	4
dane	7

(a)

Terms in Y	ID Lists
area	5, 6, 7
lake	4, 6
mendota	6, 7
monona	4, 5, 6
research	5
university	4
dane	7

(b)

FIGURE 4.17 The inverted indexes over (a) the prefixes of size $|y| - (k-1)$ of all $y \in Y$ and (b) all $y \in Y$. The former is often significantly smaller than the latter in practice.

Consider for example $x = \{$mendota, lake$\}$, and therefore $x' = \{$mendota$\}$. Using mendota to look up the inverted index in Figure 4.17(a) yields y_6. Thus, FindCands returns y_6 as the sole candidate that may match x. Note that if we check the overlap between x' and the entire y, then y_7 is also returned. Thus, checking the overlap between prefixes can reduce the size of the resulting set. In practice, this reduction can be quite significant.

It is also important to note that the size of the inverted index is much smaller. For comparison purposes, Figure 4.17(b) shows the inverted index for the entire sets $y \in Y$ (reproduced from Figure 4.15(c)). The index we create here does not contain an entry for the term lake, and its index list for mendota is also smaller than the same index list in the entire-sets index.

Applying Prefix Filtering to the Jaccard Measure
The following equation enables us to extend the prefix filtering method to the Jaccard measure.

$$J(x,y) \geq t \Leftrightarrow O(x,y) \geq \alpha = \frac{t}{1+t} \cdot (|x| + |y|) \tag{4.4}$$

The equation shows how to convert the Jaccard measure to the overlap measure, except for one detail. The threshold α as defined above is not a constant and depends on $|x|$ and $|y|$. Thus, we cannot build the inverted index over the prefixes of $y \in Y$ using α. To address this, we index the "longest" prefixes. In particular, it can be shown that we only have to index the prefixes of length $|y| - \lceil t \cdot |y| \rceil + 1$ of the $y \in Y$ to ensure that we do not miss any correct matching pairs.

4.3.4 Position Filtering

Position filtering further limits the set of candidate matches by deriving an upper bound on the size of the overlap between a pair of strings. As an example, consider the two strings $x = \{$dane, area, mendota, monona, lake$\}$ and $y = \{$research, dane, mendota, monona, lake$\}$.

Suppose we are considering $J(x,y) \geq 0.8$. In prefix filtering we will index the prefix of length $|y| - \lceil t \cdot |y| \rceil + 1$ of y, which is $y' = \{research, dane\}$ in this case (because $5 - \lceil 5 \cdot 0.8 \rceil + 1 = 2$). Similarly, the prefix of length $|x| - \lceil t \cdot |x| \rceil + 1$ of x is $x' = \{dane, area\}$. Since x' overlaps y', in prefix filtering we will return the above pair (x,y) as a candidate pair.

However, we can do better than this. Let x'' be the rest of x, after x', and similarly let y'' be the rest of y, after y'. Then it is easy to see that

$$O(x,y) \leq |x' \cap y'| + min\{|x''|, |y''|\} \tag{4.5}$$

Applying this inequality to the above example, we have $O(x,y) \leq 1 + min\{3,3\} = 4$. However, using Equation 4.4 we have $O(x,y) \geq \frac{t}{1+t} \cdot (|x| + |y|) = \frac{0.8}{1+0.8} \cdot (5+5) = 4.44$. Hence, we can immediately discard the pair (x,y) from the set of candidate matches. More generally, position filtering combines the constraints from Equation 4.5 and Equation 4.4 to further reduce the set of candidate matches.

4.3.5 Bound Filtering

Bound filtering is an optimization for computing the generalized Jaccard similarity measure. Recall from Section 4.2.3 that the generalized Jaccard measure computes the normalized weight of the maximum-weight matching M in the bipartite graph connecting x and y:

$$GJ(x,y) = \frac{\sum_{(x_i,y_j) \in M} s(x_i, y_j)}{|B_x| + |B_y| - |M|}$$

In the equation, s is a secondary similarity measure, $B_x = \{x_1, x_2, \ldots, x_n\}$ is the set of tokens that corresponds to x, and $B_y = \{y_1, y_2, \ldots, y_m\}$ is the set that corresponds to y.

Computing $GJ(x,y)$ in a straightforward fashion would require computing the maximum-weight matching M in the bipartite graph, which can be very expensive. To address this problem, given a pair (x,y) we compute an upper bound $UB(x,y)$ and a lower bound $LB(x,y)$ on $GJ(x,y)$. FindCands uses these bounds as follows: if $UB(x,y) \leq t$, then we can ignore (x,y) as it cannot be a match; if $LB(x,y) \geq t$, then we return (x,y) as a match. Otherwise, we compute $GJ(x,y)$.

The upper and lower bounds are computed as follows. First, for each element $x_i \in B_x$, we find an element $y_j \in Y$ with the highest element-level similarity, such that $s(x_i, y_j) \geq \alpha$ (recall from the description of $GJ(x,y)$ that we consider only matches between $x_i \in B_x$ and $y_j \in B_y$ such that $s(x_i, y_j) \geq \alpha$). Let S_1 be the set of all such pairs.

For example, consider the two strings x and y together with the similarity scores between their elements in Figure 4.18(a) (reproduced from Figure 4.12(a)). Figure 4.18(b) shows the set $S_1 = \{(a,q), (b,q)\}$. Note that for element $c \in B_x$, there is no element in B_y such that the similarity score between them equals or exceeds α, which is 0.5 in this case.

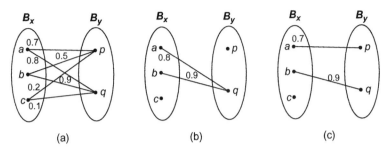

FIGURE 4.18 An example of computing an upper and lower bound for the generalized Jaccard measure.

Similarly, for each element $y_j \in B_y$, we find an element $x_i \in X$ with the highest element-level similarity, such that $s(x_i, y_j) \geq \alpha$. Let S_2 be the set of all such pairs. Continuing with our example, Figure 4.18(c) shows $S_2 = \{(a, p), (b, q)\}$.

The upper bound for $GJ(x, y)$ is given by the following formula:

$$UB(x, y) = \frac{\sum_{(x_i, y_j) \in S_1 \cup S_2} s(x_i, y_j)}{|B_x| + |B_y| - |S_1 \cup S_2|}$$

Note that the numerator of $UB(x, y)$ is at least as large as that of $GJ(x, y)$, and that the denominator of $UB(x, y)$ is no larger than that of $GJ(x, y)$. The lower bound is given by the following formula:

$$LB(x, y) = \frac{\sum_{(x_i, y_j) \in S_1 \cap S_2} s(x_i, y_j)}{|B_x| + |B_y| - |S_1 \cap S_2|}$$

Continuing with our example, $UB(x, y) = \frac{0.8 + 0.9 + 0.7 + 0.9}{3 + 2 - 3} = 1.65$ and $LB(x, y) = \frac{0.9}{3 + 2 - 1} = 0.225$.

4.3.6 Extending Scaling Techniques to Other Similarity Measures

So far we have discussed scaling techniques for the Jaccard measure or overlap measure. We now describe how to extend these techniques to multiple similarity measures. First, as noted earlier, we can easily prove that

$$J(x, y) \geq t \Leftrightarrow O(x, y) \geq \alpha = \frac{t}{1 + t} \cdot (|x| + |y|)$$

by replacing $|x \cup y|$ in $J(x, y)$ with $|x| + |y| - |x \cap y|$. Thus, if a technique works for the overlap measure $O(x, y)$, there is a good chance that we can also extend it to work for the Jaccard measure $J(x, y)$, and vice versa. For example, earlier we described how to extend the prefix filtering technique originally developed for the overlap measure to the Jaccard measure.

In general, a promising way to extend a technique T to work for a similarity measure $s(x, y)$ is to translate $s(x, y)$ into constraints on a similarity measure that already works well with T. For example, consider edit distance. Let $d(x,y)$ be the edit distance between x and y, and let B_x and B_y be the corresponding q-gram sets of x and y, respectively. Then we can show that

$$d(x,y) \leq \epsilon \Rightarrow O(x,y) \geq \alpha = (\max\{|B_x|, |B_y|\} + q - 1) - q\epsilon$$

Given the above constraint, we can extend prefix filtering to work with edit distance by indexing the prefixes of size $q\epsilon + 1$.

As yet another example, consider the TF/IDF cosine similarity $C(x,y)$. We can show that

$$C(x,y) \geq t \Leftrightarrow O(x,y) \geq \lceil t \cdot \sqrt{|x||y|} \rceil$$

Given this, we can extend prefix filtering to work with $C(x,y)$ by indexing the prefixes of size $|x| - \lceil t^2 |x| \rceil + 1$ (this can be further optimized to just indexing the prefixes of size $|x| - \lceil t|x| \rceil + 1$). Finally, the above constraints can also help us extend position filtering to work with edit distance and cosine similarity measures.

Bibliographic Notes

Durbin et al. [196] provide an excellent description of the various edit distance algorithms, together with HMM-based probabilistic interpretations of these algorithms. Further discussion of string similarity measures and string matching can be found in [146, 204, 280, 370, 455]. Tutorials on string matching include [355, 563]. The Web site [118] describes numerous string similarity measures and provides open-source implementations.

Edit distance was introduced in [376]. The basic dynamic programming algorithm for computing edit distance is described in [455]. Variations of edit distance include Needleman-Wunsch [456], affine gap [566], Smith-Waterman [526], Jaro [331], and Jaro-Winkler [575]. Learning the parameters of edit distance and related similarity measures was discussed in [84, 86, 497].

The Jaccard measure was introduced in [329]. The notion of TF/IDF originated from the information retrieval community [414], and TF/IDF-based string similarity measures are discussed in [31, 120, 145, 264, 352]. Soft TF/IDF was introduced in [86, 148]. Generalized Jaccard was introduced in [469]. The Monge-Elkan hybrid similarity measure is introduced in [442]. Cohen et al. [86, 148] empirically compare the effectiveness of string similarity measures over a range of matching tasks.

The Soundex measure was introduced in [500, 501]. Other phonetic similarity measures include New York State Identification and Intelligence System (NYSIIS) [537], Oxford Name Compression Algorithm (ONCA) [250], Metaphone [477], and Double Metaphone [478].

The material on scaling up string matching in Section 4.3 was adapted from [370]. Building inverted indexes to scale up string matching was discussed in [508]. The technique of size filtering was discussed in [34]. Prefix indexes were introduced in [124]. Bayardo et al. [59] discuss how to combine these indexes with inverted indexes to further scale up string matching. On et al. [469] discuss bound filtering, and Xiao et al. [582] discuss position indexes.

Gravano et al. [265] discuss q-gram-based string matching in RDBMSs. Koudas, Marathe, and Srivastava [354] discuss the trade-offs between accuracy and performance. Vernica, Carey, and Li [559] discuss string matching in the map reduce framework. Further techniques to scale up string matching were discussed in [388, 423, 548].

5

Schema Matching and Mapping

In Chapter 3 we described formalisms for specifying source descriptions and algorithms that use these descriptions to reformulate queries. To create the source descriptions, we typically begin by creating semantic matches. The matches specify how the elements of the source schemas and the mediated schema semantically correspond to one another. Examples include "attribute name in one source corresponds to attribute title in another," and "location is a concatenation of city, state, and zipcode." In the next step we elaborate the matches into semantic mappings, which are typically structured queries written in a language such as SQL. The mappings specify how to translate data across the sources and the mediated schema. The above two steps are often referred to as *schema matching* and *schema mapping*, respectively, and are the focus of this chapter.

In practice, creating the matches and mappings consumes quite a bit of the effort in setting up a data integration application. These tasks are often difficult because they require a deep understanding of the semantics of the schemas of the data sources and of the mediated schema. This knowledge is typically distributed among multiple people, including some who may no longer be with the organization. Furthermore, since the people who understand the meaning of the data are not necessarily database experts, they need to be aided by others who are skilled in writing formal transformations between the schemas.

This chapter describes a set of techniques that helps a designer create semantic matches and mappings. Unlike the algorithms presented in previous chapters, the task we face here is inherently a heuristic one. There is no algorithm that will take two arbitrary database schemas and flawlessly produce correct matches and mappings between them. Our goal is thus to create tools that significantly *reduce* the time it takes to create matches and mappings. The tools can help the designer speed through the repetitive and tedious parts of the process, and provide useful suggestions and guidance through the semantically challenging parts.

5.1 Problem Definition

We begin by defining the notion of schema element, semantic mapping, and semantic match. Let S and T be two relational schemas. We refer to the attributes and tables of S as the *elements* of S, and those of T as the *elements* of T, respectively.

■ ■ ■ ━━━

Example 5.1

Consider the two schemas in Figure 5.1. Schema DVD-VENDOR belongs to a vendor of DVDs and consists of three tables. The first table, **Movies**, describes the details of the movies themselves, while the remaining two, **Products** and **Locations**, describe the DVD products and the sale locations, respectively. Schema AGGREGATOR belongs to a shopping aggregation site. Unlike the individual vendor, the aggregator is not interested in all the details of the product, but only in the attributes that are shown to its customers, as captured in table **Items**.

Schema DVD-VENDOR has 14 elements: 11 attributes (e.g., id, title, and year) and three tables (e.g., **Movies**). Schema AGGREGATOR has five elements: four attributes and one table.

━━━ ■ ■ ■

DVD-VENDOR
Movies(id, title, year)
Products(mid, releaseDate, releaseCompany, basePrice, rating, saleLocID)
Locations(lid, name, taxRate)

AGGREGATOR
Items(name, releaseInfo, classification, price)

FIGURE 5.1 Example of two database schemas. Schema DVD-VENDOR belongs to a DVD vendor, while AGGREGATOR belongs to a shopping site that aggregates products from multiple vendors.

5.1.1 Semantic Mappings

As described in Chapter 3, a *semantic mapping* is a query expression that relates a schema *S* with a schema *T*. Depending on the formalism used for source descriptions, the direction of the semantic mapping can differ.

■ ■ ■ ━━━

Example 5.2

The following semantic mapping expresses the fact that the title attribute of the **Movies** relation in the DVD-VENDOR schema is the name attribute in the **Items** table in the AGGREGATOR schema.

```
SELECT name as title
FROM Items
```

The following semantic mapping goes in the reverse direction. It shows that to obtain the price attribute of the **Items** relation in the AGGREGATOR schema we need to join the **Products** and **Locations** tables in the DVD-VENDOR schema.

```
SELECT (basePrice * (1 + taxRate)) AS price
FROM Products, Locations
WHERE Products.saleLocID = Locations.lid
```

The previous two mappings obtain a single attribute of a relation. The following semantic mapping shows how to obtain an entire tuple for the **Items** table of the AGGREGATOR schema from data in the DVD-VENDOR schema:

```
SELECT title AS name, releaseDate AS releaseInfo, rating AS
    classification, basePrice * (1 + taxRate) AS price
FROM Movies, Products, Locations
WHERE Movies.id = Products.mid AND Products.saleLocID = Locations.lid
```

Given two schemas S and T, our goal is to create a semantic mapping between them.

Example 5.3

Consider building a system that integrates two data sources: a DVD vendor and a book vendor, with source schemas DVD-VENDOR and BOOK-VENDOR, respectively. Assume we use the schema AGGREGATOR in Figure 5.1 as the mediated schema.

If we use the Global-as-View (GAV) approach to relate the schemas, we need to describe the **Items** relation in the AGGREGATOR as a query over the source schemas. We would proceed as follows. We create an expression m_1 that specifies how to obtain tuples of **Items** from tuples of the DVD-VENDOR schema (this is the last expression in Example 5.2) and create an expression m_2 that shows how to obtain tuples of **Items** from relations in the BOOK-VENDOR schema. Finally, we return the SQL query (m_1 UNION m_2) as the GAV description of the **Items** table.

If we use the Local-as-View (LAV) approach, we would create an expression for every relation in the source schemas specifying how to obtain tuples for it from the **Items** relation.

5.1.2 Semantic Matches

A *semantic match* relates a set of elements in schema S to a set of elements in schema T, without specifying in detail (to the level of SQL queries) the exact nature of the relationship. The simplest type of semantic matches is *one-to-one matches*, such as

$$\textbf{Movies}.\text{title} \approx \textbf{Items}.\text{name}$$

$$\textbf{Movies}.\text{year} \approx \textbf{Items}.\text{year}$$

$$\textbf{Products}.\text{rating} \approx \textbf{Items}.\text{classification}.$$

An example of more complex matches is

$$\textbf{Items}.\text{price} \approx \textbf{Products}.\text{basePrice} * (1 + \textbf{Locations}.\text{taxRate})$$

We call such matches *one-to-many matches*, because they relate one element in schema S to multiple elements in schema T. Conversely, matches that relate multiple elements in schema *S* to one element in schema *T* are called *many-to-one matches*. Finally, *many-to-many matches* relate multiple elements in *S* to multiple elements in *T*.

5.1.3 Schema Matching and Mapping

To create the descriptions of data sources, we often begin by creating semantic matches, then elaborate the matches into mappings. These two tasks are often referred to as *schema matching* and *schema mapping*, respectively.

The main reason that we begin by creating semantic matches is that such matches are often easier to elicit from designers. For example, it may be easy for the designer to glean from their domain knowledge that price in AGGREGATOR is a function of basePrice and taxRate in DVD-VENDOR. Thus the designer can create the semantic match price ≈ basePrice * (1 + taxRate).

This semantic match for price specifies the functional relationship between basePrice and taxRate. But it does not specify which data values of basePrice should be combined with which data values of taxRate. Thus the match cannot be used to obtain data for price. In the next step, a schema mapping system takes the match as the input and elaborates it into a semantic mapping by filling in the missing details:

```
SELECT (basePrice * (1 + taxRate)) AS price
FROM Product, Location
WHERE Product.saleLocID = Location.lid
```

This semantic mapping combines a value x of basePrice with a value y of taxRate (to obtain a value for price) only if x and y come from tuples p and q of **Products** and **Locations**, respectively, such that p.saleLocID = q. lid.

Thus, in a sense, by supplying the semantic match, the designer supplies the SELECT and FROM clauses of the semantic mapping. The subsequent schema mapping system only has to create the WHERE clause, a far easier job than if the system were to start from scratch.

In practice, finding semantic matches is often already quite difficult. So the designer often employs a schema matching system to find the matches, verifies and corrects the matches, then employs a schema mapping system to elaborate the matches into the mappings. Even in such cases, breaking the overall process into the matching and mapping steps is still highly beneficial, because it allows the designer to verify and correct the matches, thus reducing the complexity of the overall process.

5.2 Challenges of Schema Matching and Mapping

As described, a schema matching and mapping system needs to reconcile the heterogeneity between the disparate schemas. Such heterogeneity arises in multiple forms. First, the table and attribute names could be different in the schemas even when they refer to the same underlying concept. For example, the attributes rating and classification both refer to the rating assigned to the movie by the Motion Picture Association of America. Second, in some cases multiple attributes in one schema correspond to a single attribute in the other. For example, basePrice and taxRate from the vendor schema are used to compute the value of price in the AGGREGATOR schema. Third, the tabular organization of the schemas is different. The aggregator only needs a single table, whereas the DVD vendor requires three. Finally, the coverage and level of details of the two schemas are different. The DVD vendor models details such as releaseDate and releaseCompany, whereas the aggregator does not.

The underlying reason for semantic heterogeneity is that schemas are created by different people whose tastes and styles are likely to be different. We see the same phenomenon when comparing computer programs written by different programmers. Even if two programmers write programs that behave exactly the same, it is likely that they will structure the programs differently, and certainly name variables in different ways. Another fundamental source of heterogeneity is that disparate databases are rarely created for the *exact* same purpose. In our example, even though both schemas model movies, the DVD vendor is managing its inventory, while the aggregator is concerned only with customer-facing attributes.

Reconciling the semantic heterogeneity between the schemas is difficult for several reasons:

- **The semantics is not fully captured in the schemas:** In order to correctly map between the schemas, the schema mapping system needs to understand the intended semantics of each schema. However, a schema itself does not completely describe its full meaning. A schema is a set of symbols that represent some model that was in the mind of the designer, but does not fully capture the model. For example, the name of the attribute rating in schema DVD-VENDOR does not convey the information that this is the rating by the Motion Picture Association of America, not the rating by the customers. In some cases, elements of the schema are accompanied by textual descriptions of their intent. However, these descriptions are typically partial at best, and even then, they are in natural language, making it hard for a program to understand.

- **Schema clues can be unreliable:** Since the semantics is not fully captured in the schemas, to perform adequately, the schema mapping system must glean enough of the semantics of the schema from both its formal specification, such as names, structures, types, and data values, and any other clues that may accompany the schema, such as text descriptions and the way the schema is used. However, such specification and clues can be unreliable. Two schema elements may share the same name and yet refer to different real-world concepts. For example, attribute name in schema DVD-VENDOR refers to the name of the sale location, whereas attribute name in schema AGGREGATOR refers to the name of the movie. Conversely, two attributes with different names, such as rating and classification, can refer to the same real-world concept.

- **Intended semantics can be subjective:** Sometimes it is difficult to decide whether two attributes should match. For example, a designer may think that attribute plot-summary matches attribute plot-synopsis, whereas another designer may not. In certain schema mapping applications (e.g., in military domains), it is not uncommon to have a committee of experts voting on such issues.
- **Correctly combining the data is difficult:** It is difficult not just to find the semantic matches, but also to elaborate the matches into mappings. When elaborating matches into mappings, the designer must find the correct way to combine the data values of the various attributes, typically using a join path coupled with various filtering conditions. Consider, for example, the semantic match

$$\text{Items.price} \approx \text{Products.basePrice} * (1 + \text{Locations.taxRate})$$

When elaborating this match into a mapping for price, the designer must decide how to join the two tables **Products** and **Locations** and whether any filtering condition should be applied to the join result. In practice, numerous join paths can exist between any two tables, and even after the designer has decided on a join path, there are still many possible ways to perform the join (e.g., full outer join, left outer join, right outer join, inner join). To decide which combination is correct, the designer often must examine a large amount of data in both schemas, in an error-prone and labor-intensive process.

A NOTE ON STANDARDS

It is tempting to argue that a natural solution to the heterogeneity problem is to create standards for every conceivable domain and encourage database designers to follow these standards. Unfortunately, this argument fails in practice for several reasons. It is often hard to agree on standards since some organizations are already entrenched in particular schemas and there may not be enough of an incentive to standardize. But more fundamentally, creating a standard is possible when data are used for the same purposes. But, as the above examples illustrated, uses of data vary quite a bit, and therefore so do the schemas created for them.

A second challenge to standardization is the difficulty of precisely delineating domains. Where does one domain end and another begin? For example, imagine trying to define a standard for the domain of people. Of course, the standard should include attributes such as name, address, phone number, and maybe employer. But beyond those attributes, others are questionable. People play many roles, such as employees, students (or alumni), bank account holders, moviegoers, and coffee consumers. Each of these roles can contribute more attributes to the standard, but including them all is clearly not practical. As another example, consider modeling scientific information, beginning with genes and proteins. We would also like to model the diseases they are linked to, the medications associated with the diseases, the scientific literature reporting findings related to the diseases, etc. There is no obvious point at which we can declare the end of this domain.

In practice, standards work for very limited use cases where the number of attributes is relatively small and there is strong incentive to agree on them (e.g., if exchanging data is critical for business processes). Examples include data that need to be exchanged between banks or in electronic commerce and medical data about vital signs of patients. Even in these cases, while the data may be *shared* in a standardized schema, each data source models the data internally with a different schema.

Before we proceed, we emphasize that heterogeneity appears not just at the schema level, but also at the data level. For example, two databases may each have a column named companyName but use different strings to refer to the same company (e.g., IBM vs. International Business Machines or HP vs. Hewlett Packard). We defer the discussion of data-level heterogeneity to Chapter 7.

5.3 Overview of Matching and Mapping Systems

We now outline the different components of matching and mapping systems. In what follows, we will use the terms "match" and "correspondence" interchangeably, when there is no ambiguity.

5.3.1 Schema Matching Systems

The goal of a schema matching system is to produce a set of matches, i.e., correspondences, between two given schemas S and T. One solution is to provide the designer a convenient graphical user interface to specify correspondences manually, but this chapter focuses on how to *automatically* create such correspondences that are then validated by a designer.

We begin by considering matching systems that produce one-to-one matches, such as title $\approx$ name and rating $\approx$ classification. The first observation from our DVD example is that no *single* heuristic is guaranteed to yield accurate matches. One set of heuristics is based on examining the similarities between the names of the schema elements. Using such heuristics, we may be able to infer that attribute releaseInfo in schema AGGREGATOR matches either attribute releaseDate or attribute releaseCompany in schema DVD-VENDOR, but we do not know which one.

Another set of heuristics examines the similarities between the data values when they are available. For example, suppose that releaseInfo specifies the year in which the DVD is released, and so does releaseDate. Then by examining the data values, we may be able to infer that releaseInfo matches either attribute releaseDate of table **Products** or attribute year of table **Movies**, but again we do not know which one. Other clues we may consider are the

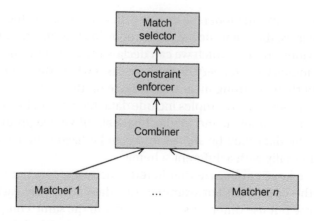

FIGURE 5.2 The components of a typical schema matching system.

proximity of attributes to each other or how attributes are used in queries. But again, none of these clues by itself is likely to produce good matches for all attributes.

On the other hand, by combining multiple clues, we can improve matching accuracy. For example, by examining both the names and the data values of the attributes, we can infer that releaseInfo is more likely to match releaseDate than releaseCompany and year.

The variety of available clues and heuristics and the need to exploit all of them to maximize matching accuracy motivate the architecture of a schema matching system, shown in Figure 5.2. A typical schema matching system consists of the following components:

- *Matchers (schemas → similarity matrix):* A matcher takes two schemas S and T and outputs a similarity matrix, which assigns to each element pair s of S and t of T a number between 0 and 1. The higher this number, the more confident the matcher is that the match $s \approx t$ is correct. Each matcher is based on a certain set of heuristics and, as a result, exploits a certain kind of clues. For example, a matcher may compare the similarities of the names of schema elements, while another matcher may compare the data values. The matching system employs several such matchers, and we describe several common types of matchers in Section 5.4.
- *Combiner (matrix × … × matrix → matrix):* A combiner merges the similarity matrices output by the matchers into a single one. Combiners can take the average, minimum, maximum, or a weighted sum of the similarity scores. More complex types of combiners use machine learning techniques or elaborate handcrafted scripts. We describe several types of combiners in Section 5.5.
- *Constraint enforcer (matrix × constraints → matrix):* In addition to clues and heuristics, domain knowledge plays an important role in pruning candidate matches. For example, knowing that many movie titles contain four words or more, but most location names do not, can help us guess that **Items.** name is more likely to match

Movies.title than **Locations**.name. Hence, the third component of the schema matching system, the *constraint enforcer*, enforces such constraints on the candidate matches. In particular, it transforms the similarity matrix produced by the combiner into another one that better reflects the true similarities. We describe several techniques to enforce constraints in Section 5.6.

- *Match selector (matrix → matches):* The last component of the matching system produces matches from the similarity matrix output by the constraint enforcer. The simplest selection strategy is thresholding: all pairs of schema elements with similarity scores exceeding a given threshold are returned as matches. More complex strategies include formulating the selection as an optimization problem over a weighted bipartite graph. We describe common selector types in Section 5.7.

Schema matching tasks are often repetitive, such as matching a mediated schema to the schemas of tens to hundreds of data sources. Section 5.8 describes a set of methods based on machine learning techniques that enable the schema matching system to reuse previous matches, that is, to learn from them to match new schemas. Section 5.9 then describes how to discover complex semantic matches, which require a more complex matching architecture, compared to the architecture of finding one-to-one matches that we described above.

5.3.2 Schema Mapping Systems

Once the matches have been produced, our task is to create the actual mappings. Here, the main challenge is to find how tuples from one source can be translated into tuples in the other. For example, the mapping should specify that in order to compute the price attribute in the **Items** table, we need to join **Products** with **Locations** on the attribute saleLocation = name and add the appropriate local tax. The challenge faced by this component is that there may be more than one possible way of joining the data. For example, we can join **Products** with **Movies** to obtain the origin of the director, and compute the price based on the taxes in the director's country of birth.

In Section 5.10, we describe how a mapping system can explore the possible ways of joining and taking unions of data and help the designer by proposing the most likely operations and by creating the actual transformations.

5.4 Matchers

The input to a matcher is a pair of schemas S and T. In addition, the matcher may consider any other surrounding information that may be available, such as data instances and text descriptions. The matcher outputs a similarity matrix that assigns to each element pair s of S and t of T a number between 0 and 1 predicting whether s corresponds to t.

There are a plethora of techniques for guessing matches between schema elements, each based on a different set of heuristics and clues. In this section we describe a few common basic matchers. We describe two classes of matchers: those that compare the names of schema elements and others that compare the data instances. It is important to keep in mind that for specific domains it is often possible to develop more specialized and effective matchers.

5.4.1 Name-Based Matchers

An obvious source of matching heuristics is based on comparing the names of the elements, in the hope that the names convey the true semantics of the elements. However, since names are seldom written in the exact same way, the challenge is to find effective similarity measures that reflect the similarity of element meanings. In principle, any of the techniques for string matching described in Chapter 4, such as edit distance, Jaccard measure, or the Soundex algorithm, can be used for name matching.

It is very common for element names to be composed of acronyms or short phrases. Hence, it is typically useful to normalize the element names before applying the similarity measures. We describe several common normalization procedures below, and note that some of them require domain-specific dictionaries.

- Split names according to certain delimiters, such as capitalization, numbers, or special symbols. For example, saleLocID would be split into sale, Loc, and ID, and agentAddress1 would be split to agent, Address, and 1.
- Expand known abbreviations or acronyms. For example, Loc may be expanded into Location, and cust may be expanded into customer.
- Expand a string with its synonyms. For example expand cost into price.
- Expand a string with its hypernyms. For example, product can be expanded into book, dvd, cd.
- Remove articles, propositions, and conjunctions, such as in, at, and.

■ ■ ■ ━━━━━━━━━━━━━━━━━━━━━━━━━━━━━━━━━━━━━━

Example 5.4

Consider again the two schemas DVD-VENDOR and AGGREGATOR, which are reproduced in Figure 5.3(a) for ease of exposition. To match the schemas, we can employ a name-based matcher that normalizes the names of the schema elements, then uses a set-based similarity measure such as the Jaccard measure or TF/IDF measure to compute the similarities between the names.

Figure 5.3(b) shows the similarity matrix produced by the name-based matcher. The figure shows the matrix in a compact fashion, by showing only schema element pairs with nonzero similarity scores and grouping these pairs by the first attribute. The first group, name ≈ ⟨name: 1,

DVD-VENDOR
Movies(id, title, year)
Products(mid, releaseDate, releaseCompany, basePrice, rating, saleLocID)
Locations(lid, name, taxRate)

AGGREGATOR
Items(name, releaseInfo, classification, price)

(a)

name-based matcher: name $\approx$ ⟨name: 1, title: 0.2⟩
releaseInfo $\approx$ ⟨releaseDate: 0.5, releaseCompany: 0.5⟩
price $\approx$ ⟨basePrice: 0.8⟩

(b)

data-based matcher: name $\approx$ ⟨name: 0.2, title: 0,8⟩
releaseInfo $\approx$ ⟨releaseDate: 0.7⟩
classification $\approx$ ⟨rating: 0.6⟩
price $\approx$ ⟨basePrice: 0.2⟩

(c)

average combiner: name $\approx$ ⟨name: 0.6, title: 0.5⟩
releaseInfo $\approx$ ⟨releaseDate: 0.6, releaseCompany: 0.25⟩
classification $\approx$ ⟨rating: 0.3⟩
price $\approx$ ⟨basePrice: 0.5⟩

(d)

FIGURE 5.3 (a) Two schemas (reproduced from Figure 5.1); (b)-(c) the similarity matrices produced by two matchers for the above two schemas; and (d) the combined similarity matrix.

title: 0.2), states that attribute name in schema AGGREGATOR matches name in DVD-VENDOR with score 1 and matches title in DVD-VENDOR with score 0.2. The remaining two groups are similarly interpreted.

■ ■ ■

With all of the above techniques, it is important to keep in mind that element names in schemas do not always convey the entire semantics of the element. Commonly, the element names will be ambiguous because they already assume a certain context that would convey their meaning to a human looking at the schema. An example of an especially ambiguous element name is name. In one context, name can refer to a book or a movie, in another to a person or animal, and in yet another to a gene, chemical, or product. Further exacerbating the problem is the fact that schemas can be written in multiple languages or using different local or industry conventions. Of course, in many cases, the designers of the schema did not anticipate the need to integrate their data with others and therefore did not carefully think of their element names beyond their immediate needs.

5.4.2 Instance-Based Matchers

Data instances often convey a significant amount of meaning of schema elements. We now describe several common techniques for predicting correspondences based on analyzing data values. Keep in mind that not all schema matching scenarios have access to instance data.

Creating Recognizers

The first technique is to build *recognizers* that employ dictionaries or rules to recognize the data values of certain kinds of attributes. Consider, for example, attribute classification in schema AGGREGATOR. A recognizer for this attribute employs a small dictionary that lists all possible classification values (G, PG, PG-13, R, etc.). Given a new attribute, if most of its values appear in the dictionary, then the recognizer can conclude that the new attribute is likely to match classification. Other examples include using dictionaries to recognize U.S. states, cities, genes, and proteins and using relatively simple rules to recognize prices and zip codes.

In general, given two schemas S and T, a recognizer for an element s of S produces a similarity matrix. In this matrix, each cell (s, t_i), where t_i ranges over all elements of T, is assigned a similarity score. All other cells are assigned the special value "n/a," because the recognizer is not designed to make predictions for these cells.

Measuring the Overlap of Values

The second technique is based on measuring the overlap of values appearing in the two schema elements and applies to fields whose values are drawn from some finite domain, such as movie ratings, movie titles, or country names. The Jaccard measure is commonly used for this purpose (see Chapter 4).

■ ■ ■ ▬▬▬▬▬▬▬▬▬▬▬▬▬▬▬▬▬▬▬▬▬▬▬▬▬▬▬▬▬

Example 5.5

Continuing with Example 5.4, to match the two schemas DVD-VENDOR and AGGREGATOR, we can employ a data-based matcher that measures the overlap of values using the Jaccard measure. Figure 5.3(c) shows the similarity matrix produced by this matcher, again in a compact format.

Consider the first group in the output, name ≈ ⟨name: 0.2, title: 0.8⟩. Attribute name of schema AGGREGATOR (which refers to DVD titles) shares few values with name of DVD-VENDOR (which refers to the names of the sale locations), resulting in the low similarity score of 0.2. In contrast, name shares many values with title (both referring to DVD titles), resulting in the high similarity score of 0.8.

▄ ▄ ▄

Using Classifiers

The third technique builds classifiers on one schema and uses them to classify the elements of the other schema. Classifier techniques commonly used are naive Bayes, decision trees, rule learning, and support vector machines. We will discuss classifiers in more detail in Section 5.8, but we give a brief example here. For each element s_i of schema S, we train a classifier C_i to recognize the instances of s_i. To do this, we need a training set of positive and negative examples. We build this training set by taking all data instances of s_i (that are available) to be positive examples and taking all data instances of other elements of schema S to be negative examples.

After we have trained classifier C_i on the training set, we are ready to use it to compute the similarity score between element s_i of schema S and each element t_j of schema T. To do this, we apply the classifier C_i to the data instances of t_j. For each data instance of t_j, the classifier C_i will produce a number between 0 and 1 that indicates how confident it is that the data instance is also a data instance of s_i. We can then aggregate these confidence scores to obtain a number that we return as the similarity between elements s_i and t_j. A simple way to perform the aggregation is to compute the average confidence score over all the data instances of t_j.

▄ ▄ ▄ ▬▬▬▬▬▬▬▬▬▬▬▬▬▬▬▬▬▬▬▬▬▬▬▬▬▬▬

Example 5.6

If s_i is address, then positive examples may include "Madison WI" and "Mountain View CA," and negative examples may include "(608) 695 9813" and "Lord of the Rings." Now suppose that element t_j is location and that we have access to three data instances of this element: "Milwaukee WI," "Palo Alto CA," and "Philadelphia PA." Then the classifier C_i may predict confidence scores 0.9, 0.7, and 0.5, respectively. In this case we may return the average confidence score of 0.7 as the similarity score between s_i = address and t_j = location.

▄ ▄ ▄

In practice, the designer decides which schema should play the role of schema S (on which we build the classifiers) and which schema should play the role of schema T (the data instances to which we apply the classifiers). For example, if a schema is the mediated schema (such as AGGREGATOR), then it may be more appropriate to build the classifiers on that schema. This allows us to reuse the classifiers when we match the mediated schema with the schemas of new data sources.

In certain cases, such as when matching taxonomies of concepts, we may want to do it both ways: build classifiers on taxonomy S and use them to classify the data instances of taxonomy T, then build classifiers on taxonomy T and use them to classify the instances of S. The bibliographic notes provide pointers to such cases as well as to more techniques that examine data values to match schemas.

5.5 Combining Match Predictions

A combiner merges the similarity matrices output by the matchers into a single one. Simple combiners can take the average, minimum, or maximum of the scores. Specifically, if the matching system uses k matchers to predict the scores between the element s_i of schema S and the element t_j of schema T, then an average combiner will compute the score between these two elements as

$$combined(i,j) = \left[\sum_{m=1}^{k} matcherScore(m,i,j) \right] /k$$

where $matcherScore(m,i,j)$ is the score between s_i and t_j as produced by the mth matcher. The minimum combiner will compute the score between elements s_i and t_j to be the minimum of the scores produced by the matchers for the pair s_i and t_j, and the maximum combiner can be defined similarly.

■ ■ ■ ▬▬▬

Example 5.7

Continuing with Example 5.5, Figure 5.3(d) shows the similarity matrix produced by the average combiner, by merging the matrix of the name-based matcher in Figure 5.3(b) and the matrix of the data-based matcher in Figure 5.3(c).

▬▬▬ ■ ■ ■

The average combiner can be used when we do not have any reason to trust one matcher over the others. The maximum combiner is preferable when we trust a strong signal from the matchers. That is, if a matcher outputs a high value, then we are relatively confident that the two elements match. In that way, if the other matchers are neutral, then the strong signal would be reflected in the combination. The minimum combiner can be used when we want to be more conservative. That is, we require high similarity scores from all of the matchers in order to declare a match.

A more complex type of combiner uses elaborate hand-crafted scripts. For example, the script may specify that if s_i = address, then return the score of the data-based matcher that uses the naive Bayes classification technique; otherwise, return the average score of all matchers.

Another complex type of combiner, weighted-sum combiners, gives *weights* to each of the matchers, corresponding to their importance. While in some cases a domain expert may be able to provide such weights, in general it may be hard to specify them. Furthermore, the weights may differ depending on some characteristics of the elements being matched. In Section 5.8 we describe techniques that *learn* appropriate weights by inspecting the behavior of the schema matching system.

5.6 Enforcing Domain Integrity Constraints

During the process of schema matching the designer often has domain knowledge that can be naturally expressed as *domain integrity constraints*. The constraint enforcer can exploit these constraints to prune certain *match combinations*. Conceptually, the enforcer searches through the space of all match combinations produced by the combiner to find the one with the highest aggregated confidence score that satisfies the constraints. The following example illustrates the above idea.

■ ■ ■ ▬▬▬▬▬▬▬▬▬▬▬▬▬▬▬▬▬▬▬▬▬▬▬▬▬▬▬▬▬▬▬

Example 5.8
Recall from Example 5.7 that the average combiner produces the following similarity matrix:

$$name \approx \langle name : 0.6, title : 0.5 \rangle$$

$$releaseInfo \approx \langle releaseDate : 0.6, releaseCompany : 0.25 \rangle$$

$$classification \approx \langle rating : 0.3 \rangle$$

$$price \approx \langle basePrice : 0.5 \rangle$$

In this matrix, the attributes name and releaseInfo each have two possible matches, resulting in a total of four match combinations, $M_1 - M_4$. The first combination M_1 is the set of matches {name $\approx$ name, releaseInfo $\approx$ releaseDate, classification $\approx$ rating, price $\approx$ basePrice}. The second combination M_2 is the same as M_1 except that it matches name with title, and so on.

For each match combination M_i, we can compute an aggregated score that captures the confidence of the combiner that M_i is correct. A straightforward way to compute this score is to multiply the scores of the matches in M_i, making the simplifying assumption that these scores have been produced independently of one another. Taking this approach, the score of the combination M_1 is $0.6 \cdot 0.6 \cdot 0.3 \cdot 0.5 = 0.054$, and the score of M_2 is $0.5 \cdot 0.6 \cdot 0.3 \cdot 0.5 = 0.045$, and so on.

Now suppose the designer knows that attribute name in schema AGGREGATOR refers to movie titles and that many movie titles contain at least four words. Then she can specify a constraint such as "if an attribute A matches name, then in any random sample of 100 data values of A, at least 10 values must contain four words or more."

The constraint enforcer searches for the match combination with the highest score that satisfies the above constraint. A simple way to do so is to check the combination with the highest score, then the one with the second highest score, and so on, until we find a combination that satisfies the constraint. In our example the combination with the highest score is M_1. M_1 specifies that attribute name of schema DVD-VENDOR matches name of AGGREGATOR. Since attribute name of DVD-VENDOR refers to the city names of the sale locations, the vast majority of its data values contain fewer than four words. Thus, the enforcer can quickly discover that M_1 does not satisfy the constraint.

The enforcer then considers M_2, the match combination with the second highest score, and finds that M_2 satisfies the constraint. So it selects M_2 as the desired match combination and produces the following similarity matrix as the output:

$$\text{name} \approx \langle \text{title} : 0.5 \rangle$$
$$\text{releaseInfo} \approx \langle \text{releaseDate} : 0.6 \rangle$$
$$\text{classification} \approx \langle \text{rating} : 0.3 \rangle$$
$$\text{price} \approx \langle \text{basePrice} : 0.5 \rangle$$

We have described the conceptual working of the constraint enforcer. In practice, enforcing the constraints is significantly more complex. First, we have to handle a variety of constraints, some of which can only be satisfied to a certain degree. Second, the space of match combinations is often quite large, so we have to find ways to search it efficiently. We now elaborate on these challenges.

5.6.1 Domain Integrity Constraints

We distinguish between *hard constraints* and *soft constraints*. Hard constraints must be applied. The enforcer will not output any match combination that violates them. Soft constraints are of a more heuristic nature and may actually be violated in correct match combinations. Hence, the enforcer will try to minimize the number (and weight) of the soft constraints being violated, but may still output a match combination that violates one or more of them. Formally, we attach a *cost* to each constraint. For hard constraints, the cost is ∞, while for soft constraints, the cost can be any positive number.

Example 5.9

Figure 5.4 shows two schemas, BOOK-VENDOR and DISTRIBUTOR, and four common constraints. As the example shows, constraints typically rely on the structure of schemas (e.g., proximity of schema elements, whether an attribute is a key) and on special properties of attributes in a particular domain.

The constraint c_1 is a hard constraint. c_1 states that any attribute mapped to code in Items must be a key. The constraint c_2 is a soft constraint. It states that any attribute mapped to desc is likely to have an average length of at least 20 words, because descriptions tend to be long textual fields.

The constraint c_3 is a soft constraint. It captures the intuition that related attributes often appear in close proximity to one another in a schema; hence matches involving these attributes also often appear close to one another.

For example, suppose that $A_1 = \text{publisher} \approx B_1 = \text{brand}$ and $A_2 = \text{location} \approx B_2 = \text{origin}$. Here B_2 is next to B_1, but A_2 is not next to A_1. Then the constraint states that there is no attribute $A*$ next to A_1 (e.g., pubCountry) that also closely matches B_2 (i.e., $|sim(A*, B_2) - sim(A_2, B_2)| \leq \epsilon$ for

BOOK-VENDOR
Books(ISBN, publisher, pubCountry, title, review)
Inventory(ISBN, quantity, location)

DISTRIBUTOR
Items(code, name, brand, origin, desc)
InStore(code, availQuant)

	Constraint	Cost
c_1	If $A \approx$ Items.code, then A is a key.	∞
c_2	If $A \approx$ Items.desc, then any random sample of 100 data instances of A must have an average length of at least 20 words.	1.5
c_3	If $A_1 \approx B_1$, $A_2 \approx B_2$, B_2 is next to B_1 in the schema, but A_2 is not next to A_1, then there is no $A*$ next to A_1 such that $|sim(A*, B_2) - sim(A_2, B_2)| \le \epsilon$ for a small prespecified ϵ.	2
c_4	If more than half of the attributes of Table U match those of Table V, then $U \approx V$.	1

FIGURE 5.4 Two schemas with integrity constraints over the matches between them.

a small prespecified ϵ). This is because if such $A*$ exists, we would rather match it, instead of A_2, to B_2, to keep the matches of A_1 and A_2 close to one another.

Finally, c_4 is also a soft constraint, which involves the matches at the table level. ■ ■ ■

Each constraint is specified only once by the designer during the matching process. The exact formalism in which constraints are represented is unimportant. The only requirement we impose is that given a constraint c and a match combination M, the constraint enforcer must be able to efficiently decide whether M violates c, given all the available data instances of the schemas.

It is important to note that just because the available data instances of the schemas conform to a constraint, that still does not mean that the constraint holds for other samples of data instances. For example, just because the current data values of an attribute A are distinct, that does not mean that A is a key. In many cases, however, the data instances that are available will be enough for the constraint enforcer to quickly detect a violation of such a constraint.

5.6.2 Searching the Space of Match Combinations

We now describe two algorithms for applying constraints to the similarity matrix output by the combiner. The first algorithm is an adaptation of A* search and is guaranteed to find the optimal solution but is computationally more expensive. The second algorithm, which applies only to constraints in which a schema element is affected by its neighbors (e.g., c_3 and c_4), is faster in practice but performs only local optimizations. We describe only the key ideas of the algorithms. The bibliographic notes provide pointers to the details.

Applying Constraints with A* Search

The A* algorithm takes as input the domain constraints $c_1, \ldots, c_p$ and the similarity matrix *combined*, produced by the combiner. The similarity matrix for our example is shown in Table 5.1. The algorithm searches through the possible match combinations and returns the one that has the lowest cost. The cost is measured by the likelihood of the match combination and the degree to which the combination violates the constraints.

Before we discuss the application of A* to constraint enforcement, we briefly review the main concepts of A*. The goal of A* is to search for a *goal state* within a set of states, beginning from an initial state. Each path through the search space is assigned a cost, and A* finds the goal state with the cheapest path from the initial state. A* performs a *best-first* search: start with the initial state, expand this state into a set of states, select the state with the smallest *estimated cost*, expand the selected state into a set of states, again select the state with the smallest estimated cost, and so on.

The estimated cost of a state n is computed as $f(n) = g(n) + h(n)$, where $g(n)$ is the cost of the path from the initial state to n, and $h(n)$ is a *lower bound* on the cost of the cheapest path from n to a goal state. Hence, the estimated cost $f(n)$ is a lower bound on the cost of the cheapest solution via n. A* terminates when it reaches a goal state, returning the path from the initial state to that goal state.

The A* algorithm is guaranteed to find a solution if one exists. When $h(n)$ is indeed a lower bound on the cost to reach a goal state, A* is also guaranteed to find the cheapest solution. The efficiency of A*, measured as the number of states that it needs to examine to reach the goal state, depends on the accuracy of the heuristic $h(n)$. The closer $h(n)$ is to

Table 5.1 The *Combined* Similarity Matrix for the Two Schemas in Figure 5.4

Items		code	name	brand	origin	desc	**InStore**	code	availQuant
Books	0.5	0.2	0.5	0.1	0	0.4	0.1	0	0
ISBN	0.2	0.9	0	0	0	0	0	0.1	0
publisher	0.2	0.1	0.6	0.75	0.4	0.2	0	0.1	0
pubCountry	0.3	0.15	0.3	0.5	0.7	0.3	0.05	0.15	0
title	0.25	0.1	0.8	0.3	0.45	0.2	0.05	0.1	0
review	0.15	0	0.6	0.1	0.35	0.65	0	0.05	0
Inventory	0.35	0	0.25	0.05	0.1	0.1	0.5	0	0
ISBN	0.25	0.9	0	0	0	0.15	0.15	0.9	0
quantity	0	0.1	0	0	0	0	0	0.75	0.9
location	0.1	0.6	0.6	0.7	0.85	0.3	0	0.2	0

the actual lowest cost, the fewer states A* needs to examine. In the ideal case where $h(n)$ is the lowest cost, A* marches straight to the goal with the lowest cost.

We now describe applying A* to match schema S_1, whose attributes are $A_1, \ldots, A_n$, with schema S_2, whose attributes are $B_1, \ldots, B_m$. We note that the method below is not the only way to apply A* to constraint enforcement.

STATES

We define a state to be a tuple of size n, where the ith element either specifies a correspondence for A_i or is a wildcard *, representing that the correspondence for A_i is undetermined. Thus, a state can be interpreted as representing the *set* of match combinations that are consistent with the specifications. For example, suppose $n = 5$ and $m = 3$; then state $(B_2, *, B_1, B_3, B_2)$ represents three match combinations $(B_2, B_1, B_1, B_3, B_2)$, $(B_2, B_2, B_1, B_3, B_2)$, and $(B_2, B_3, B_1, B_3, B_2)$. We refer to a state as an *abstract state* if it contains wildcards, and a *concrete state* otherwise. A concrete state is a match combination.

INITIAL STATE

The initial state is defined to be $(*, *, \ldots, *)$, which represents all possible match combinations.

GOAL STATES

The goal states are the states that do not contain any wildcards, and hence completely specify a candidate match combination.

We now describe how the A* algorithm computes costs for goal states and then for abstract states.

EXPANDING STATES

To expand an abstract state, we choose a wildcard at position i and create the set of states in which the wildcard is replaced by the possible correspondences for the attribute in position i. The main decision to be made here is which of the multiple wildcards to choose. Clearly, the positions for which only one correspondence exists should be chosen first. After that, we may want to prefer the wildcards for which there is a correspondence that has a much higher score than the others.

COST OF GOAL STATES

The cost of a goal state combines our estimate of the likelihood of the combination and the degree to which it violates the domain constraints. Specifically, we evaluate a combination M as follows:

$$cost(M) = -LH(M) + cost(M, c_1) + cost(M, c_2) + \cdots + cost(M, c_p) \tag{5.1}$$

In the equation, $LH(M)$ represents the likelihood of M according to the similarity matrix, and $cost(M, c_i)$ represents the degree to which M violates the constraint c_i. In practice, we also typically assign to each component of the sum a weight, to represent the trade-offs among the cost components, but we omit this detail here.

The term $LH(M)$ is defined as $log\ conf(M)$, where $conf(M)$ is the confidence score of the match combination M. We compute the confidence as the product of the confidence scores of all the matches in M. Specifically, if $M = (B_{l_1}, \ldots, B_{l_n})$, where the B_{l_i} are the elements of schema S_2, then

$$conf(M) = combined(1, l_1) \times \cdots \times combined(n, l_n)$$

The formula for $conf(M)$ effectively assumes that the confidence scores of the matches in M are independent of one another. This assumption is clearly not true, because in many cases the appropriate match for one attribute depends on the matches of its neighbors. However, we make this assumption to reduce the cost of our search procedure. Note also that the definition of $LH(M)$ coupled with Equation 5.1 implies that we prefer the combination with the highest confidence score, all other things being equal.

■ ■ ■ ▬▬▬▬▬▬▬▬▬▬▬▬▬▬▬▬▬▬▬▬▬▬▬▬▬▬▬▬▬▬

Example 5.10

Consider the goal state corresponding to the following match combination (highlighted in boldface in Table 5.1).

Books ≈ Items

Books.ISBN ≈ Items.code

Books.title ≈ Items.name

Books.publisher ≈ Items.brand

Books.pubCountry ≈ Items.origin

Books.review ≈ Items.desc

Inventory ≈ InStore

Inventory.ISBN ≈ InStore.code

Inventory.quantity ≈ InStore.availQuant

The cost of this state is the degree to which the combination violates the integrity constraints minus the likelihood of the combination. The likelihood of the combination is the log of the product of the boldface values in Table 5.1. This particular match combination satisfies all the integrity constraints in Figure 5.4 and therefore incurs no additional cost.

In contrast, consider the match combination in which **Books**.review ≈ **Items**.desc is replaced by **Books**.title ≈ **Items**.desc, and **Books**.pubCountry ≈ **Items**.origin is replaced by **Inventory**.location ≈ **Items**.origin. This combination would violate the two integrity constraints c_2 and c_3. Hence, the combination would incur an additional cost of 3.5.

▬▬▬▬▬▬▬▬▬▬▬▬▬▬▬▬▬▬▬▬▬▬▬▬▬▬▬ ■ ■ ■

COST OF ABSTRACT STATES

The cost of an abstract state s is the sum of the cost of the path from the initial state to s, denoted by $g(s)$, and an estimate of the cost of the path from s to a goal state, denoted by $h(s)$. The estimate $h(s)$ must be a lower bound on the cost of the cheapest path from s to a goal state.

The cost of the path from the initial state to s is computed in a similar fashion to the cost of a path to a goal state, except that we ignore the wildcards.

■ ■ ■ ▬▬▬▬▬▬▬▬▬▬▬▬▬▬▬▬▬▬▬▬▬▬▬▬▬▬▬▬▬▬▬▬▬▬▬▬

Example 5.11
Consider the abstract state with the following partial matches:

Books ≈ Items	Books.review ≈ Items.desc
Books.ISBN ≈ Items.code	Books.publisher ≈ Items.brand
Books.pubCountry ≈ Items.origin	Books.title ≈ Items.name

Given the similarity values in Table 5.1, the cost from the initial state to the above abstract state is $-log(0.5 * 0.9 * 0.7 * 0.65 * 0.75 * 0.8)$.

▬▬▬▬▬▬▬▬▬▬▬▬▬▬▬▬▬▬▬▬▬▬▬▬▬▬▬▬▬▬▬ ■ ■ ■

The cost $h(s)$ of the path from s to a goal state is estimated as the sum of two factors $h_1(s)$ and $h_2(S)$. The factor $h_1(s)$ is computed to be a lower bound on the cost of expanding all wildcards in s. For example, suppose that $s = (B_1 B_2 * * B_3)$; then the estimated cost $h_1(s)$ is

$$h_1(s) = -(log[\max_i combined(3, i)] + log[\max_i combined(4, i)])$$

■ ■ ■ ▬▬▬▬▬▬▬▬▬▬▬▬▬▬▬▬▬▬▬▬▬▬▬▬▬▬▬▬▬▬▬▬▬▬

Example 5.12
Continuing with Example 5.11, the wildcards are the assignment to **Inventory** and its attributes. The estimate is the product of the highest values in each of their corresponding rows, i.e., $-log(0.5 * 0.9 * 0.9 * 0.85)$.

▬▬▬▬▬▬▬▬▬▬▬▬▬▬▬▬▬▬▬▬▬▬▬▬▬▬▬▬▬▬▬ ■ ■ ■

The term $h_2(s)$ is an estimate on the degree to which goal states reachable from s violate the constraints. It is defined to be the sum $\Sigma_{i=1}^{p} cost(s, c_i)$, where $cost(s, c_i)$ is the estimate for the constraint c_i. To estimate the degree to which an abstract state violates a constraint, the algorithm assumes a best-case scenario—if it cannot show that *all* goal states reachable from s violate c_i, then it assumes that c_i is not violated. In Example 5.11, it is easy to show that at least one goal state reachable from the abstract state does not violate the constraints. Thus, the h_2 value of this abstract state is 0.

The specific method for determining whether the possible goal states violate c_i depends on the type of constraint of c_i. For example, consider $s = (B_1, B_2, *, *, B_3)$ and the hard constraint $c =$ "at most one attribute matches B_2." Clearly there are goal states that are represented by s and satisfy c, such as goal state $(B_1, B_2, B_3, B_1, B_3)$, and therefore we say that s satisfies c. Consider $s' = (B_1, B_2, *, *, B_2)$. Since any goal state represented by s' violates the hard constraint c, we set $cost(s', c) = \infty$.

It is trivial to show that the cost $f(s) = g(s) + h(s)$ is a lower bound on the cost of any goal state that is in the set of concrete states represented by s, and therefore A* will find the cheapest goal state.

Applying Constraints with Local Propagation

The second algorithm we describe is based on propagating constraints locally from elements of the schema to their neighbors until we reach a fixed point. As before, we describe an algorithm that can be instantiated in a variety of ways.

■ ■ ■ ▬▬▬▬▬▬▬▬▬▬▬▬▬▬▬▬▬▬▬▬▬▬▬▬▬▬▬▬▬▬▬▬▬▬▬▬

Example 5.13

In Figure 5.4, constraints c_3 and c_4 involve computing correspondences based on properties of an element's neighbors. To apply them with the algorithm we describe now, we need to rephrase them to be stated from the perspective of a pair of nodes, one from S_1 and one from S_2.

Constraint c_3 can be stated as follows. If $sim(A_1, B_1) \leq 0.9$ and A_1 has a neighbor A_2 such that $sim(A_2, B_2) \geq 0.75$, and B_1 is a neighbor of B_2, then increase $sim(A_1, B_1)$ by α.

Constraint c_4 can be stated as follows. Let $R_1 \in S_1$ and $R_2 \in S_2$ be two tables, and suppose the number of neighbors they have is within a factor of 2. (The neighbors of a table node include all nodes that represent the attributes of the table.) Then, if $sim(R_1, R_2) \leq 0.9$ and at least half of the neighbors of R_1 are in the set $\{A_i \in attributes(R_1) \mid \exists B_j \in attributes(R_2) \text{ s.t. } sim(A_i, B_j) \geq 0.75\}$, increase the similarity $sim(R_1, R_2)$ by α.

▬▬▬▬▬▬▬▬▬▬▬▬▬▬▬▬▬▬▬▬▬▬▬▬▬▬▬▬▬▬▬▬▬▬▬▬ ■ ■ ■

INITIALIZATION

We begin by representing the schemas S_1 and S_2 as graphs. In the case of relational schemas, the graph representation is a tree (see Figure 5.5). The root of the tree is the schema node, its children are the relation names, and the leaves are their respective attributes. Other data models (e.g., XML, object-oriented) also have natural representations as graphs. Intuitively, edges in the graph represent neighborhood relations in the schema.

The algorithm computes a similarity matrix *sim* that is initialized to be the *combined* matrix. Recall that $combined(i, j)$ is the estimate that $A_i \in S_1$ corresponds to $B_j \in S_2$.

ITERATION

The algorithm proceeds by iteratively selecting a node s_1 in the graph of S_1 and updating the values in *sim* based on the similarities computed for its neighbors. A common method for tree traversal is bottom-up, starting from the leaves and going up to the root.

When we select a node $s_1 \in S_1$, we need to apply constraints that involve a node $s_2 \in S_2$. Since we do not want to compare every pair of nodes, the algorithm checks constraints only on pairs of elements that pass some filter. For example, the nodes need to have the same number of neighbors within a factor of 2. (Note that this filter is already built into the constraint c_4.) The algorithm applies the constraint, modifying the similarities if necessary, and proceeds to the next node.

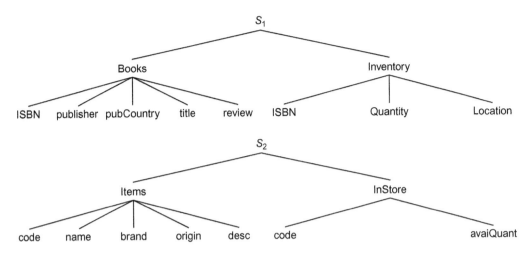

FIGURE 5.5 Tree representation of the schemas in Figure 5.4.

TERMINATION

The algorithm terminates either after a fixed number of iterations or when the changes to *sim* are smaller than a predefined threshold.

■ ■ ■

Example 5.14

In our example, let α be 20%. When we choose the node pubCountry in **Books**, we will consider the pair (pubCountry, origin) because it has the highest value in the row of pubCountry. Since pubCountry is a neighbor of publisher, and origin is a neighbor of brand, and the similarity score between publisher and brand is 0.75, constraint c_3 dictates that we increase the similarity between pubCountry and origin by 20% to 0.84. When we consider the nodes **Items** and **Books**, constraint c_4 will cause us to increase their similarity by 20% to 0.6.

The algorithm will terminate after a few iterations because the constraints c_3 and c_4 can only cause the similarities to increase, and both of them do not apply once the similarity is over 0.9.

■ ■ ■

5.7 Match Selector

The result of the previous components of the schema matcher is a similarity matrix for the schemas of S and T. The matrix combines the predictions of multiple matchers and the knowledge expressed as domain constraints. The last component of the matching system, the match selector, produces matches from the similarity matrix.

The simplest selection strategy is *thresholding:* all pairs of schema elements with similarity score equaling or exceeding a given threshold are returned as matches. For instance, in Example 5.8 the constraint enforcer produces the following matrix:

$$name \approx \langle title : 0.5 \rangle$$

$$releaseInfo \approx \langle releaseDate : 0.6 \rangle$$

$$classification \approx \langle rating : 0.3 \rangle$$

$$price \approx \langle basePrice : 0.5 \rangle$$

Given the threshold 0.5, the match selector produces the following matches: name ≈ title, releaseInfo ≈ releaseDate, and price ≈ basePrice.

More sophisticated selection strategies produce the top few match combinations. This is so that when the user makes a particular choice, the other suggested matches can be adjusted accordingly. For example, suppose that the match selector produces the top-ranked match combination

$$phone \approx shipPhone, \; addr \approx shipAddr$$

and the second-ranked match combination

$$phone \approx billPhone, \; addr \approx billAddr$$

Then once the designer has selected phone ≈ billPhone as a correct match, the system may recommend addr ≈ billAddr, even though this match may have a lower score than addr ≈ shipAddr.

There are a variety of algorithms that can be used to select match combinations. A common algorithm formulates the match selection problem as an instance of finding a *stable marriage*. Specifically, imagine the elements of S to be men and the elements of T to be women. Let the value $sim(i,j)$ be the degree to which A_i and B_j desire each other (note that in the world of schema matching A and B desire each other equally, though we can consider asymmetric correspondences, too). Our goal is to find a stable match between the men and the women. A match would be unstable if there are two couples $A_i \approx B_j$ and $A_k \approx B_l$ such that A_i and B_l would clearly want to be matched with each other, that is, $sim(i,l) > sim(i,j)$ and $sim(i,l) > sim(k,l)$.

We can produce a match combination without unhappy couples as follows. Begin with match={}, and repeat the following. Let (i,j) be the highest value in sim such that A_i and B_j are not in match. Add $A_i \approx B_j$ to match.

In contrast to the stable marriage, we can consider a match combination that maximizes the sum of the correspondence predictions. For example, in Figure 5.6, matching A to C and B to D forms a stable marriage match. However, matching A to D and B to C maximizes the total confidences of the correspondences.

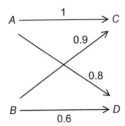

FIGURE 5.6 Matching A to C and B to D is a stable marriage match. However, matching A to D and B to C maximizes the total confidences of the correspondences.

5.8 Reusing Previous Matches

Schema matching tasks are often repetitive. For example, in the context of data integration, we are creating matches from data sources in the *same* domain to a single mediated schema. Similarly, in the enterprise context, we often have to update the semantic matches because one of the schemas has changed.

More generally, working in a particular domain, the same concepts tend to recur. As the designer works in the domain, he or she starts identifying how common domain concepts get expressed in schemas. As a result, the designer is able to create schema matches more quickly over time. For example, in the domain of real estate, one learns very quickly the typical concepts (e.g., house, lot, agent), the typical attributes of the concepts, and the properties of these attributes (e.g., the field that has numbers in the thousands is the price of the house, and the field that has longer text descriptions with words like "wonderful" and "spacious" is the description of the house).

Hence, an intriguing question is whether the schema matching system can *also* improve over time. Can a schema matching system learn from previous experience? In this section we describe how machine learning techniques can be applied to schema matching and enable the matching system to improve over time. We describe these techniques in the context of data integration, where the goal is to map a large number of data sources to a single mediated schema.

5.8.1 Learning to Match

Suppose we have n data sources, $S_1, \ldots, S_n$, and our goal is to map them to the mediated schema G. Recall that G is the schema used to formulate queries over the data integration system. We would like to *train* the system by manually providing it with semantic matches on a small number of data sources, say $S_1, \ldots, S_m$, where m is much smaller than n. The system should then *generalize* from these training examples and be able to *predict* matches for the sources $S_{m+1}, \ldots, S_n$.

We proceed by learning classifiers for the elements of the mediated schema. As explained in Section 5.4, a classifier for a concept C is an algorithm that identifies instances of C from those that are not. In this case, the classifier for an element e in the mediated schema will examine an element in a source schema and predict whether it matches e or not.

To create classifiers, we need to employ some machine learning algorithm. Like matchers, any machine learning algorithm also typically considers only one aspect of the schema and has its strengths and weaknesses. Hence, we combine multiple learning methods with a technique called *multi-strategy learning*. The training phase of multi-strategy learning works as follows:

- Employ a set of *learners*, $l_1, \ldots, l_k$. Each learner creates a classifier for each element e of the mediated schema G from the training examples of e. The training examples are derived using the semantic matches between G and the training data sources $S_1, \ldots, S_m$.
- Use a *meta-learner* to learn weights for the different learners. Specifically, for each element e of the mediated schema and each learner l, the meta-learner computes a weight $w_{e,l}$.

■ ■ ■ ▬▬▬▬▬▬▬▬▬▬▬▬▬▬▬▬▬▬▬▬▬▬▬▬▬▬▬▬

Example 5.15

Suppose the mediated schema G has three elements e_1, e_2, and e_3. Suppose further that we employ two instance-based learners: naive Bayes and decision tree (which we will describe shortly). Then the naive Bayes learner will create three classifiers, $C_{e_1,NB}$, $C_{e_2,NB}$, and $C_{e_3,NB}$, for the three elements e_1, e_2, and e_3, respectively. The goal of the classifier $C_{e_1,NB}$ is to decide whether a given data instance belongs to element e_1. The goals of classifiers $C_{e_2,NB}$ and $C_{e_3,NB}$ are similar.

To train the classifier $C_{e_1,NB}$, we have to assemble a set of positive and negative training examples. In principle, we can take all available data instances of element e_1 to be positive examples and all available instances of the other elements of the mediated schema to be negative examples. However, the mediated schema is virtual, so it has no data instances.

This is where the training sources $S_1, \ldots, S_m$ come in. Suppose when matching these sources to the mediated schema G, we have found that only two elements a and b of the sources match the element e_1 of the mediated schema. Then we can view the available data instances of a and b as the data instances of e_1, and hence as positive examples. We create negative examples in a similar fashion, using the instances of the elements (of the training data sources) that we know do not match e_1. We train the classifiers $C_{e_2,NB}$ and $C_{e_3,NB}$ in a similar fashion.

The decision tree learner creates three classifiers, $C_{e_1,DT}$, $C_{e_2,DT}$, and $C_{e_3,DT}$, and they can be trained analogously.

Finally, training the meta-learner means computing a weight for each pair of mediated-schema element and learner, for a total of six weights: $w_{e_1,NB}$, $w_{e_1,DT}$, $w_{e_2,NB}$, $w_{e_2,DT}$, $w_{e_3,NB}$, and $w_{e_3,DT}$.

▬▬▬▬▬▬▬▬▬▬▬▬▬▬▬▬▬▬▬▬▬▬▬▬▬▬▬▬ ■ ■ ■

Given the trained classifiers, the matching phase of multi-strategy learning works as follows. When presented with a schema S whose elements are $e'_1, \ldots, e'_n$:

- Apply the learners to $e'_1, \ldots, e'_n$. Denote by $p_{e,l}(e')$ the prediction of learner l on whether e' matches e.
- Combine the learners: $p_e(e') = \sum_{i=1}^{k} w_{e,l_i} * p_{e,l_i}(e')$.

The learners act as matchers, and the meta-learner acts as a combiner. Thus, the output of the meta-learner is a combined similarity matrix, which can be fed into a constraint enforcer, then a match selector, as described earlier.

■ ■ ■ ▬▬▬▬▬▬▬▬▬▬▬▬▬▬▬▬▬▬▬▬▬▬▬▬▬▬▬▬▬▬

Example 5.16
Continuing with Example 5.15, let S be a new data source with two elements e'_1 and e'_2. Then the naive Bayes learner will apply

- the classifier $C_{e_1,NB}$ to make predictions $p_{e_1,NB}(e'_1)$ and $p_{e_1,NB}(e'_2)$,
- the classifier $C_{e_2,NB}$ to make predictions $p_{e_2,NB}(e'_1)$ and $p_{e_2,NB}(e'_2)$, and
- the classifier $C_{e_3,NB}$ to make predictions $p_{e_3,NB}(e'_1)$ and $p_{e_3,NB}(e'_2)$.

The above six predictions form a similarity matrix, which can be viewed as the similarity matrix produced by the naive Bayes learner. A similar matrix is produced by the decision tree learner.

The meta-learner then combines the above two similarity matrices. Specifically, it computes the combined similarity score between e_1 and e'_1 to be the sum of the similarity scores, weighted by the learners:

$$p_{e_1}(e'_1) = w_{e_1,NB} * p_{e_1,NB}(e'_1) + w_{e_1,DT} * p_{e_1,DT}(e'_1)$$

The rest of the combined similarity scores are computed in a similar fashion.

▬▬▬▬▬▬▬▬▬▬▬▬▬▬▬▬▬▬▬▬▬▬▬▬▬ ■ ■ ■

In the next two sections we describe two common learners and how to train the meta-learner.

5.8.2 Learners

A variety of classification techniques have been employed as learners for schema matching. In what follows we describe two common learners: a rule-based learner and the naive Bayes learner.

Rule-Based Learner

A rule-based learner examines a set of training examples and computes a set of rules that can be applied to test instances. The rules can be represented as simple logical formulas or as decision trees. A rule-based learner works well in domains where there exists a set of rules, based on features of the training examples, that accurately characterize the instances of the class, such as identifying elements that adhere to certain formats. When the learned rules are applied to an instance, we return 1 if the instance satisfies the rules and 0 otherwise.

Consider the example of a rule learner for identifying phone numbers (for simplicity, we restrict our attention to American phone numbers). Example instances of strings that can be fed into the learners are "(608) 435-2322," "849-7394," and "5549902." For each string, we first identify whether it is a positive or negative example of a phone number, and then extract values for a set of features we deem important. In our example, the features are "Does the string have 10 digits?", "Does the string have 7 digits?", "Is there a '(' in position 1?", "Is there a ')' in position 5?", and "Is there a '-' in position 4?"

A common method to learn rules is to create a decision tree. Figure 5.7 shows an example decision tree for recognizing phone numbers. Informally, a decision tree is created as follows. We first search for a feature of the training data that most distinguishes between positive and negative examples. That feature becomes the root of the tree, and we divide the training instances into two sets, depending on whether they have the feature or not. We then continue recursively and build decision trees of the two subsets of instances. In Figure 5.7 we first distinguish between the instances that have 10 digits from those that do not. The next important feature for the 10-digit instances is the position of the '('.

As described, the above decision tree encodes rules such as "if an instance i has 10 digits, a '(' in position 1, and a ')' in position 5, then i is a phone number," and "if i has 7 digits, but no '-' in position 4, then i is not a phone number."

The Naive Bayes Learner

The naive Bayes learner examines the tokens of a given instance and assigns to the instance the most likely class, given the occurrences of tokens in the training data. Specifically, given an instance, the learner converts it into a *bag of tokens*. The tokens are generated by parsing and stemming the words and symbols in the instance. For example, "RE/MAX Greater Atlanta Affiliates of Roswell" becomes "re / max greater atlanta affili of roswell."

Suppose that $c_1, \ldots, c_n$ are the elements of the mediated schema and that the learner is given a test instance $d = \{w_1, \ldots, w_k\}$ to classify, where the w_i are the tokens of the instance. The goal of the naive Bayes learner is to assign d to the element c_d that has

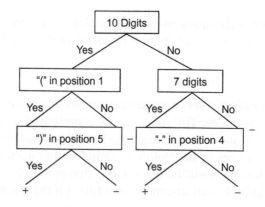

FIGURE 5.7 A decision tree for phone numbers.

the highest posterior probability given d. Formally, this probability is defined as $c_d = arg\ max_{c_i}\ P(c_i|d)$. To compute this probability, the learner can leverage Bayes' Rule, which states that $P(c_i|d) = P(d|c_i)P(c_i)/P(d)$. Using this rule, we have

$$c_d = arg\ max_{c_i}\ [P(d|c_i)P(c_i)/P(d)]$$

$$= arg\ max_{c_i}\ [P(d|c_i)P(c_i)]$$

Hence, to make its prediction, the naive Bayes learner needs to estimate $P(d|c_i)$ and $P(c_i)$ from the training data. It approximates the probability $P(c_i)$ as the portion of training instances with label c_i. To compute $P(d|c_i)$, we assume that the tokens w_j appear in d *independently* of each other given c_i (this is where naive Bayes becomes naive). With this assumption, we have

$$P(d|c_i) = P(w_1|c_i)P(w_2|c_i)\cdots P(w_k|c_i)$$

We estimate $P(w_j|c_i)$ as $\frac{n(w_j,c_i)}{n(c_i)}$, where $n(c_i)$ is the total number of tokens in the training instances with label c_i, and $n(w_j, c_i)$ is the number of times token w_j appears in all training instances with label c_i.

Even though the independence assumption is typically not valid, the naive Bayes learner still performs surprisingly well in many domains. In particular, it works best when there are tokens that are strongly indicative of the correct label, by virtue of their frequencies. For example, it can effectively recognize house descriptions in real-estate listings, which frequently contain words such as "beautiful" and "fantastic"—words that seldom appear in other elements. The naive Bayes learner also works well when there are only weakly suggestive tokens, but many of them. In contrast, it fares poorly for short or numeric fields, such as color, zip code, or number of bathrooms.

5.8.3 Training the Meta-Learner

The meta-learner decides the weights to attach to each of the learners. The weights can be different for every mediated-schema element. To compute these weights, the meta-learner asks the learners for predictions on the training examples. Since the meta-learner knows the correct matches for the training examples, it is able to judge how well each learner performs with respect to each mediated-schema element. Based on this judgment, the meta-learner assigns to each combination of mediated-schema element e and base learner l a weight $w_{e,l}$ that indicates how much it *trusts* learner l's predictions regarding e.

Specifically, to learn the weights for a mediated-schema element e, the meta-learner first creates a set of training examples. Each training example is of the form $(d, p_1, \ldots, p_k, p*)$, where

- d is a data instance of a training source S_i, $1 \leq i \leq m$,
- each p_j is the prediction that the learner l_j made for the pair (d, e), and
- $p*$ is the correct prediction for the data instance d.

The meta-learner then applies a learning method, such as linear regression, to the above set of training examples, to learn the weights for e.

■ ■ ■ ▬▬▬▬▬▬▬▬▬▬▬▬▬▬▬▬▬▬▬▬▬▬▬▬▬▬▬▬▬▬▬▬▬▬▬▬▬

Example 5.17

Continuing with Examples 5.15–5.16, our goal is to learn the six weights $w_{e_1,NB}$, $w_{e_1,DT}$, $w_{e_2,NB}$, $w_{e_2,DT}$, $w_{e_3,NB}$, and $w_{e_3,DT}$.

We begin by learning the two weights $w_{e_1,NB}$ and $w_{e_1,DT}$ for the mediated-schema element e_1. To do so, we create a set of training examples. Each example is of the form $(d, p_{NB}, p_{DT}, p*)$, where (a) d is a data instance from a training source, (b) p_{NB} and p_{DT} are the confidence scores of the naive Bayes learner and the decision tree learner, respectively, that d matches e_1 (i.e., d is an instance of e_1), and (c) $p*$ is 1 if d indeed matches e_1 and 0 otherwise.

We then apply linear regression to compute the weights $w_{e_1,NB}$ and $w_{e_1,DT}$ that minimize the squared error $\sum_d (p* - [p_{NB} * w_{e_1,NB} + p_{DT} * w_{e_1,DT}])^2$, where the term after $\sum_d$ ranges over all training examples.

We compute the remaining four weights $w_{e_2,NB}$, $w_{e_2,DT}$, $w_{e_3,NB}$, and $w_{e_3,DT}$ in a similar fashion.

▬▬▬▬▬▬▬▬▬▬▬▬▬▬▬▬▬▬▬▬▬▬▬▬▬▬▬▬▬▬▬▬▬▬▬▬▬ ■ ■ ■

5.9 Many-to-Many Matches

Until now we have focused on schema matches where all the correspondences are one-to-one. In practice, there are many correspondences that involve multiple elements of one schema or both. For example, consider the simplified SOURCE and TARGET schemas in Figure 5.8. The price attribute in the Items table corresponds to basePrice * (1 + taxRate) in the Books table; the author attribute in the Items table corresponds to concat(authorFirstName, authorLastName) in the Books table. Hence, we need to consider similarity also among *compound elements* of the two schemas. A compound element is constructed by applying a function to multiple attributes.

In this section we discuss how to extend schema matching techniques to capture many-to-many correspondences. The main challenge is that there are too many compound elements, and therefore too many candidate correspondences, to test. Whereas in the case of one-to-one matches, at worst we need to test similarity of the cross product of elements from both schemas, the number of compound elements is potentially very large or even unbounded. For example, there are many ways to concatenate multiple string attributes in

SOURCE

Books(title, basePrice, taxRate, quantity, authorFirstName, authorLastName)

TARGET

Items(title, price, inventory, author, genre)

FIGURE 5.8 Two simple schemas between which several many-to-many matches exist.

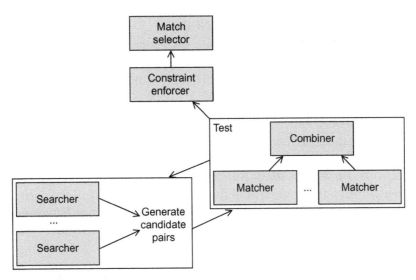

FIGURE 5.9 To discover correspondences among compound attributes, we employ several searchers to create candidate correspondences. We test them with the matchers and the combiner, as discussed earlier in the chapter. We terminate the searches when the quality of the predicted correspondences does not change significantly.

a schema, and there is an unbounded number of functions that involve multiple numerical elements of a schema.

We treat the problem of finding correspondences as a search problem (see Figure 5.9). We generate candidate element pairs, where one or both of them may be compound elements. We iteratively generate the pairs and test them as we test other candidate correspondences.

To generate candidate pairs, we employ several *specialized* searchers. Each specialized searcher focuses on a specific data type (e.g., text, string, numeric) and considers only compound elements appropriate for that type. Note that this strategy is very extensible. For example, it is easy to add another searcher that specializes in address fields and combinations thereof, or in particular ways of combining name-related fields.

A searcher has three components: a search strategy, a method for evaluating its candidate matches, and a termination condition. We explain each below.

SEARCH STRATEGY

The search strategy involves two parts. First, we define the set of candidate correspondences that a searcher will explore with a set of operators that the searcher can apply to build compound elements (e.g., concat, +, *). Second, the searcher needs a way to control its search, since the set of possible compound elements may be large or unbounded. A common technique is to use use *beam search*, which keeps the k best candidates at any point in the search.

EVALUATING CANDIDATE CORRESPONDENCES

Given a pair of compound elements, one from each schema, we evaluate their similarity using the techniques described previously in this chapter. As before, the result of the evaluation is a prediction on the correspondence between the pair. The type of searcher may dictate which matchers are more appropriate.

TERMINATION CONDITION

While in some cases the search will terminate because the set of possible compound elements is small, we need a method for terminating when the set is unbounded or too large. We terminate when we witness *diminishing returns*. Specifically, in the ith iteration of the beam search algorithm, we keep track of the highest score of any of the correspondences we have seen to that point, denoted by Max_i. When the difference between Max_{i+1} and Max_i is less than some prespecified threshold δ, we stop the search and return the top k correspondences.

■ ■ ■ ━━

Example 5.18

To discover many-to-many matches between the schemas SOURCE and TARGET in Figure 5.8, we employ two searchers. The first is a string searcher. The searcher considers attributes of type string, and tries to combine them by concatenation. The second is a numeric searcher that considers numerical fields and tries to combine them using arithmetic operations such as addition and multiplication, and some constants, such as 32, 5/9 (for Fahrenheit to Celsius), and 2.54 (for converting inches to centimeters).

When the algorithm looks for a match for the author attribute of Items, it will consider the elements title, authorFirstName, authorLastName, concat(title, authorFirstName), concat(authorFirstName, authorLastName), concat(authorLastName, authorFirstName), etc. When the algorithm looks for a match for the price attribute of Inventory, it tests many combinations including basePrice + taxRate, basePrice * taxRate, basePrice * (1 + taxRate), basePrice + quantity, and taxRate * quantity.

━━ ■ ■ ■

5.10 From Matches to Mappings

Recall from Section 5.1 that to create the descriptions of data sources, we often begin by creating semantic matches, then elaborate the matches into mappings. The reason we begin by creating the matches is that matches are often easier to elicit from designers, because they require the designer to reason about *individual* schema elements. As we have seen so far, there are also techniques that enable the system to guess matches.

In elaborating matches into mappings, the key challenge is to flesh out the matches and put all of them together into a coherent whole. This involves specifying the operations that need to be performed on the source or target data so they can be transformed from one to the other. In particular, creating the mapping requires aligning the tabular organization of the data in the source and the target by specifying joins and unions. It also involves specifying other operations on the data such as filtering columns, applying aggregates, and unnesting structures.

Given the complexity of creating mappings, the process needs to be supported by a very effective user interface. For example, the designer should be able to specify the mapping using a graphical user interface, and the system should generate the mapping expressions automatically, thus saving the designer significant effort. In addition, at every step the system should show the designer example data instances to verify that the transformation she is defining is correct and should allow her to correct errors when necessary.

This section describes how to explore the space of possible schema mappings. Given a set of matches, we describe an algorithm that searches through the possible schema mappings that are consistent with the matches. We show that we can define the appropriate search space based on some very natural principles of schema design. Furthermore, these principles also suggest methods for ranking the possible mappings when they are presented to a designer. We begin with an example that illustrates the intuition underlying these concepts.

■ ■ ■ ▬▬▬▬▬▬▬▬▬▬▬▬▬▬▬▬▬▬▬▬▬▬▬▬▬▬▬▬▬▬▬▬

Example 5.19

Figure 5.10 shows a subset of the schema match produced between a source university schema (on the left) and an accounting schema.

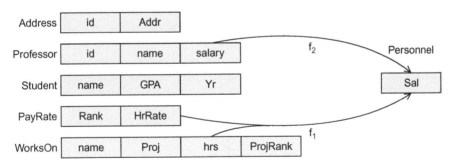

FIGURE 5.10 Combining correspondences from multiple tables. The correspondence f_1 states that the product of HrRate and hrs corresponds to Sal of **Personnel**, but the question is which tables to join to create a table that includes the two attributes. The correspondence f_2 states that salary also corresponds to Sal, and the question is whether to union professor salaries with employee salaries or to join salaries computed from the two correspondences.

The correspondence f_1 states that the product of HrRate from the **PayRate** relation and the Hrs attribute from the **WorksOn** relation corresponds to the Sal attribute in the target **Personnel** relation.

The schema mapping needs to specify how to join the relations in the source in order to map data into the target, and this choice is far from obvious. In the example, if the attribute ProjRank is a foreign key of the relation **PayRate**, then the natural mapping would be

```
SELECT P.HrRate * W.Hrs
FROM PayRate P, WorksOn
W WHERE P.Rank = W.ProjRank
```

However, suppose that ProjRank is not declared as a foreign key, and instead, the name attribute of **WorksOn** is declared as a foreign key of **Student** and the Yr attribute of **Student** is declared as a foreign key of **PayRate**. That is, the salary depends on the year of the student. In that case, the following join would be the natural one:

```
SELECT P.HrRate * W.Hrs
FROM PayRate P, WorksOn W, Student S
WHERE W.Name=S.Name AND S.Yr = P.Rank
```

If all three foreign keys are declared, then it is not clear which of the above joins would be the right one. In fact, it is also possible that the correct mapping does not do a join at all, and the mapping is a cross product between **PayRate** and **WorksOn**, but that seems less likely.

Suppose the correct mapping for the first correspondence, f_1, involves joining tables **PayRate**, **WorksOn**, and **Student**. Now consider the second correspondence, f_2, which states that the salary attribute of **Professor** maps to Sal in the target. One interpretation of f_2 is that the values produced from f_1 should be joined with those produced by f_2. However, that would mean that most of the values in the source database would not be mapped to the target. Instead, a more natural interpretation is that there are two ways of computing the salary for employees, one that applies to professors and another that applies to other employees. The mapping describing this interpretation is the following.

```
(SELECT P.HrRate * W.Hrs
 FROM PayRate P, WorksOn W, Student S
 WHERE W.Name=S.Name AND S.Yr = P.Rank)
UNION ALL
(SELECT Salary
 FROM Professor)
```

The above example illustrates two principles. First, while the space of possible mappings given a set of matches may be bewildering, there is some structure to it. In particular, the first choice we made considered how to join relations, while the second choice considered how to take the union of multiple relations. These two choices form the basis for the space of mappings we will explore in the algorithm that we will describe shortly.

The second principle illustrated by the example is that while the choices we made above seem to be of heuristic nature, they are actually grounded in solid principles from database design. For example, the fact that we preferred the simple join query when only one foreign key was declared is based on the intuition that we are reversing the data normalization performed by the designer of the source data when we map it to the target. The fact that we prefer the join mappings over the Cartesian product is based on the intuition that we do want to lose any relationships that exist between source data items. The fact that we prefer

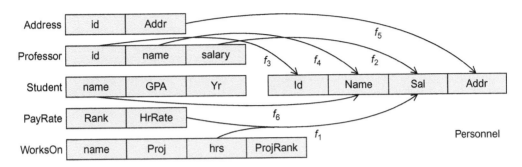

FIGURE 5.11   The full set of correspondences for Figure 5.10.

to union the data from **Professor** and **PayRate** is based on the intuition that every item from the source data should be represented *somewhere* in the target, unless it is explicitly filtered out. These principles will be the basis for ranking possible mappings in the algorithm.

Before we turn to the algorithm, we complete our example. Figure 5.11 shows our example with a few more correspondences:

f_3:   *Professor(id)* ≈ *Personnel(Id)*
f_4:   *Professor(name)* ≈ *Personnel(Name)*
f_5:   *Address(Addr)* ≈ *Personnel(Addr)*
f_6:   *Student(name)* ≈ *Personnel(Name)*

These correspondences naturally fall into two sets. The first set of f_2, f_3, f_4, and f_5 maps from **Professor** to **Personnel** and intuitively specifies how to create tuples for **Personnel** for professors. The second set of f_1 and f_6 specifies how to create tuples of **Personnel** for other employees. In the algorithm, each of these sets will be called a *candidate set*. The algorithm explores the possible joins within each candidate set, and then considers how to union the transformations corresponding to each candidate set.

The most intuitive mapping given these correspondences is the following:

```
(SELECT P.id, P.name, P.salary, A.Addr
 FROM Professor P, Address A
 WHERE A.id = P.id)
UNION ALL
(SELECT NULL AS Id, S.name, P.HrRate*W.hrs, NULL AS Addr
 FROM Student S, PayRate P, WorksOn W
 WHERE S.name = W.name AND S.Yr = P.Rank)
```

However, there are many other possible mappings, including the following one, which does not perform any joins at all and seems rather unintuitive:

```
(SELECT NULL AS Id,  NULL AS Name, NULL AS Sal, Addr
 FROM Address )
```

```
UNION ALL
(SELECT P.id, P.name, P.salary, NULL as Addr
 FROM Professor P)
UNION ALL
(SELECT NULL AS Id,  NULL AS Name, NULL AS Sal, NULL AS Addr
 FROM Student S)
...
```

Searching a Set of Possible Schema Mappings

We now describe an algorithm for searching the space of possible schema mappings given an input set of matches. For simplicity, we describe the algorithm for the case where the target consists of a single relation (as in our example). Extending the algorithm to the multi-relation case is left as a simple exercise for the reader.

The algorithm we describe is fundamentally an interactive one. The algorithm explores the space of possible mappings and proposes the most likely ones to the user. In the description of the algorithm we refer to several heuristics. These heuristics can be replaced by better ones if they are available. Though it is not reflected in our description, we assume that at every step the designer can provide feedback on the decisions made by the algorithm, therefore steering it in the right direction.

The input is specified as a set of correspondences: $M = \{f_i : (\bar{A}_i \approx B_i)\}$, where $\bar{A}_i$ is a set of attributes in the source, S_1, and B_i is an attribute of the target, S_2. We also allow the matches to specify filters on source attributes. The filters can specify a range restriction on an attribute or on an aggregate of an attribute (e.g., avg, sum, min). Algorithm 9, the FindMapping algorithm, operates in four phases.

In the first phase, we create all possible *candidate sets*, which are subsets of S_2 where each attribute of M is mentioned at most once. We denote the set of candidate sets by $\mathcal{V}$. Intuitively, a candidate set in $\mathcal{V}$ represents one way of computing the attributes of S_2. Note that sets in $\mathcal{V}$ do not need to cover all attributes of S_2, as some may be not be computed by the ultimate mapping. If a set does cover all attributes of S_2, then we call it a complete cover. Also note that the elements of $\mathcal{V}$ need not be disjoint—the same correspondence can be used in multiple ways to compute S_2.

■ ■ ■ ▬▬▬▬▬▬▬▬▬▬▬▬▬▬▬▬▬▬▬▬▬▬▬▬▬▬▬▬▬▬▬▬▬

Example 5.20

Suppose we had the correspondences

$$f_1 : S1.A \approx T.C, f_2 : S2.A \approx T.D, f_3 : S2.B \approx T.C$$

Then the complete candidate sets are $\{\{f_1, f_2\}, \{f_2, f_3\}\}$. The singleton sets $\{f_1\}$, $\{f_2\}$, and $\{f_3\}$ are also candidate sets.

▬▬▬▬▬▬▬▬▬▬▬▬▬▬▬▬▬▬▬▬▬▬▬▬▬▬▬▬▬▬▬▬▬ ■ ■ ■

Algorithm 9. FindMapping: Searches through possible schema mappings.

Input: correspondences between schemas S_1 and S_2, $M = \{f_i : (\bar{A}_i \approx B_i)\}$ (when $\bar{A}_i$ has more than one attribute, it is of the form $g(\bar{A}_i)$ where g is the function that combines the attributes); *filter$_i$*: the set of filters associated with f_i. **Output:** mapping in the form of a query.

{**Phase 1**: Create candidate sets}

Let $\mathcal{V} := \{v \subseteq M \,|\, v$ does not mention an attribute of S_2 more than once$\}$

{**Phase 2:**}

Let $\mathcal{G} := \mathcal{V}$

for every $v \in \mathcal{V}$ **do**

    if $(\bar{A}_i \approx B_i) \in v$ and includes attributes from multiple relations in S_1 **then**

        use Heuristics 1 and 2 to find a single join path connecting the relations mentioned in $\bar{A}_i$

        if there is no join path **then**

            remove v from $\mathcal{G}$

        end if

    end if

end for

{**Phase 3:**}

Let *Covers* := $\{\Gamma \,|\, \Gamma \subseteq \mathcal{G}, \Gamma$ mentions all $f_i \in M$ and no subset of Γ mentions all $f_i \in M\}$

Let *selectedCover* := the cover $c \in$ *Covers* with the fewest candidate paths

if *Covers* has more than one cover **then**

    select one with Heuristic 3

end if

{**Phase 4:**}

for each $v \in$ *selectedCover* **do**

    create a query Q_v of the following form:

        `SELECT` *vars*

        `FROM` $t_1, \ldots, t_k$

        `WHERE` $c^1, \ldots, c^j, p_1, \ldots, p_m$

    where

        vars are the attributes mentioned in the correspondences in v

        $t_1, \ldots, t_k$ are the relations of S in the join paths found for v

        $c^1, \ldots, c^j$ are the join conditions for the join paths in v

        filter$_1$, ..., *filter$_m$* are the filters associated with the correspondences in v

end for

return the query

    Q_1 `UNION ALL`...`UNION ALL` Q_b

    where $Q_1, \ldots, Q_b$ are the queries created above

In the second phase of the algorithm we consider the candidate sets in $\mathcal{V}$ and search for the best set of joins within each candidate set. Specifically, consider a candidate set $v \in \mathcal{V}$ and suppose $(\bar{A}_i \approx B_i) \in v$, and that $\bar{A}_i$ includes attributes from multiple relations in

S_1. We search for a join path connecting the relations mentioned in $\bar{A}_i$ using the following heuristic.

Heuristic 1 (Finding a Join Path). A join path can be

- a path through foreign keys,
- a path proposed by inspecting previous queries on S, or
- a path discovered by mining the data for joinable columns in S.   □

The set of candidate sets in $\mathcal{V}$ for which we find join paths is denoted by $\mathcal{G}$. When there are multiple join paths (as in Example 5.19), we select among them using the following heuristic.

Heuristic 2 (Selecting of Join Paths). We prefer paths through foreign keys. If there are multiple such paths, we choose one that involves an attribute on which there is a filter in a correspondence, if such a path exists. To further rank paths, we favor the join path where the estimated difference between the outer join and inner join is the smallest. This last heuristic favors joins with the least number of dangling tuples.   □

The third phase of the algorithm examines the candidate sets in $\mathcal{G}$ and tries to combine them by union so they cover all the correspondences in M. Specifically, we search for *covers* of the correspondences. A subset Γ of $\mathcal{G}$ is a cover if it includes all the correspondences in M and it is minimal, i.e., we cannot remove a candidate set from Γ and still obtain a cover.

In Example 5.20, $\mathcal{G} = \{\{f_1, f_2\}, \{f_2, f_3\}, \{f_1\}, \{f_2\}, \{f_3\}\}$. Possible covers include $\Gamma_1 = \{\{f_1\}, \{f_2, f_3\}\}$ and $\Gamma_2 = \{\{f_1, f_2\}, \{f_2, f_3\}\}$. When there are multiple possible covers, we select one using the following heuristic.

Heuristic 3 (Selecting of the Cover). If there are multiple possible covers, we choose the one with the smallest number of candidate sets with the intuition that a simpler mapping may be more appropriate. If there is more than one with the same number of candidate sets, we choose the one that includes more attributes of S_2 in order to cover more of that schema.   □

The final phase of the algorithm creates the schema mapping expression. Here we describe the mapping as an SQL query. The algorithm first creates an SQL query from each candidate set in the selected cover, and then unions them.

Specifically, suppose v is a candidate set. We create an SQL query Q_v as follows. First, the attributes of S_2 in v are put into the SELECT clause. Second, each of the relations in the join paths found for v are put into the FROM clause, and their respective join predicates are put in the WHERE clause. In addition, any filters associated with the correspondences in v are also added to the WHERE clause. Finally, we output the query that takes the bag union of each of the Q_v's in the cover.

Bibliographic Notes

The areas of schema matching and schema mapping have been the topic of research for decades. The survey [487] summarizes the state of the art circa 2001 and covers some of the early work such as [68, 111, 434, 465, 472]. The survey [179] and special issues [180, 463] discuss work up to 2005, while the book [61] discusses work up to 2010 (see also `http://dbs.uni-leipzig.de/file/vldb2011.pdf` for a presentation that summarizes recent work). Other books on the topic include [214, 241].

The architecture presented in this chapter is based on the LSD system [181] and the COMA system [178] (see also [371, 511] for further details). The algorithms described often combine different components of the architecture we describe, but do not tease them apart. For example, the Similarity Flooding algorithm [427] used string-based similarity to give initial values to correspondences, and then used a local propagation algorithm to spread the estimates across the graph.

The work [140] exploits multiple heuristics to match schemas. The work [178, 181] introduced the idea of leveraging the combination of multiple matchers in a schema matching system. A similar idea was proposed in [212]. Applying machine learning techniques to schema matching was introduced in [384]. The LSD system [181] introduced the use of multiple base learners and combining them via learning. The system used a technique called stacking [549, 576] to combine the predictions of the base learners. Further explanation of the naive Bayes learner and an analysis for why it works well in practice can be found in [187]. More background on learning techniques and, in particular, rule-based learning can be found in [438]. The paper [570] presents a unified approach to schema matching and data matching, using a machine learning technique called conditional random field.

The LSD system introduced the idea of learning from past matches. The COMA system [178] considered a simple form of reusing past matches (without learning from them), and also considered composing multiple past matches. The paper [339] uses information-theoretic techniques to match schemas. The papers [206, 208] utilize query logs for hints about related schema elements (e.g., in join clauses).

Corpus-based schema matching [406] showed how to leverage a corpus of schemas and mappings in a particular domain to improve schema matching. The paper [295] looks at statistical properties of collections of Web forms in order to predict a mediated schema for a domain and mappings from the data sources to the mediated schema. The paper [581] discusses how to match a corpus of schemas via interactive clustering. The paper [510] discusses ranking of clustering alternatives based on probabilistic mappings.

Several schema matching systems considered how to apply domain constraints to prune and improve schema matches [181, 183, 407, 427]. The neighborhood-adaptation algorithm we described in Section 5.6 is adapted from [407], and the A* algorithm is from [181]. The paper [183] describes a relaxation labeling algorithm that exploits a broad range of domain constraints to match taxonomies.

User interaction in schema matching systems and incremental schema matching were discussed in [78, 181, 222, 240, 581]. The papers [420, 421] discuss a crowdsourcing approach to schema matching.

The iMap system [372] addressed the problem of searching for complex mappings. Other works that find complex matches with subsumption relationships and with conditionals include [92, 251]. Techniques to match large schemas are discussed in [25, 43, 289, 306]. Gal [240] discusses the complexity of finding the top-k schema matches.

Schema matching systems typically come with myriad knobs, and tuning these knobs is well-known to be difficult. Such tuning issues are discussed in [62, 201, 371, 511].

The paper [410] discusses how the task of building a deep Web crawler can use semantic matches "as is," without having to elaborate them into semantic mappings.

The Clio system was the first to look at the problem of generating schema mappings given schema matches [302, 432]. The algorithm we described in Section 5.10 and the running example there are taken from [432]. These references also describe how to extend the algorithm to mappings with aggregation and how to create illustrative examples of the instance data that can help the designer find the correct mapping. Subsequent work on the topic includes [21, 23, 24, 30, 220, 254].

Finally, the related issue of ontology matching and mapping has also received significant attention. See [183] for an early system that employs an architecture that is similar to the architecture proposed in this chapter to match ontologies. The book [214] discusses the state of the art up to 2007, and the Web site http://ontologymatching.org contain a wealth of current information on this active area.

6

General Schema Manipulation Operators

In the last chapter, we saw techniques for taking two schemas and finding matches and mappings between them. Mappings and matches are directly useful for translating data from one schema to another, which is the focus of a good deal of this book. However, we may wish to do more with schemas than simply map data from one to the other. For instance, it may be useful to take two schemas and create a single merged schema that can represent all of their data. We may wish to translate a schema from one data model to another (e.g., relational to XML). Given three schemas A, B, and C and mappings $A \rightarrow B$ and $B \rightarrow C$, we may wish to compose the mappings to create a mapping $A \rightarrow C$.

In general, one can define an algebra of generic operators that could be applied to schemas and mappings across a broad range of applications. The operators would take as input schemas and/or mappings, and return schemas or mappings. Such an algebra would be analogous to the algebra we have for operating on data itself and which powers all modern query processors. This algebra has been termed the set of *model management operators*: model is a more general term referring to a schema, a set of classes in an object-oriented language, an ontology, etc.

We illustrate the use of a generic set of model management operators in the context of data integration with the following example.

Example 6.1

Consider the process of setting up a data integration application and maintaining it over time (see Figure 6.1). Suppose that our goal is to build a data integration application that spans two sources, S_1 and S_2.

We start by creating a mediated schema that contains the information in S_1 and S_2 and mappings from each of the sources to the mediated schema. We could proceed in two steps. First, we use the model management match operator (which does schema matching and mapping as discussed in Chapter 5) to create a schema mapping, M_{12}, between S_1 and S_2 (see Figure 6.1(1)). Second, we create a mediated schema, G, by applying a schema merge operator to schemas S_1 and S_2 and the mapping M_{12} (Figure 6.1(2)). The merge operator will create a schema that includes all the information in S_1 and S_2, but that combines any information present in both schemas so it is not duplicated. The merge operator will also create mappings from S_1 and S_2 to G, M_{1G}, and M_{2G}.

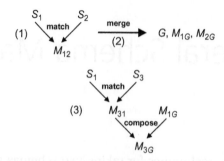

FIGURE 6.1 Common tasks in data integration can be modeled as sequences of model management operators. To set up an integration application involving S_1 and S_2 we first create a mapping between them (1), and then merge the two schemas with the **merge** operator to create the mediated schema, G (2). To add a new source S_3, we can first **match** it to one of the existing ones (S_1) and **compose** the mappings to obtain a mapping from S_3 to G (3).

Now suppose we need to add another source, S_3, to our system, and suppose that S_3 is very similar to S_1. We could add S_3 in two steps: (1) since S_3 and S_1 are relatively similar, it would be easy to use match to create a mapping, M_{31}, between S_1 and S_3, and (2) use a compose operator to create a mapping M_{3G} by composing mappings M_{31} and M_{1G} (Figure 6.1(3)).

Data integration, whether virtual or using a warehouse, is a key application for the model management operators. However, there are other tasks in which the generic operators are also useful:

- **Message-passing systems**: A message-passing system expects messages to be passed in particular formats (e.g., a particular XML schema), but the data itself typically reside in back-end systems such as relational databases. Hence, the data need to be transformed from the model and schema in which it is stored into the target message format. On the recipient side, the reverse transformation needs to be performed. Web services and message queueing middleware are commonly used instances of message passing systems.
- **Wrapper generation tools** (Chapter 9): A wrapper needs to transform the data from one data model to another and possibly apply a schema mapping. For example, a common scenario is to translate between an object model in a programming language into a relational schema.

A significant amount of labor in enterprises is spent on manually performing these operations in the tasks above and others. Developing a generic set of model management operators can significantly simplify these tasks.

6.1 Model Management Operators

We begin by describing the basic terminology of model management and presenting its main operators. Model management operators manipulate two kinds of objects:

models and *mappings* between models. Models describe the data representation used in a particular application (e.g., a relational schema of a data source). Models are specific instances of a particular representation system, which is called a *meta-model*: for instance, the relational data model, the XML data model, and the Java object model. Common language encodings of meta-models include relational DDLs, XML schemas, Java class definitions, entity-relationship models, and RDF. For example, the relational meta-model specifies that a schema include a set of relations, each of which consists of a set of typed attributes. In this chapter we will encode all models as directed graphs whose nodes are elements. The edges in the graph represent binary relationships between the elements, such as is-a; has-a and type-of represent the different constructs of the meta-models. For example, a relation element will have a has-a relationship with the attributes it contains.

Mappings describe the semantic relationship between a pair of models. Mappings are used to translate data instances from one model into another or to reformulate queries posed on one model into queries on another. Mappings can be described in a variety of formalisms, such as the GLAV formalism we described in Section 3.2.4.

The model management operators should be composable so that sequences of operators can be executed as scripts on behalf of the user. Some of the operators of model management are completely automatic (e.g., compose), while others might require some human feedback (e.g., match and merge). The goal of model management is not to completely automate these tasks, but to remove as much of the human labor as possible. We describe the most commonly studied operators below, and toward the end of the chapter we describe the ultimate vision of building a general-purpose *model management system* that is an "engine" for these operators.

Match: takes as input two models S_1 and S_2 and produces a schema mapping, M_{12}, between them. As explained in Chapter 3, a mapping expresses a constraint on which pairs of instances of S_1 and S_2 are consistent with each other. The match operator assumes that the two input models are in the same meta-model. The system may solicit some feedback from the user in the process of creating the model. Chapter 5 describes techniques for the match operator.

Compose: takes as input a mapping M_{12} between models S_1 and S_2 and a mapping M_{23} between models S_2 and S_3 and outputs a direct mapping M_{13} between S_1 and S_3. As discussed in Section 17.5, the algorithms for the compose operator are highly dependent on the particular meta-model.

Merge: takes as input two models S_1 and S_2 and a mapping M_{12} between S_1 and S_2. merge outputs a combined model S_3 that contains all the information modeled by S_1 and S_2 but but does not duplicate information that is present in both models. We discuss merge in Section 6.2.

ModelGen: takes as input a model S_1 in a given meta-model $\mathcal{M}_1$ and creates a model S_2 in a different meta-model, $\mathcal{M}_2$. For example, modelGen may translate a relational model into XML or an Java object model into a relational schema. We describe modelGen in Section 6.3.

Invert: takes as input a mapping M_{12} from S_1 to S_2 and outputs a mapping M_{21} from S_2 to S_1. The mapping M_{21} should be able to take an instance of S_2 and compute an instance of S_1. We discuss invert in Section 6.4.

We now discuss these model management operators in more detail. The bibliographic notes contain references to other works in the literature. It should be noted that our list of operators is not exhaustive. For instance, there have been proposals for a diff operator that returns the difference between two schemas.

6.2 Merge

The merge operator takes as input two models, S_1 and S_2, and a mapping M_{12} between them, and outputs a model that contains the union of the information in S_1 and S_2, but collapses the information that is present in both. The mapping M_{12} determines which information exists in both models and which does not.

Figure 6.2 depicts an example that illustrates some of the decisions that need to be made when we merge two models. Figure 6.2 shows two models of actor entities and a mapping between them. We depict each of the models as a graph of elements. The solid lines indicate the has-a relationship between the actor element and its subelements. The dashed lines depict the attribute correspondences that make up the mapping between the two models. The graph representation is agnostic of a particular meta-model. Hence, for example, the graph may be a depiction of a relational schema of an actor table or an XML schema where the element actor has the specified subelements.

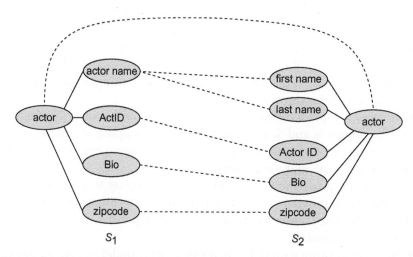

S_1 S_2

FIGURE 6.2 Two models of actors that need to be merged. The models are depicted as graphs of elements. The solid lines indicate the **has-a** relationship between the **actor** element and its subelements. The dashed lines depict the attribute correspondences that make up the mapping between the two models.

The merge operator illustrates the challenges involved in defining a *generic* model management operator. At first glance, the merge operator needs to address three kinds of conflicts. We consider each in turn.

The first conflict that the merge operator needs to consider is a *representational conflict.* In our example, the name of the actor is represented as a single field in one model and as a pair of fields in the other. This conflict is not inherent to merge and really depends on the mapping between the two models. For example, the mapping will specify whether first name and last name are subelements of name, or whether the concatenation of first name and last name are equivalent to name. In fact, different mappings between the input models can result in different merged models. This is the reason that merge is defined to take a mapping as input. In addition to the mapping, the input to merge may include rules stating that one model should be preferred over the other when we encounter representational conflicts. For example, if we merge the schema of a data source into the mediated schema, we prefer that the mediated schema changes as little as possible.

The second kind of conflict that merge needs to deal with is a meta-model conflict. For example, suppose that S_1 in our example is an XML schema and S_2 and the merged model are relational. Since relational schemas do not have the notion of a subattribute, there is no obvious way of mapping S_1 into the merged model.

The mismatch at the meta-model level is also not inherent to the merge operator. In fact, the problem of translating models from one meta-model to another occurs quite frequently. For that reason, model management includes a separate operator, modelGen, to do the specific task of converting between meta-models.

Finally, the third kind of conflict is one that is fundamental to merge and hence the focus of the generic merge algorithms proposed in the literature. The fundamental conflicts are considered with respect to the common representation we use to encode all of the models (and which must be able to capture all of the aspects of their meta-models)—sometimes this is termed the *meta-meta-model*. The meta-meta-model is the representation system used by the model management operators. In our running example, a fundamental conflict involves the modeling of zipcode in the merged model. Suppose that in S_1 zipcode is an integer, while in S_2 it is a string. Our meta-meta-model only allows attributes to have a single type, and therefore we have a conflict.

The main thrust of algorithms for merge have been on identifying fundamental conflicts and devising rules for resolving them. We give a couple of examples below.

Cardinality constraints: A cardinality constraint on a relationship R in the meta-meta-model restricts the number of elements, y, for which $R(x, y)$ holds for a given x. For example, in the relational model, the cardinality constraint requires that every element be the origin of at most one type-of relationship (i.e., have a single type). Note that cardinality constraints can provide either lower or upper bounds on the cardinality.

One solution to a violation of such a constraint is to create a new type that inherits from more than one. For example, we would create a new type in our meta-meta

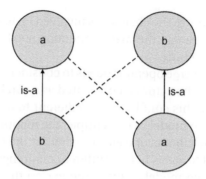

FIGURE 6.3 A cycle resulting from a merge.

model that inherits from both string and integer, and we would declare the attribute zipcode to be of the new type.

Acyclicity constraints: A meta-meta-model may require that certain relationships be acyclic. For example, the is-a relationship is required to be acyclic in our meta-meta-model. However, consider the simple example in Figure 6.3. In the schema on the left b is said to be a subset of a, while in the schema on the right the opposite is-a relationship is asserted. If we merge the two models and inherit both of these relationships, we will get an is-a cycle between a and b.

A typical solution to resolving cycle constraints is to collapse all the elements in the cycle into one element in the merged model. In our example, we would merge a and b into a single element. Of course, we may have a domain-specific rule that specifies a different solution.

6.3   ModelGen

The modelGen operator takes a model in one meta-model and translates it into another meta-model. Translations between meta-models are ubiquitous in model management scenarios because we typically handle data from a variety of sources. Other model management operators, such as match and merge, often assume that modelGen has been applied to their inputs or that it will be applied to their result if needed. The most common scenarios of modelGen are translating between XML and relational models or between object models of a programming languages (such as Java or C#) and a relational schema.

Figure 6.4 depicts an example that demonstrates some of the challenges that modelGen needs to address. The figure shows two models of companies and their suppliers. On the left, the figure shows the source model, a set of Java class definitions, that is the input to modelGen. Our goal is to generate the relational schema shown on the right of the figure.

The challenges for modelGen arise because some of the constructs of the source meta-model are not supported in the target meta-model. In our example, we have the following difficulties:

```
                                    CREATE TABLE Company(
                                    Name varchar(50),
                                    oid int NOT NULL PRIMARY KEY)

public class Company {
   public string name;           CREATE TABLE Supplier(
}                                 oid int NOT NULL PRIMARY KEY,
                                    isSameAs int NOT NULL UNIQUE
public class Supplier             FOREIGN KEY REFERENCES Company
     extends Company {              (oid))
   public item[] parts;
}                                 CREATE TABLE PartsArray(
                                    Supplier int NOT NULL
                                    FOREIGN KEY REFERENCES Company
                                      (oid),
public class Item {               itemISBN varchar(50),
   public string ISBN;            itemCost int)
   public int Cost;
}
```

FIGURE 6.4 The operator **modelGen** will translate the Java class hierarchy on the left to the relational schema on the right.

1. To begin, since there is no notion of classes in SQL, the target schema needs to encode classes as relational tables.
2. Furthermore, SQL does not support inheritance. In our example, the class Supplier is a subclass of Company. The target schema needs to encode inheritance in relations (using one of several known encodings).
3. Finally, SQL does not support array types. However, in the input model, the class Supplier has an attribute parts that is an array of items.

To translate the Java model into a relational schema, modelGen needs to perform the following transformations.

T1. Create relational structures from classes. For example, instead of a class Company, the resulting schema will have a table Company with an attribute denoting an object ID and the name as a field.
T2. The inheritance relation between Company and Supplier is represented using vertical partitioning. Specifically, the resulting schema will include a table Supplier that contains the attributes that are specific to Supplier. Each supplier will also be represented in the Company table, and there is a foreign key relationship from the Supplier table to the Company table. Therefore, getting all the information about a supplier requires accessing attributes from both the Company and Supplier tables.
T3. The parts array is represented as a join relationship. The table PartsArray includes a tuple for every (supplier, part) pair. The supplier is represented as an attribute (Supplier) that is a foreign key into the Company table, and the part is represented by its two attributes, ISBN and cost.

Continuing with the goal of developing generic model management operators, the approach taken to modelGen is based on identifying a *super-model*. The super-model is a meta-model that includes all the features of the meta-models we expect to encounter. (Clearly, there cannot be a super-model that includes all features, so the super-model is designed with a set of meta-models in mind.) The super-model knows which of its constructs are supported in each of the possible input and output meta-models. For example, the super-model will know that relational schemas include relations and their attributes, while object-oriented schemas are composed of classes with inheritance.[1]

The modelGen operator receives as input a model M in meta-model $\mathcal{M}_1$ and an output meta-model, $\mathcal{M}_2$, into which to translate M. Algorithms for modelGen will proceed in the following three steps:

Step 1: Translate the input model M into the super-model. Denote the result by M'.
Step 2: While the model M' includes a construct that is not supported in the output meta-model $\mathcal{M}_2$, apply transformations that remove the unsupported constructs.
Step 3: If Step 2 was successful in removing all the unsupported constructs, translate M' into $\mathcal{M}_2$.

Hence, the crux of the modelGen algorithm is to express the required transformations, such as T1-T3 above, in the super-model. An additional challenge that the modelGen operator needs to address is to generate a transformation that takes the data in an instance of M in $\mathcal{M}_1$ and produces an instance of it in $\mathcal{M}_2$.

6.4 Invert

In some contexts, such as data exchange, schema mappings are considered to be *directional*, defining a transformation from source schema to a target schema. In these contexts, an important question that arises is whether we can invert the schema mapping. An inverse schema mapping should be able to take an instance of the target and produce the appropriate instance of the source schema. Algorithms for inverting schemas are highly dependent on the precise formalism for specifying mappings. In this section we assume a relational meta-model and mappings that are specified as tuple-generating dependencies (which are an equivalent formalism to GLAV formulas described in Section 3.2.4).

One of the main challenges is to find a definition of invert that is theoretically sound and useful in practice. Let us consider a few definitions.

As a first definition, consider two schemas, S and T, and let M be a mapping from S to T. Recall that M defines a binary relation specifying which pairs of models of S and T are consistent with each other w.r.t. the mapping. Specifically, M defines a relation (I, J), where I is an instance of S and J is an instance of T. When (I, J) is in the relation defined

---

[1]Note the distinction between the super-model and the meta-meta-model. The super-model is a meta-model that includes the features of many other meta-models. The meta-meta-model is a language for describing meta-models.

by M, we say that $M \models (I,J)$. Hence, a seemingly natural definition is the following. The inverse of M, M^{-1}, is the mapping that defines the relation (J,I), where $M \models (I,J)$.

However, it is easy to see that under this definition, we cannot find inverse mappings that can be expressed as tuple-generating dependencies. Any relation that is defined by a set of tuple-generating dependencies is guaranteed to be *closed down* on the left and *closed up* on the right. Specifically, if I' is a subinstance of I (i.e., I' is a subset of the tuples of I) and J is a subset of the tuples of J', then $M \models (I,J)$ implies that $M \models (I',J')$. But this would mean that the inverse relation would be closed down on the right and closed up on the left, and hence cannot be expressed by tuple-generating dependencies.

A second definition of inverse mapping is based on mapping composition. Specifically, we define M' to be the inverse of M if the composition of M with M' produces the identity mapping. However, this definition turns out to be rather limiting. In particular, it can be shown that a mapping M has an inverse if and only if the following holds: whenever I_1 and I_2 are two distinct instances of S, then their targets under M are also distinct sets. As a consequence, even simple mappings such as the following two mappings do not have inverses:

$M_1 \colon \mathsf{P(x,y)} \to \mathsf{Q(x)}$
$M_2 \colon \mathsf{P(x,y,z)} \to \mathsf{Q(x,y)} \wedge \mathsf{R(y,z)}$

A more useful definition is based on *quasi-inverses*. Quasi-inverses are also based on the composition being the identity mapping, but in a slightly more relaxed way. Consider a more relaxed equivalence relationship between instances, defined as follows. We define $I_1 \approx I_2$ w.r.t. a mapping M if for every target instance J, $M \models (I_1,J)$ if and only if $M \models (I_2,J)$.

Example 6.2
Consider the mapping M_1 above. Let I_1 be the instance that includes only the tuple $P(1,2)$, and I_2 be the instance that includes only the tuple $P(1,3)$. They are equivalent w.r.t. the mapping M_1.

We now define a mapping M' to be a quasi-inverse of M if the composition of M and M' maps every instance I of S to an instance I' of S, such that $I \approx I'$. The following example illustrates the difference between inverses and quasi-inverses.

Example 6.3
The following mapping is a quasi-inverse of M_1 above:

$M_1' \colon \mathsf{Q(x)} \to \exists\, y\, \mathsf{P(x,y)}.$

Consider the instance I_1 of S that includes the tuple $P(1,2)$. Applying M_1 to I_1 results in the instance J_1 of the target that includes $Q(1)$.

Now, if we apply M_1' to J_1 we'll get the instance I_2 of the source with the tuple $P(1,A)$, where A is an arbitrary constant.

The instances I_1 and I_2 are different from each other, and therefore M_1' could not be considered a strict inverse of M_1. However, $I_1 \approx I_2$, and in fact, the same would hold if we apply M_1 and then M_1' to any instance of S, and therefore M_1' is a quasi-inverse of M_1.

■ ■ ■

In a sense, a quasi-inverse precisely restores the contents of the source that were relevant to the target. In our example, only the first argument of the relation P is relevant to the target.

Remark 6.1 (Inverses and Data Integration).   As noted earlier, the invert operator is motivated in contexts where schema mappings are assumed to be directional. In our discussion of mappings in Chapter 3 we did not assume that mappings are directional. We focused on the relation that the mappings define between the source instances and the mediated schema instances. However, much of the work on query answering in data integration is very related to inverting mappings. In particular, when source descriptions are described in Local-as-View (see Section 3.2.3), the algorithms for answering queries effectively invert the view definitions in order to produce tuples of the mediated schema. One of the key differences is that the algorithms for answering queries described in Chapter 3 invert the views only with respect to the particular query posed to the data integration system.   □

6.5 Toward Model Management Systems

One of the original goals underlying the study of the various model management operators was to build a general-purpose model management system that operates on schemas and mappings. This system would support the creation, reuse, evolution, and execution of mappings between models and be able to interact with individual data management systems that store their own schemas and mappings.

Building such a system remains the goal of ongoing research. One of the challenges in developing a model management system is that implementing the operators is often very dependent on the details of the meta-model, and therefore it is hard to build a system that is agnostic to the particular models. One of the areas in which the meta-models differ considerably is the types of integrity constraints they are able to express and the languages they use to express them.

Bibliographic Notes

While isolated work on different model management operators has gone on for a while, the vision for an algebra of operators and a model management system that encapsulates them all was first laid out by Bernstein et al. [72, 76]. In a more recent paper [77], Bernstein and Melnik refine the vision of model management to focus more on semantics of complex mappings and on paying attention to the run-time support of model management.

The run-time support involves applying schema mappings to data instances efficiently and managing updates to data and to schemas. Melnik et al. [428] describes a first model management system, and in [426] they propose semantics of model management operators.

The earliest work related to merge is by Buneman et al. [99], where the semantics of a merged model was specified by the least upper bound in a lattice of models. However, they required the resulting model to adhere to a particular meta-model. Pottinger and Bernstein [481] defined merge in a generic fashion as part of a model management algebra. They identified the different conflicts and proposed a generic merge algorithm that solves the fundamental conflicts for a broader set of cases. The examples in this chapter are taken from [481].

The basic approach to modelGen that we described in Section 6.3 was introduced by Atzeni et al. [40]. Mork et al. [445] extended the work of [40] in several ways. In particular, the modelGen algorithm proposed by Mork et al. produced a translation of data instances that did not have to go through the intermediate super-model and is therefore much more efficient. In addition, their algorithm enabled the designer to explore a much richer set of transformations from class hierarchies to relational schemas. In some sense, one can view object-relational mapping systems (ORMs), such as Hibernate, as special-case instances of modelGen.

Fagin [215] initially studied the invert operator and showed that inverse mappings exist under very limited conditions. Quasi-inverses were described by Fagin et al. [219].

One area closely related to model management, although it tends to use more operational semantics, is that of supporting schema evolution. Schema modification operators [444] capture a record of schema changes and can be used to do a variety of query rewrites [157, 369].

7

Data Matching

Data matching is the problem of finding structured data items that describe the same real-world entity. In contrast to string matching (see Chapter 4), where we tried to decide whether a pair of strings refer to the same real-world entity, here the entity may be represented by a tuple in a database, an XML element, or a set of RDF triples. For example, we would like to determine whether the tuples (David Smith, 608-245-4367, Madison WI) and (D. M. Smith, 245-4367, Madison WI) refer to the same person.

The problem of data matching arises in many integration situations. In the simplest case, we may be merging multiple databases with identical schemas, but without a unique global ID, and want to decide which rows are duplicates. The problem is complicated when we need to join rows from sources that have different schemas. Data matching may also arise at query time. For example, a query may often imprecisely refer to a particular data item, e.g., a query asking for the phone number of a David Smith who lives in Madison. We need to employ data matching techniques to decide which tuples in the database match the query. In this chapter we begin by defining the problem of data matching and then describe the techniques for addressing it.

7.1 Problem Definition

We consider the following problem. Suppose we are given two relational tables X and Y. In some cases we will assume that X and Y have identical schemas, but in the general case they will not. We assume that each of the rows in X and Y describes some properties of an entity (e.g., person, book, movie). We say a tuple $x \in X$ *matches* a tuple $y \in Y$ if they refer to the same real-world entity. We call such a pair (x, y) a match. Our goal is to find *all* matches between X and Y. For example, given the two tables X and Y in Figures 7.1(a-b), whose tuples describe properties of people, specifically their names, phone numbers, cities, and states, we want to find the matches shown in Figure 7.1(c). The first match (x_1, y_1) states that (Dave Smith, (608) 395 9462, Madison, WI) and (David D. Smith, 395 9426, Madison, WI) refer to the same real-world person. Of course, while we consider the data matching problem in the context of relational data, it also arises in other data models.

The challenges of data matching are similar in spirit to those of string matching: how to match accurately and to scale the matching algorithms to large data sets. Matching tuples accurately is difficult due to variations in formatting conventions, use of abbreviations,

Table X

	Name	Phone	City	State
X_1	Dave Smith	(608) 395 9462	Madison	WI
X_2	Joe Wilson	(408) 123 4265	San Jose	CA
X_3	Dan Smith	(608) 256 1212	Middleton	WI

(a)

Table Y

	Name	Phone	City	State
Y_1	David D. Smith	395 9426	Madison	WI
Y_2	Daniel W. Smith	256 1212	Madison	WI

(b)

Matches

(X_1, Y_1)
(X_3, Y_2)

(c)

FIGURE 7.1 An example of matching relational tuples that describe persons.

shortening, different naming conventions, omission, nicknames, and errors in the data. We could, in principle, treat each tuple as a string by concatenating the fields, and then apply string matching techniques described in Chapter 4. While effective in certain cases, in general it is better to keep the fields apart, since more sophisticated techniques and domain-specific knowledge can then be applied to the problem. For example, when the entities are represented as tuples we can write a rule that states that two tuples match if the names and phones match exactly.

We cover several classes of solutions to the data matching problem. The first kind employs handcrafted rules to match tuples. These techniques typically make heavy use of domain-specific knowledge in domains where the complexity of the rules is manageable. The next kind of solution learns the appropriate rules from labeled examples, using supervised learning. The third kind, clustering does not use training data. Instead, it iteratively assigns tuples to clusters, such that all tuples within a single cluster match and those across clusters do not.

The fourth kind of solution, probabilistic approaches, models the matching domain using a probability distribution, and then reasons with the distribution to make matching decisions. As such, these approaches can naturally incorporate a wide variety of domain knowledge, leverage the wealth of probabilistic representation and reasoning techniques that have been developed in the past two decades, and provide a frame of reference for understanding other matching approaches.

The above approaches match tuple pairs independently. The last kind of approach we consider, known as collective matching, considers correlations among tuples to improve the accuracy of its matching decisions. For example, suppose that "David Smith" is a coauthor of "Mary Jones" and that "D. M. Smith" is a coauthor of "M. Jones." Then if we have successfully matched "David Smith" with "D. M. Smith," we should have increased confidence that "Mary Jones" matches "M. Jones." Collective matching will propagate the result of one matching decision into others in an iterative fashion.

We cover the above matching techniques in the following sections and discuss scaling up in Section 7.7.

7.2 Rule-Based Matching

We begin by covering approaches that employ handcrafted matching rules. For this discussion we assume that we are matching tuples from two tables with the same schema, but generalizing to other contexts is straightforward. A simple yet popular type of rule computes the similarity score between a pair of tuples x and y as a *linearly weighted combination* of the individual similarity scores:

$$sim(x,y) = \sum_{i=1}^{n} \alpha_i \cdot sim_i(x,y) \tag{7.1}$$

where n is the number of attributes in each of the tables X and Y, $s_i(x,y) \in [0,1]$ is a similarity score between the ith attributes of x and y, and $\alpha_i \in [0,1]$ is a prespecified weight that indicates the importance of the ith attribute to the overall similarity score, such that $\sum_{i=1}^{n} \alpha_i = 1$. We declare x and y matched if $sim(x,y) \geq \beta$ for a prespecified threshold β, and not matched otherwise.

Consider matching the tuples of the tables X and Y in Figure 7.1 using a linearly weighted rule. We start by selecting similarity functions for name, phone, city, and state. To match names, we can define a similarity function $s_{name}(x,y)$ that is based on the Jaro-Winkler distance (see Chapter 4). To match phone numbers, we can define a function $s_{phone}(x,y)$ that is based on the edit distance between the phone number of x (after removing the area code because it does not appear in table Y) and the phone number of y. To match cities, we can again use edit distance. Finally, to match states, we can perform an exact match that returns 1 if the two state strings are equivalent and 0 otherwise. Now we can write a rule such as

$$sim(x,y) = 0.3s_{name}(x,y) + 0.3s_{phone}(x,y) + 0.1s_{city}(x,y) + 0.3s_{state}(x,y) \tag{7.2}$$

Intuitively, this rule states that in order to match, it is important that the names, phones, and states match, whereas it is less important that the cities match (perhaps because people often write down the name of the suburb where they live instead of the name of the city, and vice versa). We then select $\beta = 0.7$, say, and declare two persons matched if $sim(x,y) \geq 0.7$, and not matched otherwise.

Note that the decision of the matching system can be used in several ways in the user interface. For example, the system may still let a human judge inspect all matching pairs whose score is between 0.5 and 0.8, even if the threshold is 0.7.

LOGISTIC REGRESSION RULES

A linearly weighted rule has the property that an increase Δ in the value of any individual similarity function s_i will result in a *linear* increase $\alpha_i \Delta$ in the value of the overall similarity function s. This may seem counterintuitive in certain scenarios, where after a certain threshold an increase in s_i should count less (known as the principle of *diminishing*

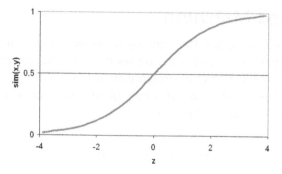

FIGURE 7.2 The general shape of the logistic regression (also known as sigmoid) function.

returns). For example, if $s_{name}(x,y)$ is already 0.95, then it may be the case that the names already very closely match. Thus, any further increase in $s_{name}(x,y)$ should contribute only minimally to $s(x,y)$.

Logistic regression matching rules try to capture this intuition. A logistic regression rule has the form

$$sim(x,y) = 1/(1 + e^{-z}) \tag{7.3}$$

where $z = \sum_{i=1}^{n} \alpha_i \cdot sim_i(x,y)$. Here we do not constrain the α_i to be in the range $[0,1]$ and sum to 1. Thus we do not limit the value of z to the range $[0,1]$. Figure 7.2 shows that as z increases from $-\infty$ to $+\infty$, $sim(x,y)$ gradually increases, but minimally so after z has exceeded a certain value, achieving our goal of diminishing returns.

Logistic regression rules are also very useful in situations where firing (producing similarity scores close to 1) of a small proportion of the individual similarity functions is sufficient to achieve a high enough similarity score. Specifically, suppose we have a large number of individual component functions in the similarity score (e.g., 10–15), but only few of them fire for any instance. However, suppose the similarity is such that as long as a reasonable number of them produce high similarity, we are already confident that the two tuples match. In such cases, logistic regression rules ensure that after a reasonable number of individual functions have produced a high similarity score, we have achieved a sufficiently high overall similarity score and the remaining individual functions only contribute in a "diminishing return" fashion to this score.

MORE COMPLEX RULES

Both linearly weighted and logistic regression matching rules are relatively easy to construct and understand. But they do not work in cases where we want to encode more complex matching knowledge, such as two persons match if the names match approximately and *either* the phones match exactly *or* the addresses match exactly. In such cases we must create more complex matching rules, which can take any form and typically involve the individual similarity functions. For example, suppose $e_{phone}(x,y)$ returns true only if the phone numbers of x and y match exactly, and similarly for $e_{city}(x,y)$

and $e_{state}(x, y)$. Then we can encode the above matching knowledge using the following rules:

1. If $s_{name}(x, y) < 0.8$ then return "not matched."
2. Otherwise, if $e_{phone}(x, y) = true$ then return "matched."
3. Otherwise, if $(e_{city}(x, y) = true) \wedge (e_{state}(x, y) = true)$ then return "matched."
4. Otherwise, return "not matched."

Many real-world data matching systems employ such rules, which are often written in a high-level declarative language to make them easier to understand, debug, modify, and maintain (compared to writing them in procedural languages such as Perl and Java).

While very useful, rule-based approaches can be difficult to use. This may be because it is labor intensive to write good matching rules with the appropriate weights, or it is not even clear how to write such rules because the domain is too complex. Learning-based approaches, which we discuss next, address these issues.

7.3 Learning-Based Matching

In this section we describe approaches that use supervised learning to automatically create matching rules from labeled examples. In the next section we will discuss clustering approaches, which are a form of unsupervised learning.

Informally, in supervised learning, we learn a *matching model M* from the training data, then apply M to match new tuple pairs. The training data takes the form

$$T = \{(x_1, y_1, l_1), (x_2, y_2, l_2), \ldots, (x_n, y_n, l_n)\}$$

where each triple (x_i, y_i, l_i) consists of a tuple pair (x_i, y_i) and a label l_i that is "yes" if x_i matches y_i and "no" otherwise.

Given the training data T, we define a set of *features* $f_1, f_2, \ldots, f_m$, each of which quantifies one aspect of the domain judged possibly relevant to matching the tuples. Specifically, each feature f_i is a function that takes a tuple pair (x, y) and produces a numeric, categorical, or binary value. We simply define all features that we think *may* be relevant to matching. The learning algorithm will use the training data to decide which features are actually relevant.

In the next step, we convert each training example (x_i, y_i, l_i) in the set T into a pair

$$(\langle f_1(x_i, y_i), f_2(x_i, y_i), \ldots, f_m(x_i, y_i) \rangle, c_i)$$

where $v_i = \langle f_1(x_i, y_i), f_2(x_i, y_i), \ldots, f_m(x_i, y_i) \rangle$ is a feature vector that "encodes" the tuple pair (x_i, y_i) in terms of the features, and c_i is an appropriately transformed version of label l_i (e.g., being transformed into "yes"/"no" or 1/0, depending on what kind of matching model we want to learn, as we detail below). Thus, the training set T is converted into a new training set $T' = \{(v_1, c_1), (v_2, c_2), \ldots, (v_n, c_n)\}$.

We can now apply a learning algorithm such as decision trees or support vector machines (SVM) to T' to learn a matching model M, then apply M to the task of matching new tuple pairs. Given a new pair (x, y), we transform it into a feature vector

$$v = \langle f_1(x,y), f_2(x,y), \ldots, f_m(x,y) \rangle$$

then apply model M to v to predict whether x matches y.

■ ■ ■ ▬▬▬▬▬▬▬▬▬▬▬▬▬▬▬▬▬▬▬▬▬▬▬▬▬▬▬▬▬▬▬▬▬

Example 7.1

Consider applying the above algorithm to learning a linearly weighted rule to match the tables X and Y in Figure 7.1 (learning a logistic regression rule can be carried out in a similar fashion). Suppose the training data consist of the three examples in Figure 7.3(a). In practice, a training set typically contains hundreds to tens of thousands of examples.

Suppose also that we have defined six possibly relevant features $s_1 - s_6$. Features $s_1(a, b)$ and $s_2(a, b)$ compute similarity scores based on Jaro-Winkler and edit distance between the person names of tuples a and b, respectively. This is because we do not know *a priori* whether Jaro-Winkler or edit distance works best for this matching scenario, so we "throw" both in and let the learning algorithm decide.

Feature $s_3(a, b)$ computes an edit distance-based similarity measure between the phone numbers (ignoring the area code of a, as this area code does not appear in the phone number of b). Features $s_4(a, b)$ and $s_5(a, b)$ return 1 if the city names and the state names, respectively, match exactly, and 0 otherwise.

Finally, feature $s_6(a, b)$ encodes a heuristic constraint that we believe may be useful in this matching scenario. To explain, consider tuples a_1 and b_1 in Figure 7.3(a). The city of tuple a_1 is Seattle, whereas the city of b_1 is Redmond, an incompatibility. However, the phone number

<a₁ = (Mike Williams, (425) 247 4893, Seattle, WA), b₁ = (M. Williams, 247 4893, Redmond, WA), yes>
<a₂ = (Richard Pike, (414) 256 1257, Milwaukee, WI), b₂ = (R. Pike, 256 1237, Milwaukee, WI), yes>
<a₃ = (Jane McCain, (206) 111 4215, Renton, WA), b₃ = (J. M. McCain, 112 5200, Renton, WA), no>

(a)

match names   match phones   match cities   match states   check area code against city

$v_1 = \langle [s_1(a_1,b_1), s_2(a_1,b_1), s_3(a_1,b_1), s_4(a_1,b_1), s_5(a_1,b_1), s_6(a_1,b_1)], 1 \rangle$

$v_2 = \langle [s_1(a_2,b_2), s_2(a_2,b_2), s_3(a_2,b_2), s_4(a_2,b_2), s_5(a_2,b_2), s_6(a_2,b_2)], 1 \rangle$

$v_3 = \langle [s_1(a_3,b_3), s_2(a_3,b_3), s_3(a_3,b_3), s_4(a_3,b_3), s_5(a_3,b_3), s_6(a_3,b_3)], 0 \rangle$

(b)

FIGURE 7.3 (a) The original training data; (b) the transformed training data for learning linearly weighted and logistic regression rules.

425 247 4893 of a_1 has area code 425, which is actually Redmond's area code. Furthermore, the names and phone numbers (without area code) match quite closely. This suggests that a_1 and b_1 may be the same person and that a_1 lives in Redmond, but lists his or her city as the nearby city of Seattle instead. To capture such scenarios, we define feature $s_6(a, b)$ to return 1 if the area code of a is an area code of the city of b, and return 0 otherwise. As we explained earlier, we leave it up to the learning algorithm to decide if this feature can be useful for matching purposes.

After defining the features $s_1 - s_6$, we transform the training examples in Figure 7.3(a) into those in Figure 7.3(b). Here each feature vector $v_1 - v_3$ has six values, as returned by the feature functions. Furthermore, since our goal is to learn a linearly weighted similarity function $s(a, b)$ that returns a *numeric* similarity score between a and b, we have to convert the labels "yes"/"no" into numeric similarity scores. In this case, we simply convert "yes" into 1 and "no" into 0, as shown on the right-hand side of Figure 7.3(b).

Now we are ready to learn from the training set in Figure 7.3(b). Our goal is to learn the weight α_i, $i \in [1, 6]$ that would give us a linearly weighted matching rule of the form $s(a, b) = \sum_{i=1}^{6} \alpha_i s_i(a, b)$. To do this, we perform a least-squares linear regression on the data set in Figure 7.3(b). This regression finds the weights α_i that minimize the squared error $\sum_{i=1}^{3} (c_i - \sum_{j=1}^{6} \alpha_j s_j(v_i))^2$, where c_i is the label associated with feature vector v_i (this label is 0 or 1 in this case), and $s_j(v_i)$ is the value of the jth element of feature vector v_i.

All that remains from the learning process is to learn a threshold β, so that given a new tuple pair (a, b), we can predict matched if $s(a, b) \geq \beta$ and not matched otherwise. We can also learn β from the training data, for example, by setting β at the value that lets us minimize the number of incorrect matching predictions.

■ ■ ■

Example 7.2

As another example to illustrate supervised learning algorithms, consider applying a decision tree learning algorithm to the training examples in Figure 7.3(a). To do this, we first convert these training examples into those in Figure 7.4(a), assuming the same features $s_1 - s_6$. Note that now the labels remain "yes"/"no," because our goal is to learn a decision tree that predicts whether a tuple pair match (rather than learning a function that produces numeric similarity scores, as in the case of linearly weighted and logistic regression rules). Then, after applying a standard decision tree algorithm (such as the well-known C4.5 algorithm) to this training data, we may learn a decision tree such as the one in Figure 7.4(b). This tree states that a tuple pair (a, b) match if the names and the phone numbers match closely, or if the names match closely, the phones do not match very well, but the cities and the states match closely. Note that the tree does not use $s_2(a, b)$ and $s_6(a, b)$. Using the training data, the learning algorithm has decided that these features are irrelevant to making matching decisions.

■ ■ ■

As described, supervised learning approaches have two major advantages compared to rule-based ones. First, in rule-based approaches we have to *manually* decide if a particular feature is useful for the matching process, a difficult and time-consuming decision.

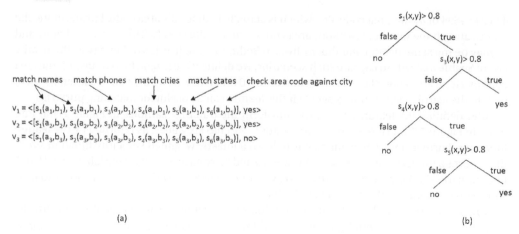

(a)

(b)

FIGURE 7.4 (a) The training data for the decision tree learning algorithm and (b) a sample decision tree learned by the algorithm.

This also limits us to examining only a relatively small set of features. In contrast, learning approaches can *automatically* examine a large set of features to select the most useful ones. The second advantage is that learning approaches can construct very complex "rules" (such as those produced by decision tree and SVM algorithms) that are difficult to construct by hand in rule-based approaches.

Supervised learning approaches, however, often require a large number of training examples, which can be hard to obtain. In the next section we describe unsupervised learning approaches that address this problem.

7.4 Matching by Clustering

In this section we describe the application of clustering techniques to the problem of data matching. Many of the commonly known clustering techniques have been applied to data matching, including agglomerative hierarchical clustering, k-means, and graph-theoretic clustering. Here we focus on agglomerative hierarchical clustering (AHC), a relatively simple yet very commonly used method. We show how AHC works, then use it to illustrate the key ideas that underlie clustering-based approaches to data matching.

Given a set of tuples D, the goal of AHC is to partition D into a set of clusters, such that all tuples in each cluster refer to a single real-world entity, while tuples in different clusters refer to different entities. AHC begins by putting each tuple in D into a single cluster. Then it iteratively merges the two most similar clusters, where similarity is computed using a similarity function. This continues until a desired number of clusters has been reached or until the similarity between the two closest clusters falls below a prespecified threshold. The output of AHC is the set of clusters when the termination condition is reached.

■ ■ ■ ━━━━━━━━━━━━━━━━━━━━━━━━━━━━━━━━━━━━━━━

Example 7.3

To illustrate, suppose we want to cluster the six tuples $x_1 - x_6$ shown in the bottom of Figure 7.5(a). We begin by defining a similarity function $s(x, y)$ between the tuples. For instance, if the tuples describe persons and have the same format as those in Figures 7.1(a-b), then we can use the linearly weighted function in Equation 7.2, reproduced here:

$$sim(x, y) = 0.3s_{name}(x, y) + 0.3s_{phone}(x, y) + 0.1s_{city}(x, y) + 0.3s_{state}(x, y)$$

In iteration 1 we compute $sim(x, y)$ for all tuple pairs and merge the two most similar tuples, which are x_1 and x_2. They have been merged into cluster c_1. In iteration 2 we merge x_4 and x_5 into cluster c_2, and in iteration 3 we merge x_3 and c_2 into cluster c_3. We now have three clusters: c_1, c_3, and x_6 (which is its own cluster), as shown in Figure 7.5(a).

At this point, suppose that no two clusters have a similarity score exceeding β, a prespecified threshold, so we stop and return c_1, c_3, and x_6. This clustering effectively specifies that x_1 and x_2 match, any two tuples of x_3, x_4, and x_5 match, while x_6 does not match any other tuple. Figure 7.5(b) visually depicts the bottom-up merging process and illustrates the "hierarchical" nature of AHC.

━━━━━━━━━━━━━━━━━━━━━━━━━━━━━━━━━━━━━━━ ■ ■ ■

To complete the description of the clustering approach we need to explain how to compute a similarity score between two clusters. Methods typically used in practice include the following:

Single link: The similarity score between clusters c and d is the minimal score between all tuple pairs $x_i \in c$ and $y_j \in d$: $s(c, d) = \min_{x_i \in c, y_j \in d} sim(x_i, y_j)$.

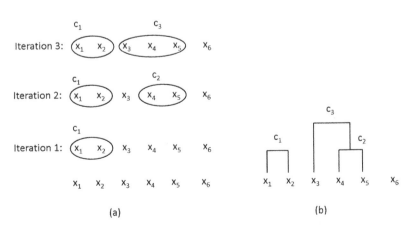

FIGURE 7.5 An example to illustrate agglomerative hierarchical clustering.

Complete link: We compute the maximal score between pairs of tuples in c and d:
$s(c, d) = \max_{x_i \in c, y_j \in d} sim(x_i, y_j)$.

Average link: We compute $s(c, d) = \sum_{x_i \in c, y_j \in d} sim(x_i, y_j)/n$, where n is the total number of pairs $x_i \in c$ and $y_j \in d$.

Canonical tuple: We create a canonical tuple that represents each cluster. The similarity between a pair of clusters is defined to be the similarity between their canonical tuples. The canonical tuple is created from the attribute values of the tuples in the cluster. For example, if the names in cluster c are "Mike Williams" and "M. J. Williams," we may merge them to generate the canonical name "Mike J. Williams." If the phone numbers are "425 247 4893" and "247 4893," we may select the longer number "425 247 4893" to be the canonical phone number, and so on.

In general, selecting a good cluster similarity method is application dependent and requires careful consideration from the application builder.

Before continuing to other approaches, it is important to emphasize the new perspectives that the clustering approach introduces to the data matching problem:

1. We view matching tuples as the problem of *constructing entities* (that is, clusters), with the understanding that only tuples within a cluster match.
2. The process is *iterative*: in each iteration we leverage what we have known so far (in the previous iterations) to build "better" entities.
3. In each iteration we *"merge"* all matching tuples within each cluster to construct an "entity profile," then use this profile to match other tuples. This is most clearly seen in the case of generating a canonical tuple, which can be viewed as an entity profile. As such, clustering introduces the novel aspect of merging then exploiting the merged information to help matching.

We will see the same principles appear in other approaches as well.

7.5 Probabilistic Approaches to Data Matching

Probabilistic approaches to data matching model the matching decision as a set of variables over which there is a probability distribution. For example, there would be a variable for whether two person names match and a variable for whether two tuples match. These approaches make matching decisions by reasoning about these variables.

The key benefit of probabilistic approaches to data matching is that they provide a principled framework that can naturally incorporate a wide variety of domain knowledge. In addition, these methods can leverage the wealth of probabilistic representation and reasoning techniques that have been developed in the past two decades in the artificial intelligence and database communities. Finally, probabilistic methods provide a frame of reference for comparing and explaining other matching approaches.

Probabilistic approaches suffer from certain disadvantages. Chief among these is that they often take far longer to run than nonprobabilistic counterparts. Another disadvantage is that it is often hard to understand and debug matching decisions of probabilistic approaches, even though the ability to do so is crucial in real-world applications.

Currently, most probabilistic approaches employ *generative models*, which encode full probability distributions and describe how to generate data that fit the distributions. Consequently, we will focus on these approaches and describe in particular three approaches that employ increasingly sophisticated generative models. In what follows we explain Bayesian networks, a relatively simple type of generative model, then use the ideas underlying Bayesian networks to explain the three approaches.

7.5.1 Bayesian Networks

We begin by describing Baysian networks, a probabilistic reasoning framework on which several of the matching approaches are based. Let $X = \{x_1, \ldots, x_n\}$ be a set of *variables*, each of which models a quantity of interest in the application domain and takes values from a prespecified set. For example, the variable *Cloud* can be *true* or *false*, and *Sprinkler* can be *on* or *off*. In our discussion we consider only variables with discrete values, but continuous variables can also be modeled (see Section 7.7.2). We define a *state* to be an assignment of values to all variables in X. For example, given $X = \{Cloud, Sprinkler\}$, we have four states, one of which is $s = \{Cloud = true, Sprinkler = on\}$.

Let S be the set of all states. A *probability distribution P* is a function that assigns to each state $s_i \in S$ a value $P(s_i) \in [0, 1]$ such that $\sum_{s_i \in S} P(s_i) = 1$. We call $P(s_i)$ the *probability* of s_i. The table in Figure 7.6 specifies a probability distribution over the states of *Cloud* and *Sprinkler* (here t and f are shorthands for *true* and *false*, respectively).

Our goal in reasoning over probabilistic models is to answer queries such as "what is the probability of $A = a$, $P(A = a)$", or "what is the probability of $A = a$ given that we know that the value of B is b, $P(A = a|B = b)$"? In both of these queries, A and B are subsets of the variables in the model. We typically abbreviate the queries as $P(A)$ and $P(A|B)$.

Probability theory gives us precise semantics for such queries. For example, to compute $P(Cloud = t)$ we simply sum over the first two rows of the table in Figure 7.6 to obtain 0.6.

States		Probabilities
Cloud	*Sprinkler*	
t	*on*	0.3
t	*off*	0.3
f	*on*	0.3
f	*off*	0.1

FIGURE 7.6 An example of a probability distribution over four states.

To compute $P(Cloud = t|Sprinkler = off)$, we first compute $P(Cloud = t, Sprinkler = off)$ and then divide it by $P(Sprinkler = off)$ to obtain 0.75.

Unfortunately, it is often impractical to specify a probability distribution by explicitly enumerating *all* states, as we do in Figure 7.6. This is because the number of possible states grows exponentially with the number of variables. Real-world applications often use hundreds or thousands of variables, and thus we cannot enumerate all states. The key idea underlying Bayesian networks is that they provide a compact representation of a probability distribution. We now explain how to represent and reason with Bayesian networks and how to learn them from data.

Representing and Reasoning with Bayesian Networks

A *Bayesian network* is an acyclic directed graph whose nodes denote the variables and whose edges encode probabilistic dependencies among the variables. Figure 7.7(a) shows such a graph over four nodes *Cloud, Sprinkler, Rain,* and *WetGrass*. Given a Bayesian network *G*, we say that node *A* is a parent of node *B* if there is a directed edge from *A* to *B*, and that node *C* is an ancestor of *B* if there is a directed path from *C* to *B*.

Informally, an edge from node *A* to node *B* can be interpreted as stating that *B* is dependent on *A*. For example, wet grass is dependent on whether the sprinkler is on and on whether it is raining. The graph *G* then encodes the following assertion: each node in *G* is probabilistically independent of its nondescendants given the values of its parents. This assertion is the key for compactly representing a probability distribution using a Bayesian network. For example, in Figure 7.7(a) the value of *WetGrass* is independent of *Cloud* given the values of *Sprinkler* and *Rain*, and the value of *Sprinkler* is independent of *Rain* given the value of *Cloud*. Given the above independence assertion, we can compute the probability distribution specified by *G* as a product of "local probabilities."

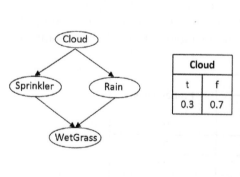

Cloud	Sprinkler	
	on	off
t	0.2	0.8
f	0.8	0.2

Cloud	
t	f
0.3	0.7

Cloud	Rain	
	t	f
t	0.6	0.4
f	0.3	0.7

Sprinkler	Rain	WetGrass	
		t	f
on	t	1	0
on	f	1	0
off	t	1	0
off	f	0.1	0.9

(a)   (b)

FIGURE 7.7 A sample Bayesian network: (a) the directed acyclic graph and (b) the conditional probability tables (CPTs).

■ ■ ■ ━━

Example 7.4

Consider the graph in Figure 7.7(a). Let C, S, R, and W be shorthands for *Cloud*, *Sprinkler*, *Rain*, and *WetGrass*, respectively, and let a term such as $P(C, S, R, W)$ denote the probability of a state on these four variables, such as $P(C = t, S = on, R = f, W = t)$. Then using the chain rule of probability we have

$$P(C, S, R, W) = P(C) \cdot P(S|C) \cdot P(R|S, C) \cdot P(W|R, S, C)$$

Since a node is probabilistically independent of its nondescendants given its parents, we can simplify $P(R|S, C)$ as $P(R|C)$, and $P(W|R, S, C)$ as $P(W|R, S)$. This gives

$$P(C, S, R, W) = P(C) \cdot P(S|C) \cdot P(R|C) \cdot P(W|R, S)$$

Thus, to compute $P(C, S, R, W)$, we only need to know four *local distributions*: $P(C)$, $P(S|C), P(R|C)$, and $P(W|R, S)$. Figure 7.7(b) shows an example of these local distributions, where $P(C = t) = 0.3$ and $P(S = on|C = t) = 0.2$.

━━ ■ ■ ■

In general, local distributions specify conditional probabilities of a node given its parents and are called *conditional probability tables*, or *CPTs* for short, one CPT per node. Note that to specify a CPT, we need to specify only half of the probabilities in the CPT, the other half can be easily inferred. For example, to specify the CPT of *Cloud*, we only have to specify $P(C = t)$, then infer $P(C = f) = 1 - P(C = t)$.

As described, given a graph and a corresponding set of CPTs, a Bayesian network fully specifies a probability distribution, and does so compactly. For example, the Bayesian network in Figures 7.7(a-b) uses only nine probability statements to specify the CPTs, whereas an explicit representation that enumerates all states would use $2^4 = 16$ statements. In general, a Bayesian network can take exponentially less space than the explicit representation of the probability distribution.

Performing inference with a Bayesian network means computing probabilities such as $P(A)$ or $P(A|B)$ where A and B are subsets of variables. In general, performing exact inference is NP-hard, taking exponential time in the number of variables of the network in the worst case. Data matching approaches address this problem in three ways. First, under certain restrictions on the structure of the Bayesian network, inference is computationally cheaper, and there are polynomial-time algorithms or closed-form equations that will return the exact answers. Second, data matching algorithms can use standard approximate inference algorithms for Bayesian networks that have been described in the literature. Finally, we can develop approximation algorithms that are tailored to a particular domain at hand. We illustrate these inference solutions in Sections 7.5.2–7.5.4, when we describe three representative probabilistic matching approaches.

Learning Bayesian Networks

To use a Bayesian network, current data matching approaches typically require a domain expert to create a directed acyclic graph (such as the one in Figure 7.7(a)), then learn the associated CPTs (e.g., Figure 7.7(b)) from the *training data*. The training data consist of a set of states that we have observed in the world. For example, suppose that on Monday we observed that it was cloudy and raining, that the sprinkler was off, and that the grass was wet; then the tuple $d_1 = (Cloud = t, Sprinkler = off, Rain = t, WetGrass = t)$ forms an observed state of the world. Suppose we also observed $d_2 = (Cloud = t, Sprinkler = off, Rain = f, WetGrass = f)$ on Tuesday, and $d_3 = (Cloud = f, Sprinkler = on, Rain = f, WetGrass = t)$ on Wednesday. Then the tuples $d_1 - d_3$ form a (tiny) set of training data, from which we can learn the CPTs of the graph in Figure 7.7(a). In practice, a training set typically contains hundreds to thousands of such training examples.

LEARNING WITH NO MISSING VALUES

We begin with the case in which the training examples do not have missing values. We illustrate the learning on the example in Figure 7.8. Given the graph in Figure 7.8(a) and the training data in Figure 7.8(b), we want to learn the CPTs in Figure 7.8(c). Note that a training example such as $d_1 = (1,0)$ specifies $A = 1$ and $B = 0$. Note also that we only have to learn probabilities $P(A = 1), P(B = 1|A = 1)$, and $P(B = 1|A = 0)$. From these we can easily infer the other probabilities of the CPTs.

Let θ denote the probabilities to be learned. In the absence of any other evidence, we want to find a $\theta*$ that maximizes the probability of observing the training data D:

$$\theta* = \arg\max_{\theta} P(D|\theta)$$

It turns out that $\theta*$ can be obtained by simple counting over the training data D. For example, to compute probability $P(A = 1)$, we simply count the number of training examples

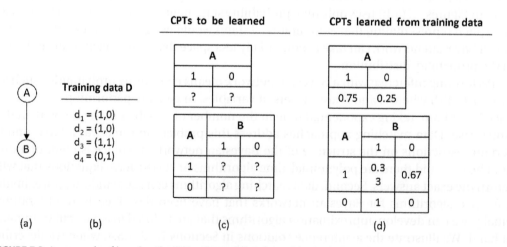

(a)   (b)   (c)   (d)

FIGURE 7.8 An example of learning the CPTs using training data with no missing values.

where $A = 1$, then divide that number by the total number of examples. In our case, we get $P(A = 1) = 0.75$. To compute $P(B = 1|A = 1)$, we divide the number of examples where $B = 1$ and $A = 1$ by the number of examples where $A = 1$, and so on. Applying this counting procedure to the example in Figures 7.8(a-c), we obtain the CPTs in Figure 7.8(d).

The tricky case is where we do not have sufficient data for certain states. Suppose that the training data D include only the three examples $d_1 - d_3$. In this case it is not clear how to compute $P(B = 1|A = 0)$, because the number of examples where $A = 0$ is 0, and we cannot divide by 0.

To address this problem, we can use a method called *smoothing of the probabilities*. A common smoothing method is the m-estimate of probability, defined as follows. Let X and Y be two variables. Consider computing the m-estimate of a probability that involves both X and Y, say $P(Y = 1|X = 0)$. Suppose we count x examples where $X = 0$ and y examples where $Y = 1$ and $X = 0$; then instead of returning y/x as an estimation of this probability, as before, we return $(y + mp)/(x + m)$, where p is our prior estimate of the probability $P(Y = 1|X = 0)$ and m is a prespecified constant. In the absence of any other information, a common method for choosing p is to assume uniform priors. For example, if Y has two possible values, then we would choose $p = 0.5$. The constant m determines how heavily to weigh p relative to the observed data and can be viewed as augmenting the x actual examples where $X = 0$ with m virtual examples where $x = 0$ and where a p fraction of these examples has $Y = 1$.

Note that when applying the m-estimate method, we apply it to all probabilities that we want to compute. For example, consider again the case where the training data consist of only three examples $d_1 - d_3$. Assuming $m = 1$ and $p = 0.5$, we have $P(B = 1|A = 1) = (1 + 1 \cdot 0.5)/(3 + 1) = 0.375$, and $P(B = 1|A = 0) = (0 + 1 \cdot 0.5)/(0 + 1) = 0.5$.

LEARNING WITH MISSING VALUES

Training examples may contain missing values. For instance, the example $d = (Cloud = ?, Sprinkler = off, Rain = ?, WetGrass = t)$ has no values for *Cloud* and *Rain*. The values may be missing because we failed to observe a variable (e.g., we slept and did not observe whether it rained). It may also be the case that the variable by its nature is unobservable. For example, if we are werewolves who only venture out of the house on dark moonless nights, then we can observe if it rains, if the sprinkler is on, and if the grass is wet, but we can never tell if the sky is cloudy. Regardless of the reason, missing values cause considerable complications for learning.

We explain how to learn in the presence of missing values using the tiny example in Figures 7.9(a-b). Here the graph is the same as the graph in Figure 7.8(a), but the training data $D = \{d_1, d_2, d_3\}$ has missing values. In particular, the value of variable A is missing from all three examples.

Given the missing values, we cannot proceed as before to use counting over D to compute the CPTs. Instead, we use an expectation-maximization (EM) algorithm (see Figure 7.9(c)). The basic idea behind this algorithm is the following. There are two unknown quantities: (1) θ, the probabilities in the CPTs that we want to learn, and (2) the

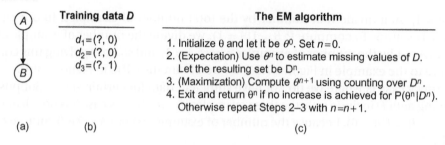

FIGURE 7.9 Learning the CPTs using training data with missing values.

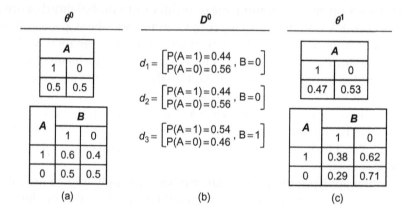

FIGURE 7.10 Applying the EM algorithm to the example in Figures 7.9(a-b).

missing values in D. The EM algorithm iteratively estimates these two quantities by using one to predict the other and vice versa until a convergence condition is met.

More specifically, we initialize θ to a value θ^0 (Step 1 in Figure 7.9(c)). Then we use θ^0 and the input graph G to estimate the missing values in the training data D. We compute the missing values by computing some conditional probabilities using the Bayesian network specified by θ and G (Step 2).

Let D^0 be the resulting training data (with no missing values). We can now reestimate θ using counting over D^0 (Step 3). Let the resulting θ be θ^1. We repeat Steps 2–3 until a convergence criterion is met, such as the absolute difference between $P(D^n|\theta^n)$ and $P(D^{n+1}|\theta^{n+1})$ is less than a prespecified ϵ (Step 4). Here $P(D^n|\theta^n) = \prod_d P(d|\theta^n)$, where d ranges over all training examples in D_n, and $P(d|\theta^n)$ is the probability of the state specified by d, given the Bayesian network specified by the input graph G and the probabilities θ^n.

■ ■ ■ ▬▬▬▬▬▬▬▬▬▬▬▬▬▬▬▬▬▬▬▬▬▬▬▬▬

Example 7.5

Figure 7.10 illustrates how the above EM algorithm is applied to the example in Figures 7.9(a-b). We start by randomly initializing $P(A = 1) = 0.5, P(B = 1|A = 1) = 0.6$, and $P(B = 1|A = 0) = 0.5$, then filling in all the other probabilities of the CPTs. Figure 7.10(a) shows the resulting CPTs, denoted as θ^0.

Next, we use θ^0 and the graph in Figure 7.9(a) to estimate the missing values in the training data. Consider tuple $d_1 = (?, 0)$ in Figure 7.9(b). Here the value of variable A is missing. Estimating this value means estimating $P(A = 1|B = 0)$ and $P(A = 0|B = 0)$. While estimating these two probabilities is standard inference operation in Bayesian networks, here we can compute them directly using the laws of probabilities. Specifically, we have

$$P(A = 1|B = 0) = P(B = 0|A = 1)P(A = 1)/P(B = 0) \qquad (7.4)$$

where

$$P(B = 0) = P(B = 0|A = 1)P(A = 1) + P(B = 0|A = 0)P(A = 0) \qquad (7.5)$$

Substituting appropriate probabilities from θ^0 in Figure 7.10(a) into Equations 7.4 and 7.5, we obtain $P(A = 1|B = 0) = 0.44$, and thus $P(A = 0|B = 0) = 0.56$. Figure 7.10(b) shows the resulting training data D^0 after we have estimated all missing values. Note that each example in D^0 specifies a probability distribution over the values of variable A.

Next, we use the counting algorithm over D^0 to estimate θ^1. This counting is necessarily fractional, given the probabilistic nature of the training examples. For instance, to estimate $P(A = 1)$, we count the number of examples where $A = 1$. We note that $A = 1$ for a 0.44 fraction of d_1, a 0.44 fraction of d_2, and a 0.54 fraction of d_3. So $P(A = 1) = (0.44 + 0.44 + 0.54)/3 = 0.47$. Similarly, consider computing $P(B = 1|A = 1) = P(B = 1, A = 1)/P(A = 1)$. We have $B = 1$ and $A = 1$ in only a 0.54 fraction of d_3. Thus $P(B = 1, A = 1) = 0.54/3 = 0.18$. We already know that $P(A = 1) = 0.47$. Thus, $P(B = 1|A = 1) = 0.18/0.47 = 0.38$. Figure 7.10(c) shows the resulting θ^1. In the next step, we use θ^1 to estimate the missing values in D, to compute D^1, and so on.

■ ■ ■

As described, the EM algorithm finds θ that maximizes $P(D|\theta)$, just like the counting approach in the case of no missing values. However, it may not find the globally maximal $\theta*$, converging instead to a local maximum in most cases.

Bayesian Networks as Generative Models

Generative models encode full probability distributions and specify how to generate data that fit such distributions. Bayesian networks are well-known examples of such models. Consider, for example, the familiar Bayesian network in Figures 7.7(a-b). This network specifies that, to generate a state of the world, we begin by selecting a value for variable *Cloud*, according to the CPT *P(Cloud)* in Figure 7.7(b). Suppose we have selected *Cloud* = *t*. Next, we select a value for variable *Sprinkler*, according to the probability *P(Sprinkler|Cloud* = *t)*, then a value for *Rain*, according to the probability *P(Rain|Cloud* = *t)*. Suppose we have selected *Sprinkler* = *on* and *Rain* = *f*. Then finally we select a value for *WetGrass* according to the probability *P(WetGrass|Sprinkler* = *on*, *Rain* = *f)*.

Taking a perspective on how the data are generated helps guide the construction of the underlying Bayesian network, discover what kinds of domain knowledge can be naturally incorporated into the network structure, and explain the network to the users.

In the rest of this section we will describe three probabilistic approaches to data matching that employ increasingly complex generative models. We begin with an approach that employs a relatively simple Bayesian network that models domain features judged relevant to matching but assumes no correlations among the features. Next, we extend the model to capture such correlations. Finally, we consider matching data tuples embedded in text documents and show how to construct a model that captures the pecularities of that domain.

7.5.2 Data Matching with Naive Bayes

We begin with a relatively simple approach to data matching that is based on Bayesian networks. We formulate the matching problem in terms of probabilistic reasoning by defining a variable M that represents whether two tuples a and b match. Our goal is to compute $P(M|a,b)$. We declare a and b matched if $P(M = t|a,b) > P(M = f|a,b)$, and not matched otherwise.

We assume that $P(M|a,b)$ depends only on a set of features $S_1,\ldots,S_n$, each of which takes a and b as the inputs and returns a discrete value. In the context of matching tuples describing people, example features include whether the two last names match, and the edit distance between the two social security numbers. Given this, we can write $P(M|a,b) = P(M|S_1,\ldots,S_n)$, where S_i is a shorthand for $S_i(a,b)$.

Next, using a well-known law of probability called Bayes' Rule, we have

$$P(M|S_1,\ldots,S_n) = P(S_1,\ldots,S_n|M)P(M)/P(S_1,\ldots,S_n) \tag{7.6}$$

If we assume that the features $S_1,\ldots,S_n$ are independent of one another given M, then we can write $P(S_1,\ldots,S_n|M) = \prod_{i=1}^{n} P(S_i|M)$. Further, observe that the denominator of the right-hand side of Equation 7.6 can be expressed as

$$P(S_1,\ldots,S_n) = P(S_1,\ldots,S_n|M = t)P(M = t) + P(S_1,\ldots,S_n|M = f)P(M = f) \tag{7.7}$$

Thus, it follows that to compute $P(M|S_1,\ldots,S_n)$ (that is, $P(M|a,b)$), we only need to know $P(S_1|M),\ldots,P(S_n|M)$ and $P(M)$.

The model we have just described is shown in the Bayesian network in Figure 7.11(a). The graph models the quantities of interest using the variables M, S_1, S_2, and S_3 (here for concreteness we consider only three variables S_1-S_3). The main simplifying assumption that we made about the nature of data matching is that S_1-S_3 are independent of one another given M. This assumption is often referred to as the *naive Bayes* assumption. The naive Bayes assumption often does not hold in the real world, but making that assumption tends to work surprisingly well in practice. Note that the probabilities $P(S_1|M),\ldots,P(S_n|M)$

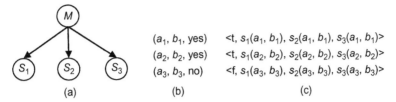

(a)   (b)   (c)

FIGURE 7.11 Learning the CPTs of the naive Bayesian approach to data matching when we have training data. Note that the "yes" and "no" in part (b) have been converted into the "t" and "f" in part (c) to generate training data (a set of states in this case) for the Bayesian network in part (a).

(a_4, b_4) $<?, s_1(a_4, b_4), s_2(a_4, b_4), s_3(a_4, b_4)>$
(a_5, b_5) $<?, s_1(a_5, b_5), s_2(a_5, b_5), s_3(a_5, b_5)>$
(a_6, b_6) $<?, s_1(a_6, b_6), s_2(a_6, b_6), s_3(a_6, b_6)>$

(a)   (b)

FIGURE 7.12 Learning the CPTs of the naive Bayesian approach to data matching when we have no training data. The set of tuples to be matched (part (a)) is converted into training data with missing values for the Bayesian network in Figure 7.11(a).

and $P(M)$ that we want to learn in order to compute $P(M|a, b)$ form the CPTs of this Bayesian network.

Learning these CPTs is straightforward if we have training data such as the three tuples in Figure 7.11(b), where tuple (a_1, b_1, yes), for example, states that a_1 matches b_1. We simply convert each such tuple into a feature vector. For example, (a_1, b_1, yes) is converted into $\langle t, s_1(a_1, b_1), s_2(a_1, b_1), s_3(a_1, b_1) \rangle$, which represents a state of the world that assigns values $t, s_1(a, b), s_2(a, b)$, and $s_3(a, b)$ to nodes M, S_1, S_2, and S_3, respectively. After converting the tuples in Figure 7.11(b) into the feature vectors in Figure 7.11(c), we can apply learning with no missing values as described in Section 7.5.1 to these feature vectors, to learn the CPTs of the graph in Figure 7.11(a).

Once we have learned the CPTs, we can apply the Bayesian network to match a new pair of tuples. Given a pair of tuples (a_4, b_4), we compute $P(M = t|a_4, b_4)$ and $P(M = f|a_4, b_4)$, using Equations 7.6–7.7, and declare "matched" if $P(M = t|a_4, b_4) > P(M = f|a_4, b_4)$ and "not matched" otherwise. Note that in practice, the denominator $P(S_1, \ldots, S_n)$ in the right-hand side of Equation 7.6 is the same for both cases of $M = t$ and $M = f$. Thus we only need to compare the numerators of the right-hand side of Equation 7.6.

Learning the CPTs becomes more involved when we have no training data. In this case, we convert the tuple pairs to be matched into training data with missing values and apply the EM algorithm as described in Section 7.5.1. To illustrate, suppose we want to match the three tuple pairs in Figure 7.12(a). We first convert them into the three feature vectors in Figure 7.12(b). Each of these vectors specifies a value for the variables M, S_1, S_2, and S_3 of the Bayesian network in Figure 7.11(a). However, since we do not yet know the value for variable M, this value is missing from all three feature vectors. Therefore, we apply the

EM algorithm to these feature vectors to learn the CPTs. After computing the CPTs we can make matching decisions.

7.5.3 Modeling Feature Correlations

The approach we described above was naive in the sense that it assumes no correlation among the features $S_1, \ldots, S_n$, given the "match" variable M. While the naive Bayesian approach works surprisingly well in many domains, there are domains in which accurate matching decisions require that we capture the correlations among the features involved.

The Bayesian network in Figure 7.13(a) attempts to model such correlations by adding directed edges among the feature nodes. Suppose that node S_1 models whether the social security numbers match, and node S_3 models whether the last names match. Then we may want to create an edge from S_1 to S_3, because if the two social security numbers match, then it is very likely that the two last names also match.

The problem with adding such edges is that it may quickly "blow up" the number of probabilities in the CPTs. For example, suppose that on average each node has q parents and d values; then the number of probabilities in the CPTs for the n feature nodes is $O(nd^q)$. In contrast, for the naive Bayesian network in Figure 7.11(a), we need only $2dn$ probabilities ($2d$ for each feature node). The more probabilities we have in the CPTs, the more training data we need to learn accurately, and the longer it takes to learn.

The Bayesian network in Figure 7.13(b) reduces the size of the required CPTs but with some loss of expressive power. Suppose each tuple to be matched has k attributes. Then here we will consider only k features $S_1, \ldots, S_k$, each of which takes as input the values of only one attribute, then outputs a discrete value. For example, if each tuple has only two attributes, *name* and *address*, then we consider two features: the first one compares the two names and the second one compares the two addresses. Note that in contrast, earlier we considered also features that can relate different attributes, such as a zip code with an area code.

Figure 7.13(b) assumes there are four attributes, and shows four features $S_1 - S_4$. For each attribute S_i we introduce a binary variable X_i. The X_i variables model whether the

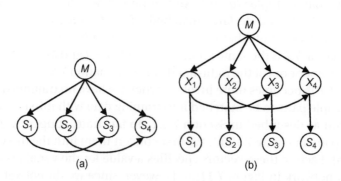

(a)   (b)

FIGURE 7.13 Sample Bayesian networks of approaches that model feature correlations.

attributes should match, given that the input tuple pair match. For example, if X_1 is about social security numbers, then X_1 models whether the social security numbers match given that the tuples match. It is likely that the value of $P(X_1 = t|M = t)$ would be high in the CPT. Now suppose S_1 returns the edit distance between the social security numbers (i.e., a number between 0 and 9). Then $P(S_1 = 0|X_1 = t)$ and $P(S_1 = 1|X_1 = t)$ would likely be high, to reflect the domain knowledge that if two social security numbers match, then the edit distance between their appearances in the data should be relatively small (i.e., 0 or 1).

In the final step of creating the network in Figure 7.13(b) we model correlations only at the $X_1 - X_4$ level (thus assuming that the $S_1 - S_4$ are independent of one another given the $X_1 - X_4$). For example, suppose again that X_1 is about social security numbers and X_3 is about last names. Then we create an edge from X_1 to X_3 to capture the knowledge that if the social security numbers match, then it is highly likely that the last names also match.

The network in Figure 7.13(b) requires far fewer probabilities in the CPTs. Assume that on average each node has q parents. Then the total number of probabilities required for the nodes $X_1 - X_k$ is $O(k2^q)$ (recall that these are binary nodes, with only two values t and f). If each feature node has d values, then we need only $2kd$ probabilities for these nodes. Thus the total is $O(k2^q + 2kd)$, far less than the number of probabilities required for the Bayesian network in Figure 7.13(a). The key to achieving this gain is to push dependency modeling from a level where each node can have many values (d on average) to a level where each node can have only two values. Of course, we pay for this gain by the fact that the graph in Figure 7.13(b) is less expressive in that it cannot model arbitrary features.

A key lesson to take away from this discussion is that constructing a Bayesian network for a matching problem is an "art" that must consider the trade-offs among many factors, including how much domain knowledge can be captured, how accurately we can learn the network, and how efficiently we can do so. The next section shows an even more complex example.

7.5.4 Matching Mentions of Entities in Text

In this section we describe a data matching example that requires a more complex generative model. Instead of considering the problem of matching tuples, as we have done so far, we consider the problem of matching *entity mentions* (e.g., "Michael Jordan," "M. Jordan," and "Mike I. Jordan") in text documents.

PROBLEM DEFINITION
Let D be a set of text documents, and M be a set of entity mentions in D, where each *mention m* is a string that occurs in a document and refers to a real-world entity. Such mentions can be discovered by applying information extraction techniques to the documents. Our goal is to decide, for any two mentions m_i and m_j in M, whether they refer to the same real-world entity. For example, consider the six mentions (the underlined strings) in the three documents $d_1 - d_3$ in Figure 7.14(a). We want to know, for instance, that mention "Michael Jordan" in d_1 matches "Mike" in d_1 and "Michael J. Jordan" in d_2, but not "Prof. M. I. Jordan" in d_3.

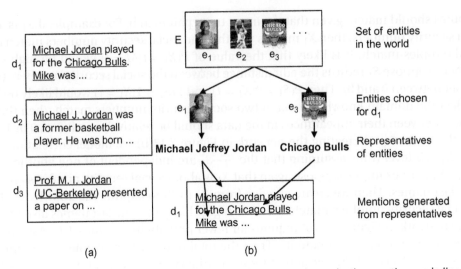

FIGURE 7.14 (a) A tiny collection of three text documents with person and organization mentions underlined; (b) a generative model to generate the mentions of a document.

THE GENERATIVE MODEL

To develop a matching algorithm, we create a generative model for how entity mentions are generated in text. We assume that the world consists of a set of entities E, such as Michael Jordan the bastketball player, Michael Jordan the researcher, and the Chicago Bulls basketball team. We generate the mentions of a document d in the following steps:

1. We select a number K that will represent the number of entities mentioned in the document d. We select K according to a distribution $P(K)$.
2. We select K entities from E, according to a distribution $P(E)$.
3. For each selected entity e, we select a string r called a *representative* of e, according to a distribution $P(r|e)$.
4. We select a number L that represents the number of mentions of entity e. We select L according to a distribution $P(L)$. Then we perturb r to generate L mentions $m_1, \ldots, m_L$, according to a distribution $P(m|r)$.
5. Finally, we "sprinkle" the mentions $m_1, \ldots, m_L$ in the document d.

Figure 7.14(b) illustrates generating the mentions of document d_1. We first select two entities e_1 and e_3, then two representatives "Michael Jeffrey Jordan" and "Chicago Bulls." Intuitively, each representative is the "full name" of the respective entity. Next, we perturb the representatives to generate mentions. For example, we drop the middle name from the representative "Michael Jeffrey Jordan" to obtain mention "Michael Jordan," drop both middle and last names, then transform the first name into a nickname, to obtain mention "Mike." Finally we sprinkle these mentions into d_1.

As described, the set of parameters θ of our generative model consists of (1) probability distributions $P(K)$ and $P(L)$ that specify how to select the number of entities and the number of mentions of each entity (respectively), (2) a set of entities E and a distribution $P(E)$ that specifies how to select entities, and (3) distributions $P(r|e)$ and $P(m|r)$ that specify how to select representatives and mentions (respectively).

Before we discuss how to learn this model from the data, we show how the model can be used for a data-matching algorithm.

USING THE MODEL TO MATCH MENTIONS

Given a document d with a set of mentions M_d, we want to apply the generative model to match M_d. Intuitively, this means finding the set of entities E_d*, the set of representatives R_d* in d, and the assignments of the mentions in M_d to E_d* and R_d*. We declare two mentions matched if and only if they are assigned to the same entity. Formally, we want to find the most likely E_d* and R_d*, that is:

$$(E_d*, R_d*) = \arg\max_{E_d, R_d} P(E_d, R_d | M_d)$$

$$= \arg\max_{E_d, R_d} P(E_d, R_d, M_d)$$

$$= \arg\max_{E_d, R_d} P(E_d)P(R_d|E_d)P(M_d|R_d) \tag{7.8}$$

Equation 7.8 assumes conditional independence between M and E given R and ignores the probabilities on the number of entities and the number of mentions, as they can be omitted in computing argmax. Solving Equation 7.8 by considering all possible combinations of E_d and R_d is clearly infeasible. Therefore, we resort to an approximation algorithm.

In the first step, we find R_d* directly by sequentially clustering the mentions M_d. We initialize the clustering algorithm by selecting the longest mention in M_d as the first representative. For each mention $m \in M_d$, we compute $P(m|r)$ for each representative r that has already been created. We use a fixed threshold to decide whether to add m to an existing group that maximizes $P(m|r)$ or to create a new group for m. We always select the longest mention in each group as its representative.

In the second step, once we have found the set of representatives R_d*, we assign each representative $r \in R_d*$ to the entity $e* = \arg\max_e P(e)P(r|e)$. By composing the mapping from mentions to representatives with the mapping from representatives to entities, we have created a mapping from mentions to entities for a single document d.

We can proceed similarly to match a set of new documents $d_1,\ldots,d_n$ with mentions $M_1,\ldots,M_n$. Specifically, once we have assigned mentions to representatives and representatives to entities, then two mentions (from the same document or across documents) match if and only if they refer to the same entity.

Learning the Generative Model

We now describe how to learn the generative model. As before, we distinguish the case in which we have training data from the case in which we do not.

CASE 1: WHEN WE HAVE TRAINING DATA

To simplify our discussion, we assume that $P(K)$ and $P(L)$ are uniform probability distributions over small plausible numeric ranges. For example, we can define $P(K)$ to be a uniform distribution over the range $[1,8]$, on the assumption that each document mentions anywhere between 1 and 8 entities. Given this, we only have to learn the set E and the distributions $P(E), P(r|e)$, and $P(m|r)$.

Let the training data be a set D of documents, and we assume the following. First, we have identified all mentions M of the target entity types (e.g., if we want to match person names and organization names, then we have identified all person and organization mentions in D). Second, we have partitioned M into n clusters such that mentions within each cluster (and only these mentions) refer to a single real-world entity.

Learning E and P(E): Given the training data, we can create n entities $e_1, \ldots, e_n$, one for each cluster, and let this set of entities be E. Assuming that entities are *independently* chosen into a document, we can learn $P(E)$ by computing $P(e_i)$, $i \in [1, n]$, as the number of mentions in the cluster of e_i divided by the total number of mentions in M. The probability of any subset F of E is then $P(F) = \prod_{e \in F} P(e)$.

Learning P(m|r): To learn $P(m|r)$, we begin by assuming that each mention m and each representative r are associated with a set of attributes $a_1, \ldots, a_p$. For example, each person mention may have the attributes *title, firstName, middleName,* and *lastName.* Thus, mention "Michael Jeffrey Jordan" can be converted into a tuple (*title* = *null, firstName* = *Michael, middleName* = *Jeffrey, lastName* = *Jordan*).

Suppose $m = (a_1 = v_1, \ldots, a_p = v_p)$ and $r = (a_1 = v'_1, \ldots, a_p = v'_p)$. Then we model $P(m|r)$ as the product of the transformation probabilities from the v'_k's to the v_k's. Specifically,

$$P(m|r) = \prod_{k=1}^{p} P(a_k(m) = v_k | a_k(r) = v'_k)$$

where $P(a_k(m) = v_k | a_k(r) = v'_k)$ is the probability that the kth attribute of m is v_k, given that the corresponding attribute of r is v'_k.

Instead of computing $P(a_k(m) = v_k | a_k(r) = v'_k)$ directly, we distinguish four types of perturbations, and we compute the probability of each one of the perturbation types. We denote the probability that the perturbation of the kth attribute is of type t by $P(k, t)$.

The four types of perturbations are *copy, missing, typical,* and *atypical.* If $v_k = v'_k$, then we say the perturbation type is *copy.* If $v_k = null$, then the type is *missing.* If v_k is obtained from v'_k in a perturbation that is typically expected for the attribute, then we say the type is *typical;* otherwise, it is *atypical.* For example, if the attribute is *firstName,* then abbreviating a first name to the first character is typical, while to the first three characters is not.

To compute the probability of each of the perturbations, we first manually collect typical and atypical perturbations for common attributes. For example, for attributes such as *title, firstName, middleName, lastName,* and *organizationName* we can collect perturbation using multiple data sources such as the U.S. government census and online dictionaries. For other attributes such as *age,* we classify all perturbations that are not *copy* or *missing* as *atypical.*

Given the perturbation types, we can model $P(a_k(m) = v_k|a_k(r) = v'_k)$ as $P(k,t)$, the probability that the perturbation of the kth attribute is of type t. If we know where the representatives are in the training data D, then it is easy to estimate $P(k,t)$. Consider all pairs of the form (r,m) in D, where m is generated from r. Then $P(k,t)$ is the number of pairs where the perturbation of $a_k(r)$ into $a_k(m)$ is of type t, divided by the total number of pairs. (We perform smoothing for perturbation types unseen in the training data, in a way similar to the smoothing discussed in Section 7.5.1.)

Thus we can learn $P(k,t)$ if we know the representatives. The training data D, however, does not specify the representatives, only the mentions and the clusters (i.e., the entities). To address this problem, from the set of all mentions in a document d that correspond to an entity e, we select the one with the largest length as the representative r of e. This heuristic is based on the assumption that a representative r in a document d is the "full name" of an entity e and that all mentions of e in d are obtained by perturbing this full name.

Learning $P(r|e)$: The same process can be applied in a similar fashion to learn $P(r|e)$. The only missing piece is how to obtain the attribute values for the entities. Again, from the set of all mentions (across all documents) that refer to an entity e, we can select the one with the largest length as the "full name" of e, then process this full name to obtain the attribute values.

CASE 2: WHEN WE DO NOT HAVE TRAINING DATA

In this case we apply the EM algorithm. Let D be a set of documents and M be a set of mentions in D. We apply the EM algorithm to match M as follows.

1. *Initialization:* We assign an initial (E_d^0, R_d^0) to each document $d \in D$ (i.e., assigning each mention in d to a representative in a set R_d^0 and each representative to an entity in a set E_d^0), as described below. Let $D^0 = \{(E_d^0, R_d^0, M_d)|d \in D\}$, where M_d is the set of mentions in document d. That is, D^0 is the set D where each mention in each document $d \in D$ has been assigned to a representative and each representative has been assigned to an entity.

2. *Maximization:* We compute the parameter θ^{t+1} that maximizes $P(D^t|\theta)$. This amounts to learning the model parameters when we have training data. So we compute θ^{t+1} using the techniques described in Case 1 above.

3. *Expectation:* For each document $d \in D$, we compute (E_d^{t+1}, R_d^{t+1}) that maximizes $P(D^{t+1}|\theta^{t+1})$, where $D^{t+1} = \{(E_d^{t+1}, R_d^{t+1}, M_d)|d \in D\}$. This amounts to using the model

to match mentions, that is, assign mentions to representatives and entities, as described earlier.

4. *Convergence:* Exit if $P(D^t|\theta^t)$ does not increase; otherwise, repeat Steps 2–3.

We note that the above EM algorithm differs from the standard EM algorithm described in Figure 7.9(c) in that in Step 3 it finds the most likely E^d and R^d for each document d, rather than finding probability distributions over all possible E^d and R^d. Since the set of all entities and representatives can be large, finding and storing distributions over them would have been impractical in this case. Note also that once the algorithm terminates, it returns the assignments from mentions to representatives and from representatives to entities. This amounts to solving the mention matching problem.

Finally, we complete our description of the above EM algorithm by describing the initialization step. Given a document d, we compute E_d^0 and R_d^0 as follows. First, we treat each mention in d as a string, then use the soft TF/IDF string similarity measure (see Chapter 4) to cluster mentions into groups. Next, we select the longest mention in each group as a representative and create an entity (with the same full name) for the group. The sets of all representatives and entities so created become R_d^0 and E_d^0, respectively.

7.6 Collective Matching

The matching approaches that we have discussed so far make independent matching decisions. That is, they decide whether any two tuples a and b match *independently* of whether any two other tuples c and d match. In many real-world scenarios, however, matching decisions are intuitively *correlated*, and by exploiting such correlations we may be able to improve matching accuracy.

To illustrate, suppose we want to match the authors of the four papers listed in Figure 7.15(a). We may start by extracting their names and creating the table shown in Figure 7.15(b), where each tuple in the table lists the first name, middle name, and last name of an author. We can apply one of the methods described so far to match the tuples. However, by doing so we cannot exploit the coauthor relationships that are present in the data, because such relationships are not captured in the table.

To see the potential benefits of such relationships for the matching process, consider Figure 7.15(c). The figure visually depicts the input data as a hypergraph, whose nodes specify the authors, and whose hyperedges connect the coauthors. Suppose we have determined that nodes $a_3 : A.\ Ansari$ and $a_5 : A.\ Ansari$ match, then intuitively that should boost the likelihood that nodes $a_1 : W.\ Wang$ and $a_4 : W.\ Wang$ match, as they share the same name and same coauthor relationship to the same author.

A simple way to exploit the extra information is to add an attribute called *coAuthors* to the tuples in Table 7.15(b). For example, tuple a_1 would have *coAuthors* = {*C. Chen,A. Ansari*}; tuple a_4 (for author $W.\ Wang$ in the second paper) would have *coAuthors* = {*A. Ansari*}. We can then apply existing matching methods, but make sure that they take into account the similarity between the *coAuthors* attributes. For example, we

W. Wang, C. Chen, A. Ansari, A mouse immunity model
W. Wang, A. Ansari, Evaluating immunity models
L. Li, C. Chen, W. Wang, Measuring protein-bound fluxetine
W. J. Wang, A. Ansari, Autoimmunity in biliary cirrhosis

(a)

	First initial	Middle inititial	Last name
a_1	W		Wang
a_2	C		Chen
...	...	...	...
a_9	W	J	Wang
a_{10}	A		Ansari

(b)

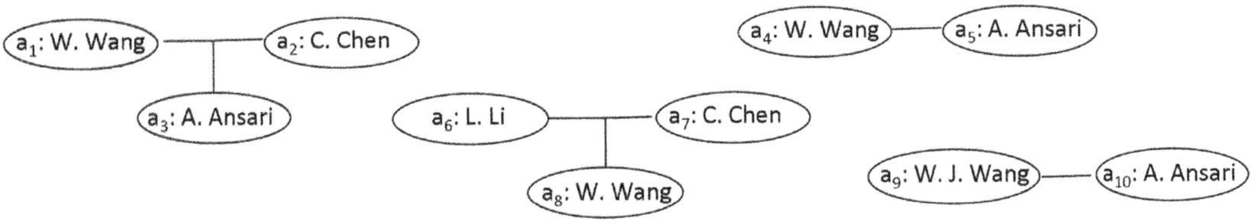

(c)

FIGURE 7.15 (a) Four publications that contain a set of author mentions that we want to match, (b) converting the mentions into relational tuples, (c) viewing the mentions as nodes in a hypergraph, whose hyperedges denote coauthor relationships among the mentions.

can compute a Jaccard similarity score between these attributes. Given $coAuthors(a_1) = \{C.\ Chen, A.\ Ansari\}$ and $coAuthors(a_4) = \{A.\ Ansari\}$, we have

$$JaccardSim_{coAuthors}(a_1, a_4) = \frac{|coAuthors(a_1) \cap coAuthors(a_4)|}{|coAuthors(a_1) \cup coAuthors(a_4)|}$$

$$= 1/2 \qquad (7.9)$$

This solution, however, can be misleading. Suppose authors $a_3 : A.\ Ansari$ and $a_5 : A.\ Ansari$ share the same name but do not match. In this case the above solution would still assume they match. That is, it still assumes the strings *A. Ansari* in $coAuthors(a_1)$ and $coAuthors(a_4)$ refer to the same author. Thus, it would incorrectly "boost" the similarity score between $a_1 : W.\ Wang$ and $a_4 : W.\ Wang$. In a sense, the source of the problem is that by treating the coauthors as a feature, string equality is already taken as a matching decision.

To avoid this problem, we want to conduct several matching decisions in parallel. Intuitively, we want to match $a_3 : A.\ Ansari$ and $a_5 : A.\ Ansari$, then use that information to help match $a_1 : W.\ Wang$ and $a_4 : W.\ Wang$. But, of course, we also want the opposite, namely, match a_1 and a_4, then use that information to help match a_3 and a_5. This suggests that we may want to match tuples in a *collective* fashion, all at once and iteratively, so that we can leverage the correlations across matching decisions to improve the overall matching accuracy. In what follows we describe two approaches that are based on this intuition. The first approach employs clustering to match tuples, and the second approach extends the probabilistic generative model of Section 7.5.4 to collectively match entity mentions in text documents.

7.6.1 Collective Matching Based on Clustering

We assume that our input is a graph whose nodes specify tuples to be matched and whose edges specify relationships among the tuples. Figure 7.15(c) shows such an input graph, with the edges depicting the coauthor relationship among the nodes. For ease of exposition, we will consider just one type of relationship here, but the approach can be generalized to work with multiple types of relationships.

To match the tuples, we perform agglomerative hierarchical clustering (AHC), exactly as described in Section 7.4, except that here we modify the similarity measure to take into account the correlations among the tuples. Specifically, let A and B be two clusters of nodes. Then we define

$$sim(A, B) = \alpha \cdot sim_{attributes}(A, B) + (1 - \alpha) \cdot sim_{neighbors}(A, B)$$

where α is a predefined coefficient. The measure $sim_{attributes}(A, B)$ computes a similarity score between A and B based only on the attributes of the nodes in A and B. Section 7.4 discusses several such scores, such as *single link, complete link*, and *average link*.

The measure $sim_{neighbors}(A, B)$ computes a similarity score between the neighborhood of A and B. Recall that we assume a single relationship R on the edges of the input graph. We define $\mathcal{N}(A)$, the neighborhood of A, to be the bag of the cluster IDs of all nodes that are in the relationship R with some node in A. For example, suppose cluster A has two nodes a and a', and suppose a is in the coauthor relationship with a node b with cluster ID 3, and that a' is in the coauthor relationship with a node b' with cluster ID 3 and another node b'' with cluster ID 5. Then $\mathcal{N}(A) = \{3, 3, 5\}$. We define $\mathcal{N}(B)$ similarly. Now we can define $sim_{neighbors}(A, B)$ using $\mathcal{N}(A)$ and $\mathcal{N}(B)$, such as

$$sim_{neighbors}(A, B) = JaccardSim(\mathcal{N}(A), \mathcal{N}(B)) = \frac{|\mathcal{N}(A) \cap \mathcal{N}(B)|}{|\mathcal{N}(A) \cup \mathcal{N}(B)|} \tag{7.10}$$

Contrast the above equation with Equation 7.9. Both equations define Jaccard similarity measures over the "neighborhoods." However, Equation 7.9 exploits only the "strings" in the neighborhoods, whereas the above equation exploits the matching decisions in the neighborhoods. More specifically, Equation 7.10 is based on similarity of cluster IDs, which encode matching decisions because two tuples that share the same cluster ID must match.

Note that in Equation 7.10 we can replace the Jaccard measure with whatever similarity measure deemed appropriate for the problem at hand (see Section 7.7.2 for other similarity functions that compare neighborhoods). Note also that the notion $\mathcal{N}(A)$ as defined above technically covers only the "neighhood of radius 1" of A. We can also define higher order neighborhoods and incorporate them into the definition of $sim_{neighbors}(A, B)$.

Figure 7.16 illustrates how AHC works on the input graph in Figure 7.15(c). Initially, we place each node into a singleton cluster, resulting in ten clusters $c_1 - c_{10}$ shown in

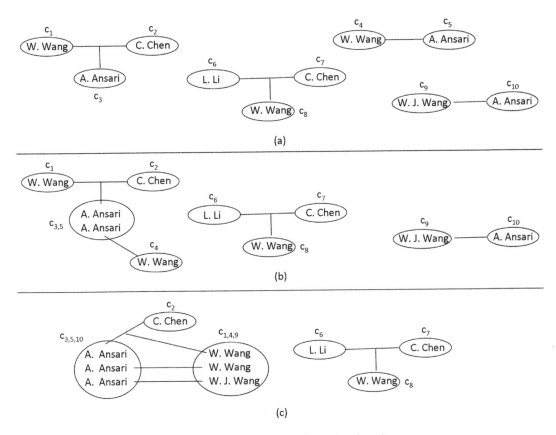

FIGURE 7.16 An example of collectively matching author mentions using clustering.

Figure 7.16(a). Next, we compute cluster similarities and merge the two most similar clusters, c_3 and c_5, into cluster $c_{3,5}$ in Figure 7.16(b). Next, we recompute cluster similarities. In computing the similarities for cluster $c_{3,5}$, we will have to compute $\mathcal{N}(c_{3,5})$, its neighborhood, which is $\{c_1, c_2, c_4\}$, according to Figure 7.16(b). Then we merge the two most similar clusters, and so on. Figure 7.16(c) shows the final clusters.

7.6.2 Collectively Matching Entity Mentions in Documents

In Section 7.5.4 we considered the problem of matching entity mentions in text documents. There, our solution employs a probabilistic generative model. Given a document d, the model selects a set of entities, generates representatives and mentions, then sprinkles the mentions into d.

An important limitation of that model is that it selects the entities of d *independently*: each entity e according to a probability $P(e)$ that does not depend on any other entities.

This independence assumption often does not hold in practice. For example, a document that mentions Michael Jordan and the basketball team Chicago Bulls is more likely to mention the Los Angeles Lakers, another basketball team, than the Los Angeles Philharmonic. Thus, there are often correlations among the entities, and a collective approach that finds and exploits these correlations can help improve matching accuracy.

We now describe a collective matching approach that extends the approach in Section 7.5.4 in a relatively simple fashion. The basic idea is to select entities sequentially, with the probability of selecting an entity depending on which entities have been selected so far. Specifically, given a document d, suppose we have selected the entities $E_d^{i-1} = \{e_1, \ldots, e_{i-1}\}$. Then next we will select entity e_i with the probability $P(e_i|E_d^{i-1})$. We now consider how this new "twist" changes the approach in Section 7.5.4.

We first must learn the model. Let us first consider the case in which we have training data. Let E be the set of all entities that appear in the training data. Instead of learning $P(e)$ for each $e \in E$, as before, now we would have to learn $P(e|S)$, for each $S \subseteq E$. However, when $|E|$ is large we would have to learn too many probabilities, and for many of them we would not have sufficient training data.

We could reduce the number of probabilities we compute by approximating $P(e|S)$ as $\max_{s \in S, s \neq e} P(e|s)$. In this case we still have to learn $|E|^2$ probabilities, possibly a huge number in practice. Consequently, we further approximate $P(e|s)$ as 1 if e and s co-occur in any document in the training data, and as $P(e)$ otherwise. We can now modify the counting procedure in Section 7.5.4 in a relatively straightforward fashion to learn $P(e|s)$ for all e and s in E.

Once we have learned the model, we use it to match mentions. Consider the problem of matching a set of mentions M_d in a new document d. In Section 7.5.4 we cast this problem as finding a set of entities E_d and a set of representatives R_d that maximize $P(E_d)P(R_d|E_d)P(M_d|R_d)$ (see Equation 7.8). To do this, we first find R_d directly, by sequentially clustering the mentions M_d, and then we find E_d that maximizes $P(E_d)P(R_d|E_d)$. Since the entities in E_d are probabilistically independent, this amounts to finding for each $r \in R_d$ the entity e that maximizes $P(e)P(r|e)$, a computationally tractable step.

In the new setting of collective matching, we still seek to find E_d that maximizes $P(E_d)P(R_d|E_d)$. Unfortunately, now the entities in E_d are correlated. So we cannot maximize $P(E_d)P(R_d|E_d)$ by maximizing $P(e)P(r|e)$ for each $r \in R_d$ in isolation, as described above. On the other hand, maximizing $P(E_d)P(R_d|E_d)$ by explicitly enumerating all possible values of E_d would be practically infeasible. Thus, we approximate this step by considering only a relatively small set of promising values for E_d. Specifically, for each $r \in R_d$ we find the top k entities that maximize $P(e)P(r|e)$ (where k is prespecified). Then we consider only those values for E_d that come from the Cartesian product of these top k lists.

In the case where we do not have the training data, we use the EM algorithm as described earlier, except that whenever we have to learn the model and use the model to match mentions, we use the modified algorithm we just described.

7.7 Scaling Up Data Matching

We now turn to the question of how to scale up the approaches to data matching that we described.

7.7.1 Scaling Up Rule-Based Matching

The key challenges in scaling rule-based matching are minimizing the number of tuple pairs to be matched and minimizing the time it takes to match each pair. We describe several techniques to address the first challenge.

Hashing: We scan and hash the tuples into "buckets," then match only tuples within each bucket. This technique works well if the hashing function spreads the tuples over a large number of buckets such that tuples in different buckets are unlikely to match. For example, suppose we are matching house listings that come from multiple real-estate Web sources, but we are confident that the zip codes are correct. In that case, we can hash the listings by zip code and match houses within each bucket to remove duplicate listings.

Sorting: We use a key to sort the tuples, then scan the sorted list and match each tuple with only the previous $(w - 1)$ tuples, where w is a prespecified "window size." The key should be strongly *discriminative*, in that using it to sort "brings together" tuples that are likely to match and "pushes apart" tuples that are not likely to match. Example keys include social security numbers, student IDs, last names, and the Soundex value of last names. Sorting clearly employs a stronger heuristic than hashing in that it also requires that tuples that are likely to match must be within a "window" of size w of one another. When this heuristic holds, however, sorting is often faster than hashing because it would match fewer tuple pairs.

Indexing: We index the tuples such that given any tuple a, we can use the index to quickly locate a relatively small set of tuples that are likely to match a. For example, suppose we have built an inverted index on names. Then, given tuple a with the name "Michael Jordan," we can look up the index to find all tuples whose names contain "Michael" and all tuples whose names contain "Jordan." We then match a with only tuples in the union of these two sets, using the heuristic that if two tuples match, their names must share at least one term.

Canopies: We use a computationally cheap similarity measure to quickly group tuples into overlapping clusters called *canopies* (or *umbrella sets*). We then use a different (and typically far more expensive) similarity measure to match tuples within each canopy. For example, if two strings differ by at least 3 in length, then their edit distance cannot be smaller than 3. Thus, we can use length comparison to quickly group tuples into canopies, then use the more expensive edit distance measure to match tuples within each canopy. As another example, we can use the TF/IDF measure to create canopies, then use more expensive similarity measures to match tuples within each canopy. Note that unlike buckets in the hash technique that are disjoint, here the canopies can overlap, and often do.

Using representatives: This technique is applied during the matching process. We assign tuples that have been matched into groups such that tuples within a group match and tuples across groups do not match. Next, we create a representative for each group, either by selecting a tuple in the group, or by "merging" tuples in the groups. When we consider a new tuple a, we only try to match it with the representatives of the groups. The rationale is that if a does not match a representative r, then it is unlikely to match any tuple in the group that contains r. A variation of this technique is often used to match Web-scale data, as we describe later in this section.

Combining the techniques: Each of the techniques we described above uses a heuristic to "bring together" candidate tuple pairs, then match only those. However, using just a single heuristic runs the risk of missing tuple pairs that should be matched but are not. For example, if we only hash and match houses based on their zip codes, then we may miss houses that match but happen to have different zip codes due to spelling mistakes (e.g., 53705 versus 53750). To minimize this risk, we can conduct multiple runs, each of which uses a different heuristic. For example, in addition to hashing house listings based on zip code, we may also hash separately based on agent name, relying on the heuristic that each house is typically represented by just one agent. The final set of matching tuples is then the union of the results of all runs.

The above techniques can be also combined in flexible ways, based on the nature of the data set. For example, we may hash houses into buckets using zip codes, then sort houses within each bucket using street names, before matching them using a sliding window. As another example, we can use hashing, sorting, or indexing to speed up the application of the cheap similarity measure in the canopy technique.

Once we have minimized the number of tuple pairs to be matched, we must minimize the time it takes to match each pair. If we use a simple rule-based approach, such as matching individual attributes then combining their scores using weights, as described in Equation 7.1, then we can use the technique of "short circuiting" the matching process: we stop the computation of the similarity score if it is already so low that the tuple pair cannot match, even if all the remaining attributes match perfectly. We discuss other optimization methods in Section 7.7.2.

7.7.2 Scaling Up Other Matching Methods

Learning, clustering, and probabilistic approaches to data matching face similar scalability challenges to rule-based approaches and can benefit from the techniques described above. Collective matching algorithms incorporate many aspects of the above matching approaches, and hence often benefit from the scalability techniques we have just described.

Probabilistic approaches, however, raise additional scalability challenges. In particular, if a probabilistic model has too many parameters, then it is difficult to learn it efficiently, and we would also need a large number of training data to learn it accurately. One approach to scale probabilistic matching methods is to make independence assumptions to reduce the number of parameters (as illustrated in Sections 7.5.2–7.5.4). Of course, such assumptions may affect matching accuracy, and the trade-offs must be evaluated carefully on a case-by-case basis. Once the model is learned, inference with the model can also often be very time consuming. One could use approximate inference algorithms or simplify the model so that these probabilities can be computed using closed form equations (e.g., see the naive Bayesian approach in Section 7.5.2). When no training data is available, we have to use unsupervised approaches such as the EM algorithm described in Section 7.5.1, which can be expensive. To address this problem, we can "truncate" the EM algorithm by computing only the maximum-likelihood probabilities instead of the entire expected distributions (see Section 7.5.4) and by initializing the EM algorithm as accurately as possible, to "encourage" faster convergence.

Finally, we note that large-scale data matching often employs parallel processing. For example, we can hash the tuples into buckets, then match within each bucket in parallel. As another example, Web-scale applications often match tuples against a taxonomy of entities (e.g., a product or Wikipedia-like concept taxonomy), in a parallel fashion. Two tuples are then declared matched if they get assigned to the same taxonomic node. The taxonomy is typically maintained semi-automatically. Matching against a taxonomy is a variant of the approach of using representatives described earlier in this section.

Bibliographic Notes

Data matching has had a long history, dating back to the late 1950s (see [143, 205, 248, 351, 353, 453, 573] for recent books, surveys, and tutorials). In 1959 Newcombe et al. [458] introduced the record linkage problem and suggested many matching ideas: use of Soundex to handle spelling errors, blocking to reduce the number of tuple comparisons, multiple blocking rules to increase the number of matches found, and estimating match probabilities using independence assumptions. This is perhaps the first well-known work in data matching.

In 1969 Fellegi and Sunter followed up the above work with an influential theory of record linkage [224]. Among others, the theory introduces what is roughly the naive Bayesian matching model described in Section 7.5.2. Later, Winkler et al. [572, 574, 575] extended the model in substantial ways to capture additional domain knowledge and proposed using the EM algorithm to learn the model.

These early works originated from the statistics community. Starting in the 1980s, however, data matching also received increasing attention in the database, data mining, and AI communities. Initial approaches assumed tuples that represent the same entity in different databases share a common key (e.g., the Multi-Base project by Dayal [165], [168]). The Pegasus project [19] asked the users to specify the equivalence among object instances (e.g., as a table that maps local object IDs to global object IDs). Monge and Elkan [443] proposed matching whole tuples as strings, using a variant of the Smith-Waterman string similarity measure (see Chapter 4). Dey et al. employed linearly weighted and logistic regression rules to match tuples [175, 176]. Hernandez and Stolfo [300, 301] described a rule-based approach that sorts and matches the tuples using a sliding window. Other works that employ handcrafted rules include [119, 390, 484, 564]. Lawrence, Giles, and Bollacker [249] in particular described handcrafting rules to match citations in the well-known Citeseer system. See Tejada, Knoblock, and Minton [545] for further discussion of rule-based approaches.

Learning matching rules from training data using methods such as decision tree, naive Bayes, and support vector machines (SVMs) was considered in Tejada, Knoblock, and Minton [545] and Sarawagi and Bhamidipaty [507]. Bilenko and Mooney [85, 86] used small corpora of hand-labeled examples to learn appropriate string similarity measures for each attribute pair, then applied SVMs to learn how to combine these measures. Other learning approaches include [141, 243, 479].

McCallum, Nigam, and Ungar [418] described an agglomerative hierarchical clustering approach to data matching and introduced the idea of applying a cheap similarity measure to quickly group tuples into overlapping clusters called canopies. Cohen and Richman [144] show how to make generic clustering methods adaptive to the problem at hand using training.

Probabilistic approaches (which dated back to the work of Newcombe, Fellegi, Sunter, and others, as described above) saw a resurgence in the mid-1990s, and have since become quite popular. Koller and Friedman [348] cover in detail graphical probabilistic models, including Bayesian networks, variables with continuous values, and the EM algorithm. The two matching approaches that use Bayesian networks in Sections 7.5.2–7.5.3 come from Ravikumar and Cohen [494] (which also discusses the case of variables with continuous values), while the generative model for matching entity mentions in text in Section 7.5.4 builds on the work of Li, Morie, and Roth [385, 386]. Generative models encode *full* probability distributions, and learning such models often means learning a large number of probabilities. This is difficult and often requires a large amount of training data. Consequently, recent work (e.g., [156, 416, 524]) has explored using *discriminative models* such as conditional random fields (CRF) [363], which encode only the probabilities that are necessary for matching (e.g., the probability of a label given a tuple pair), and try to learn them directly from the data.

Collective approaches to data matching emerged in the early 2000s. The rule-based approach described in Section 7.6.1 comes from Bhattacharya and Getoor [82]. Other rule-based collective approaches include the Semex system by Dong and Halevy [188], work by Ananthakrishna, Chaudhuri, and Ganti [31], and by Kalashnikov, Mehrotra, and Chen [338]. Probabilistic collective matching approaches include Pasula et al. [475], Li, Morie, and Roth [385], McCallum and Culotta [156], Singla and Domingos [524], and Bhattacharya and Getoor [81].

Several works have considered matching data in nonrelational formats. The Semex system [188] matches entities in personal information management settings, where attributes are frequently missing. The work [485, 567] matches entities represented as complex XML elements. Li, Morie, and Roth [385, 386] match entity mentions in text documents, as described in Section 7.5.4.

It is often the case that different parts of the data have different degrees of heterogeneity and hence may require different matching methods. Consequently, a matching workflow may employ multiple matchers, each for a different part of the data. Papers that consider this idea include [170, 520]. The work [182, 546] shows that even matching the same part of the data also benefits from using multiple matchers, each exploiting a different heuristic.

Work that exploits domain constraints to improve matching accuracy includes [126, 521]. Work that discusses active learning for data matching includes [35, 507]. Bhattacharya and Getoor [83] discuss data matching at run-time. Several works have considered data matching in the context of data cleaning, data matching operators, and declarative data matching languages [66, 100, 124, 491, 584]. The important challenges of distributed processing, secondary storage, negative information, evolving matching rules, and pay-as-you-go data matching are discussed in the SERF project [65, 66, 568].

8

Query Processing

One might assume that query processing in a data integration system differs little from query processing in a traditional DBMS. After all, the query language (whether SQL, datalog, or XQuery) is based on standard relational (or extended relational) operations. Its goal remains to find an *efficient* executable plan for the query. While data integration queries often process distributed data, even this problem has been studied in the context of distributed and federated database systems. Despite these cursory similarities, data integration actually offers a number of challenges that require novel solutions.

◾ ◾ ◾ ━━

Example 8.1

To ground this discussion, let us consider, as the central example in this chapter, a query to look for well-reviewed movies with one of the more prolific actors of our time, Morgan Freeman.

```
SELECT title, startTime
FROM Movie M, Plays P, Reviews R
WHERE M.title = P.movie AND M.title = R.movie AND
    P.location="New York" AND M.actor="Morgan Freeman"
    AND R.avgStars >= 3
```

━━━ ◾ ◾ ◾

As we execute this query in a data integration context, we may run into a number of challenges that would not emerge in a traditional DBMS setting.

SOURCE QUERY CAPABILITIES AND LIMITED DATA STATISTICS

DBMS performance is enabled by accurate cost estimation, which ultimately means that the DBMS cost estimator needs to have a good model of I/O and processing rates. Even in a distributed or federated architecture, we assume that the query optimizer can obtain good information from the individual sites. However, a data source in the integration scenario might not be a DBMS: it can range from text or HTML sources, to spreadsheets or XML, to a variety of repository formats, to a relational, hierarchical, or XML DBMS. Some of these sources might not have capabilities for keeping statistics on the data or estimating their own performance. As a result, query optimization in data integration may need to be done with no information. Moreover, some data sources might not be able to execute arbitrary full relational algebra expressions, meaning that the (global) query optimizer cannot naively assign portions of the query to each source. For our example, perhaps the Movies source provides direct access to an XML file (with no query processing capabilities) and the `Plays` source provides a forms-based interface that can perform certain selection operations.

INPUT BINDING RESTRICTIONS

Some data sources may need to be given input data in order to return results, as described in Section 3.3. For example, our `Plays` data source may not return all movie information, but only information about movies playing based on movie and director. The `Reviews` site may need the name of a movie to return its reviews.

VARIABLE NETWORK CONNECTIVITY AND SOURCE PERFORMANCE

Especially over Web sources, network bandwidth and round-trip times may be highly variable. This makes it difficult to predict the access cost for each source and may even require failure handling capabilities. Moreover, the data source may itself be a query processor that is shared with other applications and requests, and its performance in returning results might vary even from one data-fetch request to the next.

NEED FOR FAST INITIAL ANSWERS

Finally, many information integration applications have an interactive "flavor," and the goal is to optimize the creation of the first screenful of answers — as opposed to *all* of the answers, as a traditional DBMS emphasizes.

We discuss how each of these requirements impacts the design of a data integration query processor in this chapter. We first briefly review the basics of conventional DBMS query processing in Section 8.1, and then examine how such techniques have been extended to distributed databases in Section 8.2. A reader familiar with relational query engines may be able to skim at least the first of these two sections.

Once the stage has been set, we present the basic architecture of a data integration query processor in Section 8.3, which incorporates query optimization and execution in an *adaptive loop*. This loop consists of several stages. Section 8.4 describes how the initial query plan gets created. Then Section 8.5 presents the query execution runtime system, which is significantly more complex than a conventional engine. The runtime system participates in *adaptive query processing*, described in Section 8.6, which we divide into two main classes: *event-driven adaptivity* (Section 8.7) and *performance-driven adaptivity* (Section 8.8).

8.1 Background: DBMS Query Processing

To understand query processing in data integration, it is useful first to review the architecture and the basic techniques used in a standard DBMS.

An architectural diagram of a basic DBMS query processor is shown in Figure 8.1. A query in SQL is first **parsed** and converted into an *abstract syntax tree* or a conceptual representation. Then, if the query is posed over (virtual) views whose definition is stored in the system catalog it gets **unfolded** and possibly simplified, forming a *logical*

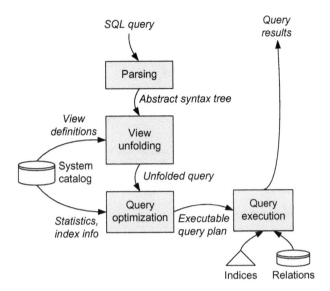

FIGURE 8.1 Modules in a conventional query processor.

query plan. Next, the unfolded query is sent to the **query optimizer**, which consults *statistics* and *index information* from the system catalog in order to choose an *executable query plan* that is predicted to perform well. This plan is fed to the **query execution engine**, which accesses indices and the relation contents, performs a series of operations over this data, and returns query results.

8.1.1 Choosing a Query Execution Plan

Traditional query optimization in a DBMS is based on several fundamental assumptions. First, costs are predictable: we can estimate the number of disk I/Os required to load a table or index, and the access costs are fixed; we can also estimate CPU performance adequately. Second, once data are loaded off disk, pipelined query processing is CPU-bound: the internal implementations of query operators are "tight loops" that have been heavily tuned, and the assumption is that the CPU will be fully occupied in executing them.

Consider how to optimize our movie example from earlier in this chapter. The first step will be to take the query and *unfold* any views — if `Movie`, `Plays`, or `Reviews` were views rather than base relations, their definitions would be expanded. A *query unfolding* stage would create a single logical expression representing the query over the outputs of the views. Then, in some systems, a *query rewrite* stage might attempt to unnest or decorrelate the query expression, such that there is a single select-project-join (SPJ) expression over a series of base tables, rather than an SPJ expression over the output of another SPJ expression.

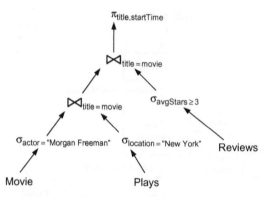

FIGURE 8.2   Example logical query plan for Example 8.1.

In our example, there are no view definitions and hence the logical expression is a single SPJ expression, namely, the simple plan shown in Figure 8.2. This SPJ expression is run through a *cost-based optimizer* that seeks to find the most efficient combination of *physical operators* to produce the expression's output. Cost-based optimization can be divided into two main problems.

Enumeration ("Search")

Plan enumeration iterates over physical query plans equivalent to the original logical plan and estimates their cost. Virtually all optimizers use a combination of *pruning heuristics* to reduce the search space over certain plans that are unlikely to yield good results, plus *exhaustive enumeration* for the remainder of the query plan space.

Modern database optimizers still have options to employ the pruning heuristics used in the original (System R) cost-based query optimizer: searching *left-linear* plans (plans in which every join can only have join expressions on its left input) and only considering cross-products when all join predicates have been evaluated. Within the pruned search space, these optimizers will enumerate all potential join orderings, as well as the different indices available and the different join algorithms.

Optimizers build upon one of the major breakthroughs in the 1970s: the observation that, under certain conditions, query execution costs follow the *principle of optimality*. In general, the optimal join query plan for, say, a 3-way join must make use of the optimal join query plan for a 2-way join. This led to the use of *dynamic programming* when enumerating n-way join plans:

- First (base case), the various access methods to each of the base tables are considered, with selection conditions and projections evaluated as early as possible.
- Next (recursive case), starting with $i = 2$ and increasing to n, possible joins of i relations are considered, by combining optimal $(i - 1)$-way join expressions with one additional relation. For each such combination, the most efficient i-way physical plan

is recorded in a dynamic programming table. Again, selection and projection operations, if applicable to the *i*-way join, are applied.

- Once all joins have been computed, similar enumeration is done over cross-products.
- Finally, any remaining grouping and aggregation operations (GROUP BY) and post-aggregation selection conditions (HAVING) are applied.

A variant of the above strategy is to use *top-down* exploration (recursion with memoization) of the same search space. Here, we start with a complete query expression, consider each potential way of decomposing it into substeps (e.g., by finding the different subexpressions that can be joined), and for each such case, we make a recursive call to enumerate each of the subexpressions. Each call will memoize the plan determined to have the lowest cost, such that repeated calls with the same subexpression simply return the memoized results. Recall from your study of algorithms that recursion with memoization and dynamic programming are equivalent. The advantage of the top-down approach is that it enables more possibilities in pruning.

INTERESTING ORDERS

The above strategy ignores the fact that certain operations — sorts (and, as we will discuss later, data shipment across a network) — can be costly but have benefits that are amortized across multiple subsequent operations.

For instance, suppose that `Plays` and `Reviews` returned data sorted by movie title. Then if we were to sort the `Movie` relation by title, we could use the merge join algorithm to perform both joins within the query. Perhaps the sort of the `Movie` relation costs too much to break even with the benefits of doing a merge join with `Plays`. But once we consider the benefits of doing a *second* merge join (with `Reviews`), it is possible that the sort is a good idea after all!

Unfortunately, our dynamic programming strategy as outlined above will not consider this scenario: it will find that the optimal plan for joining `Movie` with `Plays` is *not* to sort and then do a merge join; hence it will discard this plan alternative for the 2-way join. When the 3-way `Movie-Plays-Reviews` join is considered, it will only make use of the 2-way joins in the dynamic programming table.

What is the solution? In essence, we must expand the dynamic programming (or memoization) table to consider sort orders as special cases. The query optimizer first goes over the query to find all potentially useful sort orderings (*interesting orderings*) that might be exploited by join algorithms, the ORDER BY clause, and the GROUP BY clause. In our example, the interesting ordering is on the movie title (called `title` for `Movie` and `movie` for `Plays` and `Reviews`). At each step in plan enumeration, the optimizer will record an entry for the optimal subexpression *for each ordering* (adding a sort operation if necessary to create this ordering) and *independent of ordering*. At the end of the day, the optimizer chooses the cheapest among the different orderings and the order-independent plan (unless, of course, the query had a final ORDER BY clause, in which case it will choose the appropriately ordered plan).

Cost and Cardinality Estimation

Cost and cardinality estimation are closely related: for each algorithm, the query optimizer has a *cost formula* (generally posed in terms of time units) that captures how expensive it is to evaluate a given operation, given its expected input and output sizes. For instance, the cost formula may consider how many disk pages need to be retrieved for a given size of a relation, or how many times a hash function needs to be invoked to look items up in a hash table. (The cost formula usually also has a series of *calibration parameters* that are set during DBMS configuration, to match the speed of the current hardware on which the DBMS is operating.)

Cardinality estimation relies on information gathered by the DBMS offline (and periodically refreshed). The query optimizer can typically look up the cardinality of every base relation (from the system catalog and/or the existing indices), and for indexed attributes, it also can determine the minimum and maximum values. Additionally, the DBMS "tuning wizard" or human administrator may have created *data distribution* information — typically histograms and the number of unique values — over some of the attributes in the tables. Finally, the DBMS integrity constraints (particularly key, unique, and foreign key constraints) may allow the system to infer information about the distributions of certain attribute values.

Based on this information, the query optimizer can attempt to estimate how many values satisfy a selection predicate (by determining which histogram buckets, and subsets thereof, are likely to satisfy the predicate) or a join condition (by intersecting histograms). When multiple predicates exist within a query, the optimizer must typically make simplifying assumptions, e.g., that attributes are independent. In practice, the optimizer's assumptions typically are fairly error prone but the hope is that they at least ensure the optimizer will not choose exceptionally bad plans.

8.1.2 Executing a Query Plan

The execution engine takes the physical plan, which specifies a series of algorithms to apply, and performs the desired operations over the source relations. Here there are several options with respect to *granularity of processing* and *control flow*. We discuss each of these, and their design goals, next.

Granularity of Processing

When we learn the relational algebra, we tend to think of the query operations (select, project, join, etc.) as atomic operations that take in relations and produce relations. In reality, this is seldom the way a query execution engine will do the computation, for two main reasons. First, the intermediate relation produced by each operator can be larger than memory, and it may be quite expensive to buffer this intermediate table and spool it to (and then from) disk. Perhaps more importantly, we might want multiple operations in the query plan to execute *in parallel*, to reduce the latency to the first query answer.

Hence, most query engines support *pipelining* during query processing. Each operator reads enough input tuples to produce a single output tuple. Then it passes this to the next stage (its parent operator in the query evaluation plan). This process repeats as operators successfully produce output. If that operator is able to produce an output tuple, it passes this to *its* parent operator, and so forth. (We discuss control flow among the operators next.)

Of course, it is not always feasible to pipeline all of the operators in a query plan. First, many operators (particularly some join, grouping, and sort implementations) require significant memory, to buffer all of the input tuples they have encountered. There may not be enough memory to give to all of the operators at the same time. Second, some operators (e.g., sorting, grouping over a nonsorted attribute) are naturally *blocking*: they cannot begin producing output data until they have "seen" their input in its entirety. Finally, sometimes the query optimizer decides it is advantageous to compute and save an intermediate result (e.g., to share it across multiple subexpressions or queries). In all of these cases, a *materialization point* appears in the query plan: the intermediate relation at this point is computed, buffered, and, if necessary, saved to disk.

■ ■ ■

Example 8.2

The query plan of Figure 8.3 contains a hash join operation (HJoin), which is a *partly blocking* operator. Hash join consists of two stages: a *build* stage, in which one of its inputs (in our example, the right relation, Reviews) is read into a hash table; then the *probe* stage, in which input tuples are pipelined from the left input, joined against the contents of the hash table, and output to the next pipeline stage. The build stage blocks execution of the remainder of the plan until its input has been consumed; the probe stage is fully pipelined.

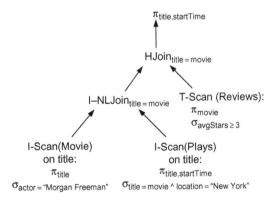

FIGURE 8.3 Example executable (physical) query plan corresponding to Figure 8.2, where **I-Scan** represents an index scan, **T-Scan** represents a table scan, **I-NLJoin** represents an index nested loops join, and **HJoin** represents a hash join.

The materialization point marks the highest point in the query plan where tuples will have been received: the operators above the materialization point will only receive input tuples once the materialized result has been fully computed. Thus one can think of a materialization point as a "barrier" dividing one stage of query processing (where all operators are working in the same pipeline) from the next.

Control Flow

There are a variety of methods by which the query operator algorithms can be scheduled. At one extreme, one could simply place each operator in its own thread (or on a separate processor), and operators could send tuples to one another through queues. At the other extreme, there could be a single execution thread, which carefully controls when each operator gets cycles.

On a single machine, the traditional DBMS architecture more closely resembles the latter: it uses a top-down *iterator*-based architecture, in which each operator calls its child operators to retrieve a tuple at a time, then performs operations over such tuples, and returns the results to its parent operator(s) or to the query output buffer. The iterator model has key advantages in a CPU-bound setting: it eliminates the overhead of context switching among threads, and it generally obviates the need for copying data items into and out of queues.

In distributed and parallel DBMS settings (which we discuss further in the next section), query processing is often I/O-bound: many I/O operations may be occurring simultaneously, and the goal is to free the CPU to work on data values as they come in. For these architectures, the *dataflow* or bottom-up architecture is popular. Here, there may be many query operator threads, each of which is event-driven. As an input tuple becomes available, it is fed to the query operator thread, which consumes it, processes it, and outputs it to some other thread's input queue.

In recent years, hybrid architectures have been extensively studied. Rather than propagating tuples one at a time in the pipelined model, various systems attempt to propagate and operate on *batches* of tuples: this has advantages in terms of cache behavior and CPU scheduling. Additionally, hybrid schemes combining the iterator model with a limited number of threads (e.g., for data prefetching) have been employed for handling external data.

8.2 Background: Distributed Query Processing

Of course, conventional databases were not solely limited to single server settings; distributed DBMSs have been studied for many years. We will highlight here some of the key innovations required to move to the distributed context, as each of these innovations came to influence work in the data integration realm.

PARALLEL VS. DISTRIBUTED DBMSs

On first impression, parallel and distributed DBMSs seem quite similar: both involve taking multiple compute and data storage nodes and coordinating the various machines in order to handle queries. However, the basic assumptions and approaches used to address these two problem spaces are quite different. In parallel DBMSs the nodes are typically assumed to be homogeneous and connected to a global storage system by a fast network. The main goal is to partition the data across machines and run the same operations in parallel across many machines, such that load is balanced and high speedups are achieved. In distributed DBMSs, different machines may have very different performance characteristics, network performance is likely to be slower and may vary widely across the system, and some data sources may only be accessible from certain machines. The challenge is to determine *which operations* should be executed on *which machines*, in order to optimize for performance. We shall focus our discussion on this latter case.

8.2.1 Data Placement and Shipment

In general, the administrator of a distributed DBMS must consider the problem of *data placement*: how to lay out data across a set of distributed machines. There are a variety of options: data may be partitioned by *relations*, such that certain tables are on one machine and others are on a different machine; by *horizontal partitioning*, meaning that different rows from the same table are placed on different machines; or by *vertical partitioning*, meaning that different columns from the same table are placed on different machines. Each has different performance ramifications: relation partitioning may allow different query subexpressions in the same plan to be computed in parallel on different machines; horizontal partitioning may allow the same query subexpression to be computed in parallel on different data located on different machines; vertical partitioning may allow for computing different query predicates in parallel on different machines. Of course, in addition to partitioning the data, one may also *replicate* and index it: this is likely to improve query performance, but increase the cost and other resources (space, possibly network bandwidth) required by updates.

Centralized DBMSs had one important property that greatly impacted performance: namely, the ordering (or lack thereof) of a query subresult. Distributed databases add a second such property, *location* (or, in the horizontally partitioned case, the set of locations). To compute a join or an aggregate, all data with the same (join or grouping) key must be co-located on the same query processing node.

These requirements have led to two new physical-level query operators: *ship*, which takes the output of a query subexpression and routes it (perhaps using buffering and batching) to the input of a query plan on another node, and *exchange*, which runs across many horizontally partitioned data nodes in parallel and "exchanges" tuples among the set nodes according to a partitioning function over a key, until data with the same key is co-located. The partitioning of data with the exchange operator can, in principle, be done by dividing ranges across the machines, by hashing keys to machines, or by performing some sort of load balancing. A hash-based exchange scheme is sometimes called a *rehash* operation.

Of course, if we are introducing new physical-level query operators, we naturally need to estimate their costs in the query optimizer. Historically, this has proven to be surprisingly difficult in the real world, as performance on the Internet is often unpredictable. The cost of one link does not necessarily tell us much about the cost of other links (even links to closer sites!). Hence, early work on distributed query processing was primarily targeted at local area or enterprise networks, where costs were fairly uniform. Today, as bandwidth on the Internet has increased both on the backbone and at the end points, performance seems much more stable.

8.2.2 Joining in Two Phases

Given the ship (and possibly exchange) operators, one can build a complete distributed query processor that can execute SQL queries over data that are distributed across machines, even if they are partitioned. However, an efficiency issue arises: if we are given two tables, each located on a different machine, then computing the join is quite expensive. We must ship the entire contents of one table to the other machine (or both to a third machine) to do the computation. In many cases, a significant portion of the data may not even join; yet we still ship it.

This observation has led to work on computing distributed joins in two phases. Here, we ship a "summary" of the join keys for the first relation, R, to the second node. We use this to "prescreen" tuples from the second relation, S: those that appear to join with R (as determined by probing R's summary using the join keys from S) will be collected and sent back to the first node. The first node will then do the actual join of tuples from R and the subset of S it receives.

Using this scheme, we can often significantly reduce network bandwidth utilization, because R's summary is smaller than R itself, and we only transmit the subset of S that appears to join with R. Of course, the summary must satisfy certain properties if we are to use it: specifically, a probe against the summary must never have false negatives, i.e., if the values actually join, the probe must return **true**. Two such summaries have been considered in the literature.

TWO-WAY SEMIJOIN

The *2-way semijoin* operator makes use of the (set-semantics) projection of the join key attributes from R as its summary. The first node sends this collection to the second; when the second node probes against the collection, clearly there will be no false negatives (or false positives!). Thus, it will send back to the first node exactly the set of S tuples that join with R.

BLOOMJOIN

The 2-way semijoin can be expensive if the projection from R is large. The *Bloomjoin* reduces the size of the summary structure by instead using a *Bloom filter* of the join key attributes from R. A Bloom filter can return false positives but never false negatives. It is a bit vector V, accompanied by a set of m hash functions. Initially, all bits are set to zero. For each item x to be inserted into the Bloom filter, we set the bit at $V[h_i(x)]$ for each $1 \leq i \leq m$.

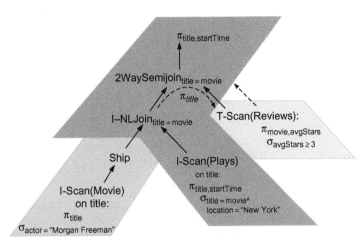

FIGURE 8.4 Example executable (physical) query plan corresponding to Figure 8.2, for query processing across three nodes. Note the use of the ship operator and the dataflow for the 2-way semijoin (indicated by dashed arrows and italicized text).

Later, we probe for an item x by computing $\bigwedge_{i=1}^{m} V[h_i(x)]$. Larger vectors, and larger values of m, result in fewer collisions (and thus fewer false positives).

Cost estimation for the 2-way semijoin and Bloomjoin is done by estimating the size of the summary of R sent in the first step, the size of S with which it joins, and the bandwidth and latency of the network. The end result is a query plan such as the one in Figure 8.4, which shows how data are shipped from the `Movie` node to the node with `Plays`. The `Plays` node also does a 2-way semijoin with the node holding `Reviews`, by sending the set of all titles and receiving the set of all reviews that match those titles. The `Plays` node does the final join and projection, returning results to the user.

8.3 Query Processing for Data Integration

At a very high level, the problem of executing queries in a data integration setting is a special case of the distributed query processing problem, in which distributed DBMS sites are replaced by distributed data sources. However, new challenges are posed by the fact that many of the data sources are located across the Internet and not simply an intranet, sources are *autonomous* and seldom designed to work in a cooperative setting, and information about source data is not readily available.

Figure 8.5 shows the overall query processing architecture that is followed by most data integration systems. As in a conventional DBMS, the first stage is query parsing. Then, rather than simply *unfolding* views, the data integration engine must *reformulate* queries using the schema mappings (see Chapter 2). Once the query has been reformulated, it needs to be optimized and executed — here, we see significant changes, not only within the optimizer and execution engine, but also in the fact that together they form a *loop* to interleave optimization and execution.

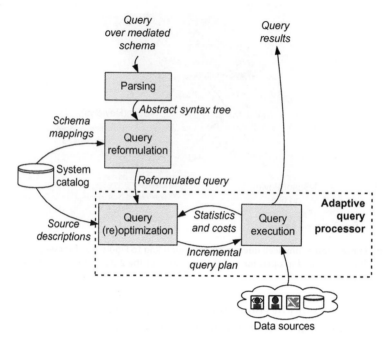

FIGURE 8.5 Modules in a data integration system.

The data sources to be integrated are generally controlled by external organizations (and, in fact, may not be DBMSs). This means that the data integration query processor must accommodate whatever interfaces a source provides to request and receive data. Simple sources may simply provide direct access to XML or HTML documents, from which the required data must be extracted. Other sources may provide a Web forms interface in which data can only be accessed by providing certain input parameters (see Section 3.3). Finally, some sources may in fact provide full SQL support (in some dialect of SQL). All of these constraints require careful treatment in the query optimizer (Section 8.4), as well as the development of custom *wrappers* that translate between a common query request/response format and those of individual sources (Chapter 9).

The fact that data integration occurs over the Internet has several ramifications. First, data transfer rates are more unpredictable, and both burstiness and limited bandwidth may be issues. Second, computation is much more likely to be I/O-bound, rather than CPU-bound, as in a local area network or a local query processor. Finally, in many Internet usage scenarios, we would like the *time to first tuple* to be low, and the output to be produced incrementally. These lead to a new style of query processing architecture and new query operators, as we discuss in Section 8.5.

Finally, in most data integration scenarios, too little information is readily available to make good optimization decisions at compile time. Actual network utilization, distributions of data at various sources, even the response times of given sources that may be serving many tasks concurrently — all of these are likely to deviate from any original estimates that a query optimizer is given as input. In fact, these characteristics might also change significantly during the execution of the query itself! Hence, as discussed in Section 8.6, for long-running queries it is important to use *adaptive* strategies during query processing, where the query plan may be adjusted in response to actual observed performance characteristics.

8.4 Generating Initial Query Plans

The problem of optimizing a data integration query can actually be extremely challenging if little information is available about costs and data distributions. However, in some settings (e.g., the corporate intranet), such information may be available. In any case, the query processor must begin somewhere, at least generating a partial query plan to start things off. Typically, this is done using a modified version of the traditional query optimizer model, with any available statistics (or ballpark estimates if statistics are unavailable).

A data integration query optimizer must deal with two restrictions that are not present in a traditional RDBMS. First, the presence of *input binding restrictions* will mean that certain query plans will become illegal, simply because they do not bind values for the input variables needed to access a particular source. Second, some data sources are capable of performing part of the query computation (e.g., they may support joins between relations supplied by the source): here it becomes essential that the optimizer be able to determine what is supported, and what cost and cardinality to expect.

The problem of reasoning about input binding restrictions is not tremendously different from what a traditional optimizer already needs to do. The optimizer already needs to reason about when certain physical or even logical plans are illegal (e.g., when input attributes to a predicate are unavailable, or when a Cartesian product is needed, but Cartesian products are only allowed *after* all join conditions are evaluated). However, it has been shown that input binding restrictions sometimes require *exhaustive* evaluation of all query plans ("bushy" enumeration) as opposed to the System-R heuristic of only using left-linear plans. Additionally, the input binding restrictions must be accommodated by using a *dependent join* operator (Section 8.5.2) rather than a more traditional join algorithm.

Optimizing a query with wrappers is somewhat more complex. The query optimizer must determine which operators are to be executed in the wrapper and which in the main query engine, and also the *cost* of the query subexpression being executed in the wrapper. This requires wrappers to have both a query execution component (the actual wrapper operator) and a query optimizer component (a plug-in module that does plan validation and cost estimation for the wrapper). The optimizer can associate with every operator a *property* specifying where the operator is to be executed (by the wrapper or the engine), and the wrapper's optimizer component will validate that a given query subexpression is actually executable within the wrapper. It will also give a cost estimate for the subexpression to be executed within the wrapper.

8.5 Query Execution for Internet Data

In the Internet setting, the CPU will often be waiting for new data to arrive before it can perform further computation. Moreover, burstiness, delays, and even failures are fairly commonplace. Additionally, a data integration engine must interface with a variety of external sources that support different protocols, and hence there is a need for special join methods that handle access pattern restrictions and wrappers that translate between a standardized request and response format and those of the specific sources.

8.5.1 Multithreaded, Pipelined, Dataflow Architecture

Data from external Internet sources often come at a relatively slow rate: this breaks the core assumption in most DBMS architectures (even those for local area networks), which is that query processing is primarily CPU-bound, and the goal is to have "tight loops" in the code that are carefully optimized. As discussed in Section 8.1.2, most conventional DBMSs use an iterator-based approach, in which the query execution algorithms in the plan determine how and when control is given to their child operators.

A data integration engine, on the other hand, typically uses a hybrid of iterator and dataflow-driven architectures: conceptually, each operator requests one data tuple at a time from its children, as in a conventional iterator model. However, the child operators may execute in threads independent from one another and from the parent (with whom they communicate via queues). Now, if one of the child operators is blocked waiting for input, the CPU can context switch to a different thread, where it may be possible to make forward progress.

THE PIPELINED HASH JOIN

The main multithreaded operator in a data integration plan tends to be the *pipelined hash join*, sometimes called the double pipelined join, the symmetric hash join, or the X-join. This algorithm constructs two hash tables, one for each input relation, and probes tuples from the opposite relation against them.

The pipelined hash join (Figure 8.7) treats each input symmetrically, simply monitoring its two input queues for available tuples. When it finds an input tuple from relation *R*, it *probes* the tuple against the hash table storing previously read results from the opposite relation *S*; it outputs each resulting tuple. Simultaneously, it adds the input tuple to the hash table for *R* (the *build* step). Upon encountering an *S* tuple, it proceeds symmetrically along the same lines. This join algorithm has several good properties: it immediately produces output the moment once it has received enough tuples to do so, and it accommodates bursty or unequal transfer rates from the sources. However, a negative property of this algorithm is that it accumulates significantly more in-memory state than many alternative algorithms. A number of sophisticated mechanisms have been developed for swapping out portions of the state from a pipelined hash join, such that it can continue to steadily produce output even for larger-than-memory datasets.

HASH-BASED OPERATORS FOR FASTER INITIAL RESULTS

Beyond the pipelined hash join, most data integration engines tend to use hash-based — as opposed to index- or sort-based — algorithms for most of their processing operations, including aggregation. Indices are seldom available in the data integration context. Sort-based methods require multiple sort passes before they can produce output, and this is contrary to the common goal of producing early output. Hash-based schemes, even in situations where the data are larger than memory, allow for tuples to be lazily swapped to disk on a bucket-by-bucket basis as more memory is needed. In most cases, some buckets do not need to be swapped out, and these can be output directly by the query before it begins swapping in the swapped-out tuples.

8.5.2 Interfacing with Autonomous Sources

At the lowest level of a physical query plan for data integration, we typically have a call to a *wrapper* operator. This operator interfaces with a source-specific wrapper or driver (see Chapter 9 for more details), which is responsible for sending requests to the data source in its native protocol and returning results in the tuple format expected by the data integration engine.

Two "generic" types of wrappers appear in most data integration systems: those for ODBC and those for XML. An ODBC (Open DataBase Connectivity) wrapper typically connects to an ODBC loadable library, which is provided by all of the major relational database vendors for their product and each host operating system. ODBC takes queries posed in XML and returns row sets that are accessed via a cursor interface. The ODBC wrapper has a fairly simple job of translating the pushed-down query operations to SQL, then reading tuples from the row set. An XML wrapper typically converts the pushed-down operations into one or more XPath patterns, makes an HTTP request to fetch the desired XML document, and evaluates the XPaths over data as they stream in. Extracted results are returned to the query plan. We discuss XML processing in more detail in Chapter 11.

WRAPPER OPERATORS

In many cases, the wrapper operator has the ability not only to fetch data, but also to pose queries that are to be executed at the source. These are typically operations that are *pushed down* by the query optimizer: selection conditions, projections, and sometimes even joins

FIGURE 8.6 Example executable (physical) query plan with dependent join.

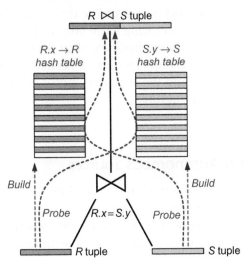

FIGURE 8.7 Internal details of a pipelined hash join. Each tuple from source R is stored in its corresponding hash table (the *build* step), then *probed* against the hash table from S to produce an $R \bowtie S$ result. Source S is processed symmetrically.

between tables that are co-located at the same source. Of course, as discussed previously in Section 8.4, the source must be capable of executing these queries.

HANDLING LIMITED ACCESS PATTERNS WITH DEPENDENT JOIN OPERATORS

As described in Sections 3.3 and 8.4, at times access to a data source must be done by sending inputs (bound variables) to the source, in order for it to return any output data. To do this for multiple sets of input values, we must use a *dependent join* operator: the dependent join fetches tuples from one of its inputs, then sends these as inputs to the source wrapper, and finally returns the cross-product of the results from the two inputs. The dependent join is a special case of the 2-way semijoin described in Section 8.2.2 and can be implemented using the same techniques. Figure 8.6 shows the dataflow of a dependent join, where Movie titles are passed to the Plays source.

8.5.3 Handling Failure

Sometimes, Web sources may become unavailable, e.g., due to a system crash or network partition. Several Web-oriented data integration systems provide for this capability by providing *event handling* capabilities: when a source failure is detected, this can trigger simple modifications to the executing query plan. Often, this involves fetching data from an alternate set of sources (e.g., a mirror or a slightly out-of-date replica). We discuss how these events can trigger adaptive behaviors in Section 8.7.

8.6 Overview of Adaptive Query Processing

Perhaps the main lesson in query processing over the Internet is that conditions constantly change or fail to match expectations: cardinalities or costs may not match optimizer predictions; data streams may get delayed; nodes may fail. Naturally, the approach to handling such issues is to develop a query processor that is capable of *adapting* its strategy in response to such conditions.

In general, this means that the dividing line between the query execution engine (which simply executes query operators) and the query optimizer (which determines strategies) starts to blur. Instead, we have a *feedback loop* in which initial cost and data distribution information is consulted; a preliminary plan is formulated based on comparing predicted costs; the plan begins executing; cost and data distribution information is updated; and we repeat the process.

All adaptive query processors must balance a number of trade-offs.

SPARSITY OF INFORMATION
In general, there are many alternative options for which plan to adapt to — but the actual information available as a basis for decision making (e.g., data distributions, correlations) tends to be limited. This often leads to a trade-off between *exploration* (spending resources to gather information) and *exploitation* (spending resources on producing results).

ANALYSIS TIME VS. EXECUTION TIME
Similarly to the above, we need to determine how many resources to spend on decision making versus execution. Adapting more frequently typically allows us to make the query plan more efficient, but also adds more overhead in continuously reoptimizing. Likewise, searching a more complex space of plan alternatives leads to more optimization time, possibly with the benefit of more efficient execution strategies.

SPACE OF TRANSFORMATIONS
Generally, the more flexibility we would like to enable in changing plans, the more overhead (whether extra memory or extra cost to redundantly compute results) is required.

THE IMPACT OF STATE, NOW AND IN THE FUTURE
Joins are inherently stateful operators, and the cost of a join increases over time (under extreme conditions, quadratically with the size of the input). We must be very careful not

to underassess the cost of a join in a way that leads to *greater* creation of state (e.g., build large intermediate results when it looks like few tuples join, then later find that we are incurring large overheads in processing these results).

We classify adaptive techniques into two broad categories: adaptivity driven by *events* in the query processing environment and adaptivity driven by *performance* monitoring and the determination that query processing should be modified. We begin with the event-driven case.

8.7 Event-Driven Adaptivity

Clearly, one of the major motivations for adaptivity in data integration, especially on the Web, is that unanticipated events may occur. For instance, sources may be unavailable, necessitating a fallback strategy; there may be delays in receiving data from a particular source or set of sources, suggesting that we may wish to prioritize some other portion of query execution; or, at the end of a pipeline stage, we may discover that our intermediate results deviate dramatically from our original expectations, suggesting that it may be beneficial to reoptimize the remainder of the query plan.

All of these can be handled through a general *event-condition-action rule framework*, in which rules may be triggered by runtime events, conditions may be evaluated, and actions may be initiated in response. Event-condition-action rules have the general form **on** *event* **if** *condition* **then** *action sequence*.

Typical events include the completion or initiation of a new pipeline stage, an error or timeout from a wrapper operator, or the processing of a certain number of tuples. For example, the following rule traps a timeout from the query operator named *wrapper1* and in response always activates operator *wrapper2*.

>   **on** timeout(wrapper1, 10 msec)   **if** true **then** activate(wrapper2)

We can model a rule as a quintuple ⟨*event, condition, action_sequence, owner, active*⟩. The *owner* is the query operator that the rule monitors. If the owner is active, and the *active* flag for the rule is also true, then an *event* can initiate or *trigger* the rule, causing it to test its *condition*. The condition is a Boolean expression with the standard operators, whose terms include integer and Boolean literals, plus predefined functions that poll query operator status: the size of intermediate state produced in an operator, cardinality of tuples read or output by the operator, how long since the operator last received a tuple, etc.

If a rule's conditions are satisfied, then the rule *fires*, i.e., the runtime system executes the actions within the *action sequence*. In an adaptive query processor, these actions may enable or disable portions of a query plan, terminate execution and report errors back to the user, or trigger a reoptimization of a portion of the query plan. A rule's *active* flag is cleared once it fires.

In the subsequent sections, we describe how rules may be used to handle a variety of events and the ensuing actions that may be taken.

8.7.1 Handling Source Failures and Delays

When a data source is completely unavailable, e.g., due to a server crash or a network partition, one option is to simply return an error to the user, stating that the query cannot be completed as specified. However, in certain cases, there may be alternative ways of getting equivalent data to what was at the original source, e.g., if mirrors exist, or if data from other semantically equivalent sources can be combined.

Conceptually, this type of task could be modeled as a relational union operator, whose inputs are the alternative data sources. However, we do not necessarily want to request data from all sources simultaneously. This can be accomplished through a *dynamic collector* operator, which is essentially a union operator with a special *policy* expressed as rules.

Finding Alternative Sources

To handle source failures, the query optimizer generates dynamic collector nodes, with multiple subtrees, each representing a different subplan for acquiring the desired data. The optimizer generates a set of rules for enabling and disabling the sources. Some of the inputs to the collector are enabled upon query start-up; then, based on events (such as timeouts, outright failures, or tuple arrivals), a set of rules associated with the dynamic collector can enable or disable the various inputs.

In the simplest case, the optimizer can generate rules for handling source failures or even timeouts. Consider the following example, where operator *coll*1 has two wrapper operators connecting to sources A (the primary source) and B (the alternative).

on timeout(A)   **if** true **then** activate(coll1,B); deactivate(coll1, A)

More elaborate event-based query processors even generate events on a per-tuple basis, enabling *competitive execution*, where we request data from more than one source in parallel and terminate the request from the slower source.

The following example illustrates a situation where initially we attempt to contact sources A and B. Whichever source sends 10 tuples earliest "wins" and "kills" the other source.

on opened(coll1)   **if** true **then** activate(coll1,A); activate(coll1,B)
on tuplesRead(A,10)   **if** true **then** deactivate(coll1,B)
on tuplesRead(B,10)   **if** true **then** deactivate(coll1,A)

The basic event handling scheme enables great flexibility in handling network issues, although it requires that the optimizer have good information about alternative means of acquiring the data.

Handling Network Delays with Rescheduling

In a complex query plan that is not fully pipelined, a delay at one of the sources can completely stall execution — even if the other data sources are available, and if some other portion of the query plan might be executable. A response is to *reschedule* query execution, such that the delayed portion of the plan is suspended but another segment of the plan can be started in the meantime.

In general, the process of rescheduling involves identifying a new *runnable subtree*, and splitting it off from the current plan — into a separate query whose output becomes a materialized table. The current query will be modified "in place" to use the results of this table. This strategy enables us to execute both the main query and the "subtree query" concurrently, and still preserve the correct semantics of operation.

We would like to consider which runnable subtrees to use by looking at their costs. Typically all rescheduling decisions are predetermined at optimization-time, with the decisions encoded as rules to be executed at runtime, specifying which subtree(s) to activate if a given pipeline stage gets stalled. This only requires minor modifications to the optimizer's existing structure: the optimizer already has estimated costs and cardinalities for each subtree, and in assessing the cost of rescheduling, it simply must also account for the costs of materializing and reading from the materialized tables. Alternative runnable subtrees can be prioritized by their *efficiency*: the ratio of how much cost they save from the existing query plan versus the cost of executing them as separate queries with materialized results. Intuitively, the most efficient runnable subtrees are ones that materialize a small amount of data, or materialize data that already gets materialized in the existing query plan.

Once a rescheduling policy has been determined, it is simple to encode it using a rule such as the following.

> **on** waiting(op1, 100 msec)   **if** true **then** reschedule(op2)

Results from the research literature show that this rescheduling technique can provide significant speedup when there are multiple pipeline stages in query execution. We note that the use of pipelined hash joins mitigates the need for rescheduling within a select-project-join query; however, for queries with aggregation, or situations in which there is insufficient memory to do a pipelined-hash-join-only query plan, rescheduling is an important technique.

8.7.2 Handling Unexpected Cardinalities at Pipeline End

Sometimes, even in data integration scenarios, query execution is divided into multiple pipeline stages — either due to a lack of memory, or because of blocking operations such as aggregation. At the end of each pipeline stage, the query processor has an opportunity to see whether the overall query plan is progressing as expected and to replace the remaining plan "for free" if not. Of course, *determining* what alternative plan to use may first require reoptimization, which in fact is not free.

The technique of *mid-query reoptimization* attempts to determine whether it is beneficial to reoptimize the remaining pipeline stages of a query plan, based on a combination of runtime statistics, heuristics, and cost estimates. There are three basic components to this technique: extending query plans with the ability to gather information (such that progress can be monitored), having the optimizer predetermine the settings under which reoptimization should be triggered, and, if necessary, reinvoking the optimizer at runtime to get a new query plan. We discuss each in turn.

Information-Gathering Query Operators

The operators in a traditional query engine do their computation "silently," in the sense that they do not provide feedback on how much data they have received, what the data distributions look like, and so forth. It is essential for an adaptive query processor to provide mechanisms for monitoring status.

In general, these come in two main forms. First, individual operators can track information about their own status and return this upon request. The most common type of status information is how many tuples each operator has processed. Maintaining such per-operator cardinalities adds a small amount of overhead to query execution, but in exchange there is the possibility of determining exact cardinalities (and thus selectivities). Other kinds of information may include execution state (open, closed, failed), and possibly even information about memory consumption.

A second kind of information is *summary* information i.e., histograms or sketches over certain attributes in the data stream. Such summary structures are typically created by special *statistics collection* operators, which are inserted into the query plan by the query optimizer. The placement and use of such operators are typically quite tricky: statistics collection is relatively expensive, and the summary structure typically is only usable *after* the pipeline containing the statistics collector operator has completed. Hence the optimizer attempts to place statistics collectors where critical attributes (e.g., join keys) are uncertain, and where a significant portion of the query plan might still be reoptimize (i.e., a good deal of the remaining query plan must not yet have been started).

Predetermined Reoptimization Thresholds

Given information from the query plan (whether cardinalities of operators or summaries from statistics collection operators), the query engine must be able to make a decision as to whether the query plan is progressing in an acceptable way (i.e., performance will be roughly along the lines of what was predicted by cost-based optimization, or better) or if it is necessary to try to find a new plan.

To change a query plan we must materialize the results of the currently executing pipeline to disk, reinvoke the optimizer over the remaining portions of the query, and execute the new query plan. Clearly, this adds two kinds of additional overhead to the overall query processing running times: that for writing and later reading the materialized results, and that for invoking the query optimizer.

The goal is to only trigger a reoptimization if the total savings will exceed this additional overhead. Of course, the challenge is that at runtime we do not have any simple way of estimating how much savings is possible: this requires the query optimizer! Hence the system must rely on heuristics to determine when to reoptimize.

Typically, the cost of optimization is fairly predictable, as is the cost of materializing and dematerializing a subresult. Let these combined costs be represented by the term C. Then the optimizer will typically be reinvoked if (1) the newly estimated cost of the query, given the new statistics gathered at runtime, exceeds the originally predicted cost by some threshold θ_1, and (2) the predicted cost of the unexecuted portion of the query exceeds C times some coefficient θ_2.

■ ■ ■ ▬▬▬▬▬▬▬▬▬▬▬▬▬▬▬▬▬▬▬▬▬▬▬▬▬▬

Example 8.3

Refer to Figure 8.8 for an instance of mid-query reoptimization for the SQL query given at the beginning of this chapter. The plan is broken into two pipelines, with a checkpoint between them. The first pipeline contains a pipelined hash join, a statistics collector, and two selection operations. At the end of the pipeline, the checkpoint operator may have a rule such as the following, which calls the optimizer to reoptimize the subsequent fragments if the estimated cardinality is significantly different from the size of the result.

on closed(join1)   **if** card(join1) > (est_card(join1) * 1.5) **then** reoptimize

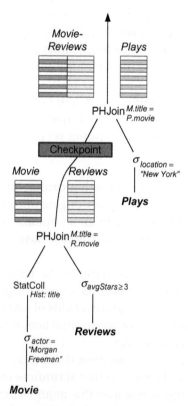

FIGURE 8.8 Example of a query plan with a reoptimization checkpoint, plus a statistics collector on the *title* attribute.

If the output of the first join is no more than 50% larger than what was expected, then the second pipeline continues unaffected. Otherwise, the second join is reoptimized (e.g., to replace the pipelined hash join with a nested loops join over the temporary table, due to lack of memory).

■ ■ ■

Runtime Reinvocation of the Optimizer

Once reoptimization is to be triggered, this requires suspension of the currently executing plan. This requires the following steps:

- Take the output from the last operator in the pipeline and materialize it to disk as a temporary table.
- Rewrite the original SQL query Q, replacing the already-executed subexpressions of the query with a reference to the temporary table, resulting in a query Q' that encapsulates the not-yet-executed operations from Q.
- Optimize Q', possibly adding statistics collection operators and reoptimization thresholds again, if Q' is to be executed in multiple pipeline stages.

The resulting plan for Q' can now be run to completion, producing the final query results. As an optimization, it is possible to *suspend* execution of the original Q before triggering reoptimization, rather than terminating it — then if Q' has approximately the same costs, it is slightly more efficient to resume computing Q than to start executing Q'.

The mid-query reoptimization approach can be quite useful if there are multiple pipeline stages in a query plan. However, in practice many data integration queries are fully pipelined, rendering the technique ineffective. This motivates the work in our next section.

8.8 Performance-Driven Adaptivity

In data integration scenarios where we do not have good cardinality estimates for base relations, the techniques of the previous subsection are generally inadequate: they can only modify portions of the query plan that are not part of the currently executing pipeline. Given that data integration queries emphasize the use of pipelined hash joins, they typically only *have* one pipeline (possibly followed by an aggregation operation). Hence there has been a great deal of interest in adaptive techniques that allow the query processor to change the execution plan for a currently executing pipeline.

All adaptive query processing systems in this vein assume that past query performance is indicative of future performance and extrapolate the overall cost and cardinality values from this. While this heuristic can be misled by variations in the data, such situations are unlikely to arise in practice: the majority of query cost tends to be in join operations, and the majority of joins are between keys and foreign keys, which may demonstrate skew but are fairly well bounded in the size of their output.

Under the covers, all of these techniques exploit a set of fundamental properties of the relational algebra — namely, the distributivity of union over select, project, and join. In general, we can take any conjunctive query expression over m relations, divide each relation into partitions, and compute the overall result as a union of conjunctive queries over the partitions:

$$\Pi_{\bar{A}}(\sigma_\theta(R_1 \bowtie \ldots \bowtie R_m)) = \bigcup_{1 \leq c_1 \leq n, \ldots, 1 \leq c_m \leq n} \Pi_{\bar{A}}(\sigma_\theta((R_1^{c1} \bowtie \ldots \bowtie R_m^{cm})))$$

where $R_j^{c_j}$ represents some subset of relation R_j.

This property is actually fundamental to the correctness of the pipelined hash join algorithm. There, at any point during the join of R_1 and R_2, we have an option about whether to read from R_1 and probe against the portion of R_2 read so far, or from R_2 and probe against the portion of R_1 that has been read. Suppose we represent the portion of R_1 that has been read as R_1^0 and, likewise, R_2's portion as R_2^0. Then the pipelined hash join can read more tuples from, say, R_1 (representing a subset R_1^1). It will join this with R_2^0, algebraically performing the operation $(R_1^0 \bowtie R_2^0) \cup (R_1^1 \bowtie R_2^0)$, but returning the same result as $(R_1^0 \cup R_1^1) \bowtie R_2^0$. Similarly, for R_2^1, we would join against R_1^0 *and* R_1^1, and so on for future subsets.

We can further exploit these algebraic equivalences to enable *inter-pipeline* adaptivity, by noting that we can evaluate each of the conjunctive queries within the union above using *any* order of evaluation. In other words, each of the different terms to be unioned might be produced by a *different* query execution plan.

The main question, then, is *which* plan to use for each of the different conjunctive expressions. Several different adaptive techniques have been proposed that opt for different points in the design space. We focus on two endpoints in the spectrum: *eddies*, a technique that enables very frequent adaptivity but makes decisions in a non-cost-based way, and an alternative strategy that makes less frequent, but cost-based decisions, called *corrective query processing*.

8.8.1 Eddies: Queueing-Based Plan Selection

Traditional DBMS query processing puts all of the "intelligence" and decision making into the query optimizer and very little intelligence in the execution engine. Operator scheduling is tightly controlled by the query plan, which consists of a tree (or, occasionally, a directed acyclic graph) of unary and binary operators.

The *eddy* approach in some sense chooses the opposite extreme: the optimizer makes very limited decisions, perhaps performing very high-level heuristics-based query rewrites, but deferring all operator ordering decisions within a select-project-join query block to runtime. Each SPJ expression gets codified into one "super-operator" called an eddy.

The eddy's functionality can be divided into a *tuple router* component and one or more *suboperators*. Suboperators can include selection and projection operators, as well as components that encapsulate join functionality (storing state for a subexpression and probing against state from a different subexpression). Tuples are fed into the eddy from the various inputs. The tuples are all annotated with special Boolean *done* flags, one for each query plan operation, to track their progress. For an initial incoming tuple, all bits are cleared.

Each suboperator has a set of *policy* rules, describing which done flags need to be set or cleared in order for the suboperator to be able to accept a tuple. No suboperator *o* will accept a tuple whose done bit for *o* is already set: this means the operator has already been applied to the tuple. Additionally, sometimes there are dependencies in the order of evaluation, and a suboperator may refuse to accept a tuple until that tuple has been processed by other suboperators first.

As a tuple comes into the eddy, its *tuple router* will typically have a choice among several destination suboperators, each of which is willing to accept the tuple. It will use a *routing policy* to choose among these destinations and send an incoming tuple to the appropriate suboperator. Any resulting output tuples from this suboperator *o* get their done bits for *o* set and also "carry forward" any set done bits from their inputs; then they are sent back to the eddy. The eddy will then consult the remaining suboperators to see which are willing to accept the tuple, and repeat the process. Once a tuple gets all of its done bits set, it is returned as output from the eddy.

■ ■ ■ ━━

Example 8.4

Refer to Figure 8.9 for an eddy corresponding to the SQL query below (repeated from the beginning of this chapter).

```
SELECT title, startTime
FROM Movie M, Plays P, Reviews R
WHERE M.title = P.movie AND M.title = R.movie AND
  P.location="New York" AND M.actor="Morgan Freeman" AND
  R.avgStars >= 3
```

The different query operations (selections and pipelined hash joins) are each encompassed as a suboperator ($o_1 \ldots o_5$) and the central router is indicated by the "R" node in the middle of the eddy. The routing constraints are indicated by connections in the "R" node between sources and suboperators. Each incoming tuple to the eddy is routed to one of the suboperators; returned results are fed back into the eddy. At each successive step through an operator o_i, the *i*th "done" bit on the output tuples is set. Once a tuple has all bits set, it is output by the eddy.

━━ ■ ■ ■

If the suboperators consist of select, project, and stateful join operations, then the eddy maintains correctness thanks to the relational algebra distributivity law properties

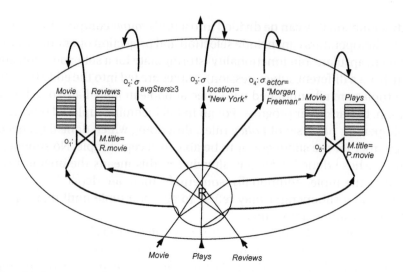

FIGURE 8.9 An eddy for our example query, showing the router ("R"), the various suboperators (o_i), and the internal hash tables in each join operation.

previously described. The major question with the eddy is what *policy* is chosen to select an order of application.

Basic Eddies: "Lottery Scheduling" Routing

The *lottery scheduling* scheme for routing is based on several observations. In general, it is too expensive to make a full cost-based comparison of alternative query plans on a tuple-by-tuple basis. However, we intuitively would prefer to send a tuple to *fast* suboperators over *slow* ones, all other things (in particular, selectivities) being equal; or to *highly selective* operators as opposed to *not very selective* ones, all other things (in particular, computation costs) being equal.

We can bias a tuple router towards fast suboperators as follows. If we place a queue in front of each suboperator, then the queue will quickly fill up for slow operators, but not for fast ones. The eddy's tuple router should *only* be able to send a tuple to a queue that is not empty, and *back pressure* from the queues will therefore bias the eddy to select fast operators.

This scheme can be extended to bias toward more selective operators through a randomized scheme. Each time a suboperator receives a tuple from the tuple router, it is given a "ticket"; each time it outputs a tuple to the router, it loses a ticket. The tuple router will choose the next destination for a tuple by conducting a "lottery" and choosing a ticket from among those for the eligible suboperator destinations.

The lottery scheduling routing scheme adds overhead, but is extremely effective in determining a good order for applying selection predicates. However, it tends to have problems with joins: the selectivity tends to diminish over time, as more tuples are "seen" by the join and added to its internal hash tables. The lottery scheme will often overestimate the selectivity of a join early in execution. Thus, rather than sending tuples first to, say, a selection predicate, the eddy may first send them to the join — creating large amounts of intermediate state. Later in execution, tuples from the other sources will need to be joined against all of that state, incurring cost that could have been avoided if the selection had been applied first (reducing the state).

Extended Eddies: State Modules

The basic eddy scheme has a bit of a quirk: it does not reflect the "stateful" properties of join operators, e.g., the fact that the rate of tuple production for a join goes up as more input tuples have been consumed. State modules or STeMs "split apart" the internal functionality of the join so an eddy can better track behavior. The STeMs' work creates *two* suboperators for each join within the eddy: one suboperator holds state and the other probes against the opposite relation's state. Now an arriving tuple must pass through both the state and the probe suboperator, in a way that ensures all results are produced: this results in a series of intricate rules on how tuples are propagated into and out of the eddy. Further details on STeMs can be found in the papers listed in the bibliographic notes of this chapter.

Eddies That Migrate State: STAIRs

Eddies, whether using the basic approach or STeMs, assume that current observed operator selectivities are good predictors for future operator selectivities. For joins this is not necessarily the case: early in execution, join operators may be extremely selective; as state is built up, they may become less so. Under extreme circumstances, a join may initially produce no results at all, but may later produce large numbers of tuples. Here, the eddy might be "misled" into accumulating state in a suboptimal way — and once that state has been built up in a suboperator, every arriving tuple must be probed against it.

STAIRs are designed to address this problem, by letting the eddy "disassemble" and move intermediate state to other suboperators (possibly being filtered in the process). This adds some overhead due to wasted work, but it can be less costly than leaving the intermediate state in its suboptimal locations. For more details on STAIRs, please consult the bibliographic references at the end of this chapter.

8.8.2 Corrective Query Processing: Cost-Based Reoptimization

Eddies perform *continuous* query reoptimization, using a data flow heuristic that adds some per-tuple overhead but enables continuous simultaneous exploration of alternative query plans. Eddies will generally avoid "worst-case" query performance, but they spend a significant time doing "exploration" of options, and hence they devote fewer resources to "exploitation" — providing peak performance — than a traditional query engine.

Corrective query processing (CQP) aims instead to dedicate the majority of computation to query answering rather than exploration of potentially better plans. It seeks to be *reactive* to bad plans, making minor course corrections, rather than *proactive* in finding better plans. Unlike eddies, which use a local heuristic, CQP seeks to perform a cost-based

evaluation of plan progress and potentially better plans. To facilitate this, the query processor periodically reruns the query optimizer's cost estimator in a low-priority background
thread with the latest runtime statistics, as query execution continues. If the optimizer
finds a plan that is substantially better, it can halt the currently executing query plan,
allow the plan to reach a *consistent* state (where all computation in the query plan, including blocking operations, has been performed on the source data that has been read), and
switch to another plan using the adaptive mechanisms described previously. The new plan
is "connected" to the input data streams, which resume where the previous plan left off.
Execution continues, potentially switching plans more than once; each sequential change
of plans is termed a *phase*. Finally, the system performs a *stitch-up phase* at the end to
compute the answers requiring data from *across* plans.

Example 8.5

Refer to Figure 8.10. Given our example query and a set of initial statistics, the query optimizer
may start execution using the query plan on the left of the figure, with Movie (M) joined with
Reviews (R) before Plays (P). We refer to the initial plan as the *phase 0* plan.

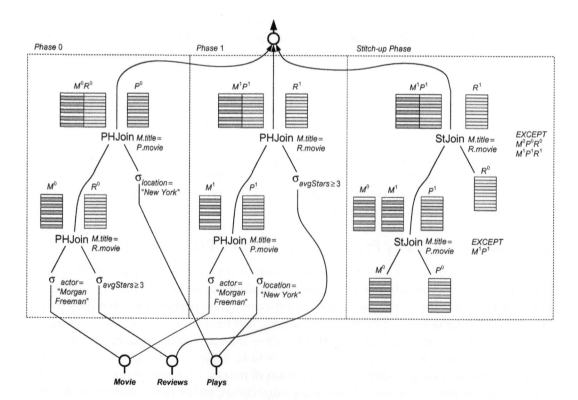

FIGURE 8.10 Corrective query processing example with two normal phases plus a stitch-up phase.

Unlike in a traditional query processor, a CQP-based query processor performs continuous monitoring on the execution of the plan. As statistics are collected and costs are reestimated, the system may trigger the query optimizer in the background, and may determine that an alternative plan is superior. The plan of the first phase is halted, and a new *phase 1* plan is initiated, indicated in the middle of the figure with `Movie` joining with `Plays` before `Reviews`. The new plan executes over the remainder of the data from the three sources: each phase has operated on a disjoint partition of the base data. We designate the first subset of each relation R as R^0 and the second subset as R^1.

The simple union of the 0th and 1st phase results returns only a subset of the desired answers. We must also join all combinations of relations *between* phases, feeding their results into the grouping operator. Omitting the join subscripts for conciseness, the remaining join expression is the following:

$$(R^0 \bowtie P^0 \bowtie R^1) \cup (R^0 \bowtie P^1 \bowtie R^0) \cup (R^0 \bowtie P^1 \bowtie R^1) \cup$$
$$(R^1 \bowtie P^0 \bowtie R^0) \cup (R^1 \bowtie P^0 \bowtie R^1) \cup (R^1 \bowtie P^1 \bowtie R^0)$$

Only when this final expression has been evaluated, in what we call the *stitch-up* phase, will query execution complete. This is done in the last query plan, where a special *stitch-up join* operator (StJoin) takes the intermediate result hash tables from previous execution and tries to use them to produce the remaining answers. This involves iterating through the contents of hash tables and joining them. In order to avoid producing duplicate results, the stitch-up join is given information about which combinations of hash tables *not* to rejoin (the "except" lists). ∎ ∎ ∎

The CQP problem poses several key challenges, first in terms of how to supplement a query engine with cost estimation and reoptimization capabilities that run during pipelined execution, and later in computing the stitch-up query plans.

Cost reestimation

The corrective query processing approach is based on performing frequent reestimations of query execution cost. The plan status is generally polled every few seconds, as new aggregate performance trends become evident. During the polling step, the system must determine (1) how the remainder of query processing will proceed (especially if the data sources' cardinalities are unknown) and (2) the costs and selectivities of alternative query plans.

Given cardinality and selectivity results from the currently executing plan, the query processor must account for the fact that the current plan only explores a very small piece of the (exponential) search space, and only gives a small amount of real information. The CQP work exploits the fact that *equivalent subexpressions* (regardless of query plan) will always have the same cardinality and selectivity. Even with this observation, the search space remains large, and the CQP cost estimator must make use of a variety of heuristics to make an estimate of the selectivities of subexpressions that it has not yet attempted to execute.

Typically, if the reestimated cost is within a small threshold of the original costs, then no reoptimization needs to be performed, i.e., the space of potential query plans does not need to be searched. However, if the cost exceeds the threshold, then reoptimization is indeed triggered.

Reoptimization

In contrast to other methods such as mid-query reoptimization, the query optimizer in CQP runs "alongside" the query engine. The reoptimizer can be patterned after any established query optimizer model: heuristics-based, randomized, dynamic programming, or top-down with memoization could all be used. The prototypical implementations have used a top-down with memoization architecture, combined with full (bushy) enumeration of alternative join trees. It is critical that the optimizer incorporate the revised cost estimates from runtime, as well as information about how much of each relation has been processed: the goal is to extrapolate the cost of executing the *remainder* of the query.

An additional cost penalty is given to changing the plan versus leaving it the same, because keeping the same plan makes the stitch-up query plan more efficient (since all subexpressions are compatible). This penalty is typically assigned in using a heuristic since the system does not yet know what the cost of the stitch-up plan will be, or even whether there will be additional query execution phases.

Creating Stitch-Up Plans

Once basic query execution has completed, if there were multiple query processing phases, then a stitch-up query plan must combine those subsets of data that had previously been partitioned to different plans. In general, for a join of m relations in n plans, there are $n^m - n$ combinations of subsets that need to be stitched together.

One underlying requirement of corrective query processing is that every plan must "buffer" the source data fed into it at the leaves, so this data can be joined with data in the other plans — this mirrors the requirement of the pipelined hash join, and in fact, since most data integration systems almost exclusively rely on pipelined hash joins, it is often trivially satisfied. Other join forms (nested loops, hybrid hash, and merge) must also be extended to do buffering.

There are several options for when corrective query processing can perform the cross-phase joins required to produce complete answers, including doing them each time a plan is changed. Existing implementations postpone all stitch-up computations to a final *stitch-up phase* at the end, after all prior plans have completed, as outlined in the earlier example.

The stitch-up plan can be computed solely from information stored in the hash tables of the various operators from the previous phases. Rather than rescanning input from the sources, CQP instead scans through the existing hash tables to obtain source tuples. The query optimizer takes into account all existing state in determining the best query plan to incorporate these hash tables — either for probing against or for scanning as inputs.

For every join operation, it estimates the cost of producing the unavailable intermediate results of the expression, rather than all answers.[1] Next, the optimizer creates an *exclusion list* that specifies which subexpressions have already been computed, can be reused, and should not be recomputed.

Finally, CQP includes a specialized variation of the join operator that efficiently incorporates tuples from multiple existing hash tables and adds lineage information to enable duplicate removal. The *stitch-up join* operator starts with an exclusion list provided by the optimizer (e.g., do not regenerate $R^0 \bowtie P^0$ in the example), plus sets of state structures containing existing results that are to be reused. The stitch-up join iterates over the combinations of existing state structures and decides at a structure-to-structure level (rather than a per-tuple level) whether this combination is in the exclusion list or needs to be generated. Moreover, it decides on a pairwise basis which state structure should be scanned for tuples and which should be probed against; if necessary for performance, it will rehash one of the structures according to the join key. Finally, the stitch-up join combines data from its inputs with that from the existing state structures, checking on a per-tuple basis whether the tuple should be created. The final result is an operator that is much more efficient at producing precisely the results needed.

Example 8.6

Refer to Figure 8.10. The stitch-up join (**StJoin**) operators reuse data from the hash tables of the prior phases, while avoiding the creation of duplicate tuples. The lower-level **StJoin** needs to produce any "missing" tuples for $M \bowtie P$. These include $M^0 \bowtie P^0$, $M^1 \bowtie P^0$, and $M^0 \bowtie P^1$, but not $M^1 \bowtie P^1$. To do this, we take the hash tables for M^0, M^1, P^0, P^1 and "attach" them to the stitch-up join. The stitch-up join operator reads from P^0 and joins against both M^0 and M^1; it reads from M^0 and joins against P^1.

The second stitch-up join performs similarly. It has existing $M^1 \bowtie P^1$ tuples in its hash table and reads the remaining $M \bowtie P$ tuples from the child expression. It also reads the R^0 tuples from a hash table created in the initial phase. The second join performs a join of all combinations of tuples except those already output.

To summarize the key differences in performance-driven adaptivity, corrective query processing takes a more conservative, cost-based approach to modifying query plans, which impacts query execution cost minimally when the plan is relatively good. Eddies take a dataflow-based approach to determining query operator ordering, and they

---

[1] Because it only considers intermediate results that are part of our current query, and since such results are only a subset of all required data, this problem is somewhat simpler than that for optimizing using materialized views, as discussed in Chapter 2.

constantly explore alternative plans as a result. The CQP approach is perhaps more suited to situations in which selectivities are stable throughout execution but initially unknown, whereas eddies are perhaps more suited to situations in which the selectivities are changing frequently.

Bibliographic Notes

Two excellent surveys of conventional query optimization appear as [121, 318]. These provide details on how plan enumeration is performed, various heuristics for pruning the search space, and the use of histograms and other techniques to estimate cardinalities. A complementary survey on query execution appears in [263], which describes hash, index, and iteration-based schemes for the basic operators.

Distributed databases were explored even in the early days of the relational DBMS field, with projects such as Distributed Ingres [530] and R* [405]. One of the first federated databases, Multi-Base, also dates back to the same time period [525]. Perhaps the most ambitious distributed (and federated) DBMS was Mariposa [532], which attempted to use simple techniques from economics to determine how to place data and where to do computation. Some of these ideas have subsequently been refined in later systems, including data integration systems.

The Bloom filter actually is named after its inventor [90]. Both the Bloomjoin and 2-way semijoin were among the earliest query execution algorithms discussed in the distributed query processing literature [73, 161, 404]. For a more comprehensive overview of distributed query processing, refer to the survey in [350] and the textbook [471]. Recent work has even considered mechanisms for doing distributed processing of correlated subqueries [328] and recursion [395].

Much of the work done on query optimization with sophisticated wrapper cost models was pioneered by IBM Almaden Research Center's Garlic system [281, 498]. Garlic was a data integration system built over the Starburst engine (the research version of DB2 UDB). A major focus of the effort was to extend the optimizer to handle heterogeneous (including nonrelational) data sources. In contrast to most of our discussion in this chapter, Garlic was focused on enterprise information integration (EII) tasks within the corporate intranet. Today, many aspects of Garlic are implemented in IBM's InfoSphere series of products.

Adaptive query processing has been the subject of intense study in the conventional database, data stream, and data integration communities. Two surveys on the topic are [48, 172]. Foundational pieces of work discussed in detail in the surveys include techniques to interleave reoptimization and execution in a conventional database context [150, 336, 556], as well as techniques for building more robust query plans [46, 138, 319]. Eddies, including their STeM and STAIR variations, are presented in [44, 171, 490]. Eddies have even been extended to a distributed context [547]. Corrective query processing was presented in [326], and a closely related technique called CAPE appears in [499]. Within the stream query processing context, adaptive techniques have been developed for load shedding [47, 543, 552] and minimizing memory usage [45, 50]. Strategies for scheduling and adaptive reordering of windowed operators were developed in [49].

Estimating latencies across the Internet has become less challenging over time as network bandwidth has increased, thus reducing latency due to router contention. The Internet measurement community has done significant work on attempting to predict latencies, and also on instrumenting the Internet with measurement infrastructure [232].

9

Wrappers

Wrappers are the components of a data integration system that communicate with the data sources. The wrapper's task involves sending queries from the higher levels of the data integration system to the sources and then converting the replies to a format that can be manipulated by the query processor. The complexity of the wrapper depends on the nature of the data source. In the simplest case, if the data source is a relational database system, then the task of the wrapper is rather simple and can involve merely interacting with a JDBC driver (which, admittedly, can often be harder than you would expect!). In more complex cases, the wrapper needs to parse semistructured data such as those found on HTML pages and transform them into a set of tuples. This chapter will focus on the latter case — efficiently building wrappers that convert semistructured data into tuples. We introduce the problems that are faced by wrappers and then discuss the different solutions that have been proposed in the literature.

9.1 Introduction

We illustrate the ideas underlying wrappers by considering data sources that consist of a set of Web pages. For each source S, we assume that each Web page displays structured data using a *schema* T_S and a *format* F_S, which are common across all pages of the source. It is important to keep in mind that the schema is not explicitly declared.

■ ■ ■

Example 9.1

Figures 9.1(a)–(c) describe three such data sources. Source *countries.com* describes basic information about countries, and Figure 9.1(a) shows a page that describes Germany. This page uses a relational schema that consists of a single table with the attributes country, capital, population, and continent. It displays country first, fully capitalized, then capital, population, and continent, prefixed with "Capital:", "Population:", and "Continent:", respectively.

   Source *easycalls.com* is about calling codes, and Figure 9.1(b) shows a page that displays a list of tuples (country, code). Each tuple is displayed on a single line, with country in bold font, followed by code in italic. Finally, Figure 9.1(c) shows a page from *greatbooks.com*, which displays a book title in bold font, one or more authors, which are underlined, then price and publisher, which are prefixed with "Price:" and "Publisher:", respectively.

■ ■ ■

   These kinds of pages are very common on the World Wide Web. They are created in sites that are powered by database systems. When a query is posed by a user, it is sent to

FIGURE 9.1 Examples of data sources, each of which displays data using a schema and a format that are common across all pages of the source.

the back-end database, which responds with a set of tuples. At that point, a Perl script or another scripting program will create HTML that looks presentable to the user.

9.1.1 The Wrapper Construction Problem

Given a source S as described above, a *wrapper* W extracts structured data from the pages of S. Formally, W is a tuple (T_W, E_W), where T_W is a *target schema*, and E_W is an *extraction program* that uses the format F_S to extract from each page a data instance conforming to T_W. The target schema E_W need not be the same as the schema used on the page, since we may want to rename the attributes or only include a subset of them in our output. The following two examples illustrate the operation of wrappers.

Example 9.2

Consider a wrapper that extracts all attributes from the pages of *countries.com* (Figure 9.1(a)). The target schema T_W is the source schema T_S = (country, capital, population, continent). The extraction program E_W may specify that, when given a page P from the source, return the first fully capitalized string as country, then the string immediately following "Capital:" as capital, and so on.

Example 9.3

Consider a wrapper that extracts only title and price from source *greatbooks.com* (Figure 9.1(c)). Here the target schema T_W is the relational schema (title, price), and the extraction program E_W returns the string in bold font as title, then the number following "$" as price.

The *wrapper construction* problem is to quickly create the pair (T_W, E_W) by inspecting the pages of the source S. Since much of the effort in this realm has focused on developing machine learning algorithms for constructing wrappers, the problem is often referred to as *wrapper learning*. Two main variants of this problem exist. In the first variant we want to learn the source schema T_S as well as a program E_W that extracts data conforming to T_S. Thus the wrapper to be constructed is $W = (T_S, E_W)$. In this case the source schema T_S is also the target schema T_W. For example, if we do not know the schema of *countries.com*, we may want to construct the wrapper in Example 9.2, in particular we want to construct both the target schema and the extraction program.

In the second variant, we want to extract only a subset of the attributes of the source schema T_S, and we already know this subset (e.g., by manually examining a set of pages of S). Then we define this subset to be the target schema T_W, and our goal is to construct only the extraction program E_W. For example, if we want to extract only title and price from *greatbooks.com*, then we may want to build the wrapper in Example 9.3, where we already know the target schema.

9.1.2 Challenges of Wrapper Construction

The above two variants of wrapper construction have been studied extensively and have proven quite challenging, for the following reasons.

LEARNING THE SOURCE SCHEMA

First, learning the source schema T_S turns out to be quite difficult. A common way to do this is to imagine that each page of S is a string generated by a grammar G. We then learn G from a set of pages and use G to infer T_S. For example, after examining a set of pages of *countries.com*, we may learn that they are generated by the following regular expression (which encodes a regular grammar):

$$R = <html>(.+?)<hr>
(.+?)
Capital: (.+?)
Population:(.+?)$$
$$
Continent: (.+?)</body></html>$$

From this regular expression we can infer the source schema (country, capital, population, continent).

Unfortunately, inferring a grammar from positive examples (i.e., the pages of S in this case) is well known to be difficult. For example, we know that regular grammars cannot be correctly identified from positive examples alone. Even with both positive and negative examples, there is no efficient algorithm to identify a reasonable grammar (e.g., to identify the minimum-state deterministic finite state automaton that is consistent with an arbitrary set of examples).

Given these limitations, current solutions consider only relatively simple regular grammars that encode either flat tuple or nested tuple schemas. But even learning simple schemas has proven quite difficult. The general approach is to use various heuristics for searching a large space of candidate schemas. However, the correctness of the discovered schemas heavily depends on the heuristics employed, as incorrect heuristics often lead to incorrect schemas. Furthermore, increasing the complexity of the schema even slightly can lead to an exponential increase in the size of the search space, resulting in an intractable learning process.

LEARNING THE EXTRACTION PROGRAM

Learning the extraction program E_W has also proven quite difficult. Ideally, E_W should be Turing-complete (e.g., as a Perl script) to have the maximal expressive power. But learning such programs is clearly impractical. Consequently, we often impose a far more restricted "computational model" on E_W, then learn only the limited set of "parameters" of the model.

Consider, for example, learning to extract country and capital from pages such as the Germany page in Figure 9.1(a). We may assume that the program E_W is specified by a tuple (s_1, e_1, s_2, e_2), whose meaning is that E_W always extracts the first string between s_1 and e_1 as country and the first string between s_2 and e_2 as capital. In this case, learning E_W reduces to learning the four parameters s_1, e_1, s_2, and e_2, and we may learn that s_1 = <hr>
, e_1 =
, s_2 = Capital:, and e_2 =
.

Even learning just parameters like these has proven quite difficult. Like the case of learning the source schema, learning the parameters often involves a search in a space of possible values, guided by heuristics. Incorrect heuristics often lead to incorrect parameter values, and the search space is often vast, making the search process time intensive and easy to go wrong.

COPING WITH EXCEPTIONS

The third reason wrapper construction is difficult is that there are often many exceptions in how data are laid out and formatted. For example, the data may normally be laid out as a tuple, say (title, author, price). However, in some cases certain attributes (e.g., price) may be missing, attribute order may be reversed (e.g., listing author before title, if the author is well known), or attribute format may be changed (e.g., price is normally listed in black font, but will be listed in red font if it is below $2).

Such exceptions are common in practice and not always apparent if we only inspect a small number of pages when we begin to create the wrapper. As such, exceptions cause numerous problems. They can invalidate assumptions regarding the schema and data format, thus producing incorrect wrappers. They can also force us to revise considerably the source schema T_S and the extraction program T_W. For instance, in the above book example, to accommodate missing attributes and different attribute orders, we must revise T_S from a flat tuple schema into a nested tuple schema with disjunction. We must also revise the program E_W to handle the many ways that price can be formatted. These revisions blow up the search space, making finding T_s and E_W far more difficult.

9.1.3 Categories of Solutions

Current approaches to constructing wrappers fall into four main groups: manual, learning, automatic, and interactive. In the *manual* approach, a developer examines a set of Web pages, then manually creates the target schema T_W and the extraction program E_W. The program E_W is typically written in a procedural language (e.g., Perl, Java) or a specialized declarative language. This approach is relatively easy to understand, implement, and debug. It also produces highly accurate wrappers. Thus, it is very commonly used in practice. However, the manual approach is labor intensive and requires highly trained developers.

In the *learning* approach, the developer creates the target schema T_W and highlights the attributes of T_W in a set of Web pages (typically using a graphical user interface that was designed for this purpose). The developer then applies a learning algorithm to these highlighted examples to automatically learn the extraction program E_W. This approach requires less work than the manual approach and can be used by users with less technical skills. However, highlighting attributes still incurs a nontrivial amount of work, and the learned program E_W is often brittle, requiring significant post-processing effort.

The *automatic* approach examines a set of Web pages to automatically infer a grammar that encodes the source schema T_S and a program E_W that extracts data conforming to T_S. Learning arbitrary grammars is impractical, as mentioned earlier. Thus this approach considers only grammars that are restricted forms of regular expressions. The approach requires virtually no developer effort and can be used by technically naive users. But like the learning approach, this approach often produces brittle wrappers, which require significant post-processing effort.

The *interactive* approach combines aspects of the learning and automatic approaches. It examines Web pages and some initial user feedback to infer a set $\mathcal{E}$ of possible extraction programs. It then interactively solicits feedback to refine and narrow $\mathcal{E}$. Example feedback includes highlighting attributes on Web pages, identifying correct extraction results, and visually guiding the process of creating extraction rules. Unlike the learning approach, in which users spend a considerable amount of effort *in advance* to highlight attributes, this approach asks for feedback only when judged necessary to make progress. Thus, it often requires less manual effort. Furthermore, it uses user feedback to guide the search process and thus is more robust than both learning and automatic approaches.

In the rest of this chapter we describe the above four approaches. For ease of exposition, we will use the phrases "wrapper" and "extraction program" as well as "developer" and "user" interchangeably, when there is no ambiguity.

9.2 Manual Wrapper Construction

Manual wrapper construction involves a developer examining a set of Web pages and then creating the target schema T_W and the extraction program E_W. The developer often writes E_W using a procedural language such as Perl. For example, given the Web page in Figure 9.2(a), Figure 9.2(b) shows a Perl program that extracts (country, code) tuples, which in this case are (Australia, 61), (East Timor, 670), and (Papua New Guinea, 675).

In the above example, the Perl program models the page as a long string. An alternative model is to consider the DOM tree of a page. For example, Figure 9.3(a) shows a DOM tree that captures the HTML structure of a movie Web page. With the DOM model, the developer can write the wrapper in Figure 9.3(b) using the XPath language. The first rule of this wrapper

$$title = /html/body/div[1]/table/td[2]/text()$$

is an XPath rule that starts from the root, and then travels through the *body* child, the first *div* child, and *table* before arriving at the second *td* child of *table* and extracting the text value of this child as a movie title. The second rule extracts rating, and the third rule extracts run time in a similar fashion.

Another option is for the developer to employ a visual model of the pages. For example, the page in Figure 9.2(a) can be visually modeled with three blocks: the header "Countries in Australia (Continent)," the region of (country, code) tuples, and the footer "Copyright easycalls.com." Given a page, the developer can use this visual model to locate the second block, then parse this block using a string model to extract (country, code) tuples. In general, visual models often provide effective ways to remove headers, footers, and ads and to locate data regions. String models then provide effective ways to parse data regions to extract the desired data.

Regardless of the page model employed, using a low-level procedural language to write extraction programs can be very laborious. In response, several high-level wrapper languages have been proposed. For example, the HLRT language that we describe in detail

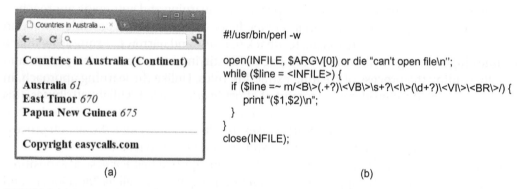

FIGURE 9.2 (a) An example page from source *easycalls.com* and (b) a manually constructed wrapper (a Perl program in this case) that extracts data from such pages.

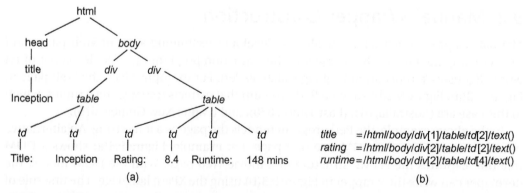

FIGURE 9.3 (a) The DOM tree of a Web page about a movie and (b) a wrapper that uses the DOM tree to extract the title, rating, and run time of the movie.

in the next section uses a tuple of $2n + 2$ values of the form $(h, t, l_1, r_1, \ldots, l_n, r_n)$ to specify a program for extracting n attributes. Given this tuple, a program E_W extracts the region between the *first* occurrence of h and the *last* occurrence of t as the data region. It then parses this region to extract strings between l_1 and r_1 as the values of the first attribute, between l_2 and r_2 as the values of the second attribute, and so on. If a developer determines that HLRT suffices for his or her needs, such as extracting (country, code) tuples from *easycalls.com*, then writing the wrapper reduces to specifying $2n + 2$ parameter values. Section 9.5 discusses other high-level wrapper languages, including datalog variants. Besides saving developer effort, wrappers written in such languages are often easier to understand, debug, and maintain than those in low-level procedural languages.

9.3 Learning-Based Wrapper Construction

While manually constructed wrappers can be very powerful, they often incur labor cost that is impractical when dealing with a large number of data sources. Learning approaches, in contrast, consider only limited wrapper types, but can automatically learn these using training examples. Providing such examples, typically by marking up a set of Web pages, can be done by technically naive users and requires far less work than manually writing the wrappers themselves.

This section explains learning approaches. We use HLRT, a simple wrapper learner, to explain the key ideas underlying wrapper learning. We then describe Stalker, a more complex wrapper learner, and use it to illustrate the full range of complexity in wrapper learning.

9.3.1 HLRT Wrappers

HLRT wrappers use string delimiters to specify how to extract relational tuples. To explain, consider again the page "Countries in Australia (Continent)," reproduced in Figure 9.4(a). Figure 9.4(b) shows the HTML text, which consists of a "head" ending with ⟨P⟩, a "tail" starting with ⟨HR⟩, and a data region in between, which lists (country, code) tuples, with country between ⟨B⟩ and ⟨/B⟩, and code between ⟨I⟩ and ⟨/I⟩.

To extract (country, code) tuples from such pages, we can write a simple wrapper that would "chop off" the head using the delimiter ⟨P⟩, "chop off" the tail using ⟨HR⟩, then scan the data region to extract strings between ⟨B⟩ and ⟨/B⟩ as countries, and between ⟨I⟩ and ⟨/I⟩ as codes. Since the head and tail may also contain strings between ⟨B⟩ and ⟨/B⟩, such as "Countries in Australia (Continent)," which is clearly not a country name, it is necessary to chop them off before scanning for countries and codes.

In HLRT (standing for "head-left-right-tail"), the above wrapper can be represented with a tuple of six strings (⟨P⟩, ⟨HR⟩, ⟨B⟩, ⟨/B⟩, ⟨I⟩, ⟨/I⟩). Formally, an HLRT wrapper that extracts n attributes $a_1, \ldots, a_n$ is a tuple of $(2n + 2)$ strings $(h, t, l_1, r_1, \ldots, l_n, r_n)$, where h marks the end of the head, t marks the start of the tail, and l_i and r_i delimit

FIGURE 9.4 An example of a Web page from which the **HLRT** wrapper model can use string delimiters to extract relational tuples (**country, code**).

attribute a_i. Such a wrapper does not have to extract *all* attributes present in a page. For example, the HLRT wrapper (`<P>`, `<HR>`, `<B>`, `</B>`) extracts only countries from the page in Figure 9.4(a).

Learning HLRT Wrappers

We now describe how to learn an HLRT wrapper for a data source S. Suppose a developer wants to extract attributes $a_1, \ldots, a_n$ from S. Suppose that after examining some pages of S the developer has established that an HLRT wrapper $W = (h, t, l_1, r_1, \ldots, l_n, r_n)$ will accurately extract these attributes.

Our goal is to learn the $(2n + 2)$ parameters $h, t, l_1, r_1, \ldots, l_n, r_n$. To do this, we label a set of pages $T = \{p_1, \ldots, p_m\}$ from source S. Labeling a page p_i means identifying in p_i the start and end positions of *all* values of the attributes $a_1, \ldots, a_n$ and is typically done using a specialized graphical user interface. For example, labeling the page in Figure 9.4(a) involves specifying that "Australia" is a country name, which starts at position 108 and ends at position 116, that "61" is a code, which starts at position 125 and ends at position 126, and so on.

The developer then feeds the labeled pages $p_1, \ldots, p_m$ into a learning module. The simplest kind of learning module systematically searches the space of all possible HLRT wrappers that are consistent with the labeled pages, as follows.

1. *Find all possible values for h:* Let x_i be the string from the beginning of page p_i until (but not including) the first occurrence of the very first attribute a_1. For example,

```
<HTML>
<TITLE>Countries in Australia (Continent)</TITLE>
<BODY>
<B>Countries in Australia (Continent)</B><P>
<B>
```

is such a string for the page in Figure 9.4(b). Clearly, the strings $x_1, \ldots, x_m$ contain the correct h. Thus, we take the set of all common substrings of $x_1, \ldots, x_m$ to be the candidate values for h.

2. *Find all possible values for t:* We can find all candidate values for t in a similar fashion.

3. *Find all possible values for each l_i:* Consider l_1, the left delimiter of attribute a_1. Clearly, l_1 must be a common suffix of all strings (in the labeled pages) that end right before a marked value of attribute a_1. Thus, we can take the set of all such suffixes to be the candidate values for l_1. We proceed similarly to find the candidate values for $l_2, \ldots, l_n$.

4. *Find all possible values for each r_i:* Similarly, we take the set of all common prefixes of all strings (in the labeled pages) that start right after a marked value of attribute a_i to be the candidate values for r_i.

5. *Search in the combined space of the above values:* We combine the above candidate values to form candidate wrappers. If a candidate wrapper W correctly extracts all values of $a_1, \ldots, a_n$ from a page p, we say W is consistent with p. As soon as we find a wrapper that is consistent with all labeled pages $p_1, \ldots, p_m$, we terminate and return that wrapper.

In the bibliographic notes we point to work that discusses how to optimize the above search, and how to select m, the number of pages to be labeled, to guarantee with a high probability that we produce a correct wrapper.

As described, HLRT wrappers are relatively easy to understand and implement. However, they have limited applicability. In particular, they assume a *flat tuple schema* and assume that all attributes can be reliably extracted using delimiting strings. In practice, many sources use more complex schemas, such as *nested tuple schemas*. For example, a page may describe a book as a tuple (title, authors, price), where the attribute authors is actually a list of tuples (first-name, last-name). Furthermore, we may not be able to extract attributes using delimiting strings, such as extracting zip codes from the addresses "4000 Colfax, Phoenix, AZ 85258" and "523 Vernon, Las Vegas, NV 89104." In what follows we describe Stalker wrappers that address these limitations.

9.3.2 Stalker Wrappers

We begin by defining nested tuple schemas, and then we discuss how Stalker learns wrappers that employ such schemas.

Nested Tuple Schemas

The Web page in Figure 9.5(a) is an example of a nested tuple schema. The page lists a restaurant's name, food type, and its multiple addresses. Each address in turn lists the street, city, state, zip code, and phone. Thus the page displays a single tuple (name, food, addresses), where addresses in turn contains multiple tuples (street, city, state, zip-code, phone).

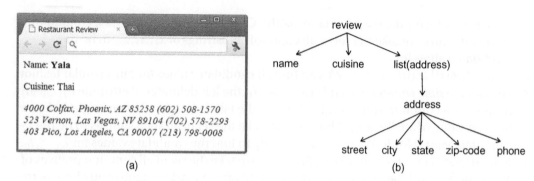

FIGURE 9.5 (a) A Web page that displays data using a nested tuple format and (b) the visualization of this format as a tree.

Nested tuples are very commonly used on Web pages because they are convenient for visual presentation. Formally, the set T of all nested tuple schemas satisfies the following properties:

- The schema that displays data as a single string belongs to T.
- If $T_1, \ldots, T_n$ belong to T, then the tuple schema $(T_1, \ldots, T_n)$, which generates tuples of the form $(t_1, \ldots, t_n)$ where t_i is an instance of T_i, $1 \leq i \leq n$, also belongs to T.
- Finally, if T belongs to T, then the list schema $\langle T \rangle$, which generates lists whose elements are instances of T, also belongs to T.

A nested tuple schema can be visualized as a tree whose leaves are strings and internal nodes are either tuple nodes or list nodes. The children of a tuple node are the different components of the tuple, while a list node has a single child that describes the type of the instances of the list. Figure 9.5(b) shows the tree that visualizes the schema of the page in Figure 9.5(a). Here a leaf node such as name is a string. The internal node list(addresses) is a list of address nodes, and each address node includes leaves such as street and city.

The Stalker Wrapper Model

A Stalker wrapper specifies a nested-tuple schema in the form of a tree and assigns to each node in the tree a set of rules that show how to extract data values for that node. Figure 9.6(a) shows a Stalker wrapper for restaurant reviews. (To avoid clutter, we omit the rules at certain leaf nodes.)

We demonstrate the wrapper in Figure 9.6(a) by showing how it is executed on the page p in Figure 9.6(b). We begin by assigning p to the root node restaurant. Then for each child node — name, cuisine, and list(address) — we execute the associated rules on the string assigned to the root node to extract the appropriate data values.

Consider executing the rules of node name. The first rule, *Start: SkipTo()*, scans p *from the start forward* until reaching a token , then marks the subsequent token as the *start* of a name. Similarly, the second rule, *End: BackTo()*, scans p *from the end backward* until , then marks the token right before as the *end* of a name. This allows

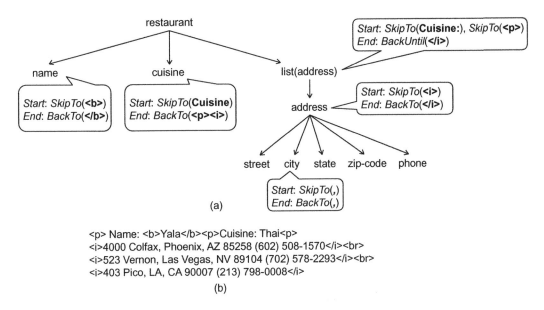

FIGURE 9.6 (a) A **Stalker** wrapper and (b) a target page.

us to pull out "Yala" as the restaurant name. We execute the rules at node cuisine similarly, to extract "Thai" as the cuisine.

Executing node list(address) is a bit more involved. Here the two rules extract the entire list, i.e., a string that contains *all* addresses. Specifically, rule *Start: SkipTo*(Cuisine:), *SkipTo*(<p>) scans *p* forward until Cuisine:, keeps scanning until <p>, then marks the next token as the start of the list. (Note that here a single *SkipTo* rule such as *Start: SkipTo*(<p>) will not correctly mark the start of the list. It will terminate well before that.) Similarly, rule *End: BackUntil*(</i>) scans *p* backward until </i>, then marks this token as the end of the list. Note that here *BackUntil*(</i>) does not consume </i> (unlike *BackTo*(</i>)). The entire list is then the string between the marks.

Next, we apply the two rules of node address to the above string to extract the addresses. Rule *Start: SkipTo*(<i>) scans the string until the first <i>, marks the next token as the start of the *first* address, then keeps scanning until the second <i>, marks the next token as the start of the *second* address, and so on. Similarly, rule *End: BackTo*(</i>) marks the ends of the addresses. We then extract the strings between the corresponding marks as the addresses.

In the next step, we apply the rules at nodes street, city, state, zip-code, and phone to each address to extract appropriate instances. For example, to extract a city, we scan an address forward until a comma, then backward until a comma, then extract the string in between.

Thus, a **Stalker** wrapper is executed in a top-down fashion. The root node is assigned a string (which is the Web page). Executing a child node of the root produces a set of substrings, which are then passed as input to the extraction rules of the children of this child node, and so on.

Stalker **EXTRACTION RULES**

We now describe the extraction rules in detail. Each rule consists of a *context* and a *sequence of commands*. Example contexts are *Start* and *End*, which we have seen earlier. Example sequences of commands are

SkipTo(<b>)
SkipTo(Cuisine:), SkipTo(<p>)

Each command takes as input a *landmark*, such as <b>, Cuisine:, <p>, or the triple (Name *Punctuation HTMLTag*).

To explain landmarks, we note that a page is viewed as a sequence of *tokens*, which are punctuation symbols, HTML tags, and alphanumeric strings (that are delimited by space, punctuation symbols, or HTML tags). A landmark is then a sequence of tokens and *wildcards*, where each wildcard such as *Punctuation* or *HTMLTag* refers to a class of tokens. A landmark can be viewed as a restricted kind of regular expression that can be matched to the page content. For example, the landmark

Name Punctuation HTMLTag

will match the string Name: <b>.

Executing a command proceeds by consuming text until reaching a string that matches the input landmark. Executing a sequence of commands means executing the commands in the listed order, with the next command starting where the previous command stopped.

To handle variations in the page format, Stalker also considers extraction rules that contain a *disjunction* of sequences of commands. For example, if restaurant names appear in bold for recommended ones and in italic otherwise, then we can use the following rule to mark the start of a restaurant:

Start : either SkipTo(<b>) or SkipTo(<i>)

This rule stops when we have consumed a <b> token or an <i> token. Similarly, the following rule marks the end of a restaurant:

End : either BackTo(</b>) or BackTo(Cuisine), BackTo(</i>)

In general, a disjunctive rule specifies an ordered list of sequences of commands. To apply the rule, we apply the sequences in order until we find a sequence that matches.

Learning Stalker Wrappers

We now describe how to learn a Stalker wrapper. The learner will take as input a nested tuple schema specified by the developer and a set of pages in which the instances of the nodes have been marked up.

FIGURE 9.7 (a) A simple address schema and (b) four addresses where the occurrences of **area-code** have been marked up.

Our goal is to use the marked-up pages to learn the rules for the nodes of the tree. Specifically, for each leaf node, such as name, we learn a start rule and an end rule, such as the two rules shown in Figure 9.6(a). For each internal node, such as list(address), we learn a start rule and an end rule for extracting the entire list. In what follows we illustrate the learning process by discussing how to learn a start rule for a leaf node.

For ease of exposition, we will consider the simple address schema in Figure 9.7(a) and the four pages E_1–E_4 in Figure 9.7(b), which shows the area codes marked up. Our goal is to use these marked-up examples to learn a start rule for area-code.

We apply a learning technique called *sequential covering*, which proceeds iteratively. The first iteration finds a rule that *covers* (i.e., correctly matches) a subset of the training examples. The second iteration finds a rule that covers a subset of the remaining training examples, and so on, until we have covered all training examples. The final rule is then a disjunction of all the rules found so far.

Continuing with the example in Figure 9.7, we first define the *prefix of an example* to be the string from the start of the example to the start of the area code. For example, the prefix of E_1 is "513 Pico, <b>Venice</b>, Phone: 1-<b>." Next, we select the example with the shortest prefix, which is E_2 in this case. The last token of the prefix is "(", which also matches two wildcards: *Punctuation* and *Anything*. (See Figure 9.8 for sample wildcards that we use in this learning scenario.) So we create three initial candidate rules:

$$R_1 = SkipTo((), R_2 = SkipTo(Punctuation), R_3 = SkipTo(Anything)$$

Rule R_1 *covers* E_2 and E_4, in that it stops right before an area code. In contrast, rules R_2 and R_3 do not cover any training example. Hence, the first iteration returns the rule R_1.

The second iteration considers the remaining examples: E_1 and E_3. E_1 has a shorter prefix, so we select E_1 and create three initial candidate rules:

$$R_4 = SkipTo(\texttt{<b>}), R_5 = SkipTo(HTMLTag), R_6 = SkipTo(Anything)$$

None of these rules covers any training example, so we select one rule to refine. We select R_4 because it uses no wildcards in the landmark. Refining R_4 produces the 18 candidate rules shown in Figure 9.8. Out of these rules, rules $R_7, R_{11}, R_{12}, R_{13}, R_{15}, R_{16}$, and R_{19} cover all the remaining examples, E_1 and E_3. Hence, we select one rule from these to return. We

Wildcards: *Anything, Numeric, AlphaNumeric, Alphabetic, Capitalized,*
AllCaps, HTMLTag, nonHTML, Punctuation

R_7: *SkipTo(-* **<b>***)* R_{16}: *SkipTo(***1***) SkipTo(***<b>***)*
R_8: *SkipTo(Punctuation* **<b>***)* R_{17}: *SkipTo(Numeric) SkipTo(***<b>***)*
R_9: *SkipTo(Anything* **<b>***)* R_{18}: *SkipTo(Punctuation) SkipTo(***<b>***)*
R_{10}: *SkipTo(***Venice***) SkipTo(***<b>***)* R_{19}: *SkipTo(HTMLTag) SkipTo(***<b>***)*
R_{11}: *SkipTo(***</b>***) SkipTo(***<b>***)* R_{20}: *SkipTo(AlphaNum) SkipTo(***<b>***)*
R_{12}: *SkipTo(:) SkipTo(***<b>***)* R_{21}: *SkipTo(Alphabetic) SkipTo(***<b>***)*
R_{13}: *SkipTo(-) SkipTo(***<b>***)* R_{22}: *SkipTo(Capitalized) SkipTo(***<b>***)*
R_{14}: *SkipTo(,) SkipTo(***<b>***)* R_{23}: *SkipTo(NonHTML) SkipTo(***<b>***)*
R_{15}: *SkipTo(***Phone***) SkipTo(***<b>***)* R_{24}: *SkipTo(Anything) SkipTo(***<b>***)*

FIGURE 9.8 A sample set of wildcards and a set of candidate rules obtained while learning a start rule for area-code.

end up selecting R_7 because it has the longest end landmark (all other rules end with a one-token landmark). Since there are no more uncovered examples, the algorithm terminates returning the disjunctive rule that combines R_1 and R_7 as the start rule for area-code:

Start : either *SkipTo(()* or *SkipTo(-<b>)*

Discussion

The wrapper model of Stalker subsumes that of HLRT, and both can be viewed as modeling finite state automata. Together, HLRT and Stalker illustrate how imposing structure on the target schema language makes learning practical. This structure can be relatively simple, as in the flat tuples of HLRT, or significantly more complex, as in the tree structure of Stalker. Regardless, the structure severely restricts the target languages and transforms the general learning problem into an easier one of learning a relatively small set of parameters, such as delimiting strings in HLRT or extraction rules in Stalker.

Even with the restricted search space, HLRT and Stalker still need to use heuristics to make learning the parameters easier. For example, in each iteration Stalker selects the example with the shortest prefix to generate candidate extraction rules. Stalker then refines each rule by expanding the landmark or adding another command (see Section 9.3.2). Even with these heuristics, we often still face a vast search space. For example, the tiny scenario in Figure 9.7 already generates 18 rules in its second iteration (see Figure 9.8). Complications such as variations in page formats further blow up the search space, making learning brittle.

9.4 Wrapper Learning without Schema

The so-called *automatic approaches* to wrapper learning take as input a set of Web pages of a source S, examine the similarities and dissimilarities across the pages, and automatically infer the schema T_S of the pages and a program E_W that extracts data conforming to T_S.

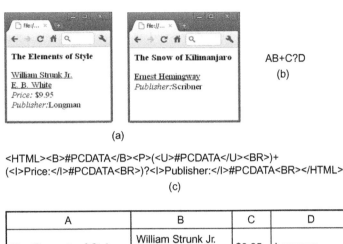

(a)

AB+C?D

(b)

```
<HTML><B>#PCDATA</B><P>(<U>#PCDATA</U><BR>)+
(<I>Price:</I>#PCDATA<BR>)?<I>Publisher:</I>#PCDATA<BR></HTML>
```

(c)

A	B	C	D
The Elements of Style	William Strunk Jr.	$9.95	Longman
	E.B. White		
The Snow of Kilimanjaro	Ernest Hemingway		Scribner

(d)

FIGURE 9.9 (a) Two Web pages from the same data source, (b) the schema T_S of the pages, expressed as a regular expression, (c) the extraction program E_W, and (d) the data extracted by E_W from the above two pages.

As an example, given the two pages that describe books in Figure 9.9(a), an automatic approach may return the schema T_S in Figure 9.9(b) and the extraction program E_W in Figure 9.9(c), both written in a regular-expression language variant. The schema T_S shows that each page lists an attribute A, one or more values of attribute B, optionally attribute C, then attribute D. The extraction program E_W shows how to parse a page to extract the data of the attributes A–D (encoded as #PCDATA in the program). Applying E_W to the two pages in Figure 9.9(a) produces the table of extracted data in Figure 9.9(d).

Thus, in contrast to the methods described in the previous sections, automatic methods do not take the target schema as input. Consequently, they cannot assign meaningful names (e.g., author, title) to the attributes of the schema they learn but only generic ones (e.g., A and B). The main advantage of automatic wrapper learners is that they require no human intervention.

We now describe RoadRunner, a representative automatic approach. We illustrate how RoadRunner models the target schema T_S and the extraction program E_W, then how it infers T_S and E_W from a set of Web pages.

9.4.1 Modeling Schema T_S and Program E_W

The Web pages of source S use the schema T_S to display data. RoadRunner models T_S as a nested-tuple schema (see Section 9.3.2). Recall that such a schema nests tuples and lists and allows certain kinds of *optionals* and *disjunctions*. RoadRunner allows *optionals* in that certain attributes (e.g., attribute C in Figure 9.9(d)) can be missing from a page. But it does not allow disjunctions. Thus, T_S can be expressed as a *union-free regular expression*, such as the one shown in Figure 9.9(b).

RoadRunner models the extraction program E_W as a regular expression that when evaluated on a Web page will extract the attributes of T_S. Figure 9.9(c) shows such a regular expression R. Given a Web page, R matches <HTML><B> from the start of the page, then matches and returns the string up to the first </B> as the value of attribute A, and so on. On the first Web page of Figure 9.9(a), for example, R would return "The Elements of Style" as the value of A. In general, the fields #PCDATA of R are the "slots" for the values of the attributes of T_S, and these values are not supposed to contain any HTML tag (such as <B>).

The assumptions of no disjunction in T_S and no HTML tag in attribute values reduce the complexity of finding T_S and E_W. But they do limit the applicability of RoadRunner. The bibliographic notes discuss works that relax these assumptions.

9.4.2 Inferring Schema T_S and Program E_W

Given a set of Web pages $\mathcal{P} = \{p_1, \ldots, p_n\}$ from the source S, RoadRunner examines $\mathcal{P}$ to infer the extraction program E_W and to infer the schema T_S from E_W. In the rest of this section we focus on the first step of inferring E_W; the second step of inferring T_S from E_W is relatively straightforward.

To infer the extraction program E_W, RoadRunner proceeds iteratively. It begins by initializing E_W to be a page from $\mathcal{P}$, say p_1. Page p_1 can clearly be viewed as a regular expression that matches only p_1. Thus at this point E_W matches only p_1. RoadRunner then takes another page from $\mathcal{P}$, say p_2, and attempts to generalize E_W so that E_W can also match p_2. Continuing in this way, in the end RoadRunner returns an E_W that has been generalized (in a minimal fashion) to match all pages in $\mathcal{P}$.

We now focus on the generalization step. To illustrate, we will use the example in Figure 9.10, where E_W has just been initialized to be the page p_1, and we have to generalize it to match a target page p_2. We proceed with the following steps.

Tokenizing the Target Page
We first convert the target page p_2 into a sequence of tokens, where each token is an HTML tag or a string (that does not contain any HTML tag). The right side of Figure 9.10 shows how p_2 has been converted into 27 tokens (one per line, except lines 09-11, 15-17, and 21-23, which contain three tokens each).

Generalizing Program E_W to Match the Target Page
Next, we apply E_W to match p_2. Continuing with our example, currently E_W is just the regular expression represented by the page p_1. To facilitate matching p_1 with p_2, we also display p_1 one token per line, as shown in the left side of Figure 9.10 (except lines 08-10 and 14-16, which contain three tokens each).

We now match p_1 with p_2 line by line, from the top down. If we reach the end of p_2, then E_W has successfully matched p_2 and does not have to be generalized. Otherwise, there is

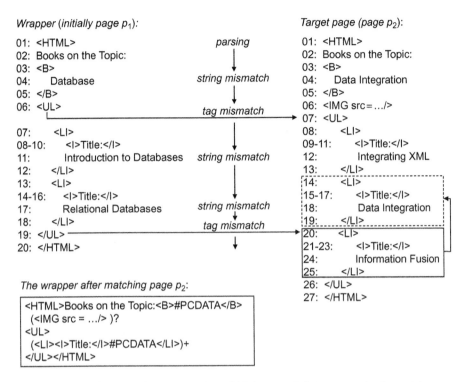

FIGURE 9.10 Generalizing the extraction program E_W, which is currently just page p_1, to also match page p_2.

a *mismatch*. A *string mismatch* involves two strings, such as "Database" on line 04 of p_1 versus "Data Integration" on line 04 of p_2. A *tag mismatch* involves an HTML tag and a string, or two tags, such as <UL> on line 06 of p_1 versus <IMG src=.../> on line 06 of p_2. We must generalize the extraction program E_W to resolve these mismatches.

It is not difficult to show that if a string mismatch happens, we have just discovered a new attribute, and the two strings are two different values of that attribute. To resolve this mismatch, we generalize E_W by adding a new #PCDATA slot to capture the new attribute. For example, after detecting the string mismatch "Database" versus "Data Integration" on line 04 of p_1 and p_2, we generalize the initial part of E_W from

```
<HTML>Books on the Topic:<B>Database</B>
```

to

```
<HTML>Books on the Topic:<B>\#PCDATA</B>
```

Resolving a tag mismatch is far more difficult. Such a mismatch happens due to either an *iterator* or an *optional*. For example, the mismatch <UL> versus <IMG src=.../> on line 06 is due to an optional image on page p_2. The mismatch </UL> on line 19 of p_1 versus <LI> on line 20 of p_2, on the other hand, is due to an iterator, and it comes from the different lengths of the book lists (two books in p_1 versus three books in p_2).

When a tag mismatch happens, we first try to find if it is due to an iterator. If it is, we generalize E_W to incorporate the iterator. Otherwise, we assume it is due to an optional and generalize E_W accordingly (later we explain why we look for iterators before optionals). We now discuss the two cases, starting with the case of optional.

RESOLVING AN OPTIONAL MISMATCH

We begin by detecting which page includes the optional by searching for the mismatched strings in the pages. Consider again the mismatch `<UL>` versus `<IMG src=.../>` on line 06 of pages p_1 and p_2. There are two cases.

1. String `<UL>` is the optional. Then after skipping it we should be able to continue by matching `<IMG src=.../>` of page p_2 with the first occurrence of `<IMG src=.../>` in the rest of p_1.
2. String `<IMG src=.../>` is the optional. Then after skipping it we can continue by matching `<UL>` of page p_1 with the first occurrence of `<UL>` in the rest of p_2.

Since `<UL>` occurs in the rest of p_2 (after `<IMG src=.../>`), and `<IMG src=.../>` does not occur in the rest of p_1 (after `<UL>`), it is clear that we are in Case 2, that is, `<IMG src=.../>` is the optional.

Once we have found which string is the optional, it is relatively straightforward to generalize E_W. Continuing with the above example, we generalize E_W by introducing the pattern `(<IMG src=.../>)?`, then resume matching at tokens `<UL>` on line 06 of p_1 and line 07 of p_2, respectively.

RESOLVING AN ITERATOR MISMATCH

An iterator repeats a pattern, which we will refer to as a *square*. For example, page p_1 contains a list of two books, where each book description is a square of the form `<LI><I>Title:</I> ... </LI>`. An iterator mismatch happens when the two lists differ in their numbers of squares. For example, pages p_1 and p_2 contain lists of two and three books, respectively. This causes an iterator mismatch at line 19 of p_1 and line 20 of p_2 (tokens `</UL>` versus `<LI>`).

To resolve such a mismatch, we must first find the squares, then use them to find the lists, then generalize E_W to account for the lists. Let the two lists be $U = u_1 u_2 \ldots u_n$ and $V = v_1 v_2 \ldots v_m$, where the u's and v's are squares. Suppose $n < m$; then by the time we run into an iterator mismatch, we can conclude that we have successfully matched u_1 with v_1, u_2 with v_2, and so on, until u_n with v_n. The mismatch happens the moment we move on to the first token of v_{n+1}.

This implies that (a) the last token right before the mismatch must be the last token of u_n and v_n, that is, *the last token of a square*, and (b) one of the mismatched tokens must be the first token of v_{n+1}, that is, *the first token of a square*. This allows us to know the overall form of the square. For example, consider the mismatch at line 19 of p_1 and line 20 of p_2. The last token right before the mismatch is `</LI>`, and the mismatched tokens are `</UL>` and `<LI>`. Thus, the square is either of the form `</UL> ... </LI>` or `<LI> ...`

</LI>. Next, we search the pages p_1 and p_2 (only the portions after the mismatch point) for square candidates of these forms. It is easy to see that there is only one square candidate, <LI> ... </LI>, spanning lines 20-25 of page p_2.

Once we have found a square candidate s, we "double check" that s is indeed a square, by matching it against the square immediately above it, in a backward fashion. In the above example, we start by matching line 25 of page p_2 with line 19 of the same page, then line 24 with line 18, and so on. If the match is successful, we declare s a true square.

Next, we generalize the extraction program E_W, by searching for contiguous repeated occurrences of s around the mismatch region, then replacing those with $(s)+$. For example, we replace squares <LI> ... </LI> with

```
<UL>
    (<LI><I>Title:</I>#PCDATA</LI>)+
</UL>
```

as shown in Figure 9.10.

We can now describe the entire process of matching pages p_1 and p_2 in Figure 9.10. The first mismatch at line 04 is a string mismatch. This is resolved by adding #PCDATA to E_W. The next mismatch at line 06 is a tag mismatch. To resolve this, we first assume that this is an iterator mismatch. This produces two square candidates: <UL> ... </B> and <IMG src=.../> ... </B>. We can quickly see that neither candidate is a true square, because the rest of page p_1 and the rest of page p_2 (after line 06) do not contain </B>. Thus, this is not an iterator mismatch. Next, we assume this is an optional mismatch, and resolve it with (<IMG src=.../>)?.

We then resume matching line 07 of p_1 with line 08 of p_2. The string mismatches at lines 11 versus 12 and lines 17 versus 18 are resolved with #PCDATA. The next mismatch at lines 19 versus 20 is a tag mismatch. We have described earlier how to resolve this as an iterator mismatch. After this, matching resumes at lines 19 versus 26 and ends at the last tokens of p_1 and p_2. At this point, the original program E_W, which is page p_1, has been successfully generalized into the program in the bottom of Figure 9.10, to match both p_1 and p_2.

The above example also makes clear why in the case of a tag mismatch, we want to look for an iterator first. Consider the tag mismatch at lines 19 versus 20 (</UL> versus <LI>). If we look for an optional first, we will generalize E_W so that it assumes each page contains two books, with a third book being optional. It will miss the list of books entirely and thus is clearly incorrect.

Finally, we note that resolving an iterator mismatch often involves *recursion*. To see this, consider a simple example in which we have found the square candidate in Figure 9.11(a). To verify that it is a true square, we want to match it against the square in Figure 9.11(b), in a backward fashion. We start out matching </LI> with </LI>, then <B>Jane Lee</B> with <B>James Madison</B>. Then we have a tag mismatch </B> versus Data Integration. This happens because each book square contains a list of authors, and the two squares in the above figure differ in the number of authors, causing the mismatch. Thus, while resolving an outer mismatch, we may run into an inner mismatch, which in turn may cause

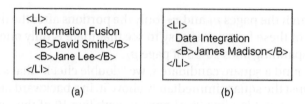

FIGURE 9.11 An example to illustrate that resolving an iterator mismatch often involves recursion.

further mismatches, and so on. Clearly, the mismatches must be resolved from inside out, in a recursive fashion.

Reducing Runtime Complexity

As described, to generalize the extraction program E_W to match a page p, we must consider the following:

- We must detect and resolve all mismatches.
- For each mismatch, we must decide if it is a string mismatch (thus introducing a new attribute), an iterator mismatch, or an optional mismatch.
- For an iterator or optional mismatch, we can search on either the side of the program E_W or the side of the target page p. For example, in the case of an optional mismatch, the optional can be either on E_W or on p.
- For an iterator or optional mismatch, even when we limit the search to just one side, there are often multiple square candidates and optional candidates to consider.
- To resolve an iterator mismatch, it may be necessary to recursively resolve multiple inner mismatches first.

As a consequence of the above points, we are typically faced with a rather large search space, with multiple options at each decision point, and when we "dead end," we must backtrack to the closest decision point and try another option. In fact, it can be shown that the above generalization algorithm incurs exponential run time with respect to the length of the inputs.

Consequently, RoadRunner employs three heuristics to reduce the run time. First, it limits the number of options at each decision point by ranking and retaining only the top k options. For example, it ranks optional candidates based on their lengths, then considers only the top four.

Second, RoadRunner does not allow backtracking at decision points where it thinks the chance that it has been wrong is very low. For example, at a decision point that considers whether the mismatch is due to an iterator or an optional, if RoadRunner has found an iterator, then it disables further backtracking. That is, it will never revisit this decision point and explore the option that the mismatch may be due to an optional.

Finally, RoadRunner ignores certain iterator and optional patterns judged to be highly unlikely. For example, it does not consider any iterator or optional pattern that is delimited on either side by an optional pattern, such as ((<HR>)?<LI>#PCDATA</LI>) and (<BR>)?(<HR>)?.

9.5 Interactive Wrapper Construction

Learning and automatic approaches to wrapper construction often use heuristics to reduce the time it takes to search the huge space of wrapper candidates. Such heuristics are not perfect, and as a result, these approaches have often been brittle: sometimes they produce correct wrappers and sometimes they do not, but we cannot use them blindly because we do not know when they are correct.

Interactive approaches address this problem by injecting user feedback into the search process. They start with little or no input from the wrapper developer and search the space of wrappers until uncertainty arises. At that point they ask for user feedback, then resume searching, until they converge on a wrapper that satisfies the user. In these systems, user feedback can come in multiple forms: users can label a new Web page, identify the correct extraction result, visually create extraction rules, answer questions posed by the system, or identify page patterns. The main challenge faced by these systems is to decide *when* to solicit feedback from the user and *what* question to pose to them.

In what follows we describe three representative works using the interactive approach. We describe only the basic ideas underlying the works and point to more elaborate descriptions in the bibliographic notes.

9.5.1 Interactive Labeling of Pages with Stalker

Recall that Stalker asks the user to label a set of Web pages, then uses these pages to search for a wrapper. We can modify Stalker to be interactive, in that it asks the user to label pages *during* the search process. Specifically, Stalker asks the developer to label a page (or a few pages) and uses this page to build an initial wrapper. Then Stalker can interleave search with soliciting user feedback until it finds a satisfactory wrapper. To decide which page to ask the user to label next, Stalker maintains two candidate wrappers and finds pages on which the two wrappers disagree. It then asks the user to label one of these "problematic" pages.

Stalker employs a form of active learning called *co-testing*, in which alternative hypotheses (wrappers in this case) are co-tested on a new page to see if they disagree. We now describe the interactive Stalker and its co-testing mechanism in detail.

1. **Initialization:** The user labels one or several Web pages. In our example, to begin extracting phone numbers of restaurants, the user would label the phone numbers in Figure 9.12.

Name:<i>Savory</i><p>Phone:<i> (608) 263-4567 </i><p>Fax:(608) 523-4917

FIGURE 9.12 To start the process of wrapper construction, the interactive **Stalker** may ask the user to label a phone number on a restaurant address.

2. **Learning two wrappers:** Next, we learn to extract phone numbers from the labeled pages. This means learning to mark the start and end of a phone number (see Section 9.3.2). For simplicity, let us focus on learning to mark the *start* of a phone number. In this case, we may learn a rule such as

$$R_1 : SkipTo(\texttt{Phone:<i>})$$

This is known as a *forward* rule in that it consumes the page forward from the start, until reaching the end of Phone:<i>. Alternatively, we can also learn a *backward* rule such as

$$R_2 : BackTo(\texttt{Fax}), BackTo(())$$

which consumes the page backward from the end (see Section 9.3.2). Both rules mark the start of phone numbers. The traditional Stalker learns just one of these rules. But the interactive Stalker will learn both, thus in a sense learning two alternative wrappers.

3. **Applying the wrappers to find a problematic page:** Next, let P be a large set of unlabeled pages available to Stalker. Stalker finds all pages in P on which the two wrappers disagree. In the above example, this means pages on which the forward and backward rules identify two different sets of the start of phone numbers. Stalker can either randomly select a page or select one with the most disagreements.

4. **Soliciting feedback and relearning:** Since the rules disagree on the selected page p, at least one of them must be wrong, and user feedback can help us identify which one. Thus, we remove p from the set of unlabeled pages P, ask the user to label it, add it to the set of labeled pages, then go back to Step 2 to relearn the rules. We repeat steps 2-4 until there are no more problematic pages in P. (If we have exhausted all pages in P, we can expand P by adding more unlabeled pages.) In the end we have two wrappers and can return as the output one or both wrappers.

9.5.2 Identifying Correct Extraction Results with Poly

The second interactive wrapper learning system we describe is Poly, and it differs from Stalker in several ways. While Poly also uses co-testing, it maintains multiple candidate wrappers instead of just two. Second, instead of asking a user to label a page, it applies the wrappers to the page, then asks the user to identify the correct extraction result. Finally, instead of using the string model, Poly uses DOM tree and visual models to build wrappers.

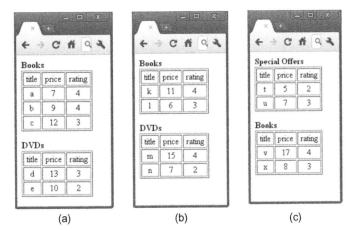

FIGURE 9.13 **Poly** starts by asking the user to highlight a tuple on the Web page in (a), then later uses pages in (b) and (c) to evaluate the generated wrappers.

1. **Initialization:** Poly assumes that there are multiple tuples per page, and that the user wants to extract a subset of these tuples. Thus, it starts by asking the user to label a target tuple on a page by highlighting the attributes of the tuple.

   Consider, for example, the Web page in Figure 9.13(a). Suppose we want to extract all tuples with rating 4 in table "Books." Then the user defines the attributes of the output schema to be *title, price*, and *rating*, and highlights these attributes in a tuple, say the first tuple $(a, 7, 4)$ in table "Books."

2. **Using the labeled tuple to generate multiple wrappers:** Next, Poly generates a set of wrappers $\mathcal{W}$, such that each wrapper extracts from the current page a set of tuples that contains the highlighted tuple. In the above example, Poly may generate wrappers that extract (1) all book and DVD tuples, (2) just book tuples, (3) book and DVD tuples with rating 4, (4) just book tuples with rating 4, (5) the first tuple of all tables, or (6) just the first tuple of the first table. All of these wrappers extract the labeled tuple $(a, 7, 4)$.

3. **Soliciting the correct extraction result:** Next, Poly shows the user the extraction results produced by wrappers in $\mathcal{W}$ on the page and asks the user to identify the correct one. Poly then removes from the set $\mathcal{W}$ all wrappers that do not produce the correct result.

   In the above example, since we want to extract book tuples with rating 4, the user would identify the set $\{(a, 7, 4), (b, 9, 4)\}$ as the correct result. This would remove wrappers such as (1) extract all book and DVD tuples, (2) just book tuples, (3) the first tuple of all tables, or (4) just the first tuple of the first table. The set $\mathcal{W}$ still contains wrappers that give correct extraction results on the current page, such as (1) all book and DVD tuples with rating 4, (2) book tuples with rating 4, and (3) all tuples with rating 4 from the first table.

4. **Evaluating the remaining wrappers on verification pages:** Next, Poly applies all wrappers in $\mathcal{W}$ to a large set of unlabeled pages Q to see if the wrappers disagree. For example, when applied to the page in Figure 9.13(b), the two wrappers "extracting all

book and DVD tuples with rating 4" and "extracting book tuples with rating 4" disagree in that they extract different sets of tuples. As another example, when applied to the page in Figure 9.13(c), the two wrappers "extracting book tuples with rating 4" and "extracting all tuples with rating 4 in the first table" disagree.

As soon as Poly finds a disagreement on a page q, it repeats Steps 3-4. That is, it asks the user to again select the correct result on q, removes from $\mathcal{W}$ all wrappers that do not produce the correct result, then evaluates $\mathcal{W}$ on pages in Q again. Poly terminates, returning $\mathcal{W}$ when all wrappers in $\mathcal{W}$ agree on all pages in Q.

We note that in Step 3 of the above algorithm, to help the user quickly find the correct result, Poly can show the results in ranked order of decreasing likelihood of being the correct result. Furthermore, if the user does not find the correct result, then he or she can edit a result shown by Poly into a correct one, or highlight another tuple on the current page.

GENERATING THE WRAPPERS

We now look in detail at how Poly generates the wrappers. Suppose the user has just high-lighted the tuple $(a, 7, 4)$ on the page in Figure 9.13(a). Poly first converts the page into a DOM tree, such as the simplified tree shown in Figure 9.14. Next, Poly identifies the nodes that correspond to the highlighted attributes. They are the three nodes marked with squares in Figure 9.14. Poly finds the least common ancestor node of these squared nodes, which is the node <tr> with ID 8 in the figure. We refer to this node as a *tuple node*, because its subtree contains the data of a single tuple.

Next, Poly creates an XPath-like expression E that denotes the path from the root to the highlighted tuple node: $E = /html/table/tr$. It applies E to the entire page to find all potential tuple nodes, which are <tr> nodes with IDs 7-13 in the figure. The intuition is that the path from the root to the potential tuple nodes must be similar to the path from the root to the highlighted tuple node.

Next, Poly creates wrappers, each of which extracts a subset of the potential tuple nodes. It does this in a top-down, level-by-level fashion, and uses an XPath-like language to encode the wrappers. At level 1, all wrappers start with $/html$.

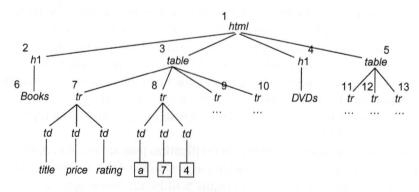

FIGURE 9.14 The DOM tree of the Web page in Figure 9.13(a).

At level 2 of the DOM tree, the wrappers must "touch" node 3 or node 5, or both of them, in order to get to the possible tuple nodes at lower levels. Thus, we refine the partial wrapper */html* into a set of wrappers: */html/table*[1] (which touches node 3), */html/table*[2] (node 5), */html/table* (both nodes), and */html/table*[*prevSibling*($h1, Books$) = *true*] (node 3), among others. Here *prevSibling* is a predefined predicate, and wrapper */html/table*[*prevSibling*($h1, Books$) = *true*] touches the node table that follows a sibling node whose name is "h1" and whose text content contains "Books."

At level 3, a wrapper may touch any subset of the potential tuple nodes, and Poly generates these wrappers accordingly. For example, it may generate wrapper */html/table*[1]*/tr*, which extracts all tuples of the first table, or it may generate wrapper */html/table*[*prevSibling*($h1, Books$) = *true*]*/tr*, which extracts all tuples of the table "Books," and so on. Poly proceeds similarly at subsequent levels. In general, the set of wrappers that Poly generates depends on the expressiveness of the internal XPath-like language that Poly uses to encode the wrappers.

To create wrappers, Poly uses a visual model of the page in addition to the DOM tree model. The visual model helps remove incorrect tuple nodes. For example, the path */html/table/tr* may extract not just true tuple nodes, but also ad nodes, which contain large advertisement regions. To remove such ad nodes, Poly can compute the visual rectangle of the rendered page that covers a tuple set, then discard this rectangle and the associated tuple set if it exceeds a prespecified size.

9.5.3 Creating Extraction Rules with Lixto

The Lixto system uses a new user interaction mode. Instead of labeling pages or selecting extraction results, users visually create extraction rules in Lixto using highlighting and dialog boxes. In addition, Lixto differs from the previous systems we described by encoding the extraction rules internally using an expressive datalog-like language, defined over both a DOM tree model and a string model of the pages.

Creating the Extraction Rules Visually
In our discussion we use the example Web page in Figure 9.15(a), which lists books being auctioned. To extract these books, a user can visually create four extraction rules. The first rule extracts the books themselves (i.e., the page regions that contain the books), and the next three rules extract the title, price, and number of bids from each book, respectively. Lixto encodes these rules internally as rules R_1–R_4 in Figure 9.15(b). We explain these rules in detail at the end of this section.

Note that in general, rules can depend on one another. For example, rule R_1 extracts books, and rule R_2 extracts titles from the result of R_1. As another example, a rule R_5 that extracts the currency (e.g., "$", "£") would depend on R_3, because R_5 would take as input prices (e.g., "$15.00"), which are the output of R_3.

We now describe how the user visually creates the rules. In the above example, the user starts by creating a rule to extract books. To do this, he or she highlights a book tuple,

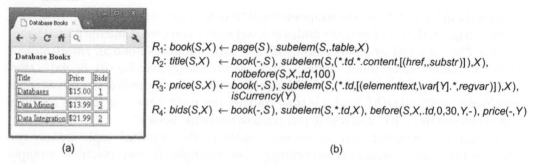

R_1: $book(S,X) \leftarrow page(S), subelem(S,.table,X)$
R_2: $title(S,X) \leftarrow book(-,S), subelem(S,(*.td.*.content,[(href,,substr)]),X), notbefore(S,X,.td,100)$
R_3: $price(S,X) \leftarrow book(-,S), subelem(S,(*.td,[(elementtext,\var[Y].*,regvar)]),X), isCurrency(Y)$
R_4: $bids(S,X) \leftarrow book(-,S), subelem(S,*.td,X), before(S,X,.td,0,30,Y,-), price(-,Y)$

(a)   (b)

FIGURE 9.15 (a) A Web page that lists a set of auctions and (b) an internal datalog-like program that **Lixto** generates to wrap such pages.

say the first tuple (i.e., "Databases") in Figure 9.15(a). Lixto maps this tuple into the corresponding subtree of the DOM tree of the page, then extrapolates from the subtree to create rule R_1 in Figure 9.15(b), which extracts the `<table>` subtrees as book tuples. Next, Lixto shows these newly extracted tuples (i.e., "Data Mining" and "Data Integration") to the user. These tuples are correct, and hence the user accepts R_1. (However, note that the user never sees R_1, which is kept internally by Lixto.)

To create a rule to extract titles, the user first specifies that this rule will extract from the book instances identified by rule R_1. Next, the user highlights a title, say the first title "Databases" in Figure 9.15(a). Lixto uses this title to create the internal rule

$$title(S,X) \leftarrow book(-,S), subelem(S, (*.td.*.content, [(href,,substr)]),X)$$

which says that if a data item is inside a `<td>` cell of a table and it is linked (i.e., it contains a "href" tag), then it is a title. Lixto uses this rule to extract, and shows the user all the titles in Figure 9.15(a).

The user realizes that this rule is too general because it extracts not only the titles but also the bids (which are also linked). Hence, the user restricts the rule by specifying that no other data cell should exist within 100 characters *before* a title. This condition removes all bids (because a price data cell exists before each bid) and generates rule R_2 in Figure 9.15(b), which is correct and is accepted by the user. The user then proceeds similarly to create rules R_3–R_4 that extract price and number of bids, respectively.

The user can iteratively restrict or relax a rule using a set of conditions defined by Lixto, such as the target instance (1) must appear before or after a specific element, or (2) must not be close to a specific element, or (3) must not contain a specific element. The user specifies these conditions with highlighting and dialog boxes.

In addition to highlighting and dialog boxes, the user can also write regular expressions or refer to real-world concepts defined by Lixto. For example, to extract the currency (e.g., "$", "£"), he or she may specify that the currency must be a substring of a price string (e.g., "$15.00"), and satisfy predicate *isCurrency*() supplied by Lixto. This allows Lixto to generate the following rule (the format of which we will explain soon):

$$R_5 : currency(S,X) \leftarrow price(-,S), subtext(S, \backslash var[Y], X), isCurrency(Y)$$

Finally, we note that to correctly extract an attribute (or a tuple), the user often writes *multiple* rules, each covering a formatting variation. For example, if book titles are either linked or in italics, we need two separate rules. The set of titles is then the union of the output of these two.

Representing the Extraction Rules

Lixto encodes an extraction rule with datalog rules in which the head predicate specifies the instance to be extracted and the body predicates, which include predicates over the DOM tree, specify constraints that must hold true.

Consider the rule R_1 in Figure 9.15(b). The head *book(S,X)* states that X is a book to be extracted and it comes from S. The body predicate *page(S)* states that S is a Web page, and *subelem(S, .table, X)* states that X is a subtree with root `<table>` in the DOM tree of S. In general, *subelem(S, P, X)* states that X is a subtree of S, with the root of the subtree being a node that satisfies the XPath-like expression P.

In rule R_2, the head *title(S,X)* states that X is a title to be extracted from S. The body predicate *book(-, S)* states that S is a book. In predicate *subelem(S, (*.td.* .content, [(href, , substr)]), X)*, the expression *(*.td.* .content, [(href, , substr)])* specifies paths in the DOM tree that lead to `<td>` nodes that contain a link (see the reference to "href" in the expression). Thus, the entire predicate says that X is a subtree of S with root `<td>` and that X contains a link. Finally, the predicate *notbefore(S, X, .td, 100)* states that there is no subtree of S with root `<td>` that exists *before* X, within a distance of 100 (for a predefined notion of distance).

Rule R_3 in Figure 9.15(b) can be explained similarly. In this rule, the predicates *subelem(S, (*.td, [(elementtext, \backslash var[Y].*, regvar)]), X)* and *isCurrency(Y)* jointly state that (a) the price X is a subtree of S with root `<td>` and (b) the text of this subtree matches the regular expression $\backslash var[Y].*$, which is a currency sign followed by zero or more characters.

Finally, in rule R_4, the predicates *before(S, X, .td, 0, 30, Y)* and *price(-, Y)* jointly state that (a) the bid X is a subtree of S with root `<td>` and (b) a price must exist within a distance 0-30 before X.

To generate rules such as the ones above, Lixto generalizes over the DOM tree of the page. For example, when the user highlights a book tuple, Lixto maps the tuple into a subtree with root `<table>`, then generates rule R_1, which says that any subtree with root `<table>` is a book tuple. As such, Lixto generates rules in a way analogous to the way Poly generates wrappers, using the DOM structure. Unlike Poly, however, Lixto can also combine a string model of the page with the DOM tree model to create rules, such as rule R_5 to extract the currency sign.

Bibliographic Notes

Work on wrapper construction dates back to 1997. Recent surveys include [115, 362, 392]. A variety of page schemas, including flat and nested tuple schemas, are discussed in [392, Chapter 9]. Gold [256, 257] shows that learning regular languages from examples alone is very difficult. Building on this work, Grumbach and Mecca [273] and subsequent work in the RoadRunner [153, 154] and ExAlg [33] projects discuss why it is difficult to apply a grammar inference approach to learn arbitrary page schemas.

Early work on wrapper construction used manual techniques. Well-known projects include W4F [503], Minerva [152], XWRAP [394], TSIMMIS [290, 291], WebOQL [39], FLORID [401], Jedi [308], and [41, 276, 292].

Wrapper construction systems that use learning techniques include SHOPBOT [195], WIEN [358, 360], Stalker [449, 450], SoftMealy [305], WL^2 [147], and [374]. The HLRT wrappers were introduced in [360] and discussed in detail in [357, 358]. The Stalker wrappers were introduced in [450]. Several works mentioned in the learning approach, such as CRYSTAL [529], WHISK [528], RAPIER [105], and SRV [151], are designed to operate primarily on free text, such as news articles. Extracting structured data from free text is referred to as *information extraction* (see [506] for a survey) and is often viewed as a problem distinct from that of wrapper construction.

Automatic approaches to wrapper construction include IEPAD [116], RoadRunner [153, 154], ExAlg [33], DeLa [562], and DEPTA [589]. RoadRunner assumed no disjunction in the target regular expression and no HTML tag in attribute values. These assumptions were subsequently relaxed by ExAlg [33].

Interactive approaches include NoDoSe [9], interactive Stalker [451], Lixto [56, 57, 262], iFlex [519], and [322]. The Poly system described in this chapter is based on the system of [322]. The systems W4F [503] and XWRAP [394] also employ user interaction.

An ontology-based approach to wrapper construction, inspired by conceptual modeling, is described in [210], and a visual approach is described in [103]. Discovering record boundaries in multiple-record Web pages is described in [211, 393]. Once discovered, free text inside each record can be segmented into separate data fields using the technique in [94].

Several works have considered wrapper construction for multiple sites or at the Web scale. Chang et al. [139] collaboratively wrap multiple data sources all at once. Dalvi et al. [158] and Gulhane et al. [274] consider how to extract structured data at the Web scale. Cafarella et al. [102] consider how to extract millions of HTML tables on the Web.

Once built, it is also critical to maintain a wrapper over time, as the underlying data source evolves. Several works attempt to detect when a wrapper is broken (i.e., extracting incorrect data) [359, 375, 419] and to repair broken wrappers [375, 429, 441, 493]. Dalvi et al. [159] and Aditya et al. [474] consider a complementary problem: building robust wrappers that are unlikely to break as the underlying data sources evolve.

10

Data Warehousing and Caching

Thus far, we have discussed the key approaches to defining schema mappings, composing queries with schema mappings (reformulation) to get queries posed directly over data sources, and query processing over remote data. These basic techniques enable us to fetch data on demand in response to user information needs, using the most up-to-date state available. However, in a variety of circumstances this *fully virtual* data integration architecture may not be ideal: we may be willing to tolerate slightly older data in exchange for better performance, better data quality, or the ability to express more complex queries or perform more sophisticated data transformations. The basic idea is to exploit *materialization* — i.e., precomputed or cached results from the integration process — to meet these goals.

In this chapter we describe various methods for storing and exploiting locally materialized data in order to answer data integrating queries. We start with an overview of the two main approaches to materialization and their respective roles. We then describe the use of *partial* materialization and caching to improve performance. Finally, we discuss an emerging "hybrid" of virtual integration and warehousing, namely, direct querying of externally materialized flat-file data, as in many Web settings today.

There are many applications where the main goal of data integration is to bring all of the data into a single, centralized system where it can be analyzed extensively. As a first example, consider a retailer that is recording each of its transactions (i.e., each purchase of an item at one of its stores) in a set of databases. These databases need to be optimized to support high throughput of transactions, effectively reducing your waiting time at the cashier — and therefore saving you from buying candy that you don't need. In addition to recording the transactions, the retailer would also like to perform deeper analysis of their sales data. For example, they would like to know whether raincoats are selling in higher numbers in Kansas so they can make sure to stock up their stores appropriately. To support such analysis, the retailer creates a separate data store, called a warehouse, that contains data that is cleaned up, aggregated, and in an appropriate form for posing complex decision-support queries. A data warehouse is typically populated not using declarative schema mappings as we have described in this book, but rather through pipelines of procedural ETL (extract/transform/load) tools. In the first phase the system extracts the data from the original sources, be they legacy systems or database systems, and converts them into a format that can be processed further. In the second phase, the system transforms the data into a form appropriate for the data warehouse. This may involve selecting a subset of rows or columns, joining data across tables, aggregating values or applying transformations to data values, applying data cleaning or normalization operations, and so on. In the third phase, the data are loaded into the warehouse, either replacing existing data or adding to it. We describe data warehouses in Section 10.1.

However, many (though not all) ETL operations can in fact be expressed through declarative means, much as in virtual data integration systems. Consider a set of scientists, each of whom is collecting data about specimens in the field, and each of whom wants to share data with the others. It is common for scientists to store their data in spreadsheets, and perhaps the frequency of their updates will be relatively low. A valuable data integration system for these scientists would be one in which they can all load their data into one repository and query across the data of all the collaborators. The process of *data exchange* results in a materialized central database, much like the data warehouse, except that the data transformations are specified declaratively as in our prior discussions of virtual data integration. As with data warehousing, the heterogeneity is resolved when the data are *uploaded* into the repository. This approach provides some of the benefits of data warehousing — query processing does not require reformulation, the ability to index the materialized data, and the fact that all data are localized to a single DBMS — while also preserving some of the benefits of virtual integration (namely, declarative mappings that the system can reason about). We describe data exchange in Section 10.2.

Of course, there are situations in which one wants some of the performance benefits of materialized data, while also getting "live" data from some of the sources. We briefly discuss opportunities for "hybrid" approaches to integration, relying on partial materialization and caching, in Section 10.3.

We wrap up the chapter with a discussion of problems such as Web traffic analysis, as is done in any advertisement-based Web platform today. Here, the goal is to bring together the Web traffic logs, particularly user click-throughs on advertisements, for every Web server owned by the service provider. Once the data are in one place, the task is to perform a variety of analytics on click-throughs: grouping by customer, by advertiser campaign, by ad type, and so on. Often the goal here is to *directly* process the Web logs "in situ" without having to first load them into a database, and to do very large-scale parallel processing of the data. The standard tools used in this context are based on Google's MapReduce framework or Apache's open-source version, Hadoop MapReduce. We discuss these cloud data processing frameworks and their role in doing integrated data analysis over locally materialized data (in delimited files) in Section 10.4.

10.1 Data Warehousing

The original, and still predominant, approach to information integration in the enterprise setting is through the definition and creation of a centralized database called a *data warehouse* (see Figure 10.1). In this model, all data needed by an organization are translated into a target schema and copied into a single (possibly parallel or distributed) DBMS, which gets periodically refreshed. Contrast that with virtual data integration, where data are requested from the *sources* on demand, or with MapReduce, where data are typically

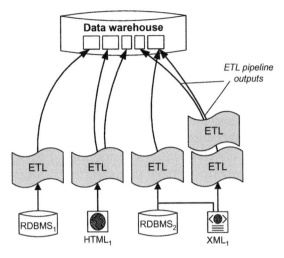

FIGURE 10.1 Logical components of a data warehouse setup. The data are loaded through a pipeline of transformations into a physical data warehouse.

external to the query system and do not support updates or random access. In addition, the transformations that are used to load the data into the warehouse are typically carried out by pipelines of *procedural* code.

Especially in business, a data warehouse serves the natural roles of *archival* and *decision support*. For a variety of reasons, enterprises may need to maintain historical data — for auditing, for analysis, and even for prediction. Simply querying over the existing state of data sources is unlikely to be sufficient — instead, the enterprise needs a master archival copy of the data at different points in time, and the warehouse accomplishes exactly this. More generally, the warehouse, as a consistent "global snapshot" of an enterprise's data with a powerful DBMS, storage system, and CPU, can often be used to perform so-called *decision-support* or *online analytic processing* (OLAP) queries — queries that look at the aggregate characteristics of the data to help form business decisions. For instance, Walmart built a very strong reputation for using sales data to forecast which items, in what quantity, to stock in each store. Such queries typically have multiple levels of aggregation and may involve data mining operations. Similarly, online shopping sites such as Amazon.com, media sites such as Netflix, and even supermarkets such as Safeway all try to build profile information on their customers in order to improve their ability to market to them.

MASTER DATA MANAGEMENT

This central role of the data warehouse has been formalized under the term *master data management* (MDM), which uses a central warehouse as a repository of knowledge about the enterprise's "critical business objects," rules, and processes. Central to MDM is a clean, normalized version of the terms used throughout the enterprise — whether addresses, names, or concepts — and information about the related metadata. Ideally, whenever business objects are used in systems throughout the enterprise, the data values used by these systems can be tied back to the master data. In many ways, a master data repository is merely a data warehouse with a particular role to play.

As with any warehouse, MDM gives the various data owners and stakeholders a bird's-eye view of all of the data entities and a common intermediate representation. However, the master data repository is also intended to be a central repository where relevant properties about data — especially constraints and assumptions — can be captured, making it the home of all *metadata* as well as data. In many cases, the master repository is made queriable to all of the data owners, such that they can directly incorporate it into their systems and processes. It is seen as a way of improving risk management, decision making, and analysis.

Finally, MDM provides a process by which the data can be overseen and managed through *data governance*. In a large enterprise, coordinating the design and evolution of data in accordance with business needs and regulations can be a challenge. Data governance refers to the process and organization put in place to oversee the creation and modification of data entities in a systematic way. Of particular importance are any reporting requirements such as those introduced by the Sarbanes-Oxley Act in the USA, which imposes responsibility and accountability provisions for public corporations that may drive data collection and representation.

Actually defining a data warehouse involves two main tasks: performing central database schema and physical design (Section 10.1.1) and defining a set of extract/transform/load (ETL) operations (Section 10.1.2).

10.1.1 Data Warehouse Design

Designing a data warehouse can be even more involved than designing a mediated schema in a data integration setting because the warehouse must support very demanding queries, possibly over data archived over time. Physical database design becomes critical — effective use of partitioning across multiple machines or multiple disk volumes, creation of indices, definition of materialized views that can be used by the query optimizer. Most data warehouse DBMSs are configured for query-only workloads, as opposed to transaction processing workloads, for performance: this disables most of the (expensive) consistency mechanisms used in a transactional database.

Since the early 2000s, all of the major commercial DBMSs have attempted to simplify the tasks of physical database design for data warehouses. Most tools have "index selection wizards" and "view selection wizards" that take a log of a typical query workload and perform a (usually overnight) search of alternative indices or materialized views, seeking to find the best combination to improve performance. Such tools help, but still there is a need for expert database administrators and "tuners" to obtain the best data warehouse performance.

10.1.2 ETL: Extract/Transform/Load

Once a data warehouse has been designed and configured, obviously it must be initially populated with data and maintained over time. The wide variety of tools used to do this are generically referred to as *ETL*, or *extract/transform/load*, tools. ETL tools address a wide variety of tasks:

IMPORT FILTERS
These include parsers for external file formats, or drivers that interact with third-party systems (whether DBMSs or other applications). Often the external data may not be coming from a relational database, whereas, in almost all cases, a data warehouse is relational.

DATA TRANSFORMATIONS
Data transformation modules typically serve a role very similar to schema mappings in a virtual data integration system: they may join, aggregate, or filter data.

DEDUPLICATION
Deduplication (or record linking) tools seek to determine when multiple records refer to the same entity — often through heuristics. The techniques are often based on the data matching techniques mentioned in Chapter 7.

PROFILING
Data profiling tools typically build up tables, histograms, or other information that summarizes the properties of the data in the warehouse.

QUALITY MANAGEMENT
In addition to deduplication tools, ETL quality management support might include testing against a master list of data values (e.g., a list of legal state/province abbreviations), testing against known business rules (e.g., constraints on combinations of values), standardization tools (e.g., postal address canonicalization), and record merging.

■ ■ ■ ▬▬

Example 10.1
Consider an e-commerce site scenario: We have a series of invoice line items from customers' purchases, as fulfilled by our warehouse. We wish to bring these into the central data warehouse, while simultaneously filtering for data entry errors.

To do this, we must assemble an ETL pipeline that performs a variety of data splitting, filtering, joining, and grouping operators. See Figure 10.2: the first operator modifies the schema by splitting a single attribute (date/time) into separate date and time attributes. Next, we filter any records with invalid date/time signatures and write them to a log. Next, we join each record with our database of items; again, we filter any invalid entries and write them to a log. Subsequently,

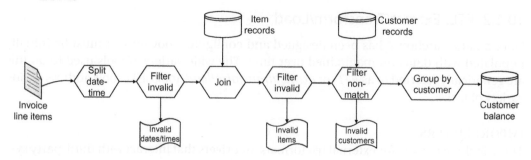

FIGURE 10.2 Example ETL pipeline for importing customer records.

we validate that each record actually corresponds to a valid customer; as has been our pattern, we write any invalid entries to a log. Finally, we group all of the records by customer and use them to update the customer's balance in our data warehouse.

∎ ∎ ∎

The above example primarily consists of operations that might be captured with declarative schema mappings. However, it should be clear from the preceding list of capabilities that ETL tools can capture functionalities beyond virtual data integration mappings. Tremendous flexibility and expressiveness are provided by the basic architecture, especially since ETL is an offline process that enables long-lived, computationally intensive tasks to be performed. Unfortunately, the flexibility has a drawback, which is that there is very little standardization among ETL tools and approaches. Different vendors' tools have entirely different interfaces and different tools for specifying workflows among the tools.

Moreover, there are cases where one might want to *optimize* the loading process, e.g., by precomputing or caching certain results or sharing work among operators. Most ETL frameworks do not have this flexibility. Hence there has been significant interest in replacing some ETL operations with declarative mappings similar to those we have seen previously in this book. This leads to the problem of computing a data warehouse using declarative mappings, termed *data exchange*, which we discuss next.

10.2 Data Exchange: Declarative Warehousing

As discussed in the previous section, the basic idea of data exchange is to support a warehouse-like setting, with declarative schema mappings specifying the data transformation. Under this model, every data source likely has a wrapper, much as in a conventional data integration scenario, but all data from the sources will be retrieved, transformed according to the schema mappings, and stored in the centralized warehouse or *target data instance* in an offline step. Users directly query the target data instance as in a data warehouse.

In specifying the data-exchange *setting*, we assume that all of the sources have been "wrapped" such that we have access to their data as relations. Moreover, we will consider *all* of these source relations to be part of a single source schema S, and all of the warehouse relations to be part of a target schema T.

Informally, given S and T, an instance, I, of schema S, and a semantic mapping between S and T, the problem of data exchange is to create an appropriate instance of T. In our context, S is the schema of a data source, and T is the schema of the mediated schema of the materialized data store. The challenge in data exchange arises because there are many possible instances of T that we may consider for a given instance, I, of S, but we want the ones that satisfy certain desirable properties. We formalize the problem below.

10.2.1 Data-Exchange Settings

In the discussion of data exchange, we follow the notation of *tuple-generating dependencies*, which were briefly introduced in Chapter 3 and are commonly used in the literature. Recall that tuple-generating dependencies are an alternative formalism for expressing GLAV mappings. Tuple-generating dependencies are formulas of the form

$$(\forall \bar{X}) s_1(\bar{X}_1), \ldots, s_m(\bar{X}_m) \rightarrow (\exists \bar{Y}) t_1(\bar{Y}_1), \ldots, t_l(\bar{Y}_l)$$

where $s_1, \ldots, s_m$ are relations in the source schema S, and $t_1, \ldots, t_l$ are relations in the target schema T. The variables $\bar{X}$ are a subset of $\bar{X}_1 \ldots \cup \ldots \bar{X}_m$, and the variables $\bar{Y}$ are a subset of $\bar{Y}_1 \ldots \cup \ldots \bar{Y}_l$. The variables $\bar{Y}$ do not appear in $\bar{X}_1 \ldots \cup \ldots \bar{X}_m$.

While we focus mostly on data-exchange settings that only involve schema mappings, in some settings we also want to ensure that the target instance satisfies certain constraints on the target schema T. To model such constraints, we introduce *target constraints* into data-exchange settings. Formally, we assume we also have a set of constraints C_T that can be of two forms:

1. Tuple-generating dependencies where the s_i's and the t_j's are relations in T, or
2. Equality-generating dependencies that are formulas of the form

$$(\exists \bar{Y}) t_1(\bar{Y}_1), \ldots, t_l(\bar{Y}_l) \rightarrow (Y_i = Y_j)$$

The formal definition of data-exchange settings is the following.

Definition 10.1 (Data-Exchange Settings). *A data-exchange setting is a tuple (S, T, M, C_T), where S is a source schema, T is a target schema, M is a set of tuple-generating dependencies describing a semantic mapping between S and T, and C_T is a set of constraints on the target schema T.* □

■ ■ ■ ━━━━━━━━━━━━━━━━━━━━━━━━━━━━━━━━━━━━

Example 10.2

Consider the following example, where the source schema S has two relations. The relation Teaches stores pairs of professor and student where the professor teaches a class taken by the student, and the relation Adviser stores pairs of (adviser, student). The target schema T has three relations: Advise is the same as Adviser, TeachesCourse represents which courses professors teach, and Takes stores the student enrollment in courses. The following are the schema mappings between S and T:

r_1 : Teaches(prof, stud) → $\exists D$ Advise(D,stud)
r_2 : Teaches(prof, stud) → $\exists C$ TeachesCourse(prof,C), Takes(C,stud)
r_3 : Adviser(prof, stud) → Advise(prof, stud)
r_4 : Adviser(prof, stud) → $\exists C, D$ TeachesCourse(D, C), Takes(C,stud)

━━━━━━━━━━━━━━━━━━━━━━━━━━━━━━━━━━━━ ■ ■ ■

10.2.2 Data-Exchange Solutions

Data-exchange solutions are instances of the target schema that satisfy the constraints in the data-exchange setting.

Definition 10.2 (Data-Exchange Solutions). *Let $D = (S, T, M, C_T)$ be a data-exchange setting. Let I be an instance of S. An instance J of T is said to be a data-exchange solution for D and I if*

1. *the pair (I, J) satisfies the schema mapping M, and*
2. *J satisfies the constraints C_T.*   □

■ ■ ■ ━━━━━━━━━━━━━━━━━━━━━━━━━━━━━━━━━━━━

Example 10.3

Consider the following instance, I, for the schema S in Example 10.2.

I = {Teaches(Ann, Bob), Teaches(Chloe, David),
        Adviser(Ellen, Bob), Adviser(Felicia, David)}

One data-exchange solution for I is the following:

J_0 = {TeachesCourse(Ann, C_1), Takes(C_1, Bob)
        TeachesCourse(Chloe, C_2), Takes(C_2, David)
        Advise(Ellen, Bob), Advise(Felicia, David)}

As seen in the example, data-exchange solutions include two kinds of values in their tuples: constants from the original instance I and new symbols that did not occur in I. Intuitively, the new symbols, which we refer to as *variables* (sometimes called *labeled nulls*), represent incomplete information we may have about the instance. More precisely, we know that the facts in which they appear hold for some substitution for the variables, but we do not know the exact substitution. For example, in J_0 the symbols C_1 and C_2 represent unknown values, describing the fact that we know there must be courses that Ann and Chloe teach, but we don't know the precise courses.

The following are also data-exchange solutions for I:

J = {TeachesCourse(Ann, C_1), Takes(C_1, Bob)
     TeachesCourse(Chloe, C_2), Takes(C_2, David)
     Advise(D_1, Bob), Advise(D_2, David)
     Advise(Ellen, Bob), Advise(Felicia, David)}

J_0' = {TeachesCourse(Ann, C_1), Takes(C_1, Bob)
     TeachesCourse(Chloe, C_1), Takes(C_1, David)
     Advise(Ellen, Bob), Advise(Felicia, David)}

The instance J has two more Advise tuples than J_0. The extra tuples contain new variables. The instance J_0' is the same as the instance J, except that instead of having two variables C_1 and C_2, it uses the same variable throughout. Later we will see that J_0 has more desirable properties than J or J_0'.

■ ■ ■

10.2.3 Universal Solutions

As we pointed out earlier, the challenge is to find the data-exchange solutions that are in some sense better than others. In this section we discuss two properties that distinguish data-exchange solutions. The first property, satisfied by *universal* solutions, guarantees that the solution does not *lose* any information. The second property, satisfied by *core universal* solutions, guarantees that the solutions are as small as possible.

■ ■ ■

Example 10.4

Returning to Example 10.3, we see that solution J_0' is not completely satisfactory. Specifically, it uses the same variable for the course taught by Ann and the course by Chloe, thereby implying that they teach the same course. However, that equality is not implied by the original instance, I, or from the schema mapping. The instance J_0' is, in some sense, more specific than the other solutions.

■ ■ ■

Intuitively, universal solutions are ones that do not lose or add any information. The way we formalize this property is to require that a universal solution can be homomorphically mapped to *any other* universal solution.

In defining homomorphisms, we denote by $\mathcal{C}$ the set of constants appearing in instances of S. In addition to constants in $\mathcal{C}$, instances of T can also include variables taken from an infinite alphabet $\mathcal{V}$ that is assumed to be disjoint from $\mathcal{C}$.

Definition 10.3 (Instance Homomorphism). *Let J_1 and J_2 be two instances of the schema T.*

- *A mapping $h : J_1 \to J_2$ is a homomorphism from J_1 to J_2 if*
  - *$h(c) = c$ for every $c \in C$,*
  - *for every tuple $R(a_1, \ldots, a_n) \in J_1$, the tuple $R(h(a_1), \ldots, h(a_n)) \in J_2$.*
- *J_1 and J_2 are homomophically equivalent if there are homomorphisms $h : J_1 \to J_2$ and $h' : J_2 \to J_1$.* □

We can now define universal solutions. In Example 10.3 the solutions J and J_0 are universal solutions, but J_0' is not.

Definition 10.4 (Universal Solutions). *Let $D = (S, T, M, C_T)$ be a data-exchange setting, and let I be an instance of S. We say that J is a universal solution for D and I if J is a data-exchange solution for D and I, and for every other data-exchange solution, J', for D and I, there exists a homomorphism $h : J \to J'$.* □

It can be shown that under very broad conditions on M and C_T, a universal solution exists if and only if there is a data-exchange solution for D and I, and that a universal solution can be constructed in polynomial time in the size of I. It is easy to verify that if C_T is empty, then there always exists a universal solution to a data-exchange problem. When C_T includes equality-generating dependencies, then situations may arise where a universal solution does not exist.

In what follows, we restrict ourselves to the case in which C_T is empty and show that we can create a universal solution using a classical algorithm called the *chase*. Informally, the chase considers every formula r of M in turn. If the algorithm finds a variable substitution for the left-hand side of r for which the right-hand side is not already in the data-exchange solution, then it adds an appropriate tuple to the solution. In creating the new tuple, the algorithm uses fresh variables to substitute for the $\bar{Y}$ variables of r. The chase is shown in Algorithm 10.

■ ■ ■ ▬▬▬▬▬▬▬▬▬▬▬▬▬▬▬▬▬▬▬▬▬▬▬▬▬▬▬▬▬▬▬▬▬▬▬▬

Example 10.5

Continuing with our running example, recall the mapping M and the instance I:

r_1 : Teaches(prof, stud) $\to \exists D$ Advise(D,stud)
r_2 : Teaches(prof, stud) $\to \exists C$ TeachesCourse(prof,C), Takes(C,stud)
r_3 : Adviser(prof, stud) $\to$ Advise(prof, stud)
r_4 : Adviser(prof, stud) $\to \exists C, D$ TeachesCourse(D, C), Takes(C,stud)

$I = \{$Teaches(Ann, Bob), Teaches(Chloe, David),
        Adviser(Ellen, Bob), Adviser(Felicia, David)$\}$

Applying the chase algorithm of Algorithm 10 on I would yield the following instance for J:

Algorithm 10. CreateUniversalSolution

Input: data exchange setting (S, T, M) and an instance I of S. **Output:** data instance J containing a universal solution.

  Let $J = \emptyset$
  while new tuples can be added to J **do**
    Let $r \in M$ be of the form $(\forall \bar{X}) s_1(\bar{X}_1), \ldots, s_m(\bar{X}_m) \rightarrow (\exists \bar{Y}) t_1(\bar{Y}_1), \ldots, t_l(\bar{Y}_l)$
    Let ψ be a mapping from $\bar{X}$ to constants in I such that $s_1(\psi(\bar{X}_1)), \ldots, s_m(\psi(\bar{X}_m)) \in S$
    Let $\bar{Y}_i' = \psi(\bar{Y}_i)$ for $1 \leq i \leq l$
    if there does not exist a mapping ϕ from $\bar{Y}'$ to the constants in J s.t. $t_1(\phi(\bar{Y}_1')), \ldots, t_l(\phi(\bar{Y}_l')) \in J$
    then
      Let μ be a mapping that maps each variable $Y' \in \bar{Y}'$ to a new variable that does not appear in J
      Insert $t_1(\mu(\bar{Y}_1')), \ldots, t_l(\mu(\bar{Y}_l'))$ into J
    end if
  end while
  return J

    {Advise(C_1, Bob), Advise(C_2, David)
    TeachesCourse(Ann, C_3), Takes(C_3, Bob),
    TeachesCourse(Chloe, C_4), Takes(C_4, David),
    Advise(Ellen, Bob), Advise(Felicia, David)}

    The first two facts are generated by r_1. The next four facts are generated by r_2, and the last two facts are generated by r_3. The mapping formula r_4 does not add new facts to the solution. ■ ■ ■

10.2.4 Core Universal Solutions

A conceptual problem with universal solutions is that they still may be of arbitrary size. To see why, consider the following set of data-exchange solutions that can be generated in our example.

$J_m = $ {TeachesCourse(Ann, C_1), Takes(C_1, Bob)
      TeachesCourse(Chloe, C_2), Takes(C_2, David)

      ...

      TeachesCourse(Ann, C_{2m-1}), Takes(C_{2m-1}, Bob)
      TeachesCourse(Chloe, C_{2m}), Takes(C_{2m}, David)
      Advise(Ellen, Bob), Advise(Felicia, David)}

    The example shows that we can actually create a universal solution of any size we want. Clearly, in a data-exchange scenario we would like to materialize the smallest universal solution. Below we define core universal solutions that are the smallest universal solutions.

    To define core universal solutions, we first define subinstances of database schemata.

Algorithm 11. CreateCoreUniversalSolution

Input: data exchange setting $D = (S, T, M)$; an instance I of S; a universal solution J for D and I.
  Output: updated data instance J containing a core universal solution.
  while there is a tuple $\bar{t} \in J$ such that $\{J - \bar{t}\}$ satisfies M **do**
    Remove $\bar{t}$ from J
  end while
  return J

Definition 10.5 (Subinstances).   *Let the relations in the schema T be $T_1, \ldots, T_m$, and let J be an instance of T that for $1 \leq i \leq m$ contains the tuples $\bar{t}_i$ for the relation T_i. Let A be the set of constants and variables mentioned in tuples of J.*

Let J' be an instance of T with relation instances $\bar{t}'_1, \ldots, \bar{t}'_m$ and let B be the constants and variables mentioned in J'.

We say that J' is a subinstance of J if $B \subseteq A$ and $t'_j \subseteq t_j$ for $1 \leq j \leq m$. J' is a proper subinstance of J if one of the inclusions is strict. ☐

We define core universal solutions to be solutions for which there is no substructure instance that is also a solution.

Definition 10.6 (Core Universal Solutions).   *Let $D = (S, T, M, C_T)$ be a data-exchange setting and let I be an instance of S. We say that J is a core universal solution for D and I if J is a universal solution to D and I, and if there is no proper sub-instance of J that is also a universal solution for D and I.* ☐

It can be shown that the core universal solutions for a data-exchange setting are unique up to an isomorphism. While, in general, finding a core universal solution is intractable, there is a broad range of cases where it can be done in polynomial time in the size of I. One of these cases is when C_T is empty, and Algorithm 11 shows a greedy algorithm for finding the core universal solution in this case. More efficient algorithms for finding core universal solutions have been proposed in the literature, but the greedy one illustrates the key ideas best.

■ ■ ■ ▬▬▬▬▬▬▬▬▬▬▬▬▬▬▬▬▬▬▬▬▬▬▬▬▬▬▬▬▬▬▬▬▬▬▬

Example 10.6

Consider applying the greedy algorithm in Algorithm 11 to the universal solution created in Example 10.5.

  {Advise(C_1, Bob), Advise(C_2, David)
  TeachesCourse(Ann, C_3), Takes(C_3, Bob),
  TeachesCourse(Chloe, C_4), Takes(C_4, David),
  Advise(Ellen, Bob), Advise(Felicia, David)}

The facts Advise(C_1, Bob) and Advise(C_2, David) will be removed because r_1 is satisfied without them. All the other facts must remain in J.

▬▬▬▬▬▬▬▬▬▬▬▬▬▬▬▬▬▬▬▬▬▬▬▬▬▬▬▬▬▬▬▬▬▬▬ ■ ■ ■

10.2.5 Querying the Materialized Repository

We now have the necessary machinery to create the materialized repository from a set of data sources described by GLAV schema mappings. The materialized repository is the data-exchange solution, where S is a data source and T is the schema of the materialized repository. We can create such as solution for every source in isolation and take their union.

The final problem we need to address is how to *query* the materialized repository. Fortunately, the machinery developed for query reformulation and inverse rules (Section 2.4.5) applies. Specifically, the following theorem shows that we can answer queries by evaluating them on the materialized repository and keeping only the answer tuples that do not contain variables. The theorem follows from Theorem 3.3.

Theorem 10.1. *Let S be a set of data sources and T be the schema of the materialized repository. Let M be a set of GLAV mappings between S and T. Let I be an instance of S and let J be a universal data-exchange solution for (S, T, M) and I.*

Let Q be a union of conjunctive queries without interpreted predicates over T. Let $Q(J)$ be the result of applying Q to J, and let $Q(J)'$ be the subset of $Q(J)$ that includes tuples that contain only constants from I.

Then, $Q(J)'$ is precisely the certain answers to Q. □

10.3 Caching and Partial Materialization

Compared to a virtual integration system, materialization enables us to execute more computationally and disk-intensive queries, over larger amounts of (especially historical) data. However, on the flip side, materialization often imposes a *delay* between when a source is updated and when the updated results appear in the integrated data instance — and hence in users' query results. This may be a problem in settings like *customer relationship management*, where we may need to join the state of multiple internal and external databases, as well as Web services from shipping companies, suppliers, etc.

Naturally, in practice there are many "hybrid" approaches to addressing these problems. Often, some data sources and relations are updated more frequently than others: for instance, the business vocabulary in a Master Data Management system is unlikely to change at a high rate, even if individual line items in a billing system are frequently updated.

Thus, in practice most deployed integration systems — whether designed as warehouses or virtual integration ("Enterprise Information Integration," or EII) systems — exploit *caching* and *partial materialization* over those results that may not need to be 100% up to date or that seldom change and use virtual integration over the other sources. We briefly discuss a variety of potential approaches to "hybrid" models, where queries may be answered over data materialized at the central integration system, rather than being reformulated over remote sources.

CACHING AND DIRECT REUSE IN A VIRTUAL INTEGRATION SCENARIO
A simple, low-maintenance approach to get some of the benefits of materialization in a virtual integration system is to directly *cache* the results of queries and to use answering-queries-using-views algorithms (Chapter 2) to rewrite subsequent queries to reuse the data. One challenge is that the cached entries must be assigned a *time-to-live* after which they should be expired, in the event that the source data have changed. However, this approach otherwise requires little direct intervention from the user or administrator. It is sometimes termed *mid-tier* or *middle-tier caching*.

ADMINISTRATOR-SELECTED VIEW MATERIALIZATION
The database administrator may determine that certain data change slowly and may manually specify how to materialize them — using either ETL or declarative mappings. User queries will be posed over a combination of materialized relations plus virtual relations, and query reformulation will take this into account.

AUTOMATED VIEW SELECTION
A more sophisticated approach is to have the data integration system choose what to materialize, given a set of declarative (not ETL!) mappings, a *query workload*, and perhaps a specification of what source data are relatively static. From this, automated view selection algorithms, using techniques similar to those in the "tuning wizards" of commercial DBMSs, can be used to identify common query expressions and to materialize them.

10.4 Direct Analysis of Local, External Data

Thanks to the preponderance of Web-based applications in which logs are processed to detect patterns — ad click-throughs, site visit patterns, page co-views — and the popularity of Google's MapReduce programming paradigm for doing distributed computation, there are a wide number of commercial platforms for processing data stored not in database tables but simply in flat files with delimiters. Such data may come from a wide variety of Web server logging platforms and application modules, and they are generally append-only logs describing behavior over time. Thus most of the benefits of a transactional DBMS storage system are less pertinent. In some sense, these logs already represent a locally materialized data warehouse, merely one where the data are stored outside a DBMS. In such settings — unless there is a strong need for indexing — it becomes more desirable to simply process data directly from the files, rather than first importing the data and then querying them. Furthermore, many of the queries of interest are transient, so there is little benefit in setting up a database system to store and query the data.

The integration task in these contexts is generally to perform aggregation queries — somewhat less structurally complex ones than in data warehouse (OLAP) settings, though sometimes computations that require custom logic (what in the database world we would call "user-defined functions" written in a language like Java, C, or Python). For instance, a social network advertiser might want to know the performance of certain ad campaigns, by type of ad, region, demographic, etc., or may want to make friend recommendations based on commonly visited pages.

For such tasks, the Google MapReduce programming model (often implemented in the open-source Apache Hadoop MapReduce platform) is commonly used. MapReduce provides a particular programming "template" for parallel analysis of large-scale data sets; it is roughly analogous to a single SQL query block. The basic programming model is as follows:

- A function called *map* — provided by the user — is given input records (typically in the form of lines of text from a file) one at a time. Its tasks are to (1) parse the records, (2) extract the relevant information from the records, (3) filter data based on the records, and (4) output for each record one or more subresults. One can think of it as primarily serving the role of the WHERE clause in SQL, with user-defined predicates. However, it can also split records, derive new values, and so on.
- The outputs of the map computations are grouped together according to *keys*. This is done through a *shuffle* stage. By default, the shuffle stage *sorts* the data according to the key.
- For each group of map outputs with the same key, a user-provided *reduce* computation is invoked. This computation can output zero or more values. One can think of this as being equivalent to an SQL GROUP BY on the key, followed by a user-defined aggregate function over the group.

Oddly to a database audience, the core MapReduce framework does not directly support the composition of analysis queries with one another. However, in practice one can "string together" multiple MapReduce stages, with each reading the results of the previous, to accomplish composition. For even more complex analysis (performing recursive or iterative computations like link analysis), it is common practice to repeatedly invoke a MapReduce computation within a loop in a shell script or a Java program.

■ ■ ■ ━━━━━━━━━━━━━━━━━━━━━━━━━━━━━━━━━━

Example 10.7

Suppose we are running a large, multisite Web property, and our goal is to count the number of visits to each Web page. To do this, we need to extract requests from our various Web server logs, which are generally created on a daily basis per machine. We then want to group them together by URL and count them. If the log were a relational table, this query would be trivial to express as a GROUP BY/COUNT query in SQL.

In MapReduce we write two functions, *map*, shown in Algorithm 12, and *reduce*, shown in Algorithm 13. As we can see, these functions are both quite brief, given that the task is so simple. The *map* function is called once per line of a log file; it is also given information about the byte position of the line in the log (which it ignores). It outputs a pair (*key, value*), using *url* as the key and the number 1 as the value.

Algorithm 12. User-provided *map* for grouping Web-log URLs

Input: string *line*; logfile position *position*; target *output*. **Output:** writes a record to *output*.
Let url := extractUrlFromLine(line)
Call output.emit(url,1)

Algorithm 13. User-provided *reduce* for counting Web-log requests per URL

Input: key *url*; set of counts *valueSet*; target *output*. **Output:** writes a record to *output*.
Call output.emit(url,valueSet.size())

Now the MapReduce framework performs its *shuffle* stage, sorting all *map* output to group by key. It then invokes the *reduce* code over each key (URL) value, as well as the set of all values matching the key. The cardinality of this set is precisely the count, so we can output that. ■ ■ ■

One might ask the question: Why is MapReduce so popular in the Web world? In part it is because the framework makes it easy to do large-scale processing of external data, while also implementing custom filtering or aggregation functions. Unlike with SQL, one can seamlessly incorporate user-defined code in C, Java, or Python with little effort. In contrast, many DBMS and data warehouse platforms have fairly awkward and arcane methods of integrating user-defined functions with SQL: often the administrator must first register the functions in SQL DDL, ensure that paths are properly set up, and so on.

Perhaps more importantly, MapReduce provides a level of dependability and scalability that is unmatched in most DBMSs. A MapReduce job can be executed in parallel across thousands of nodes in a cluster (multiple *map* and *reduce* operations run simultaneously over different portions of the data). MapReduce is incredibly resilient to machine *failures*, which are surprisingly likely to occur when thousands of machines are involved. If a node dies, MapReduce will automatically reallocate its tasks to other machines and will recompute any work that was in progress at the node during the crash. MapReduce's absolute performance has sometimes been questioned, but it works quite well if the results are needed, e.g., overnight.

Some developers have felt that MapReduce provides a frustratingly low-level way of writing complex queries. This has led to a series of higher-level, compositional programming languages that compile down to MapReduce: one can get the benefits of MapReduce's "run and forget about it" execution across a cluster, while also having more natural abstractions. The Pig Latin language, for instance, is commonly used to do SQL-like queries, expressed as a nondeclarative pipeline of operators. Going even further, companies like Facebook have developed SQL translation layers (in particular, Apache Hive) to let their customers and developers pose queries in a variant of SQL, but then to run those in Hadoop over flat files.

Clearly, flat-file-based data analysis is only a small subclass of information integration, and systems based on the approach are limited in their ability to manage and integrate heterogeneous data. However, due to their simplicity, MapReduce and its relatives are rather effective in tying together data from multiple autonomous systems, and they are highly scalable. They therefore serve a very important role in the back ends of many Web-based systems and services.

Increasingly, some organizations have begun to use MapReduce not to do the actual data analysis, but to do data *transformation* in order to load the data into a data warehouse: this is a different way of performing ETL.

Bibliographic Notes

The data warehouse has been the traditional approach to data integration from the early days, largely because the early applications revolved around online analytic processing (OLAP), forecasting, and data mining. An excellent survey by Chaudhuri and Dayal appears in [122]. A major challenge in data warehousing is that of incrementally maintaining the data warehouse; this was the focus of the Stanford WHIPS project [129, 447, 486, 596].

Fagin et al. [216] first introduced the notion of data exchange and defined its semantics. An excellent overview of the data-exchange literature appears in the book [36]. The work on data exchange was originally motivated by the Clio System [302], which we discussed in Chapter 5. In [216] they introduced universal solutions and showed that they are homomorphically equivalent to each other and that certain answers can be obtained by any universal solution. Core universal solutions were introduced by Fagin et al. [217]. Both of these papers show precise conditions under which we can find universal and core universal solutions efficiently, and in particular how it depends on the form of the mappings between the source and target schemas and on the constraints present on target schema. They also describe an algorithm for finding the core universal solution that is more efficient than the greedy algorithm we presented. Afrati and Kolaitis showed how to answer aggregation queries in the data-exchange setting in [15], which is important in a data warehouse/OLAP setting.

It is interesting to note that the process of creating a universal solution for a data-exchange problem is similar in spirit to applying the Inverse-Rules Algorithm (Section 2.4.5) on a set of data sources in the context of virtual data integration. The two processes produce a materialized instance of the target schema where some of the tuples have variables. The difference is that in the data-exchange context the goal is to produce the materialized instance of the schema T, whereas in the virtual data integration context the goal is to answer the query that is posed over the mediated schema. Hence, in that context the inverse rules are part of the rewriting of the query using the source descriptions, but the hope is that the query optimizer will find a plan that does not require materializing a complete instance of T.

The problems of caching at an integration or middleware layer have been studied in a variety of contexts and generally are labeled "mid-tier caching" [402]. Commercial implementations are typically based on relatively simple matching templates. One of the first systems to look at a combination of virtual and materialized data integration together was the H2O project [592].

The specific problem of choosing *what* views to materialize, given a workload and a set of database statistics, has been extensively studied in a wide variety of contexts. Among the earliest work on this problem was that of Gupta [276, 277]. Chirkova et al. studied the theoretical complexity of the problem, showing that it can be exponential in the size of the views [134] — but that the problem is often polynomial when standard estimation heuristics are used. More recently, the view selection problem has been incorporated into a multiple query optimizer [437]. The problem of maintaining materialized warehouse views was studied in [149, 398]. View materialization for aggregate queries was considered in [14]. The Active XML [4] project focused on how to decompose integration tasks over Web services into virtual and materialized components.

At the time of the writing of this book, the use of MapReduce in database-style applications was attracting significant interest in the database community. A variety of projects have explored combining MapReduce and SQL database techniques, including HadoopDB [8]. In [531], Stonebraker et al. have also suggested that MapReduce should primarily be considered as complementary to data warehousing, for instance, as an ETL tool framework. In fact, there do exist ETL frameworks written over MapReduce, such as ETLMR [396].

Integration with Extended Data Representations

11

XML

As described in the previous chapters of this book, most research on data integration has centered on the relational model. In many ways, the relational model and the datalog query language are the simplest and cleanest formalisms for data and query representation, so many of the fundamental issues were considered first in that setting.

However, as such techniques are adapted to meet real-world needs, they typically get adapted to incorporate XML (or its close cousin JSON[1]). For instance, IBM's Rational Data Architect or Microsoft's BizTalk Mapper both use XML-centric mappings.

The reason for this is straightforward. XML has become the default format for data export from both database and document sources, and many additional tools have been developed to export to XML from legacy sources (e.g., COBOL files, IMS hierarchical databases). Prior to XML's adoption, data integration systems needed custom wrappers that did "screen scraping" (custom HTML parsing and content extraction) to extract content from the Web, and that translated to the proprietary wire formats of different legacy tools. Today, we can expect most sources to have an XML interface (URIs as the request mechanism and XML as the returned data format), and thus the data integrator can focus on the semantic mappings rather than the low-level format issues.

We note that XML brings standardization not only in the actual data format, but also in terms of an entire ecosystem of interfaces, standards, and tools. See Figure 11.1 for an illustration. XML serves as a common format over database, document, and even Web service data. It is typically accompanied by DTD and XML Schema for specifying schemas, and most commonly XML is requested via the HTTP protocol that underlies the Web. DOM and SAX provide language-neutral parser interfaces for XML data. If one wishes to query XML declaratively, this can be achieved with XPath and XQuery (which, in turn, are implemented over SAX or DOM interfaces). Finally, Web services use XML, XML Schema, and HTTP as core technologies within the WSDL and SOAP as well as the REST interfaces for remote procedure calls. Of course, there are also a wide variety of text editors, integrated development environments, and browsers with built-in support for XML creation, display, and validation. Any tool that produces and consumes XML automatically benefits from having these other components. While XML in itself is not meant to directly resolve semantic heterogeneity or introduce standard schemas in any domains, it enables domain experts to more easily focus on the semantic issues rather than on lower-level data encoding issues.

---

[1] JSON, the JavaScript Object Notation, can be thought of as a "simplified XML," although it also closely resembles previous *semistructured data* formats like the Object Exchange Model.

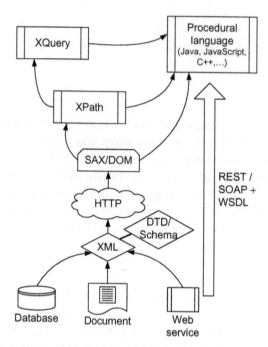

FIGURE 11.1 A diagram of the relationship among various XML-related technologies.

This book does not attempt to cover all of the details of XML, but rather to provide the core essentials. In this chapter, we focus first on the XML data model in Section 11.1 and the schema formalisms in Section 11.2. Section 11.3 presents several models for querying XML, culminating in the XQuery standard that is implemented in many XML database systems. Section 11.4 discusses XML query processing for data integration, and Section 11.5 discusses the subsets of XQuery typically used for XML schema mappings.

11.1 Data Model

Like HTML (HyperText Markup Language), XML (eXtensible Markup Language) is essentially a specialized derivative of an old standard called SGML (Structured Generalized Markup Language). As with these other markup standards, XML encodes document metainformation using *tags* (in angle brackets) and *attributes* (attribute-value pairs associated with specific tags).

XML distinguishes itself from its predecessors in that (if correctly structured, or *well-formed*) it is *always parsable* by an XML parser — regardless of whether the XML parser has any information that enables it to interpret the XML tags. To ensure this, XML has strict rules about how the document is structured. We briefly describe the essential components of an XML document.

```
<?xml version="1.0" encoding="ISO-8859-1" ?>
<dblp>
  <mastersthesis mdate="2002-01-03" key="ms/Brown92">
    <author>Kurt P. Brown</author>
    <title>PRPL: A Database Workload Specification Language</
    title>
    <year>1992</year>
    <school>Univ. of Wisconsin-Madison</school>
  </mastersthesis>
  <article mdate="2002-01-03" key="tr/dec/SRC1997-018">
    <editor>Paul R. McJones</editor>
    <title>The 1995 SQL Reunion</title>
    <journal>Digital System Research Center Report</journal>
    <volume>SRC1997-018</volume>
    <year>1997</year>
    <ee>db/labs/dec/SRC1997-018.html</ee>
    <ee>http://www.mcjones.org/System_R/SQL_Reunion_95/</ee>
  </article>
  ...
</dblp>
```

FIGURE 11.2 Sample XML data from the DBLP Web site.

PREAMBLE: PROCESSING INSTRUCTIONS TO AID THE PARSER

The first line of an XML file tells the XML parser information about the character set used for encoding the remainder of the document; this is critical since it determines how many bytes encode each character in the file. Character sets are specified using a *processing-instruction*, such as `<?xml version="1.0" encoding="ISO-8859-1"?>`, which we see at the top of the example XML fragment in Figure 11.2 (an excerpt from the research paper bibliography Web site DBLP, at `dblp.uni-trier.de`). Other processing instructions may specify constraints on the content of the XML document, and we will discuss them later.

TAGS, ELEMENTS, AND ATTRIBUTES

The main content of the XML document consists of tags, attributes, and data. XML tags are indicated using angle brackets and must come in pairs: for each open tag `<tag>`, there must be a matching close tag `</tag>`. An open tag/close tag pair and its contents are said to be an *XML element*. An element may have one or more *attributes*, each with a unique name and a value specified within the open tag: `<tag attrib1="value1" attrib2="value2">`. An element may contain nested elements, nested text, and a variety of other types of content we will describe shortly. It is important to note that every XML document must contain a single *root element*, meaning that the element content can be thought of as a tree and not a forest.

■ ■ ■ ━━

Example 11.1

Figure 11.2 shows a detailed fragment of XML from DBLP. The first line is a processing instruction specifying the character set encoding. Next comes the single *root element*, dblp. Within the DBLP element we see two subelements, one describing a mastersthesis and the other an article. Additional elements are elided.

Both the MS thesis and article elements contain two attributes, mdate and key. Additionally, they contain subelements such as author or editor. Note that ee appears twice within the article. Within each of the subelements at this level is *text content*, each contiguous fragment of which is represented in the XML data model by a text node.

━━ ■ ■ ■

NAMESPACES AND QUALIFIED NAMES

Sometimes an XML document consists of content merged from multiple sources. In such situations, we may have the same tag names in several sources and may wish to differentiate among them. To do so, we can give each of the source documents a *namespace*: this is a globally unique name, specified in the form of a Uniform Resource Indicator (URI). (The URI is simply a unique name specified in the form of a qualified path and does not necessarily represent the address of any particular content. The more familiar Uniform Resource Locator, or URL, is a special case of a URI where there is a data item whose content can be retrieved according to the path in the URI.) Within an XML document, we can assign a much shorter name, the *namespace prefix*, to each of the namespace URIs. Then, within the XML document, we can "qualify" individual tag names with this prefix, followed by a colon, e.g., <ns:tag>. The *default namespace* is the one for all tags without qualified names.

Namespace prefixes (and the default namespace) are assigned to URLs using a reserved XML attribute (xmlns for the default namespace, xmlns:*name* for any namespace prefix). The namespace assignment takes effect *with the parent element of the attribute*.

■ ■ ■ ━━

Example 11.2

Consider the following XML fragment:

```
<root xmlns="http://www.first.com/aspace" xmlns:myns="http://
  www.fictitious.com/mypathY">
  <tag>
  <thistag>is in the default namespace (aspace)</thistag>
  <myns:thistag>is in myns</myns:thistag>
  <otherns:thistag xmlns:otherns="http://somewhere">is in
    otherns</otherns:thistag>
  </tag>
</root>
```

Here, the element root gets associated with the default namespace defined with the xmlns attribute; it also defines the namespace prefix myns. The descendant elements tag and thistag remain with the default namespace. However, myns:thistag is in the new namespace at pathY.

Finally, `otherns:thistag` introduces the namespace prefix `otherns`, to which the element itself belongs.

■ ■ ■

DOCUMENT ORDER

XML was designed to serve several different roles simultaneously: (1) extensible document format generalizing and replacing HTML, (2) general-purpose markup language, and (3) structured data export format. XML distinguishes itself from most database-related standards in that it is *order-preserving* and generally *order-sensitive*. More specifically, the order between XML elements is considered to be meaningful and is preserved and queriable through XML query languages. This enables ordering among paragraphs in a document to be maintained or tested. Perhaps surprisingly, XML *attributes* (which are treated as properties of elements) are *not* order-sensitive, although XML tools will typically preserve the original order.

At the logical level, we typically represent an XML document as a tree, where each XML node is represented by a node in the tree, and parent-child relationships are encoded as edges. There are seven node types, briefly alluded to above:

- **Document root**: This node represents the entire XML document and generally has as its children at least one processing instruction representing the XML encoding information and a single **root element**. Observe that the *document root* represents the entire document, whereas the root element only contains the element structure.
- **Processing instruction**: These nodes instruct the parser on character encodings, parse structure, etc.
- **Comment**: As with HTML comments, these are human-readable notes.
- **Element**: Most data structures are encoded as XML elements, which include open and close tags plus content. A content-free element may be represented as a single *empty tag* of the form `<tag/>`, which is considered equivalent to an open tag/close tag sequence.
- **Attribute**: An attribute is a name-value pair associated with an element (and embedded in its open tag). Attributes are not order-sensitive, and no single tag may have more than one attribute with the same name.
- **Text**: A text node represents contiguous data content within an element.
- **Namespace**: A namespace node qualifies the name of an element within a particular URI. This creates a *qualified name*.

Each node in the document has a unique identity, as well as a relative ordering and (if a schema is associated with the document) a data type. A depth-first, left-to-right traversal of the tree representation corresponds to the node ordering within the associated XML document.

■ ■ ■

Example 11.3

Figure 11.3 shows an XML data model representation for the document of Figure 11.2. Here we see five of the seven node types (comment and namespace are not present in this document).

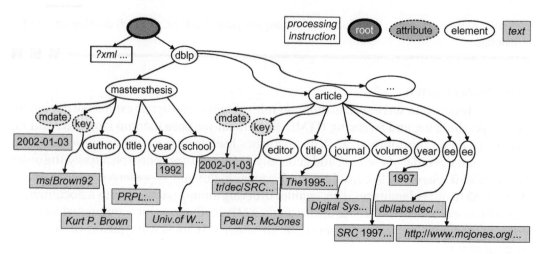

FIGURE 11.3 Example data model representation for the XML fragment of Figure 11.2. Note that the different node types are represented here using different shapes.

11.2 XML Structural and Schema Definitions

In general, XML can be thought of as a semistructured hierarchical data format, whose leaves are primarily string (text) nodes and attribute node values. To be most useful, we must add a *schema* describing the semantics and types of the attributes and elements — this enables us to encode nonstring datatypes as well as inter- and intra-document links (e.g., foreign keys, URLs).

11.2.1 Document Type Definitions (DTDs)

When the XML standard was introduced, the focus was on document markup, and hence the original "schema" specification was more focused on the legal structure of the markup than on specific datatypes and data semantics. The *document type definition,* or DTD, is expressed using processing instructions and tells the XML parser about the structure of a given element.

In DTD, we specify for each element which subelements and/or text nodes are allowed within an element, using EBNF notation to indicate alternation or nesting. A subelement is represented by its name, and a text node is designated as #PCDATA ("parsed character" data).

Example 11.4

Figure 11.4 shows a fragment of a DTD for our running example in this section. We focus in this portion of the example on the element definitions (ELEMENT processing instructions). The DBLP element may have a sequence of mastersthesis and article subelements, interleaved in any order. In turn the mastersthesis has mandatory author, title, year, and school subelements, followed by zero or more committeemembers. Each of these subelements contains text content.

```
<!ELEMENT dblp((mastersthesis | article)*)>
<!ELEMENT mastersthesis(author,title,year,school,
   committeemember*)>
<!ATTLIST mastersthesis(mdate    CDATA   #REQUIRED
                        key      ID      #REQUIRED
                        advisor  CDATA   #IMPLIED>
<!ELEMENT author(#PCDATA)>
<!ELEMENT title(#PCDATA)>
<!ELEMENT year(#PCDATA)>
<!ELEMENT school(#PCDATA)>
<!ELEMENT committeemember(#PCDATA)>
  . . .
```

FIGURE 11.4 Fragment of an example DTD for the XML of Figure 11.2. Note that each definition here is expressed using a processing instruction.

■ ■ ■

Attributes are specified in a series of rows within the ATTLIST processing instruction: each attribute specification includes a name, a special type, and an annotation indicating whether the attribute is optional (#IMPLIED) or mandatory (#REQUIRED). The types are as follows: text content is called CDATA ("character data"), which is somewhat more restricted than the PCDATA allowed in elements; ID designates that the attribute contains an *identifier* that is globally unique within the document; IDREF or IDREFS specifies that the attribute contains a *reference* or space-separated references, respectively, to ID-typed attributes within the document. IDs and IDREFs can be thought of as special cases of keys and foreign keys, or anchors and links.

■ ■ ■

Example 11.5
Figure 11.4 defines three attributes related to the mastersthesis. The mdate is mandatory and of text type. The key is also mandatory, but a unique identifier. Finally, the advisor string is optional.

■ ■ ■

Oddly enough, the DTD does not specify which element is the root within a document. The root element is instead specified within the processing instruction *in the source XML* that references the DTD. The DTD can be directly embedded within the document using a syntax like

```
<?xml version="1.0" encoding="ISO-8859-1" ?>
<!DOCTYPE dblp [
   <!ELEMENT dblp((mastersthesis | article)*)>
```

```
    <!ELEMENT mastersthesis(author,title,year,school,
      committeemember*)>
    ...
  ]>
<dblp>
  ...
```

but more commonly, the DTD is in a separate file that must be referenced using the SYSTEM keyword:

```
<!DOCTYPE dblp SYSTEM "dblp.dtd">
<dblp>
  ...
```

In both cases, the first parameter after DOCTYPE is the name of the root element, and the XML parser will parse the DTD before continuing beyond that point.

PROS AND CONS OF DTD

DTD, as the first XML schema format, is very commonly used in practice. It is relatively simple to understand and concise (if syntactically awkward), it is supported by virtually every XML parser in existence, and it is sufficient for most document structural specifications. Unfortunately, it has many limitations for data interchange. One cannot directly map the database concepts of key and foreign key to ID and IDREFS (there is no support for compound keys, and the value of a key must be *globally unique* within a document, even to the exclusion of ID-typed attributes with other names). The concept of null values does not map to any aspect of DTD-based XML, meaning that relational database export is awkward. Primitive datatypes such as integers and dates are not possible to specify.

All of these limitations, as well as a variety of other desiderata, led to the development of a newer specification in the early 2000s, called XML Schema.

11.2.2 XML Schema (XSD)

XML Schema (commonly abbreviated to its standard three-letter file extension, XSD) is an extremely comprehensive standard designed to provide a superset of DTD's capabilities, to address the limitations mentioned in the previous section, and to itself be an XML-encoded standard.

Since an XML Schema is itself specified in XML, we will always be dealing with (at least) two namespaces: the namespace for XML Schema itself (used for the built-in XSD definitions and datatypes) and the namespace being defined by the schema. Typically, we will use the default namespace for the tags defined in the schema and will use a prefix (commonly xs: or xsd:) associated with the URI www.w3.org/2001/XMLSchema to refer to the XML Schema tags.

Beyond the use of XML tags, XML Schema differs significantly from DTD in two respects. First, the notion of an *element type* has been separated from the *element name*. Now we define an element type (either a complexType representing a structured element or a `simpleType` representing a scalar or text node) and later associate it with one or more element names. Second, the use of EBNF notation has been completely eliminated; instead, we group sequences of content using `sequence` or `choice` elements and specify a number of repetitions using `minOccurs` and `maxOccurs` attributes.

■ ■ ■ ▬▬▬▬▬▬▬▬▬▬▬▬▬▬▬▬▬▬▬▬▬▬▬▬▬▬▬▬▬▬▬▬▬▬▬▬

Example 11.6

Figure 11.5 shows an XML Schema fragment for our running example. We see first that the schema definition has a root tag `schema` within the XML Schema namespace (abbreviated here as `xsd`).

The fragment shows the definition of a complex element type for a thesis. Associated with this element type are three attributes (`mdate`, `key`, and optional `advisor`). Observe that each of the attributes has a particular type (one of the built-in XML Schema *simple types*): date, string, and string, respectively. Within the `ThesisType` is a sequence of subelements: an `author` string, a `title` string, a `year` integer, a school `string`, and a sequence of zero or more `committeemember`s of a complex type called `CommitteeType`. The `ThesisType` can be used for

```
<xsd:schema xmlns:xsd="http://www.w3.org/2001/XMLSchema">
 ...
 <xsd:complexType name="ThesisType">
  <xsd:attribute name="key" type="xsd:string"/>
  <xsd:attribute name="mdate" type="xsd:date"/>
  <xsd:attribute name="advisor" type="xsd:string" minOccurs="0
    "/>
  <xsd:sequence>
   <xsd:element name="author" type="xsd:string"/>
   <xsd:element name="title" type="xsd:string"/>
   <xsd:element name="year" type="xsd:integer"/>
   <xsd:element name="school" type="xsd:string"/>
   <xsd:element name="committeemember" type="CommitteeType"
              minOccurs="0" maxOccurs="unbounded"/>
  </xsd:sequence>
 </xsd:complexType>
 <xsd:complexType name="CommitteeType">
  ...
 </xsd:complexType>
 ...
 <xsd:element name="dblp">
  <xsd:sequence>
   <xsd:element name="mastersthesis" type="ThesisType"/>
   ...
  </xsd:sequence>
 </xsd:element>
 ...
</xsd:schema>
```

FIGURE 11.5 Example XML Schema fragment corresponding to the XML of Figure 11.2. This excerpt focuses on defining the structure of the `mastersthesis`.

more than one element; we finally associated it with the `mastersthesis` near the bottom of the figure.

━━ ■ ■ ■

XML Schema allows for the definition of both keys and foreign keys, which we shall discuss later in this chapter when we have introduced XPath. It also has many features that we do not discuss at all: it is possible to define simple types that restrict the built-in types (e.g., positive integers, dates from 2010 to 2020, strings starting with "S"), to make use of inheritance in defining types, and to create reusable structures. For more detail, we suggest consulting the many resources available on the Web.

XML Schema and its associated data model are the "modern" schema format for XML and are used by most XML-related Web standards. Examples include SOAP, the Simple Object Access Protocol used to pass parameters across systems; WSDL, the Web Service Description Language; the data type primitives of RDF Schema, the schema language for the Resource Description Framework used in the Semantic Web (see Section 12.3); and XQuery, the XML query language we describe later in this chapter.

11.3 Query Language

Given that XML represents documents and data in a standard way, it quickly became apparent that applications and developers would need standardized mechanisms for extracting and manipulating XML content.

Over the years, models emerged for parsing XML into objects (DOM) and messages (SAX), the XPath primitive, and ultimately the XQuery language. We discuss the parsing standards in Section 11.3.1, XPath in Section 11.3.2, and XQuery in Section 11.3.3. Another XML transformation language, XSLT (XML Stylesheet Language: Transformations), is used in many document and formatting scenarios, but is not well-suited to data manipulation, and hence we do not discuss it in this book.

11.3.1 Precursors: DOM and SAX

Prior to the creation of XML query primitives, the XML community established a series of language-independent APIs for parsing XML: the goal was that any parser would implement these APIs in a consistent way, making it easy to port code to a variety of platforms and libraries.

The first standard, the Document Object Model, or DOM, specifies a common object-oriented hierarchy for parsed HTML and XML. DOM actually emerged from the internal object models supported by HTML Web browsers, but it was generalized to XML as well. DOM establishes a common interface, the DOM node, to encompass all of the various XML node types; instances include the Document node, Element node, and Text node. A DOM parser typically builds an in-memory object tree representing a parsed document and returns the document root node to the calling program. From here, the application can traverse the entire document model. Every DOM node has methods for traversing to the node's parent and children (if applicable), testing the node type, reading the text value of the node, and so on. An interface also exists to retrieve nodes directly by their name, rather than through the document hierarchy. Later versions of DOM also support *updates* to the in-memory document model.

DOM is a fairly heavyweight representation of XML: each node in an XML document is instantiated as an object, which typically consumes significantly more space than the original source file. Moreover, early versions of DOM were not in any way *incremental*: no processing would happen until the entire document was parsed. To meet the needs of applications that only wanted to manipulate a small portion of an XML document — or to incrementally process the data — SAX, Simple API for XML, was created. SAX is not an object representation, but rather a standard parser API. As an XML parser reads through an input XML file, it *calls back* to user-supplied methods, notifying them when a new element is beginning, when an element is closing, when a text node is encountered, etc. The application can take the information provided in the callback and perform whatever behaviors it deems appropriate. The application might instantiate an object for each call-back, or it might simply update progress information or discard the callback information entirely.

Both SAX and DOM are designed for developers in object-oriented languages to manipulate XML; they are not declarative means for extracting content. Of course, such declarative standards have also been developed, and we discuss them next.

11.3.2 XPath: A Primitive for XML Querying

XPath was originally developed to be a simple XML query language, whose role was to extract subtrees from an individual XML document. Over time it has become more commonly used as a building block for other XML standards. For example, XPath is used to specify keys and foreign keys in XML Schema, and it is used to specify collections of XML nodes to be assigned to variables in XQuery (described below).

XPath actually has two versions in active use, the original XPath 1.0 and the later XPath 2.0. The original version is limited to expressions that do not directly specify a source XML document (i.e., one needs to use a tool to apply the XPath to a specific XML file). Version 2.0 was created during the development of XQuery, in order to make XPath a fully integrated subset of that language. It adds a number of features, with the most notable being the ability to specify the source document for the expression and a data model and type system matching that of XQuery.

PATH EXPRESSIONS

The main construct in XPath is the *path expression*, which represents a sequence of *steps* from a *context node*. The *context node* is by default the root of the source document to which the XPath is being applied. The result of evaluating the path expression is a *sequence of nodes* (and their subtree descendants), with duplicates removed, returned in the order they appear in the source document. For historic reasons, this sequence is often termed a "node set."

THE CONTEXT NODE

XPaths are specified using a Unix path-like syntax. As in Unix, the *current* context node is designated by "." If we start the XPath with a leading "/", then this node starts at the document root. In XPath 2.0, we can also specify a particular source document to use as the context node: the function `doc("URL")` parses the XML document at *URL* and returns its document root as the context node.

From the context node, an XPath typically includes a sequence of *steps* and optional *predicates*. If we follow the usual interpretation of an XML document as a tree, then a step in an XPath encodes a *step type* describing how to traverse from the context node, and a *node restriction* specifying which nodes to return. The *step type* is typically a delimiter like "/" or "//" and the *node restriction* is typically a label of an element to match; we specify these more precisely in a moment.

By default, traversal is downward in the tree from nodes to their descendants. We can start at the context node and traverse a *single level* to a child node (specified using the delimiter "/") or through *zero or more descendant subelements* (specified using "//"). We can restrict the matching node in a variety of ways:

- A step "···/label" or "···//label" will only return child or descendant elements, respectively, with the designated label. (Any intervening elements are unrestricted.)
- A step with a "*" will match any label: "···/*" or "···//*," will return the set of all child elements, or descendant elements, respectively.
- A step "···/@label" will return attribute nodes (including both label and value) that are children of the current element, which match the specified label. The step or "···//@label" will return attribute nodes of the current *or any descendant element*, if they have the specified label.
- A step "···/@*" or "···//@*" will return any attribute nodes associated with the current element, or the current and any descendant elements, respectively.
- A step "/.." represents a step up the tree to the *parent* of each node matched by the previous step in the XPath.
- A step with a *node-test* will restrict the type of node to a particular class: e.g., ···/text() returns child nodes that are text nodes; ···/comment() returns child nodes that are comments; ···/processing-instruction() returns child nodes that are processing instructions; ···/node() returns any type of node (not just elements, attributes, etc.).

■ ■ ■ ▬▬▬▬▬▬▬▬▬▬▬▬▬▬▬▬▬▬▬▬▬▬▬▬▬▬▬▬▬▬▬▬▬▬▬▬▬▬

Example 11.7

Given the data of Figure 11.2, the XPath `./dblp/article` would begin with the document root as the context node, traverse downward to the `dblp` root element and any `article` sub-elements, and return an XML node sequence containing the `article` elements (which would still maintain all attachments to its subtree). Thus, if we were to serialize the node sequence back to XML, the result would be

```
<article mdate="2002-01-03" key="tr/dec/SRC1997-018">
  <editor>Paul R. McJones</editor>
  <title>The 1995 SQL Reunion</title>
  <journal>Digital System Research Center Report</journal>
  <volume>SRC1997-018</volume>
  <year>1997</year>
  <ee>db/labs/dec/SRC1997-018.html</ee>
  <ee>http://www.mcjones.org/System_R/SQL_Reunion_95/</ee>
</article>
...
```

Note that if there were more than one `article`, the result of the XPath would be a *forest* of XML trees, rather than a single tree. Hence the output of an XPath is often not a legal XML document since it does not have a single root element.

■ ■ ■

■ ■ ■

Example 11.8
Given the example data, the XPath `//year` would begin at the document root (due to the leading "`/`"), traverse any number of subelements downward, and return

```
<year>1992</year>
<year>1997</year>
...
```

where the first `year` comes from the `mastersthesis` and the second from the `article`.

■ ■ ■

■ ■ ■

Example 11.9
Given the example data, the XPath `/dblp/*/editor` would begin at the document root, traverse downward to match first the `mastersthesis`, and look for an `editor`. No such match is found, so the next traversal will occur in the `article`. From the `article`, an `editor` can be found, and the result would be

```
<editor>Paul R. McJones</editor>
...
```

where, of course, further results might be returned if there were matches among the elided content in the document.

■ ■ ■

MORE COMPLEX STEPS: AXES
While they are by far the most heavily used step specifiers, "`/`" and "`//`" are actually considered to be a special *abbreviated syntax* for a more general XML traversal model called *axes*. Axes allow an XPath author to specify a traversal to not only a descendant node, but also an ancestor, a predecessor, a successor, etc. The syntax for axes is somewhat

cumbersome: instead of using "/" or "//" followed by a node restriction, we instead use "/" followed by an *axis specifier* followed by "::", then the node restriction. The axes include:

- `child`: traverses to a child node, identically to a plain "/"
- `descendant`: finds a descendant of the current node, identically to a plain "//"
- `descendant-or-self`: returns the current node or any descendant
- `parent`: returns the parent of the current node, identically to ".."
- `ancestor`: finds any ancestor of the current node
- `ancestor-or-self`: returns the current node or an ancestor
- `preceding-sibling`: returns any sibling node that appeared earlier in the document order
- `following-sibling`: returns any sibling node that appeared later in the document order
- `preceding`: returns any node, at any level, appearing earlier in the document
- `following`: returns any node, at any level, appearing later in the document
- `attribute`: matches attributes, as with the "@" prefix
- `namespace`: matches namespace nodes

■ ■ ■ ▬▬▬▬▬▬▬▬▬▬▬▬▬▬▬▬▬▬▬▬▬▬▬▬▬▬▬▬

Example 11.10

The XPath of Example 11.7 could be written as
```
./child::dblp/child::article
```
and Example 11.8 as
```
/descendant::year
```
An XPath to return *every* XML node in the document is
```
/descendant-or-self::node()
```

▬▬▬▬▬▬▬▬▬▬▬▬▬▬▬▬▬▬▬▬▬▬▬▬▬▬▬▬ ■ ■ ■

PREDICATES

Often we want to further restrict the set of nodes to be returned, e.g., by specifying certain data values we seek. This is where XPath *predicates* come in. A predicate is a Boolean test that can be attached to a specific step in an XPath; the Boolean test is applied to each result that would ordinarily be returned by the XPath. The Boolean test may be as simple as the existence of a path (this enables us to express queries that test for specific *tree patterns* as opposed simply to paths), it could be a test for a particular value of a text or attribute node, etc.

Predicates appear in square brackets, [and]. The expression within the brackets has its context node set to the node matched by the previous step in the XPath.

■ ■ ■ ▬▬▬▬▬▬▬▬▬▬▬▬▬▬▬▬▬▬▬▬▬▬▬▬▬▬▬▬

Example 11.11

If we take the XPath expression `/dblp/*[./year/text()="1992"]` and evaluate it against Figure 11.2, then first `mastersthesis` is matched (the context node becomes the mastersthesis), and then the predicate expression is evaluated. Since it returns true, the mastersthesis node is returned. When the article node is matched (becoming the context node for the predicate), the predicate is again evaluated, but this time it fails to satisfy the conditions.

■ ■ ■

PREDICATES REFERRING TO POSITION

Predicates can also be used to select only specific values from a node set, based on the index position of the nodes. If we use an integer value *i* as the position, e.g., p[5], this selects the *i*th node in the node sequence. We can also explicitly request the index of a node with the position() function and the index of the *last* node in the node sequence with the last() function. (The corresponding first() function also exists.)

■ ■ ■

Example 11.12

To select the last article in the XML file of Figure 11.2, we could use the following XPath:

```
//article[position()=last()]
```

■ ■ ■

NODE FUNCTIONS

Sometimes we wish to test or restrict the value of a particular node's name or its namespace. The function name takes as an argument a (nontext) node and returns the node's fully qualified name. local-name just returns the name without its namespace prefix; namespace-uri returns the URI of the associated namespace. (All of these functions will also take node collections as inputs and will merely return their results for the first element in the collection.)

REVISITING XML SCHEMA: KEYS AND KEYREFS

Now that we have seen the basics of XPath, we revisit the notion of keys and foreign keys in XML Schema. Figure 11.6 shows an expanded version of Figure 11.5 where we have added a number of keys and foreign keys.

Let us begin with the notion of a key, as captured in line 31 (as well as 25). The first thing we note is that each key receives its own name: this name does not manifest itself within the structure of the XML document, but rather is used so a foreign key can link to this key. Most readers unfamiliar with XML Schema may also find it odd and unnatural that the keyref is defined not with respect to the complexType (mastersthesis or school), but in fact *outside* the place where an element of that complexType is introduced. Recall that a *key* is a special case of a functional dependency, where an attribute or set of attributes determines an entire element in a collection. In the relational world, this element was a tuple and the collection was a table. Here, the element determined by the key must be specified: this is the role of the xsd:selector. The set of all elements matching the selector is the collection over which the key is defined. Then, within the selected element, a set of attributes must be identified to form the key: this is the xsd:field.

```
 1  ...
 2  <xsd:complexType name="ThesisType">
 3   <xsd:attribute name="key" type="xsd:string"/>
 4   ...
 5   <xsd:sequence>
 6    ...
 7    <xsd:element name="school" type="xsd:string"/>
 8    ...
 9   </xsd:sequence>
10  </xsd:complexType>
11  ...
12  <xsd:complexType name="SchoolType">
13   <xsd:attribute name="key" type="xsd:string"/>
14    ...
15  </xsd:complexType>
16  ...
17  <xsd:element name="dblp">
18   <xsd:sequence>
19    <xsd:element name="mastersthesis" type="ThesisType">
20      <xsd:keyref name="schoolRef" refer="schoolId">
21        <xsd:selector xpath="."/>
22        <xsd:field xpath="./school"/>
23      </xsd:keyref>
24    </xsd:element>
25    <xsd:key name="mtId">
26      <xsd:selector xpath="mastersthesis"/>
27      <xsd:field xpath="@key"/>
28    </xsd:key>
29    <xsd:element name="university" type="SchoolType"> ...
30    </xsd:element/>
31    <xsd:key name="schoolId">
32      <xsd:selector xpath="university"/>
33      <xsd:field xpath="@key"/>
34    </xsd:key>
35    ...
```

FIGURE 11.6 XML Schema excerpt with keys and keyrefs.

Once we understand how a key is defined, the foreign key or keyref, in line 20, should be straightforward. keyrefs also have a name, but this is not as significant as the refer attribute, which names the key pointed to by the foreign key.

11.3.3 XQuery: Query Capabilities for XML

The XPath language is not expressive enough to capture the kinds of data transformations that are employed in a typical database query or schema mapping. For instance, XPath does not support cross-document joins, changing of labels, or restructuring. To address these needs, the XQuery language was developed. Intuitively, XQuery is the "SQL of XML": the single standard language that is intended to be implemented by XML databases and document transformation engines.

XQuery currently consists of a core language plus a series of extensions: the core language provides exact-answers semantics and supports querying and transformation. There exist extensions for full-text querying with ranked answers (XQuery Full Text) and for XQuery updates (the XQuery Update Facility). In this book we focus on the "core" XQuery.

Basic XQuery Structure: "FLWOR" Expressions

SQL is well-known for its basic "`SELECT...FROM...WHERE`" pattern for describing query blocks (with an optional "`ORDER BY`" and "`GROUP BY...HAVING`". XQuery similarly has a basic form for a query block, called a FLWOR (indeed, pronounced "flower") expression. FLWOR is an acronym for "`for...let...where...order by...return`." (Note that XQuery keywords must be in lowercase, in contrast to SQL, which is case-insensitive.) In reality, the different XQuery clauses can be interleaved in a variety of orders, and several clauses are optional, but the FLWOR ordering is by far the prevalent one.

Intuitively, the XQuery `for` and `let` clauses together correspond to the `FROM` clause in SQL; the XQuery `where` corresponds to its namesake in SQL; and the `return` clause corresponds to the `SELECT` clause in SQL. However, there are a number of key differences in the semantics of the clauses. The relational model consists of tables and tuples, with completely different operators that apply to each. In XML, a document or any subtree is represented as a node with a set of subtrees. Hence XQuery distinguishes between nodes, scalar types, and collections, and operators are defined in a relatively clean way over these. XQuery also allows for the outputs of multiple (possibly correlated) queries to be nested, in order to form nested output. We consider each FLWOR clause in turn.

`for`: ITERATION AND BINDING OVER COLLECTIONS

The most common way of specifying an input operand for a query is to *bind* a variable to each node matching a pattern. The `for` clause allows us to define a variable that ranges over a node sequence returned by an XPath. The syntax is `for` *$var* `in` *XPath-expression*. To bind multiple variables, we can nest `for` clauses. For each possible valuation of the variables, the XQuery engine will evaluate the `where` condition(s) and optionally `return` content.

■ ■ ■ ━━━━━━━━━━━━━━━━━━━━━━━━━━━━━━━━━━

Example 11.13

Suppose we have a document called `dblp.xml` located on the `my.org` server. If we use the following sequence of nested `for` clauses:

```
for $docRoot in doc("http://my.org/dblp.xml")
  for $rootElement in $docRoot/dblp
    for $rootChild in $rootElement/article
```

then the variable `$docRoot` will take on a single value, that of the document root node of the XML source file. The variable `$rootElement` will iterate over the child elements of the document root — namely, the (single) root element of the XML file. Next, `$rootChild` will iterate over the child element nodes of the root element.

We can abbreviate nested `for` clauses using an alternate form, in which a comma is used to separate one expression from the next, and the second `for` clause is omitted.

Example 11.14

The above example can be rewritten as in lines 1–4 of Figure 11.7.

```
1 for $docRoot in doc("http://my.org/dblp.xml"),
2   $rootElement in $docRoot/dblp,
3     $rootChild in $rootElement/article
4 let $textContent := $rootChild//text()
5 where $rootChild/author/text() = "Bob"
6 order by $rootChild/title
7 return <BobResult>
8             { $rootChild/editor }
9             { $rootChild/title }
10            { for $txt in $textContent
11              return <text> { $txt } </text>
12            }
13        </BobResult>
```

FIGURE 11.7 Simple XQuery example.

`let`: ASSIGNMENT OF COLLECTIONS TO VARIABLES

Unlike SQL, XQuery has a notion of collection-valued variables, where the collection may be a sequence of nodes or of scalar values. The `let` clause allows us to assign the results of any collection-valued expression (e.g., an XPath) to a variable. The syntax is `let` *$var* := *collection-expression*.

Example 11.15

Continuing our example from above, the first 4 lines of Figure 11.7 will assign a different value to `$textContent` for each value of `$rootChild`, namely, the set of *all* text nodes that appear in the element's subtree.

`where`: EVALUATION OF CONDITIONS AGAINST BINDINGS

For each possible valuation of the variables in the `for` and `let` clauses, the XQuery engine will attempt to evaluate the predicates in the `where` clause. If these are satisfied, then the `return` clause will be invoked to produce output. We can think of XQuery's execution model as being one in which "tuples of bindings" (one value for each variable from each source) are joined, selected, and projected; the `where` clause performs the selection and join operations.

■ ■ ■ ━━

Example 11.16

We can restrict our example from above to only consider `$rootChild` elements that have `editor` subelements with value "Bob," as seen in lines 1–5 of Figure 11.7.

━━ ■ ■ ■

`return`: OUTPUT OF XML TREES

The `return` clause gets invoked each time the `where` conditions are satisfied, and in each case it returns a fragment of output that is typically an XML tree. The content output by the `return` clause may be literal XML, the results of evaluating some expression (even XPath expression) based on bound variables, or the results of evaluating a nested XQuery.

If a `return` clause begins with an angle bracket or a literal value, the XQuery engine assumes that it is to output whatever it reads as literal text. To instead force it to interpret the content as an expression, we use the *escape* characters { and } around the expression.

`order by`: CHANGING THE ORDER OF RETURNED OUTPUT

The `order by` clause allows us to change the order content is returned, according to one or more sort keys (specified as a list of XPaths relative to bound variables).

■ ■ ■ ━━

Example 11.17

The full query in Figure 11.7 completes our example, where we return an XML subtree each time "Bob" is matched. Within the subtree, we output the editor and title within the `$rootChild` subtree. Then we use a nested XQuery to iterate over all of the text nodes in `$textContent`, outputting each in an element labeled `text`.

━━ ■ ■ ■

Aggregation and Uniqueness

SQL allows the query author to specify duplicate removal using a special `DISTINCT` keyword in the `SELECT` clause or an aggregate function (e.g., `COUNT DISTINCT`). In XQuery, the notion of computing distinct values or items is handled as a collection-valued function, which essentially converts an ordered sequence into an ordered set. There are two functions in most XQuery implementations, `fn:distinct-values` and `fn:distinct-nodes`, which take node sequences, and remove items that match on value equality or node identity, respectively. These functions can be applied to the results of an XPath expression, to the output of an XQuery, etc.; `fn:distinct-values` can even be applied to a collection of scalar values.

As with computing unique values, aggregation in XQuery is accomplished in a way that is entirely different from SQL. In XQuery, there is no GROUP BY construct, and hence aggregate functions are not applied to attributes in grouped tables. Instead, an aggregate function simply takes a collection as a parameter and returns a scalar result representing the result of the function: fn:average, fn:max, fn:min, fn:count, fn:sum.

■ ■ ■ ▬▬▬▬▬▬▬▬▬▬▬▬▬▬▬▬▬▬▬▬▬▬▬▬▬▬▬▬▬▬▬▬▬▬▬▬

Example 11.18

Suppose we want to count the number of theses or articles written by each author (assuming author names are canonicalized) for a document of the form shown in Figure 11.2. Rather than using a GROUP BY construct, we express this by computing the set of all authors, then finding the papers for each author.

```
let $doc := doc("dblp.xml")
let $authors := fn:distinct-values($doc//author/text())
for $auth in $authors
return <author>
          { $auth }
          { let $papersByAuth := $doc/*[author/text() =
                                        $auth]
         return <papers>
                  <count>
                    { fn:count(papersByAuth) }
                  </count>
                  <titles>
                    { $papersByAuth/title }
                  </titles>
                </papers> }
       </author>
```

Here, the inner query computes the set of all papers by the author, then returns the count as well as the complete list of titles.

▬▬▬▬▬▬▬▬▬▬▬▬▬▬▬▬▬▬▬▬▬▬▬▬▬▬▬▬▬▬▬▬▬▬ ■ ■ ■

Data to and from Metadata

An extremely important aspect of XQuery for data integration — one that has no relational equivalent — is that of converting between data and element or attribute names. Recall from Section 11.3.2 that we can use XPath functions like name, local-name, and namespace-uri to retrieve the name and/or namespace information associated with an element or attribute node. In XQuery, such functions can be used not only within the XPaths associated with the for or let clauses, but as general predicates anywhere in the query.

Moreover, in the return clause we can use the *computed constructors* element (which takes a name and structured content) and attribute (which takes a name and a string value). By default, the name is treated as literal text, so expressions must be enclosed in braces.

■ ■ ■ ▬▬▬▬▬▬▬▬▬▬▬▬▬▬▬▬▬▬▬▬▬▬▬▬▬▬▬▬▬▬▬▬▬▬▬▬

Example 11.19

Consider the following XML:

```
for $x in doc ("dblp.xml")/dblp/*,
    $year in $x/year,
    $title in $x/title/text()
        where local-name($x) <> "university"
return
    element { name($x) } {
    attribute key { $x/key }
    attribute { "year-" + $year } { $title }
}
```

It makes use of several operations for querying and constructing metadata. Initially, we bind $x to any subelements of the root element but use a condition on the local-name to restrict our search to subelements that are not universities. In the return clause, we output a computed element whose name is *the same* as the initial $x but with different content. The new element has two computed attributes: one is key with the value of the original key attribute, and the other is an attribute whose name consists of the string "year-" concatenated with the value to which $year is bound.

▬▬▬▬▬▬▬▬▬▬▬▬▬▬▬▬▬▬▬▬▬▬▬▬▬▬▬▬▬▬▬▬▬▬▬▬ ■ ■ ■

Functions

XQuery does not expressly have the notion of a view, as in SQL. Rather, XQuery supports arbitrary *functions* that can return scalar values, nodes (as the roots of XML trees), or collections (of scalars or XML nodes/trees). Since a function can return an XML forest or tree, one can think of it as a view that might optionally be parameterized.

Note that XQuery allows for recursion as well as if/else and iteration within functions, hence the language is Turing-complete, unlike SQL. A function in XQuery is specified using the keywords declare function, followed by the function name, its parameters and their types, the keyword as, and the function return type. Note that the types for the parameters and return type are the XML Schema types. If there is no accompanying schema, a generic element can be specified using element(), and an untyped element with a particular name *n* can be specified using element(*n*).

■ ■ ■ ▬▬▬▬▬▬▬▬▬▬▬▬▬▬▬▬▬▬▬▬▬▬▬▬▬▬▬▬▬▬▬▬▬▬▬▬

Example 11.20

The following function returns all authors in the dblp.xml document. Note that we have placed the function into the namespace "my," which is presumably defined elsewhere.

```
declare function my:paperAuthors() as element(author)* {
  return doc("dblp.xml")//author
};
```

Note that the return type here is specified to be zero or more elements (hence the asterisk) called `author`, for which we may (or may not) have an accompanying XML Schema type.

■ ■ ■

■ ■ ■

Example 11.21

The following function returns the number of coauthors who wrote an article with the author whose name is specified as an input parameter $n. It does this by finding the sets of authors for each article authored by $n, then doing duplicate removal, and finally counting the number of entries and then subtracting 1 to avoid counting $n him- or herself.

```
let $authors := doc("dblp.xml")/article[author/text()=$n]/
    author
return fn:count(fn:distinct-values($authors)) - 1
}
```

Note that the return type here is specified to be zero or more elements (hence the asterisk) called `author`, for which we may (or may not) have an accompanying XML Schema type.

■ ■ ■

11.4 Query Processing for XML

Now that we are familiar with the form of XML and its query languages, we consider the problem of *processing* queries expressed in XPath and XQuery over XML data. Inherently, XML is a tree-structured, *non-first-normal-form* data format. The bulk of work on large-scale XML query processing, especially in terms of matching XPaths over the input, has focused on settings in which the data are *stored on disk*, e.g., in a relational DBMS. Here the challenges are how to break up the XML trees and index them (if using a "native" XML storage system) or how to "shred" the XML into relational tuples.

For the latter case, intuitively the goal is to take each XML node and create a corresponding tuple in a relational table. Each such tuple is encoded in a way that enables it to be joined with its parent (and possibly ancestors) and children (and possibly descendants). A common approach is to annotate each tuple T with an *interval code* describing the position of the first and last item in the tree rooted at the node corresponding to T: then we can compare the intervals of tuples T_1 and T_2 for containment to see if one tree is a subtree of the other.

In data integration, the time-consuming portion of evaluation is often *reading an XML source file* and extracting subtrees that match particular XPath expressions. Rather than *store* the XML before extracting relevant trees, our goal is to, in a *single pass*, read, parse, and extract XPath matches from each source document. This is often referred to as "streaming XPath evaluation."

Streaming XPath evaluation relies on two critical observations:

1. SAX-style XML parsing very efficiently matches against XML as it is read from an input stream (e.g., across a network) and uses a callback interface to trigger an

event handler whenever specific content types, start tags, or end tags are encountered. This enables parsing as data are being pipelined into the query processor's system.

2. A large subset of XPath expressions can be mapped to regular expressions, where the alphabet consists of the set of possible edge labels plus a wildcard character. In general, we end up with a set of *nested* regular expressions for each XPath (since, e.g., predicates must be separately matched).

These observations have led to a variety of XML *streaming XPath* matchers, based on event handlers and modified finite state machines. A streaming XPath matcher typically returns sets of nodes, or, if it matches multiple XPaths simultaneously as for XQuery, *tuples of bindings to nodes* (i.e., tuples in which there exists one attribute per variable, whose value is a reference to a node, or a set of references to nodes). These tuples of bindings are typically processed by an extended version of a relational-style query processor, which has the standard set of operators (e.g., select, project, join) as well as a few new ones, such as evaluating an XPath against a tree-valued attribute in a tuple, adding XML tags, and collecting sequences or sets of tuples into an XML tree. Finally, XML content is assembled at the end and output in the form of a tree, using a combination of tagging and grouping operators.

■ ■ ■ ━━━━━━━━━━━━━━━━━━━━━━━━━━━━━━━━━━━━━━━

Example 11.22

We see an example of a typical query plan for XML data in Figure 11.8, corresponding to the query of Figure 11.7. Starting from the bottom, we see a streaming XPath operator that fetches `dblp.xml` and begins parsing it, looking for trees corresponding to the root element, its child, and any descendent text content. This operator returns tuples with values for `rootElement`, `rootChild`, and `textContent`, of which the first two are trees and the last is a forest. These tuples are then left outer joined with a nested expression. The nested expression matches an XPath against the forest in `textContent` and returns a sequence of tuples with values for `txt`. These tuples are tagged within `text` elements, then grouped into a single forest. The results of the left outer join are then fed into further XPath matching, which extracts the `editor` and `title` from the `rootChild`. After further projection, the element `BobsResult` is created for each tuple, and its children are set to be the `editor`, `title`, and results of the nested expression. The result is a sequence of `BobsResult` tuples that can be written to disk, a data stream, etc.

━━━━━━━━━━━━━━━━━━━━━━━━━━━━━━━━━━━━ ■ ■ ■

Let us now look at the specifics of how the operators are implemented.

11.4.1 XML Path Matching

The XML path matching operator appears in two guises, one based on streaming evaluation over incoming data and the other based on traversal of the tree representation within an attribute of a binding tuple. Both can be implemented using the same mechanisms, as handlers to an event-driven XML tree parser.

A variety of design points have been considered for XML path matchers.

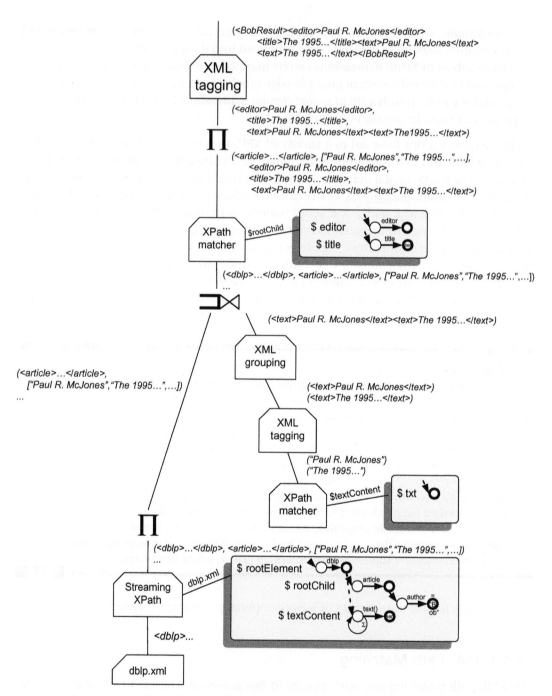

FIGURE 11.8 Sketch of a query plan for the query of Figure 11.7. Most of the engine remains a tuple processor, where tuples are no longer in first normal form, but rather *binding tuples* containing (references to) trees.

TYPE OF AUTOMATON

In general, within a single XPath segment (series of steps separated by / or //), the presence of wildcards or the // step allows for multiple matches at each level. This introduces *nondeterminism* into the picture, and several schemes have been considered to process data in this context. The first involves building a single nondeterministic finite state machine (NFA) for the XPath and keeping track of multiple possible matches simultaneously. The second method is to convert the expression to a deterministic finite state machine (DFA). The third method builds on the previous ones by creating an NFA that is "lazily" expanded to a DFA as needed (where portions of the expansion are cached).

■ ■ ■ ▬▬▬▬▬▬▬▬▬▬▬▬▬▬▬▬▬▬▬▬▬▬▬

Example 11.23

We can see the NFAs for two of the example XPaths of Examples 11.7 and 11.8 in Figure 11.9. Depending on the specific style of XPath match, this NFA might be directly represented in memory and used to match against events from input, or it might be converted to a DFA (either eagerly or lazily) and used to match.

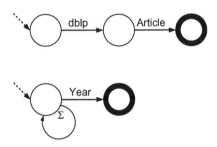

FIGURE 11.9 Nondeterministic finite automata for the XPaths /dblp/article and //year. Note that the Σ on the edge label in the automata represents the alphabet of all possible labels, i.e., a wildcard.

▬▬▬▬▬▬▬▬▬▬▬▬▬▬▬▬▬▬▬▬▬▬▬ ■ ■ ■

DIFFERENT SCHEMES FOR EVALUATING SUBPATHS

Many XPaths have "subsidiary" segments — for instance, nested paths within predicates. One can create a single automaton with different final states indicating which XPaths have been matched, or one can create a series of nested automata, where matching one automaton activates the others.

PREDICATE PUSH-DOWN AND SHORT-CIRCUITING

In any case, predicates may include operations beyond simple path-existence tests, which can often be "pushed" into the path-matching stage. Here the XPath matcher must invoke subsidiary logic to apply predicates such as testing for value equality of a text node. Any nonmatch must be discarded.

XPATH VERSUS XQUERY

If the query processor is computing XPath queries, then the XPath matcher's goal is to return a node set for each query. Sometimes, however, the goal is to provide a set of *input binding tuples* for the `for` (or, in some cases, `let`) clauses of an XQuery. Here, we want the Cartesian product of the possible node matches to a set of XPaths. The *x-scan* operator combines XPath matching with an extension of the pipelined hash join, such that it can incrementally output tuples of bindings to be evaluated.

■ ■ ■ ▬▬

Example 11.24

In evaluating an XQuery within a streaming operator, the first stage simultaneously matches a hierarchy of XPaths corresponding to `for` and `let` expressions (see Figure 11.10, which corresponds to the leftmost leaf operator from Figure 11.8). For this streaming XPath matcher, reaching the final state in one NFA may trigger certain behaviors. One such behavior is that a match to the first NFA may activate other, nested NFAs, corresponding to nested XPaths. Moreover, upon matching a particular pattern we may need to test the match against a particular value (a predicate push-down, indicated in the test for `author = ''Bob''`), and we may add matches to a set, rather than adding one binding per match (as is needed for the `$rootElement//text()` `let` clause, versus the other `for` clauses).

The output of the streaming operator for this collection of NFAs will be a sequence of binding tuples for the variables `rootElement`, `rootChild`, and (collection-typed) `textContent`. Example 11.22 describes in more detail how the output from the streaming XPath evaluator is propagated through the other operators in the query plan.

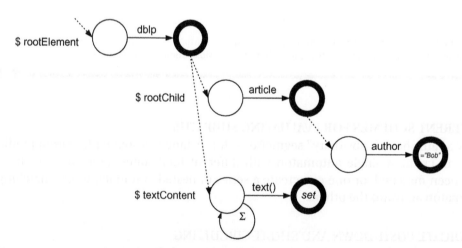

FIGURE 11.10 Hierarchy of nondeterministic finite automata for matching the set of XPaths in the XQuery of Figure 11.7. Note that upon reaching the final state of one machine, we may activate other (nested) XPaths, and we may need to test the match against a value or collect it within a set.

11.4.2 XML Output

The process of creating XML within a tuple is typically broken into two classes of operations.

TAGGING
Takes an attribute (which is already tree-valued) and "wraps" it within an XML element or attribute. In certain cases well-structured properties may need to be tested (e.g., certain kinds of content are illegal within an attribute).

GROUPING
Takes a set of tuples (with some common key attributes) and combines their results, typically within a single collection-valued attribute. It is analogous to SQL GROUP BY, except that instead of computing a scalar aggregate value over an attribute, it instead collects all of the different attribute values into a single XML forest.

Of course, another key component of XQuery processing tends to be nesting within the return clause. This is typically accomplished using the **left outer join** operator, as in Example 11.22.

The focus of this chapter has been on implementing the SQL-like "core" of XQuery. Support for recursive functions and some of XQuery's more advanced features typically requires additional operators, for instance, some form of function invocation plus an if/else construct that helps determine when to terminate, the ability to query nodes for their XML Schema types, and support for calling library functions.

11.4.3 XML Query Optimization

For the core parts of the language, XQuery optimization is little different from conventional relational optimization: there is a process of enumeration and cost and cardinality estimation. The challenges tend to lie in the unique properties of XML. XQuery is much more expressive than SQL, and in general XQuery cost-based optimizers are most effective on subsets of the overall language. Even for subsets, there are often many more potential rewrites than in the normal SQL case.

Moreover, the cardinalities (and hence costs) of XPath matching tend to be more difficult to determine: it becomes essential to estimate "fan-outs" of different portions of an XML document. New metadata structures have been developed to try to help estimate branching factors.

With functions, XQuery is in fact Turing-complete — necessitating an approach to optimizing XQuery function calls that more closely resembles optimizing functional programming languages. All of these techniques are beyond the scope of this textbook.

11.5 Schema Mapping for XML

Not surprisingly, XML introduces new complexities in terms of *schema mappings*. The two main ones are as follows.

- XML is *semistructured*, meaning that different XML elements (even of the same type) may have variations in structure. Moreover, XML queries contain multiple path expressions with optional wildcards and recursion. Hence the conditions for query containment are somewhat different.
- XML contains nesting, and the specific nesting relationships may be *different* between a source instance and a target instance. Hence it becomes necessary to specify nesting relationships, and optionally merge operations on nodes, within XML mappings.

Moreover, under different conditions we may wish to output an XML element for each occurrence of a data value, and in others we may wish to output an XML element for each *unique* occurrence — roughly analogous to bag versus set semantics.

We discuss specific methods of specifying XML schema mappings, as well as for reformulating queries over them, in this section.

11.5.1 Mappings with Nesting

As a hierarchical data model with a complex schema language, XML makes the schema mapping problem significantly more complex than in the relational model. Even for the relational model, we did not seek to support arbitrary SQL as a mapping language. Rather, we focused on a subset, namely, conjunctive queries in LAV, GAV, or GLAV formulations (where the latter may be expressed using tgds rather than GLAV rules).

Similarly, for XML schema mappings, it is intractable to use the full power of XQuery. Rather, we use a simplified mapping language that has as its underpinnings the notion of *nested tgds*. In this section, we explain the basics of XML mapping using one such language, that of Piazza-XML, and then we explain the nested tgd formulation.

Piazza-XML Mappings

The Piazza-XML mapping language is derived from a subset of XQuery. It consists of a series of nested XML elements and attributes with optional *query annotations* enclosed in {::} escapes. Each query annotation may define variable bindings using XPath expressions, following the same semantics as the `for` clause in XQuery, as well as conditions, specified with a `where` clause as in XQuery. Within each instance of the *parent* element, each annotated element gets produced once per binding combination that satisfies the associated query annotation. Bound variables are scoped to be visible to any descendant elements and their query annotations. We illustrate with an example.

■ ■ ■ ━━━

Example 11.25

Suppose we want to map between two sites: a target that contains `books` with nested `authors` and a source that contains `authors` with nested `publications`. We illustrate partial schemas for these sources in Figure 11.11, using a format in which indentation indicates nesting and a * suffix indicates "0 or more occurrences of...," as in a BNF grammar.

Assume we know that the input `pub-type` must be `book`, and the publisher has a name that is not present in the input document. The corresponding Piazza-XML schema mapping is shown in Figure 11.12. Observe that the `pubs` element is unannotated as it appears only once. Then the `book` element is produced once per combination of `$a`, `$t`, and `$type` in the annotation. Nested within `book`, the verb—title— and `author name` have nested XPath/XQuery expressions within braces, whose output is directly embedded, XQuery style.

Target:
```
pubs
  book*
    title
    author*
      name
    publisher*
      name
```

Source:
```
authors
  author*
    full-name
    publication*
      title
      pub-type
```

FIGURE 11.11 Example of two schemas (target and source) for XML mapping.

```
<pubs>
  <book>
    {: $a IN doc("source.xml")/authors/author,
       $t IN $a/publication/title/text(),
       $typ IN $a/publication/pub-type
       WHERE $typ = "book" :}
    <title>{ $t }</title>
    <author>
      <name> { $a/full-name/text() } </name>
    </author>
  </book>
</pubs>
```

FIGURE 11.12 Piazza-XML mapping for Example 11.11.

■ ■ ■

It can be observed from the example that the Piazza-XML language allows for multiple nesting levels, with correlation among nested expressions. This language of nested queries can be connected to our prior mapping formalisms of Chapter 3.

One challenge with the above example is that if, say, a book has two publishers, we will actually produce two book elements. To get around this, the Piazza-XML language has a special reserved tag, `piazza:id`, which defines a set of grouping terms. One instance of the annotated element will be produced *per parent element* per combination of values in the `piazza:id`.

■ ■ ■

Example 11.26

Figure 11.13 shows a refined version of the mapping, this time generating a single `book` element and a single `title` for each unique book title. An `author` element will be generated for each book, for each author.

```
<pubs>
  <book piazza:id={$t}>
    {: $a IN doc("source.xml")/authors/author,
       $t IN $a/publication/title/text(),
       $f IN $a/full-name/text(),
       $typ IN $a/publication/pub-type
       WHERE $typ = "book" :}
     <title piazza:id={$t}>{ $t }</title>
     <author piazza:id={$t $a}>
       <name> { $a } </name>
     </author>
  </book>
</pubs>
```

FIGURE 11.13 Improved Piazza-XML mapping with duplicate elimination.

■ ■ ■

Nested tgds

Recall from Section 3.2.5 that tuple-generating dependencies are one way of expressing Global-and-Local-as-View mappings. As we have described it to this point, the tgd is an assertion about relational instances. An interesting application of such constraints is discussed in Section 10.2. For this chapter, however, our interest is not in relational instances, but instances with hierarchical nesting, i.e., XML.

Definition 11.1 (Nested Tuple-Generating Dependency). *A nested tuple-generating dependency (nested tgd) is an assertion about the relationship between a source data instance and a target data instance, of the form*

$$\forall \bar{X}, \bar{Y}, \bar{S}(\phi(\bar{X}, \bar{Y}) \wedge \bar{\Phi}(\bar{S}) \rightarrow \exists \bar{Z}, \bar{T}(\psi(\bar{X}, \bar{Z}) \wedge \bar{\Psi}(\bar{T})))$$

where $\bar{X}, \bar{Y}, \bar{Z}$ are variables representing attributes; ϕ and ψ are atomic formulas over source and target instances, respectively; $\bar{S}$ and $\bar{T}$ are set-valued variables representing nested relations; and $\bar{\Phi}$ and $\bar{\Psi}$ are sets of atomic formulas, one for each of the respective variables of $\bar{S}$ and $\bar{T}$. Each set-valued variable in $\bar{T}$ must also have a grouping key, to which a variable-specific Skolem function is applied to uniquely specify the desired output set — such that multiple matches to the rhs of the tgd must use the same set.

The grouping key mentioned above is in effect the same as the `piazza:id` used in the Piazza-XML mapping language. We can express the schema mapping of Example 11.26 as follows.

■ ■ ■

Example 11.27

Define a nested tgd as follows, where we omit universally quantifiers (implicit for all variables that appear on the lhs), where boldface indicates a set-typed (relation) variable, and where an atom subscripted with a variable name specifies the grouping key:

$$\textbf{authors}(\textbf{author}) \wedge \textbf{author}(f, \textbf{publication}) \wedge \textbf{publication}(t, book) \rightarrow$$
$$\exists p(\textbf{pubs}(\textbf{book}) \wedge \textbf{book}_t(t, \textbf{author'}, \textbf{publisher}) \wedge \textbf{author'}_{t,f}(f) \wedge \textbf{publisher}_t(p))$$

In this formulation, we treat the output XML structure (expressed using the Piazza-XML language with different elements and their annotations) as a series of nested relations, reflecting the hierarchical structure.

The use of the grouping keys specifies when the *same* node in the target must be used to satisfy the rhs, as with `piazza:id`. In the output, we create a single `pubs` root element, then nest within it a `book` element for each unique title; within the book we add an `author` (created for each title-author combination) and a single "unknown" `publisher` entry (created separately for each title).

■ ■ ■

The example above hints at two constraints on the parameters for the grouping keys, which is also true in Piazza-XML, although often implicit. First, if a parent element (e.g., `book`) has a particular variable as a grouping key, then all descendant elements must also inherit this variable as a grouping key. This ensures a tree structure, as different parent elements will not share the same descendant. Second, as in `publisher`, existential variables are not included in the grouping keys.

A common use of nested tgds — like traditional tgds — is as constraints that are used to *infer* tuples in a target instance. In essence, we populate the target instance with any tuples that are needed to satisfy the constraint, using a procedure called the *chase*. This is called *data exchange* and is described in Section 10.2. However, we can also use nested tgds in query reformulation, as we describe next.

11.5.2 Query Reformulation with Nested Mappings

In query reformulation, we are given a query over the target schema and we need to use the semantic mappings to translate it to a query that refers to the sources. The XML mappings discussed in this section can be viewed as a version of GAV mappings, and hence we simply need to do view unfolding to rewrite a query Q posed over the target schema into a query Q' posed over the source schema(s).

This is essentially the same process as the one used in a standard XQuery engine. It can get quite complex in the presence of grouping (e.g., due to `piazza:id` or Skolems) and in the presence of complex XPath expressions in the query Q. Thus we limit our discussion here to a simple setting.

■ ■ ■

Example 11.28

Suppose we are given the query

```
<results> {
for $b in doc("target.xml")/pubs/book
where $b/author/name="Jones"
```

```
    return <match> { $b/title } </match>
} </results>
```

over our Example 11.25 mapping without grouping. Then the query processor will determine that variable $b corresponds to the book element output once by the mapping for each source author, that $b/author/name corresponds to the source full-name, and that $b/title corresponds exactly to the title element with value $t output by the mapping. We will get a rewritten query like the following:

```
<results> {
  for $b in doc("source.xml")/authors/author,
      $t in $b/publication/title/text(),
      $typ in $b/publication/pub-type
  where $typ = "book" and $b/full-name="Jones"
  return <match> <title> { $t } </title></match>
} </results>
```

■ ■ ■

Beyond GAV-style reformulation, some XML schema mapping systems have supported reformulation with *bidirectional* mappings, where a query over the target schema can be answered using source schema data. We leave this as a topic for advanced study and refer the reader to the bibliographic notes.

Bibliographic Notes

XML, XPath, and XQuery are discussed in great detail in the official W3C recommendations, at www.w3.org. For a more readable (though slightly dated) introduction to XQuery, consult [96]. XML's relationship to semistructured data is discussed in significant detail in some of the early works on adapting semistructured languages and databases to XML, such as those from the Lore project [258] and the XML-QL [173] language derived from StruQL [225]. Such works tended to abstract away many of the details of XML's data model (e.g., ordering) but laid the foundation for studying XML as a data model rather than a file format.

The properties of XPath and query containment for XPath have been extensively studied in the literature. A good survey appears in [516], with notable papers on the topic being [430] and [457], and with [517] showing how to validate that streaming XML conforms to a schema. Streaming XPath evaluation has also been the subject of a great deal of study, with early work being that of XFilter [26] (which supported Boolean XPath queries) and x-scan [325] (which supported evaluation of the for clause in an XQuery). Some other notable streaming evaluation schemes include [270], which espoused the use of *lazy DFAs*, and YFilter [177], which looked at distributing and coordinating XFilter-like computation. The work of [476] used a push-down transducer instead of a DFA. Another interesting alternative was to assume the use of multiple concurrent streams (as one might get if the document stored locally in partitioned form) that must be combined in evaluating an XPath. This has resulted in a strong body of work on "twig joins" [97, 131, 272]. This latter body of work is more applicable to conventional databases than to data integration; hence we do not discuss it in this chapter, but for that area the approach has been quite effective.

Of course, streaming XPath/XQuery evaluation is not appropriate for all settings. Commercial IBM DB2, which contains both relational and native XQuery engines, uses a construct very similar to x-scan called TurboXPath [335] to process hierarchical "native XML" data pages written to disk. Earlier efforts to incorporate XML into commercial database systems tended to use the "shredding" approach (normalizing the XML tree into multiple relations) espoused by [542]. A number of fully native XQuery engines have been studied in the research community, including MonetDB/XQuery [590] (based on the MonetDB column-store architecture), Natix [340], and TIMBER [20]. Active XML [3, 5] includes XML with embedded function calls to enable new kinds of data sharing and integration in distributed environments.

Schema mappings for XML have been proposed in a variety of settings. The Piazza-XML language is based on mappings for the Piazza PDMS [287], whose underpinnings are essentially the same as nested tgds, introduced for IBM's Clio project [237]. Clio also used a "friendlier" language over the nested tgds, XQuery-like `for`/`where` syntax. Clio does not do query reformulation but rather data exchange (see Section 10.2). Piazza does XML-based query reformulation, and the discussion in this chapter is based on the Piazza work. Piazza also supports the use of mappings bidirectionally, where a query over the source could be reformulated in terms of the target. Other reformulation work for XML includes the chase-based reasoning used in the MARS (Mixed and Redundant Storage) project [174].

12 ⚏ Ontologies and Knowledge Representation

Knowledge representation (KR) systems are an important component of many artificial intelligence applications, such as planners, robots, natural language processors, and game-playing systems. The KR system stores the underlying model of the domain that is employed by the application. In contrast to database systems, KR systems need to represent more complex and possibly incomplete domain models. KR systems use reasoning techniques to answer queries about the knowledge. Knowledge representation is the branch of artificial intelligence that studies the design and expressive power of KR languages, the computational properties of their associated reasoning problems, and effective implementation of KR systems.

Some aspects of data integration can also be viewed as a knowledge representation problem. Data sources and their contents lend themselves to rather complex modeling. Determing the relationships between data sources, or between a data source and a mediated schema, often requires subtle reasoning. For these reasons researchers have considered applying knowledge representation techniques to data integration from the very early days of the field. This chapter describes some of the principles of knowledge representation and how they apply to data integration.

Section 12.1 motivates the use of knowledge representation in data integration with an example. In Section 12.2 we describe description logics, which is the main family of KR languages that has been employed in the context of data integration. Description logics offer a set of logical formalisms for defining a domain *ontology*: a description of the entities in the domain, relationships between them, and any other known constraints. The key question explored in description logics is the trade-off between expressive power and the complexity of performing inference.

In recent years, much of the work in knowledge representation has been conducted under the umbrella of the *Semantic Web*. The Semantic Web is a vision that calls for associating semantic markup with content on the Web. The markup can be used to enhance the accuracy of search and to enable novel services that combine information from multiple sources on the Web. Section 12.3 describes the Semantic Web vision and gives an overview of some of the standards that have been developed to enable the vision, such as the Resource Description Language (RDF) and the Web Ontology Language (OWL), which is based on description logics.

12.1 Example: Using KR in Data Integration

We begin with an example that illustrates the power of knowledge representation and reasoning in data integration. In the example we use a few technical terms informally, but we explain them in later sections.

Consider an ontology of movies, shown in Figure 12.1. The ontology has the class Movie representing the set of all movies. The class Movie has two subclasses: Comedy and Documentary, and they are declared to be disjoint from each other. Note that ontologies permit overlapping classes, whereas object-oriented database models typically do not. The ontology also includes a set of properties, representing relationships between pairs of objects in the domain. In our example, we have the properties award and oscar, and we declare that oscar is a subproperty of award.

The ontology will serve as the mediated schema of the data integration system. Hence, we describe data sources in terms of the classes and properties in the ontology and pose queries using these terms as well. Let us consider several queries and data sources and see how reasoning serves as a mechanism for determining when a data source is relevant to a given query.

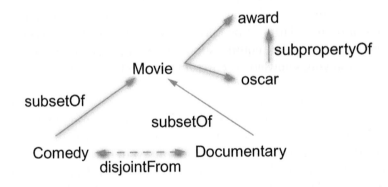

FIGURE 12.1 The figure shows a simple ontology of movies, with subclasses for comedies and documentaries. Note that the concepts **Comedy** and **Documentary** are stated to be disjoint. The property **oscar** is a subproperty of **award**. Given this ontology, the system can reason about the relevance of individual data sources to a query. For example, **S1** is relevant to a query asking for all movies, but **S2** is not relevant to a query asking for comedies. Sources **S3** and **S4** are relevant to queries asking for all movies that won awards, and **S4** is relevant to a query asking for movies that won an Oscar.

In the simplest example, consider the data source S_1 that provides comedies, as specified by the following LAV description, and the query Q_1 asking for all movies:

$S_1(X) \subseteq$ Comedy(X)
$Q_1(X)$:- Movie(X)

Since Comedy is a subclass of Movie, simple reasoning will deduce that data source S_1 is relevant to Q_1. In a similar fashion, we can infer that certain sources can be pruned from consideration. For example, suppose we have a data source S_2 containing documentaries and a query Q_2 asking for comedies. We can deduce that S_2 is irrelevant to Q_2.

$S_2(X) \subseteq$ Documentary(X)
$Q_2(X)$:- Comedy(X)

The two examples above only involved reasoning about basic classes and the relationships between them. We can go further and reason about *complex class expressions*. Suppose we have the data source S_3 that contains movies that won at least two awards, and a query, Q_3, asking for all movies that won an award:

$S_3(X) \subseteq$ Movie$(X) \sqcap (\geq 2$ award$)(X)$
$Q_3(X)$:- Comedy(X), award(X, Y)

The reasoning system can translate the query into the expression Movie $\sqcap (\geq 1$ award$)$, i.e., movies that won at least *one* award. Therefore, since the class of movies that won two awards is a subset of the class of movies that won at least one award, the system can deduce that source S_3 is relevant to the query Q_3. Note that numerical restrictions can also be used to derive disjointness between classes. For example, suppose we had a data source that supplied only movies without awards, described by the complex class expression Movie $\sqcap (\leq 0$ award$)$. We would be able to prune this source from consideration for Q_3.

Finally, the system can also use relationships between properties in its reasoning. For example, suppose we have a data source, S_4, that only contains Oscar-winning comedies.

$S_4(X) \subseteq$ Comedy$(X) \sqcap (\geq 1$ oscar$)(X)$

We could still deduce that S_4 is relevant to Q_3 because Comedy is a subclass of Movie and oscar is a subproperty of award.

As we can see from the above examples, the ontology can represent fairly complex relationships between data sources, the mediated schema, and queries. The inference engine can reason about these relationships to decide whether data sources are relevant to given queries. In the next section we describe more formally how these services are achieved.

12.2 Description Logics

Description logics are a family of languages for defining ontologies that vary in their expressive power. They range from languages with limited expressive power for which reasoning is very efficient, to very expressive languages for which reasoning is intractable or even undecidable. Formally, a description logic is a subset of first-order logic that is restricted to unary relations (called concepts or classes) and binary relations (called roles or properties). The concepts describe sets of individuals in the domain, and the roles describe binary relationships between individuals.

A description logic knowledge base contains two parts: a *Tbox*, which is a set of statements defining concepts and roles, and an *Abox*, which is a set of assertions on individuals in the domain. The Tbox defines two kinds of concepts, *base* concepts and *complex* concepts, that are defined from the base concepts using a set of *constructors*. For example, the concept Comedy $\sqcap$ (≥ 1 award) denotes the individuals that are comedies and won at least one award and is defined using the constructors $\sqcap$ (denoting conjunction) and ($\geq n$ R) (denoting number restrictions).

Description logics differ from each other on the set of constructors they allow to define complex concepts and roles. In principle, every choice of constructors leads to a different language, though some combinations of constructors can lead to languages that are equivalent in expressive power. The set of constructors allowed by a description logic has significant impact on the complexity of the reasoning tasks offered by the logic.

In what follows we describe a relatively simple description logic, $\mathcal{L}$, for which reasoning is tractable. We begin with describing the syntax of $\mathcal{L}$.

12.2.1 Syntax of Description Logics

A knowledge base, Δ, in $\mathcal{L}$ is composed of a Tbox, $\Delta_{\mathcal{T}}$ and an Abox $\Delta_{\mathcal{A}}$. Assertions in $\Delta_{\mathcal{T}}$ have two possible forms: definitional assertions of the form A := C or inclusion assertions of the form A $\sqsubseteq$ C. In both cases, we require that the left-hand side, A, be a base concept, while C can be a complex concept. More expressive description logics allow both sides of an assertion to be complex concepts.

Complex concepts are defined using the following grammar, where A denotes a base concept and C, D denote complex concepts:

$$
\begin{array}{ll}
C, D \to A \,| & \text{(base concept)} \\
\quad \top \,| & \text{(top, the set of all individuals)} \\
\quad C \sqcap D \,| & \text{(conjunction)} \\
\quad \neg A \,| & \text{(complement)} \\
\quad \forall R.C \,| & \text{(universal quantification)} \\
\quad (\geq n R) \,|\, (\leq n R) & \text{(number restrictions)}
\end{array}
$$

■ ■ ■ ▬▬▬▬▬▬▬▬▬▬▬▬▬▬▬▬▬▬▬▬▬▬▬

Example 12.1

Consider the following ontology, δ, of movies. The following are assertions in its Tbox, $\delta_{\mathcal{T}}$:

a_1. Italian $\sqsubseteq$ Person
a_2. Comedy $\sqsubseteq$ Movie
a_3. Comedy $\sqsubseteq$ ¬Documentary

a_4. Movie $\sqsubseteq$ ($\le$ 1 director)

a_5. AwardMovies := Movie $\sqcap$ ($\ge$ 1 award)

a_6. ItalianHits := AwardMovie $\sqcap$ ($\forall$director.Italian)

The first assertion defines Italians to be a subset of people. Assertions a_2 and a_3 specify that comedies are movies and they are disjoint from documentaries. The assertion a_4 specifies that movies have at most one director. The concept AwardMovies is defined, by a_5, to be the set of movies that won at least one award, and a_6 defines the concept ItalianHits to be all the movies that won at least one award for which all directors are Italian.

■ ■ ■

Assertions in the Abox, $\triangle_\mathcal{A}$, are statements about individuals in the domain, much like tuples in a database with arity of 1 or 2. There are two kinds of assertions. The first kind, of the form C(a), asserts that the individual a is an instance of the concept C. The second kind of assertion, of the form R(a,b), asserts that the role R holds between the objects a and b. The constant b is called a *filler* of the role R for a.

An important difference between Aboxes and databases is that an assertion of the form C(a) can involve a complex concept C. In effect, asserting C(a) is akin to stating that an individual a is in the extension of a view. As we discuss later, we can draw several conclusions from such assertions.

■ ■ ■

Example 12.2

Consider an Abox, $\delta_\mathcal{A}$, for the Tbox defined in Example 12.1:

Comedy(LifeIsBeautiful)

director(LifeIsBeautiful, Benigni)

Italian(Benigni)

award(LifeIsBeautiful, Oscar1997)

ItalianHits(LaStrada)

The reasoning engine would be able to deduce from the first four assertions that the movie LifeIsBeautiful is an instance of the concept ItalianHits. The last assertion only tells us that LaStrada is a member of the concept ItalianHits, but does not tell us who the director is or what awards the movie received. However, we do know that the director is Italian and it won at least one award.

■ ■ ■

12.2.2 Semantics of Description Logics

The semantics of description logic knowledge bases are given via *interpretations*. An interpretation, I, contains a nonempty domain of objects, $\mathcal{O}^I$. The interpretation assigns an object a^I to every individual a mentioned in $\triangle_\mathcal{A}$. Description logics make the *unique-names assumption*: for any distinct pairs of individuals, a and b, $a^I \ne b^I$. (Note that databases also make the unique-names assumption.)

The interpretation I assigns a unary relation, C^I, to every concept in Δ_T and a binary relation, R^I, over $\mathcal{O}^I \times \mathcal{O}^I$ to every role R in Δ_T. The extensions of concept and role descriptions are given by the following equations ($\sharp\{S\}$ denotes the cardinality of a set S):

$$\top^I = \mathcal{O}^I,$$
$$(C \sqcap D)^I = C^I \cap D^I,$$
$$(\neg A)^I = \mathcal{O}^I \setminus A^I,$$
$$(\forall R.C)^I = \{d \in \mathcal{O}^I \mid \forall e : (d,e) \in R^I \rightarrow e \in C^I\}$$
$$(\geq nR)^I = \{d \in \mathcal{O}^I \mid \sharp\{e \mid (d,e) \in R^I\} \geq n\}$$
$$(\leq nR)^I = \{d \in \mathcal{O}^I \mid \sharp\{e \mid (d,e) \in R^I\} \leq n\}$$

For example, the first two lines define the extension of $\top$ to be the set of all objects in $\mathcal{O}^I$, and the extension of $(C \sqcap D)$ to be the intersection of the extensions of C and D. The extension of $(\forall R.C)$ is the set of objects in the domain for which all the fillers on the role R are members of C. The extension of $(\geq nR)$ is the set of objects in the domain that have at least n fillers on the role R.

The assertions in a knowledge base specify a set of constraints on the interpretations. The interpretations that satisfy these constraints are called *models*. Intuitively, models describe states of the domain that are possible given the assertions in the knowledge base.

Definition 12.1 (Containment and Equivalence). *An interpretation, I, for a knowledge base Δ is a model of Δ if*

- $A^I \subseteq C^I$ *for every inclusion $A \sqsubseteq C$ in Δ_T,*
- $A^I = C^I$ *for every statement $A := C$ in Δ_T,*
- $a^I \in C^I$ *for every statement $C(a)$ in Δ_A, and*
- $(a^I, b^I) \in R^I$ *for every statement $R(a,b)$ in Δ_A.* □

■ ■ ■ ▬▬▬▬▬▬▬▬▬▬▬▬▬▬▬▬▬▬▬▬▬▬▬▬▬▬▬▬▬▬▬

Example 12.3

Consider the following interpretation for our example knowledge base δ. For simplicity, assume that I is the identity mapping on the constants in δ. Let $\mathcal{O}$ be the set

{LifeIsBeautiful, LaStrada, Benigni, Director1, Oscar1997, Award1, Actor1, Actor2}.

Note that Director1, Award1, Actor1, and Actor2 are not mentioned in the Abox of δ but are necessary in $\mathcal{O}$ in order to obtain a model. Consider the following extensions for the concepts in δ_T (we omit the parentheses around unary tuples):

Movie^I:	{LifeIsBeautiful, LaStrada}
Comedy^I:	{LifeIsBeautiful}
Documentary^I:	∅
Person^I:	{Benigni, Director1}
Italian^I:	{Benigni, Director1}
award^I:	{(LifeIsBeautiful, Oscar1997), (LaStrada, Award1)}
director^I:	{(LifeIsBeautiful, Benigni), (LaStrada, Director1)}
actor^I:	{(LaStrada, Actor1), (LaStrada, Actor2)}

The reader can verify that all the assertions in the Tbox and Abox are satisfied, and therefore I is a model of δ. Two points are worth noting. First, we do not know who the director of LaStrada is or the award it received, so the interpretation I only includes the constants that are needed to satisfy the Tbox. Also, note that LifeIsBeautiful is a member of Comedy, which is not asserted in the knowledge base but is consistent with it. If we remove LifeIsBeautiful from the extension of Comedy, we will still have a model of δ.

Small changes to I would preclude it from being a model of δ. For example, if we add LifeIsBeautiful to the extension of the concept Documentary then a_3 would no longer be satisfied, and if we add another director to either of the movies, then a_4 would no longer be satisfied.

∎ ∎ ∎

12.2.3 Inference in Description Logics

A description logic system supports two main kinds of inference: subsumption and query answering.

Subsumption: Given two concepts, C and D, the fundamental question is whether C is subsumed by D. Intuitively, C is subsumed by D if in every model of the knowledge base, the instances of C are always guaranteed to be instances of D. As we discuss later, subsumption is much like query containment (see Chapter 2), but the reasoning patterns are somewhat different. Formally, subsumption is defined as follows.

Definition 12.2 (Subsumption). *We say that the concept C is subsumed by the concept D w.r.t. a Tbox Δ_T if $C^I \subseteq D^I$ in every model I of Δ_T.* ☐

∎ ∎ ∎

Example 12.4
The concept Movie $\sqcap$ (≥ 2 award) is subsumed by AwardMovies in δ, but it is not subsumed by ItalianHits. The concept Movie $\sqcap$ ($\forall$director.Person) subsumes the concept ItalianHits, because the restriction on the director is weaker, and there is no restriction on the number of awards.

∎ ∎ ∎

As we saw earlier, subsumption can be used to infer relationships between pairs of data sources, between a concept in the mediated schema and a data source, or between a query and a data source. For example, if we pose a query on the data integration system to find all Italian movies, and we have a source S providing instances of the concept ItalianHits, then we can infer that S is relevant to the query. On the other hand, if the query asks for Italian movies that received at least two awards, then we can only use S if it also provides the number of awards won by each movie, so we can filter those that have at least two awards.

In the logic $\mathcal{L}$ that we described above, subsumption can be done in time that is polynomial in the size of the Tbox. However, slight additions to the logic would cause subsumption to be intractable or even undecidable. As a simple example, if we allow the disjunction constructor that defines a complex concept to be the union of two other concepts, then reasoning becomes NP-complete. Adding negation on complex concepts would have the same effect. Some of the other constructors that have been considered are existential quantification: (∃R C) specifying that at least one of the fillers of R needs to be a member of C; and sameAs specifying that the fillers on role-chain $P_1,...,P_n$ need to be the same as the fillers on the role-chain $R_1,...,R_n$. In fact, if the sameAs constructor is allowed on nonfunctional roles, then subsumption becomes undecidable.

Query answering: The second class of inference problems considers the Tbox and Abox. The most basic reasoning task is *instance checking*. We say that $C(a)$ is entailed by a knowledge base Δ, denoted by $\Delta \models C(a)$, if in every model I of Δ, $a^I \in C^I$.

When description logics are used for data integration, more attention has been paid to the more general inference problem of answering conjunctive queries over knowledge bases. Formally, the problem is defined as follows.

Definition 12.3 (conjunctive queries over Description Logic knowledge bases).   *Let Δ be a knowledge base, and let Q be a conjunctive query of the form*

$$q(\bar{X}) :\text{-} \; p_1(\bar{X}_1), ..., p_n(\bar{X}_n)$$

where $p_1,...,p_n$ are either concepts or roles in Δ_T.

The set of answers to Q over Δ is defined as follows. Given an interpretation I of Δ we can evaluate Q over I as if it were a database. We denote by Q(I) the set of tuples obtained by evaluating Q over I. A tuple $\bar{t}$ of constants in Δ_A is in the answer of Q over Δ if for every model, I, of Δ, $\bar{t} \in Q(I)$.   □

The reader should observe the similarity between Definition 12.3 and the definition of certain answers in Chapter 3.2.1.

■ ■ ■ ━━

Example 12.5

Consider a simple example where we have the query

Q1(X) :- Comedy(X), ItalianHits(X), award(X, Y)

and suppose we have the Abox with the following facts:

ItalianHits(LifeIsBeautiful), Comedy(LifeIsBeautiful)

If we simply apply the query to the Abox, there will be no answers, because we do not have facts for the award relation. However, ItalianHits implies that the movie has at least one award, and therefore that the subgoal award(X, Y) will be satisfied in every model of the knowledge base. Hence, LifeIsBeautiful should be in the answer to Q1.

The example above can be handled by removing subgoals of the query that can be deemed redundant based on the ontology (in this example, award(X, Y) is entailed by ItalianHits(X) and therefore is redundant). However, consider the following query that is a union of two conjunctive queries.

Q2(X) :- Movie(X), ≥ 1 award(X)
Q2(X) :- Comedy(X), ∀director.Italian(X), ≤ 0 award(X)

Now suppose we have the following Abox:

> Comedy(LaFunivia), director(LaFunivia, Antonioni), Italian(Antonioni)

The first conjunctive query will not yield any answers, even if we realize that a comedy is also a movie, because we know nothing about the awards that LaFunivia won. The second conjunctive query will also yield no answers but for a different reason: just because the Abox does not contain any awards for LaFunivia does not mean that the movie did not win any awards! However, by reasoning about *both* queries together, we can infer that the following conjunctive query can be added to *Q2* without losing correctness.

> Q2(X) :- Comedy(X), ∀director.Italian(X)

The correctness of the last conjunctive query is established by reasoning by cases. If a movie is an Italian comedy, it has either no awards or at least one award. In the first case, it would satisfy the second conjunctive query, and in the second case it would satisfy the first conjunctive query. Hence, it does not matter how many awards an Italian comedy has.

Applying the new conjunctive query to the Abox would still not yield LaFunivia as an answer. First, the system would need to infer that (∀director.Italian(LaFunivia)) holds, from the fact that the movie has exactly one director and he is known to be Italian. ■ ■ ■

Finding all the answers for a conjunctive query over a description logic knowledge base can be rather tricky. While it can still be done in polynomial time in the size of the Abox for fairly expressive description logics, it requires more complex algorithms. Answering recursive datalog queries is even more complicated. In fact, even for $\mathcal{L}$, answering recursive queries is undecidable.

12.2.4 Comparing Description Logics to Database Reasoning

To conclude this section, it is worthwhile to consider more carefully the relationship between description logics and view mechanisms in database systems. Complex concepts are similar to views in the sense that they are defined by a set of constructors from base relations. In the case of relational views, the constructors are join, selection, projection, union, and some forms of negation. The analog of subsumption reasoning is query containment, which we covered in Chapter 2.3. There are, however, significant differences between the two formalisms.

The first difference is that the set of constructors used in description logics enable defining views that are impossible or complicated to define in datalog or SQL. For example, description logics enable stating that one concept is the complement of another, which is not possible with database views. One can define a view to be the complement of another by using negation, but then query containment becomes quickly undecidable. Similarly, universal restrictions, such as (∀ director.Italian), also require negation and composition in a database view language. Finally, number restrictions (≥ 3 actor) and (≤ 2 actor) are difficult to specify with views. We can specify minimal cardinality restrictions, (≥ n R), with a conjunctive query using the ≠ predicate, but the length of the expression is dependent on n. Specifying maximal cardinality restrictions, ($\leq$ n R), requires negation and a similarly long expression.

On the other hand, conjunctive queries enable defining views with arbitrary joins and are not limited to unary and binary relations. In description logics the only join relationships possible are constructed by following role paths. Hence, the main lesson from description logics is that by restricting attention to unary and binary predicates, and by limiting the joins one can perform, description logics offer a view definition language for which containment is decidable (and often efficient) for a class of views for which it would not be possible otherwise.

The second difference is that in a description logic Abox we assert facts about *any* concept, whether it is a base concept or complex one. In the latter case, asserting a fact is akin to stating that a tuple is in the instance of a view. The description logic is able to make inferences about such facts as well. For example, consider the concept ItalianHits in our running example. In δ we asserted that LaStrada is an instance of ItalianHits. The system can infer that if LaStrada has a director, then that director is an instance of the concept Italian even though we do not know who the director is. Similarly, we can deduce that the movie won at least one award, even if we do not know which. Relatedly, unlike database systems, description logic knowledge bases make the *open-world assumption*. If a fact is not explicitly in the knowledge base, that does not mean that the fact does not hold.

The analog to reasoning about instances of complex concepts in database formalisms would be techniques for answering queries using views, which we covered in Chapter 2.4. For example, we could have a view for Italian hits that includes the instance LaStrada. Techniques for answering queries using views would be able to conclude that LaStrada would be in the answer to the query asking for all movies that won at least one award. As before, description logics offer a setting in which we can use a rich set of constructors and still be able to develop algorithms for answering queries using views.

The final difference we mention is that description logics unify the schema definition language with the constraint language. For example, some description logics allow arbitrary inclusion statements of the form C $\sqsubseteq$ D, where both C and D are complex concepts. The reasoning algorithms would consider these constraints as well in making inferences, whereas query containment under constraints is fairly limited.

It is also worthwhile to compare object-oriented database schemas and description logics. While both formalisms model domains in terms of classes of objects and their properties, there are fundamental differences between them. Object-oriented schemas focus on the physical properties of objects. They define which properties are attached to an instance of a class. The only form of reasoning is inheritance of properties from classes to their subclasses. Furthermore, in most OODB formalisms an object can be a member of at most one class (and its superclasses). Description logics focus on providing a language for expressing relationships between classes and making inferences based on partial information. As a result, objects can belong to multiple classes. Description logic knowledge bases specify very little about the physical properties of the objects or how they are to be stored.

12.3 The Semantic Web

The Semantic Web is a vision in which documents on the Web have annotations that make their meanings explicit. Today, the Web is largely text and links between HTML *pages*. However, the entities and the relationships that are the subjects of the pages are not clearly described. The lack of such annotations hinders the accuracy of search and the ability to create more advanced services. The following example illustrates the potential of such annotations.

■ ■ ■ ▬▬▬▬▬▬▬▬▬▬▬▬▬▬▬▬▬▬▬▬▬▬▬▬▬▬▬▬▬▬

Example 12.6

Consider pages concerning movies and their reviews on the Web. For the most part, a page would come up in an answer to a query if the words on the page match the words in the query. Furthermore, the proximity between the occurrences of the query words on the page would also be an important feature in ranking the page. Consider a page that has multiple movie reviews, ordered alphabetically by the title of the movie, but the word "review" only appears once near the top of the page. The page is unlikely to come up in the answer to the query "review zanzibar," because the words "review" and "zanzibar" occur far away from each other on the page, and the search engine doesn't *know* that the page contains review objects.

Suppose that in addition to the text on the page, we would also add an annotation to each review specifying that it is a movie review, along with the title of the movie, the name of the reviewer, and possibly even the sentiment of the review. We could now add functionality to search engines to exploit these annotations for more accurate retrieval of reviews. If the practice of annotation were prevalent, we could even support queries such as "find all reviews of zanzibar," which would retrieve the appropriate segments of *multiple* pages on the Web. In addition, we can relate the review information to other data relating to the movie, such as playing times, trailers, and information about the actors.

▬▬▬▬▬▬▬▬▬▬▬▬▬▬▬▬▬▬▬▬▬▬▬▬▬▬▬▬▬▬ ■ ■ ■

The vision of the Semantic Web is clearly a very ambitious one, and that ambition has led to quite a bit of criticism. There are two main challenges faced by the Semantic Web. The first challenge is to entice people to invest the extra effort to create these annotations without an immediate reward. The second challenge concerns the semantic heterogeneity issues that will arise when so many people create structured representations of data. While it seems like a long shot that the vision, in its entirety, will be fulfilled, there have been some developments that facilitate structural markup on the Web. These developments have had an impact in certain domains and within enterprises. At the core of these developments is the Resource Description Framework (RDF) for semantic markup and its associated schema languages, RDF Schema (RDFS) and the Web Ontology Language (OWL). These standards are built on the principles of knowledge representation languages and adapt them to the context of the Web, where knowledge is authored in a decentralized fashion by many participants. We describe the key ideas from these standards in the next few sections.

12.3.1 Resource Description Framework

RDF is a language for describing resources on the Web. Initially, RDF was developed in order to add metadata to resources that can be physically found on the Web, such as documents. With RDF, one would describe the author of a document, its last modification time, and the subject of the document. However, RDF has been generalized to also describe objects that are not on the Web but are referenced on the Web, such as people and products. RDF describes the objects and the relationships between them and is complemented by RDF Schema and OWL, which describe the schema-level elements mentioned in RDF files. In the terminology of the previous section, RDF can be viewed as the Abox, while RDFS and OWL are the Tbox. In fact, OWL is based on description logics.

Conceptually, RDF contains statements about resources. Each statement provides a value for one of the resource's properties. A statement is a triple of the form (subject, predicate, object). As we see soon, the names of resources can get rather long. Therefore, to make the notation more palatable, we use the common practice of defining qualified names (qnames), which are shorter codes for prefixes of resources. In the example below, `ex:` is the qname for `http://www.example.org/` and `exterms:` is the qname for `http://www.example.org/terms`. Hence, `ex:movie1` is a shorthand for `http://www.example.org/movie1`.

■ ■ ■ ▬▬▬▬▬▬▬▬▬▬▬▬▬▬▬▬▬▬▬▬▬▬▬▬▬▬▬▬▬▬▬▬▬▬▬▬▬▬

Example 12.7

The following triples specify that the title of the movie identified by `http://www.example.org/movies/movie1` is "Life Is Beautiful" and that the subject of the review is identified by `http://www.example.org/review1.html` is the movie identified by ex:movie1. The third triple specifies the date on which the review was written.

```
ex:movie1 exterms:title "Life Is Beautiful"
ex:review1.html exterms:movieReviewed ex:movie1
ex:review1.html exterms:written-date "August 15, 2008"
```

▬▬▬▬▬▬▬▬▬▬▬▬▬▬▬▬▬▬▬▬▬▬▬▬▬▬▬▬▬▬▬▬▬▬▬▬▬▬ ■ ■ ■

Hence, RDF is a language for expressing unary and binary relations. The correspondence between RDF statements and Abox assertions is straightforward. RDF specifications can be (and often are) modeled as graphs. Figure 12.2 shows the graph representation of the three triples in Example 12.7. The *RDF/XML specification* shows how to serialize a set of RDF statements as XML and includes a few shortcuts that make it more parsimonious.

■ ■ ■ ▬▬▬▬▬▬▬▬▬▬▬▬▬▬▬▬▬▬▬▬▬▬▬▬▬▬▬▬▬▬▬▬▬▬▬▬▬▬

Example 12.8

The following XML is a serialization of three RDF statements that have the same subject, `ex:review1.html`. Note that RDF/XML enables all the properties of `ex:review1.html` to be

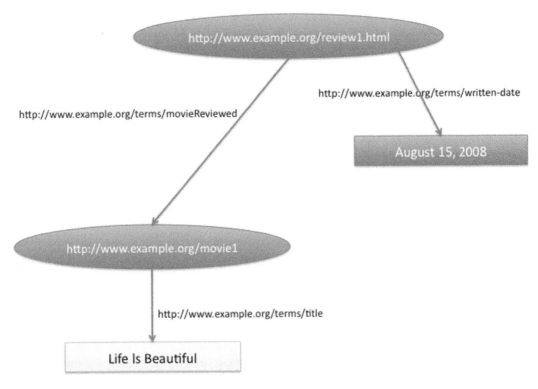

FIGURE 12.2 A graph representation of RDF triples.

nested in one XML element whose `about` value is the subject (lines 5-9), rather than having to repeat the subject three times.

```
1. <?xml version="1.0"?>
2. <rdf:RDF xmlns:rdf="http://www.w3.org/1999/02/22-rdf-syntax-ns#"
3.          xmlns:dc="http://purl.org/dc/elements/1.1/"
4.          xmlns:exterms="http://www.example.org/terms/">
5.    <rdf:Description rdf:about="http://www.example.org/review1.html">
6.       <exterms:written-date>August 15, 2008</exterms:creation-date>
7.       <exterms:movieReviewed  rdf:resource="http://www.example.org/movie1/>
8.       <exterms:writtenBy  rdf:resource="http://www.example.org/staffID/23440>
9.    </rdf:Description>
10. </rdf:RDF>
```

We will not discuss all the details of RDF here, but below we explain some of its most important features and explain how it is designed to support large-scale knowledge sharing.

UNIFORM RESOURCE IDENTIFIERS

Statements in RDF include two kinds of constants: Uniform Resource Identifiers (URIs) and literals. The subject and predicate of an RDF statement are required to be URIs (except for blank nodes, which we discuss shortly) and the object can be either a URI or a literal.

A URI is a reference to a resource on the Web and therefore provides a more global mechanism for referring to entities. Consider, for example, a reference to a person. In a traditional knowledge base, we may have a string denoting her name, such as MarySmith. However, that string and even an internal unique identifier are only meaningful *within* the database or knowledge base. In RDF, we can refer to `www.example.com/staffID/5544`, and that reference is available to anyone who wants to refer to the same individual. Similarly, we can have common references to predicates, such as `www.example.com/exterms/writtenBy`, or values such as `www.example.com/exvalues/Blue`.

RDF's use of URIs is one of the crucial aspects of the language and makes it suitable for data integration and sharing. Except for providing a more global mechanism for referring to entities, it also encourages data authors to converge on a common terminology, since they can reuse existing terms. It is important to emphasize that the ability to refer to URIs does not *force* authors to confirm to standards, but *encourages* them to do so.

LITERALS IN RDF

RDF does not have its own set of built-in data types. Instead, it includes a mechanism for specifying which data type a particular literal is drawn from. These data types are also referred to by URIs, thereby creating an open type system. For example, the following statements specify the age and birth date of two staff members. The first statement specifies that the age is given as an integer, and the second specifies that the birth date is given as a date.

```
exstaff:23440   exterms:age   "42"^^xsd:integer
exstaff:54322   exterms:birthdate  "1980-05-06"^^xsd:date
```

BLANK OBJECTS

As mentioned above, RDF can represent binary relationships between objects. However, binary relations are not always sufficient. Consider representing the address of Mary from the previous example. The address is a structured object that contains multiple fields, such as street, city, country, and zip code. Representing each of these as a property of Mary is unnatural. Instead, RDF allows *blank nodes*, which are nodes without a specific identifier. In our example, shown in Figure 12.3, we would use a blank node to represent the address object of Mary, and the blank node would have the specific address properties.

Blank nodes do not have unique IDs. We can assign them IDs within an RDF document in cases where we want to refer to them more than once (e.g., if the address represents both the billing and shipping address of an order), but the IDs are meaningless across documents. Hence, if we merge two RDF graphs we need to ensure *a priori* that the IDs

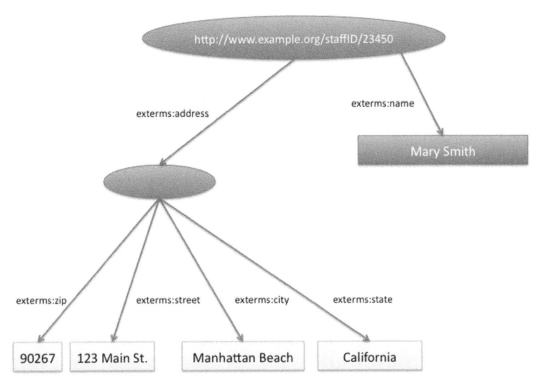

FIGURE 12.3 Blank nodes in RDF graphs.

of their blank nodes are disjoint. RDF also has constructs for representing bags, lists, and alternatives.

REIFICATION

As we will discuss in Chapter 14, it is often important to know the *provenance* of data on the Web. The provenance includes where the data came from and when (see Chapter 14). RDF provides a mechanism for reification of statements, which enables stating facts about them. Specifically, we reify an RDF triple by referring to it as a resource.

■ ■ ■ ▬▬▬▬▬▬▬▬▬▬▬▬▬▬▬▬▬▬▬▬▬▬▬▬▬▬▬▬▬▬▬▬

Example 12.9

The following RDF triples reify the statement about the title of `movie1`. The first statement gives the reified statement a name (`triple12345`), and the next three statements specify its properties.

```
moviedb:triple12345    rdf:type       rdf:Statement.
moviedb:triple12345    rdf:subject    ex:movie1.
moviedb:triple12345    rdf:predicate  exterms:title.
moviedb:triple12345    rdf:object     "Life Is Beautiful"
```

Given the reification, we can now assert additional facts about the statement. Below we specify who entered the triple into the movie database and when.

```
moviedb:triple12345    exterms:entered-by  ex:staffID/23340
moviedb:triple12345    exterms:entered-date "2007-07-07"^^xsd:date
```

■ ■ ■

12.3.2 RDF Schema

RDF Schema (RDFS) provides constructs for defining classes, hierarchies on classes, and membership of resources in classes. RDF Schema also allows declaring restrictions on the domains and ranges of properties. RDF Schema preceded the Web Ontology Language, which we cover shortly, and has gained adoption on its own. It is important to note that RDF does not *enforce* any of the semantics of its constructs. RDF is just a language, and it is up to the implementation of RDF systems to utilize their semantics.

The constructs of RDF Schema are themselves described by an RDF vocabulary at `http://www.w3.org/2000/01/rdf-schema#`, and its qualified name is rdfs:. The most basic construct of RDFS is `rdfs:type`, which is used to denote membership of a resource in a class. The following states that Movie is a class, by specifying that it has type `rdfs:class`.

```
ex:Movie rdfs:type rdfs:class
```

The same construct is used to specify instances of the class. Here, movie1 is asserted to be a movie:

```
ex:movie1 rdfs:type ex:Movie
```

These two statements illustrate a very powerful feature of RDFS: a resource that is a class can itself be a member of another class! Hence, we can have the following scenario:

■ ■ ■

Example 12.10

The following triples state that Corolla is a class with instance car11. However, Corolla is also a member of the class CarModels.

```
ex:Corolla rdfs:type rdfs:Class
ex:car11 rdfs:type ex:Corolla
ex:CarModels rdfs:type rdfs:Class
ex:Corolla rdfs:type ex:CarModels
```

It is important to note the difference between the statements above and the scenario in which we could declare Corolla to be a *subclass* of CarModels. In the latter case, we make a clear distinction between schema elements and data elements. Individual cars are data elements, and the collection of Corollas and car models are schema. However, what if we want to describe aspects of Corollas, such as how many of them were sold in the last year? This is an attribute of Corollas as a class, not of its individual instances. Hence, RDF offers greater modeling flexibility.

■ ■ ■

Subclasses in RDFS can be declared using the `rdfs:subclassOf` construct, as in the following:

```
ex:Comedy rdfs:subclassOf ex:Movie
```

Note that multiple statements are interpreted as conjunction. Hence, if we added

```
ex:Comedy rdfs:subclassOf ex:LaughProvokingEvents
```

then `Comedy` is asserted to be in the intersection of `Movie` and `LaughProvokingEvents`.

Finally, properties in RDFS are described using the following constructs. In the statements below we define `actor` to be a property with subproperty `leadActor`. The range of `actor` is `Person` and its domain is `Movie`.

```
exterms:actor rdfs:type rdfs:Property
exterms:leadActor rdfs:subPropertyOf exterms:actor
exterms:actor rdfs:range exterms:Person
exterms:actor rdfs:domain exterms:Movie
```

12.3.3 Web Ontology Language (OWL)

RDF Schema provides constructs that are very similar to object-oriented database schemas. OWL is inspired by the types of reasoning supported in description logics and was developed to carry such inferences over to the Semantic Web, in the spirit of the example in Section 12.1.

As described in Section 12.2, description logics are a family of languages, each with some set of constructors (and hence different computational properties). Therefore, selecting one particular description logic to be the basis for OWL would be somewhat arbitrary. Instead, the OWL standard proposes three versions: (1) OWL-Lite, which is meant to capture a very small subset of description logics but for which reasoning is very efficient, (2) OWL-DL, a version of OWL that includes a rich set of constructors found in description logics but whose computational complexity is very high, and (3) OWL-Full, which allows reification of statements in addition to the constructs of OWL-DL. Below we describe the schema-level constructs in OWL.

OWL-Lite: Unlike description logics, the OWL languages do not make the unique-names assumption. Indeed, on the Web, entities are likely to have more than one name. Hence, OWL-Lite enables specifying that two entities are the same (`sameAs`) or that they are different (`differentFrom`). It also includes the construct `allDifferent` for specifying that a set of objects is pairwise different from each other.

OWL-Lite is designed so that reasoning and question answering are very efficient, even in the presence of a large number of individuals. The main constructs included in OWL-Lite are the following:

- all the constructs of RDF Schema that we described above,
- some constructs from the language $\mathcal{L}$ that we described in Section 12.2, including the conjunction operator on classes ($\sqcap$), universal quantification ($\forall R.C$), and number restrictions; number restrictions are limited to only use 0 or 1,
- existential quantification on properties ($\exists R.C$); as an example, with this constructor we can describe the set of movies that have at least one actor who is female,
- a few constructs for specifying constraints on properties: `TransitiveProperty`, `SymmetricProperty`, `FunctionalProperty`, and `InverseFunctionalProperty`.

OWL-DL: OWL-DL allows the following constructs in addition to those of OWL-Lite:

- arbitrary cardinality restrictions,
- union, complement, and intersections of arbitrary concept descriptions,
- disjointness: specifying that two classes A and B are disjoint from each other,
- oneOf: describing a concept composed of an enumeration of several individuals; for example, WeekDay can be defined as oneOf(Sunday, Monday, Tuesday, Wednesday, Thursday, Friday, Saturday),
- hasValue: describing a concept that must have a particular value as a filler on a role; for example, (nationality Vietnam) describes the set of individuals that have Vietnam as one of the fillers on their nationality role. Note that the role need not be functional.

In summary, OWL is an adaptation of description logics to the context of the Web. It adopts the use of URIs to allow more global references to terms. Like description logics, OWL is based on the open-world assumption, which is appropriate for the Web context. Finally, unlike description logics, OWL does not make the unique-names assumption, since on the Web there are likely to be many ways of referring to the same entity.

12.3.4 Querying RDF: the SPARQL Language

SparQL is a language for querying repositories of RDF triples. SparQL borrows ideas from other database query languages but provides a native RDF query language. The language is based on matching patterns of triples expressed by variables and constants, and the result of a query can be either a set of tuples or an RDF graph.

■ ■ ■ ▬▬▬▬▬▬▬▬▬▬▬▬▬▬▬▬▬▬▬▬▬▬▬▬▬▬▬▬

Example 12.11

Consider querying the following four RDF triples.

```
exstaff:23440   exterms:name   exstaff:person1
exstaff:23440   exterms:city   "New York"
```

```
exstaff:23444   exterms:name   exstaff:person2
exstaff:23444   exterms:city   "San Francisco"
```

The query below selects the people living in New York. Note that the variable ?d needs to match two triples.

```
SELECT ?d ?person
WHERE
     {?d exterms:city "New York"} .
      ?d exterms:name ?person}
```

The result is a table with two columns.

?d	?person
exstaff:23440	exstaff:person1

Using CONSTRUCT, it is possible to create an RDF graph as output. The following outputs a graph with the exterms:city predicates renamed into exterms:livesIn.

```
CONSTRUCT {?d exterms:livesIn ?city }
WHERE
   { ?d exterms:city ?city }

exstaff:23440   exterms:livesIn   "New York"
exstaff:23444   exterms:livesIn   "San Francisco"
```

Bibliographic Notes

The application of knowledge representation techniques to data integration was investigated from the early days of the field. Catarci and Lenzerini [112] were the first to articulate how description logics can be used to model data sources and reason about relationships between them. Some systems used AI planning techniques to perform reasoning after describing the sources and mediated schema in description logics [37, 38, 361]. The Information Manifold System combined description logics with Local-as-View descriptions [380], and [60, 107] explore the complexity of answering queries using views in the presence of description logics.

The handbook of description logics [1] provides a comprehensive guide to the theory underlying description logics, the systems used to implement the logics, and some of their applications. A shorter paper that provides some of the complexity analysis of different logics is [192]. Borgida [93] describes the relevance of description logics to data management in general.

Several works have tried combining description logics with datalog. In [193] the authors explored adding unary predicates to datalog programs, where the unary predicates were classes defined in description logics. The CARIN languages [377] extended that work by considering both unary and binary predicates in datalog rules, both of which are defined in a description logic's Tbox. In [377] the authors show tight conditions on when reasoning with a combination of description logics and datalog is decidable. Several other systems incorporated description logics into data integration and peer-data management systems, such as [11, 255, 367].

The vision of the Semantic Web was first outlined in [71]. Since then, there has been an annual conference dedicated to advances on the topic. Noy [466] surveys the approaches to semantic integration based on ontologies. Given that ontologies are more expressive than schemas, there has also been work in the community on *ontology alignment*, which has the same goal as schema mapping, but applied to ontologies. Work on this topic includes [183, 440, 464]. In fact, there are annual competitions comparing ontology alignment algorithms. The Linked Data effort [88] focuses on a subset of the Semantic Web vision. The focus is on ensuring that data sets are linked via shared identifiers, making it possible to programmatically traverse relationships across multiple data sources. The current state of the effort can be investigated at http://linkeddata.org.

Detailed specifications of the RDF, RDFS, SPARQL, and OWL standards can be found on the World Wide Web Consortium Web site at www.w3.org. There are multiple other standards related to the Semantic Web, such as OWL2 (a newer version of OWL) and the Rules Interchange Format (for specifying datalog-style and business rules). http://swoogle.umbc.edu offers a search engine over a large collection of ontologies found on the Web.

13

Incorporating Uncertainty into Data Integration

Database systems typically model only certain data. That is, if a tuple is in the database, then it is true in the real world. There are many contexts in which our knowledge of the world is uncertain, and we would like to model that uncertainty in the database and be able to query it. For example, consider situations like the following:

- We are collecting information about theft sightings, and a witness does not remember whether the thief had blond or brown hair.
- We are recording temperature measurements from sensors in the field, and the accuracy of the sensors has a certain error bound or measurements may even be completely wrong if a sensor's battery is low.
- We are integrating data across multiple sites, and the answer to a query requires a join. This join includes an approximate string matching condition, which may yield a certain number of false positives.

The field of uncertain data management develops models for representing uncertainty in databases, semantics for query answering over such databases, and techniques for efficient query evaluation. Uncertainty can be introduced in multiple aspects of data integration:

DATA
To begin, some of the data may be extracted from unstructured data (as described in Chapter 9), and we may be uncertain about the accuracy of extraction. Furthermore, when we integrate data from many sources, they may be inconsistent with each other, because some of them are inaccurate or simply out of date. Even in enterprise settings, it is common for informational data about customers, such as gender and income level, to be dirty or missing, even when the data about the actual transactions concerning these customers are precise.

SCHEMA MAPPINGS
As described in Chapter 5, schema mappings may be generated using semiautomatic techniques. If we are dealing with a very large number of sources (e.g., on the World Wide Web) we may not have the resources to validate all these mappings. In other cases, we may not know the exact schema mapping because the meaning of the data may be ambiguous. Hence, uncertainty about schema mappings can be very common in data integration applications.

QUERIES

Some data integration contexts cannot assume that the users are familiar with the schema or that they have the skills to pose structured queries. Hence, the system may need to offer the user a keyword-query search interface, as we discuss in Chapter 16. The system needs to translate the keyword queries into some structured form so they can be reformulated onto the data sources. The translation step may generate multiple candidate structured queries, and therefore there will be uncertainty about which is the intended user query.

MEDIATED SCHEMA

When the domain of the integration system is very broad, there may even be some uncertainty about the mediated schema itself. As a simple example, if our mediated schema attempts to model all the disciplines of computer science, there will be uncertainty about the precise interpretation of each discipline and about the overlap between disciplines. For example, there may be overlap between the fields of databases and artificial intelligence, but quantifying the overlap may be difficult. In general, as we attempt to model broader domains, the terms in the domain may become more vague.

A data integration system that manages uncertainty would be able to model uncertain data, uncertain schema mappings, and uncertain queries. The system should attach probabilities to every object it manipulates and should incrementally produce *ranked* answers rather than finding all the certain answers.

Many of these challenges are the subject of ongoing research. This chapter introduces many of the basic concepts, especially as they pertain to data integration. Section 13.1 introduces the topic of modeling uncertainty associated with data. Section 13.2 then describes how uncertainty can be attached to schema mappings. We conclude with a brief discussion about the close connections between uncertainty and data provenance in Section 13.3. Further information on uncertainty as it pertains to queries in the context of keyword search, as well as general techniques for merging ranked results, can be found in Chapter 16. Finally, we refer the reader to the bibliographic references at the end of this chapter for more information about probabilistic modeling in databases and about how probabilities can be computed for the outputs of semiautomated schema matching techniques.

13.1 Representing Uncertainty

In general, uncertain data management is formulated in terms of *possible worlds*: instead of the database representing a single certain data instance, an uncertain database instead represents a set of possible instances or worlds. Each such instance may have some likelihood of being correct.

Uncertainty may be modeled to different degrees, depending on the circumstances.

- In perhaps the simplest form, we may know that there are several possible worlds, but we do not have any idea about the relative likelihood of each. Here we will often use *condition variables* to represent the set of possible values for an attribute (attribute A has values a_1, a_2, or a_3) or as Boolean conditions under which a tuple exists (tuple t exists if condition c_1 is true).

- In some cases, as in a Web search engine, we may annotate each data item with a score, whose value comes from a hand-tuned combination of factors. Here the rules for combining and composing scores may be fairly ad hoc.
- It is often desirable to have clean rules for *composing* scores as we apply query operations to tuples and tuple combinations. This leads to more formal models for computing and combining measures of uncertainty. A natural model is that of probabilities, which have a bounded range (the interval [0,1]) and can be cleanly composed even under negation (complement).

Our focus in this chapter will be on the last of these three cases, namely, using probabilistic models for uncertain data.

TYPES OF UNCERTAINTY

Uncertain data modeling generally considers two kinds of uncertainty. In *tuple-level uncertainty*, we do not know whether a data instance contains a tuple or not. We can consider the presence of the tuple to be a random variable that is true if the tuple is in the instance, or false if the tuple is not present in the instance. Alternatively, in *attribute-level uncertainty*, the value of an attribute is itself a random variable, whose domain is the set of values allowed for that tuple.

For regularity, we often convert attribute-level uncertainty into tuple-level uncertainty, as follows. For each possible value of attribute A, say a_1, a_2, a_3, in tuple t, we create a copy t_1, t_2, t_3 with attribute A set to a_1, a_2, a_3, respectively. Then we assign to each copied tuple t_i the probability of attribute A being a_i. Finally, we constrain t_1, t_2, t_3 to be mutually exclusive.

■ ■ ■ ▬▬▬▬▬▬▬▬▬▬▬▬▬▬▬▬▬▬▬▬▬▬▬▬▬▬▬▬▬▬▬▬▬▬▬▬

Example 13.1

Suppose for a theft sighting database, we are given that the witness is 60% confident he or she saw the thief, although the person who was seen might have been an innocent bystander. The person witnessed had blond hair. We can represent this using a tuple ($thief_1$, *Blondhair*) with tuple-level probability 0.6.

Alternatively, the witness may have directly seen the thief stealing an item, but due to the lighting, may not be certain about the thief's hair color (with 50% confidence it was brown, but with a 20% chance it was black and a 30% chance it was blond). We can represent this using attribute-level uncertainty given a tuple ($thief_1$, X). Random variable X is given the value *Brown* with probability 0.5, *Black* with probability 0.2, and *Blond* with probability 0.3.

Alternatively, we can convert the last case to a set of tuple-level probabilities given a data representation where we can mark tuples as mutually exclusive. We create the tuples

$t_1 = (thief_1, Brown)$ with probability 0.5, $t_2 = (thief_1, Black)$ with probability 0.2, and $t_3 = (thief_1, Blond)$ with probability 0.3. Then we make t_1, t_2, t_3 mutually exclusive.

■ ■ ■

This last example brings up a natural question, which is how to represent mutual exclusion among tuples and other kinds of constraints over how tuples may appear within possible worlds. From this point forward (given that we have the above conversion process), let us assume tuple-level uncertainty in our discussion.

13.1.1 Probabilistic Data Representations

In the database world, the starting point for uncertain data representations is that of the *conditional table* (c-table). In conditional tables every tuple is annotated with a Boolean condition over a set of variables. The tuple is present in the table if the condition evaluates to true, and absent if it evaluates to false. The c-table gives us a means of representing a set of possible worlds, which are the set of instances that arise due to different combinations of valuations to the variables. The various conditions restrict which combinations of tuples are allowed in the instances.

■ ■ ■

Example 13.2

Suppose Alice wishes to go on a vacation with Bob. They have two options as destinations, Tahiti and Ulaanbaatar. A third traveler, Candace, will be going to Ulaanbaatar. We can model this set of vacations as

Vacationer	Destination	Condition
Alice	Tahiti	x
Bob	Tahiti	x
Alice	Ulaanbaatar	$\neg x$
Bob	Ulaanbaatar	$\neg x$
Candace	Ulaanbaatar	true

where x represents the condition that they jointly choose Tahiti. Observe that there are only two possible worlds in the above table.

■ ■ ■

We can generalize the notion of the conditional table to the *probabilistic conditional table*, or pc-table, by letting the variables in the c-table be random variables and assigning a probability distribution to the random variables and their possible values.

■ ■ ■ ▬▬▬▬▬▬▬▬▬▬▬▬▬▬▬▬▬▬▬▬▬▬▬▬▬▬▬▬▬▬

Example 13.3

Given the above data instance, we might see Alice with a tan and know that it is winter. Hence odds are 80% that Alice and Bob went to Tahiti and not to Ulaanbaatar. We assign a probability of 0.8 to x.

▬▬▬▬▬▬▬▬▬▬▬▬▬▬▬▬▬▬▬▬▬▬▬▬▬▬▬▬ ■ ■ ■

The pc-table is an elegant abstraction for capturing probabilistic information, although it leaves open precisely how we capture the probability distributions of the variables. One possibility is to use concepts from machine learning such as graphical models (Markov networks, Bayesian networks, and their relatives), which capture the correlation structure among random variables. Significant work has been done on building database query models and systems that return probabilistic results under such models.

Sometimes we use much simpler models, which greatly limit the set of possible worlds that can be captured — but which make the query answering problem much more tractable. We briefly describe two such models that are often used.

THE TUPLE-INDEPENDENT MODEL

The simplest probabilistic representation of a set of possible worlds uses a separate Boolean variable to annotate each tuple in a pc-table. We then assign a probability to each variable separately: this probability is with respect to the *event* that the tuple is a member of the instance. Observe that since each tuple has its own variable, there are no correlations among the tuples. Hence we can find the set of possible models by enumerating all possible subsets of tuples from the relation and computing the probability of each instance as the product of all of the probabilities of the member tuples. The resulting model is, rather naturally, called the *tuple-independent* model.

The tuple-independent model is, unfortunately, too simple to capture correlations or mutual exclusions. In our vacationers example, there is no way of indicating that Alice can only go to one of Tahiti or Ulaanbaatar, as opposed to having some independent probability of going to each. There is also no way of capturing the fact that Alice and Bob will go together. The next model captures mutual exclusions, although it still cannot express correlations.

THE BLOCK-INDEPENDENT-DISJOINT (BID) MODEL

Here we divide the table into a set of *blocks*, each of which is independent of the others. Any instance of the table must have a tuple from each block, and each tuple in the block is a *disjoint* (i.e., mutually exclusive) probabilistic event. We can think of this as assigning a random variable x_b to each block b, and annotate each tuple in the block $t_1, t_2, t_3, \ldots$ with the condition $x_b = 1$, $x_b = 2$, $x_b = 3, \ldots$, respectively. Since each random variable only appears once per block, in writing the BID table, we will typically replace the condition $x_b = y$ with its associated event probability.

■ ■ ■

Example 13.4

We can capture the various choices with the following BID table, where the long horizontal lines separate the different blocks.

Vacationer	Destination	Probability
Alice	Tahiti	0.8
Alice	Ulaanbaatar	0.2
Bob	Tahiti	0.8
Bob	Ulaanbaatar	0.2
Candace	Ulaanbaatar	1.0

However, we still cannot constrain Alice and Bob to go to the same destination. Graphical models offer a more powerful formalism for capturing correlations between tuples. We discuss them briefly in the bibliographic notes.

■ ■ ■

13.1.2 From Uncertainty to Probabilities

A probabilistic model for representing uncertainty has many positives. However, a natural question is how one goes from confidence levels in data, mappings, queries, or schemas to actual probability values. After all, for example, converting a string edit distance score to a probability requires a model of how typographical errors or string modifications are introduced. Such a model is likely highly dependent on the particular data and application — and thus unavailable to us.

The answer to the question of where probabilities come from is typically application specific, and often not formally justified. In the best cases, we do have probabilistic information about distributions, error rates, etc. to build from. In a few of these cases, we may even have models of how data values correlate.

However, in many other cases, we only have a subjective confidence level that gets converted to a [0,1] interval and gets interpreted as a probability. Much as in Web search, the ultimate question is whether the system assigns a higher score to answers composed from good (high-confidence) values than to poor ones — not whether we have a mathematically solid foundation to the generation of the underlying scores.

Within this section, our focus has been on representing uncertainty associated with data. We next describe how we can ascribe uncertainty to another key ingredient in data integration, namely, schema mappings.

13.2 Modeling Uncertain Schema Mappings

Schema mappings describe the relationship between the terms used in the mediated schema and the terms used in the sources. In this section we describe probabilistic schema mappings (p-mappings) that are intended to capture uncertainty on mappings.

We describe the possible semantics of probabilistic mappings and their effect on the complexity of query answering.

For brevity, we consider very simple schema mappings here, specified as attribute correspondences. Specifically, a mapping consists of a set of *attribute correspondences*. An attribute correspondence is of the form $c_{ij} = (s_i, t_j)$, where s_i is a *source attribute* in the schema S and t_j is a *target attribute* in the schema T. Intuitively, c_{ij} specifies that there is a relationship between s_i and t_j. The correspondence may specify that the two attributes are equal to each other or that there may be a transformation function involved (e.g., from Celsius to Fahrenheit). We consider simple schema mappings defined as follows.

Definition 13.1 (Schema Mapping).   *Let $\bar{S}$ and $\bar{T}$ be relational schemas. A relation mapping M is a triple (S, T, m), where S is a relation in $\bar{S}$, T is a relation in $\bar{T}$, m is a set of attribute correspondences between S and T, and each source and target attribute occurs in at most one correspondence in m.*

A schema mapping $\overline{M}$ is a set of relation mappings between relations in $\bar{S}$ and in $\bar{T}$, where every relation in either $\bar{S}$ or $\bar{T}$ appears at most once.   □

■ ■ ■ ▬▬▬▬▬▬▬▬▬▬▬▬▬▬▬▬▬▬▬▬▬▬▬▬▬▬▬▬▬▬

Example 13.5

Consider a data source S that describes a person by her email address, current address, and permanent address, and the mediated schema T that describes a person by her name, email, mailing address, home address, and office address (both of these schemas include a single relation):

```
S=(pname, email-addr, current-addr, permanent-addr)
T=(name, email, mailing-addr, home-addr, office-addr)
```

The following is a possible relation mapping between S and T.

```
{
    (pname, name),
    (email-addr, email),
    (current-addr, mailing-addr),
    (permanent-addr, home-addr)
}
```

▬▬▬▬▬▬▬▬▬▬▬▬▬▬▬▬▬▬▬▬▬▬▬▬▬▬▬ ■ ■ ■

13.2.1 Probabilistic Mappings

As described earlier, we may not be sure about the mapping between two schemas. Continuing with Example 13.5, a semiautomatic schema mapping tool may generate three possible mappings between S and T, assigning each a probability, as shown in Figure 13.2. Whereas the three mappings all map pname to name, they map other attributes in the source and the target differently. For example, mapping m_1 maps current-addr to mailing-addr, but mapping m_2 maps permanent-addr to mailing-addr. Because of the uncertainty about which mapping is correct, we would like to consider all of these mappings in query answering.

We can now formalize the notion of p-mappings. Intuitively, a p-mapping describes a probability distribution over a set of *possible* schema mappings between a source schema and a target schema.

Definition 13.2 (Probabilistic Mapping).   *Let $\bar{S}$ and $\bar{T}$ be relational schemas. A probabilistic mapping (p-mapping), pM, is a triple $(S, T, \mathbf{m})$, where $S \in \bar{S}$, $T \in \bar{T}$, and $\mathbf{m}$ is a set $\{(m_1, Pr(m_1)), \dots, (m_l, Pr(m_l))\}$, such that*

- *for $i \in [1, l]$, m_i is a mapping between S and T, and for every $i, j \in [1, l]$, $i \neq j \Rightarrow m_i \neq m_j$.*
- *$Pr(m_i) \in [0, 1]$ and $\sum_{i=1}^{l} Pr(m_i) = 1$.*

A schema p-mapping, $\overline{pM}$, is a set of p-mappings between relations in $\bar{S}$ and in $\bar{T}$, where every relation in either $\bar{S}$ or $\bar{T}$ appears in at most one p-mapping.   □

13.2.2 Semantics of Probabilistic Mappings

Given a p-mapping, *pM*, there are (at least) two ways to interpret uncertainty about schema mappings:

1. a single mapping in *pM* is the correct one and it applies to all the data in the source *S*, or
2. several mappings in *pM* are *partially* correct and each is suitable for a different subset of tuples in *S*. Furthermore, we do not know which mapping is the right one for a specific tuple.

In our running example, both interpretations are equally valid. While one of the mappings may be correct for all the data, it may also be true that some people may choose to use their current address as their mailing address while others use their permanent address as their mailing address. In the latter case, the correct mapping depends on the particular tuple.

We define query answering semantics with respect to two interpretations, *by-table* semantics and *by-tuple* semantics. The two semantics turn out to have different computational properties. Note that the needs of the application dictate which is the appropriate semantics.

The by-table and by-tuple semantics are natural extensions of certain answers (see Section 3.2.1). We first briefly review certain answers in our simplified context. Recall that a mapping defines a relationship between instances of *S* and instances of *T* that are *consistent* with the mapping.

Definition 13.3 (Consistent Target Instance).   *Let $M = (S, T, m)$ be a relation mapping and D_S be an instance of S.*

An instance D_T of T is said to be consistent with D_S and M if for each tuple $t_s \in D_S$, there exists a tuple $t_t \in D_T$, such that for every attribute correspondence $(a_s, a_t) \in m$, the value of a_s in t_s is the same as the value of a_t in t_t.   □

■ ■ ■

Example 13.6

In Figure 13.1, (a) is an instance of the source that is consistent with (b) under the mapping m_1 and is consistent with (c) under the mapping m_2.

pname	email-addr	current-addr	permanent-addr
Alice	alice@	Mountain View	Sunnyvale
Bob	bob@	Sunnyvale	Sunnyvale

(a)

name	email	mailing-addr	home-addr	office-addr
Alice	alice@	Mountain View	Sunnyvale	office
Bob	bob@	Sunnyvale	Sunnyvale	office

(b)

name	email	mailing-addr	home-addr	office-addr
Alice	alice@	Sunnyvale	Mountain View	office
Bob	bob@	Sunnyvale	Sunnyvale	office

(c)

FIGURE 13.1   (a) is an instance of the source schema, and (b) and (c) are instances of the target schema. (a) is consistent with (b) and (c) under different schema mappings.

■ ■ ■

For a relation mapping M and a source instance D_S, there can be an infinite number of target instances that are consistent with D_S and M. We denote by $Tar_M(D_S)$ the set of all such target instances. The set of answers to a query Q is the intersection of the answers on all instances in $Tar_M(D_S)$:

Definition 13.4 (Certain Answer).   *Let $M = (S, T, m)$ be a relation mapping. Let Q be a query over T and let D_S be an instance of S.*

A tuple t is said to be a certain answer of Q with respect to D_S and M if for every instance $D_T \in Tar_M(D_S)$, $t \in Q(D_T)$.   □

13.2.3 By-Table Semantics

We now generalize certain answers to the probabilistic setting, beginning with the by-table semantics. Intuitively, a p-mapping pM describes a set of possible worlds. In each of these worlds, a different mapping in pM applies to the source. The worlds are weighted by the probability of each mapping in pM. Following this intuition, we define target instances that are *consistent with* the source instance.

Definition 13.5 (By-Table Consistent Instance).   *Let $pM = (S, T, \mathbf{m})$ be a p-mapping and D_S be an instance of S.*

An instance D_T of T is said to be by-table consistent with D_S and pM if there exists a mapping $m \in \mathbf{m}$ such that D_S and D_T satisfy m.   □

■ ■ ■

Example 13.7

In Figure 13.1, both (b) and (c) are by-table consistent with (a) with respect to the probabilistic mappings in Figure 13.2.

Possible Mapping		Prob
$m_1 =$	{(pname, name), (email-addr, email), (current-addr, mailing-addr), (permanent-addr, home-addr)}	0.5
$m_2 =$	{(pname, name), (email-addr, email), (permanent-addr, mailing-addr), (current-addr, home-addr)}	0.4
$m_3 =$	{(pname, name), (email-addr, mailing-addr), (current-addr, home-addr)}	0.1

(a)

FIGURE 13.2 A probabilistic mapping, consisting of three alternative relation mappings.

■ ■ ■

Given a source instance D_S and a possible mapping $m \in \mathbf{m}$, there can be an infinite number of target instances that are consistent with D_S and m. We denote by $Tar_m(D_S)$ the set of all such instances.

In the probabilistic context, we assign a probability to every answer. Intuitively, we consider the certain answers with respect to each possible mapping in *isolation*. The probability of an answer t is the sum of the probabilities of the mappings for which t is deemed to be a certain answer. We define by-table answers as follows:

Definition 13.6 (By-Table Answer). *Let $pM = (S, T, \mathbf{m})$ be a p-mapping. Let Q be a query over T and let D_S be an instance of S.*

Let t be a tuple. Let $\bar{m}(t)$ be the subset of $\mathbf{m}$, such that for each $m \in \bar{m}(t)$ and for each $D_T \in Tar_m(D_S)$, $t \in Q(D_T)$.

Let $p = \sum_{m \in \bar{m}(t)} Pr(m)$. If $p > 0$, then we say (t, p) is a by-table answer of Q with respect to D_S and pM. □

■ ■ ■

Example 13.8

Consider the query that retrieves all the mailing addresses in the target relation. Figure 13.3(a) shows the answers to the query under by-table semantics. As an example, for tuple $t =$('Sunnyvale'), we have $\bar{m}(t) = \{m_1, m_2\}$, so the possible tuple ('Sunnyvale', 0.9) is an answer.

■ ■ ■

13.2.4 By-Tuple Semantics

Whereas by-table semantics modeled a possible world for each choice of mapping in $\mathbf{m}$, by-tuple semantics need to consider that each tuple may choose a different mapping. Hence, a possible world is an assignment of a possible mapping in $\mathbf{m}$ to each tuple in D_S.

Tuple (mailing-addr)	Prob
('Sunnyvale')	0.9
('Mountain View')	0.5
('alice@')	0.1
('bob@')	0.1

(a)

Tuple (mailing-addr)	Prob
('Sunnyvale')	0.94
('Mountain View')	0.5
('alice@')	0.1
('bob@')	0.1

(b)

FIGURE 13.3 Finding all the mailing addresses according to by-table semantics (a) and according to by-tuple semantics (b).

Formally, the key difference in the definition of by-tuple semantics from that of by-table semantics is that a consistent target instance is defined by a mapping *sequence* that assigns a (possibly different) mapping in **m** to each source tuple in D_S. We assume, without loss of generality, that we have an ordering on the tuples in D_S.

Definition 13.7 (By-Tuple Consistent Instance).   *Let d denote the number of tuples in D_S. Let pM = (S, T, **m**) be a p-mapping and let D_S be an instance of S with d tuples.*

An instance D_T of T is said to be by-tuple consistent with D_S and pM if there is a sequence $\langle m^1, \ldots, m^d \rangle$ such that for every $1 \le i \le d$,

- $m^i \in \mathbf{m}$, *and*
- *for the ith tuple of D_S, t_i, there exists a target tuple $t'_i \in D_T$ such that for each attribute correspondence $(a_s, a_t) \in m^i$, the value of a_s in t_i is the same as the value of a_t in t'_i.*   □

Given a mapping sequence $seq = \langle m^1, \ldots, m^d \rangle$, we denote by $Tar_{seq}(D_S)$ the set of all target instances that are consistent with D_S and *seq*. Note that if D_T is by-table consistent with D_S and *m*, then D_T is also by-tuple consistent with D_S and a mapping sequence in which each mapping is *m*.

We can think of every sequence of mappings $seq = \langle m^1, \ldots, m^d \rangle$ as a separate event whose probability is $Pr(seq) = \Pi_{i=1}^{d} Pr(m^i)$. If there are *l* mappings in *pM*, then there are l^d sequences of length *d*, and their probabilities add up to 1. We denote by $\mathbf{seq}_d(pM)$ the set of mapping sequences of length *d* generated from *pM*.

Definition 13.8 (By-Tuple Answer).   *Let pM = (S, T, **m**) be a p-mapping. Let Q be a query over T and D_S be an instance of S with d tuples.*

Let t be a tuple. Let $\overline{seq}(t)$ be the subset of $\mathbf{seq}_d(pM)$, such that for each $seq \in \overline{seq}(t)$ and for each $D_T \in Tar_{seq}(D_S)$, $t \in Q(D_T)$.

Let $p = \sum_{seq \in \overline{seq}(t)} Pr(seq)$. If $p > 0$, we call (t, p) a by-tuple answer of Q with respect to D_S and pM.   □

■ ■ ■ ▬▬▬

Example 13.9
Continuing with Example 13.8, Figure 13.3(b) shows the answers to the query under by-tuple semantics. Note that the probability of tuple t=('Sunnyvale') in the by-table answers is different from that in the by-tuple answers.

▬▬▬ ■ ■ ■

Remark 13.1 (Computational Complexity). By-table semantics have an attractive property: it can be shown that we can find all the certain answers to a select-project-join query in time that is polynomial in the size of the data and the mappings. By-tuple semantics do not enjoy the same computational properties as by-table semantics. It can be shown that in general, finding all the certain answers under by-tuple semantics is #P-complete with respect to the size of the data.   □

13.3 Uncertainty and Data Provenance

Ultimately, particularly in a data integration scenario, the score (whether a probability or some other measure) associated with a tuple should depend on a wide variety of factors: the probability of correctness of the query, the probability of correctness of individual schema mappings, the probability of correctness of the source data, and in fact the overall sample space (the set of possible worlds).

As has been observed by many researchers in the probabilistic and data integration realms, there is a very close tie between the provenance of query answers, i.e., the explanations for how the answers were produced and from where, and the scores assigned to the answers. A variety of techniques have been proposed for separately computing query results with provenance, and then computing probabilities over these results. Other techniques have been proposed for learning the scores for individual data sources, schema mappings, or queries, given a correct ranking of the query answers, as well as provenance information that explains the relationships among sources and results. Work continues in this very rich area. We discuss data provenance in Chapter 14, and we detail how it is useful in computing and learning scores in Chapter 16.

Bibliographic Notes

An excellent overview text about probabilistic databases appears in [535]. Our discussion of probabilistic data modeling is heavily inspired by that text. Some of the foundational work includes representations for incomplete information, including c-tables, in [313], as well as the early probabilistic database work in [236, 364] and the model of pc-tables from [271]. More recently, a wide variety of work on probabilistic data management has arisen in the database, rather than data integration, context. Several well-known recent systems include Trio [67], MystiQ [95, 160, 496], MaybMS [32], PrDB [518], and BayesStore [561]. A popular scheme for computing approximate results, first used in MystiQ and studied in greater detail in MCDB [330] and [569], is to use Monte Carlo simulation. One motivating application for such systems is to support the execution of probabilistic computations such as information extraction from text or Web pages [560].

Managing and mining uncertain data have been a subject of research for quite some time. Some recent progress is described in a collection of articles edited by Aggrawal [17].

The by-table and by-tuple semantics for probabilistic schema mappings were introduced in [189]. That paper also establishes the complexity results on answering queries in the presence of p-mappings. There have been various models proposed to capture uncertainty on mappings between attributes. Gal et al. [239] propose keeping the top-K mappings between two schemas, each with a probability (between 0 and 1) of being true. In [242] they propose assigning a probability for matching of every pair of source and target attributes. A more comprehensive treatment of the topic can be found in the book [241].

Magnani and Montesi [411] have empirically shown that top-k schema mappings can be used to increase the recall of a data integration process, and Gal [238] described how to generate top-k schema matchings by combining the matching results generated by various matchers. Nottelmann and Straccia [462] proposed generating probabilistic schema matchings that capture the uncertainty on each matching step.

He and Chang [293] considered the problem of generating a mediated schema for a set of Web sources. Their approach was to create a mediated schema that is statistically maximally *consistent* with the source schemas. To do so, they assume that the source schemas are created by a *generative model* applied to some mediated schema, which can be thought of as a probabilistic mediated schema. Magnani et al. [412] proposed generating a set of alternative mediated schemas based on probabilistic relationships between *relations* (such as an Instructor relation intersects with a Teacher relation but is disjoint with a Student relation) obtained by sampling the overlapping of data instances.

Chiticariu et al. [135] studied the generation of multiple mediated schemas for an existing set of data sources. They consider multitable data sources and explore interactive techniques that aid humans in arriving at the mediated schemas.

Lu et al. [399] describe a system in which multiple data owners can share data, each using their own terminology. The data are inserted into a *wide table* that has a column for each attribute of each data provider. The system automatically determines the similarity between pairs of tags used by multiple data providers by inspecting the data itself and represents the similarity with a probability. Users can ask queries using any schema they want, and the system uses probabilistic query answering to retrieve data that do not conform to the schema used in the query.

14 ⋮⋮⋮

Data Provenance

The majority of this book has focused on how to take data from a plethora of sources and formats and integrate it into a single homogeneous view — such that it becomes indistinguishable from data with other origins. Sometimes, however, we would still like to be able to take a tuple from an integrated schema and determine *where it came from* and how it came to be.

This motivates a topic of study called *data provenance*, or sometimes *data lineage* or *data pedigree*. A data item's provenance is a record of how it came to be. In the broadest sense, this provenance may include a huge number of factors, e.g., who created the initial data, when they created them, or what equipment they used. Typically, however, in the database community we model provenance of derived data strictly in terms of how it was derived from the original base tuples in the original source databases. We leave it to individual applications to keep records of any additional information appropriate for the problem domain, like how and when the original base tuples were created, by whom, and so forth.

■ ■ ■ ━━

Example 14.1
Consider a situation where a scientific data warehouse imports data from multiple sources S_1, S_2. If a data conflict arises, the users and administrators of the data warehouse would like to know which source provided which data, and also which mappings were used to convert the data. If one source is known to be more authoritative than the other, then perhaps the conflict can be resolved simply by knowing the sources. Likewise, if a schema mapping is known to be error-prone, it would be useful to identify which tuples it produced.

━━ ■ ■ ■

We start in Section 14.1 by describing two different viewpoints on what provenance is: a set of annotations describing where data came from, or a set of relationships among data. Each viewpoint is very natural in certain settings. Section 14.2 provides an overview of the many applications of data provenance. Section 14.3 discusses a formal model for data provenance, that of *provenance semirings*, which captures the full detail of select-project-join-union queries. We briefly discuss how provenance can be stored in a database system in Section 14.4.

14.1 The Two Views of Provenance

Provenance, as the means of describing how data are derived, can be thought of in two different, complementary ways. Typically one thinks of provenance in the first representation when reasoning about the existence or value of particular data items, whereas one thinks of provenance in the second representation when *modeling* it with respect to an entire database. Both views are equivalent, and one can convert from one to the other as convenient. Most systems that manipulate data provenance use both representations.

14.1.1 Provenance as Annotations on Data

Perhaps the most natural way to conceptualize provenance is as a series of annotations describing how each data item was produced. These annotations can be placed on different portions of the data. In the relational model, this means tuples or fields within a tuple may be annotated. For instance, the provenance of tuple t might be the set of tuples t_1, t_2, t_3 that were joined together to produce t. In a more complex model such as that of XML, provenance annotations might appear on (sub)trees. Such annotations could describe the tuple in terms of the transformations (mappings and/or query operations) and sources of the data.

■ ■ ■ ━━

Example 14.2

Refer to Figure 14.1 for a sample database instance, with two base data instances (tables R and S). Here we have a view V_1 computed using the relational algebra expression $R \bowtie S \cup S \bowtie S$. We can annotate each tuple in V_1 with an "explanation" of how it was produced; see the "directly derivable by" column in the figure. For instance, $V_1(1,3)$ is derivable in two alternative ways, where the first is the join of $R(1,2)$ with $S(2,3)$ and the second is the join of $R(1,4)$ with $S(4,3)$.

Relation R

A	B
1	2
1	4

Relation S

B	C
2	3
3	2
4	3

View $V_1 := R \bowtie S \cup S \bowtie S$

A	C	directly derivable by...
1	3	$R(1,2) \bowtie S(2,3) \cup R(1,4) \bowtie S(4,3)$
2	2	$S(2,3) \bowtie \rho_{B \to A, C \to B} S(3,2)$
3	3	$S(3,2) \bowtie \rho_{B \to A, C \to B} S(2,3)$

FIGURE 14.1 Two example base relation instances and a view instance (with definition shown in relational algebra).

━━ ■ ■ ■

This view of provenance is extremely convenient when one wishes to use the provenance to assign some sort of score or confidence assessment to a tuple. In essence, the provenance annotation gets treated as an expression whose value is the score.

As we shall see shortly, the notion of annotations can even be generalized to support recursive dependencies, e.g., due to a recursive view or cyclic set of schema mappings.

14.1.2 Provenance as a Graph of Data Relationships

There are other situations where it is more natural to think about provenance as a means of connecting source and derived tuples via particular mappings: in other words, to think of provenance as a sort of graph. Such a graph is a very natural way to visualize provenance and in fact also to store provenance information.

More specifically, we model provenance as a hypergraph, with tuples as vertices. Each direct derivation of a tuple from a set of source tuples is a *hyperedge* connecting the source and derived tuples. In datalog parlance, a direct derivation of one tuple from a set of source tuples is called an *immediate consequent* of a particular rule.

■ ■ ■ ▬▬▬▬▬▬▬▬▬▬▬▬▬▬▬▬▬▬▬▬▬▬▬▬▬▬▬▬▬▬▬▬▬▬▬▬▬▬

Example 14.3
Refer again to Figure 14.1. We can restate the relational algebra expression for V_1 in datalog:

$$V_1(x,z):- \quad R(x,y), S(y,z)$$

$$V_1(x,x):- \quad S(x,y), S(y,x)$$

Each tuple in V_1's view instance is derivable as an immediate consequent from other tuples, i.e., it is directly derived by applying the datalog rule to those tuples. We see in the figure that the first tuple of V_1 can actually be derived by joining two different combinations of tuples from R and S. Meanwhile, the second and third tuples in V_1's instance are derived simply by doing a self-join on S. We can visualize the relationships between the tuples using the hypergraph of Figure 14.2.

In this example, the name of the derivation (V_1) and the relation for the resulting tuple $(V_1(a,b))$ are the same. In more general data integration settings, however, we may have multiple mappings or rules expressing constraints between source and target instances. Here,

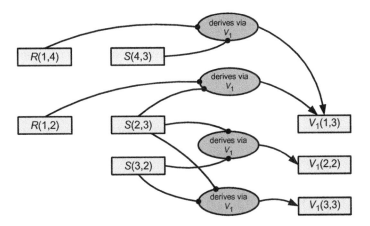

FIGURE 14.2 Example hypergraph of relationships between tuples in a database (and view) instance, where tuples are indicated by rectangular nodes and derivation hyperedges are represented by ellipses with incoming and outgoing arcs.

the rules or mappings may each receive a unique name, which is distinct from the output relation name.

■ ■ ■

14.1.3 Interchangeability of the Two Views

It is worth noting that any provenance graph can be equivalently represented using annotations on tuples, with a slight generalization of the form discussed in the previous section. In particular, if we want to support recursive derivations as in the graph, then we assign to each tuple a corresponding *provenance token*. For base tuples, this is a *base token* representing a known base value. For all other cases, we use a *result token* whose (derived) value is computed through a *provenance expression* over other provenance tokens. The set of all provenance tokens then forms a system of equations, whose solution may have an infinite expansion in the presence of recursion. Fortunately, as we shall discuss in Section 14.3, if we assign the right semantics to the mathematical structure in which the equations are represented, then we can manipulate and reason about the annotations in a tractable way.

■ ■ ■

Example 14.4

We illustrate the intuition of the system of equations in Figure 14.3. This is Figure 14.1 redrawn so all tuples are annotated with provenance tokens, which represent either base values or expressions over other provenance tokens.

Relation R

A	B	annotation
1	2	r_1
1	4	r_2

Relation S

B	C	annotation
2	3	s_1
3	2	s_2
4	3	s_3

View V_1

A	C	annotation
1	3	$v_1 = r_1 \bowtie s_1 \cup r_2 \bowtie s_3$
2	2	$v_2 = s_1 \bowtie s_2$
3	3	$v_3 = s_2 \bowtie s_1$

FIGURE 14.3 Figure 14.1 with provenance as a system of annotation equations over provenance tokens. Each tuple is annotated with a token, whose value is an expression over other tokens. We use join and union informally here and provide a formal framework in Section 14.3.

■ ■ ■

Under this model, each product term, which is now expressed in terms of the tuples from which the tuple was directly derived, corresponds exactly to a hyperedge in the graph.

14.2 Applications of Data Provenance

Provenance, as a means of explaining answers, can be useful in many contexts. Motivations for storing and examining provenance can generally be split into three classes:

explaining a data item, scoring a data item, or reasoning about interactions among tuples.

EXPLANATIONS

There are a variety of contexts where an end user or data integrator may wish to see an "explanation" of a tuple in the output. Perhaps the tuple looks erroneous: we may need to see which mapping produced it in order to debug the mapping or clean the source. We may want an audit trail showing how the data came to be, including the operations applied. Alternatively, we may wish to see an explanation of where the data came from and how the tuple was produced in order to better assess the evidence in support of the answer. In such settings, our goal is probably to see a diagram, e.g., a directed graph, representing the dataflow and operations that produced a tuple.

SCORING

In a variety of cases it is possible to assign a base score to raw data, to mappings, and to computations like joins or unions. The base score can represent a confidence level, author-authoritativeness score, likelihood of landing on a node in a random walk, or similarity metric. In these cases, given provenance and a scheme for combining scores, we can automatically derive a score for the derived data values, in the form of an annotation. For instance, we can automatically derive probabilistic event expressions (describing the conditions under which a joint event is true) or negative log likelihood scores (describing the logarithm of the likelihood a joint event is true) from provenance information. A closely related kind of score might be an access level: if source data are known to have a particular set of access privileges associated with them, we may be able to automatically determine that derived data should have *at least* the same amount of protection.

REASONING ABOUT INTERACTIONS

Sometimes there is a need not merely to look at the provenance of a tuple, but to understand the relationship between different tuples. For instance, we might want to know whether two different tuples are independently derivable, whether one tuple is dependent on the presence of another, or whether two tuples share a mapping. Here we may want to see a set of data items for which the relationship holds, or possibly a graphical representation of the connections between the data items.

14.3 Provenance Semirings

Since the early 2000s, many different formulations of data provenance have been developed, each with the ability to capture certain levels of detail in explaining a tuple. The culmination of this work was the provenance semirings formalism, which is the most general representation of the relationships among tuples derived using the core relational algebra (select, project, join, union). Provenance semirings also provide two very useful properties: (1) different, algebraically equivalent relational expressions[1] produce algebraically equivalent provenance; (2) one can use the same formalism to compute a wide variety of score types to a derived result in a materialized view simply based on its provenance annotation, i.e., without recomputing the result. Recent research has extended the provenance semiring model to richer query languages (e.g., with support for aggregation), but we focus on the core relational algebra here.

14.3.1 The Semiring Formal Model

If one looks at a tuple produced by a query in the relational algebra, there are two basic ways tuples get combined: through join or Cartesian product, resulting in a "joint" tuple, and via duplicate elimination in a projection or union operation, resulting in a tuple that was derived in more than one "alternative" way. Moreover, there are certain equivalences that hold over these operations, thanks to the relational algebra. For instance, union is commutative, and join distributes through union. The semiring model is designed to capture these equivalences, such that algebraically equivalent query expressions produce equivalent provenance annotations. Put in more dramatic terms, the semiring captures cases in which the query optimizer can choose different plans for evaluating a query, without affecting the provenance.

The basic provenance semiring formalism consists of the following:

- A set of *provenance tokens* or tuple identifiers K, which uniquely identify the relation and value for each tuple. Consider, for example, a relation ID and key as a means of obtaining a provenance token. Tokens are divided into base tokens, representing base values, and result tokens, representing the results of provenance expressions over other tokens.
- An abstract *sum* operator, $\oplus$, which is associative and commutative, and with an identity element $\mathbf{0}$ ($a \oplus \mathbf{0} \equiv a \equiv \mathbf{0} \oplus a$).
- An abstract *product* operator, $\otimes$, which is associative and commutative, which distributes through the sum operator, and for which there is an identity element $\mathbf{1}$ such that $a \otimes \mathbf{1} \equiv \mathbf{1} \otimes a \equiv a$. Moreover, $a \otimes \mathbf{0} \equiv \mathbf{0} \otimes a \equiv \mathbf{0}$.

More formally, $(K, \oplus, \otimes, \mathbf{0}, \mathbf{1})$ form a *commutative semiring* and $(K, \oplus, \mathbf{0})$ and $(K, \otimes, \mathbf{1})$ form *commutative monoids*, where $\otimes$ is distributive over $\oplus$.

Intuitively, if each element of K is a tuple ID, then $\oplus$ captures settings where the same result is derived by unioning or projecting from multiple expressions. The $\otimes$ operator corresponds to joining the results of multiple expressions or applying a given mapping rule.

---

[1] Here, we refer to equivalent with the "standard" relational algebraic transformations used in an optimizer, hence the set of query plans that might be produced for any query. See the bibliographic notes for details on some subtleties.

■ ■ ■

Example 14.5

Suppose we assign a provenance token $X_{y,z}$ to each tuple of the form $X(y,z)$ in Figure 14.1. For instance, tuple $R(1,2)$ receives token $R_{1,2}$. Then the provenance of tuples in view V_1 would be as follows:

A	C	*provenance expression*
1	3	$V_{1,3} = R_{1,2} \otimes S_{2,3} \oplus R_{1,4} \otimes S_{4,3}$
2	2	$V_{2,2} = S_{2,3} \otimes S_{3,2}$
3	3	$V_{3,3} = S_{3,2} \otimes S_{2,3}$

■ ■ ■

EXTENSION: TOKENS FOR MAPPINGS

It is sometimes convenient to also assign a provenance token to each mapping or rule (or even *version* of a mapping or rule definition) in a derivation. This enables us to track not only the data items but also the mappings used to create a tuple. We might ultimately want to assign a score to each mapping, e.g., based on its likelihood of correctness, and to include the mapping's score in our computation of an annotation. Chapter 13 discusses how we can use *by-table* semantics to assign probabilistic scores to schema mappings.

■ ■ ■

Example 14.6

Let us expand Example 14.5 to a scenario where we are uncertain about the quality of view V_1. We assign a token v_1 to the view V_1, representing our confidence in the quality of the view's output. Then the provenance of tuples in view V_1 would be as follows:

A	C	*provenance expression*
1	3	$V_{1,3} = v_1 \otimes [R_{1,2} \otimes S_{2,3} \oplus R_{1,4} \otimes S_{4,3}]$
2	2	$V_{2,2} = v_1 \otimes [S_{2,3} \otimes S_{3,2}]$
3	3	$V_{3,3} = v_1 \otimes [S_{3,2} \otimes S_{2,3}]$

■ ■ ■

Note from the example that we define the provenance of a tuple as a polynomial expression over the provenance tokens of other tuples. This model is general enough to capture complex provenance relationships, including recursive relationships. There is a direct translation to and from the hypergraph representation of Figure 14.1, as well: each provenance token for a tuple is encoded as a tuple node in the hypergraph; each provenance token for a mapping becomes a hyperedge, connecting from the tuple nodes for the tokens being multiplied and connecting to the tuple node(s) for the resulting (output) provenance tokens.

14.3.2 Applications of the Semiring Model

One application of data provenance is simply to help the end user visualize how a tuple was derived, e.g., to perform debugging or to better understand the data. Figure 14.4 shows an example of this, with the provenance visualizer used in the ORCHESTRA system. The visualizer uses rectangles to represent tuples within relations. Derivations are indicated by diamonds, such as the derivation through mapping M5 (labeled as such). Additionally, insertions of source data are indicated with "+" nodes.

The true power of the provenance semiring formalism occurs in its ability to assign scores to tuples by giving an interpretation to the $\oplus$, $\otimes$ operators and a score to the base provenance tokens. By performing an evaluation over the provenance representation, we can automatically derive the score. Moreover, the same stored provenance representation can be directly used in all of the applications — we do not need a different stored representation for, say, visualizing provenance versus assigning scores or counts to tuples.

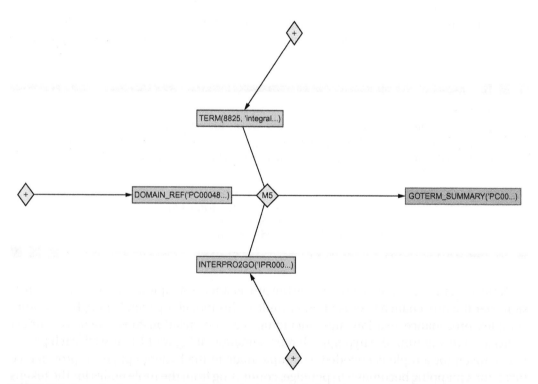

FIGURE 14.4 Example of provenance visualization as a hypergraph, from the ORCHESTRA system. "+" nodes represent insertions of source data. Rectangles represent tuples within relations, and diamonds, such as the one labeled "M5," represent derivations through schema mappings.

■ ■ ■

Example 14.7

Suppose we have a simple scoring model in which the score of a tuple is computed based on the number of times it is derived. Let the value of each base tuple $R_{x,y}$ or $S_{y,z}$ be the integer 1, let $\otimes$ be arithmetic multiplication, and let $\oplus$ be arithmetic sum. Assign the **1** element to be the integer value 1 and the **0** element to be the integer value 0. Finally, let the value of v_1 be the integer value 1.

Then we get the following for V_1:

A	C	*evaluation of provenance expression*
1	3	$V_{1,3} = 1 \cdot 1 \cdot 1 + 1 \cdot 1 \cdot 1 = 2$
2	2	$V_{2,2} = 1 \cdot 1 \cdot 1 = 1$
3	3	$V_{3,3} = 1 \cdot 1 \cdot 1 = 1$

■ ■ ■

■ ■ ■

Example 14.8

Suppose we have a slightly more complex scoring model that is commonly used in information retrieval: each tuple receives a score that is its *negative log likelihood*, i.e., the negation of the log of its probability. Assuming independence of all tuples, the negative log likelihood of a join result is the sum of the negative log likelihoods of the expressions being joined. When a tuple has two different derivations, we will pick the most likely of the cases (i.e., the smallest of the negative log likelihoods).[2]

We can compute negative log likelihood annotations for each tuple as follows. Let the value of each base tuple $R_{x,y}$ or $S_{y,z}$ be the negative log likelihood of the tuple; let $\otimes$ be the arithmetic sum, and let $\oplus$ be the the operator *min*. Assign the **1** element to be the real value 1 and the **0** element to be the real value 0. Finally, let the value of v_1 be the negative log likelihood of the view being correct. As we combine these components, we will receive a single score. In many cases, we may wish to return only the *top k-scoring* tuples in the view (See Section 16.2 for more details).

■ ■ ■

Beyond these simple examples, there are a wide variety of commutative semirings that have been shown to be useful. See Table 14.1 for a list of the operators and base value assignments. The derivability semiring assigns true to all base tuples and determines whether a tuple (whose annotation must also be true) can be derived from them. Trust is very similar, except that we must check each base (EDB) tuple to see whether it is trusted, annotating it with true or false. Moreover, each mapping may be associated with the

---

[2]Note that this does not compute the probabilistically correct answer. However, it is a tractable approximation often used in machine learning, since computing the true probabilities is a #P-complete problem.

Table 14.1   Some Useful Assignments of Base Values and Operations in Evaluating Provenance Expressions to Compute Scores

Use case	Base value	Product $R \otimes S$	Sum $R \oplus S$
Derivability	true	$R \wedge S$	$R \vee S$
Trust	trust condition result	$R \wedge S$	$R \vee S$
Confidentiality level	tuple confidentiality level	more_secure (R, S)	less_secure (R, S)
Weight/cost	base tuple weight	$R + S$	$min(R, S)$
Lineage	tuple ID	$R \cup S$	$R \cup S$
Probabilistic event	tuple probabilistic event	$R \wedge S$	$R \vee S$
Number of derivations	1	$R \cdot S$	$R + S$

The term "lineage" actually has three distinct meanings, as described in the bibliographic notes. Here we refer to the original definition.

multiplicative identity value true, not affecting the value of the other terms with which it is multiplied; or may be associated with the untrusted value false, returning false when multiplied with any term. Any derived tuples with annotation true are trusted. The confidentiality level semiring assigns a confidentiality access level to a tuple derived by joining multiple source tuples. For any join, it assigns the highest (most secure) level of any input tuple to the result; for any union, it assigns the lowest (least secure) level required. The weight/cost semiring, used in the previous example, is useful in ranked models where output tuples are given a cost, evaluating to the sums of the individual scores or weights of atoms joined (and to the lowest cost of different alternatives in a union). This semiring can be used to produce ranked results in a keyword search or to assess data quality. The probability semiring represents probabilistic event expressions that can be used for query answering in probabilistic databases.[3] The lineage semiring corresponds to the set of all base tuples contributing to some derivation of a tuple. The number of derivations semiring, used in our first example, counts the number of ways each tuple is derived, as in the bag relational model.

Semiring provenance has also been extended to support nested data, such as XML (see the bibliographic notes).

14.4   Storing Provenance

The hypergraph representation of provenance semirings can be very naturally encoded using relations. Suppose we have a set of relational tuples and want to also encode their provenance. Each tuple node in the graph can be encoded, of course, by a tuple in a table within the database. Each type of provenance hyperedge (conjunctive rule within a view)

[3]Computing actual probabilities from these event expressions is in general a #P-complete problem; the provenance semiring model does not change this.

has its own schema, comprising a set of typed input and output tuple IDs that are foreign keys to tuples in the DBMS; each instance of this hyperedge type can be stored as a tuple within the database.

■ ■ ■

Example 14.9

For the running example in this chapter we can create two provenance tables, $P_{V1-1}(R.A, R.B, S.B, S.C, V1.A, V1.C)$ and $P_{V1-2}(S.B, S.C, S.B', S.C', V1.A, V1.C)$, representing the first and second conjunctive queries within V_1, with the following content to describe the specific hyperedges comprising derivations through V_1

P_{V1-1}

R.A	R.B	S.B	S.C	V1.A	V1.C
1	2	2	3	1	3
1	4	4	3	1	3

P_{V1-2}

S.B	S.C	S.B'	S.C'	V1.A	V1.C
2	3	3	2	2	2
3	2	2	3	3	3

■ ■ ■

One can in fact further optimize this storage scheme by observing that in many cases, the various relations in a derivation have overlapping (shared) attributes. For instance, most of the output attributes should be derived from input attributes; and most likely, we only combine input tuples based on equality of certain attributes. A provenance table only needs to contain one copy of each of these attributes.

■ ■ ■

Example 14.10

We refine the previous schemas to $P_{V1-1}(A, B, C)$ and $P_{V1-2}(B, C, C')$ with the following content:

P_{V1-1}

A	B	C
1	2	3
1	4	3

P_{V1-2}

B	C	C'
2	3	2
3	2	3

where we know that in the rule of V_1, $R.A = V.A = A$, $R.B = S.B = B$, and $S.C = V_1.C = C$; and in the second rule of V_1, for the first atom $S.B$ is equal to $V_1.A$ and column B, $S.C$ in the first atom matches $S.B$ in the second atom and has value C, and for the second atom $S.C = V_1.C = C'$.

Bibliographic Notes

As of the writing of this book, data provenance remains an area of intensive research in the database community. A major point of active work is capturing more expressive queries (e.g., negation, aggregation) for querying and indexing provenance storage and for understanding data provenance's relationship with the problem of encoding provenance of workflow systems. (In the latter case, a workflow system is generally a pipeline of stages in which little is known about their semantics.)

Provenance (sometimes called pedigree or lineage) has been a topic of interest in the scientific research community for many years. Perhaps the earliest formalisms for provenance in the database community date back to the early 2000s. Cui and Widom first proposed a notion of *lineage* for data warehouses, where the lineage of a tuple in a view consisted of the IDs of the set of source tuples or *witnesses* [155]. Roughly concurrently, Buneman et al. proposed notions of *why-* and *where-provenance* in [98]. Why-provenance contains a *set of sets* of base tuple IDs; each "inner" set represents a combination of tuples that can derive the tuple of interest in the view, and the different sets represent different possible derivations. Where-provenance, rather than annotating tuples, instead drills down to annotate an individual field. Work on the Trio system developed a different formalism for lineage, approximately equivalent to bags of sets of source tuples, described in [67]. Finally, the lineage term has also recently been used to refer to probabilistic event expressions, as in [535]. See [267] for more details on the relationship among the majority of different provenance formalisms.

The provenance semiring formalism has seen extensive study in recent years. A major reason is that it preserves the commonly used relational algebra equivalences that hold over bag semantics. It should be noted, however, that there are certain relational algebra equivalences that hold in set semantics but not bag semantics, such as join and union idempotence — such properties do not hold in the semiring model. See [28, 267] for more details. While we do not expressly discuss it in this book, the provenance semiring formalism has been extended to support provenance annotations over hierarchical data, as in where-provenance or the XML data model [231]. Extensions have also been developed to support queries with aggregation [29].

A provenance model similar to that of semirings, but focused on supporting several other operators such as semijoins, is that of Perm [252, 253]. Building upon Perm, the TRAMP model [254] distinguishes among data, query, and mapping provenance.

Others have looked at a concept closely related to provenance — that of explaining why an answer is *not* produced or why an answer is ranked higher than others [117, 307, 372]. Finally, connections have been made to the notion of *causality* in determining *which* part of provenance "best explains" a result [424, 425].

Recent work on the Trio [67] and ORCHESTRA [324] projects motivated a new study of provenance with greater ability to capture alternative derivations. In Trio, probabilities are assigned to a derived tuple by first computing the *lineage* (expression over probabilistic events). In ORCHESTRA, trust levels or ranks are computed for output tuples depending on how they are derived. See [67] and [231, 267, 269], respectively, for more detail. An excellent survey of data provenance as a field appears in [133].

Provenance has been studied within the database community for a more expressive set of operators within the context of scientific workflow systems. Here, a workflow consists of "black box" operators strung together in a pipeline (possibly with control structures such as iteration). In contrast to data provenance, which exploits our knowledge of relational operator semantics, workflow provenance must assume that few if any equivalences hold. Hence provenance is purely a graph representing connections between data inputs, tools, and data products. The workflow provenance community has been at the core of the development of the Open Provenance Model [470]. The scientific workflow system that has the most comprehensive integration with data provenance is VisTrails [58], which is a workflow system for producing scientific visualizations. VisTrails enables users to examine and query provenance [513, 522], and even to generalize it into workflows. Other workflow systems such as Taverna [468] and Kepler [400] also have support for provenance. An emerging topic in the workflow provenance space is the notion of *securing* or abstracting away portions of a provenance graph [87, 164]. Recent work has proposed a model for unifying database and workflow provenance [27].

Related forms of data provenance are also studied outside the database community. Two prominent areas include those of provenance for filesystems [448] and work on dependency analysis in programs [132]. Recently, work on declarative techniques for describing network protocols [397] has led to a notion of *network provenance* [595]. Building upon these ideas, new forms of provenance for recording dynamic events in a system [594], and for ensuring that distributed provenance is unforgeable [593], have been developed. Others have examined provenance's connections to the Semantic Web and Linked Open Data efforts [387, 436, 591].

Finally, given that provenance has its own data model (as a hypergraph or system of semiring equations) and operations (projecting portions of a graph, computing annotations) — as well as value to end users — a natural question is how to store and query it. An initial provenance query language and storage scheme was proposed in [343].

Novel Integration Architectures

15 ::::

Data Integration on the Web

The World Wide Web offers a vast array of data in many forms. The majority of this data is structured for presentation not to machines but to humans, in the form of HTML tables, lists, and forms-based search interfaces. These extremely heterogeneous sources were created by individuals around the world and cover a very broad collection of topics in over 100 languages. Building systems that offer data integration services on this vast collection of data requires many of the techniques described thus far in the book, but also raises its own unique challenges.

While the Web offers many kinds of structured content, including XML (discussed in Chapter 11) and RDF (discussed in Chapter 12), the predominant representation by far is HTML. Structured data appears on HTML pages in several forms. Figure 15.1 shows the most common forms: HTML tables, HTML lists, and formatted "cards" or templates. Chapter 9 discusses how one might extract content from a given HTML page. However, there are a number of additional challenges posed by Web data integration, beyond the task of wrapping pages.

SCALE AND HETEROGENEITY

According to conservative estimates, there are at least a billion structured HTML data sets on the Web. Naturally, the quality of the data varies — it is often dirty, wrong, out of date, or inconsistent with other data sources. As discussed previously, the data may be in different languages. In many cases, we must have general and scalable techniques to make use of the data without requiring large amounts of human-administrator input.

MINIMAL STRUCTURAL AND SEMANTIC CUES

While to a viewer these data sets appear structured, a computer program faces several challenges to extract the structure from the Web pages. First, the visual structure evident in an HTML page may not be mirrored by consistent structure in the underlying HTML. Second, HTML tables are used primarily as a formatting mechanism for *arbitrary* data, and therefore the vast majority of the content that is formatted as HTML tables is actually not what we would consider high-quality structured data. When tabular data does appear on the Web, it comes with very little schema. At best, tables will have a header row with column names, but often it is tricky to decide whether the first row is a header row. The relations represented by the table are typically explained in the surrounding text and hard to extract. For example, the table on the bottom left of Figure 15.1 describes the list of winners of the Boston Marathon, but that fact is embedded somewhere in the surrounding text. Lists on Web pages present additional challenges. They have no schema at all, and every item in a list represents an entire row in a database. Hence, we need to first segment

Rank	Country	GDP (millions of USD)
—	World	60,689,812[4]
—	European Union	18,394,115[4]
1	United States	14,264,600
2	Japan	4,923,761
3	China (PRC)	4,401,614[h]
4	Germany	3,667,513
5	France	2,865,737
6	United Kingdom	2,674,085
7	Italy	2,313,893
8	Russia	1,676,586
9	Spain	1,611,767
10	Brazil	1,572,839

2004 — Timothy Cherigat, Kenya, 2:10:37

2003 — Robert Cheruiyot, Kenya, 2:10:11

2002 — Rodgers Rop, Kenya, 2:09:02

2001 — Lee Bong-ju, South Korea, 2:09:43

2000 — Elijah Lagat, Kenya, 2:09:47

1999 — Joseph Chebet, Kenya, 2:09:52

1998 — Moses Tanui, Kenya, 2:07:34

1997 — Lameck Aguta, Kenya, 2:10:34

1996 — Moses Tanui, Kenya, 2:09:16

195 N California Ave, Palo Alto CA — FEATURED — obeo.com
$1,899,000
4 br 2 ba 1,930 sqft $984/sqft
Single-Family Home
Old Palo Alto
▶ Preview   Save   Price Alerts

3901 Fabian Way, Palo Alto CA — FEATURED — newhomesource.com NewHome SOURCE
$999,999
2 br 2 ba
Multi-Family Home
▶ Preview   Save   Price Alerts

2079 Edgewood Dr, Palo Alto CA — FEATURED — Intero Real Estate
$1,299,000
4 br 2 ba 2,000 sqft $650/sqft
Single-Family Home
Duveneck-St. Francis
▶ Preview   Save   Price Alerts

840 Hamilton Ave, Palo Alto CA — Alain Pinel Realtors
$2,239,000
4 br 2 ba 2,288 sqft $979/sqft
Single-Family Home
Crescent Park
▶ Preview   Save   Price Alerts

771 Coastland Dr, Palo Alto CA — bhgrealestate.com
$1,599,000
4 br 4 ba 2,115 sqft $756/sqft
Single-Family Home
Midtown
▶ Preview   Save   Price Alerts

FIGURE 15.1 The different kinds of structured data on the Web. The top left shows an HTML table of country GDPs, and the bottom left shows part of an HTML list of the winners of the Boston Marathon. On the right, we see a search result for real estate listings, where each result is formatted as a card.

each list item into a row of cells. Cards display the attributes of an object in a template that is repeated for every object. To extract the data, we must know the template's specific layout structure.

DYNAMIC CONTENT, ALSO KNOWN AS THE "DEEP WEB"

Many of the pages containing structured data are generated dynamically in response to user queries that are posed using HTML forms. A few example forms are shown in Figure 15.2. In some domains, such as cars, jobs, real estate, public records, events, and patents, there may be hundreds or thousands of forms in each domain. However, there is also a *long tail* effect — a large number of domains for which there are few forms. Examples of more exotic domains include quilts, horses for sale, and parking tickets in particularly well-organized municipalities.

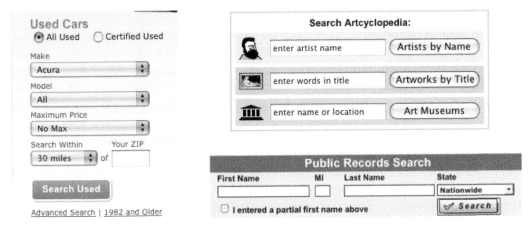

FIGURE 15.2 Sample HTML forms from the Web. The form on the left enables searching for used cars. The form on the top right is for searching art works, and the one on the bottom right is for searching public records.

Since form-based sources offer a structured query interface, much of the work on data integration on the Web is focused on providing uniform access to a multitude of forms. Accessing this data conveniently is even more important because the data are often hidden from Web search engines. Specifically, crawlers of Web search engines typically collect pages by following hyperlinks from pages they have already indexed. However, pages generated by form invocations are dynamically created on the fly, and typically have no incoming links. For this reason, this content has been referred to as the *deep Web* or *invisible Web*, and contrasted with the *surface Web*. The number of such form sources is estimated to be in the tens of millions, and estimates of the amount of content on the deep Web vary from being the size of the surface Web to being two orders of magnitude bigger.[1]

15.1 What Can We Do with Web Data?

In contrast to other types of data integration, Web sources often provide greater heterogeneity, fewer cues that help an automated system reason about what to do, and larger scale. Worse, at scale, we are often limited in the amount of human or even automated processing we can do on an individual source. So a natural question is whether and how we can harness Web data.

The answer is that broadly, we can use data sources on the Web for a variety of services, ranging from data integration to improving search. Before describing the specific techniques for extracting and querying such data, it is instructive to first consider the possible uses of structured data on the Web.

[1] These are estimates of sheer size, not of useful content.

DATA INTEGRATION

A natural goal in the presence of many data sources on a particular topic is to provide a single query interface that retrieves data from all these sources. For example, instead of expecting users to visit multiple job search sites, we can create a single site that integrates the data from multiple sites. Such engines are typically referred to as *vertical-search* engines.

A slightly different goal is to create a *topical portal* that integrates all the data on a particular domain. For example, consider a site that integrates all the information about the database research community, including its researchers, conferences, and publications. Here, different aspects of the data come from different sites. For example, data about researchers may come from one set of sources, while data about publications will come from another. In contrast, a vertical-search engine typically integrates data from multiple sites that all offer the same kind of information (e.g., cars for sale).

A third category is transient or "one-off" data integration tasks. Here, we may combine data from multiple sources in order to create a data set that will only be needed briefly. For example, consider a disaster relief effort where we need to rapidly create an online map displaying shelters with their contact details, or a student working on a course project who needs to collect information about water availability and GDP for various countries. Unlike the first two data integration tasks, here we do not expect technically skilled users, which leads to a different system design.

IMPROVED WEB SEARCH

There are several ways to use structured data to improve Web search. One can think of Web search as a special case of data integration, where no joins are performed (only unions).

As noted above, the deep Web, whose contents are not available to search engines, presents a significant gap in the coverage of search engines and therefore in search quality. Another opportunity lies in using the layout structure as a relevance signal. For example, if we find a page with a table that has a column labeled population and a row that has Zimbabwe in the left column, then that page should be considered relevant to the query "zimbabwe population" even if the occurrence of population on the page is far from the occurrence of Zimbabwe.

Another long-standing goal for Web search is to return facts as answers. For example, if the user queries for "zimbabwe population" and the appropriate answer exists in a table, we can return that number with a pointer to the source data. We can be even more ambitious and return *derived* facts. For example, for the query "africa population" we could calculate the answer from a table that contains the populations of all countries. Today's Web search engines offer factual answers to queries in very limited domains (e.g., weather, sports results) and with the support of contracted data sources.

Finally, often the intention of our search is to find structured data. For example, as part of a class assignment we may be looking for a data set containing crime rates in different American cities. Today there is no explicit way of telling the search engine that we are looking for a table of data, and therefore we are limited to the tedious process of scanning the results manually for those containing structured data.

We now discuss several bodies of work that try to provide the services described above. Section 15.2 describes two bodies of work for leveraging the content of the deep Web: search engines (e.g., cars for sale), which apply many of the ideas of virtual data integration systems, and deep-Web surfacing, which attempts to crawl through forms and find useful HTML pages. Section 15.3 discusses topical portals that attempt to assemble a broad range of data on a particular domain (e.g., find all that is known about database researchers). Finally, Section 15.4 discusses the common case of data integration on the Web where users need to integrate data sets for transient tasks (e.g., correlating coffee production of a country with its population).

15.2 The Deep Web

The deep Web contains data on a broad range of domains and in many languages. Users access content on the deep Web by filling out forms. When a query is submitted, an answer page is dynamically generated. Our discussion here is focused on deep-Web sources that provide data on a particular domain (e.g., cars, patents) and not on forms that provide generic search (e.g., www.google.com) or forms that provide a "search this site" functionality.

Before we describe how to integrate data across deep-Web sites, we review the basic constructs of Web forms. An HTML form is defined within a special HTML form tag (see Figure 15.3 for the HTML specifying the form shown in Figure 15.4). The action field identifies the server that will perform the query processing in response to the form submission. Forms can have several input controls, each defined by an input tag. Input controls can be of a number of types, the prominent ones being text boxes, select menus (defined in

```
<form action="http://jobs.com/find" method="get">
  <input type="hidden" name="src" value="hp"/>
  Keywords: <input type="text" name="kw"/>
  State: <select name="st">
            <option value="Any"/>
            <option value="AK"/>
            <option value="AL"/>
            . . .
        </select>
  Sort By: <select name="sort">
            <option value="salary"/>
            <option value="startdate"/>
            . . .
          </select>
  <input type="submit" name="s" value="go"/>
</form>
```

FIGURE 15.3 HTML for defining a form. The form defines the set of fields, their types, menu options, and the server that will process the request.

Keywords: [＿＿＿＿＿] State: [＿ ⬍] Sort By: [＿ ⬍] (go)

FIGURE 15.4 The rendering of the form specified in Figure 15.3.

a separate select tag), check boxes, radio buttons, and submit buttons. Each input has a name, which is typically not the name that the user sees on the HTML page. For example, in Figure 15.3 the user will see a field Keywords, but the name by which it can be identified by the browser or a Javascript program is kw. Users select input values either by entering arbitrary keywords into text boxes or by selecting from predefined options in select menus, check boxes, and radio buttons. In addition, there are hidden inputs whose values are fixed and are not visible to users interacting with the form. These are used to provide the server additional context about the form submission (e.g., the specific site from which it came). Our discussion focuses on the select menus and text boxes. Check boxes and radio buttons can be treated in the same way as select menus.

The example in Figure 15.3 includes a form that lets users search for jobs. When a form is submitted, the Web browser sends an HTTP request with the inputs and their values to the server using one of two methods: GET or POST. With GET, the parameters are appended to the action and included as part of the URL in the HTTP request. For example, the URL

```
http://jobs.com/find?src=hp&kw=chef&st=Any&sort=salary&s=go
```

defines the query looking for chef positions in *any* state and sorting the results by salary. With POST, the parameters are sent in the body of the HTTP request and the URL is simply the action (e.g., `http://jobs.com/find`). Hence, the URLs obtained from forms that use GET are unique and encode the submitted values, while the URLs obtained with POST are not. One reason that this distinction is important is that a search engine index can treat a GET URL as any other page, thereby storing result pages for specific queries.

There are two main approaches for querying on the deep Web. The first (Section 15.2.1) builds vertical-search engines that integrate data on very narrow domains from thousands of deep-Web sources. The second (Section 15.2.2) attempts to crawl past forms and add pages to the search engine index from millions of sites on any domain.

15.2.1 Vertical Search

We begin by describing vertical-search engines, whose goal is to provide a single point of access to a set of sources in the same domain. In the most common domains of vertical search, such as cars, jobs, real estate, and airline tickets, there are thousands of sites with possibly relevant content. Even after restricting to sites that are relevant to a particular metropolitan area, there may be several tens of relevant sites — too many to browse manually. Figure 15.5 illustrates that even for simple domains such as job search, there is

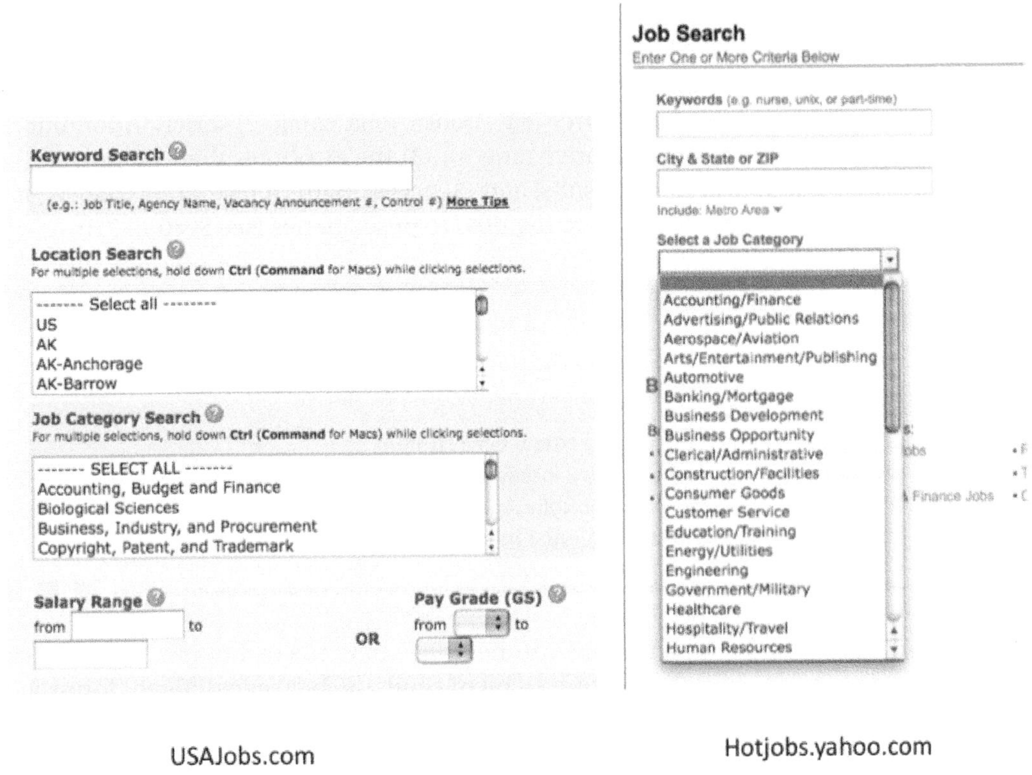

FIGURE 15.5 Two different Web forms for searching job listings.

significant variability between the fields of different forms. Hence, a vertical-search engine needs to resolve heterogeneity. As such, vertical-search engines are a specialization of virtual data integration systems as we have described in earlier chapters. We consider each of their components in turn.

MEDIATED SCHEMA

The mediated schema of a vertical-search engine models the important properties of the objects under consideration. Some of the attributes in the mediated schema will be *input attributes* and will appear in the form that the users access. Other attributes will be *output attributes* and will only be seen in the search results pages. For example, a mediated schema for job search that integrates data from the two sources shown in Figure 15.5 would include the attributes shown in the form, such as category, keywordDescription, city, state, and the attributes openingDate and employingAgency that are only shown with the results. Note that in some cases, the attributes shown on the form may be minimum and maximum values for attributes of the schema (e.g., minPay).

SOURCE DESCRIPTIONS

The source descriptions in a vertical-search engine are also relatively simple because logically the sources expose a single relation. Hence, the main components of the source descriptions are (1) contents of the source (e.g., books, jobs, cars), (2) selection conditions (e.g., relevant geographical location, price ranges), (3) the attributes that can be queried on, (4) attributes that appear in the results, and (5) access-pattern restrictions, i.e., which input fields, or combinations thereof, are required to pose queries (see Section 3.3).

■ ■ ■ ▬▬▬▬▬▬▬▬▬▬▬▬▬▬▬▬▬▬▬▬▬▬▬▬▬▬▬▬▬

Example 15.1

A source description for the USAJobs.com site shown in Figure 15.5 would look as follows:

Contents:	jobs
Constraints:	employer = USA Federal Government
Query attributes:	keywords, category, location, salaryRange, payGrade
Output attributes:	openingData, employingAgency
Access restrictions:	at least one field must be given

▬▬▬▬▬▬▬▬▬▬▬▬▬▬▬▬▬▬▬▬▬▬▬▬▬▬ ■ ■ ■

Constructing the source descriptions can be done using the techniques described in Chapter 5. In particular, since there is quite a bit of similarity between different forms in a particular domain, schema matching techniques based on learning from experience (see Section 5.8) are especially effective.

The type of heterogeneity we see on the Web does present some unique challenges to query reformulation. In particular, forms often use drop-down menus to enable the user to make selections. For example, a real estate site may have a drop-down menu specifying the kind of property to search for (single-family home, condo, vacation property, etc.). However, these categories do not always line up with each other easily. For example, in some cities the site may feature the option lakefront property, and there will be no corresponding category in other cities. A similar challenge is dealing with ranges (e.g., price ranges). The ranges of the mediated schema may not map nicely onto ranges in each of the data sources, and therefore the system may need to reformulate a single range into a union of ranges.

WRAPPERS

There are two components to the wrappers of vertical-search engines: (1) posing the query to the underlying site and (2) processing the returned answer. Posing the query is relatively simple. After determining which query needs to be posed on a particular site, the system needs to create the HTTP request that would have been generated if the user posed the appropriate query directly on that site. For sites that use the HTML GET method for querying back-end databases, this amounts to creating a URL that contains the query parameters. For sites using POST, the query parameters need to be sent as part of the HTTP request.

There is an interesting wrinkle here, though, because some sites have more complex interactions. For example, it is common for real estate sites to guide the user through several steps until she can query for houses. In the first step the user will select a state, and in the second step she will select a county from that state. Finally, the third page the user encounters allows her to query for houses in the chosen county. Of course, the goal of the vertical-search engine is to abstract all these details from the user. Hence, if the user poses a query on a particular city, then the system needs to know how to arrive at the appropriate county search page.

In terms of processing the HTML pages returned for queries, we have two main options. We can either present the HTML page to the user as is (with an option of easily navigating between answers from different Web sites), or try to extract structured results from the returned page. The former option is much easier to implement and also has the advantage of being more friendly to the underlying sources. Many Web sites rely on ad revenue to support their operation and would greatly prefer that the vertical-search engine drive traffic to their site. Parsing the results from the answer pages requires applying information extraction techniques (see Chapter 9). However, these techniques typically require training machine learning algorithms per site, making it harder to scale the system up to a large number of sources.

15.2.2 Surfacing the Deep Web

Conceivably, we could follow the approach of building vertical-search engines for each of the thousands of domains that exist on the deep Web. However, such an approach would be impractical for several reasons. First, the human effort to create such a broad schema covering many domains would be prohibitive. In fact, it is not clear that such a schema can be built. In addition to covering many domains, the schema would have to be designed and maintained in over 100 languages and account for subtle cultural variations. Trying to break down the problem into smaller pieces is also tricky, because the boundaries of domains are very loosely defined. For example, starting from the domain of biology, it is easy to drift into medicine, pharmaceuticals, etc. Of course, the cost of building and maintaining source descriptions for millions of sources is also prohibitive. Finally, since we cannot expect users to be familiar with the mediated schema, or even easily find the one domain in which they are interested out of the thousands available, the system must be designed to accept keyword queries in arbitrary structure and on any domain. The problem of deciding whether a keyword query can be reformulated into a structured query in one of these many domains is a challenging and yet-unsolved problem.

A more practical approach to providing access to the full breadth of the deep Web is called *surfacing*. In this approach, the system guesses a relevant set of queries to submit to forms that it finds on the Web. The system submits these queries and receives HTML pages that are then entered into the search-engine index (hence, they become part of the surface Web). At query time, the surfaced pages participate in ranking like any other page in the index.

Except for freeing us from the effort of building a mediated schema and mappings, the main advantage of the surfacing approach is that it leverages the indexing and ranking systems of the search engine, which have become carefully tuned large software systems. The URLs that are stored in the index are the dynamic URLs associated with specific queries on the forms. Hence, when a user clicks on a result that is a surfaced page, she will be directed to a page that is created dynamically at that moment.

The main disadvantage of the surfacing method is that we lose the semantics associated with the page. Suppose we surfaced pages based on filling a form on a patents Web site and entering "chemistry" into the topic field. The word "chemistry" may not appear on some of the resulting pages, and therefore they may not be retrieved for a query asking for "chemistry patents." While this problem may be alleviated by adding the word "chemistry" into the document when it is indexed, it would be impractical to add all of chemistry's subfields (e.g., material science, polymers) or related fields.

Surfacing a deep-Web site requires an algorithm that examines an HTML form and returns a set of relevant and well-formed queries to submit to it. To scale to millions of forms, such an algorithm cannot involve any human intervention. We now describe the two main technical challenges that such an algorithm faces: (1) determining which subsets of fields to use for providing inputs and (2) determining good values to put into text fields.

(1) Determining input combinations: HTML forms typically have more than one input field. Hence, a naive strategy of enumerating the entire Cartesian product of all possible values of all inputs can result in a very large number of queries being posed. Submitting all these queries would drain the resources of the Web crawler and may often pose an unreasonable load on Web servers hosting the HTML forms. Furthermore, when the Cartesian product is very large, it is likely that a large number of the result pages are empty and hence useless from an indexing standpoint. As an example, a particular search form on cars.com has five inputs and a Cartesian product yields over 240 million URLs, though there are fewer than a million cars for sale on cars.com.

A heuristic for choosing input combinations that has proved useful in practice is to look for *informative inputs*. Intuitively, a field f (or a set of fields) in a form is informative if we obtain qualitatively different pages when we vary the values of f and hold all the other values constant. Consider a job search site that has, among others, the input fields state and sort by. Filling in the different values for state would lead to fetching pages that contain jobs in different states and would probably be relatively different from each other. In contrast, filling in the different values for the sort by field would only change the order of the results on the page; the content of the page would remain relatively the same.

Finding good input combinations can be done in a bottom-up fashion. We first consider each of the fields in the form in isolation and determine which ones are informative. We then consider pairs of fields, where at least one of them is informative, and check which pairs are informative. Continuing, we consider sets of three fields that contain an informative pair, and so on. In practice, it turns out that we rarely need to consider combinations that include more than three fields, though we may have to consider a few field combinations for a particular form.

(2) **Generating values for text fields:** When a field is a drop-down menu, the set of values we can provide it is given. For text fields, we need to generate relevant values. The common method of doing so is based on *iterative probing*. Initially, we predict candidate keywords by analyzing the text on pages from the site containing the form page that are available in the index. We test the form with these candidate keywords, and when valid form submissions result, we extract more keywords from the resulting pages. This iterative process continues until either new candidate keywords cannot be extracted or a prespecified target number of words is reached. The set of all candidate keywords can then be pruned to select a smaller subset that ensures diversity of the exposed database contents.

COVERAGE OF THE CRAWL

The surfacing algorithm will get some of the data from the deep-Web site, but does not provide any guarantees as to how much of the site it has covered. In fact, typically we do not know how much data exist in a deep-Web database, so it would be impossible to check if we have it all. In practice it turns out that it suffices to surface some of the content from the deep-Web site, even if it is not complete. With a good enough sample of the site's content, there is a substantial increase in the number of relevant queries that get directed to that site. Moreover, once some of the site is surfaced, the search engine's crawler will discover new deep-Web pages by following links from the surfaced pages. Finally, we note that the surfacing technique is limited to deep-Web sites that are powered by the GET method, not POST. In practice, many sources that accept POST also accept GET requests.

15.3 Topical Portals

A topical portal offers an integrated view of an entire topic. For example, consider a portal that pulls together all the information about researchers in a particular research community. The site would fuse data about individuals in the field, their advisers and students, their respective publications, the conferences and journals in the field, and members of program committees of conferences. As an example, the site can create *superpages* for individuals, as shown in Figure 15.6.

Topical portals are different from vertical-search engines in the type of integration they perform. Conceptually, the data underlying both types of sites are a table. A vertical-search engine integrates *rows* from different sources (i.e., a union of many sites). For example, each deep-Web site contributes a set of job listings, each represented as a row in the table. In contrast, a topical portal integrates *columns* from different sites (i.e., a join of many sites). For example, the column about publications could come from one site, while the column about affiliation would come from another. Hence, somewhat ironically,

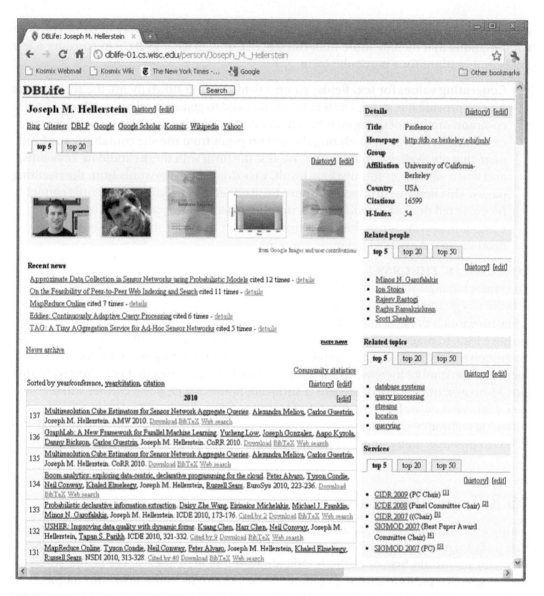

FIGURE 15.6 A superpage created by integrating many sources of information about Joseph M. Hellerstein.

vertical-search engines perform horizontal integration, while portal sites perform vertical integration.

A typical, but somewhat naive, approach to building a topical portal would be the following. First, conduct a *focused crawl* of the Web that looks for pages that are relevant to the topic. To determine whether a page is relevant, the crawl can examine the words on the page, the entities mentioned in it, or links to and from the page. Second, the system would apply a variety of general information extraction techniques (see Chapter 9) to find facts on the pages. For example, the system would try to extract relations such as advisedBy and authoredBy. Finally, given all the facts that were extracted from the pages, the system would put them together into a coherent knowledge base. The main challenge in this step is to reconcile multiple references to the same real-world objects, a topic we discussed in detail in Chapter 7.

A more effective approach to building topical portals relies on the observation that there is a collection of a few sites that provide most of the high-quality information in the domain. Furthermore, these sites are typically known to experts in the field. In our example, the combination of the DBLP[2] Web site, the sites of the top conferences and journals in the field, and the homepages of several hundreds of the top researchers in the field already provide a significant portion of the information about the database research community. Based on this approach, building the site proceeds in two steps.

INITIAL SETUP

We begin by deciding on the main sets of entities and relationships that we want our site to model. In our example, the entity sets may be person, conference, programCommittee, and publication, and the relationships can be authoredBy, advisedBy, and memberOf. We then select an initial set of sources in the domain, denoted by S_{int}.

We create extractors for each of the entity sets and relationships. These extractors will be more accurate than general-purpose extraction algorithms because they are aware of the specific patterns relevant to the relationships they are meant to extract. Therefore, we obtain a seed of accurately extracted entities and relationships. Moreover, if we want even more accurate data, we can tailor the extractors to be aware of the specific structure of particular sites. For example, an extractor that is aware of the DBLP site can yield a very high-quality database of authors and their publications. Another side benefit of this approach is that the problem of reference reconciliation from such sites also tends to be easier because these sites are more careful about maintaining unique naming conventions for individuals.

EXTENDING THE PORTAL

We consider two of the many methods to extend the data coverage of the portal. The first method relies on the heuristic that any important piece of information related to the topic will ultimately appear on one of the sites in S_{int} or on a page that is linked from a page in S_{int}. For example, if a new workshop is being organized on a novel area of database research, it is likely that we will find a pointer to it from one of our core sites. Hence, to extend the portal we monitor the initial collection of sites on a regular basis to expand it by finding new pages that are reachable from these sites.

The second method is based on *collaboration* among the users of the portal site. The portal provides a set of mechanisms that allow the users to correct data and add new data to the system. For example, users can be asked whether two strings refer to the individual or to correct an erroneous extraction. One of the key challenges in providing these mechanisms is to offer incentives for members of the community to collaborate. A simple

---

[2]A well-known site that lists publications in computer science conferences and journals.

kind of incentive is immediate positive feedback: the user should instantly see how his correction improves the site. A second set of incentives is based on publicly recognizing major contributors. Finally, the system must also ensure that it is not easily misled by erroneous or malicious contributions (e.g., from graduate students seeking a premature promotion).

15.4 Lightweight Combination of Web Data

The rich collection of structured data sources on the Web offers many opportunities for ad hoc data integration. For example, consider a coffee enthusiast who wants to compile a list of cafes with their various quality ratings, using data of the type shown in Figures 15.7 and 15.8, or a disaster relief effort where we need to rapidly create an online map displaying shelters with their contact details and respective capacity. Similarly, consider a journalist who wants to add a data visualization to a news story that has a lifetime of a few days. In some scenarios we may integrate only data that are available on the Web, while in others we may integrate Web data with our own private data. Such combinations of data are often called *mashups*, and they have become a common way of providing data services on the Web.

Unlike standard data integration applications where it is expected that many similar queries will be posed against a relatively stable federation of sources for an extended period of time, the kinds of data integration we discuss here may be transient or even "one-off" tasks. The disaster relief mashup will hopefully be needed for only a short amount of time, and the coffee enthusiast may only need the list of cafes during his trip to the area. Hence, the challenge of lightweight data integration on the Web is to radically reduce the time and effort needed to set up the integration. In fact, there should not even be an explicit setup stage — data discovery, collection, cleaning, and analysis should be seamlessly intertwined.

Rank	Name (Sort By Last Update)	Address	Neighborhood	Espresso [info]	Cafe [info]	Overall
1.	Blue Bottle Cafe	66 Mint St.	SOMA	8.60	8.80	8.700
2.	Coffee Bar	1890 Bryant St.	Potrero Hill	8.50	8.50	8.500
3.	Blue Bottle Coffee Co.	315 Linden St.	Hayes Valley	8.40	8.20	8.300
	Blue Bottle Coffee Co.	1 Ferry Building	Embarcadero	8.40	7.80	8.100
	Epicenter Cafe	764 Harrison St.	SOMA	8.40	8.20	8.300
	Ritual Coffee Roasters	1026 Valencia St.	Mission	8.40	8.20	8.300
	Ritual Coffee Roasters	1634 Jerrold Ave.	Bayview	8.40	8.00	8.200
8.	Cafe Capriccio	2200 Mason St.	North Beach	8.30	7.80	8.050
	Gilt Edge Creamery (aka "The Creamery")	685 4th St.	China Basin	8.30	8.00	8.150
10.	Cafe Algiers	50 Beale St. #102	SOMA	8.20	8.00	8.100
	Trouble Coffee	4033 Judah St.	Outer Sunset	8.20	8.20	8.200
12.	Piccino Cafe	807 22nd St.	Dogpatch	8.10	7.80	7.950
13.	Bar Bambino	2931 16th St.	Mission	8.00	7.80	7.900
	Bittersweet - The Chocolate Café	2123 Fillmore St.	Fillmore	8.00	7.50	7.750

FIGURE 15.7 A table of cafe ratings that can be found on an HTML page.

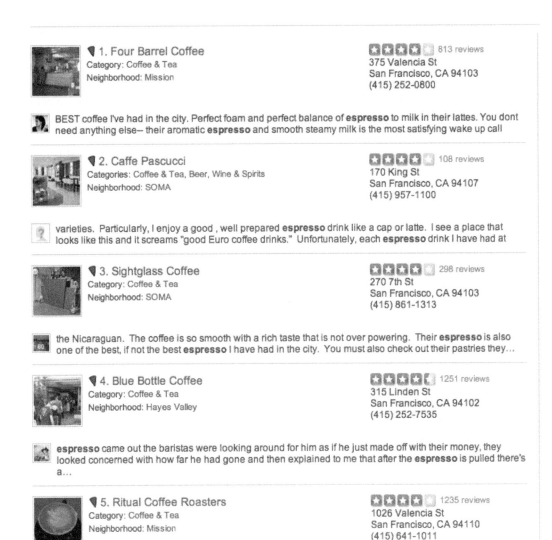

FIGURE 15.8 A list of cafes in San Francisco from yelp.com.

As mentioned earlier, the data integration problem is further complicated by the fact that the data are only partially structured. For example, tables, which constitute one of the main sources of structured data on the Web, have relatively little in the way of schema. We may know the headers of the columns if the first row is clearly marked (as in Figure 15.7), but often it is tricky to decide whether the first row (or rows) is a header row. Other elements of schema, such as the table name or data types, are nonexistent. The relation represented by the table is typically clear from the surrounding text to a person looking at it. Data types can sometimes be inferred by the data itself. Lists on the Web present additional challenges. As shown in Figure 15.9, every item in a list represents an entire row in a table. To convert the list into a table we need to segment each list item into multiple cells, which can be tricky. In addition, lists do not typically have a header row with attribute names.

We divide the data integration challenge into three components: locating the data on the Web, importing the data into a structured workspace, and combining data from multiple sources.

- Daniel Abadi (Yale University, USA)
- Gustavo Alonso (Swiss Federal Institute of Technology, Switzerland)
- Shivnath Babu (Duke University, USA)
- Elisa Bertino (Purdue University, USA)
- Peter Boncz (CWI, Netherlands)
- Nico Bruno (Microsoft Research, USA)
- Barbara Catania (Università di Genova, Italy)
- Chee Yong Chan (National University of Singapore, Singapore)
- Surajit Chaudhuri (Microsoft Research, USA)
- Yi Chen (Arizona State University, USA)
- Lei Chen (Hong Kong University of Science and Technology, China)
- Ming-Syan Chen (National Taiwan University, Taiwan)
- Reynold Cheng (Hong Kong Polytechnic University, China)
- Junghoo Cho (University of California, Los Angeles, USA)
- Nilesh Dalvi (Yahoo! Research, USA)
- Amol Deshpande (University of Maryland, College Park, USA)
- Yanlei Diao (University of Massachusetts Amherst, USA)
- Jens Dittrich (Swiss Federal Institute of Technology, Switzerland)
- Wei Fang (Vienna University of Technology, Austria)
- Christos Faloutsos (Carnegie Mellon University, USA)
- Wenfei Fan (University of Edinburgh, UK)
- Johann-Christoph Freytag (Humboldt University, Germany)
- Floris Geerts (University of Edinburgh, UK)
- Minos Garofalakis (Yahoo! Research, USA)
- Johannes Gehrke (Cornell University, USA)

FIGURE 15.9 An HTML list containing some of the program committee members of VLDB 2008.

15.4.1 Discovering Structured Data on the Web

The first step in data integration is to locate the relevant structured data on the Web. Data discovery typically starts by posing keyword queries, but search engines have been designed to index large collections of text files and turn out to be much less effective at searching for tables or lists. There is no way for the user to specify to the engine that she is interested in structured data. Without special support, the only option available to the user is to tediously scan the search results one by one for those containing structured data.

To support searches specifically for structured data, we need to discover which Web pages contain high-quality structured data and to mark those documents in the Web index (or create a separate repository of these documents). The discovery problem is challenging because many Web page designers use the HTML table construct to format unstructured data content nicely (e.g., forum responses, calendars, table of contents). In fact, less than 1% of the HTML tables on the Web contain high-quality tabular data.

Once we have a corpus of structured data, ranking results needs to consider *where* the keywords in the query match on the page. Two important kinds of hits are on the *header* row and on the *subject* column. Hits on the header row, which presumably includes the attribute names, should be given more weight because the attribute name applies to *all* the rows in the table. For example, if we search for "country olympic medals," then a hit on a column name olympic medals would be more meaningful than other occurrences of the phrase. The majority of tables on the Web have a subject column, which is a column that contains the entities the table is about (e.g., countries). If we search for "population zimbabwe," then a table that contains Zimbabwe in the subject column would be better than one that contains Zimbabwe elsewhere in the table. The latter table may actually be about cities and have a column for their country or may be describing different variants of corn and include a column describing in which countries they are grown. The subject column tends to be closer to the left-hand side of the table (except, of course, for tables in Hebrew and Arabic), but finding it algorithmically (when it exists) can be tricky. Needless to say, like any ranking signal, these are merely heuristics that need to be combined with other signals to arrive at a final ranking. In general, any preprocessing that can recover the semantics of the table, such as phrases describing the sets of objects represented in the table and the relationships modeled in the table will be extremely useful in ranking. In particular, the relationships modeled by a table are notoriously hard to discover. For example, a table describing the coffee production of different countries may have column headers such as name, 2001, 2002, ..., 2010. Deeper analysis is required to infer that the column 2001 describes the coffee production of the country in the name column for 2001.

15.4.2 Importing Data

Once we locate the data, we need to import them into a workspace where the data are put into tabular form and proper column headers are assigned. In some cases, such as the table shown in Figure 15.7, we may be lucky because the structure is nicely reflected in the HTML. However, consider the data shown in Figure 15.8. The data are structured but organized into cards, where each attribute appears in a particular place in the card. Extracting the different parts of each card requires knowledge of the card's internal structure. Similarly, if we import data from a list, we need to segment each list item into a row of cells. We consider two sets of methods for importing data: fully automatic and user supervised.

Fully automatic techniques for extracting data rows from cards or lists consider several aspects of the data, such as punctuation marks, changes in data type, and identifying entities that commonly appear elsewhere on the Web. Note that neither of these cues would work well in isolation, and they may not even suffice when applied together. In Figure 15.9, punctuation will enable separating the name of the program committee member from the affiliation. However, the punctuation within the affiliations is not consistent across the list items. Most of the list items have a comma separating the institution name from the country, but in some cases (e.g., University of California, Los Angeles) there is an additional comma that would confuse the importer. To resolve such ambiguities, an import algorithm can benefit from looking at the entire list as a whole. In our example, by looking at the entire list we can notice that there is always a country name before the right parenthesis, so we can use that signal to align the rest of the affiliations. Another powerful heuristic is to use the appearance of strings in table cells on the Web as a signal that these strings refer to entities. Specifically, if a particular string (e.g., University of California, Los Angeles) appears by itself in many cells of tables on the Web, that is a pretty good signal that it refers to an entity in the world. The wrapper construction techniques discussed in Chapter 9 are often applicable in this context as well.

User-supervised techniques are based on generalizing import patterns that are *demonstrated* by users and bear some resemblance to techniques for training wrappers (Chapter 9.3). Consider the data in Figure 15.8. The user would begin by selecting "Four Barrel Coffee" and pasting it into the leftmost cell of the workspace. The system would attempt to generalize from this example and propose other cafe names, such as Sightglass and Ritual. By doing so, the system will propose additional data rows. Next, the user will select the address of Four Barrel Coffee and paste it into the second column, to the right of the name. Similarly, she will copy and paste the phone number into the third column and the number of reviews into the fourth. The system will generalize from these examples and will fill in the other rows in the table with the corresponding data.

COLUMN HEADERS

After importing the data into a table, we need to propose headers for the columns of the resulting table if they do not already exist in the data. In some cases, such as phone numbers or addresses, it is possible to analyze the values in a column and propose a header. In other cases, we may consult a repository of tables that do have column headers. To find a header for a column C, we search for columns C' that have significant overlap of values with C and choose the most common column header among that set. For example, in the list shown in Figure 15.9, we can propose the column header country for the last column after noticing that it has high overlap with other columns with the same column header.

Another technique for proposing headers is to mine the Web for particular text patterns. For example, phrases of the form "countries such as France, Italy, and Spain" will appear very frequently on the Web. From this sentence we will be able to mine with high degree of confidence that France is a country. Using the same technique we will be able to derive that France is a European country and even a Western European country. If the same class (e.g., country) applies to a majority of the values in a particular column, we can propose the class as a label for the column. In general, we want to attach to the column any label that will help to retrieve it in response to relevant queries.

15.4.3 Combining Multiple Data Sets

Once we have the data, there are two challenges in combining multiple data sources. Since the collection of data sources is huge, the first challenge is to find *what* to combine your data with. Since the data are not always completely structured, the second challenge is to specify *how* to combine the data.

To find related data, we can consider two cases: adding more rows by union or adding more columns by join. To add more rows to a table T, the system needs to find tables that have the same columns as T, even if the column headers do not match up exactly. To find more columns, the system first needs to find the interesting join columns in T, and then find other tables that have a column that overlaps with the join column. For example, to find tables that join with the coffee data in Figure 15.7, the system would first postulate that the column with cafe names is a likely join column, and then search for tables that have overlapping values.

To specify how to join the data, we can employ the principle of demonstration by example again. Consider the task of joining the coffee data in Figure 15.7 with the data in Figure 15.8 after they have been imported. The user would highlight the cell with the value "Ritual Coffee" in the table created from Figure 15.7 and drag it onto the corresponding cell created for the data in Figure 15.8. By doing so, the user has told the system which columns she wishes to join. The user can also drag other columns of the row of Ritual Coffee into the appropriate row in the table to specify which columns should be kept in the joined table. The system can generalize from this example and apply the same process to other rows.

15.4.4 Reusing the Work of Others

As we consider data integration tasks on the Web, it is important to keep in mind that many people are trying to access the *same* data sources and perform similar, if not identical, tasks. If we can leverage the collective work of many people, we can develop very powerful techniques for managing structured data on the Web. For example, when a person makes the effort to extract a structured data set from a Web page and import it into a spreadsheet or database, we can use that as a signal that the data set is a valuable one and record the spreadsheet name and column headers she gave in the spreadsheet. When someone manually combines two data sets, we can infer that the two sources are related to each other and that the pair of columns used for the join are from the same domain, even if they are not identical. When someone transforms an HTML list into a table, that effort can also be recorded for future uses even if the data change a bit over time. The same transformation may be applicable to other lists on the Web with similar characteristics. Of course, the key to enabling these heuristics is to record actions across a large number of users, while being sensitive to privacy concerns. Cloud-based tools for data management have the potential for providing such services since they log the activities of many users.

15.5 Pay-as-You-Go Data Management

Data integration on the Web is an extreme example motivating pay-as-you-go data management. In contrast to the kinds of data integration systems described thus far in the book, pay-as-you-go systems try to avoid the need for the initial setup phase that includes creating the mediated schema and source descriptions. Instead, the goal is to offer a system that provides useful services on a collection of heterogeneous data with very little up-front effort. The following example illustrates a different kind of motivating scenario.

■ ■ ■ ▬▬▬

Example 15.2

Consider an example of a nonprofit organization trying to collect data about the world's water resources. Initially, the engineers at the organization will be handed a collection of data sources (typically in the form of spreadsheets or CSV files). There are several challenges they need to face. First, they will be unfamiliar with the data. They will not know all the terminology used to collect data about water, nor will they know the contents of the data sources and the relationships between them. Second, some of the sources may be redundant, out of date, or subsumed by others and therefore not of much use.

Hence, the first step in creating a data integration application is to explore the data in a rather unstructured fashion. The mediated schema can only be created after they have some familiarity with the data. They will only create semantic mappings to the select set of data sources they deem useful. Of course, they will also spend significant effort to clean the data and reconcile references where needed.

▬▬▬ ■ ■ ■

The above scenario is very typical in domains where data have been collected by independent experts who want to start collaborating. The key observation is that requiring the engineers to put all the effort of setting up the data integration system up front may not be practical or even possible. Instead, the system should enable the engineers to only invest the effort where the return on the investment is clear, while still providing value even when all the sources are not integrated.

Dataspace systems have been proposed as a concept for supporting pay-as-you-go data management systems. Broadly, there are two main components to such a system:

bootstrapping the system with useful services with no or little human intervention and guiding the user to improve the semantic coherence over time.

For the first component, providing keyword search over a collection of data coupled with effective data visualization is already a useful step. Going further, dataspace systems can employ the techniques we described for automatic schema matching, clustering of data sources, and automatic extraction of metadata.

For the second component the challenge is to channel the attention of the users to opportunities for improving the metadata in the system. Improvements to metadata could be to validate schema mappings, spend some effort on reference reconciliation, or improve the results of information extraction. As we described earlier, reusing the work of others and crowdsourcing some tasks are two powerful methods that can be employed here. Some of these ideas are discussed in the next chapter.

Bibliographic Notes

The Web has been one of the main driving forces behind research on data integration. In fact, the inspiration behind the initial work of the authors of this book was Web data integration [181, 323, 381]. A survey on data integration and management in the early days of the Web is given in [229]. Some of the early research prototypes that attempted to integrate information from deep-Web sources are [37, 199, 244, 361, 381], and more recent work in this area is described in [294, 296, 297, 581]. Junglee and Netbot were two early startups in the area of vertical search, focusing on job search and integrating data from shopping sites. Later, vertical-search engines appeared in other commercially viable domains, such as airline tickets and other categories of classified ads.

Several papers have offered estimates of the size of the deep Web [70, 409]. In [163] the authors describe methods for estimating the size of a given database on the hidden Web. The work we described on surfacing the deep Web is based on the surfacing in the Google search engine [410]. According to [410], their system was able to surface pages from millions of forms, from hundreds of domains, and in over 40 languages. The pages it surfaced were served in the top-10 results for over 1000 queries per second on the Google search engine at the time of writing. One of the main lessons learned from that work is that deep-Web content was especially helpful for long-tail queries rather than the most popular ones, for which there was sufficient data on the surface Web. Earlier work on iterative probing, one of the techniques used for surfacing Web pages, includes [55, 106, 321, 467]. Relatedly, in [550] the authors describe a technique that takes text as input and decides how to use the text to fill the fields of an HTML form.

The investigation of tables on the Web began with the works of [247, 565]. The first investigation of the entire collection of HTML tables on the Web was described in [101, 102]. That work showed that there are over 150 million high-quality HTML tables on the Web, even when restricting attention content to English. The authors collected these tables into a corpus and built a search engine that incorporated some of the ranking methods we described in this chapter. They also showed that the collection of schemas of these tables is a unique resource. For example, synonyms for column headers on the Web can be mined from this collection and used as a component of schema matching. Subsequent work on tables tried to recover the semantics of the tables. In [391] the authors describe an algorithm that maps cells in the table to objects in the YAGO ontology, while proposing categories in YAGO for the columns and binary relations for pairs of columns in the table. In [558] the authors describe a technique that mines phrases on the Web that mention values in table cells (as described in Section 15.4.2) to guess labels for columns and relationships for pairs of columns. Techniques for segmenting HTML lists into tables are described in [207].

Querying large collections of tables presents new challenges. On the one hand, users should be able to specify queries with structure, as they would do in a database system. On the other hand, users cannot be expected to know the schemas of millions of tables, and therefore keyword queries are more appropriate. In [483] the authors propose a query language that allows the user to specify some structure in the query but still have the benefit of using keyword queries. In [509] the authors describe a method of annotating keyword queries with mappings to tables in a corpus. The query annotator is created by learning from a query log and a collection of tables. When a new query arrives, the annotator is able to efficiently propose possible annotations, each with a confidence score. In [413] the authors describe techniques for clustering large collections of schemas into domains based on attribute names in tables.

DBLife [170, 185] introduced the methodology we described for creating topical portals. In [170] the authors show that it is beneficial to start from a few select sites rather than crawl the Web looking for any site relevant to the topic. Earlier topical sites include [356, 417, 461]. As we discussed, topical portals present an opportunity for members of the community to contribute content to the portal and improve its content, in a crowdsourcing fashion. Methods for enticing individuals to contribute content are described in [422]. Techniques to allow both algorithms and humans to contribute to building structured portals are described in [113, 169, 421].

The problem of building and maintaining product catalogs for shopping sites is clearly of major commercial interest. Building such a catalog is challenging because the taxonomy of products is very broad and products are often distinguished by tangential properties (e.g., accessories) that make it hard to reconcile references to the same product. In [460] the authors describe a system that takes as input product offerings on the Web and reconciles them against an evolving product taxomomy.

Several tools have been proposed to help users create mashups easily [194, 314–316, 553, 577]. The approach of demonstrating data import and integration is based on the Karma and CopyCat systems [327, 553]. CopyCat also advocated not separating between the setup phase and querying phase of data integration.

Google Fusion Tables [261] is a cloud-based system that facilitates integration of data on the Web. Users of Fusion Tables can upload data sets (e.g., CSV files or spreadsheets) and share them with collaborators or make them public. They can easily create visualizations that can be embedded on Web pages and merge data sets that others have made public. Fusion Tables and tools like it (e.g., Tableau Software [536], Socrata [527], InfoChimps [317]) are being used by individuals who have relatively little technical skills but want to make data available to the public. In particular, journalists have been using Fusion Tables quite aggressively to add data and interactive visualizations to their news stories.

One of the challenges when dealing with data on the Web is that data are often copied from one source to another. Hence, seeing a particular data fact on many sites does not necessarily indicate independent sources of validity. The Solomon Project [79, 190] developed techniques for detecting copying relationships between sources, thereby finding the true number of independent occurrences of facts. Redundancy on the Web can also be a benefit. The work of [473] develops wrappers for Web sites that expose structured content by relying on the fact that (1) each site publishes many pages with the same templates and (2) many objects are described on multiple sites. Hence, accurate wrappers that are created for one site can be used to improve the accuracy of sites with overlapping content.

The vision for dataspace systems was described in [233, 286] as a new abstraction around which to unify many strands of database research. Some of the early dataspace systems were outgrowths of systems for personal information management [91, 191, 504]. In [333] the authors describe a decision-theoretic framework for improving a dataspace with time. In particular, they show how to use decision theory to select the most beneficial question that can be posed to a human to improve the semantic relationships in a dataspace. The decision is based on the utility that the answer has on improving the quality of results returned by the system.

In [162] the authors show how to bootstrap a dataspace system by automatically creating a mediated schema for a given set of sources and then computing approximate schema mappings between the mediated schema and the sources. They show that it is beneficial to create a *probabilistic mediated schema* in the bootstrapping process, which is a set of alternative mediated schemas, each with an associated probability. A keyword query is then reformulated on each of the individual mediated schemas, and the probabilities of the answers are computed by further weighing the probability of each mediated schema.

A recent body of work attempts to build knowledge bases from the Web. For example, mining the Web for linguistic patterns of the form "X such as Y and Z" (known as Hearst patterns [299]) can yield a database of pairs (X, Y) where X is an instance of Y. For example, by seeing patterns like "cities such as Berlin, Paris, and London" on the Web we can infer that Berlin, Paris, and London are cities and even European capitals. Mirroring the broad scope of content on the Web, such knowledge bases cover many domains at fine granularity, but may also contain many incorrect facts. Furthermore, the coverage of such a knowledge base is very *culturally aware:* Berlin, Paris, and London can also be found to be instances of Important European Capitals.

Building such knowledge bases can often significantly benefit from crowdsourcing. See [186] for a survey of work in this area up to 2011.

Open information extraction (OpenIE), pioneered by the TextRunner System [54], is a set of techniques for mining (typically binary) relations between entities without specifying ahead of time the relation or set of relations to be extracted. For example, OpenIE techniques can extract facts such as *Einstein bornIn Ulm* or *Google headquarteredIn Mountain View*. OpenIE systems extract both the relation name and its two arguments using self-supervised machine learning techniques that use heuristics to generate labeled data for training the extractor. For example, TextRunner uses a small set of handwritten rules to heuristically label training examples from sentences in the Penn Treebank. The Nell system [110] demonstrates an architecture for continuously learning many classifiers at once from primarily unlabeled data, coupling the learning of these classifiers in order to improve accuracy. Additional work in this area includes [303, 580].

A second approach to building knowledge bases from the Web is to expand Wikipedia, which itself was created by contributions of many. The YAGO system [534] extends the Wordnet ontology [431] with facts extracted from Wikipedia and has very high precision. The set of binary relationships in YAGO is defined in advance and relatively small. In [578] the authors describe the Kylin system, which leverages the infoboxes in Wikipedia, the set of facts shown on many Wikipedia pages. Kylin uses these facts as training data for learning how to extract additional facts from Wikipedia pages, thereby considerably increasing the coverage of infoboxes in Wikipedia. In [579] they show how to extend the ontology of Wikipedia. In [435] the authors use pairs of entities related in the Freebase ontology and find all the patterns in text (in Wikipedia) that relate these pairs. From these patterns in text, their system learns how to extract additional pairs of the same relation. DBPedia [42] extracts the infoboxes in Wikipedia into a structured form for querying.

16

Keyword Search:
Integration on Demand

Traditionally, data integration is used to either build applications (whether Web-based or more traditional) that provide cross-source information access or to build ad hoc query interfaces for data exploration by relatively sophisticated users. However, a more recent focus has been to enable "average" (non-database-expert) users to pose ad hoc queries over structured, integrated data via a familiar interface: keyword search. However, keyword search in this model is a good deal more complex than in a typical information retrieval system or search engine: it does not merely match against single documents or objects. Intuitively, the set of keyword terms describes a set of concepts in which the user is interested. The data integration system is tasked with the job of finding a way of relating the tables or tuples relating to these concepts, e.g., through a series of joins.

In this chapter, we first describe the abstract problem of keyword search over structured data in Section 16.1, then some popular algorithms for returning ranked results in Section 16.2. Finally, we describe some of the issues in implementing keyword search over data integration applications in Section 16.3.

16.1 Keyword Search over Structured Data

In information retrieval, keyword search involves finding a *single* document with matches to all of the keywords. In a relational or XML setting, the goal is typically to find *different* data items matching the different keywords and to return ways these matches can be *combined* to form an answer.

The general approach to answering keyword queries over structured data sources is to represent the databases as a *data graph* relating data and/or metadata items. Nodes represent attribute values and in some cases metadata items such as attribute labels or relations. Directed edges represent conceptual links between the nodes, where the links in a traditional DBMS include foreign key, containment, and "instance-of" relationships.

A query consists of a set of terms. Each term gets matched against the nodes in the graph, and the highest-scoring trees (with leaf nodes matching the search terms) are returned as answers. A variety of scoring or ranking models have been developed, with slightly different semantics and different levels of efficiency of evaluation.

We now describe the data graph, scoring models, and basic algorithms for computing results with top scores in more detail. The basic model and many of the techniques apply equally to a single-database setting or a data integration setting. Moreover, with minor variations the same techniques can be applied not only to relational databases, but also to XML or RDF (or even object, network, or hierarchical) databases.

16.1.1 Data Graph

A variety of different graph representations have been proposed for representing the database(s). In the most general form, we have a graph with weighted nodes and weighted directed edges. Nodes may represent specific attribute values within tuples, composite objects such as sets or XML trees, attribute labels, and even relations. In some cases these nodes may be annotated with weights representing authoritativeness, trust, etc.

Directed edges in the graph model the relationships among nodes. Some examples include containment of a value node within a node representing a collection or a tuple; "instance-of" relationships between a label and a data value; foreign key-to-key references; or even relationships based on similarity. In general, these directed edges may also be weighted, indicating the strength of the relationship.

Note that this graph is typically a logical construct used for defining the semantics of query answering; for efficiency reasons it is generally computed lazily.

■ ■ ■ ▬▬▬▬▬▬▬▬▬▬▬▬▬▬▬▬▬▬▬▬▬▬▬

Example 16.1

An example of a data graph that includes schema components appears in Figure 16.1. This graph represents an excerpt of a bioinformatics setting with four tables (focusing on gene-related terms, protein-related entries, and protein-related publications), indicated as rounded

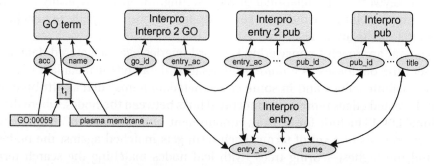

FIGURE 16.1 Example schema/data graph for a set of relations in the bioinformatics domain. This example includes nodes representing relations (rounded rectangles), attribute labels (ellipses), tuples (t_1), and attribute values (rectangles); and edges representing membership (small directed arrows) as well as foreign key or predicted cross-reference (bidirectional arrows).

rectangles. We show the attribute labels for each table (ellipses), member tuples (rectangles such as node t_1), and attribute values (rectangles with text labels). Edges in this example include foreign keys (shown as bidirectional thick arrows), as well as membership (small directed arrows). In many settings, both edges and nodes might be annotated with weights.

■ ■ ■

A natural question is how to set the weights in a data graph. In general, the weights on data or metadata nodes represent authoritativeness, reliability, accuracy, or trustworthiness. Typically the weights on edges represent similarity or relatedness.

Node weights are generally assigned using one of three approaches:

- **Graph random-walk algorithms.** Inspired by link analysis algorithms such as PageRank, some systems look at the edge connectivity in the graph to assign a score to each node. A popular algorithm here is called ObjectRank, which is a modification of PageRank to a linked-object setting.
- **Voting or expert rating.** In certain settings, especially in scientific data sharing, there may be an advisory board who assigns scores to certain nodes. Alternatively, it is possible to have the entire user community vote on authoritativeness.
- **Query answer-based feedback.** Later in this chapter we discuss an approach whereby the system takes feedback on the quality of specific *query results* to learn authoritativeness assignments to nodes.

In a single-database context, edge weights are typically assigned based on known relationships such as integrity constraints (specifically foreign keys). In the more general data integration setting, edges may need to be inferred, as we discuss in Section 16.3.

16.1.2 Keyword Matching and Scoring Models

Given a set of keyword terms and a data graph, a keyword search system will match each keyword against nodes in the graph and compute a similarity score or weight. We can model this as adding a node for each keyword into the graph, and then adding weighted edges to each (possibly approximately) matching node in the data graph.

■ ■ ■

Example 16.2

Figure 16.2 shows an example of a *query graph* where nodes and similarity edges have been added into the data graph of Figure 16.1. The keyword nodes are represented in italics, with dashed directed edges to the matching nodes in the data graph. In general, each keyword node may have edges going to multiple nodes in the data graph, and each edge might be annotated with a similarity score or other weight.

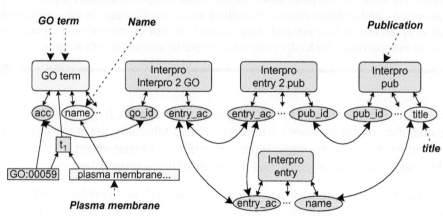

FIGURE 16.2 Example of matching keywords against the schema/data graph.

■ ■ ■

Under this model, the actual query processing computation finds the sets of trees from the data graph — with keyword nodes as leaf nodes — and returns the top-scoring trees. We describe two of the more popular scoring models next.

SCORE AS SUM OF WEIGHTS IN THE QUERY TREE

One popular approach is to assume that the weights within the tree, including the weights on edges between keyword nodes and data or metadata nodes, are effectively costs or prestige scores, where higher values represent greater distance or less value. This model has a probabilistic interpretation: if each weight represents the negative log likelihood of the probability of its correctness and/or relevance, then the sum of the weights of all of the edges in the tree represents the overall negative log likelihood of tree's correctness or relevance, under an assumption of probabilistic independence. If we only have weights on the edges, then the k highest scoring Steiner trees in the graph represent the k best answers. (A Steiner tree is a tree whose edge weights sum to the smallest value, which connects a designated set of leaf nodes.)

If nodes do have weights, then one option is to simply "convert" these into edge weights in a modified graph, as follows: take each weighted node n_i and split it into nodes n_i and n'_i, then add an edge from n_i to n'_i with weight equal to the original $weight(n_i)$ times some scale factor α. Then, as before, a Steiner tree algorithm run over the modified graph will return the top answers.

In certain situations, the query tree is considered to have a *root* (which takes into account the directionality of the edges), and the root may itself be given a score that needs to be scaled and added to the tree score. Again, this can be incorporated into the Steiner tree algorithm: add one additional leaf node R to the modified graph and an edge between

R and each potential root node, with a weight equal to the score the node would receive as root. Then add node *R* to the set of leaf nodes in the Steiner tree.

SCORE AS SUM OF ROOT-LEAF COSTS
The previous scoring model takes into account sharing among edges: each edge's weight is only counted once. Moreover, a root node may be shared across multiple result trees. An alternative scoring model assumes that there should only be one answer per candidate root node and that the score of a tree rooted at node *R* should be based on the sum of the costs of the shortest paths between *R* and the closest node matching each keyword term. Under this model, shared edges are counted multiple times, but there is a computational advantage that each path can be computed separately. As with the previous model, it is straightforward to also incorporate weights on the graph nodes and an additional weight assignment when a node becomes the root.

16.2 Computing Ranked Results

Given a method for assigning scores to possible matches of a keyword query against a data graph, the next challenge is to compute the top-k-ranking answers. Computing top-k answers is a heavily studied topic in the database research literature, so new techniques continue to be developed. We briefly sketch some of the common techniques used here and refer the reader to the bibliographic references for a more comprehensive treatment.

16.2.1 Graph Expansion Algorithms

As described previously, a query result in the keyword search setting is derived from a Steiner tree over a graph. In some systems, the graph represents the entire database and the Steiner tree is itself an answer. In other systems, the Steiner tree is over the schema (or a combination of schema and data), and thus the tree represents a particular join query to be executed. In either case, Steiner tree computation is an NP-hard problem, hence it is not feasible to use exact Steiner tree algorithms to compute top-scoring results over a large graph.

Instead, the most popular means of computing answers is that of heuristics-based graph expansion, which generally consists of finding a spanning tree and then iteratively refining it. Often the assumption is that the data are to be returned as a tree with a root: this tree's structure is based on the directionality of key-foreign key relationships.

BACKWARDS EXPANSION
One popular scheme, called *backwards expansion*, is to build a complete graph over the terminal (leaf) nodes as follows. Match the search keywords against the set of nodes using an inverted index or similar structure: each match becomes a leaf node. From each such leaf node, create a cluster for the single-source shortest path and populate it with the leaf node. Expand each cluster by following foreign-key edges backwards from existing nodes

in the cluster, according to a lowest-cost-first strategy (using any of the cost models of Section 16.1). Ultimately, the clusters will intersect, meaning that the algorithm has found intersecting paths forming a spanning tree. Such paths can be returned in increasing order of cost.

BIDIRECTIONAL EXPANSION

Sometimes backward expansion can be very expensive, especially if most nodes have high degree, so *bidirectional expansion* refines this. Here, the expansion of clusters is done in a prioritized way. It can be performed in the forward direction from candidate root nodes, as well as through backwards expansion from the leaves. Bidirectional expansion uses a heuristic called *spreading activation*, which prioritizes nodes of low degree and edges with low weights.

COST-BASED BACKWARDS EXPANSION

This technique improves on backwards expansion but requires a cost model where the score is a sum of root-leaf costs as opposed to a sum of edge weights in the query tree (see Section 16.1, and recall that the former model will "double-count" edges shared by shortest paths between the root and multiple leaf nodes). As before, exploration is done in terms of clusters that orginate from leaf nodes. The choice of which cluster to expand next depends on the cardinality of the cluster: the cluster with the fewest items is the one to be expanded, and the nearest node to the cluster (by the cost model) is added to that cluster. The algorithm's running times are further improved by partitioning the graph into blocks and preindexing each block.

Generally, the nodes in the graph represent values or tuples within relational tables, and multiple rows within the same table may match the same keyword. Thus it is often advantageous to "batch" the computation of results as a series of select-project-join queries to compute sets of partial results simultaneously. Such subresults are typically termed *candidate networks*. Results from candidate networks are typically combined using threshold-based merging techniques, discussed next.

16.2.2 Threshold-Based Merging

A key technique in providing the top-scoring query answers — so-called top-k query processing — is that of merging several streams of partial results. Most of the algorithms for doing this are derived from the Threshold Algorithm (TA).

In our context, the goal is to rank a set of tuples where the score of every tuple is computed as a function of multiple base scores. For example, we may be ranking restaurants based on a combined score of their rating and their price range.

For each of the base scoring functions x_i, we have an index L_i through which we can access the tuples in nonincreasing order of the value of x_i. Furthermore, the combined scoring function $t(x_1, \ldots, x_m)$ is monotone, i.e., $t(x_1, \ldots, x_m) \le t(x'_1, \ldots, x'_m)$ whenever $x_i \le x'_i$ for every i. Moreover, assume that given a value of x_i for the ith index, we can access all the tuples that contain x_i via random access.

As its name suggests, the Threshold Algorithm is based on the notion of the threshold, which refers to the maximum score of any tuple we have not yet encountered by reading from the various indices. Once we have encountered k tuples whose scores are higher than the threshold, we know that we do not need to read further to return the top-k-scoring answers. At initialization the threshold is set to a maximum value. Each time we read a tuple from one of the indices L_i, this either keeps the threshold the same (if x_i is the same as in the previous tuple read from L_i) or lowers it (if x_i is smaller).

In this context, the Threshold Algorithm can be expressed as follows.

1. In parallel, read each of the m indices $L_1, \ldots, L_m$. As a tuple R is retrieved from one of the lists, do random access and any required joins to produce the set of tuples $\mathcal{R}$ that have the same value for x_i on R. For each $R' \in \mathcal{R}$, compute the score $t(R')$. If R' is one of the k highest combined scores we have seen, then remember R' and $t(R')$ (breaking ties arbitrarily).

2. For each index L_i, let $\underline{x_i}$ be the lowest value of x_i sequentially read from the index. Define a *threshold value* τ to be $t(\underline{x_1}, \underline{x_2}, \ldots, \underline{x_m})$. Note that none of the tuples that have not been seen by the algorithm yet can have a combined score of more than τ. While we have not seen k objects whose score is at least equal to τ, the algorithm continues reading from the indices (and as a result, τ will decrease). Once k objects have been seen whose score is at least equal to τ, halt and return the k highest-scoring tuples that have been remembered.

We can see this more formally specified in Algorithm 14.

Algorithm 14. Threshold Algorithm (TA)

Input: table-valued input T; indices over T, each in descending order of associated score attribute x_i: $L_1 \ldots L_i \ldots L_m$; number of tuples k; cost function t. **Output**: top-k answers.

    Create priority queue Q of size k

    repeat

        for all $i := 1 \ldots m$ in parallel **do**

            Read $R_i :=$ next entry in index L_i

            Let $\underline{x_i}$ be the value of the scoring attribute for R_i

            Let $\mathcal{T}_i := retrieve(R_i)$

            {Retrieve tuples from T indexed by R_i}

            for all $T_i \in \mathcal{T}_i$ **do**

                Compute score $t(T_i)$

                Enqueue T_i into Q; if Q is already full, discard lowest-scoring result, which might be T_i

            end for

        end for

        Set threshold $\tau = t(\underline{x_1}, \ldots, \underline{x_m})$

    until k tuples in Q score above τ

    Dequeue and output all elements of Q

Many variations of this core algorithm have been proposed, including approximation algorithms and algorithms that do not require random access over the source data (if joins are not required). Moreover, a wide variety of "ranked join" algorithms have been developed using the core ideas of the Threshold Algorithm.

■ ■ ■ ▬▬▬▬▬▬▬▬▬▬▬▬▬▬▬▬▬▬▬▬▬▬▬▬▬▬▬▬▬▬▬▬▬▬

Example 16.3

Suppose we are given a relation *Restaurants* with two scoring attributes, *rating* and *price*, as shown in Table 16.1. Each restaurant (we shall use its name as its ID) has a rating on a scale of 1 to 5 (where 5 is better) and a price on a scale of 1 to 5 (where 5 is most expensive).

Now assume a user wants to find the most promising restaurants and has decided that the rating should be based on a scoring function $score \cdot 0.5 + (5 - price) \cdot 0.5$. If we wish to use the Threshold Algorithm to efficiently retrieve the top three restaurants, we would proceed as follows. First, construct two indices over the table, as shown in Table 16.2: one index is based on the ratings, in decreasing order; the other index is based on the value $(5 - price)$, also in decreasing order.

Table 16.1   Example Restaurants, Rated and Priced

Name	Location	Rating	Price
Alma de Cuba	1523 Walnut St.	4	3
Moshulu	401 S. Columbus Blvd.	4	4
Sotto Varalli	231 S. Broad St.	3.5	3
McGillin's	1310 Drury St.	4	2
Di Nardo's Seafood	312 Race St.	3	2

Table 16.2   Score Attribute Indices over Restaurants

Rating	Name
4	Alma de Cuba
4	Moshulu
4	McGillin's
3.5	Sotto Varalli
3	Di Nardo's Seafood

(a) Ratings index

(5 - price)	Name
3	McGillin's
3	Di Nardo's Seafood
2	Alma de Cuba
2	Sotto Varalli
1	Moshulu

(b) Price index

Execution proceeds as follows. We read the top-scoring items in the *ratings* index, resulting in **Alma de Cuba**, and in the *price* index, resulting in **McGillin's**. Retrieving **Alma de Cuba** we compute a score of $4 \cdot 0.5 + 2 \cdot 0.5 = 3$. **McGillin's** receives a score of 3.5. We add these two results to a priority queue, prioritizing according to their scores. We set our threshold value τ to the cost function over the lowest scores read sequentially over the indices: $4 \cdot 0.5 + 3 \cdot 0.5 = 3.5$. Nothing exceeds our threshold, so we must read more values.

Suppose we next read **Moshulu** (score = 2.5) and **Di Nardo's Seafood** (score = 2.5). The threshold still has not changed at this point, so we cannot output any results, but we enqueue these (breaking ties arbitrarily). Next we read **Sotto Varalli** (score = 2.75) from both of the lists and add it to the priority queue, and the threshold gets lowered to 2.75. Now we have three items in the priority queue that all match or exceed 2.75: namely, **Alma de Cuba**, **McGillin's**, and **Sotto Varalli**. We output these and are done.

■ ■ ■

16.3 Keyword Search for Data Integration

Like many topics in data integration, the keyword search problem in this setting builds heavily on techniques applied to single databases. However, data integration exacerbates two challenges:

- In a single database, we can often rely on foreign keys to serve as the only edge types in the data graph. Across databases, we must typically *discover* edges through string matching techniques (Chapter 4) and other approaches resembling those of schema matching (Chapter 5). This may require additional processing to infer possible edges based on the query, and it results in a larger search space of potential query trees. Moreover, some of the inferred edges may in fact be incorrect.
- Across many databases, some sources are likely to represent different viewpoints and be of higher or lower relevance to a given query, based on the user's context and information need. Note that this is somewhat different from the general notion of authoritativeness or data quality, which can often be formulated in a query-independent way.

Hence the work on keyword-driven data integration typically considers how to tractably infer edges and how to use feedback on query results to correct edges or learn source relevance.

16.3.1 Scalable Automatic Edge Inference

Perhaps the most critical issue faced in providing keyword search in a data integration setting is that of discovering potential cross-source joins, such that user queries might integrate data from multiple sources. Unlike in a conventional data integration scenario, there is typically no mediated schema and no schema mappings — hence the search system may need to work directly on the contents of the data sources.

Naturally, keyword-search-based data integration systems typically include a pre-indexing and preprocessing step, whose tasks include indexing search terms, searching for possible semantically meaningful joins that also produce answers, and creating data structures that describe the potential edges in the data graph. There may also be capabilities for incrementally updating the data graph as new sources are discovered.

Conceptually, the task of finding semantically meaningful joins is very close to the problem of schema matching and, more specifically, finding an alignment between attributes in different schemas. The goal is to find attributes that match semantically and in terms of datatypes.

However, there are some key differences that in fact make the problem slightly simpler in this context. In both cases the goal is to find attributes that capture the same semantic concept. However, the join discovery problem is seeking key/foreign-key relationships between conceptually heterogeneous tuples to be joined, whereas the schema matching problem is one of trying to find a transformation that lets us convert tuples into a homogeneous form that can be unioned together. Moreover, in schema matching there is often a problem that the actual data values between a pair of source attributes may be non-overlapping (e.g., because the sources have complementary data that can be unioned together), whereas for join discovery we are only looking for situations in which there is overlap (hence joining on the attributes produces answers).

The task of discovering possible joins can be broken into two subtasks whose results are to be combined: discovering compatible data values and considering semantic compatibility.

DISCOVERING COMPATIBLE DATA VALUES
The first task seeks to identify which attributes come from the same general value domain, in effect clustering by the value domain. A challenge lies in how to do efficient comparisons of data values at scale. One approach is to compute statistical synopses of the values (using hashing, histograms, sketches, etc.) and another is to partition the data values across multiple machines and use parallel processing (map/reduce or alternatives) to compute the ratio of values that overlap.

CONSIDERING SEMANTIC COMPATIBILITY
Sometimes, attributes can have overlapping values without being semantically related (e.g., many attributes may be integer-valued). Here, we would like to consider other sources of evidence for compatibility, e.g., relatedness of attribute names. Such information can be obtained from schema mapping tools.

COMBINING EVIDENCE
The simplest means of combining data value compatability and semantic compatibility is as a weighted sum of the component scores. Alternatively, one can use link analysis techniques from recommendation systems, like label propagation. Specifically, we create a graph encoding of the data-to-data relationships and the metadata-to-metadata relationships and use the label propagation algorithm to combine the results and create a combined prediction of overlap.

16.3.2 Scalable Query Answering

Given a data graph with appropriate weights, there can often be a challenge in computing the top-scoring or top-k query answers: there may be a need to pose large numbers of queries simultaneously. The approaches described in Section 16.2 remain useful here, but the challenge is in how to only execute the work needed. If we have information about the values at the sources, we can often estimate a score range for certain queries or subqueries. Then during the generation and execution of top-k queries, we will only enumerate or execute the subqueries if they are able to contribute to the final answer.

16.3.3 Learning to Adjust Weights on Edges and Nodes

Earlier in this section, we described several means of precomputing weights for the edges and nodes in a data graph. One major issue is that it may be difficult to make correct assignments without involving data or domain experts and seeing how relevant a given source's data are with respect to a particular question. Recent work has shown that it is possible to make weight assignments *at query time* instead of purely during preprocessing. The idea is to provide "most likely" answers to user queries and request that the users (who may often be able to assess the plausibility of a query answer) provide feedback on any answers they know to be good or bad.

The system can then generalize from the feedback using machine learning techniques and will adjust certain "score components" that make up the weights on some of the edges in the data graph. More formally, the process is an instance of so-called *online* or *semi-supervised* learning (learning incrementally based on multiple feedback steps), and the "score components" are called features in the machine learning literature. A given edge in the data graph receives its weight as a particular combination of weighted features, e.g., the weight assigned to an edge between two metadata items may represent a weighted linear combination of (1) Jaccard distance between sets of values for these metadata items, (2) the string edit distance between the labels, or (3) the authoritativeness of the sources of the two metadata items and their values. Observe that some of these features might be specific to the edge between the nodes, and others might be shared with other edge weights (e.g., the source authoritativeness). The right set of features allows the system to generalize feedback on a single answer to other, related answers.

Two technical challenges must be solved in making this approach work.

It Must be Possible to go from Tuple Answers to the Features Forming the Tuple Score
Given a query result tuple, it is vital to be able to identify how and from where the tuple was produced and the individual features and weights that formed the score of the query result. The vector of features and weights, as well as feedback on the correct answers, will be given

to the online learning algorithm. Data provenance (Chapter 14) annotations on the output tuples can provide this capability of looking up feature values from query results.

The Scoring Model and Learning Algorithm Must be Closely Related

There are a wide variety of techniques used for online learning. However, in general it should be the case that the scoring model used to compute ranked results and the learning algorithm are compatible. When the scoring model is based on a weighted linear combination of components (the most popular model used in keyword search over databases), it is possible to use learning algorithms that rely on linear combinations of features, such as the Margin-Infused Ranking Algorithm (MIRA) to make weight adjustments. MIRA takes feedback in the form of constraints over output tuple scores ("the 5th-ranking answer should score higher than the 2nd-ranking answer") and adjusts feature weights to satisfy the constraint.

It has been shown that the learning techniques of this section can effectively address a variety of weight-adjustment problems for keyword-based data integration: learning node weights (e.g., source authoritativeness) across all queries, learning the relevance of nodes and edges to *specific* queries posed with a specific context, and learning the correct similarity score on an edge in the graph, e.g., to "repair" a bad value alignment.

Bibliographic Notes

Keyword search and its relationship to databases and data integration have been studied in a wide variety of ways. Yu, Lu, and Chang [587] provide a recent overview of work in the broader keyword search-over-databases field. Early systems included DISCOVER [304] and DbXplorer [18], which focused on SQL generation for keyword search but used very simple ranking schemes derived from the structure of the query tree itself. SPARK [403] proposed a scoring scheme that was motivated by techniques from information retrieval.

Algorithms for scaling up search over databases remain a key focus. BANKS [80] developed the techniques for backwards graph expansion described in this chapter and adopted a very general tree-based scoring model. A refined version of BANKS developed the more general bidirectional search strategy [337]. BLINKS [298] used the root-to-path-based scoring model described in this chapter and showed that there were complexity bound benefits. The STAR [344] Steiner Tree approximation algorithm exploits an existing taxonomic tree to provide improved performance beyond the methods described in this chapter and even gives an approximation guarantee in this setting. It focuses on supporting keyword search in the YAGO project [534], also discussed in Chapter 15. The work in [51] seeks to scale up keyword search in the DISCOVER system by requiring results to be returned within a time budget, and then to point the user toward a list of other resources for more specialized information, such as query forms matching the keywords [137, 492].

Other work has explored broader sets of operations in the keyword search context. SQAK [540] incorporates aggregation operations. The Précis system [523] developed a semantics that enabled combinations of keywords using Boolean operators. Work on product search [509, 583] has explored taking keyword search terms and expanding them into selection predicates over multiple attributes, for a single table.

One of the major ingredients of keyword search systems is top-k query processing algorithms. Fagin's Threshold Algorithm and numerous variants appear in [221]. There are also a wide variety of approaches to performing joins in a ranked model, including [226, 266, 310, 415, 514, 515]. Since a top-k query should *only* execute to the point where it has generated k answers, specialized techniques [109, 311, 383] have been developed for query optimization in this setting and for estimating how much input actually gets consumed. Techniques have also been developed for storing indices over which top-k queries may be computed, while eliminating the need for random accesses [334]. The work [52] discusses how to build industrial-strength keyword search systems.

In the data integration setting, one task is to identify the domain of the query, and then separate its different components. For example, to answer the query "vietnam coffee production," we would first need to identify that the query is about the coffee domain, then translate it to a query of the form **CoffeeProduction(vietnam)**. We then need to find a table that is relevant to the property **CoffeeProduction** (which is likely to be called something very different in the table) and has a row for Vietnam. Initial work in this topic is described in [167]. The Kite system [512] developed techniques for using synopses to discover join relationships and to iteratively generate queries during top-k computation. The Q system [538, 539] developed the feedback-based learning approach described here. Work by Velegrakis et al. [69] considered the issue of how to perform ranked keyword search when only metadata are available for querying, as in certain data integration scenarios. Several works discussed in Chapter 15 addressed the problem of keyword queries on the collection of HTML tables found on the Web [101, 102, 391].

Naturally, there are connections between search, ranking, and probabilistic data (Chapter 13). Details on the use of probabilistic ranking schemes are provided in [312].

17

Peer-to-Peer Integration

In all the structured query-based data integration and warehousing architectures we have described so far in this book, one must create a mediated schema or centralized database for the domain of the data integration application, before any queries may be posed. This task requires significant modeling, maintenance, and coordination effort among the owners of the data sources. In particular, creating a mediated schema entails that the *scope* of the domain be well defined and that there exists a clearly identifiable schema for it, which is not necessarily true. For example, consider data sharing in a scientific context, where data may involve scientific findings from multiple disciplines, such as genomic data, diagnosis and clinical trial data, bibliographic data, and drug-related and clinical trial data. Each discipline may have its own way of conceptualizing the domain. Hence, attempting to create a single mediated schema that covers all of these topics is likely to fail.

There are an increasing number of scenarios in which owners of data sources want to collaborate, but without any central authority and global standardization. The collaboration may start with two or three data sources wanting to exchange their data, and then it may grow as new data sources become available or as the requirements change. However, the owners of the data might not want to explicitly create a mediated schema that defines the entire scope of the collaboration and a set of terms to which every data source owner needs to map.

These problems of decentralized collaboration have become a recent emphasis in the data integration literature. In this chapter we focus on how one enables decentralized, collaborative querying of data that are of high quality, through a variety of different schemas. Chapter 18, particularly in Section 18.4, builds upon many of these ideas to support scenarios where data are of nonuniform quality and may be subject to updates.

The basic approach of *peer data management systems*, or PDMSs, is to eliminate the reliance on a central, authoritative mediated schema. Rather, each *participant* or *peer* in the system has the ability to define its own schema, both for its source data (*stored relations*) and for integrated querying of the data (*peer relations*). This model is conceptually related to the notion of peer-to-peer computing, in that all participants are peers who provide resources in the form of tuples, schemas, and query processing and who consume resources by posing queries. In the PDMS the participants need not have any broad consensus on an integrated view of the data; rather, they must instead come to a limited number of local (e.g., pairwise) agreements about how to map data from one schema to another. These *peer mappings* define the semantic relationships between peers. A query is always posed with respect to a specific peer's schema, and query answering is recursively reformulated in terms of the schemas of the "neighboring" peers, who can then reformulate it onto their neighbors, and so on — thereby following paths in the network. In this way, local semantic relationships give rise to data sharing among peers farther apart in the network.

The PDMS makes data transformations more local and modular, in that collaborating data sources can create local mappings between pairs (or small sets) of data sources. These mappings can be specialized to the particular collaboration needs the data owners may have. Over time, collaborators can grow these local mappings either by extending the scope of the data they are sharing or by adding new collaborators with data sets. Data sharing proceeds by reformulating queries over these local mappings and by following *mapping paths* to connect far-flung collaborators in the network.

17.1 Peers and Mappings

A PDMS is composed of a set of peers and two kinds of mappings: storage descriptions, which specify how to map source data into the PDMS, and peer mappings, which relate the schemas of different peers. See Figure 17.1 for an example. Each peer in a PDMS has a peer schema that is composed of a set of *peer relations*. The peer schema is the schema

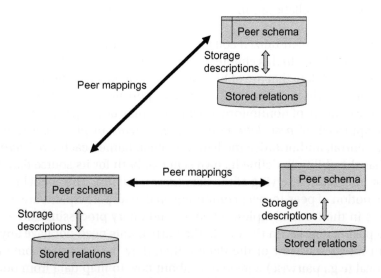

FIGURE 17.1 The structure of a PDMS. Each peer has a peer schema, and peer mappings relate the schemas of multiple peers. The data at each peer are stored in the stored relations, and the storage descriptions are semantic mappings between the stored relations and the peer schema.

that is visible to other peers in the PDMS. Peers typically also have their own data in the form of (instances of) stored relations. The storage descriptions are semantic mappings that relate the schema of the stored relations to the peer schema. The peer mappings are semantic mappings that relate schemas of multiple peers.

Each peer may hide quite a bit of complexity. For example, a peer may be a local data integration system that offers access to multiple sources and exposes the mediated schema to other peers. In some cases, a peer may not have any data and only serve the purpose of mediating among other peers.

A query to a PDMS is posed over the peer schema of one of the peers. In general, each peer relation is "namespaced" or prefixed with a unique identifier corresponding to the peer, making it easy to determine the peer schema. Following this convention, we will name all peer and stored relations in this chapter using a peer-name.relation-name syntax.

A query over a peer schema is reformulated by using the peer mappings and the storage descriptions, and the result of the reformulation is a query that refers only to the stored relations in the PDMS.

■ ■ ■ ━━━

Example 17.1

Figure 17.2 illustrates a PDMS for coordinating emergency response. Relations listed near the rectangles are peer relations, and those listed near the cylinders are stored relations. Lines between peers illustrate that there is a peer mapping between those peers (which we describe in more detail later).

On the left side of the figure, we see a set of peers with data from Oregon. Stored relations containing actual data are provided by the hospitals and fire stations (the FH, LH, PFD, and VFD peers). The two fire services peers (PFD and VFD) can share data because there are mappings between their peer relations. Additionally, the FS peer provides a uniform view of all fire services data, but note that it does not have any data of its own. Similarly, H provides a unified view of hospital data. The 911 Dispatch Center (9DC) peer unites all emergency services data.

On the right side of the figure, we see a set of peers with data from the state of Washington. The power of the PDMS becomes evident when an earthquake occurs: the Earthquake Command Center (ECC) and other related peers from Washington can join the Oregonian system. Once we provide peer mappings between the ECC and the existing 911 Dispatch Center, queries over *either* the 9DC or ECC peers will be able to make use of *all* of the source relations.

━━━ ■ ■ ■

We now formally describe the language we use for storage descriptions and for peer mappings. The language we describe is based on schema mapping languages from Chapter 3 and combines the features of Global-as-View and Local-as-View. In a sense, the language we describe below extends GAV and LAV from a two-tiered architecture that includes sources and a mediated schema to our more general network of peers that can form an arbitrary graph.

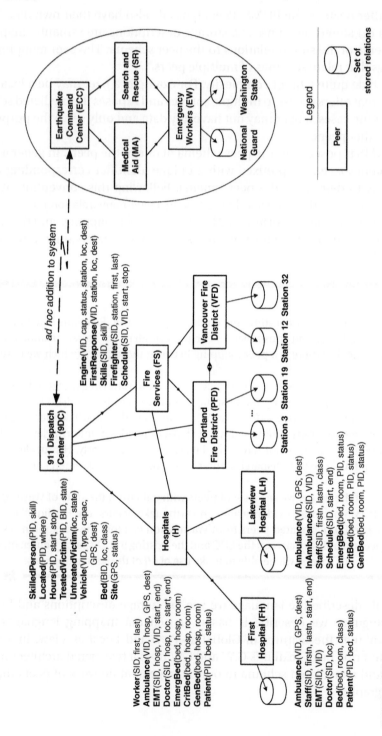

FIGURE 17.2

PDMS for coordinating emergency response in the states of Oregon and Washington. Arrows indicate that there is (at least a partial) mapping between the relations of the peers.

STORAGE DESCRIPTIONS

Each peer contains a (possibly empty) set of storage descriptions that specify which data it actually stores. The storage descriptions are semantic mappings that relate the stored relations with the peer relations. Formally, a storage description for a peer A is of the form

$$A.R = Q \text{ or } A.R \subseteq Q$$

R is a stored relation at peer A, and Q is a query over the peer schema of A. We refer to storage descriptions with $=$ as *equality descriptions* and those with $\subseteq$ as *containment descriptions*. An equality description specifies that A stores in relation R the result of the query Q over its schema, and a containment description specifies that R is a subset of the result of the query Q over its schema, thereby expressing an open-world semantics.

■ ■ ■ ▬▬▬▬▬▬▬▬▬▬▬▬▬▬▬▬▬▬▬▬▬▬▬▬▬▬▬▬▬▬

Example 17.2

An example storage description might relate stored doctor relations at First Hospital to the peer relations.

doc(sid, last, loc) $\subseteq$ FH.Staff(sid, f, last, s, e), FH.Doctor(sid, loc)
sched(sid, s, e) $\subseteq$ FH.Staff(sid, f, last, s, e), FH.Doctor(sid, loc)

▬▬▬▬▬▬▬▬▬▬▬▬▬▬▬▬▬▬▬▬▬▬▬▬▬▬▬▬▬ ■ ■ ■

PEER MAPPINGS

Peer mappings semantically relate the schemas of different peers. We describe two types of peer mappings. The first kind is *equality* and *inclusion* mappings that are similar to GLAV descriptions in data integration. The second kind is *definitional mappings* that are essentially datalog programs.

Equality and inclusion peer mappings have the following forms:

$Q_1(\bar{A}_1) = Q_2(\bar{A}_2)$ (equality mappings)
$Q_1(\bar{A}_1) \subseteq Q_2(\bar{A}_2)$ (inclusion mappings)

where Q_1 and Q_2 are conjunctive queries with the same arity and $\bar{A}_1$ and $\bar{A}_2$ are *sets* of peers. Query Q_1-can refer to any of the peer relations in $\bar{A}_1$ (and the same for Q_2 and $\bar{A}_2$, respectively).

Intuitively, such a mapping states that evaluating Q_1 over the peers $\bar{A}_1$ will always produce the same answer (or a subset in the case of inclusions) as evaluating Q_2 over $\bar{A}_2$. Note that by "evaluating" here we consider data retrieved from other peers as well, not only from the peer being queried.

Definitional mappings are datalog rules whose relations (both head and body) are peer relations. We distinguish definitional mappings for two reasons. First, as we see later, the complexity of answering queries when equality mappings are restricted to being definitional is more attractive than the general case. Second, definitional mappings can easily express disjunction (as we see in the example below), which cannot be done with GLAV mappings.

■ ■ ■ ━━

Example 17.3

We can use the inclusion mappings to specify the Lakeview Hospital peer relations as views over the relations of the peer H that mediates data from multiple hospitals. This is especially convenient in this scenario because the peer H may eventually mediate between many hospitals, and hence LAV-type descriptions are more appropriate.

LH.CritBed(bed, hosp, room, PID, status) ⊆
                    H.CritBed(bed, hosp, room), H.Patient(PID, bed, status)
LH.EmergBed(bed, hosp, room, PID, status) ⊆
                    H.EmergBed(bed, hosp, room), H.Patient(PID, bed, status)
LH.GenBed(bed, hosp, room, PID, status) ⊆
                    H.GenBed(bed, hosp, room), H.Patient(PID, bed, status)

The 911 Dispatch Center's SkilledPerson peer relation, which mediates hospital and fire services relations, may be expressed using the definitional mappings below. The definition specifies that SkilledPerson in the 9DC is obtained by a union over the H and FS schemas.

9DC.SkilledPerson(PID, "Doctor") :- H.Doctor(SID, h, l, s, e)
9DC.SkilledPerson(PID, "EMT") :- H.EMT(SID, h, vid, s, e)
9DC.SkilledPerson(PID, "EMT") :- FS.Schedule(PID, vid),
                    FS.1stResponse(vid, s, l, d), FS.Skills(PID, "medical")

━━ ■ ■ ■

17.2 Semantics of Mappings

We now define the semantics of mappings in PDMS in the same spirit that we defined semantics for mappings in virtual data integration systems. In Section 3.2.1 we defined the set of *certain answers* for a query Q. The certain answers are the ones that hold in *every* instance of the mediated schema that is consistent with the data in the sources.

In the context of PDMS, we look at instances of the peer relations in all the peers instead of looking at instances of the mediated schema. To be a consistent instance, the extensions of the peer relations need to satisfy the peer mappings and storage descriptions with respect to the contents of the stored relations.

Formally, we assume that we are given a PDMS, $\mathcal{P}$, and an instance for the stored relations, D. The instance D assigns a set of tuples, $D(R)$, to every stored relation in $R \in \mathcal{P}$. A *data instance*, I, for a PDMS $\mathcal{P}$ is an assignment of a set of tuples $I(R)$ to each relation in $\mathcal{P}$. Note that I assigns a set of tuples to the peer relations as well as the stored relations. We denote by $Q(I)$ the result of computing the query Q over the instance I.

Intuitively, a data instance *I* is consistent with $\mathcal{P}$ and *D* if it describes *one* possible state of the world (i.e., an extension for the relations in $\mathcal{P}$) that is allowable given *D*, the storage descriptions, and the peer mappings.

Definition 17.1 (Consistent Data Instance). *Let I be a data instance for a PDMS, $\mathcal{P}$, and let D be an instance for the stored relations in $\mathcal{P}$. The instance, I, is said to be consistent with $\mathcal{P}$ and D if*

- *for every storage description $r \in \mathcal{P}$, if r is of the form $A.R = Q_1$ ($A.R \subseteq Q_1$), then $D(R) = Q_1(I)$ ($D(R) \subseteq Q_1(I)$).*
- *for every peer description in $r \in \mathcal{P}$,*
  - *if r is of the form $Q_1(\mathcal{A}_1) = Q_2(\mathcal{A}_2)$, then $Q_1(I) = Q_2(I)$,*
  - *if r is of the form $Q_1(\mathcal{A}_1) \subseteq Q_2(\mathcal{A}_2)$, then $Q_1(I) \subseteq Q_2(I)$,*
  - *if r is a definitional description whose head predicate is p, then let $r_1, \ldots, r_m$ be all the definitional mappings with p in their head, and let $I(r_i)$ be the result of evaluating the body of r_i on the instance I. Then $I(p) = I(r_1) \cup \ldots \cup I(r_m)$.* □

We define the certain answers to be the answers that hold in *every* consistent data instance:

Definition 17.2 (Certain Answers in PDMS). *Let Q be a query over a PDMS $\mathcal{P}$, and let D be an instance of the stored relations of $\mathcal{P}$. A tuple $\bar{a}$ is a certain answer to Q w.r.t. D if $\bar{a} \in Q(I)$ for every data instance that is consistent with $\mathcal{P}$ and D.* □

Note that in the last bullet of Definition 17.1 we did not require that the extension of *p* be the least fixed point model of the datalog rules. However, since we defined certain answers to be those that hold for *every* consistent data instance, we will actually get only the ones that are satisfied in the least fixed point model.

17.3 Complexity of Query Answering in PDMS

We now consider the problem of finding all the certain answers to a query posed on a PDMS. As we will soon see, the complexity of the problem depends on the properties of the mappings. We consider the computational complexity of query answering in terms of the size of the data and the size of the PDMS. One of the important properties in determining the computational complexity is whether the mappings are *cyclic*.

Definition 17.3 (Acyclic Inclusion Peer Mappings). *A set $\mathcal{L}$ of inclusion peer mappings is said to be acyclic if the following directed graph, G, is acyclic.*

The nodes in G are the peer relations mentioned in $\mathcal{L}$. There is an arc in G from the relation R to the relation S if there is a peer mapping in $\mathcal{L}$ of the form $Q_1(\bar{A}_1) \subseteq Q_2(\bar{A}_2)$, where R appears in Q_1 and S appears in Q_2. □

The following theorem characterizes two extreme cases of query answering in PDMS:

Theorem 17.1. *Let P be a PDMS, and let Q be a conjunctive query over P.*

1. *The problem of finding all certain answers to Q is undecidable.*
2. *If P includes only inclusion storage descriptions and peer mappings, and the peer mappings are acyclic, then Q can can be answered in polynomial time in the size of P and the stored relations in P.*   □

The difference in complexity between the first and second statements shows that the presence of cycles is the culprit for achieving efficient query answering in a PDMS. The next section describes a query-answering algorithm that completes in polynomial time when the PDMS satisfies the conditions of the second statement of Theorem 17.1. The proof of the first statement of the theorem is based on a reduction from the implication problem for functional and inclusion dependencies.

It is interesting to note how Theorem 17.1 is an extension of the results concerning GLAV reformulation (Section 3.2.4). The theorem in Section 3.2.4 shows that LAV and GAV reformulation can be combined by applying one level of LAV followed by one level of GAV. Theorem 17.1 implies that under certain conditions, LAV and GAV can be combined an arbitrary number of times.

17.3.1 Cyclic PDMS

Acyclic PDMSs may be too restrictive for practical applications. One case of particular interest is *data replication*: when one peer maintains a copy of the data stored at a different peer. For example, in the example in Figure 17.2, the Earthquake Command Center may wish to replicate the 911 Dispatch Center's Vehicle table for reliability, using an expression such as

$$\text{ECC.vehicle}(vid, t, c, g, d) = \text{9DC.vehicle}(vid, t, c, g, d)$$

To express replication, we need equality descriptions that, in turn, introduce cycles into the PDMS. While, in general, query answering in the presence of cycles is undecidable, it becomes decidable when equalities are projection-free, as in this example. The following theorem shows an important special case where answering queries on a PDMS is tractable even in the presence of cycles in the peer descriptions.

Theorem 17.2. *Let P be a PDMS for which all inclusion peer mappings are acyclic, but which may also contain equality peer mappings. Let Q be a conjunctive query over P. Suppose the following two conditions hold:*

- *whenever a storage description or peer mapping in P is an equality description, it does not contain projections, i.e., all the variables that appear on the left-hand side appear on the right-hand side and vice versa, and*

- *a peer relation that appears in the head of a definitional description does not appear on the right-hand side of any other description.*

Then, finding all certain answers to a Q can be done in polynomial time in the size of the data and the PDMS. □

A further generalization to a specific class of cyclic mappings, called *weakly acyclic* mappings, can also be made using a query reformulation algorithm different from the one presented in this chapter. This is discussed in Section 18.4.

17.3.2 Interpreted Predicates in Peer Mappings

As we saw in Chapter 3, the complexity of answering queries can change if mappings include interpreted predicates. The following theorem characterizes the effect of interpreted predicates on query answering in a PDMS.

Theorem 17.3. *Let $\mathcal{P}$ be a PDMS satisfying the same conditions as the first bullet of Theorem 17.2, and let Q be a conjunctive query over $\mathcal{P}$.*

1. *If interpreted predicates appear only in storage descriptions or in the bodies of definitional mappings, but not in Q, then finding all the certain answers to Q can be done in polynomial time.*
2. *Otherwise, if either the query contains interpreted predicates or interpreted predicates appear in nondefinitional peer mappings, then the problem of deciding whether a tuple $\bar{t}$ is a certain answer to Q is co-NP-complete.* □

17.4 Query Reformulation Algorithm

We now describe an algorithm for query reformulation in PDMSs. The input to the algorithm is a PDMS, $\mathcal{P}$, with its storage descriptions and its peer mappings, and a conjunctive query Q over $\mathcal{P}$. The algorithm outputs a reformulation of Q onto the stored relations in $\mathcal{P}$, i.e., an expression, Q', that refers *only* to stored relations at the peers. To answer Q we need to evaluate Q' over the stored relations, which can be done with the techniques described in Chapter 8.

The algorithm we describe has two properties relating it to our previous discussion on computational complexity. First, the algorithm is sound: evaluating Q' on the stored relations will produce *only* certain answers to Q. Second, the algorithm is complete in the sense that when peer descriptions are acyclic, then evaluating Q' will produce *all* the certain answers to Q.

In the input of the algorithm, we assume that every peer mapping in $\mathcal{P}$ of the form $Q_1 = Q_2$ has been replaced by the pair of mappings $Q_1 \subseteq Q_2$ and $Q_1 \supseteq Q_2$. We also assume that left-hand sides of the inclusion dependencies have a single atom. We can easily achieve that by replacing any description of the form $Q_1 \subseteq Q_2$ by the pair $V \subseteq Q_2$ and $V :\!- Q_1$, where V is a new predicate name that appears nowhere else in the PDMS.

The key challenge in developing the reformulation algorithm is that we need to interleave reformulation of definitional mappings, which require query unfolding (in the style of GAV reformulation), with reformulation of inclusion mappings, which require algorithms for answering queries using views (in the style of LAV reformulation). Before we discuss how to combine these two kinds of reformulation, let us first briefly consider each one in isolation in the PDMS setting.

Consider a PDMS in which all peer mappings are definitional. In this case, a reformulation algorithm is a simple construction of a *rule-goal tree*. A rule-goal tree has *goal nodes*, labeled with atoms of the peer relations (for the inner nodes) and stored relations (for the leaves), and *rule nodes*, labeled with peer mappings or storage descriptions (see Figure 17.3). The root of the tree is the goal node representing the head of the query Q. The algorithm proceeds by expanding each goal node in the tree with the definitional mappings whose head unifies with the goal node. When none of the nodes of the tree can be expanded with peer mappings, we consider the storage descriptions and create the leaves of the tree.

■ ■ ■ ▬▬▬▬▬▬▬▬▬▬▬▬▬▬▬▬▬▬▬▬▬▬▬▬▬▬

Example 17.4

Consider the example in Figure 17.3. The root of the tree is the query, and its children are its conjuncts. Each of the conjuncts is expanded with a peer mapping (r_0 and r_1, respectively), resulting in four subgoals. These are then reformulated using the storage descriptions r_2 and r_3. The resulting reformulation is the conjunction of leaves in the tree.

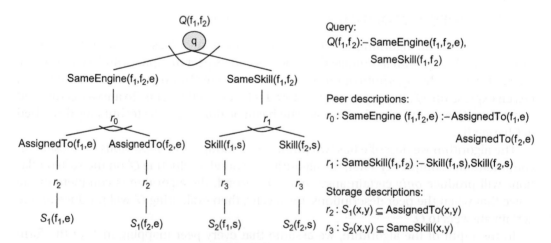

FIGURE 17.3 A rule-goal tree for a PDMS with only definitional peer mappings.

■ ■ ■

Now consider a PDMS whose peer mappings are all inclusions. In this case, we begin with the query subgoals and apply an algorithm for answering queries using views (as in Section 3.2.3). Here, we may take a set of subgoals and replace them by a single subgoal.

■ ■ ■ ▬▬▬▬▬▬▬▬▬▬▬▬▬▬▬▬▬▬▬▬▬▬▬▬▬▬▬▬▬▬▬▬

Example 17.5

As a simple example, suppose we have the query

$Q(f_1, f_2) \text{ :- } \mathsf{SameEngine}(f_1, f_2, e), \mathsf{Skill}(f_1, s), \mathsf{Skill}(f_2, s)$

and the peer mapping

$\mathsf{SameSkill}(f_1, f_2) \subseteq \mathsf{Skill}(f_1, s), \mathsf{Skill}(f_2, s)$

The first step of reformulation would replace two subgoals in the query with a single subgoal of SameSkill.

$Q'(f_1, f_2) \text{ :- } \mathsf{SameEngine}(f_1, f_2, e), \mathsf{SameSkill}(f_1, f_2)$

▬▬▬▬▬▬▬▬▬▬▬▬▬▬▬▬▬▬▬▬▬▬▬▬▬▬▬▬▬▬▬▬ ■ ■ ■

We apply such reformulation steps until we can no longer reformulate any peer relations, and then, as in the previous algorithm, we consider the storage descriptions. Hence, the key difference between these two kinds of reformulation is that while one reformulation replaces a single subgoal with a set of subgoals (definitional reformulation), the other reformulation replaces a set of subgoals with a single subgoal (inclusion reformulation). The algorithm will combine the two types of reformulation by building a rule-goal tree, but in that tree certain nodes will be marked as covering their *uncle* nodes in the tree. We illustrate the algorithm first with an example.

■ ■ ■ ▬▬▬▬▬▬▬▬▬▬▬▬▬▬▬▬▬▬▬▬▬▬▬▬▬▬▬▬▬▬▬▬

Example 17.6

Figure 17.4 shows an example of the operation of the reformulation algorithm. The query, Q, asks for firefighters with matching skills riding in the same engine. The query Q is expanded into its three subgoals, each of which appears as a goal node. The SameEngine peer relation (indicating which firefighters are assigned to the same engine) is involved in a single definitional peer description, r_0; hence we expand the SameEngine goal node with the rule r_0, and its children are two goal nodes of the AssignedTo peer relation (each specifying an individual firefighter's assignment).

The Skill relation appears on the right-hand side of an inclusion peer description, r_1. Hence, we expand $\mathsf{Skill}(f1,s)$ with the rule node r_1, and we create a child node for it that is labeled with the left-hand side of r_1, $\mathsf{SameSkill}(f_1, f_2)$. However, in doing so, we realize that the SameSkill atom also covers the subgoal $\mathsf{Skill}(f_2, s)$, which is the uncle of the node r_1. In the figure, this covering is annotated by a dashed line, but in the algorithm we will denote the covering with the relation *unc*.

Since the peer relation Skill is involved in a single peer description, we do not need to expand the subgoal $\mathsf{Skill}(f2,s)$ any further. Note, however, that we must apply description r_1 a second

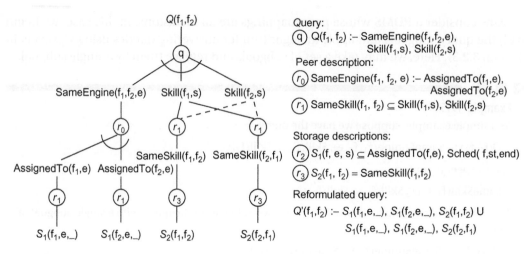

FIGURE 17.4 Reformulation rule-goal tree for the Emergency Services domain. Dashed lines represent nodes that are included in the *unc* label.

time with the head variables reversed, since **SameSkill** may not be symmetric (because it is $\subseteq$ rather than $=$).

At this point, since we cannot reformulate the peer mappings any further, we consider the storage descriptions. We find stored relations for each of the peer relations in the tree (S_1 and S_2) and produce the final reformulation. In this simple example, our reformulation involves only one level of peer mappings, but in general, the tree may be arbitrarily deep.

■ ■ ■

The first step of the algorithm, shown in Algorithm 15, builds a rule-goal tree starting from the query definition. The algorithm expands goal nodes with either definitional or inclusion mappings until it reaches the stored relations. The labels on the nodes indicate which ancestor and uncle subgoals are covered by each expansion. Note that in order to avoid cycles, the algorithm never uses the same peer mapping more than once in any path down the tree.

When the algorithm considers inclusion mappings, it creates MCDs. Recall from the description of the MiniCon Algorithm (Section 2.4.4) that when we consider a conjunctive query Q and a view V, an MCD is the smallest set of subgoals in Q that will be covered by V if V is used in the rewriting of Q. The other atoms in the MCD are going to be uncles of the rule node in the tree, and we mark those with the *unc* label.[1]

The second step of the algorithm, shown in Algorithm 16, constructs the reformulation from the rule-goal tree T. The solution is a union of conjunctive queries over the stored

---

[1] We note that in some cases, an MCD may cover cousins or uncles of its father node, not only its own uncles. For brevity of exposition, we ignore this detail in our discussion. However, we note that we do not compromise completeness as a result. In the worst case, we obtain conjunctive rewritings that contain redundant atoms.

Algorithm 15. PDMS-Build-Tree: Build a reformulation rule-goal tree.

Input: PDMS $\mathcal{P}$; conjunctive query Q over $\mathcal{P}$. **Output:** A rule-goal tree.

  // Create rule-goal tree T

  Add a goal node as the root of T, $root(T)$, labeled with $Q(\bar{X})$

  Add a child r to $root(T)$ and label it with the rule defining the query $Q(\bar{X})$

  for every subgoal, g, of Q **do**

    Create a rule-goal child for r labeled with g

  end for

  while goal nodes in T can be expanded **do**

    Let n be a leaf goal node in T whose label is $l(n) = p(\bar{Y})$, and p is not a stored relation

    if p appears in the head of a definitional description r **and** r is not an ancestor of n in T **then**

      // definitional expansion

      Let r' be the result of unifying $p(\bar{Y})$ with the head of r

      Create a child rule node n_r with $l(n_r) = r'$

      Create a child goal node for n_r for every subgoal, g, of r' with $l(g) = g$

    else if p appears in the right-hand side of an inclusion description or storage description r of the form $V \subseteq Q_1$ **and** r is not an ancestor of n in T **then**

      // inclusion expansion

      Let $n_1, \ldots, n_m$ be the children of the father node of n, and $p_1, \ldots, p_m$ be their corresponding labels

      for every MCD that can be created for $p(\bar{Y})$ w.r.t. $p_1, \ldots, p_m$ and r **do**

        Let $V(\bar{Z})$ be the atom created by the MCD

        Create a child rule node, n_r, for n labeled with r, and a child goal node, n_g, for n_r labeled with $V(\bar{Z})$

        Set $unc(n_g)$ to be the set of subgoals covered by the MCD

      end for

    end if

  end while

  return T

---

relations. Each of these conjunctive queries represents one way of obtaining answers to the query from the relations stored at peers. Each of them may yield different answers unless we know that some sources are exact replicas of others.

Let us first consider the simple case where only definitional mappings are used. In this case, the reformulation would be the union of conjunctive queries, each with head $Q(\bar{X})$ and a body that can be constructed as follows. Let T' be a subset of the leaves of T constructed by traversing the tree top-down and choosing a *single* child at every goal node and all the children for a given rule node. The body of a conjunctive query is the conjunction of all the nodes in T'.

To accommodate inclusion expansions, we create the conjunctive queries as follows. In creating T's we still choose a single child for every goal node. This time, we do not necessarily have to choose *all* the children of a rule node g. Instead, given a rule node g, we need

---

Algorithm 16. PDMS-Construct-Reformulation: Create the output PDMS reformulation.

Input: a rule-goal tree constructed by Algorithm PDMS-Build-Tree. **Output:** a set of conjunctive queries.

Let $A = \emptyset$

Add to A any conjunctive query of the form $Q(\bar{X})$:- B, where B is a conjunction of subgoals that can be created as follows

Initialize s to be a list containing the root node of T

while the list contains nonleaf nodes in T **do**

    Let g be a nonleaf node in s

    Remove g from s

    if g is a goal node **then**

        Choose one child of g and add it to s

    else if g is a definitional rule node **then**

        Add all the children of g to s

    else if g is an inclusion rule node **then**

        Choose a subset of the children of $g, g_1, \ldots, g_l$, where $unc(g_1) \cup \ldots \cup unc(g_l)$ includes all of the children of g

        Add $g_1, \ldots, g_l$ to s

    end if

end while

return A

---

to choose a subset of the children $g_1, \ldots, g_l$ of g, such that $unc(g_1) \cup \ldots \cup unc(g_l)$ includes all of the children of g.

17.5 Composing Mappings

The reformulation algorithm we described above builds a rule-goal tree that can get very large in a PDMS with many nodes and many peer mappings. To answer queries efficiently in a PDMS, multiple optimizations are needed. For example, we need to intelligently *order* how we expand nodes in the tree, be able to *prune* paths in the tree that yield only redundant results, and apply *adaptive* methods (as described in Chapter 8) to provide results to the user in a streaming fashion.

Another important optimization is to *compose* peer mappings in order to compress longer paths into single edges in the PDMS. Composing mappings saves in reformulation time and also enables us to prune paths that may look good initially but turn out to yield nothing ultimately. In fact, composing schema mappings is an interesting problem in its own right from a logical point of view. It is also important in the context of data exchange (Section 10.2) when data exchange may span longer paths across multiple systems.

Informally, the problem of composing schema mappings is the following. Suppose we have sources A, B, and C and mappings M_{AB} between A and B and M_{BC} between B and C.

Our goal is to find a mapping, M_{AC}, between A and C that will always give the same answers as following the mappings M_{AB} and then M_{BC}.

In the formal definition of composition, recall that a schema mapping, M, between sources A and B defines a binary relation, M^R, between the instances of A and the instances of B. The relation M^R contains pairs (a, b), where $a \in I(A)$ and $b \in I(b)$ and where a and b are consistent with each other under the mapping M (Section 3.2.1). The formal definition requires that M_{AC} be the join of the relations M_{AB} and M_{BC}.

Definition 17.4 (Mapping Composition).   *Let A, B, and C be data sources, and let M_{AB} be a mapping between A and B and M_{BC} be a mapping between B and C. A mapping M_{AC} is said to be a composition of M_{AB} and M_{BC} if*

$$M_{AC}^R = M_{AB}^R \times M_{BC}^R$$

☐

Finding the composition of mappings turns out to be rather tricky. The following examples illustrate why.

■ ■ ■

Example 17.7

Consider the following schema mappings, where each source has a single relation A, B, and C, respectively.

$$M_{AB}\quad \mathsf{A(x,z), A(z,y) \subseteq B(x,y)}$$

$$M_{BC}\quad \mathsf{B(x,z), B(z,y) \subseteq C(x,y)}$$

Each relation can be thought of as storing the set of edges in a directed graph. The mapping M_{AB} states that paths of length two in A are a subset of edges in B, and M_{BC} says that paths of length two in B are a subset of the edges in C.

It is easy to verify that the following mapping represents the composition of M_{AB} and M_{BC}. The mapping states that paths of length four in A are a subset of edges in C.

$$M\quad \mathsf{A(x,z_1), (z_1,z_2), A(z_2,z_3), A(z_3,y) \subseteq C(x,y)}$$

■ ■ ■

In Example 17.7 we were able to express the composition with a mapping in GLAV, i.e., in the same language as the mappings being composed. A natural question is whether a language for expressing mappings is closed under composition. In particular, is it always possible to express the composition of GLAV mappings in GLAV?

The answer to this question depends in subtle ways on the form of the mappings being composed. In Example 17.7, the mappings did not introduce any new existential variables. Specifically, all the variables that appeared on the right-hand side of the mappings also appear on the left-hand side. As it turns out, this condition is crucial in order to express the composition of GLAV mappings in GLAV. We state the following theorem without proof (see the bibliographic notes for more detail).

In the theorem, we say that a formula in a GLAV schema mapping is a *full* formula if the right-hand side of the mapping does not have variables that do not appear on the left-hand side.[2]

Theorem 17.4. *Let M_{AB} and M_{BC} be mappings, each specified by a finite set of GLAV mappings. If all the formulas in M_{AB} are full formulas, then the composition of M_{AB} and M_{BC} can be represented by a finite set of GLAV formulas. Deciding whether a GLAV formula f is in the composition of M_{AB} and M_{BC} can be done in polynomial time.* □

In fact, as we show below, Theorem 17.4 describes a rather tight condition on when composition can be computed efficiently. The following example shows that a composition of two finite GLAV mappings may require an *infinite* number of formulas.

■ ■ ■ ▬▬▬▬▬▬▬▬▬▬▬▬▬▬▬▬▬▬▬▬▬▬▬▬▬▬▬▬

Example 17.8

In this example, source B has two relations, R and G, representing red and green edges, respectively. Sources A and C also have two relations each. Consider the following mappings:

$$M_{AB} \quad \{A_{rg}(x,y) \subseteq R(x,x_1), G(x_1,y)$$

$$A_{gg}(x,y) \subseteq G(x,x_1), G(x_1,y)\}$$

$$M_{BC} \quad \{R(x,x_1), G(x_1,x_2), G(x_2,y) \subseteq C_{rgg}(x,y)$$

$$G(x,x_1), G(x_1,y) \subseteq C_{gg}(x,y)\}$$

The relation A_{rg} is a subset of the node pairs in B with red-green paths. The other relations A_{gg}, B_{rgg}, and C_{gg} can be described similarly. Observe that the following infinite sequence of formulas are all in the composition of M_{AB} and M_{BC}:

$$A_{gg}(x,y) \subseteq C_{gg}(x,y) \tag{17.1}$$

$$A_{rg}(x,x_1), A_{gg}(x_1,x_2) \subseteq C_{rgg}(x,y_1) \tag{17.2}$$

$$A_{rg}(x,x_1), A_{gg}(x_1,x_2), A_{gg}(x_2,x_3) \subseteq C_{rgg}(x,y_1), C_{gg}(y_1,y_2) \tag{17.3}$$

$$\cdots$$

$$A_{rg}(x,x_1), A_{gg}(x_1,x_2), \ldots, A_{gg}(x_n,x_{n+1}) \subseteq C_{rgg}(x,y_1), C_{gg}(y_1,y_2), \ldots, C_{gg}(y_{n-1},y_n) \tag{17.4}$$

---

[2]As noted earlier, GLAV formulas are similar to tuple-generating dependencies. In that terminology, a full formula is a full dependency.

The sequence is infinite. Each equation in the infinite sequence says that a path comprising one red (R) edge followed by $2n + 1$ green (G) edges (the query over A) is contained within a path comprising a red edge followed by $2n + 2$ green edges (the query over C). None of them can be expressed in terms of the others. For example, Formula 17.3 is not implied by Formulas 17.1 and 17.2.

■ ■ ■

The following theorem formalizes the intuition of Example 17.8 and shows that whenever M_{AB} may have existential variables on the right-hand side of the formulas, the composition may not be definable by a finite set of GLAV formulas.

Theorem 17.5. *There exist mappings, M_{AB} and M_{BC}, where M_{AB} is a finite set of GLAV formulas and M_{BC} is a finite set of full GLAV formulas, such that the composition of M_{AB} and M_{BC} is not definable by a finite set of GLAV formulas but is definable by an infinite set of GLAV formulas.* □

In practice, it is possible to compute efficiently the compositions of peer mappings. However, it is important that compositions be used judiciously in query answering, because they can also cause the search space of possible plans to grow further.

17.6 Peer Data Management with Looser Mappings

So far we have discussed peer data management as a generalization of data integration systems. The system is based on peer mappings that are specified between pairs (or small sets) of peers, rather than mappings between data sources and a mediated schema. As described, the system already provides quite a bit more flexibility than virtual data integration systems. However, to obtain these benefits, the collaborators must still create schema mappings, which may be a labor-intensive task.

In this section we describe two looser models for collaboration among multiple parties that do not require full peer mappings. Of course, with less precise specification of relationships between peers, the queries that can be specified and the accuracy of the results obtained will be diminished. However, in some applications, getting *some* data from other peers may be much better than nothing.

In the first method we describe, relationships between peers are *inferred* via approximate techniques (in the spirit of Chapter 5). In the second method, mappings are specified at the data level only with *mapping tables*. Of course, in practice, we may have a system that includes precise mappings in some places and uses a combination of the techniques we describe below in others.

17.6.1 Similarity-Based Mappings

Consider a PDMS where each peer, n, has a *neighborhood* of peers that are the peers with which n can communicate. However, we do not necessarily have peer mappings between

---

Algorithm 17. PDMS-Similarity: Compute PDMS similarity. The function *sim* computes similarity between pairs of relation names or attribute names. The parameter τ is a similarity threshold.

Input: PDMS $\mathcal{P}$; node n from $\mathcal{P}$; query $Q(\bar{X})$ on $\mathcal{P}$; (initially empty) accumulator for result $\mathcal{R}$.
Output: $\mathcal{R}$ contains final result.
Let $Q(\bar{X})$ be of the form $p(\bar{X})$, where p is a relation in the schema of n, and $A_1, \ldots, A_l$ are the attributes of p
Evaluate $Q(\bar{X})$ on the stored relations of n; add the results to $\mathcal{R}$
for every neighbor n_1 of n **do**
   Let $sim(r, p)$ denote be the similarity between the relation $r \in n_1$ and p
   Let $sim(A_i, B)$ be the similarity between an attribute A_i and an attribute B in n_1
   for every atom $r(B_1, \ldots, B_j)$ where $sim(r, p), sim(B_1, A_1), \ldots, sim(B_k, A_k) \geq \tau$ **do**
      Call **PDMS-Similarity**($\mathcal{P}$, $r(B_1, \ldots, B_j), n_1, \mathcal{R}$)
   end for
end for

---

n and its neighbors, and therefore reformulation and query answering will proceed by approximate mappings between schema elements of n and of its neighbors.

Specifically, suppose a user poses an atomic query $p(\bar{X})$ on n, and let n_1 be a neighbor of n. We can compute a similarity measure between the relation names of n and the relation names of n' and similarity values between the attribute names of p and the attribute names in n'. If we find a relation $p' \in n'$ that has high similarity to p, and we can find attributes $B_1, \ldots, B_k$ of p' that are similar to $A_1, \ldots, A_j$ of p, respectively, then we can formulate the query $p(\bar{X})$ as a query of the form $p'(\bar{Y})$. Note that we do not need to cover all the attributes of p in order for this to be useful. If p' does not have attributes corresponding to each of the attributes of p, then the reformulation ignores the missing attributes. Algorithm 17 describes the algorithm based on such a reformulation strategy.

We can continue this process recursively with neighbors of n_1 to obtain more answers. Note that since we may not always find all the attributes of the reformulated query, as the path gets longer the resulting tuples will be narrower, and possibly empty.

17.6.2 Mapping Tables

The second mechanism involves describing only correspondences at the data level. As described in Chapter 7, data-level mappings are often crucial to data integration because data sources often refer to the same real-world object in different ways, and in order to integrate data we must know which values match up.

In this context we can make broader use of mapping tables. In the simplest case, mapping tables can specify correspondences between different references to the same real-world objects. Going one step further, mapping tables can be used to describe correspondences between different lexicons. For example, suppose we are given two airlines' flight tables, shown in Figure 17.5. The mapping table in Figure 17.6 describes the mapping that is necessary for the airlines to code-share flights. We can go even further and create mapping tables that describe correspondences between elements in completely *different*

UnitedFlights

flightNum	origin	destination	departure	arrival
UA292	JFK	SFO	8AM	11:30AM
UA200	EWR	LAX	9AM	12:30PM
UA404	YYZ	SFO		

(a)

AirCanadaFlights

flightID	origin	dest	depTime	arrivalTime	aircraft
AC543	JFK	SFO	8AM	11:30AM	Boeing 747
AC505	EWR	LAX	9AM	12:30PM	Airbus 320
UA404	YYZ	SFO	8AM	1PM	Airbus 320

(b)

FIGURE 17.5 Tables of flights for two different peers (United Airlines and Air Canada).

FlightCodeMapping

UnitedFlightCode	AirCanadaFlightCode
UA292	AC543
UA200	AC505
UA404	AC303
v - {UA001 − UA500}	v - {CA001 − CA500}

FIGURE 17.6 A mapping table for the tables shown in Figure 17.5.

domains. For example, when sharing biological data, we can create a mapping table that relates gene IDs to related proteins.

Intuitively, a mapping table represents a possible join between tables in different peers. By following such joins, a user at one peer can obtain data from other peers without the need for schema mappings. For example, the table in Figure 17.5(a) shows flights for United Airlines and Figure 17.5(b) shows flights for Air Canada. Note that United Airlines does not store the aircraft for the flight (or perhaps it stores the aircraft for its own flights in a different table). A user can query for all the information for flight UA404 at the United Airlines peer. With a mapping table, the system will reformulate the query on the Air Canada peer, with flight ID 303. The Air Canada peer does store the aircraft.

More formally, we define a mapping table M between two relations R_1 and R_2. We assume the table M has two attributes A_1 and A_2, where A_1 is assumed to be an attribute of R_1 and A_2 is assumed to be an attribute of R_2. In principle, M can have any number of attributes, mapping projections of tuples in R_1 with projections of tuples in R_2, but we consider the simple case here for brevity. We denote the domain of A_1 by D_1 and the domain of A_2 by D_2. We also assume there is an alphabet of variables, $\mathcal{V}$, that is disjoint from $D_1 \cup D_2$.

Definition 17.5 (Mapping Tables). *A mapping table, M, between two relations R_1 and R_2 is a table with two attributes A_1 and A_2, where the values in columns can be as follows:*

- *values in D_1 (in the A_1 column) or values in D_2 (in the A_2 column), or*
- *a variable $v \in \mathcal{V}$, or*

- *an expression of the form $v - C$, where C is a finite set of values D_1 (in A_1) or C is a finite set of values for D_2 (in A_2).*

We assume that every variable appears in at most one tuple in M.   □

■ ■ ■ ▬▬▬▬▬▬▬▬▬▬▬▬▬▬▬▬▬▬▬▬▬▬▬▬▬▬▬▬▬▬▬▬▬▬▬▬▬▬▬

Example 17.9

Consider the mapping table in Figure 17.6. The first three rows specify correspondences between specific flights of United Airlines and Air Canada. The fourth row is a succinct way of specifying that for flights whose number is greater than 500, the codes of the two airlines are identical. In fact, the tuple (x, x) can be used to specify that any time the same value appears in both tables, they can map to each other.

▬▬▬▬▬▬▬▬▬▬▬▬▬▬▬▬▬▬▬▬▬▬▬▬▬▬▬▬▬▬▬▬▬▬▬▬▬▬▬ ■ ■ ■

We now consider the semantics of mapping tables, which is based on valuations. A valuation for a tuple in a mapping table is the result of substituting values for the variables. We can substitute a value in D_1 for a variable that appears in the left column and a value from D_2 for a variable that appears in the right column. Of course, if the tuple does not have any variables, then the tuple is unchanged.

The formal definition of a mapping table specifies a subset of the Cartesian product of R_1 and R_2 that is consistent with the mapping.

Definition 17.6 (Mapping Table Semantics).   *Let $M(A_1, A_2)$ be a mapping table between R_1 and R_2. A tuple t in $R_1 \times R_2$ is consistent with M if and only if there is a tuple, t', in M and a variable substitution, τ, such that $\Pi_{A_1, A_2}(t) = \tau(t')$.*   □

Mapping tables are interesting subjects of study in themselves. As with schema mappings, an interesting question that arises is whether they can be composed to discover new mapping tables, and whether a set of mapping tables is consistent with each other. We comment on these properties in the bibliographic notes.

Bibliographic Notes

The emergence of of peer-to-peer file sharing systems inspired the data management research community to consider P2P architectures for data sharing. Some of the systems that were built in this spirit were [74, 283, 309, 346, 433, 459, 544, 585]. Connections have also been made between PDMSs and architectures for the Semantic Web [2, 10, 287].

The language for describing peer mappings in PDMSs and the query reformulation algorithm are taken from [288], describing the Piazza PDMS. Optimization algorithms, including methods for ignoring redundant paths in the reformulation and the effect of mapping composition, are described in [288, 541].

The problem of composing schema mappings was initially introduced by Madhavan and Halevy [408]. In that paper, composition was defined to hold w.r.t. a class of queries and several restricted cases where composition can be computed were identified. They also showed that compositions of GLAV mappings may require an infinite number of formulas. The definition we presented is based on the work of Fagin et al. [218], and Theorems 17.4 and 17.5 are also taken from there. Interestingly, Fagin et al. also showed that composition of GLAV formulas can always be expressed as a finite number of *second-order* tuple-generating dependencies, where relation names are also variables. Nash et al. [452] present more complexity results regarding composition, and in [75] Bernstein et al. describe a practical algorithm for implementing composition. A variant on the notion of composition is to merge many partial specifications of mappings, as is done in the work on the MapMerge operator [22].

The looser architectures we described in Section 17.6 are from [2, 346, 459]. In particular, the similarity-based reformulation is described in more detail in [459]. Mapping tables were introduced in [346], where the Hyperion PDMS is described. That paper considers several other interesting details concerning mapping tables. First, the paper considers two semantics for mapping tables – the open-world semantics and the closed-world semantics. In the closed-world semantics, the presence of a pair (X, Y) in the mapping table implies that X (or Y) cannot be associated with any other value, while in the open-world assumption they can. The semantics also differ on the meaning of a value *not* appearing in the mapping table. Second, the paper considers the problem of composing mapping tables and determining whether a set of mapping tables is consistent and shows that in general, the problem is NP-complete in the size of the mapping tables. Another related idea is that of update coordination across parties with different levels of abstraction, studied in [368]. One means of propagating such updates is via triggers [341].

The Orchestra system [268, 544] takes PDMSs one step further and focuses on *collaboration* among multiple data owners. To facilitate collaboration, users need to be able to manage their data independently of others, propagate updates as necessary, track the provenance of the data, and create and apply *trust* conditions on which data they would like to import locally. We touch on some of these issues in more detail in Chapter 18.

18

Integration in Support
of Collaboration

Up to this point in the book, we have focused on data integration scenarios where data creation and editing (at the sources) and data *usage* (via querying) are separate: those who query the data through the integration system are generally not able to *create* and update data. Under such scenarios, the users are primarily concerned with being able to pose queries, get results, and act upon those results. In the business world, the users might be account representatives who contact clients; in the scientific realm, the users might be biologists who need to consult protein and gene databases to conduct an experiment.

Of course, Web 2.0 applications, particularly Wikipedia, have shown an entirely different class of usage scenario, in which the users are themselves the primary data creators, curators, and maintainers. In fact, such scenarios are also commonplace in more focused settings, such as scientific research communities — where scientists publish data, import data from one another as well as large organizational repositories, and make revisions to this data. Under these *collaborative* scenarios, we must consider a variety of issues beyond those in traditional data integration, ranging from handling of updates and annotations to handling conflicting data and different user perspectives.

18.1 What Makes Collaboration Different

We begin with an overview of the major challenges encountered when supporting collaboration. Many of these are not exclusive to the collaborative setting and exist to a limited extent in other contexts — but they must be dealt with in a much more systematic fashion in collaborative settings, because of the greater diversity and dynamicity in the system.

EMPHASIS ON DATA CREATION/EDITING
Often the goal of a collaboration is to allow different users to jointly add and edit data, possibly in response to what they see in their existing query results. Sometimes the data to be shared simply come from tables or XML documents contributed by a single user, but in many cases the users need to be able to edit one another's contributed data. Ultimately, this property leads to issues such as concurrency and conflict management (different users may make incompatible updates to the same data), incremental change propagation and even data provenance (a topic discussed in Chapter 14).

REPAIR VIA USER FEEDBACK

Individual actions from a particular user may be subject to error or even malicious behavior. Many collaborative tools, borrowing from the ideas underlying popular services such as Wikipedia, support correction and undo mechanisms for edits.

NEED FOR DATA ANNOTATION

In sharing data, collaborators will often want to make comments or *annotations*, attached to particular subsets of the data. Such annotations can be arbitrarily complex, depending on the situation, including attachments, discussion threads, and provenance. They are not direct modifications to the database data, but rather additional metadata to be overlaid.

DIFFERENT INTERPRETATIONS, BELIEFS, AND VALUE ASSESSMENTS

In a collaborative setting, different users may have different beliefs about the data domain, different standards for believing or disbelieving a claim, and different hypotheses about observed phenomena. For instance, in science there are typically many competing theories. Likewise, in intelligence or business forecasting there may be multiple perspectives or predictions. A system for facilitating collaboration must take this into account, for instance, by assigning relevance or trustworthiness scores to data based on user perspective or authority, or by managing conflicts in a standardized way.

A variety of approaches have been attempted to address these issues. We divide our discussion of these topics into three broad categories. In Section 18.2, we focus on systems where the data are primarily obtained through automated Web crawling or from external sources but are repaired via user feedback or input. Next, in Section 18.3, we consider situations where users primarily add curation, in the form of annotations and discussions. Finally, Section 18.4 describes the handling and propagation of user updates to the data.

18.2   Processing Corrections and Feedback

There are a variety of settings in which information is widely available across the Internet, from sources of differing degrees of quality or ease of extraction, and users would like to see a bird's-eye view of the data. Of particular note are the following:

- **Topic-specific portals**, where data are automatically extracted from different sources and used to generate pages, such as a portal on the database research community or a portal that provides access to thousands of job search sites (see Sections 15.2.1 and 15.3 for techniques used in generating these portals).
- **Local search services** provided by various search engines such as Google, Yahoo!, and Bing, which in fact are looking increasingly like topic-specific portals in the sense that they present restaurants, businesses, tourist attractions, and other items that are oriented around a specific locale. Moreover, the search providers increasingly are trying to take semantics into account for local search.

- **Bioinformatics or medical informatics repositories**, which often incorporate data from a variety of public sources and provide a Web interface around a query system.

In all of these contexts, some of the data shown to the user population is likely to be incorrect — whether because the source data included errors (as is often the case with life sciences data), because the data were automatically extracted through an imperfect process, or because the data were combined through mappings or joins that were incorrectly formulated. We describe two different models for making corrections to such data. In both of these models, we assume that updates can only be made by individuals with authority to do so, or that there is another module that verifies the truth or popularity of an update before applying it.

18.2.1 Direct User Updates Propagated Downstream

One approach that is commonly used in topic-specific portals generalizes the direct-edit model used in Wikis. At selected stages in the data gathering and integration pipeline, e.g., after various information extraction routines are run, views are presented to the end user. These views are predefined by an administrator and limited to selection and projection operations, and these views are constrained to include any key attributes in the base relations. This set of restrictions ensures that the views are updatable.

Now the user may make direct updates to the content of the views. These updates will then get materialized and also propagated "downstream" to any derived data products. The source data remain unchanged, but relevant updates will continue to be applied even as the source data get refreshed.

This basic approach allows for "persistent" user-provided updates, whenever the administrator chooses to enable such a capability. However, the updates are not seen by the original data provider or the author of the information extractor.

18.2.2 Feedback or Updates Propagated Back Upstream

Naturally, an alternative approach is to try to make revisions to the actual source data — or the formulation of the source queries — in response to user feedback. If the user feedback comes in the form of updates to data values, then one common approach is to support *view update* operations, where an update to a query's output is transformed to a series of operations over the view's data sources. The view update problem has been studied extensively since the 1980s, with the challenge being that updates might cause side effects. In essence a side effect refers to a situation in which, if we are to accomplish the desired change to a view's output, we must change at least one of the source tuples. Yet if the view is recomputed in response to this change, additional tuples will be changed in the output (not in accordance with the user's feedback). For example, tuples that are created as a result of joining the modified tuple may also be affected. Early work explored the constraints under which views are always updatable without unpredictable side effects. More recently, data provenance (Section 14) was shown to be effective in determining whether a specific update (even to a generally nonupdatable view) will actually cause side effects. This enables a "best effort" model of update propagation.

In some cases, a user deletion should not be interpreted merely as the desire to remove a source tuple but, rather, as feedback that a specific set of results should never have been generated. For instance, when automatic schema alignments or extraction rules are used to produce output, a bad alignment or rule will result in invalid results. Here the system should learn not to use the specific alignment or rule that produced the output result. This can be accomplished as follows. Suppose each rule or alignment is given a score or cost, and query results are each given scores composed from these underlying values. Given feedback on the query results, it is possible to use online learning algorithms to adjust the base scores, ultimately moving them beyond some threshold so they do not appear in the output.

18.3 Collaborative Annotation and Presentation

There are a variety of settings where the assembly of content is done in a highly distributed way, possibly even over time. This is especially true in the *pay-as-you-go* information integration context, where the system starts with very limited ability to extract structured information from the sources, find mappings to semantically related sources, and query the data.

Perhaps over time, multiple users extract and refine data from certain sources. Others may collect data or suggest sources. Still others may provide comments about specific data. In this section we consider scenarios supporting pay-as-you-go integration through collaborative annotations, including annotations that define mappings as well as those that are simply comments. Other aspects of pay-as-you-go and lightweight data integration are discussed in Chapter 15.

18.3.1 Mappings as Annotations: Trails

Within any collection of data, some specific data items are likely to be of use to many users, even if those users have different information needs. Intuitively, if one user defines a way of extracting or mapping such a data item into their query, it would be nice to be able to "capture" this, such that a future user might be able to make use of the work done by the first user. This is the intuition behind *trails*.

A trail is a Global-as-View mapping over XML data in an extended dialect of XPath that supports both keywords and path expressions. One can use it to map a keyword search to a path query and vice versa, or to map from one path to another. Trails might be created by using mining techniques or by looking at how users are mapping data items through a graphical tool.

We illustrate trails with a few examples, rather than presenting a full language syntax. Recall that basic XPath is discussed in Section 11.3.2.

■ ■ ■ ▬▬▬▬▬▬▬▬▬▬▬▬▬▬▬▬▬▬▬▬▬▬▬▬▬▬▬▬▬▬▬▬▬

Example 18.1

Consider an repository of photos that is either on the Web or part of a personal collection and assume that the metadata about the photos are stored as XML elements. Suppose we want to query for all data about digital photos received yesterday. The following trails might be useful.

First, the keyword "photo" might refer to any filename ending with ".jpeg":

$photo \rightarrow //*.jpeg$

Second, the keyword "yesterday" should be macro-expanded into a query over the date property and the yesterday() function:

$yesterday \rightarrow date = yesterday()$

Finally, we might declare that the property "date" should also be expanded to mean the "modified" or "received" properties. In trails, the attributes or properties associated with an XML element can be specifically requested using the *.tuple.{attribute}* syntax. Hence we can enter the following:

$//*.tuple.date \rightarrow //*.tuple.received$

which means that we will macro-expand the "date" property into a "received" property.

▬▬▬▬▬▬▬▬▬▬▬▬▬▬▬▬▬▬▬▬▬▬▬▬▬▬▬▬▬ ■ ■ ■

Of course, multiple trails may match a given query, and in general each must be expanded to produce candidate answers. In any practical setting, trails may be given different scores, and we may wish to return the top-scoring answers rather than all answers.

Assuming that users are willing to share their query or mapping operations (i.e., they do not have any expectation of confidentiality), trails are a promising mechanism for pay-as-you-go integration, in that they let future users benefit from the work of past users.

18.3.2 Comments and Discussions as Annotations

Sometimes, the task of integrating data involves contributions by different data owners and users. It may be that the data need to be understood and assessed by multiple people in order to be integrated, or certain data items need to be corrected along the way. One of the necessary capabilities in such scenarios is the ability to annotate data — attributes, tuples, trees — with comments and possibly even discussion threads. Such annotations would be combined with provenance information (as described in Chapter 14) to help the collaborators with their tasks. We briefly discuss two different contexts in which these capabilities have been offered.

WEB END USER INFORMATION SHARING

One setting in which annotations are employed is that of supporting end user data integration and sharing on the Web. Here, the system provides an intuitive AJAX-based browser interface that enables users to import and merge multiple spreadsheets or tables on the Web, through joins and unions. Within this interface, a user may highlight a specific cell, row, or column and add a discussion thread to that item. The annotation will show up as a highlight in the Web interface and includes the time of the post as well as the user.

In the Web context, discussion items are not propagated to derived (or base) data, rather, annotations are kept local to the view in which they were defined. The rationale for this is that other versions of the data may be for very different purposes; hence it might be undesirable to see the comments. In essence, annotations are associated with the *combination* of the view and the data.

SCIENTIFIC ANNOTATION AND CURATION

In the scientific data sharing setting, annotations are generally closely associated with the data, and the view simply becomes a means of identifying the data. Scientific data management systems thus follow a more traditional database architecture and include the ability to propagate annotations to derived views in a controlled fashion.

To help a database administrator control annotation propagation from base to derived data, language extensions to SQL, called pSQL, have been developed. In some cases, attributes from multiple source relations might be merged into the same column (e.g., during an equijoin), and there are several options for which annotations are shown.

pSQL has three modes of propagation, specifiable through a new PROPAGATE clause: *default*, which only propagates annotations from the attributes specifically named to be output in the query; *default-all*, which propagates annotations from *all* equivalent query formulations; and *custom*, where the user determines which annotations to propagate.

■ ■ ■ ▬▬▬▬▬▬▬▬▬▬▬▬▬▬▬▬▬▬▬▬▬▬▬▬▬▬▬▬▬▬▬▬▬

Example 18.2

The two SQL queries

```
SELECT   R.a                                    SELECT   S.b
FROM     R, S                                    FROM     R, S
WHERE    R.a = S.b                               WHERE    R.a = S.b
```

are equivalent in standard semantics. However, according to pSQL they are not, because *R.a* might have different annotations from *S.b*.

In pSQL:

- The PROPAGATE DEFAULT clause will propagate only *R.a*'s annotation for the query on the left and *S.b*'s annotation for the query on the right.
- The PROPAGATE DEFAULT-ALL clause will copy annotations from both sources.
- If the SELECT clause were changed to "SELECT X" and a custom clause such as PROPAGATE R.a TO X were added, then only *R.a* will be output.

▬▬▬▬▬▬▬▬▬▬▬▬▬▬▬▬▬▬▬▬▬▬▬▬▬▬▬▬▬▬▬▬ ■ ■ ■

While this syntax is relatively straightforward, pSQL queries must be rewritten into common SQL in a way that brings together all of the potential annotations. This typically requires a union of multiple possible rewritings (each of which retrieves a subset of the annotations).

18.4 Dynamic Data: Collaborative Data Sharing

Increasingly, progress in the sciences, medicine, academia, government, and even business is being facilitated through sharing large structured data resources, such as databases and object repositories. Some common examples include highly curated experimental data, public information such as census or survey data, market forecasts, and health records. A major challenge lies in how to enable and foster the sharing of such information in a collaborative fashion. Most effective data-centric collaborations have a number of key properties that one would like to promote with any technical solution:

1. They generally **benefit all parties**, without imposing undue work or restrictions on anyone. In other words, there is a low barrier to entry and a noticeable payoff.
2. They include parties with **diverse perspectives**, in terms of both how information is modeled or represented and what information is believed to be correct.
3. They may involve **differences of authoritativeness** among contributors. In some sense, this is a generalization of the notions of authoritativeness considered by PageRank and other link analysis mechanisms in search engines — with the extra wrinkle being that a result in a database system may come from multiple joined or unioned sources.
4. They support an **evolving understanding of a dynamic world** and hence include data that change.

In this section we consider one type of data that forms a collaboratively maintained, publicly available resource: scientific data from the field of bioinformatics.

Example Application
In bioinformatics there are a plethora of different databases, each focusing on a different aspect of the field from a unique perspective, e.g., organisms, genes, proteins, and diseases. Associations exist between the different databases' data, such as links between genes and proteins, or gene homologs between species. Multiple standardization efforts have resulted in large data warehouses, each of which seeks to be the definitive portal for a particular bioinformatics subcommunity. Each such warehouse provides three services to its community:

1. A data representation, in the form of a schema and query interface with terminology matched to the community.
2. Access to data, in the form of both raw measurements and statistically or heuristically derived diagnoses and links, e.g., a gene that appears to be correlated with a disease.

3. Cleaning and curation of data produced locally, as well as data that have possibly been imported from elsewhere.

There are occasionally disputes about which data are correct among the different warehouses. Yet some of the databases import data from one another (typically using custom scripts), and each warehouse is constantly updated, with corrections and new data typically published on a weekly, monthly, or on-demand basis.

Observe that the usage model here is update-centric and requires support for multiple schemas and multiple data versions, across different participating organizations. This is quite different from most of the data integration scenarios described in this book, even going beyond peer data management systems (Chapter 17), in that updates and data conflicts need to be managed. That has motivated the development of the *collaborative data sharing system* (CDSS), which builds upon data integration techniques to provide a principled semantics for exchanging data and updates among autonomous sites. The CDSS models the exchange of data among sites as *update propagation among peers*, which is subject to transformation (through schema mappings), content filtering (based on policies about source authority), and local, per-participant revision or replacement of data.

Each participant or *peer* in a CDSS controls a local database instance, encompassing all data it wishes to manipulate (possibly including data that originated elsewhere), in the format that the peer prefers. The participant normally operates in "disconnected" mode for a period of time, querying over the local DBMS and making local modifications. As edits are made to this database, they are logged. This enables users to make modifications without (yet) making them visible to the external world. There are many scenarios where individual participants ultimately want to share their data but need to keep it proprietary for a short time, e.g., to publish a paper on their results or to ensure the data are consistent and stable.

At the users' discretion, the *update exchange* capability of the CDSS is invoked, which publishes the participant's previously invisible updates to "the world" at large and then translates others' updates to the participant's local schema — also filtering which ones to apply and reconciling any conflicts, according to the local administrator's unique trust policies, before applying them to the local database.

Schema mappings, resembling those of the PDMS (Chapter 17), specify one participant's schema-level relationships to other participants. Schema mappings may be annotated with trust policies that specify filter conditions about which data should be imported to a given peer, as well as precedence levels for reconciling conflicts. Trust policies take into account the provenance as well as the values of data.

■ ■ ■ ━━

Example 18.3

Figure 18.1 shows a simplified bioinformatics collaborative data sharing system. GUS, the Genomics Unified Schema, contains gene expression, protein, and taxon (organism)

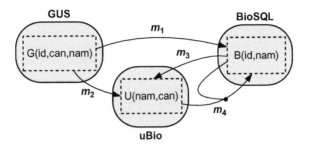

FIGURE 18.1 Example collaborative data sharing system for three bioinformatics sources. For simplicity, we assume one relation at each participant (**GUS, BioSQL, uBio**). Schema mappings are indicated by labeled arcs.

information; BioSQL contains very similar concepts; and uBio establishes synonyms and canonical names for taxa. Instances of these databases contain taxon information that is autonomously maintained but of mutual interest to the others. Suppose that BioSQL wants to import data from GUS, as shown by the arc labeled m_1, but the converse is not true. Similarly, uBio wants to import data from GUS, along arc m_2. Additionally, BioSQL and uBio agree to mutually share some of their data, e.g., uBio imports taxon names from BioSQL (via m_3) and BioSQL uses mapping m_4 to add entries for synonyms to any organism names it has in its database. Finally, each participant may have a certain trust policy about what data it wishes to incorporate. For example, BioSQL may only trust data from uBio if they were derived from GUS entries. The CDSS facilitates dataflow among these systems, using mappings and policies developed by the independent participants' administrators. ■ ■ ■

18.4.1 Basic Architecture

We begin with an overview of the CDSS architecture. The CDSS is designed to build over, rather than replace, collaborators' existing DBMS infrastructure. The CDSS runtime sits above an existing DBMS on every participant's machine (peer) P and manages the exchange and permanent storage of updates. It implements a fully peer-to-peer architecture with no central server. In general, each peer represents an autonomous domain with its own unique schema and associated local data instance (managed by the DBMS). The users located at P typically query and update the local instance in a "disconnected" fashion. Periodically, upon the initiative of P's administrator, P invokes the CDSS. This publishes P's local edit log, making it globally available. This also subjects P to the effects of update exchange, which fetches, translates, and applies updates that other peers have published (since the last time P invoked the CDSS). After update exchange, the initiating participant will have a data instance incorporating the most trusted changes made by participants transitively reachable via schema mappings. Any updates made locally at P can modify data imported (by applying updates) from other peers.

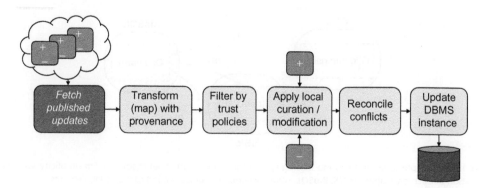

FIGURE 18.2 CDSS stages for importing updates to a peer.

Publishing and Archiving Update Logs

The first stage of sharing updates with other peers in a CDSS is to publish the updated data into a permanent, archived, always-available repository. The full version history of all data is kept in this repository, such that different versions can be compared and changes can be traced or even rolled back. In principle, the storage system could be any sort of highly available server infrastructure or a cloud storage system such as Amazon's SimpleDB. Some implementations even use reliable peer-to-peer storage infrastructure, such that the data are partitioned and replicated among the participants' own servers. That involves fairly complex engineering, and we refer the interested reader to the bibliographic references for more details.

Transforming and Filtering Updates

The most intricate aspects of the CDSS model revolve around how updates are processed, filtered, made consistent, and applied to a given participant's database instance. Figure 18.2 shows the basic data processing "pipeline" from the perspective of a given peer. Initially, all updates published by other peers, but not yet seen by the peer, are fetched from the aforementioned update log storage system. Next, update exchange (Section 18.4.2) is performed, consisting of two aspects: transforming or mapping the updates using schema mappings while recording the mapping steps as data provenance (Chapter 14), and then filtering trusted vs. untrusted updates based on their provenance, according to local trust policies. Now, any modifications made by local users are additionally considered, forming a set of candidate updates. These candidate updates may be grouped into transactions, which may have data dependencies. The reconciliation process (Section 18.4.3) arbitrates among the possible updates and determines a consistent set to apply to the peer's database instance.

18.4.2 Mapping Updates and Materializing Instances

Updates published by the various participants will typically have different schemas and identifiers. Some of these updates may conflict with updates from other peers either due to concurrent changes or due to disagreement about facts. Moreover, each participant may have some assessment of the authoritativeness of the other participants, and this may vary from one peer to another. The update exchange operation involves translating updates across schema mappings (and possibly identifiers), tracking provenance of those updates, and filtering according to trust policies. Moreover, the peer's users may override data imported by update exchange through local curation (updates). Finally, the set of imported and local updates may not in fact be mutually compatible; thus, update exchange is followed by reconciliation (Section 18.4.3).

The Update Exchange Process

Logically, the process of translating updates in a CDSS is a generalization of *data exchange* (see Section 10.2). If we take the data locally inserted by each peer to be the source data in the system, then (in the absence of deletions or trust conditions) each peer should receive a materialized data instance capable of providing all of the certain answers entailed by the data in the CDSS and the constraints implied by the schema mappings. This is the same query answering semantics supported by the PDMS. To achieve this, we must compute a canonical universal solution, using a process similar to the chase, described in Section 10.2.

Of course, there are many additional subtleties introduced by deletions, the computation of provenance, and trust conditions. We provide a brief overview of the update exchange process here, and provide detailed references in the bibliographic notes.

The CDSS uses a set of schema mappings specified as tuple generating dependencies (tgds), as introduced in Section 3.2.5.

■ ■ ■ ━━

Example 18.4

Refer to Figure 18.1. Peers GUS, BioSQL, and uBio have one-relation schemas describing taxon IDs, names, and canonical names: GUS(id,can,nam), BioSQL(id,nam), and uBio(nam,can). Among these peers are mappings:

$$m_1 \quad \text{GUS}(i, c, n) \rightarrow \text{BioSQL}(i, n)$$

$$m_2 \quad \text{GUS}(i, c, n) \rightarrow \text{uBio}(n, c)$$

$$m_3 \quad \text{BioSQL}(i, n) \rightarrow \exists c \, \text{uBio}(n, c)$$

$$m_4 \quad \text{BioSQL}(i, c) \wedge \text{uBio}(n, c) \rightarrow \text{BioSQL}(i, n)$$

Observe that m_3 has an existential variable: the value of c is unknown (and not necessarily unique). The first three mappings all have a single source and target peer, corresponding to the left-hand side and the right-hand side of the implication. In general, relations from multiple peers may occur on either side, as in mapping m_4, which defines data in the BioSQL relation based on its own data combined with tuples from uBio.

━━ ■ ■ ■

DATA EXCHANGE PROGRAMS

Let us focus initially on how the CDSS model extends the data exchange paradigm to compute instances. Data exchange typically uses the schema mappings with a procedure called the *chase* to compute a canonical universal solution. Importantly, this solution is not a standard data instance, but rather a *v-table*, a representation of a set of possible database instances. For instance, in m_3 in the above example, the variable c may take on many different values, each resulting in a different instance.

In order to make the process of computing a canonical universal solution feasible using standard DBMS techniques, rather than a custom chase implementation, a relational-model CDSS translates the schema mappings into a program in an extended version of datalog, which includes support for Skolem functions that take the place of existential variables like c. The resulting (possibly recursive) program computes a canonical universal solution as well, but has benefits arising from the fact that it is a query as opposed to a procedure. The program greatly resembles that of the inverse-rules query answering scheme (Section 2.4.5), with a key difference that we do not drop results that contain Skolem values in the distinguished variables. Instead, we must actually materialize the Skolem values.

■ ■ ■ ▬▬▬▬▬▬▬▬▬▬▬▬▬▬▬▬▬▬▬▬▬▬▬▬▬▬▬▬▬

Example 18.5

The update exchange datalog program for our running example includes the following rules (note that the order of the source and target is reversed from the tgds):

$$\text{BioSQL}(i, n) \text{ :- } \text{GUS}(i, c, n)$$

$$\text{uBio}(n, c) \text{ :- } \text{GUS}(i, c, n)$$

$$\text{uBio}(n, f(i, n)) \text{ :- } \text{BioSQL}(i, n)$$

$$\text{BioSQL}(i, n) \text{ :- } \text{BioSQL}(i, c), \text{uBio}(n, c)$$

This program is recursive (specifically, with respect to BioSQL) and must be run to fixpoint in order to fully compute the canonical universal solutions.

▬▬▬▬▬▬▬▬▬▬▬▬▬▬▬▬▬▬▬▬▬▬▬▬▬▬▬▬▬ ■ ■ ■

XML

As of the writing of this textbook, no XML implementation of a CDSS exists. However, given that data exchange, query reformulation, and incremental view maintenance techniques have all been shown to extend fairly easily to an XML model using the mapping formalisms of Section 11.5, there is a very natural path to such an implementation.

GENERALIZING FROM DATA TO UPDATE EXCHANGE

Update exchange requires the ability for each peer not simply to provide a relation with source data, but in fact to provide a set of *local updates* to data imported from elsewhere: insertions of new data as well as deletions of imported data. The CDSS models the local updates as relations. It takes the update log published by each peer and "minimizes it," removing insertion-deletion pairs that cancel each other out. Then it splits the local updates of each relation R into two logical tables: a *local contributions table*, R^l, including all inserted data, and a *local rejections table*, R^r, including all deletions of external data. It then updates the datalog rules for R by adding a mapping from R^l to R and by adding a $\neg R^r$ condition to every mapping. For instance, the first mapping in our example would be replaced with

$$\text{BioSQL}(i, n) :\text{-} \text{BioSQL}^l(i, n)$$

$$\text{BioSQL}(i, n) :\text{-} \text{GUS}(i, c, n), \neg\text{BioSQL}^r(i, n)$$

INCREMENTAL UPDATE PROPAGATION

Finally, the CDSS uses *incremental view maintenance* techniques to more efficiently update the materialized instances at each peer. Given the set of updates made by each peer, described as *delta* relations (the sets of tuples inserted and deleted), plus the contents of the existing relations, the system can use the mappings to derive the set of deltas to apply to "downstream" relations. Additionally, it is possible in many circumstances to propagate updates "upstream" along mappings, in a variant of the *view update* problem, changing the source tuples from which the modified tuple was derived.

During incremental update propagation, the CDSS will typically filter the updates being propagated according to how trusted or authoritative they are; this is based in part on data provenance. It turns out that data provenance enables more efficient deletion propagation algorithms as well. Specifically, provenance is used to determine whether view tuples are still derivable when some base tuples have been removed. Provenance can also be used to facilitate more flexible solutions to the view update problem by making it possible to determine whether a modification to a base tuple will trigger side effects.

CYCLIC MAPPINGS

To guarantee termination of the data exchange process, the standard CDSS formulation requires that the set of mappings be weakly acyclic (see Section 10.2). Intuitively, this is because non-weakly-acyclic mappings may continue to introduce new labeled null values with each iteration through the mappings, never terminating. Recent work on CDSSs has investigated a user intervention phase, where the system lets the user decide whether the new labeled null values should be unified with the previous ones, i.e., assigned the same value. This enables computation even with cyclic mappings, at the expense of additional user input and a slightly different semantics.

Data Provenance

In any sort of data integration setting where sources have data of varying quality or represent different perspectives, a major challenge is determining *why* and *how* a tuple exists in a query answer or a materialized data instance. The integrated view hides the details from us. This is where *data provenance* plays an instrumental role in the CDSS.

A CDSS creates, materializes, and incrementally maintains a representation of the provenance semiring formalism described in Chapter 14; specifically, it takes the hypergraph representation and encodes it on disk. (Current implementations use relational tables, though other representations could equally well be used.)

■ ■ ■ ━━━━━━━━━━━━━━━━━━━━━━━━━━━━━━━━━━━━

Example 18.6

Consider the mappings from our running example. The provenance of the data in the peers' instances can be captured in the hypergraph representation shown in Figure 18.3. Note that "source" tuples (insertions in the local peers' R^l relations) are highlighted using 3-D nodes and "+" derivations. Labeled nulls are indicated with the $\perp$ character.

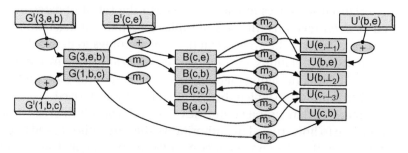

FIGURE 18.3 Provenance graph corresponding to example CDSS setting.

From this graph we can analyze the provenance of, say, B(3, 2) by tracing back paths to source data nodes — in this case through m_4 to p_1 and p_2 and through m_1 to p_3.

━━━━━━━━━━━━━━━━━━━━━━━━━━━━━━━━━━━ ■ ■ ■

An advantage of encoding the provenance information as relations is that it can be incrementally maintained along with the database instances. In essence, we can split every CDSS schema mapping $\mathcal{M}$ into partial mappings: one that takes the left-hand side of $\mathcal{M}$ and computes a provenance relation from it (materializing all variables from the left-hand side) and a second that takes the provenance relation and projects the necessary variables to obtain the right-hand side of $\mathcal{M}$.

Trust Policies and Provenance

Schema mappings describe the relationships between data elements in different instances. However, mappings are compositional, and not every peer wants to import all data that can be logically mapped to it. A peer may distrust certain sources or favor some sources over others, e.g., because one source is more authoritative. Trust policies, specified for each peer, encode conditions over the data and provenance of an update and associate a priority with the update. A priority of 0 means the update is untrusted.

■ ■ ■ ▬▬▬▬▬▬▬▬▬▬▬▬▬▬▬▬▬▬▬▬▬▬▬▬▬▬▬▬▬▬▬▬▬

Example 18.7
As examples, uBio may trust data from GUS (giving it priority 2) more than BioSQL (given priority 1). BioSQL might not trust any data from mapping m_3 with a name starting with "a" (trust priority 0).

▬▬▬▬▬▬▬▬▬▬▬▬▬▬▬▬▬▬▬▬▬▬▬▬▬▬▬ ■ ■ ■

Trust policies can be enforced directly during update exchange: as an update is propagated across a mapping, it is assigned a trust priority level for every peer. This priority level takes into account the peer's trust of the source tuples from the mapping, the trust level of the mapping itself, and the trust level of the target of the mapping. These are composed using operators conforming to one of the provenance semirings of Table 14.1 — generally the Boolean **trust** model or the **weight/cost** model.

At this stage, every tuple in every instance will conceptually be given a priority assignment for every peer. A challenge occurs if the tuples conflict with one another, especially if they are grouped into transactions: we must choose which tuples to accept and which to reject, and somehow treat all tuples within the same transaction as an atomic unit.

18.4.3 Reconciling Conflicts

The CDSS reconciliation process ensures that each peer receives a consistent (though perhaps unique) data instance. It considers not only conflicts but also transactions. The CDSS is not really intended for online transaction processing applications. However, transactions might arise when an atomic update gets mapped into a relational representation. For instance, a user of a particular application might update an XML tree, which gets mapped to a set of relation updates, of which all or none should be applied.

The CDSS defines the trust priority of a transaction in terms of its constituent updates. Many different policies are plausible. For instance, we might consider the priority of a transaction to be the minimum priority of its constituent updates or the maximum. The current state of the art considers a transaction to be untrusted if any of its member updates is untrusted (an untrusted update "taints" an entire transaction). Otherwise, it receives the highest trust priority of any contained update (we want to ensure that the most trusted data are applied).

Challenges of Transactions
Transactions introduce several challenges that do not arise in a simple delete-insert update model: (1) data dependencies (one transaction may depend on the output of another);

(2) atomicity (all updates, or none, may be applied); (3) serializability (some transactions can be applied in parallel, and others cannot).

A common approach is to assign priorities to every transaction; then, in descending order of priority, find the latest transactions of that priority that can be applied (together with any antecedent transactions needed in order to satisfy read-write or write-read dependencies). This runs in time polynomial in the number of priorities and updates and the length of the transaction chains.

Bibliographic Notes

The problems of supporting collaboration in database environments have been considered in a variety of contexts. The grassroots development of community portals is one of the major motivations, and the Cimple system [170, 184, 185] (and its accompanying DBLife portal) developed a variety of techniques for allowing user intervention and repair [113, 169]. This is also one setting considered in "in situ" pay-as-you-go data integration or *dataspaces* [233]. The iTrails system [504] discussed in this chapter was an attempt to construct a dataspace system. The notion of *data coordination*, where multiple users may wish to perform coordinated transactions (e.g., book a flight on the same plane or to the same destination), has been examined in the Youtopia system [278, 279].

A very common thread through many collaborative systems is the use of annotations and provenance. Google's Fusion Tables [260, 261], which is an implementation of an end user Web annotation system, uses both of these mechanisms. DBNotes [136], the first scientific data management system focusing on annotation propagation, and Orchestra [268, 342, 544], a collaborative data sharing system, also use annotations and provenance. Fusion Tables focuses primarily on the user-facing issues, whereas DBNotes focuses on how annotations interface with the query language, and Orchestra focuses on provenance and its interactions with update propagation. Storage schemes related to annotations have been studied in [209].

Provenance leads very naturally to work on two related notions useful in collaborative settings: trust and causality. We often wish to assign a score for how much to believe or trust a data value or a dataset, given knowledge of the trust levels of some of the input data, some of the results, or a combination thereof. A common approach is to use probabilistic models to compose trust, as discussed in Chapter 13, or machine learning techniques to determine the trust levels of different contributing factors, as discussed in Chapter 16. In many cases provenance helps us to distinguish between sources and to determine whether these sources are compatible with our beliefs. The notion of beliefs is much more deeply studied in the BeliefDB project [246], where a notion of "higher-order beliefs" (X believes Y believes something) is considered. Causality refers to finding the input "most responsible" for a given output result, e.g., an erroneous value. Recent work has examined how one might select tuples in a view and determine the input tuples that have the strongest level of causality for those results [425].

Finally, it is worth noting that both annotation and update propagation build heavily upon the ideas of view maintenance, including recursive view maintenance techniques proposed by Gupta, Mumick, and Subrahmanian [275], as well as the view update problem considered by Dayal and Bernstein [166], Keller [345], Bancilhon and Spyratos [53], and many others.

19 ▦

The Future of Data Integration

"Prediction is very difficult, especially if it's about the future."
— **Niels Bohr**

Like the entire field of data management, data integration keeps evolving as technology shifts and new applications come to the forefront. Initially, data integration was focused on challenges that occur within enterprises. As the Web emerged, new problems were introduced to data integration, such as scaling to a much larger number of sources and handling sources with less structure. We continue to see the field evolving today as data are being produced faster than ever before and in new forms. Large scientific experiments rely on data management for progress. People create data fragments (often called breadcrumbs) whenever they interact with services on the Web. Sensors are collecting data from more sources (e.g., GPS, vehicle movement, vital signs) and in higher fidelity than ever before. Since data sources are created by multiple people and organizations, new sources of data end up yielding new challenges to data integration.

As we have seen throughout the book, data integration tends to be one of the drivers of new subfields of database management and a beneficiary of techniques developed in these fields. As a few examples, we have seen this in the development of XML, uncertain databases, provenance, keyword search on databases, and Web data management, each of which was developed for independent reasons but contributed in some way to data integration.

In the following paragraphs we touch upon some of the trends we see in data integration and areas that require additional attention.

19.1 Uncertainty, Provenance, and Cleaning

In some sense, the fact that data integration takes a set of heterogenous sources, transforms and combines then, and produces a uniform result can be both a plus and a minus. Sometimes knowing where the data have come from and how they were produced is critical. Perhaps a particular information extractor turns out to have some issues. Perhaps a source is especially authoritative.

As discussed in Chapter 14, data provenance relates source data items to results, while also recording the transformations applied. Given some information about the quality of some of the source (or result) values, plus the provenance, we would like to be able to reason about the the uncertainty we should have in the other data values.

Existing work has looked at how to compute probabilistic answers given scores on the inputs, as discussed in Chapter 13. Some early work has also been done on learning from user feedback on the quality of the query results, as discussed in Chapter 16.

More generally, one would like to take a wide array of general data cleaning and update operations — deduplication, value correction, etc. — and use them, plus provenance, to revise our ranking of a source's quality (and possibly even to create general repair scripts). In general, a problem that is likely to see increasing attention is how to take usage, feedback, and data quality cues and use them to assess uncertainty and automate cleaning. A second key issue is how to develop formalisms, akin to the data models and query primitives we use over data, that can nicely capture the semantics of the uncertainty propagation operations we wish to perform.

19.2 Crowdsourcing and "Human Computing"

Inspired by the success of Amazon Mechanical Turk and Web 2.0 sites such as Wikipedia, many researchers have started investigating crowdsourcing as basic database operator. The key observation is that some conditions are hard for a computer to evaluate (e.g., whether an image contains a sunset, or whether an extraction from a Web page is correct), but can be done trivially by humans. Hence, if human evaluation can be built in to query processing (even if it takes longer), then new kinds of queries and data management services can be supported, such as finding images that satisfy a certain set of conditions and obtaining clean databases from Web pages.

A second kind of crowdsourcing requires the crowd members to be more proactive. For example, imagine building a database that contains the price of bottled water anywhere in the world, or finding which villages in Tanzania have access to clean water. Traditionally, creating such databases could take multiple years, and by the time they were completed they would be out of date. With appropriate crowdsourcing technology powered by mobile devices, such databases can be created within hours, and their effects can be transformative on people's lives.

Crowdsourcing has the potential of providing powerful solutions to traditionally hard data integration problems. For example, the quality of extractions from the Web can be verified by humans, and schemas and data can be matched by crowds. Work on this topic is in its infancy, but will undoubtedly be a focus in the upcoming years.

19.3 Building Large-Scale Structured Web Databases

In many domains there is a need to build large-scale structured Web databases by integrating data from many different sources. For example, Google Scholar integrates many bibliographic sources to build a citation database for millions of publications. As another example, biologists often want to integrate sources such as PubMed, Grants, and Clini-calTrials to build biomedial databases. As yet another example, e-commerce companies often integrate product information from vendor feeds to build giant product taxonomies for searching and advertising purposes.

Building and maintaining such databases raise numerous challenges. Many of these challenges, such as wrapper construction and schema matching, have been discussed in this book. Many others are new, and we have only begun to understand them, as we build more and more databases. For example, we need to develop a methodology for building such databases. If we are to integrate PubMed, Grants, and ClinicalTrials, how should we proceed? Should we clean each source first (e.g., via data matching), then merge them, or should we do the reverse? There are well-understood methodologies for building rela-tional databases. But no such methodology exists for building large-scale databases via integration.

As another example, when deploying such databases on the Web, we often create a "home page" for each integrated entity. However, as we gain more information, we often split or merge entities. How do we manage the IDs of such entities, and how do we pro-vide navigational pages so that users can easily find the desired entities, even after we have moved them around? Wikipedia has developed a basic solution for these problems. But can it be used in other contexts? And are there better solutions? Other challenges include incre-mentally updating the database and recycling human feedback during the update process. Current research on building portals has begun to identify and address such challenges (see Chapter 15), but far more work is necessary.

19.4 Lightweight Integration

At the other end of the spectrum, many data integration tasks are transient. We often face a task where we need to integrate data from multiple sources to answer a question that will be asked only once or twice. However, the integration needs to be done quickly and by people who may not have much technical expertise. For example, consider a disaster response situation in which reports are coming from multiple data sources in the field, and the goal is to corroborate them and quickly share them with the affected public.

In general, there are many easy-to-explain integration tasks that are surprisingly diffi-cult to perform using current tools and techniques. Beyond the major challenge of creating a data integration system that is usable by indviduals with a wide range of technical skills, lightweight integration introduces several other challenges. These include locating rele-vant data sources, assessing the quality of the sources, helping the user understand the semantics well enough so the sources can be integrated in a meaningful fashion, and supporting the process of integration.

One key to progress in this area is to focus on the task(s) the user is facing and make sure that each of the steps is easily supported. In addition, as we describe in Section 15.5, we should support pay-as-you-go data integration: this should offer an immediate and clear return on the investment in reconciling, cleaning, and integrating the data. Ideally, machine learning and other techniques can be used to amplify the effects of human input, possibly through *semi-supervised learning*, where small amounts of human data classification, plus large amounts of additional raw ("unlabeled") data, are used to train the system.

19.5 Visualizing Integrated Data

Ultimately, users do not want to view rows of data but rather visualizations that highlight the important patterns in the data and offer flexible exploration. For example, a map or a timeline can quickly reveal a hot region of interest or a point in time that requires detailed investigation. While visualization is a challenge for the entire field of data management, it becomes even more important in data integration. For example, when data come from multiple sources we would like to immediately see discrepancies between the sources. In addition, a visualization can also aid in the process of integration itself by pinpointing a subset of the data that was not reconciled correctly. As people start searching through large collections of heterogeneous data, visualizations will be key to presenting the different search results and evaluating their relevance to the task at hand. Finally, visualizations also play a key role in conveying the certainty of the integrated data and its provenance.

19.6 Integrating Social Media

Social media includes Facebook updates, tweets, user-generated videos, and blogs. Such data are exploding, and there is much interest in integrating them. One integration scenario is to discover interesting events in the Twittersphere. Examples include a recent earthquake, the emerging negative reception of a newly released product, and a planned protest in a public square. Another integration scenario is to find all social media data (e.g., tweets and videos) that are related to a particular event. Yet another integration scenario is to summarize and visualize major trends in the blogosphere.

Clearly, integrating social media can bring tremendous benefits. However, it also raises many difficult challenges, due to the particular nature of the medium. First, social media data are often noisy, full of spam and low-quality data. Second, identifying quality data and influential users in social media is often quite difficult due to the transient nature of such data and users. Third, the data often lack context, making them hard to interpret and integrate. For example, it is difficult to interpet the tweet "mel just crashed his maserati" unless we know that Mel Gibson just had an accident. Finally, social media data often arrive as high-speed streams that require very fast processing. This raises not just "big data" but also "fast data" challenges. Work on integrating social media is just emerging, but will undoubtedly be a major focus of the field of data integration in the coming years.

19.7 Cluster- and Cloud-Based Parallel Processing and Caching

The ultimate vision of the data integration field is to be able to integrate large numbers of sources with large amounts of data — ultimately approaching the scale of the structured part of the Web.

We are currently far from this vision. Most query engines, schema matchers, storage systems, query optimizers, and so forth have been developed for operation on a single server or a small set of servers and quickly run into performance limitations. Likewise, many core algorithms are based on assumptions of limited scale (e.g., they are limited to main memory).

Ultimately, the ability to scale up to more sources, as well as to spend more processing power to make more accurate matches and more extensive searches, will almost certainly require us to redesign many algorithms to exploit the power of large clusters. Problems like schema matching, entity resolution, data cleaning, indexing, and so on will likely need to be tackled in a much more parallelizable and scalable way.

Bibliography

1. *The Description Logic Handbook: Theory, Implementation and Applications, 2nd Edition.* Cambridge University Press, 2007.

2. Karl Aberer, Philippe Cudré-Mauroux, and Manfred Hauswirth. The Chatty Web: Emergent semantics through gossiping. In *12th World Wide Web Conference*, 2003.

3. Serge Abiteboul, Omar Benjelloun, Bogdan Cauytis, Ioana Manolescu, Tova Milo, and Nicoleta Preda. Lazy query evaluation for Active XML. In *SIGMOD*, June 2004.

4. Serge Abiteboul, Omar Benjelloun, and Tova Milo. The Active XML project: An overview. *VLDB J.*, 17(5), 2008.

5. Serge Abiteboul, Angela Bonifati, Gregory Cobena, Ioana Manolescu, and Tova Milo. Dynamic XML documents with distribution and replication. In *SIGMOD*, June 2003.

6. Serge Abiteboul and Oliver Duschka. Complexity of answering queries using materialized views. In *PODS*, Seattle, WA, 1998.

7. Serge Abiteboul, Richard Hull, and Victor Vianu. *Foundations of Databases*. Addison-Wesley, 1995.

8. Azza Abouzeid, Kamil Bajda-Pawlikowski, Daniel J. Abadi, Alexander Rasin, and Avi Silberschatz. HadoopDB: An architectural hybrid of MapReduce and DBMS technologies for analytical workloads. *PVLDB*, 2(1), 2009.

9. B. Adelberg. Nodose – A tool for semi-automatically extracting semi-structured data from text documents. In *SIGMOD*, 1998.

10. P. Adjiman, Philippe Chatalic, François Goasdoué, Marie-Christine Rousset, and Laurent Simon. Distributed reasoning in a peer-to-peer setting. In *ECAI*, pages 945–946, 2004.

11. Philippe Adjiman, François Goasdoué, and Marie-Christine Rousset. SomerDFsin the semantic web. *J. Data Semantics*, 8:158–181, 2007.

12. Foto Afrati, Chen Li, and Prasenjit Mitra. Rewriting queries using views in the presence of arithmetic comparisons. *Theoretical Computer Science*, 368(1-2):88–123, 2006.

13. Foto Afrati, Chen Li, and Jeffrey Ullman. Generating efficient plans for queries using views. In *Proceedings of the ACM SIGMOD Conference*, pages 319–330, 2001.

14. Foto N. Afrati and Rada Chirkova. Selecting and using views to compute aggregate queries. *J. Comput. Syst. Sci.*, 77(6), 2011.

15. Foto N. Afrati and Phokion G. Kolaitis. Answering aggregate queries in data exchange. In *PODS*, 2008.

16. Foto N. Afrati, Chen Li, and Prasenjit Mitra. On containment of conjunctive queries with arithmetic comparisons. In *EDBT*, pages 459–476, 2004.

17. Charu Aggrawal, editor. *Managing and Mining Uncertain Data*. Kluwer Academic Publishers, 2009.

18. Sanjay Agrawal, Surajit Chaudhuri, and Gautam Das. DBXplorer: A system for keyword-based search over relational databases. In *ICDE*, 2002.

19. Rafi Ahmed, Phillippe De Smedt, Weimin Du, William Kent, Mohammad A. Ketabchi, Witold A. Litwin, Abbas Rafii, and Ming-Chien Shan. The Pegasus heterogeneous multidatabase system. *IEEE Computer*, pages 19–26, December 1991.

20. Shurug Al-Khalifa, H. V. Jagadish, Nick Koudas, Divesh Srivastava, and Yuqing Wu. Structural joins: A primitive for efficient XML query pattern matching. In *ICDE*, 2002.

21. Bogdan Alexe, Laura Chiticariu, Renée J. Miller, and Wang Chiew Tan. Muse: Mapping understanding and design by example. In *ICDE*, pages 10–19, 2008.

22. Bogdan Alexe, Mauricio Hernández, Lucian Popa, and Wang-Chiew Tan. Mapmerge: Correlating independent schema mappings. *Proc. VLDB Endow.*, 3, September 2010.

23. Bogdan Alexe, Phokion G. Kolaitis, and Wang Chiew Tan. Characterizing schema mappings via data examples. In *PODS*, pages 261–272, 2010.

24. Bogdan Alexe, Balder ten Cate, Phokion G. Kolaitis, and Wang Chiew Tan. Designing and refining schema mappings via data examples. In *SIGMOD Conference*, pages 133–144, 2011.

25. Alsayed Algergawy, Sabine Massmann, and Erhard Rahm. A clustering-based approach for large-scale ontology matching. In *ADBIS*, pages 415–428, 2011.

26. Mehmet Altinel and Michael J. Franklin. Efficient filtering of XML documents for selective dissemination of information. In *VLDB*, 2000.

27. Yael Amsterdamer, Susan B. Davidson, Daniel Deutch, Tova Milo, Julia Stoyanovich, and Val Tannen. Putting lipstick on pig: Enabling database-style workflow provenance. *PVLDB*, 5(4), 2011.

28. Yael Amsterdamer, Daniel Deutch, Tova Milo, and Val Tannen. On provenance minimization. In *PODS*, 2011.

29. Yael Amsterdamer, Daniel Deutch, and Val Tannen. Provenance for aggregate queries. In *PODS*, 2011.

30. Yuan An, Alexander Borgida, Renée J. Miller, and John Mylopoulos. A semantic approach to discovering schema mapping expressions. In *ICDE*, pages 206–215, 2007.

31. Rohit Ananthakrishna, Surajit Chaudhuri, and Venkatesh Ganti. Eliminating fuzzy duplicates in data warehouses. In *VLDB*, 2002.

32. Lyublena Antova, Christoph Koch, and Dan Olteanu. 10^{10^6} worlds and beyond: Efficient representation and processing of incomplete information. In *ICDE*, 2007.

33. A. Arasu and H. Garcia-Molina. Extracting structured data from web pages. In *SIGMOD*, 2003.

34. Arvind Arasu, Venkatesh Ganti, and Raghav Kaushik. Efficient exact set-similarity joins. In *VLDB*, pages 918–929, 2006.

35. Arvind Arasu, Michaela Götz, and Raghav Kaushik. On active learning of record matching packages. In *SIGMOD Conference*, pages 783–794, 2010.

36. Marcelo Arenas, Pablo Barceló, Leonid Libkin, and Filip Murlak. *Relational and XML Data Exchange*. Synthesis Lectures on Data Management. 2011.

37. Yigal Arens, Chin Y. Chee, Chun-Nan Hsu, and Craig A. Knoblock. Retrieving and integrating data from multiple information sources. *International Journal on Intelligent and Cooperative Information Systems*, 1994.

38. Yigal Arens, Craig A. Knoblock, and Wei-Min Shen. Query reformulation for dynamic information integration. *International Journal on Intelligent and Cooperative Information Systems*, (6)2/3, June 1996.

39. Gustavo Arocena and Alberto Mendelzon. WebOQL: Restructuring documents, databases and webs. In *Proceedings of the International Conference on Data Engineering (ICDE)*, Orlando, Florida, 1998.

40. P. Atzeni and R. Torlone. Management of multiple models in an extensible database design tool. In *Proc. EDBT*, pages 79–95, 1996.

41. Paolo Atzeni, Giansalvatore Mecca, and Paolo Merialdo. To weave the web. In *Proceedings of the International Conference on Very Large Databases (VLDB)*, 1997.

42. Sören Auer, Christian Bizer, Georgi Kobilarov, Jens Lehmann, Richard Cyganiak, and Zachary G. Ives. Dbpedia: A nucleus for a web of open data. In *ISWC/ASWC*, 2007.

43. David Aumueller, Hong Hai Do, Sabine Massmann, and Erhard Rahm. Schema and ontology matching with COMA++. In *SIGMOD Conference*, pages 906–908, 2005.

44. Ron Avnur and Joseph M. Hellerstein. Eddies: Continuously adaptive query processing. In *SIGMOD*, 2000.

45. Brian Babcock, Shivnath Babu, Mayur Datar, and Rajeev Motwani. Chain: Operator scheduling for memory minimization in data stream systems. In *SIGMOD*, 2003.

46. Brian Babcock and Surajit Chaudhuri. Towards a robust query optimizer: A principled and practical approach. In *SIGMOD*, New York, NY, USA, 2005.

47. Brian Babcock, Mayur Datar, and Rajeev Motwani. Load shedding for aggregation queries over data streams. In *ICDE*, 2004.

48. Shivnath Babu and Pedro Bizarro. Adaptive query processing in the looking glass. In *CIDR*, 2005.

49. Shivnath Babu, Rajeev Motwani, Kamesh Munagala, Itaru Nishizawa, and Jennifer Widom. Adaptive ordering of pipelined stream filters. In *SIGMOD*, 2004.

50. Shivnath Babu, Utkarsh Srivastava, and Jennifer Widom. Exploiting k-constraints to reduce memory overhead in continuous queries over streams. Technical Report, Stanford University, 2002.

51. Akanksha Baid, Ian Rae, AnHai Doan, and Jeffrey F. Naughton. Toward industrial-strength keyword search systems over relational data. In *ICDE*, 2010.

52. Akanksha Baid, Ian Rae, Jiexing Li, AnHai Doan, and Jeffrey F. Naughton. Toward scalable keyword search over relational data. *PVLDB*, 3(1):140–149, 2010.

53. François Bancilhon and Nicolas Spyratos. Update semantics of relational views. *TODS*, 6(4), 1981.

54. Michele Banko, Michael J. Cafarella, Stephen Soderland, Matthew Broadhead, and Oren Etzioni. Open information extraction from the web. In Manuela M. Veloso, editor, *IJCAI*, pages 2670–2676, 2007.

55. Luciano Barbosa and Juliana Freire. Siphoning hidden-web data through keyword-based interfaces. In *SBBD*, 2004.

56. Robert Baumgartner, Sergio Flesca, and Georg Gottlob. Declarative information extraction, Web crawling, and recursive wrapping with Lixto. In *Proc. of the 6th Int Conf. on Logic Programming and Nonmonotonic Reasoning*, 2001.

57. Robert Baumgartner, Sergio Flesca, and Georg Gottlob. Visual Web information extraction with Lixto. In *VLDB*, 2001.

58. Louis Bavoil, Steven P. Callahan, Patricia J. Crossno, Juliana Freire, Carlos E. Scheidegger, Claudio T. Silva, and Huy T. Vo. VisTrails: Enabling interactive multiple-view visualizations. *IEEE Visualization*, 2005.

59. Roberto J. Bayardo, Yiming Ma, and Ramakrishnan Srikant. Scaling up all pairs similarity search. In *WWW*, pages 131–140, 2007.

60. Catriel Beeri, Alon Y. Levy, and Marie-Christine Rousset. Rewriting queries using views in description logics. In *Proceedings of the ACM Symposium on Principles of Database Systems (PODS)*, pages 99–108, Tucson, Arizona., 1997.

61. Z. Bellahsene, A. Bonifati, and E. Rahm, editors. *Schema Matching and Mapping*. Springer, 2011.

62. Zohra Bellahsene and Fabien Duchateau. Tuning for schema matching. In *Schema Matching and Mapping*, pages 293–316. 2011.

63. Randall Bello, Karl Dias, Alan Downing, James Feenan, Jim Finnerty, William Norcott, Harry Sun, Andrew Witkowski, and Mohamed Ziauddin. Materialized views in Oracle. In *Proceedings of the International Conference on Very Large Databases (VLDB)*, pages 659–664, 1998.

64. Michael Benedikt and Georg Gottlob. The impact of virtual views on containment. *PVLDB*, 3(1):297–308, 2010.

65. Omar Benjelloun, Hector Garcia-Molina, Heng Gong, Hideki Kawai, Tait Eliott Larson, David Menestrina, and Sutthipong Thavisomboon. D-swoosh: A family of algorithms for generic, distributed entity resolution. In *ICDCS*, page 37, 2007.

66. Omar Benjelloun, Hector Garcia-Molina, David Menestrina, Qi Su, Steven Euijong Whang, and Jennifer Widom. Swoosh: A generic approach to entity resolution. *VLDB J.*, 18(1):255–276, 2009.

67. Omar Benjelloun, Anish Das Sarma, Alon Y. Halevy, and Jennifer Widom. ULDBs: Databases with uncertainty and lineage. In *VLDB*, 2006.

68. Sonia Bergamaschi, Silvana Castano, and Maurizio Vincini. Semantic integration of semistructured and structured data sources. *SIGMOD Record*, 28(1):54–59, 1999.

69. Sonia Bergamaschi, Elton Domnori, Francesco Guerra, Raquel Trillo Lado, and Yannis Velegrakis. Keyword search over relational databases: A metadata approach. In *Proceedings of the 2011 International Conference on Management of Data*, SIGMOD '11, New York, NY, USA, 2011. Available from http://doi.acm.org/10.1145/1989323.1989383.

70. Michael K. Bergman. The deep web: Surfacing hidden value. *Journal of Electronic Publishing*, 2001.

71. Tim Berners-Lee, James Hendler, and Ora Lassila. The semantic web. *Scientific American*, May 2001.

72. Philip A. Bernstein. Applying model management to classical meta-data problems. In *Proceedings of the Conference on Innovative Data Systems Research (CIDR)*, 2003.

73. Philip A. Bernstein and Dah-Ming W. Chiu. Using semi-joins to solve relational queries. *J. ACM*, 28, 1981.

74. Philip A. Bernstein, Fausto Giunchiglia, Anastasios Kementsietsidis, John Mylopoulos, Luciano Serafini, and Ilya Zaihrayeu. Data management for peer-to-peer computing: A vision. In *Proceedings of the WebDB Workshop*, 2002.

75. Philip A. Bernstein, Todd J. Green, Sergey Melnik, and Alan Nash. Implementing mapping composition. In *Proc. of VLDB*, pages 55–66, 2006.

76. Philip A. Bernstein, Alon Y. Halevy, and Rachel Pottinger. A vision for management of complex models. *SIGMOD Record*, 29(4):55–63, 2000.

77. Philip A. Bernstein and Sergey Melnik. Model management 2.0: Manipulating richer mappings. In *Proc. of SIGMOD*, pages 1–12, 2007.

78. Philip A. Bernstein, Sergey Melnik, and John E. Churchill. Incremental schema matching. In *VLDB*, pages 1167–1170, 2006.

79. Laure Berti-Equille, Anish Das Sarma, Xin Dong, Amélie Marian, and Divesh Srivastava. Sailing the information ocean with awareness of currents: Discovery and application of source dependence. In *CIDR*, 2009.

80. Gaurav Bhalotia, Arvind Hulgeri, Charuta Nakhe, Soumen Chakrabarti, and S. Sudarshan. Keyword searching and browsing in databases using BANKS. In *ICDE*, 2002.

81. I. Bhattacharya and L. Getoor. A latent Dirichlet model for unsupervised entity resolution. In *Proc. of the SIAM Int. Conf. on Data Mining (SDM)*, 2006.

82. I. Bhattacharya and L. Getoor. Collective entity resolution in relational data. *ACM Transactions on Knowledge Discovery from Data*, 1(1), 2007.

83. Indrajit Bhattacharya, Lise Getoor, and Louis Licamele. Query-time entity resolution. In *KDD*, pages 529–534, 2006.

84. M. Bilenko. Learnable similarity functions and their applications to clustering and record linkage. In *AAAI*, pages 981–982, 2004.

85. M. Bilenko and R. J. Mooney. Adaptive duplicate detection using learnable string similarity measures. In *Proc. of the ACM Int. Conf. on Knowledge Discovery and Data Mining (KDD)*, pages 39–48, 2003.

86. M. Bilenko, R. J. Mooney, W. W. Cohen, P. D. Ravikumar, and S. E. Fienberg. Adaptive name matching in information integration. *IEEE Intelligent Systems*, 18(5):16–23, 2003.

87. Olivier Biton, Sarah Cohen Boulakia, Susan B. Davidson, and Carmem S. Hara. Querying and managing provenance through user views in scientific workflows. In *ICDE*, 2008.

88. Christian Bizer, Tom Heath, and Tim Berners-Lee. Linked data – The story so far. *Int. J. Semantic Web Inf. Syst.*, 5(3):1–22, 2009.

89. José A. Blakeley, Neil Coburn, and Per-Åke Larson. Updating derived relations: Detecting irrelevant and autonomously computable updates. *TODS*, 14(3), 1989.

90. Burton H. Bloom. Space/time trade-offs in hash coding with allowable errors. *CACM*, 13(7), July 1970.

91. Lukas Blunschi, Jens-Peter Dittrich, Olivier Girard, Shant Krakos Karakashian, and Marcos Antonio Vas Salles. The iMemex personal dataspace management system (demo). In *CIDR*, 2007.

92. Philip Bohannon, Eiman Elnahrawy, Wenfei Fan, and Michael Flaster. Putting context into schema matching. In *VLDB*, pages 307–318, 2006.

93. Alex Borgida. Description logics in data management. *IEEE Trans. on Know. and Data Engineering*, 7(5):671–682, 1995.

94. V. R. Borkar, K. Deshmukh, and S. Sarawagi. Automatic segmentation of text into structured records. In *SIGMOD*, 2001.

95. J. Boulos, N. Dalvi, B. Mandhani, S. Mathur, C. Re, and D. Suciu. MYSTIQ: A system for finding more answers by using probabilities. In *Proc. of ACM SIGMOD*, 2005.

96. Michael Brundage. *XQuery: The XML Query Language*. February 2004.

97. Nicolas Bruno, Nick Koudas, and Divesh Srivastava. Holistic twig joins: Optimal xml pattern matching. In *SIGMOD Conference*, 2002.

98. Peter Buneman, Sanjeev Khanna, and Wang Chiew Tan. Why and where: A characterization of data provenance. In *ICDT*, 2001.

99. Peter Buneman, Anthony Kosky, and Susan Davidson. Theoretical aspects of schema merging. In *Proc. of EDBT*, pages 152–167, 1992.

100. Douglas Burdick, Mauricio A. Hernández, Howard Ho, Georgia Koutrika, Rajasekar Krishnamurthy, Lucian Popa, Ioana Stanoi, Shivakumar Vaithyanathan, and Sanjiv R. Das. Extracting, linking and integrating data from public sources: A financial case study. *IEEE Data Eng. Bull.*, 34(3):60–67, 2011.

101. Michael J. Cafarella, Alon Halevy, Yang Zhang, Daisy Zhe Wang, and Eugene Wu. Uncovering the Relational Web. In *WebDB*, 2008.

102. Michael J. Cafarella, Alon Halevy, Yang Zhang, Daisy Zhe Wang, and Eugene Wu. WebTables: Exploring the power of tables on the web. In *VLDB*, 2008.

103. D. Cai, S. Yu, J. Wen, and W. Ma. Extracting content structure for Web pages based on visual representation. In *Proc. of the 5th Asian-Pacific Web Conference (APWeb)*, 2003.

104. Andrea Cali, Diego Calvanese, Giuseppe DeGiacomo, and Maurizio Lenzerini. Data integration under integrity constraints. In *Proceedings of CAiSE*, pages 262–279, 2002.

105. M. E. Califf and R. J. Mooney. Relational learning of pattern-match rules for information extraction. In *AAAI*, 1999.

106. James P. Callan and Margaret E. Connell. Query-based sampling of text databases. *ACM Transactions on Information Systems*, 19(2):97–130, 2001.

107. D. Calvanese, G. De Giacomo, and M. Lenzerini. Answering queries using views over description logics. In *Proceedings of AAAI*, pages 386–391, 2000.

108. D. Calvanese, G. De Giacomo, M. Lenzerini, and M. Vardi. View-based query processing for regular path queries with inverse. In *Proceedings of the ACM Symposium on Principles of Database Systems (PODS)*, pages 58–66, 2000.

109. Michael J. Carey and Donald Kossmann. On saying "enough already!" in SQL. In *SIGMOD*, 1997.

110. Andrew Carlson, Justin Betteridge, Bryan Kisiel, Burr Settles, Estevam R. Hruschka Jr., and Tom M. Mitchell. Toward an architecture for never-ending language learning. In Maria Fox and David Poole, editors, *AAAI*. AAAI Press, 2010.

111. S. Castano and V. De Antonellis. A discovery-based approach to database ontology design. *Distributed and Parallel Databases – Special Issue on Ontologies and Databases*, 7(1), 1999.

112. T. Catarci and M. Lenzerini. Representing and using interschema knowledge in cooperative information systems. *Journal of Intelligent and Cooperative Information Systems*, pages 55–62, 1993.

113. Xiaoyong Chai, Ba-Quy Vuong, AnHai Doan, and Jeffrey F. Naughton. Efficiently incorporating user feedback into information extraction and integration programs. In *SIGMOD*, New York, NY, USA, 2009.

114. A.K. Chandra and P.M. Merlin. Optimal implementation of conjunctive queries in relational databases. In *Proceedings of the Ninth Annual ACM Symposium on Theory of Computing*, pages 77–90, 1977.

115. C. Chang, M. Kayed, M. R. Girgis, and K. F. Shaalan. A survey of web information extraction systems. *IEEE Trans. Knowl. Data Eng.*, 18(10):1411–1428, 2006.

116. C. Chang and S. Lui. IEPAD: Information extraction based on pattern discovery. In *WWW*, 2001.

117. Adriane Chapman and H. V. Jagadish. Why not? In *SIGMOD Conference*, 2009.

118. Sam Chapman. Sam's string metrics. 2006. Available at `http:staffwww.dcs.shef.ac.uk/people/sam.chapman@k-now.co.uk/stringmetrics.html`.

119. A. Chatterjee and A. Segev. Data manipulation in heterogeneous databases. *SIGMOD Record*, 20(4):64–68, 1991.

120. S. Chaudhuri, K. Ganjam, V. Ganti, and R. Motwani. Robust and efficient fuzzy match for online data cleaning. In *SIGMOD*, 2003.

121. Surajit Chaudhuri. An overview of query optimization in relational systems. In *PODS*, 1998.

122. Surajit Chaudhuri and Umeshwar Dayal. An overview of data warehousing and olap technology. *SIGMOD Record*, 26(1), 1997.

123. Surajit Chaudhuri, Umeshwar Dayal, and Vivek R. Narasayya. An overview of business intelligence technology. *Commun. ACM*, 54(8):88–98, 2011.

124. Surajit Chaudhuri, Venkatesh Ganti, and Raghav Kaushik. A primitive operator for similarity joins in data cleaning. In *ICDE*, page 5, 2006.

125. Surajit Chaudhuri, Ravi Krishnamurthy, Spyros Potamianos, and Kyuseok Shim. Optimizing queries with materialized views. In *Proceedings of the International Conference on Data Engineering (ICDE)*, pages 190–200, Taipei, Taiwan, 1995.

126. Surajit Chaudhuri, Anish Das Sarma, Venkatesh Ganti, and Raghav Kaushik. Leveraging aggregate constraints for deduplication. In *SIGMOD Conference*, pages 437–448, 2007.

127. Surajit Chaudhuri and Moshe Vardi. Optimizing real conjunctive queries. In *Proceedings of the ACM Symposium on Principles of Database Systems (PODS)*, pages 59–70, Washington D.C., 1993.

128. Sudarshan Chawathe, Hector Garcia-Molina, Joachim Hammer, Kelly Ireland, Yannis Papakonstantinou, Jeffrey Ullman, and Jennifer Widom. The TSIMMIS project: Integration of heterogeneous information sources. In *Proceedings of IPSJ*, Tokyo, Japan, October 1994.

129. Sudarshan S. Chawathe and Hector Garcia-Molina. Meaningful change detection in structured data. In *SIGMOD*, pages 26–37, 1997.

130. Chandra Chekuri and Anand Rajaraman. Conjunctive query containment revisited. *Theor. Comput. Sci.*, 239(2):211–229, 2000.

131. Yi Chen, Susan B. Davidson, and Yifeng Zheng. Vitex: A streaming xpath processing system. In *ICDE*, 2005.

132. James Cheney, Umut A. Acar, and Amal Ahmed. Provenance traces. *CoRR*, abs/0812.0564, 2008.

133. James Cheney, Laura Chiticariu, and Wang Chiew Tan. Provenance in databases: Why, how, and where. *Foundations and Trends in Databases*, 1(4), 2009.

134. Rada Chirkova, Alon Y. Halevy, and Dan Suciu. A formal perspective on the view selection problem. *VLDB J.*, 11(3), 2002.

135. L. Chiticariu, P. G. Kolaitis, and L. Popa. Interactive generation of integrated schemas. In *Proc. of SIGMOD*, 2008.

136. Laura Chiticariu, Wang Chiew Tan, and Gaurav Vijayvargiya. Dbnotes: A post-it system for relational databases based on provenance. In *SIGMOD*, 2005.

137. Eric Chu, Akanksha Baid, Xiaoyong Chai, AnHai Doan, and Jeffrey F. Naughton. Combining keyword search and forms for ad hoc querying of databases. In *SIGMOD Conference*, 2009.

138. Francis C. Chu, Joseph Y. Halpern, and Johannes Gehrke. Least expected cost query optimization: What can we expect? In *PODS*, 2002.

139. S. Chuang, K. C. Chang, and C. Zhai. Collaborative wrapping: A turbo framework for Web data extraction. In *ICDE*, 2007.

140. Chris Clifton, E. Housman, and Arnon Rosenthal. Experience with a combined approach to attribute-matching across heterogeneous databases. In *DS-7*, 1997.

141. M. Cochinwala, V. Kurien, G. Lalk, and D. Shasha. Efficient data reconciliation. *Inf. Sci.*, 137(1-4):1–15, 2001.

142. Sara Cohen. Containment of aggregate queries. *SIGMOD Record*, 34(1):77–85, 2005.

143. W. Cohen. A mini-course on record linkage and matching, 2004. http://www.cs.cmu.edu/~wcohen.

144. W. Cohen and J. Richman. Learning to match and cluster large high-dimensional data sets for data integration. In *Proc. of the ACM Int. Conf. on Knowledge Discovery and Data Mining (KDD)*, pages 475–480, 2002.

145. W. W. Cohen. Data integration using similarity joins and a word-based information representation language. *ACM Trans. Inf. Syst.*, 18(3):288–321, 2000.

146. W. W. Cohen. Record linkage tutorial: Distance metrics for text. 2001. PPT slides, available at www.cs.cmu.edu/~wcohen/Matching-2.ppt.

147. W. W. Cohen, M. Hurst, and L. S. Jensen. A flexible learning system for wrapping tables and lists in HTML documents. In *WWW*, 2002.

148. W. W. Cohen, P. D. Ravikumar, and S. E. Fienberg. A comparison of string distance metrics for name-matching tasks. In *IIWeb*, 2003.

149. Latha S. Colby, Timothy Griffin, Leonid Libkin, Inderpal Singh Mumick, and Howard Trickey. Algorithms for deferred view maintenance. In *SIGMOD*, 1996.

150. Richard L. Cole and Goetz Graefe. Optimization of dynamic query evaluation plans. In *SIGMOD*, 1994.

151. Mark Craven, Dan DiPasquo, Dayne Freitag, Andrew McCallum, Tom Mitchell, Kamal Nigam, and Sean Slattery. Learning to extract symbolic knowledge from the world-wide web. In *Proceedings of the AAAI Fifteenth National Conference on Artificial Intelligence*, 1998.

152. V. Crescenzi and G. Mecca. Grammars have exceptions. *Inf. Syst.*, 23(8):539–565, 1998.

153. V. Crescenzi and G. Mecca. Automatic information extraction from large websites. *J. ACM*, 51(5):731–779, 2004.

154. V. Crescenzi, G. Mecca, and P. Merialdo. Roadrunner: Towards automatic data extraction from large web sites. In *VLDB*, 2001.

155. Yingwei Cui. *Lineage Tracing in Data Warehouses*. PhD thesis, Stanford Univ., 2001.

156. A. Culotta and A. McCallum. Joint deduplication of multiple record types in relational data. In *Proc. of the ACM Int. Conf. on Information and Knowledge Management (CIKM)*, pages 257–258, 2005.

157. Carlo Curino, Hyun Jin Moon, Alin Deutsch, and Carlo Zaniolo. Update rewriting and integrity constraint maintenance in a schema evolution support system: Prism++. *PVLDB*, 4(2), 2010.

158. N. Dalvi, R. Kumar, and M. A. Soliman. Automatic wrappers for large scale web extraction. *PVLDB*, 4(4):219–230, 2011.

159. N. N. Dalvi, P. Bohannon, and F. Sha. Robust Web extraction: An approach based on a probabilistic tree-edit model. In *SIGMOD*, 2009.

160. Nilesh Dalvi and Dan Suciu. Efficient query evaluation on probabilistic databases. In *VLDB*, 2004.

161. Dean Daniels. Query compilation in a distributed database system. Technical Report RJ 3423, IBM, 1982.

162. A. Das Sarma, L. Dong, and A. Halevy. Bootstrapping pay-as-you-go data integration systems. In *Proc. of SIGMOD*, 2008.

163. Arjun Dasgupta, Xin Jin, Bradley Jewell, Nan Zhang, and Gautam Das. Unbiased estimation of size and other aggregates over hidden web databases. In *SIGMOD Conference*, pages 855–866, 2010.

164. Susan B. Davidson, Sanjeev Khanna, Tova Milo, Debmalya Panigrahi, and Sudeepa Roy. Provenance views for module privacy. In *PODS*, 2011.

165. U. Dayal. Processing queries over generalized hierarchies in a multidatabase systems. In *Proc. of the VLDB Conf.*, pages 342–353, 1983.

166. Umeshwar Dayal and Philip A. Bernstein. On the correct translation of update operations on relational views. *TODS*, 7(3), 1982.

167. Filipe de S Mesquita, Altigran Soares da Silva, Edleno Silva de Moura, Pvel Calado, and Alberto H. F. Laender. Labrador: Efficiently publishing relational databases on the web by using keyword-based query interfaces. *Inf. Process. Manage.*, 43(4):983–1004, 2007.

168. L. G. DeMichiel. Resolving database incompatibility: An approach to performing relational operations over mismatched domains. *IEEE Transactions on Knowledge and Data Engineering*, 1989.

169. Pedro DeRose, Xiaoyong Chai, Byron J. Gao, Warren Shen, AnHai Doan, Philip Bohannon, and Xiaojin Zhu. Building community wikipedias: A machine-human partnership approach. In *ICDE*, pages 646–655, 2008.

170. Pedro DeRose, Warren Shen, Fei Chen, AnHai Doan, and Raghu Ramakrishnan. Building structured web community portals: A top-down, compositional, and incremental approach. In *Proc. of VLDB*, 2007.

171. Amol Deshpande and Joseph M. Hellerstein. Lifting the burden of history from adaptive query processing. In *VLDB*, 2004.

172. Amol Deshpande, Zachary Ives, and Vijayshankar Raman. Adaptive query processing. *Foundations and Trends in Databases*, 2007.

173. Alin Deutsch, Mary F. Fernández, Daniela Florescu, Alon Y. Levy, and Dan Suciu. XML-QL. In *QL*, 1998.

174. Alin Deutsch and Val Tannen. MARS: A system for publishing XML from mixed and redundant storage. In *VLDB*, 2003.

175. D. Dey. Entity matching in heterogeneous databases: A logistic regression approach. *Decision Support Systems*, 44(3):740–747, 2008.

176. D. Dey, S. Sarkar, and P. De. A distance-based approach to entity reconciliation in heterogeneous databases. *IEEE Trans. Knowl. Data Eng.*, 14(3):567–582, 2002.

177. Yanlei Diao, Peter M. Fischer, Michael J. Franklin, and Raymond To. YFilter: Efficient and scalable filtering of XML documents. In *ICDE*, 2002.

178. Hong Hai Do and Erhard Rahm. COMA – A system for flexible combination of schema matching approaches. In *VLDB*, 2002.

179. A. Doan and A. Y. Halevy. Semantic integration research in the database community: A brief survey. *AI Magazine*, 26(1):83–94, 2005.

180. A. Doan, N. F. Noy, and A. Y. Halevy. Introduction to the special issue on semantic integration. *SIGMOD Record*, 33(4):11–13, 2004.

181. AnHai Doan, Pedro Domingos, and Alon Y. Halevy. Reconciling schemas of disparate data sources: A machine learning approach. In *Proceedings of the ACM SIGMOD Conference*, 2001.

182. AnHai Doan, Ying Lu, Yoonkyong Lee, and Jiawei Han. Profile-based object matching for information integration. *IEEE Intelligent Systems*, 18(5):54–59, 2003.

183. Anhai Doan, Jayant Madhavan, Pedro Domingos, and Alon Halevy. Learning to map between ontologies on the semantic web. In *11th World Wide Web Conference*, 2002.

184. AnHai Doan, Jeffrey F. Naughton, Raghu Ramakrishnan, Akanksha Baid, Xiaoyong Chai, Fei Chen, Ting Chen, Eric Chu, Pedro DeRose, Byron Gao, Chaitanya Gokhale, Jiansheng Huang, Warren Shen, and Ba-Quy Vuong. Information extraction challenges in managing unstructured data. *SIGMOD Record*, December 2008.

185. AnHai Doan, Raghu Ramakrishnan, Fei Chen, Pedro DeRose, Yoonkyong Lee, Robert McCann, Mayssam Sayyadian, and Warren Shen. Community information management. *IEEE Data Eng. Bull.*, 29(1):64–72, 2006.

186. AnHai Doan, Raghu Ramakrishnan, and Alon Y. Halevy. Crowdsourcing systems on the world-wide web. *Commun. ACM*, 54(4):86–96, 2011.

187. Pedro Domingos and Micheal Pazzani. On the Optimality of the Simple Bayesian Classifier under Zero-One Loss. *Machine Learning*, 29:103–130, 1997.

188. X. Dong, A. Y. Halevy, and J. Madhavan. Reference reconciliation in complex information spaces. In *Proc. of the SIGMOD Conf.*, pages 85–96, 2005.

189. X. Dong, A. Y. Halevy, and C. Yu. Data integration with uncertainty. In *Proc. of VLDB*, 2007.

190. Xin Dong, Laure Berti-Equille, Yifan Hu, and Divesh Srivastava. Global detection of complex copying relationships between sources. *PVLDB*, 3(1):1358–1369, 2010.

191. Xin Dong and Alon Halevy. A platform for personal information management and integration. In *Proc. of CIDR*, 2005.

192. Francesco M. Donini, Maurizio Lenzerini, Daniele Nardi, and Werner Nutt. The complexity of concept languages. In *Proceedings of KR-91*, 1991.

193. Francesco M. Donini, Maurizio Lenzerini, Daniele Nardi, and Andrea Schaerf. A hybrid system with datalog and concept languages. In E. Ardizzone, S. Gaglio, and F. Sorbello, editors, *Trends in Artificial Intelligence*, volume LNAI 549, pages 88–97. Springer Verlag, 1991.

194. Mira Dontcheva, Steven M. Drucker, David Salesin, and Michael F. Cohen. Relations, cards, and search templates: User-guided web data integration and layout. In *UIST*, pages 61–70, 2007.

195. R. B. Doorenbos, O. Etzioni, and D. S. Weld. A scalable comparison-shopping agent for the World-Wide Web. In *Agents*, 1997.

196. R. Durbin, S. Eddy, A. Krogh, and G. Mitchison. *Biological Sequence Analysis: Probabilistic Models of Proteins and Nucleic Acids*. Cambridge University Press, 1999.

197. Oliver Duschka, Michael Genesereth, and Alon Levy. Recursive query plans for data integration. *Journal of Logic Programming, special issue on Logic Based Heterogeneous Information Systems*, 43(1), 2000.

198. Oliver M. Duschka and Michael R. Genesereth. Answering recursive queries using views. In *PODS*, 1997.

199. Oliver M. Duschka and Michael R. Genesereth. Query planning in infomaster. In *Proceedings of the ACM Symposium on Applied Computing*, pages 109–111, San Jose, CA, 1997.

200. Oliver M. Duschka and Alon Y. Levy. Recursive plans for information gathering. In *Proc. of the 15th Int. Joint Conf. on Artificial Intelligence (IJCAI)*, pages 778–784, 1997.

201. Marc Ehrig, Steffen Staab, and York Sure. Bootstrapping ontology alignment methods with APFEL. In *International Semantic Web Conference*, pages 186–200, 2005.

202. Charles Elkan. A decision procedure for conjunctive query disjointness. In *Proceedings of the ACM Symposium on Principles of Database Systems (PODS)*, Portland, Oregon, 1989.

203. Charles Elkan. Independence of logic database queries and updates. In *Proceedings of the ACM Symposium on Principles of Database Systems (PODS)*, pages 154–160, 1990.

204. A. K. Elmagarmid, P. G. Ipeirotis, and V. S. Verykios. Duplicate record detection: A survey. *IEEE Trans. Knowl. Data Eng.*, 19(1):1–16, 2007.

205. A.K. Elmagarmid, P.G. Ipeirotis, and V.S. Verykios. Duplicate record detection: A survey. *IEEE Transactions on Knowledge and Data Engineering*, 19(1):1–16, 2007.

206. Hazem Elmeleegy, Ahmed K. Elmagarmid, and Jaewoo Lee. Leveraging query logs for schema mapping generation in u-map. In *SIGMOD Conference*, pages 121–132, 2011.

207. Hazem Elmeleegy, Jayant Madhavan, and Alon Y. Halevy. Harvesting relational tables from lists on the web. *PVLDB*, 2(1):1078–1089, 2009.

208. Hazem Elmeleegy, Mourad Ouzzani, and Ahmed K. Elmagarmid. Usage-based schema matching. In *ICDE*, pages 20–29, 2008.

209. Mohamed Y. Eltabakh, Walid G. Aref, Ahmed K. Elmagarmid, Mourad Ouzzani, and Yasin N. Silva. Supporting annotations on relations. In *EDBT*, 2009.

210. D. W. Embley, D. M. Campbell, Y. S. Jiang, S. W. Liddle, Y. Ng, D. Quass, and R. D. Smith. Conceptual-model-based data extraction from multiple-record web pages. *Data Knowl. Eng.*, 31(3):227–251, 1999.

211. D. W. Embley, Y. S. Jiang, and Y. Ng. Record-boundary discovery in web documents. In *SIGMOD*, 1999.

212. David W. Embley, David Jackman, and Li Xu. Multifaceted exploitation of metadata for attribute match discovery in information integration. In *Workshop on Information Integration on the Web*, pages 110–117, 2001.

213. O. Etzioni, K. Golden, and D. Weld. Sound and efficient closed-world reasoning for planning. *Artificial Intelligence*, 89(1–2):113–148, January 1997.

214. Jérôme Euzenat and Pavel Shvaiko. *Ontology Matching*. Springer, 2007.

215. Ronald Fagin. Inverting schema mappings. In *Proc. of PODS*, pages 50–59, 2006.

216. Ronald Fagin, Phokion Kolaitis, Renée J. Miller, and Lucian Popa. Data exchange: Semantics and query answering. *TCS*, 336:89–124, 2005.

217. Ronald Fagin, Phokion Kolaitis, and Lucian Popa. Data exchange: Getting to the core. *ACM Transactions on Database Systems*, 30(1):174–210, 2005.

218. Ronald Fagin, Phokion G. Kolaitis, and Lucian Popa. Composing schema mappings: Second-order dependencies to the rescue. *ACM Transactions on Database Systems*, 30(4):994–1055, 2005.

219. Ronald Fagin, Phokion G. Kolaitis, Lucian Popa, and Wang-Chiew Tan. Quasi-inverses of schema mappings. In *Proc. of PODS*, pages 123–132, 2007.

220. Ronald Fagin, Phokion G. Kolaitis, Lucian Popa, and Wang Chiew Tan. Schema mapping evolution through composition and inversion. In *Schema Matching and Mapping*, pages 191–222. 2011.

221. Ronald Fagin, Amnon Lotem, and Moni Naor. Optimal aggregation algorithms for middleware. *Journal of Computer and System Sciences*, 66(4), June 2003.

222. Sean M. Falconer and Margaret-Anne D. Storey. A cognitive support framework for ontology mapping. In *ISWC/ASWC*, pages 114–127, 2007.

223. Wenfei Fan and Floris Geerts. Capturing missing tuples and missing values. In *PODS*, pages 169–178, 2010.

224. I. P. Fellegi and A. B. Sunter. A theory for record linkage. *Journal of the American Statistical Society*, 64(328):1183–1210, 1969.

225. Mary Fernandez, Daniela Florescu, Jaewoo Kang, Alon Levy, and Dan Suciu. Catching the boat with Strudel: Experiences with a web-site management system. In *Proceedings of the ACM SIGMOD Conference*, Seattle, WA, 1998.

226. Jonathan Finger and Neoklis Polyzotis. Robust and efficient algorithms for rank join evaluation. In *SIGMOD*, New York, NY, USA, 2009.

227. Daniela Florescu, Daphne Koller, and Alon Levy. Using probabilistic information in data integration. In *VLDB*, 1997.

228. Daniela Florescu, Alon Levy, Ioana Manolesu, and Dan Suciu. Query optimization in the presence of limited access patterns. In *Proceedings of the ACM SIGMOD Conference*, 1999.

229. Daniela Florescu, Alon Levy, and Alberto Mendelzon. Database techniques for the world-wide web: A survey. *SIGMOD Record*, 27(3):59–74, September 1998.

230. Daniela Florescu, Louiqa Raschid, and Patrick Valduriez. Using heterogeneous equivalences for query rewriting in multidatabase systems. In *Proceedings of the Int. Conf. on Cooperative Information Systems (COOPIS)*, 1995.

231. J. Nathan Foster, Todd J. Green, and Val Tannen. Annotated XML: Queries and provenance. In *PODS*, 2008.

232. Paul Francis, Sugih Jamin, Cheng Jin, Yixin Jin, Danny Raz, Yuval Shavitt, and Lixia Zhang. Idmaps: A global internet host distance estimation service. *IEEE/ACM Trans. Netw.*, 9(5), 2001.

233. Michael Franklin, Alon Halevy, and David Maier. From databases to dataspaces: A new abstraction for information management. *SIGMOD Rec.*, 34(4), 2005.

234. M. Friedman and D. Weld. Efficient execution of information gathering plans. In *Proc. of the 15th Int. Joint Conf. on Artificial Intelligence (IJCAI)*, 1997.

235. Marc Friedman, Alon Levy, and Todd Millstein. Navigational Plans for Data Integration. In *Proceedings of the National Conference on Artificial Intelligence (AAAI)*, 1999.

236. N. Fuhr and T. Rölleke. A probabilistic relational algebra for the integration of information retrieval and database systems. *ACM Transactions on Information Systems*, 14(1), 1997.

237. Ariel Fuxman, Mauricio A. Hernández, C. T. Howard Ho, Renée J. Miller, Paolo Papotti, and Lucian Popa. Nested mappings: Schema mapping reloaded. In *VLDB*, 2006.

238. A. Gal. Why is schema matching tough and what can we do about it? *SIGMOD Record*, 35(4):2–5, 2007.

239. A. Gal, G. Modica, H. Jamil, and A. Eyal. Automatic ontology matching using application semantics. *AI Magazine*, 26(1):21–31, 2005.

240. Avigdor Gal. Managing uncertainty in schema matching with top-k schema mappings. *Journal of Data Semantics*, VI:90–114, 2006.

241. Avigdor Gal. *Uncertain Schema Matching*. Synthesis Lectures on Data Management. 2011.

242. Avigdor Gal, Ateret Anaby-Tavor, Alberto Trombetta, and Danilo Montesi. A framework for modeling and evaluating automatic semantic reconciliation. In *VLDB J.*, pages 50–67, 2005.

243. M. Ganesh, J. Srivastava, and T. Richardson. Mining entity-identification rules for database integration. In *Proc. of the ACM Int. Conf. on Knowledge Discovery and Data Mining (KDD)*, pages 291–294, 1996.

244. Hector Garcia-Molina, Yannis Papakonstantinou, Dallan Quass, Anand Rajaraman, Yehoshua Sagiv, Jeffrey Ullman, and Jennifer Widom. The TSIMMIS project: Integration of heterogeneous information sources. *Journal of Intelligent Information Systems*, 8(2), March 1997.

245. Hector Garcia-Molina, Jeffrey D. Ullman, and Jennifer Widom. *Database Systems: The Complete Book*. Prentice Hall, 2002.

246. Wolfgang Gatterbauer, Magdalena Balazinska, Nodira Khoussainova, and Dan Suciu. Believe it or not: Adding belief annotations to databases. *PVLDB*, 2(1), 2009.

247. Wolfgang Gatterbauer, Paul Bohunsky, Marcus Herzog, Bernhard Krüpl, and Bernhard Pollak. Towards domain-independent information extraction from web tables. In *WWW*, pages 71–80, 2007.

248. L. Getoor and R. Miller. Data and metadata alignment, 2007. Tutorial, the Alberto Mendelzon Workshop on the Foundations of Databases and the Web.

249. C. L. Giles, K. D. Bollacker, and S. Lawrence. CiteSeer: An automatic citation indexing system. In *Proc. of the ACM Int. Conf. on Digital Libraries*, pages 89–98, 1998.

250. L. E. Gill. OX-LINK: The Oxford medical record linkage system. In *Proc. of the Int Record Linkage Workshop and Exposition*, 1997.

251. Fausto Giunchiglia, Pavel Shvaiko, and Mikalai Yatskevich. S-match: An algorithm and an implementation of semantic matching. In *ESWS*, pages 61–75, 2004.

252. Boris Glavic and Gustavo Alonso. Perm: Processing provenance and data on the same data model through query rewriting. In *ICDE*, 2009.

253. Boris Glavic and Gustavo Alonso. Provenance for nested subqueries. In *EDBT*, 2009.

254. Boris Glavic, Gustavo Alonso, Renée J. Miller, and Laura M. Haas. Tramp: Understanding the behavior of schema mappings through provenance. *PVLDB*, 3(1), 2010.

255. François Goasdoué and Marie-Christine Rousset. Querying distributed data through distributed ontologies: A simple but scalable approach. *IEEE Intelligent Systems*, 18(5):60–65, 2003.

256. E. M. Gold. Language identification in the limit. *Information and Control*, 10(5):447–474, 1967.

257. E. M. Gold. Complexity of automaton identification from given data. *Information and Control*, 37(3):302–320, 1978.

258. Roy Goldman, Jason McHugh, and Jennifer Widom. From semistructured data to XML: Migrating the Lore data model and query language. In *WebDB '99*, 1999.

259. Jonathan Goldstein and Per-Ake Larson. Optimizing queries using materialized views: A practical, scalable solution. In *Proceedings of the ACM SIGMOD Conference*, pages 331–342, 2001.

260. Hector Gonzalez, Alon Y. Halevy, Christian S. Jensen, Anno Langen, Jayant Madhavan, Rebecca Shapley, and Warren Shen. Google fusion tables: Data management, integration and collaboration in the cloud. In *SoCC*, 2010.

261. Hector Gonzalez, Alon Y. Halevy, Christian S. Jensen, Anno Langen, Jayant Madhavan, Rebecca Shapley, Warren Shen, and Jonathan Goldberg-Kidon. Google fusion tables: Web-centered data management and collaboration. In *SIGMOD*, 2010.

262. Georg Gottlob, Christoph Koch, Robert Baumgartner, Marcus Herzog, and Sergio Flesca. The Lixto data extraction project — Back and forth between theory and practice. In *PODS*, 2004.

263. Goetz Graefe. Query evaluation techniques for large databases. *ACM Computing Surveys*, 25(2), June 1993.

264. L. Gravano, P. G. Ipeirotis, N. Koudas, and D. Srivastava. Text joins in an RDBMS for web data integration. In *WWW*, 2003.

265. Luis Gravano, Panagiotis G. Ipeirotis, H. V. Jagadish, Nick Koudas, S. Muthukrishnan, and Divesh Srivastava. Approximate string joins in a database (almost) for free. In *VLDB*, pages 491–500, 2001.

266. Luis Gravano, Panagiotis G. Ipeirotis, Nick Koudas, and Divesh Srivastava. Text joins in an RDBMS for web data integration. In *WWW*, 2003.

267. Todd J. Green. Containment of conjunctive queries on annotated relations. In *ICDT*, 2009.

268. Todd J. Green, Grigoris Karvounarakis, Zachary G. Ives, and Val Tannen. Update exchange with mappings and provenance. In *VLDB*, 2007. Amended version available as Univ. of Pennsylvania report MS-CIS-07-26.

269. Todd J. Green, Grigoris Karvounarakis, and Val Tannen. Provenance semirings. In *PODS*, 2007.

270. Todd J. Green, Gerome Miklau, Makoto Onizuka, and Dan Suciu. Processing XML streams with deterministic automata and stream indexes. Available from `http://www.cs.washington.edu/homes/suciu/files/paper.ps`, February 2002.

271. Todd J. Green and Val Tannen. Models for incomplete and probabilistic information. In *International Workshop on Incompleteness and Inconsistency in databases*, March 2006.

272. Nils Grimsmo, Truls A. Bjørklund, and Magnus Lie Hetland. Fast optimal twig joins. *PVLDBJ*, 3, September 2010.

273. S. Grumbach and G. Mecca. In search of the lost schema. In *ICDT*, 1999.

274. Pankaj Gulhane, Amit Madaan, Rupesh R. Mehta, Jeyashankher Ramamirtham, Rajeev Rastogi, Sandeepkumar Satpal, Srinivasan H. Sengamedu, Ashwin Tengli, and Charu Tiwari. Web-scale information extraction with vertex. In *ICDE*, pages 1209–1220, 2011.

275. Ashish Gupta, Inderpal Singh Mumick, and V. S. Subrahmanian. Maintaining views incrementally. In *SIGMOD*, 1993.

276. Himanshu Gupta. Selection of views to materialize in a data warehouse. In *Database Theory ICDT '97*, volume 1186 of *Lecture Notes in Computer Science*. 1997. Available from `http://dx.doi.org/10.1007/3-540-62222-5_39`.

277. Himanshu Gupta and Inderpal Singh Mumick. Selection of views to materialize under a maintenance cost constraint. In *ICDT*, 1999.

278. Nitin Gupta, Lucja Kot, Sudip Roy, Gabriel Bender, Johannes Gehrke, and Christoph Koch. Entangled queries: Enabling declarative data-driven coordination. In *SIGMOD Conference*, 2011.

279. Nitin Gupta, Milos Nikolic, Sudip Roy, Gabriel Bender, Lucja Kot, Johannes Gehrke, and Christoph Koch. Entangled transactions. *PVLDB*, 4(11), 2011.

280. Dan Gusfield. *Algorithms on Strings, Trees, and Sequences*. Cambridge University Press, 1999.

281. Laura M. Haas, Donald Kossmann, Edward L. Wimmers, and Jun Yang. Optimizing queries across diverse data sources. In *VLDB*, 1997.

282. Jan Hajic, Sandra Carberry, and Stephen Clark, editors. *ACL 2010, Proceedings of the 48th Annual Meeting of the Association for Computational Linguistics, July 11–16, 2010, Uppsala, Sweden*. The Association for Computer Linguistics, 2010.

283. Alon Halevy, Zachary Ives, Jayant Madhavan, Peter Mork, Dan Suciu, and Igor Tatarinov. The Piazza peer data management system. *TKDE*, 16(7), July 2004.

284. Alon Y. Halevy. Answering queries using views: A survey. *VLDB J.*, 10(4), 2001.

285. Alon Y. Halevy, Naveen Ashish, Dina Bitton, Michael J. Carey, Denise Draper, Jeff Pollock, Arnon Rosenthal, and Vishal Sikka. Enterprise information integration: Successes, challenges and controversies. In *SIGMOD Conference*, pages 778–787, 2005.

286. Alon Y. Halevy, Michael J. Franklin, and David Maier. Principles of dataspace systems. In *PODS*, 2006.

287. Alon Y. Halevy, Zachary G. Ives, Peter Mork, and Igor Tatarinov. Piazza: Data management infrastructure for semantic web applications. In *12th World Wide Web Conference*, May 2003.

288. Alon Y. Halevy, Zachary G. Ives, Dan Suciu, and Igor Tatarinov. Schema mediation in peer data management systems. In *ICDE*, March 2003.

289. Fayçal Hamdi, Brigitte Safar, Chantal Reynaud, and Haïfa Zargayouna. Alignment-based partitioning of large-scale ontologies. In *EGC (best of volume)*, pages 251–269, 2009.

290. J. Hammer, H. Garcia-Molina, S. Nestorov, R. Yerneni, M. M. Breunig, and V. Vassalos. Template-based wrappers in the tsimmis system. In *SIGMOD*, 1997.

291. J. Hammer, J. McHugh, and H. Garcia-Molina. Semistructured data: The tsimmis experience. In *Proc. of the First East-European Symposium on Advances in Databases and Information Systems (ADBIS)*, 1997.

292. Joachim Hammer, Hector Garcia-Molina, Svetlozar Nestorov, Ramana Yerneni, Markus M. Breunig, and Vasilis Vassalos. Template-based wrappers in the TSIMMIS system (system demonstration). In *Proceedings of the ACM SIGMOD Conference*, Tucson, Arizona, 1998.

293. B. He and K. C. Chang. Statistical schema matching across web query interfaces. In *Proc. of SIGMOD*, 2003.

294. Bin He and Kevin Chang. Automatic complex schema matching across web query interfaces: A correlation mining approach. *TODS*, 31(1), 2006.

295. Bin He and Kevin Chen-Chuan Chang. Statistical schema integration across the deep web. In *Proc. of SIGMOD*, 2003.

296. Bin He, Kevin Chen-Chuan Chang, and Jiawei Han. Discovering complex matchings across web query interfaces: A correlation mining approach. In *KDD*, pages 148–157, 2004.

297. Bin He, Mitesh Patel, Zeng Zhang, and Kevin Chen-Chuan Chang. Accessing the deep Web: A survey. *Communications of the ACM*, 50(5):95–101, 2007.

298. Hao He, Haixun Wang, Jun Yang, and Philip S. Yu. Blinks: Ranked keyword searches on graphs. In *SIGMOD*, 2007.

299. Marti A. Hearst. Automatic acquisition of hyponyms from large text corpora. In *COLING*, pages 539–545, 1992.

300. M. A. Hernandez and S. J. Stolfo. The merge/purge problem for large databases. In *Proc. of SIGMOD*, 1995.

301. M. A. Hernández and S. J. Stolfo. Real-world data is dirty: Data cleansing and the merge/purge problem. *Data Mining and Knowledge Discovery*, 2:9–37, 1998.

302. Mauricio A. Hernandez, Renée J. Miller, and Laura M. Haas. Clio: A semi-automatic tool for schema mapping. In *SIGMOD*, 2001.

303. Raphael Hoffmann, Congle Zhang, and Daniel S. Weld. Learning 5000 relational extractors. In Hajic et al. [282], pages 286–295.

304. Vagelis Hristidis, Yannis Papakonstantinou, and Andrey Balmin. Keyword proximity search on XML graphs. In *ICDE*, 2003.

305. C. Hsu and M. Dung. Generating finite-state transducers for semi-structured data extraction from the web. *Inf. Syst.*, 23(8):521–538, 1998.

306. Wei Hu, Yuzhong Qu, and Gong Cheng. Matching large ontologies: A divide-and-conquer approach. *Data Knowl. Eng.*, 67(1):140–160, 2008.

307. Jiansheng Huang, Ting Chen, AnHai Doan, and Jeffrey F. Naughton. On the provenance of non-answers to queries over extracted data. *PVLDB*, 1(1), 2008.

308. G. Huck, P. Fankhauser, K. Aberer, and E. J. Neuhold. Jedi: Extracting and synthesizing information from the Web. In *CoopIS*, 1998.

309. Ryan Huebsch, Brent N. Chun, Joseph M. Hellerstein, Boon Thau Loo, Petros Maniatis, Timothy Roscoe, Scott Shenker, Ion Stoica, and Aydan R. Yumerefendi. The architecture of PIER: An Internet-scale query processor. In *CIDR*, 2005.

310. Ihab F. Ilyas, Walid G. Aref, and Ahmed K. Elmagarmid. Supporting top-k join queries in relational databases. In *VLDB*, 2003.

311. Ihab F. Ilyas, Walid G. Aref, Ahmed K. Elmagarmid, Hicham G. Elmongui, Rahul Shah, and Jeffrey Scott Vitter. Adaptive rank-aware query optimization in relational databases. *ACM Trans. Database Syst.*, 31(4), 2006.

312. Ihab F. Ilyas and Mohamed Soliman. *Probabilistic Ranking Techniques in Relational Databases*. Synthesis Lectures on Data Management. 2011.

313. Tomasz Imielinski and Witold Lipski. Incomplete information in relational databases. *JACM*, 31(4), 1984.

314. IBM Inc. IBM AlphaWorks QED Wiki. http://services.alphaworks.ibm.com/qedwiki/.

315. Microsoft Inc. Popfly. http://www.popfly.com/, 2008.

316. Yahoo Inc. Pipes. http://pipes.yahoo.com/pipes/.

317. Infochimps: Smart data for apps & analytics. http://www.infochimps.com/, 2011.

318. Yannis E. Ioannidis. Query optimization. *ACM Comput. Surv.*, 28(1), 1996.

319. Yannis E. Ioannidis, Raymond T. Ng, Kyuseok Shim, and Timos K. Sellis. Parametric query optimization. *VLDB J.*, 6(2), 1997.

320. Yannis E. Ioannidis and Raghu Ramakrishnan. Containment of conjunctive queries: Beyond relations as sets. *ACM Transactions on Database Systems*, 20(3):288–324, 1995.

321. Panagiotis G. Ipeirotis and Luis Gravano. Distributed search over the hidden web: Hierarchical database sampling and selection. In *VLDB*, pages 394–405, 2002.

322. U. Irmak and T. Suel. Interactive wrapper generation with minimal user effort. In *WWW*, 2006.

323. Zachary Ives, Daniela Florescu, Marc Friedman, Alon Levy, and Dan Weld. An adaptive query execution engine for data integration. In *Proceedings of the ACM SIGMOD Conference*, pages 299–310, 1999.

324. Zachary G. Ives, Todd J. Green, Grigoris Karvounarakis, Nicholas E. Taylor, Val Tannen, Partha Pratim Talukdar, Marie Jacob, and Fernando Pereira. The ORCHESTRA collaborative data sharing system. *SIGMOD Rec.*, 2008.

325. Zachary G. Ives, Alon Y. Halevy, and Daniel S. Weld. An XML query engine for network-bound data. *VLDB J.*, 11(4), December 2002.

326. Zachary G. Ives, Alon Y. Halevy, and Daniel S. Weld. Adapting to source properties in processing data integration queries. In *SIGMOD*, June 2004.

327. Zachary G. Ives, Craig A. Knoblock, Steven Minton, Mari Jacob, Partha Pratim Talukdar, Rattapoom Tuchinda, Jose Luis Ambite, Maria Muslea, and Cenk Gazen. Interactive data integration though smart copy & paste. In *Proceedings of the Conference on Innovative Data Systems Research (CIDR)*, 2009.

328. Zachary G. Ives and Nicholas E. Taylor. Sideways information passing for push query processing. In *ICDE*, 2008.

329. P. Jaccard. Étude comparative de la distribution florale dans une portion des Alpes et des Jura. *Bulletin de la Socit Vaudoise des Sciences Naturelles*, 37:547–579, 1901.

330. Ravi Jampani, Fei Xu, Mingxi Wu, Luis Leopoldo Perez, Chris Jermaine, and Peter J. Haas. The monte carlo database system: Stochastic analysis close to the data. *ACM Trans. Database Syst.*, 36(3), 2011.

331. M. A. Jaro. Unimatch: A record linkage system: User's manual. 1976. Technical Report, U.S. Bureau of the Census, Washington D.C.

332. T. S. Jayram, Phokion Kolaitis, and Erik Vee. The containment problem for real conjunctive queries with inequalities. In *Proc. of PODS*, pages 80–89, 2006.

333. S. Jeffery, M. Franklin, and A. Halevy. Pay-as-you-go user feedback for dataspace systems. In *Proc. of SIGMOD*, 2008.

334. Wen Jin and Jignesh M. Patel. Efficient and generic evaluation of ranked queries. In *SIGMOD Conference*, 2011.

335. Vanja Josifovski, Marcus Fontoura, and Attila Barta. Querying XML streams. *The VLDB Journal*, 14(2), 2005.

336. Navin Kabra and David J. DeWitt. Efficient mid-query re-optimization of sub-optimal query execution plans. In *SIGMOD*, 1998.

337. Varun Kacholia, Shashank Pandit, Soumen Chakrabarti, S. Sudarshan, Rushi Desai, and Hrishikesh Karambelkar. Bidirectional expansion for keyword search on graph databases. In *VLDB*, 2005.

338. D. V. Kalashnikov, S. Mehrotra, and Z. Chen. Exploiting relationships for domain-independent data cleaning. In *Proc. of the SDM Conf.*, 2005.

339. Jaewoo Kang and Jeffrey F. Naughton. On schema matching with opaque column names and data values. In *SIGMOD Conference*, pages 205–216, 2003.

340. Carl-Christian Kanne and Guido Moerkotte. Efficient storage of XML data. In *ICDE*, 2000.

341. Verena Kantere, Maher Manoubi, Iluju Kiringa, Timos K. Sellis, and John Mylopoulos. Peer coordination through distributed triggers. *PVLDB*, 3(2), 2010.

342. Grigoris Karvounarakis and Zachary G. Ives. Bidirectional mappings for data and update exchange. In *WebDB*, 2008.

343. Grigoris Karvounarakis and Zachary G. Ives. Querying data provenance. In *SIGMOD*, 2010.

344. Gjergji Kasneci, Maya Ramanath, Mauro Sozio, Fabian M. Suchanek, and Gerhard Weikum. Star: Steiner-tree approximation in relationship graphs. In *ICDE*, 2009.

345. Arthur M. Keller. Algorithms for translating view updates to database updates for views involving selections, projections, and joins. In *SIGMOD*, 1985.

346. Anastasios Kementsietsidis, Marcelo Arenas, and Renée J. Miller. Mapping data in peer-to-peer systems: Semantics and algorithmic issues. In *SIGMOD*, June 2003.

347. A. Klug. On conjunctive queries containing inequalities. *Journal of the ACM*, 35(1): pages 146–160, 1988.

348. D. Koller and N. Friedman. *Probabilistic Graphical Models*. The MIT Press, 2009.

349. George Konstantinidis and José Luis Ambite. Scalable query rewriting: A graph-based approach. In *SIGMOD Conference*, pages 97–108, 2011.

350. Donald Kossmann. The state of the artin distributed query procesing. *ACM Computing Surveys*, 32(4), 2000.

351. N. Koudas. Special issue on data quality. *IEEE Data Engineering Bulletin*, 29(2), 2006.

352. N. Koudas, A. Marathe, and D. Srivastava. Flexible string matching against large databases in practice. In *VLDB*, 2004.

353. N. Koudas, S. Sarawagi, and D. Srivastava. Record linkage: Similarity measures and algorithms. Tutorial, the ACM SIGMOD Conference, 2006.

354. Nick Koudas, Amit Marathe, and Divesh Srivastava. Flexible string matching against large databases in practice. In *VLDB*, pages 1078–1086, 2004.

355. Nick Koudas and Divesh Srivastava. Approximate joins: Concepts and techniques. In *VLDB*, page 1363, 2005.

356. Andries Kruger, C. Lee Giles, Frans Coetzee, Eric J. Glover, Gary William Flake, Steve Lawrence, and Christian W. Omlin. Deadliner: Building a new niche search engine. In *CIKM*, pages 272–281, 2000.

357. N. Kushmerick. Wrapper induction for information extraction, 1997. PhD thesis, University of Washington.

358. N. Kushmerick. Wrapper induction: Efficiency and expressiveness. *Artif. Intell.*, 118(1-2):15–68, 2000.

359. N. Kushmerick. Wrapper verification. *World Wide Web*, 3(2):79–94, 2000.

360. Nick Kushmerick, Robert Doorenbos, and Daniel Weld. Wrapper induction for information extraction. In *IJCAI*, 1997.

361. Chung T. Kwok and Daniel S. Weld. Planning to gather information. In *Proc. of the 13th National Conf. on Artificial Intelligence (AAAI)*, pages 32–39, 1996.

362. A. H. F. Laender, B. A. Ribeiro-Neto, A. S. da Silva, and J. S. Teixeira. A brief survey of web data extraction tools. *SIGMOD Record*, 31(2):84–93, 2002.

363. J. D. Lafferty, A. McCallum, and F. Pereira. Conditional random fields: Probabilistic models for segmenting and labeling sequence data. In *Proc. of the Int. Conf. on Machine Learning (ICML)*, pages 282–289, 2001.

364. Laks V. S. Lakshmanan, Nicola Leone, Robert Ross, and V. S. Subrahmanian. Probview: A flexible probabilistic database system. *ACM Trans. Database Syst.*, 22(3), 1997.

365. Eric Lambrecht, Subbarao Kambhampati, and Senthil Gnanaprakasam. Optimizing recursive information gathering plans. In *Proc. of the 16th Int. Joint Conf on Artificial Intelligence (IJCAI)*, pages 1204–1211, 1999.

366. T. Landers and R. Rosenberg. An overview of multibase. In *Proceedings of the Second International Symoposium on Distributed Databases*, pages 153–183. North Holland, Amsterdam, 1982.

367. Veronique Lattes and Marie-Christine Rousset. The use of the CARIN language and algorithms for information integration: The PICSEL project. In *Proceedings of the ECAI-98 Workshop on Intelligent Information Integration*, 1998.

368. Michael K. Lawrence, Rachel Pottinger, and Sheryl Staub-French. Data coordination: Supporting contingent updates. *PVLDB*, 4(11), 2011.

369. Amy J. Lee, Andreas Koeller, Anisoara Nica, and Elke A. Rundensteiner. Data warehouse evolution: Trade-offs between quality and cost of query rewritings. In *ICDE*, 1999.

370. Dongwon Lee. Weighted exact set similarity join. Tutorial Presentation. Available from http://pike.psu.edu/p2/wisc09-tech.ppt, 2009.

371. Y. Lee, M. Sayyadian, A. Doan, and A. Rosenthal. eTuner: Tuning schema matching software using synthetic scenarios. *VLDB J.*, 16(1):97–122, 2007.

372. Yoonkyong Lee, AnHai Doan, Robin Dhamankar, Alon Y. Halevy, and Pedro Domingos. imap: Discovering complex mappings between database schemas. In *Proc. of SIGMOD*, pages 383–394, 2004.

373. Maurizio Lenzerini. Data integration: A theoretical perspective. In *Proceedings of the ACM Symposium on Principles of Database Systems (PODS)*, 2002.

374. K. Lerman, L. Getoor, S. Minton, and C. A. Knoblock. Using the structure of Web sites for automatic segmentation of tables. In *SIGMOD*, 2004.

375. K. Lerman, S. Minton, and C. A. Knoblock. Wrapper maintenance: A machine learning approach. *J. Artif. Intell. Res. (JAIR)*, 18:149–181, 2003.

376. V. Levenshtein. Binay code capable of correcting deletions, insertions, and reversals. *Doklady Akademii Nauk SSSR*, 163(4):845–848, 1965. Original in Russian–translation in *Soviet Physics Doklady*, 10(8): 707–710, 1966.

377. Alon Levy and Marie-Christine Rousset. Combining Horn rules and description logics in CARIN. *Artificial Intelligence*, 104:165–209, September 1998.

378. Alon Y. Levy. Obtaining complete answers from incomplete databases. In *Proceedings of the International Conference on Very Large Databases (VLDB)*, pages 402–412, Bombay, India, 1996.

379. Alon Y. Levy. Logic-based techniques in data integration. In Jack Minker, editor, *Logic-Based Artificial Intelligence*, pages 575–595. Kluwer Academic Publishers, Dordrecht, 2000.

380. Alon Y. Levy, Anand Rajaraman, and Joann J. Ordille. Query answering algorithms for information agents. In *Proc. of the 13th National Conf. on Artificial Intelligence (AAAI)*, 1996.

381. Alon Y. Levy, Anand Rajaraman, and Joann J. Ordille. Querying heterogeneous information sources using source descriptions. In *VLDB*, 1996.

382. Alon Y. Levy and Yehoshua Sagiv. Queries independent of updates. In *Proceedings of the International Conference on Very Large Databases (VLDB)*, pages 171–181, Dublin, Ireland, 1993.

383. Chengkai Li, Kevin Chen-Chuan Chang, Ihab F. Ilyas, and Sumin Song. RankSQL: Query algebra and optimization for relational top-k queries. In *SIGMOD*, 2005.

384. W. Li and C. Clifton. Semantic integration in heterogeneous databases using neural networks. In *VLDB*, pages 1–12, 1994.

385. X. Li, P. Morie, and D. Roth. Robust reading: Identification and tracing of ambiguous names. In *Proc. of the HLT-NAACL Conf.*, pages 17–24, 2004.

386. X. Li, P. Morie, and D. Roth. Semantic integration in text: From ambiguous names to identifiable entities. *AI Magazine*, 26(1):45–58, 2005. A. Doan and N. Noy and A. Halevy (editors).

387. Xian Li, Timothy Lebo, and Deborah L. McGuinness. Provenance-based strategies to develop trust in semantic web applications. In *IPAW*, 2010.

388. Y. Li, A. Terrell, and J. M. Patel. WHAM: A high-throughput sequence alignment method. In *SIGMOD Conference*, pages 445–456, 2011.

389. Leonid Libkin. Incomplete information and certain answers in general data models. In *PODS*, pages 59–70, 2011.

390. E. P. Lim, J. Srivastava, S. Prabhakar, and J. Richardson. Entity identification in database integration. In *Proc. of the 5th Int. Conf. on Data Engineering (ICDE-93)*, pages 294–301, 1993.

391. Girija Limaye, Sunita Sarawagi, and Soumen Chakrabarti. Annotating and searching web tables using entities, types and relationships. *PVLDB* 3(1), pages 1338–1347, 2010.

392. B. Liu. *Web Data Mining: Exploring Hyperlinks, Contents, and Usage Data. Data-Centric Systems and Applications*. Springer, 2007.

393. B. Liu, R. L. Grossman, and Y. Zhai. Mining data records in Web pages. In *KDD*, 2003.

394. L. Liu, C. Pu, and W. Han. XWRAP: An XML-enabled wrapper construction system for Web information sources. In *Proc. of the IEEE Intl Conf. on Data Engineering (ICDE)*, 2000.

395. Mengmeng Liu, Nicholas E. Taylor, Wenchao Zhou, Zachary G. Ives, and Boon Thau Loo. Recursive computation of regions and connectivity in networks. In *ICDE*, 2009.

396. Xiufeng Liu, Christian Thomsen, and Torben Bach Pedersen. Etlmr: A highly scalable dimensional etl framework based on mapreduce. In *Proceedings of the 13th International Conference on Data Warehousing and Knowledge Discovery*, DaWaK'11, Berlin, Heidelberg, 2011.

397. Boon Thau Loo, Joseph M. Hellerstein, Ion Stoica, and Raghu Ramakrishnan. Declarative routing: Extensible routing with declarative queries. In *SIGCOMM*, 2005.

398. James J. Lu, Guido Moerkotte, Joachim Schue, and V.S. Subrahmanian. Efficient maintenance of materialized mediated views. In *SIGMOD*, 1995.

399. Meiyu Lu, Divyakant Agrawal, Bing Tian Dai, and Anthony K. H. Tung. Schema-as-you-go: On probabilistic tagging and querying of wide tables. In *SIGMOD Conference*, pages 181–192, 2011.

400. Bertram Ludäscher, Ilkay Altintas, Chad Berkley, Dan Higgins, Efrat Jaeger, Matthew Jones, Edward A. Lee, Jing Tao, and Yang Zhao. Scientific workflow management and the kepler system. *Concurrency and Computation: Practice and Experience*, 2006.

401. Bertram Ludäscher, Rainer Himmeröder, Georg Lausen, Wolfgang May, and Christian Schlepphorst. Managing semistructured data with *FLORID*: A deductive object-oriented perspective. *Information Systems*, 23(8), 1998.

402. Qiong Luo, Sailesh Krishnamurthy, C. Mohan, Hamid Pirahesh, Honguk Woo, Bruce G. Lindsay, and Jeffrey F. Naughton. Middle-tier database caching for e-business. In *SIGMOD*, 2002.

403. Yi Luo, Wei Wang, and Xuemin Lin. Spark: A keyword search engine on relational databases. In *ICDE*, 2008.

404. Lothar F. Mackert and Guy M. Lohman. R* optimizer validation and performance evaluation for distributed queries. In *VLDB*, 1986.

405. Lothar F. Mackert and Guy M. Lohman. R* optimizer validation and performance evaluation for local queries. In *SIGMOD*, 1986.

406. Jayant Madhavan, Philip A. Bernstein, AnHai Doan, and Alon Y. Halevy. Corpus-based schema matching. In *Proc. of ICDE*, pages 57–68, 2005.

407. Jayant Madhavan, Philip A. Bernstein, and Erhard Rahm. Generic schema matching with Cupid. In *VLDB*, 2001.

408. Jayant Madhavan and Alon Halevy. Composing mappings among data sources. In *Proc. of VLDB*, 2003.

409. Jayant Madhavan, Shawn Jeffery, Shirley Cohen, Xin Dong, David Ko, Cong Yu, and Alon Halevy. Web-scale data integration: You can only afford to pay as you go. In *CIDR*, 2007.

410. Jayant Madhavan, David Ko, Lucja Kot, Vignesh Ganapathy, Alex Rasmussen, and Alon Halevy. Google's deep-web crawl. In *Proc. of VLDB*, pages 1241–1252, 2008.

411. M. Magnani and D. Montesi. Uncertainty in data integration: Current approaches and open problems. In *VLDB Workshop on Management of Uncertain Data*, pages 18–32, 2007.

412. M. Magnani, N. Rizopoulos, P. Brien, and D. Montesi. Schema integration based on uncertain semantic mappings. *Lecture Notes in Computer Science*, pages 31–46, 2005.

413. Hatem A. Mahmoud and Ashraf Aboulnaga. Schema clustering and retrieval for multi-domain pay-as-you-go data integration systems. In *SIGMOD Conference*, pages 411–422, 2010.

414. C. D. Manning, P. Raghavan, and H. Schütze. *Introduction to Information Retrieval*. Cambridge University Press, 2008.

415. Amélie Marian, Nicolas Bruno, and Luis Gravano. Evaluating top-k queries over web-accessible databases. *ACM Trans. Database Syst.*, 29(2), 2004.

416. A. McCallum and B. Wellner. Conditional models of identity uncertainty with application to noun coreference. In *Proc. of the Conf. on Advances in Neural Information Processing Systems (NIPS)*, 2004.

417. Andrew McCallum, Kamal Nigam, Jason Rennie, and Kristie Seymore. A machine learning approach to building domain-specific search engines. In *IJCAI*, pages 662–667, 1999.

418. Andrew K. McCallum, Kamal Nigam, and Lyle H. Ungar. Efficient clustering of high-dimensional data sets with application to reference matching. In *KDD*, 2000.

419. R. McCann, B. K. AlShebli, Q. Le, H. Nguyen, L. Vu, and A. Doan. Mapping maintenance for data integration systems. In *VLDB*, 2005.

420. Robert McCann, AnHai Doan, Vanitha Varadarajan, Alexander Kramnik, and ChengXiang Zhai. Building data integration systems: A mass collaboration approach. In *WebDB*, pages 25–30, 2003.

421. Robert McCann, Warren Shen, and AnHai Doan. Matching schemas in online communities: A web 2.0 approach. In *ICDE*, pages 110–119, 2008.

422. Luke McDowell, Oren Etzioni, Alon Halevy, Henry Levy, Steven Gribble, William Pentney, Deepak Verma, and Stani Vlasseva. Enticing ordinary people onto the semantic web via instant gratification. In *Proceedings of the Second International Conference on the Semantic Web*, October 2003.

423. C. Meek, J. M. Patel, and S. Kasetty. OASIS: An online and accurate technique for local-alignment searches on biological sequences. In *VLDB*, pages 910–921, 2003.

424. Alexandra Meliou, Wolfgang Gatterbauer, Katherine F. Moore, and Dan Suciu. The complexity of causality and responsibility for query answers and non-answers. *PVLDB*, 4(1), 2010.

425. Alexandra Meliou, Wolfgang Gatterbauer, Suman Nath, and Dan Suciu. Tracing data errors with view-conditioned causality. In *SIGMOD*, 2011.

426. Sergey Melnik, Philip A. Bernstein, Alon Y. Halevy, and Erhard Rahm. Supporting executable mappings in model management. In *Proc. of SIGMOD*, pages 167–178, 2005.

427. Sergey Melnik, Hector Garcia-Molina, and Erhard Rahm. Similarity flooding: A versatile graph matching algorithm. In *Proceedings of the 18th International Conference on Data Engineering (ICDE)*, 2002.

428. Sergey Melnik, Erhard Rahm, and Phil Bernstein. Rondo: A programming platform for generic model management. In *Proc. of SIGMOD*, 2003.

429. X. Meng, D. Hu, and C. Li. Schema-guided wrapper maintenance for Web-data extraction. In *WIDM*, 2003.

430. Gerome Miklau and Dan Suciu. Containment and equivalence for a fragment of XPath. *J. ACM*, 51(1), 2004.

431. George A. Miller. Wordnet: A lexical database for English. In *HLT*, 1994.

432. Renée J. Miller, Laura M. Haas, and Mauricio Hernandez. Schema matching as query discovery. In *VLDB*, 2000.

433. Tova Milo, Serge Abiteboul, Bernd Amann, Omar Benjelloun, and Frederic Dang Ngoc. Exchanging intensional XML data. In *Proc. of SIGMOD*, pages 289–300, 2003.

434. Tova Milo and Sagit Zohar. Using schema matching to simplify heterogeneous data translation. In *Proceedings of the International Conference on Very Large Databases (VLDB)*, 1998.

435. Mike Mintz, Steven Bills, Rion Snow, and Daniel Jurafsky. Distant supervision for relation extraction without labeled data. In Keh-Yih Su, Jian Su, and Janyce Wiebe, editors, *ACL/AFNLP*, pages 1003–1011. The Association for Computer Linguistics, 2009.

436. Paolo Missier, Satya Sanket Sahoo, Jun Zhao, Carole A. Goble, and Amit P. Sheth. *Janus*: From workflows to semantic provenance and linked open data. In *IPAW*, 2010.

437. Hoshi Mistry, Prasan Roy, S. Sudarshan, and Krithi Ramamritham. Materialized view selection and maintenance using multi-query optimization. In *SIGMOD*, 2001.

438. Tom M. Mitchell. *Machine Learning*. McGraw Hill, 1997.

439. Prasenjit Mitra. An algorithm for answering queries efficiently using views. In *ADC*, pages 99–106, 2001.

440. Prasenjit Mitra, Natasha F. Noy, and Anuj R. Jaiswal. Omen: A probabilistic ontology mapping tool. In *International Semantic Web Conference*, pages 537–547, 2005.

441. R. Mohapatra, K. Rajaraman, and S. Y. Sung. Efficient wrapper reinduction from dynamic Web sources. In *Web Intelligence*, 2004.

442. A. E. Monge and C. Elkan. The field matching problem: Algorithms and applications. In *KDD*, 1996.

443. A. E. Monge and C. P. Elkan. An efficient domain-independent algorithm for detecting approximately duplicate database records. In *Proc. of the Second ACM SIGMOD Workshop on Research Issues in Data Mining and Knowledge Discovery (DMKD-97)*, pages 23–29, 1997.

444. Hyun Jin Moon, Carlo Curino, Alin Deutsch, Chien-Yi Hou, and Carlo Zaniolo. Managing and querying transaction-time databases under schema evolution. *PVLDB*, 1(1), 2008.

445. Peter Mork, Philip A. Bernstein, and Sergey Melnik. Teaching a schema translator to produce o/r views. In *Proceedings of Entity Relationship Conference*, pages 102–119, 2007.

446. Amihai Motro. Integrity = validity + completeness. *ACM Transactions on Database Systems*, 14(4):480–502, December 1989.

447. Inderpal Singh Mumick, Dallan Quass, and Barinderpal Singh Mumick. Maintenance of data cubes and summary tables in a warehouse. In *SIGMOD*, 1997.

448. Kiran-Kumar Muniswamy-Reddy, David A. Holland, Uri Braun, and Margo I. Seltzer. Provenance-aware storage systems. In *USENIX Annual Technical Conference, General Track*, 2006.

449. I. Muslea, S. Minton, and C. A. Knoblock. A hierarchical approach to wrapper induction. In *Agents*, 1999.

450. I. Muslea, S. Minton, and C. A. Knoblock. Hierarchical wrapper induction for semistructured information sources. *Autonomous Agents and Multi-Agent Systems*, 4(1/2):93–114, 2001.

451. I. Muslea, S. Minton, and C. A. Knoblock. Active learning with strong and weak views: A case study on wrapper induction. In *IJCAI*, 2003.

452. A. Nash, P. Bernstein, and S. Melnik. Composition of mappings given by embedded dependencies. *ACM Transactions on Database Systems*, 32(1), 2007.

453. F. Naumann and M. Herschel. *An Introduction to Duplicate Detection (Synthesis Lectures on Data Management)*. Morgan & Claypool, 2010. M. Tamer Ozsu (editor).

454. Felix Naumann, Johann Christoph Freytag, and Ulf Leser. Completeness of integrated information sources. *Inf. Syst.*, 29(7):583–615, 2004.

455. G. Navarro. A guided tour to approximate string matching. *ACM Comput. Surv.*, 33(1):31–88, 2001.

456. S. Needleman and C. Wunsch. A general method applicable to the search for similarities in the amino acid sequence of two proteins. *Journal of Molecular Biology*, 48(3):443–453, 1970.

457. Frank Neven and Thomas Schwentick. XPath containment in the presence of disjunction, DTDs, and variables. In *ICDT*, 2003.

458. H. B. Newcombe, J. M. Kennedy, S. Axford, and A. James. Automatic linkage of vital records. *Science*, 130(3381):954–959, 1959.

459. W. S. Ng, B. C. Ooi, K.-L. Tan, and A. Zhou. Peerdb: A p2p-based system for distributed data sharing. In *ICDE*, Bangalore, India, 2003.

460. Hoa Nguyen, Ariel Fuxman, Stelios Paparizos, Juliana Freire, and Rakesh Agrawal. Synthesizing products for online catalogs. *PVLDB*, 4(7):409–418, 2011.

461. Zaiqing Nie, Ji-Rong Wen, and Wei-Ying Ma. Object-level vertical search. In *CIDR*, pages 235–246, 2007.

462. H. Nottelmann and U. Straccia. Information retrieval and machine learning for probabilistic schema matching. *Information Processing and Management*, 43(3):552–576, 2007.

463. N. F. Noy, A. Doan, and A. Y. Halevy. Semantic integration. *AI Magazine*, 26(1):7–10, 2005.

464. Natalya F. Noy and Mark A. Musen. PROMPT: Algorithm and tool for automated ontology merging and alignment. In *Proceedings of the National Conference on Artificial Intelligence (AAAI)*, 2000.

465. Natalya Freidman Noy and Mark A. Musen. Smart: Automated support for ontology merging and alignment. In *Proceedings of the Knowledge Acquisition Workshop, Banff, Canada*, 1999.

466. Natalya Fridman Noy. Semantic integration: A survey of ontology-based approaches. *SIGMOD Record*, 33(4):65–70, 2004.

467. Alexandros Ntoulas, Petros Zerfos, and Junghoo Cho. Downloading textual hidden web content through keyword queries. In *JCDL*, pages 100–109, 2005.

468. T. Oinn, M. Greenwood, M. Addis, N. Alpdemir, J. Ferris, K. Glover, C. Goble, A. Goderis, D. Hull, D. Marvin, P. Li, P. Lord, M. Pocock, M. Senger, R. Stevens, A. Wipat, and C. Wroe. Taverna: Lessons in creating a workflow environment for the life sciences. *Concurrency and Computation: Practice and Experience*, 18(10), 2006.

469. B. On, N. Koudas, D. Lee, and D. Srivastava. Group linkage. In *ICDE*, 2007.

470. Open provenance model. `http://twiki.ipaw.info/bin/view/Challenge/OPM`, 2008.

471. M. Tamer Ozsu and Patrick Valduriez. *Principles of Distributed Database Systems*. Springer, 2011.

472. Luigi Palopoli, Domenico Sacc, G. Terracina, and Domenico Ursino. A unified graph-based framework for deriving nominal interscheme properties, type conflicts and object cluster similarities. In *Proceedings of CoopIS*, 1999.

473. Paolo Papotti, Valter Crescenzi, Paolo Merialdo, Mirko Bronzi, and Lorenzo Blanco. Redundancy-driven web data extraction and integration. In *WebDB*, 2010.

474. A. Parameswaran, N. Dalvi, H. Garcia-Molina, and R. Rastogi. Optimal schemes for robust web extraction. In *VLDB*, 2011.

475. H. Pasula, B. Marthi, B. Milch, S. Russell, and I. Shpitser. Identity uncertainty and citation matching. In *Proc. of the NIPS Conf.*, pages 1401–1408, 2002.

476. Feng Peng and Sudarshan S. Chawathe. Xsq: A streaming xpath engine. *ACM Trans. Database Syst.*, 30(2), 2005.

477. L. Philips. Hanging on the metaphone. *Computer Language Magazine*, 7(12):39–44, 1990.

478. L. Philips. The double metaphone search algorithm. *C/C++ Users Journal*, 18(5), 2000.

479. J. C. Pinheiro and D. X. Sun. Methods for linking and mining massive heterogeneous databases. In *Proc. of the ACM Int. Conf. on Knowledge Discovery and Data Mining (KDD)*, pages 309–313, 1998.

480. Lucian Popa and Val Tannen. An equational chase for path conjunctive queries, constraints and views. In *Proceedings of the International Conference on Database Theory (ICDT)*, 1999.

481. Rachel Pottinger and Philip A. Bernstein. Merging models based on given correspondences. In *Proc. of VLDB*, pages 826–873, 2003.

482. Rachel Pottinger and Alon Halevy. Minicon: A scalable algorithm for answering queries using views. *VLDB Journal*, 2001.

483. Jeffrey Pound, Ihab F. Ilyas, and Grant E. Weddell. Expressive and flexible access to web-extracted data: A keyword-based structured query language. In *SIGMOD Conference*, pages 423–434, 2010.

484. C. Pu. Key equivalence in heterogeneous databases. In *Proc. of the 1st Int. Workshop on Interoperability in Multidatabase Systems*, 1991.

485. Sven Puhlmann, Melanie Weis, and Felix Naumann. Xml duplicate detection using sorted neighborhoods. In *EDBT*, pages 773–791, 2006.

486. Dallan Quass and Jennifer Widom. On-line warehouse view maintenance. In *SIGMOD*.

487. Erhard Rahm and Philip A. Bernstein. A survey of approaches to automatic schema matching. *VLDB Journal*, 10(4):334–350, 2001.

488. Anand Rajaraman, Yehoshua Sagiv, and Jeffrey D. Ullman. Answering queries using templates with binding patterns. In *Proceedings of the ACM Symposium on Principles of Database Systems (PODS)*, pages 105–112, San Jose, CA, 1995.

489. Raghu Ramakrishnan and Johannes Gehrke. *Database Management Systems*. McGraw Hill, 2000.

490. Vijayshankar Raman, Amol Deshpande, and Joseph M. Hellerstein. Using state modules for adaptive query processing. In *ICDE*, 2003.

491. Vijayshankar Raman and Joseph M. Hellerstein. Potter's wheel: An interactive data cleaning system. In *VLDB*, pages 381–390, 2001.

492. Aditya Ramesh, S. Sudarshan, and Purva Joshi. Keyword search on form results. *PVLDB*, 4(11), 2011.

493. J. Raposo, A. Pan, M. Álvarez, and J. Hidalgo. Automatically maintaining wrappers for semi-structured Web sources. *Data Knowl. Eng.*, 61(2):331–358, 2007.

494. P. D. Ravikumar and W. Cohen. A hierarchical graphical model for record linkage. In *Proc. of the Conf. on Uncertainty in Artificial Intelligence (UAI)*, pages 454–461, 2004.

495. Simon Razniewski and Werner Nutt. Completeness of queries over incomplete databases. *PVLDB*, 4(11):749–760, 2011.

496. Christopher Re, Nilesh N. Dalvi, and Dan Suciu. Efficient top-k query evaluation on probabilistic data. In *ICDE*, 2007.

497. E. S. Ristad and P. N. Yianilos. Learning string-edit distance. *IEEE Trans. Pattern Anal. Mach. Intell.*, 20(5):522–532, 1998.

498. Mary Tork Roth, Fatma Ozcan, and Laura M. Haas. Cost models do matter: Providing cost information for diverse data sources in a federated system. In *VLDB*, 1999.

499. Elke A. Rundensteiner, Luping Ding, Timothy M. Sutherland, Yali Zhu, Bradford Pielech, and Nishant Mehta. Cape: Continuous query engine with heterogeneous-grained adaptivity. In *VLDB*, 2004.

500. R. C. Russell. 1918. U.S. Patent 1,261,167.

501. R. C. Russell. 1922. U.S. Patent 1,435,663.

502. Y. Sagiv and M. Yannakakis. Equivalence among relational expressions with the union and difference operators. *Journal of the ACM*, 27(4):633–655, 1981.

503. A. Sahuguet and F. Azavant. Web ecology: Recycling HTML pages as XML documents using W4F. In *WebDB (Informal Proceedings)*, 1999.

504. Marcos Antonio Vaz Salles, Jens-Peter Dittrich, Shant Kirakos Karakashian, Olivier René Girard, and Lukas Blunschi. iTrails: Pay-as-you-go information integration in dataspaces. In *VLDB*, 2007.

505. Yatin Saraiya. *Subtree-elimination algorithms in deductive databases*. PhD thesis, Stanford University, Stanford, California, 1991.

506. S. Sarawagi. Information extraction. *Foundations and Trends in Databases*, 1(3):261–377, 2008.

507. S. Sarawagi and A. Bhamidipaty. Interactive deduplication using active learning. In *Proc. of the ACM Int. Conf. on Knowledge Discovery and Data Mining (KDD)*, pages 269–278, 2002.

508. Sunita Sarawagi and Alok Kirpal. Efficient set joins on similarity predicates. In *SIGMOD Conference*, pages 743–754, 2004.

509. Nikos Sarkas, Stelios Paparizos, and Panayiotis Tsaparas. Structured annotations of web queries. In *SIGMOD Conference*, 2010.

510. Anish Das Sarma, Xin Dong, and Alon Y. Halevy. Bootstrapping pay-as-you-go data integration systems. In *SIGMOD Conference*, pages 861–874, 2008.

511. M. Sayyadian, Y. Lee, A. Doan, and A. Rosenthal. Tuning schema matching software using synthetic scenarios. In *VLDB*, pages 994–1005, 2005.

512. Mayssam Sayyadian, Hieu LeKhac, AnHai Doan, and Luis Gravano. Efficient keyword search across heterogeneous relational databases. In *ICDE*, 2007.

513. Carlos Eduardo Scheidegger, Huy T. Vo, David Koop, Juliana Freire, and Cláudio T. Silva. Querying and re-using workflows with vstrails. In *SIGMOD Conference*, 2008.

514. Karl Schnaitter and Neoklis Polyzotis. Evaluating rank joins with optimal cost. In *PODS*, 2008.

515. Karl Schnaitter, Joshua Spiegel, and Neoklis Polyzotis. Depth estimation for ranking query optimization. In *VLDB*, 2007.

516. Thomas Schwentick. XPath query containment. *SIGMOD Record*, 33(1), 2004.

517. Luc Segoufin and Victor Vianu. Validating streaming XML documents. In *PODS*, 2002.

518. Prithviraj Sen and Amol Deshpande. Representing and querying correlated tuples in probabilistic databases. In *ICDE*, 2007.

519. Warren Shen, Pedro DeRose, Robert McCann, AnHai Doan, and Raghu Ramakrishnan. Toward best-effort information extraction. In *SIGMOD*, 2008.

520. Warren Shen, Pedro DeRose, Long Vu, AnHai Doan, and Raghu Ramakrishnan. Source-aware entity matching: A compositional approach. In *ICDE*, pages 196–205, 2007.

521. Warren Shen, Xin Li, and AnHai Doan. Constraint-based entity matching. In *AAAI*, pages 862–867, 2005.

522. Cláudio T. Silva, Erik W. Anderson, Emanuele Santos, and Juliana Freire. Using vistrails and provenance for teaching scientific visualization. *Comput. Graph. Forum*, 30(1), 2011.

523. Alkis Simitsis, Georgia Koutrika, and Yannis Ioannidis. Précis: From unstructured keywords as queries to structured databases as answers. *The VLDB Journal*, 17, 2008. Available from http://dx.doi.org/10.1007/s00778-007-0075-9.

524. P. Singla and P. Domingos. Object identification with attribute-mediated dependences. In *Proc. of the PKDD Conf.*, pages 297–308, 2005.

525. John Miles Smith, Philip A. Bernstein, Umeshwar Dayal, Nathan Goodman, Terry Landers, Ken W.T. Lin, and Eugene Wong. MULTIBASE – Integrating heterogeneous distributed database systems. In *Proceedings of 1981 National Computer Conference*, 1981.

526. T. Smith and M. Waterman. Identification of common molecular subsequences. *Journal of Molecular Biology*, 147(1):195–197, 1981.

527. Socrata: The social data cloud company. http://www.socrata.com/, 2011.

528. S. Soderland. Learning information extraction rules for semi-structured and free text. *Machine Learning*, 34(1-3):233–272, 1999.

529. S. Soderland, D. Fisher, J. Aseltine, and W. G. Lehnert. Crystal: Inducing a conceptual dictionary. In *IJCAI*, 1995.

530. Michael Stonebraker. *The Design and Implementation of Distributed INGRES*. Boston, MA, USA, 1986.

531. Michael Stonebraker, Daniel J. Abadi, David J. DeWitt, Samuel Madden, Erik Paulson, Andrew Pavlo, and Alexander Rasin. MapReduce and parallel DBMSs: Friends or foes? *Commun. ACM*, 53(1), 2010.

532. Michael Stonebraker, Paul M. Aoki, Witold Litwin, Avi Pfeffer, Adam Sah, Jeff Sidell, Carl Staelin, and Andrew Yu. Mariposa: A wide-area distributed database system. *VLDB J.*, 5(1), 1996.

533. V.S. Subrahmanian, S. Adali, A. Brink, R. Emery, J. Lu, A. Rajput, T. Rogers, R. Ross, and C. Ward. HERMES: A heterogeneous reasoning and mediator system. Technical Report, University of Maryland, 1995.

534. Fabian M. Suchanek, Gjergji Kasneci, and Gerhard Weikum. Yago: A large ontology from wikipedia and wordnet. *J. Web Sem.*, 6(3), 2008.

535. Dan Suciu, Dan Olteanu, Christopher Ré, and Christoph Koch. *Probabilistic Databases*. Synthesis Lectures on Data Management. 2011.

536. Tableau software. http://www.tableausoftware.com/, 2011.

537. R. L. Taft. Name search techniques. 1970. Technical Report, special report no. 1, New York State Identification and Intelligence System, Albany, N.Y.

538. Partha Pratim Talukdar, Zachary G. Ives, and Fernando Pereira. Automatically incorporating new sources in keyword search-based data integration. In *SIGMOD*, 2010.

539. Partha Pratim Talukdar, Marie Jacob, Muhammad Salman Mehmood, Koby Crammer, Zachary G. Ives, Fernando Pereira, and Sudipto Guha. Learning to create data-integrating queries. In *VLDB*, 2008.

540. Sandeep Tata and Guy M. Lohman. Sqak: Doing more with keywords. In *Proceedings of the 2008 ACM SIGMOD International Conference on Management of Data*, SIGMOD '08, New York, NY, USA, 2008. Available from http://doi.acm.org/10.1145/1376616.1376705.

541. Igor Tatarinov and Alon Halevy. Efficient query reformulation in peer data management systems. In *Proc. of SIGMOD*, 2004.

542. Igor Tatarinov, Stratis Viglas, Kevin S. Beyer, Jayavel Shanmugasundaram, Eugene J. Shekita, and Chun Zhang. Storing and querying ordered XML using a relational database system. In *SIGMOD*, 2002.

543. Nesime Tatbul, Ugur Cetintemel, Stanley B. Zdonik, Mitch Cherniack, and Michael Stonebraker. Load shedding in a data stream manager. In *VLDB*, 2003.

544. Nicholas E. Taylor and Zachary G. Ives. Reconciling while tolerating disagreement in collaborative data sharing. In *SIGMOD*, 2006.

545. S. Tejada, C. A. Knoblock, and S. Minton. Learning object identification rules for information integration. *Inf. Syst.*, 26(8):607–633, 2001.

546. Andreas Thor and Erhard Rahm. MOMA – A mapping-based object matching system. In *CIDR*, pages 247–258, 2007.

547. Feng Tian and David J. DeWitt. Tuple routing strategies for distributed eddies. In *VLDB*, 2003.

548. Y. Tian, S. Tata, R. A. Hankins, and J. M. Patel. Practical methods for constructing suffix trees. *VLDB J.*, 14(3):281–299, 2005.

549. Kai-Ming Ting and Ian H. Witten. Issues in stacked generalization. *Journal of Artificial Intelligence Research*, 10:271–289, 1999.

550. Guilherme A. Toda, Eli Cortez, Altigran S. da Silva, and Edleno de Moura. A probabilistic approach for automatically filling form-based web interfaces. *PVLDB*, 4(3):151–160, 2011.

551. Odysseas G. Tsatalos, Marvin H. Solomon, and Yannis E. Ioannidis. The GMAP: A versatile tool for physical data independence. In *Proceedings of the International Conference on Very Large Databases (VLDB)*, pages 367–378, Santiago, Chile, 1994.

552. Yi-Cheng Tu, Song Liu, Sunil Prabhakar, Bin Yao, and William Schroeder. Using control theory for load shedding in data stream management. In *ICDE*, 2007.

553. Rattapoom Tuchindra, Pedro Szekely, and Craig Knoblock. Building mashups by example. In *Proceedings of CHI*, pages 139–148, 2008.

554. Jeffrey D. Ullman. *Principles of Database and Knowledge-Base Systems, Volumes I, II*. Computer Science Press, Rockville MD, 1989.

555. Jeffrey D. Ullman. Information Integration using Logical Views. In *Proceedings of the International Conference on Database Theory (ICDT)*, 1997.

556. Tolga Urhan, Michael J. Franklin, and Laurent Amsaleg. Cost based query scrambling for initial delays. In *SIGMOD*, 1998.

557. Ron van der Meyden. The complexity of querying indefinite data about linearly ordered domains. In *Proceedings of the ACM Symposium on Principles of Database Systems (PODS)*, pages 331–345, San Diego, CA, 1992.

558. Petros Venetis, Alon Y. Halevy, Jayant Madhavan, Marius Pasca, Warren Shen, Fei Wu, Gengxin Miao, and Chung Wu. Recovering semantics of tables on the web. *PVLDB*, 4(9):528–538, 2011.

559. Rares Vernica, Michael J. Carey, and Chen Li. Efficient parallel set-similarity joins using MapReduce. In *SIGMOD Conference*, pages 495–506, 2010.

560. Daisy Zhe Wang, Michael J. Franklin, Minos N. Garofalakis, Joseph M. Hellerstein, and Michael L. Wick. Hybrid in-database inference for declarative information extraction. In *SIGMOD Conference*, 2011.

561. Daisy Zhe Wang, Eirinaios Michelakis, Minos N. Garofalakis, and Joseph M. Hellerstein. BayesStore: Managing large, uncertain data repositories with probabilistic graphical models. *PVLDB*, 1(1), 2008.

562. J. Wang and F. H. Lochovsky. Data extraction and label assignment for Web databases. In *WWW*, 2003.

563. Wei Wang. Similarity join algorithms: An introduction. Tutorial Presentation. Available from http://www.cse.unsw.edu.au/ weiw/project/tutorial-simjoin-SEBD08.pdf, 2008.

564. Y. R. Wang and S. E. Madnick. The inter-database instance identification problem in integrating autonomous systems. In *Proc. of the 5th Int. Conf. on Data Engineering (ICDE-89)*, pages 46–55, 1989.

565. Yalin Wang and Jianying Hu. A machine learning based approach for table detection on the web. In *WWW*, pages 242–250, 2002.

566. M. Waterman, T. Smith, and W. Beyer. Some biological sequence metrics. *Advances in Math*, 20(4):367–387, 1976.

567. Melanie Weis and Felix Naumann. Detecting duplicates in complex XML data. In *ICDE*, page 109, 2006.

568. Steven Euijong Whang and Hector Garcia-Molina. Developments in generic entity resolution. *IEEE Data Eng. Bull.*, 34(3):51–59, 2011.

569. Michael L. Wick, Andrew McCallum, and Gerome Miklau. Scalable probabilistic databases with factor graphs and MCMC. *PVLDB*, 3(1), 2010.

570. Michael L. Wick, Khashayar Rohanimanesh, Karl Schultz, and Andrew McCallum. A unified approach for schema matching, coreference and canonicalization. In *KDD*, pages 722–730, 2008.

571. Gio Wiederhold. Mediators in the architecture of future information systems. *IEEE Computer*, pages 38–49, March 1992.

572. W. E. Winkler. Improved decision rules in the Fellegi-Sunter model of record linkage, 1993. Technical Report, Statistical Research Report Series RR93/12, U.S. Bureau of the Census.

573. W. E. Winkler. The state of record linkage and current research problems, 1999. Technical Report, Statistical Research Report Series RR99/04, U.S. Bureau of Census.

574. W. E. Winkler. Methods for record linkage and Bayesian networks, 2002. Technical Report, Statistical Research Report Series RRS2002/05, U.S. Bureau of the Census.

575. W. E. Winkler and Y. Thibaudeau. An application of the Fellegi-Sunter model of record linkage to the 1990 U.S. decennial census. 1991. Technical Report, Statistical Research Report Series RR91/09, U.S. Bureau of the Census, Washington, D.C.

576. David Wolpert. Stacked generalization. *Neural Networks*, 5:241–259, 1992.

577. Jeffrey Wong and Jason I. Hong. Making mashups with marmite: Towards end-user programming for the web. In *CHI*, pages 1435–1444, 2007.

578. Fei Wu and Daniel S. Weld. Autonomously semantifying wikipedia. In Mário J. Silva, Alberto H. F. Laender, Ricardo A. Baeza-Yates, Deborah L. McGuinness, Bjørn Olstad, Øystein Haug Olsen, and André O. Falcão, editors, *CIKM*, pages 41–50. ACM, 2007.

579. Fei Wu and Daniel S. Weld. Automatically refining the wikipedia infobox ontology. In Jinpeng Huai, Robin Chen, Hsiao-Wuen Hon, Yunhao Liu, Wei-Ying Ma, Andrew Tomkins, and Xiaodong Zhang, editors, *WWW*, pages 635–644. ACM, 2008.

580. Fei Wu and Daniel S. Weld. Open information extraction using wikipedia. In Hajic et al. [282], pages 118–127.

581. Wensheng Wu, Clement T. Yu, AnHai Doan, and Weiyi Meng. An interactive clustering-based approach to integrating source query interfaces on the deep web. In *SIGMOD Conference*, pages 95–106, 2004.

582. Chuan Xiao, Wei Wang, Xuemin Lin, and Jeffrey Xu Yu. Efficient similarity joins for near duplicate detection. In *WWW*, pages 131–140, 2008.

583. Dong Xin, Yeye He, and Venkatesh Ganti. Keyword++: A framework to improve keyword search over entity databases. *PVLDB*, 3(1), 2010.

584. Khaled Yagoub, Daniela Florescu, Valerie Issarny, and Patrick Valduriez. Caching strategies for data-intensive web sites. In *Proceedings of the International Conference on Very Large Databases (VLDB)*, pages 188–199, Cairo, Egypt, 2000.

585. Beverly Yang and Hector Garcia-Molina. Improving search in peer-to-peer networks. In *ICDCS*, pages 5–14, 2002.

586. H. Z. Yang and P. A. Larson. Query transformation for PSJ-queries. In *Proceedings of the International Conference on Very Large Databases (VLDB)*, pages 245–254, Brighton, England, 1987.

587. Jeffrey Xu Yu, Qin Lu, and Lijun Chang. *Keyword Search in Databases*. Synthesis Lectures on Data Management. 2010.

588. Markos Zaharioudakis, Roberta Cochrane, George Lapis, Hamid Pirahesh, and Monica Urata. Answering complex SQL queries using automatic summary tables. In *Proceedings of the ACM SIGMOD Conference*, pages 105–116, 2000.

589. Y. Zhai and B. Liu. Web data extraction based on partial tree alignment. In *WWW*, 2005.

590. Y. Zhang, N. Tang, and P. A. Boncz. Efficient distribution of full-fledged XQuery. In *Engineering*, pages 565–576, April 2009.

591. Jun Zhao, Satya Sanket Sahoo, Paolo Missier, Amit P. Sheth, and Carole A. Goble. Extending semantic provenance into the web of data. *IEEE Internet Computing*, 15(1), 2011.

592. Gang Zhou, Richard Hull, Roger King, and Jean-Claude Franchitti. Data integration and warehousing using h2o. *IEEE Data Eng. Bull.*, 18(2), 1995.

593. Wenchao Zhou, Qiong Fei, Arjun Narayan, Andreas Haeberlen, Boon Thau Loo, and Micah Sherr. Secure network provenance. In *SOSP*, 2011.

594. Wenchao Zhou, Qiong Fei, Shengzhi Sun, Tao Tao, Andreas Haeberlen, Zachary G. Ives, Boon Thau Loo, and Micah Sherr. NetTrails: A declarative platform for maintaining and querying provenance in distributed systems. In *SIGMOD Conference*, 2011.

595. Wenchao Zhou, Micah Sherr, Tao Tao, Xiaozhou Li, Boon Thau Loo, and Yun Mao. Efficient querying and maintenance of network provenance at internet-scale. In *SIGMOD*, 2010.

596. Yue Zhuge, Hector Garcia-Molina, and Janet L. Wiener. Multiple view consistency for data warehousing. In *ICDE*, 1997.

Index

Page numbers followed by "*f*" indicates figures and "*t*" indicates tables.

Printed and bound by CPI Group (UK) Ltd, Croydon, CR0 4YY

03/10/2024

01040326-0017